Biplanes at War

BIPLANES AT WAR

US Marine Corps Aviation in the Small Wars Era, 1915–1934

Wray R. Johnson

UNIVERSITY PRESS OF KENTUCKY

Scholarly publisher for the Commonwealth,
serving Bellarmine University, Berea College, Centre
College of Kentucky, Eastern Kentucky University,
The Filson Historical Society, Georgetown College,
Kentucky Historical Society, Kentucky State University,
Morehead State University, Murray State University,
Northern Kentucky University, Transylvania University,
University of Kentucky, University of Louisville,
and Western Kentucky University.

Editorial and Sales Offices: The University Press of Kentucky
663 South Limestone Street, Lexington, Kentucky 40508-4008
www.kentuckypress.com

Unless otherwise noted, photographs are courtesy of the US Marine Corps.
Maps by George Stoll.

Library of Congress Cataloging-in-Publication Data

Names: Johnson, Wray R., author.
Title: Biplanes at War : US Marine Corps Aviation in the Small Wars Era, 1915–1934 / Wray R. Johnson.
Description: Lexington, Kentucky : University Press of Kentucky, 2019. | Series: Aviation & Air Power | Includes bibliographical references and index.
Identifiers: LCCN 2018056725| ISBN 9780813177045 (hardcover : alk. paper) | ISBN 9780813177069 (pdf) | ISBN 9780813177052 (epub)
Subjects: LCSH: United States. Marine Corps—Aviation—History—20th century. | Haiti—History—American occupation, 1915-1934. | Nicaragua—History—Revolution, 1926-1929.
Classification: LCC VG93 .J64 2019 | DDC 972.94/05—dc23
LC record available at https://lccn.loc.gov/2018056725

Member of the Association
of University Presses

For John E. "Johnny" Johnson Jr.,
USMC, World War II, Korean War

and

Emmett Ross Mercer

In order to secure the full measure of cooperation between the air and ground forces, it is necessary that each understands the problems of the other. The aviator must know something of the tactics of the ground patrol, and he must be ready and willing to assume any justified risk to assist the ground commander. On the other hand, the ground commander should understand the hazards and limitations imposed on aviation operating over difficult terrain, and should not expect the impossible.

Marine Corps *Small Wars Manual,* 1940

Contents

Preface

> How vain it is to sit down to write when you have not stood up to live.
>
> Henry David Thoreau

I sat down to write this story because of the marines who stood up to live, and die, in lands far away from their homes, for reasons they did not truly fathom, in flimsy flying machines that killed more of them than the enemy ever did. It is for those marines and for the marines I have taught and teach today that I wrote this book. *Semper fidelis.*

This book borrows its approach from philosopher and political theorist Michael Oakeshott, an Englishman who wrote about the philosophy of history (among other things). Oakeshott believed that experience forms a single whole that is inseparable from reality. In that regard, he likened the task of the historian in explaining experience to that of building a wall without mortar. Even if one lays the bricks or stones as closely together as possible, gaps remain. And when the builder is careless in the placement of the materials, the gaps are even wider. If the gaps are too great, our understanding of the whole is inadequate, and the wall we have built may (and very probably will) collapse. The history of Marine Corps aviation during World War I and the period between the world wars has many gaps. Fortunately, the overall picture is adequate. But here, I aim to provide a fuller (albeit still incomplete) understanding of the marines' experience.

This book also borrows from Hegel, whose philosophy of history is neatly summarized in the German phrase *Weltgeschichte ist das Weltgericht,* or "World history is a tribunal that judges the world." In other words, history judges men, their actions, their ideas, and, ultimately, how we regard them.

Many historians have condemned American intervention in Latin America between the world wars, as well as the actions of the marines who executed those interventions. Other historians have sought to explain the rationale for intervention *ex ante* rather than *ex post* and have given the marines their due for attempting to achieve positive results. Still other historians eschew interpretation in the sense of judging history. These positivists and neo-positivists oppose judgment as unscientific and therefore pretend to be neutral and objective, which I believe is impossible. To be objective is a worthy goal, and to offer a fair interpretation is equally worthy, but to claim neutrality is a lie.

I am not neutral in my approach to the history of Marine Corps aviation in the small wars era, here defined as the period beginning with the occupation of Haiti in 1915 and ending with the marines' withdrawal from Nicaragua in 1933 and Haiti in 1934. I am not neutral because I am a retired US Air Force officer who served in a small wars capacity and was one of three men in the early 1990s who built a special operations squadron specifically designed to execute a mission not unlike that of Marine Corps aviators in the Caribbean, Central America, and China. I am not neutral because my father was a marine and because I have worked for the Marine Corps as a professor in the School of Advanced Warfighting, a part of Marine Corps University, since 2007. Speaking as an airman, I believe Marine Corps aviators have not been given adequate recognition for what they accomplished between the world wars, especially when it comes to the subject of aviation in small wars.

With the above in mind, I do not pretend that this book is the full and definitive reconstruction of that experience—or, to borrow Oakeshott's analogy, of that particular wall. To achieve a reasonably definitive understanding of the marines' experience, one must commit oneself to the full depth and breadth of the literature on the subject, from politics to technology. As marine Lieutenant General Paul Van Riper likes to say: "Cast your net widely." To help readers fill in many of the gaps created by casting that net, I have included extensive notes. For those readers who do not normally peruse the notes (which is common), I highly encourage you to do so in this case.

Even though the notes are extensive, the citations in this book are by no means exhaustive. To cite every fact and datum would require a companion volume. Nevertheless, I regard the notes as a book within a book. This was a deliberate decision, for a couple of reasons. First, I wanted the book to be interesting, even entertaining. This led me to separate some of the peripheral aspects of the story from the main narrative. The recollections of many of the marines (aviators and nonaviators alike) read like adventure tales—because that is what they are. Young men left their homes and families and volunteered to fly at a time when airplanes were exceedingly difficult to get off the ground and then return them safely to the ground. Not only did they volunteer to fly these dangerous machines; they volunteered to fly them in combat, first in a world war against an enemy with equally good and often better planes and later against guerrillas who had no compunction about mutilating their bodies in the most horrific ways possible should these fliers be shot down or forced down by mechanical defect.

Second, I cite all quoted material and anything else that, for one reason or another, requires notation, amplification, or clarification or might cause a military history buff to camp out on my front lawn. In keeping with the storytelling intent, I include short stories in the notes that I could not fit into the narrative without bogging things down but struck me as worth telling. I also provide short biographies of several marines because many of these men went on to become icons in Marine Corps history, and their service deserves mention in a book such as this. Thus, I hope this book will appeal to a wide audience: scholars; those interested in military history or the history of American intervention in Latin America; those interested in the history of the Marine Corps; those interested in technology; and, last but not least, those fascinated by flying and the history of flight.

It behooves me at this point to confess to gaps in my wall, as well as to arranging its stones in such a fashion that might offend the sensibilities of some. So be it. My emphasis is on the yarn as much as on the history, but I have tried to keep Oakeshott and Hegel in mind throughout. To borrow from Samuel Huntington: "We need a map that portrays reality and simplifies reality in a way that best serves our purposes."

More than a century has passed since the period covered by this book began. It is time to make a fresh inquiry into what the marines accomplished and failed to accomplish, and what they learned along the way. It is also time to emphasize what Marine Corps aviators pioneered, and what was later ignored or subsumed within the broader history of air power. Today, the US Marines Corps, US Army, US Navy, and police departments across the United States refer to aviation rather than air power. That is because air power includes aviation but pretends to much, much more. Even in my air force days, we referred to special operations aviation, not special operations air power.

Aviation is about airplanes (manned or unmanned), whereas air power refers to a vision if not a theory of war waged in the third dimension, easily summarized in a pseudo-syllogism: that air power is inherently offensive; that it is manifestly strategic; and by that fact (and in order to fully realize its offensive and strategic possibilities) must, necessarily, be independent. Marine Corps aviation has never been independent; it was always meant to support marines on the ground, and beginning in the small wars era, it did just that.

Thus, this book is not about air power. It is about the utility of aviation in small wars as pioneered by the Marine Corps between the world wars. I pray that I have provided an entertaining story as well as a description of the experience that closely matches reality and therefore serves as a useful example of what aviation can and cannot do in small wars today and in the future.

In closing, I would be remiss not to acknowledge the assistance I received while writing this book. First, I must thank Marine Corps University and the School of Advanced Warfighting for giving me the time to write this book. I also thank everyone who helped me in the Marine Corps History Division and the Marine Corps Historical Research Center. It is remarkable how shallow most of the secondary literature is on this subject, and the employees of the History Division in particular pointed me to relevant files that proved crucial to my storytelling. I thank George Stoll for his wonderful maps and for his patience as the maps were developed. In addition, I thank those whose encouragement kept me going in this process, for there were times that I wanted to quit. Of course, my acknowledgment of these individuals' support in no way implies any responsibility on their part for this book's content or for any infelicitous errors that might have crept in.

Finally, I thank my bride of over thirty years, Marcia, who put up with my being home too much or being away too much while writing this book. She never once complained and has always been my copilot, keeping me on vector and reminding me that if you look up and see trees, you are upside down.

On June 19, 1930, Marine Corps aviator Captain Byron Johnson, flying a Vought 02U Corsair in a two-ship mission, encountered a large group of Sandinista "bandits" on Saragossa Mountain of the *Cordillera de Amerrisque*. He attacked with bombs and machine gun fire. Although his airplane was struck six times by ground fire and the leading edge of the lower wing was crushed in a collision with a vulture, he continued the attack until his ammunition was exhausted. On the same day he led a second six-ship mission, and his airplane was struck by four bullets. The guerrilla band subsequently dispersed. For these actions Captain Johnson received the Distinguished Flying Cross. (Painting by John J. Capolino. Art Collection, National Museum of the Marine Corps, Triangle, VA)

Introduction

> You can land a Sailor or Marine and it is not considered war; but if you land one section of the Army that is war.
>
> Rear Admiral John Pillsbury, 1909

Going Aloft

Marines of the British Royal Navy were the inspiration for the United States Marine Corps (USMC). As a result, the American marines adopted many of the customs and traditions of the British marines, including the fact that marines were not seamen and therefore were not required to go "aloft" in the ship's rigging to work the sails.[1] That said, both British and American marines were expected to climb the rigging to the "tops" to fight,[2] that is, to rain down suppressing fire onto the deck of an enemy ship. Moreover, British regulations encouraged marines to go aloft to learn seagoing skills and to help their shipmates. American regulations offered similar encouragement and stated, "Cases may arise to make it important and necessary" to go aloft.[3] Thus, although they were not required to go aloft to perform sailors' tasks, marines were expected to go aloft to fight and were encouraged to go aloft as seafaring men. Not surprisingly, then, US marines have been going aloft since the formal establishment of the Marine Corps in 1798, and it should come as no surprise that marines would be more than willing to rise above the rigging in "flying machines" to support their brothers in arms on the deck—whether at sea or on land.[4]

In the United States, early aeronautical literature used the term "flying machine" to mean a motor-driven, heavier-than-air craft. Indeed, Orville and

Wilbur Wright described their own invention as the Wright Flyer, and when the US Army Signal Corps solicited bids for a heavier-than-air craft in December 1907, it specifically called for a powered flying machine.[5] The British adopted the term "aëroplane" (from the French *aéroplane*) for flying machines, and for a time, so did American publications. But perhaps because American Linotype typesetting machines generally did not include the diaeresis, the diacritic was dropped and the term became "aeroplane."[6] Then, in 1918, the National Advisory Committee for Aeronautics recommended use of the word "airplane," at which point aeronautical publications in the United States quickly adopted the two-syllable term (and its derivatives such as "aircraft") and occasionally shortened it to "plane." This study uses these terms interchangeably, as they all mean the same thing, except that "aeroplane" is used when discussing the earliest years of American military aviation, as that was the term in use at the time.

American military aviation in the United States began during the early part of the Civil War, when Union forces used hydrogen-filled captive balloons with baskets slung underneath for observation purposes. Balloon operations ceased in 1863 and did not resume until Congress made the Signal Corps responsible for the collection and transmission of information within the US Army in 1890, and the chief signal officer, Brigadier General Adolphus Greely, requested funding to establish a balloon corps. In 1891 the army purchased a French balloon, and by 1892 a balloon section was established. Following the loss of that balloon, a second was constructed at Fort Logan, Colorado, by William Ivy, an army sergeant and well-known stunt balloonist, and his wife. The second balloon was used on several occasions during the Spanish-American War, including to adjust artillery fire at the Battle of San Juan Hill, made famous by the charge of Theodore "Teddy" Roosevelt's Rough Riders. By 1906 the Balloon Section had eight captive balloons. Two years later the army acquired a rigid airship. Two years after that the army acquired its first heavier-than-air flying machine.

The Wright brothers famously inaugurated motor-driven, heavier-than-air flight on December 17, 1903, at Kitty Hawk, North Carolina. The brothers tried to attract the attention of the US Army but had no success until foreign governments took an interest, at which point newly elected President Theodore Roosevelt ordered Secretary of War William Howard Taft to investigate the military potential of the Wrights' creation. Consequently, Brigadier General James Allen, chief of the Signal Corps, issued specifications for a military flying machine and solicited bids in 1907. Of the forty-one bids received, only three complied with the specifications. The Wright brothers secured the contract after the other two bidders failed to deliver a machine on the date specified. The first army airplane (a Wright A) was delivered to Fort Meyer, Virginia, on August 20, 1908.

With regard to the US Navy, during the Civil War some of the balloons employed by Federal forces were tethered to barges or specially constructed boats and can be regarded as forerunners of the navy's lighter-than-air craft and, arguably, naval aviation. But the navy lost interest in aircraft until the Wright brothers' feat, after which its leadership became keenly interested in both heavier-than-air and lighter-than-air craft (especially dirigibles and other steerable airships). Indeed, Captain Mark Bristol, the second head of naval aviation, believed aeroplanes operating from ships and from shore in coordination with airships and warships would be especially useful against submarines. But no serious thought was given to the employment of aeroplanes (operating aboard ships or from the water) except as the "eyes" of the fleet. Envisioning a wider combat role for powered heavier-than-air craft was beyond the ken of most navy officers of the time. The same was true of most Marine Corps officers.

A Brief History of the US Marine Corps

From 1783 (when the last American fighting ship of the War of Independence was sold) to 1797, the United States was without a navy or marines.[7] But soon after American independence, European warships (in particular, those of France and Great Britain), as well as Mediterranean pirates, began harassing American merchant vessels. Thus, on March 27, 1794, the US Congress commissioned six frigates to be constructed to patrol trade routes and protect American shipping interests. With the authorization for these ships, Congress initiated a process that would lead to the revival of the American navy and marines. On May 10, 1797, the USS *United States* was launched; it would serve for sixty years until lost at Norfolk, Virginia, in 1861.[8] The following July, President John Adams authorized marines to serve aboard the new ships. Three months later the USS *Constitution* was launched and remains commissioned today. On April 3, 1798, the Department of the Navy was established, and three months after that the US Marine Corps was officially created by an act of Congress.

By the time the War of 1812 commenced, the organization of the marines was firmly established. At the top was the commandant of the Marine Corps, although he was then a lieutenant colonel and not a general. Both then and now, the commandant resided at the Marine Barracks in Washington, DC. Public law provided for the commandant to have a staff that consisted of an adjutant, a paymaster, and a quartermaster. There was also a sergeant major and a quartermaster sergeant, as well as a fife major and a drum major (the Marine Corps Band was created in 1798). The first commandant was William Ward Burrows, a South Carolinian who had been educated in England and had seen little military service during the War of Independence. When war was declared on England on June 18, 1812, the Marine Corps was undermanned, with some 1,200 of the 2,000 men authorized scattered on sixteen oceangoing ships and various gunboats and at navy yards and stations in Boston, New York, Philadelphia, Norfolk, New Orleans, and Washington, DC. There were also handfuls of marines at smaller stations in Baltimore and Charleston, as well as aboard the brig USS *Oneida* on Lake Ontario. And there was a company-sized detachment of marines on Cumberland Island in the St. Mary's River between Georgia and Florida. The size of the detachments aboard ship varied, from perhaps a corporal and one other marine serving on a gunboat to the 55 marines of the ship's company of 450 men on the USS *Constitution.*

As noted earlier, marines were not required to perform sailors' tasks on ships, but in times of battle, predetermined teams of marines would climb the rigging to the tops. On the large frigates these teams ranged in size from twelve men in the main top to seven in the foretop and five in the mizzen top. The teams generally chose the best marksmen among them to fire on the enemy, and the remainder would hand loaded muskets to the shooters. The targets for these sharpshooters were enemy officers, helmsmen, ships' boys, gunners, and opposing marines and sailors in the rigging. Firefights between marines were common. If two ships came together, the marines' responsibility was to repel boarders from the enemy ship, using muskets and bayonets as well as the cutlass and pike. If the commander chose to board the enemy vessel, the marines were required by regulations to remain in place in the event the assault failed and they had to defend their ship from enemy boarders. Nonetheless, marines regularly took part in boarding parties, and Lieutenant William Bush, the senior marine officer on board the *Constitution,* was killed in a fight with the British warship HMS *Guerriere* off Halifax, Nova Scotia, during the War of 1812 when he leaped to the taffrail crying, "Shall I board her, Sir?"[9]

Although understrength at the outbreak of the War of 1812, the new Marine Corps comprised many combat veterans. Before the war the United States had been embroiled in efforts to remove the threat of the Barbary pirates to American commercial shipping, including the so-called Tripolitanian War. The marines took part in two notable combat operations during this period: a commando-type raid led by navy lieutenant Stephen Decatur that resulted in the burning of the captured American sloop of war USS *Philadelphia* at Tripoli, and an overland attack by a mixed force led by marine lieutenant Presley O'Bannon on the Tripolitan port of Derna.[10]

The end of the War of 1812 ushered in an era of relative peace and maritime expansion for the United States. By the late 1830s the US Navy was building steam-powered warships and sending its squadrons around the globe to execute an emergent naval strategy born of far-flung American trade. To support this strategy, Congress and the navy established a Board of Naval Commissioners (three US Navy captains) to plan and supervise navy acquisition and other programs as well as to oversee operations at sea. The board served in this role until 1842, when five functional bureaus were created: Naval Yards and Docks; Construction, Equipment, and Repairs; Provisions and Clothing; Ordnance and Hydrography; and Medicine and Surgery. In 1862 the bureaus were reorganized and expanded: Yards and Docks, Provisions and Clothing, Ordnance, Equipment and Recruiting, Construction and Repair, Steam Engineering (later, Engineering), Navigation, and Medicine and Surgery. But the bureaus were not obligated to cooperate or plan with one another. As a result, there was considerable overlap and friction until the General Board of the US Navy was created in March 1900. Although the bureaus cared little about the Marine Corps, the General Board would have considerable impact on the organization, training, roles, and missions of the Corps.

William Burrows was replaced as Marine Corps commandant by Franklin Wharton in 1804. Wharton was succeeded by Anthony Gale in 1820, after which Archibald Henderson took charge, serving for the next thirty-eight years. According to Allan Millett, Henderson was no "slouch as a bureaucratic infighter and schemer. . . . but moderated his capacity for dissimulation and his burning ambition with equally real moral probity, devotion to his Corps, and love of soldiering."[11] Henderson recognized that marines were useful as landing parties, in addition to their routine "constable" duties aboard ships at sea. In the 1820s the marines of the West India Squadron went ashore in antipiracy operations. In the 1830s navy-marine landing parties went ashore in the Falkland Islands (Malvinas) as well as in Peru and Argentina. In 1832 Commodore John Downes sent 250 sailors and marines ashore from the frigate USS *Potomac* to "chastise" the population of Quallah Battoo, Sumatra.[12] Marines were also used to suppress the Atlantic slave trade. But according to critics, in all these activities "they showed little more aptitude for such operations than the sailors."[13]

Not surprisingly, then, many navy officers believed there was no need for marines aboard ships, and if they were used for anything, it should be to guard shore facilities. Some navy officers went so far as to call for the abolition of the Marine Corps, a theme that reoccurs throughout Marine Corps history. Noting the hostility and threat, Commandant Henderson took every opportunity to demonstrate the contributions marines could make to national strategy and security. Therefore, marines took part in the Indian Wars in the southeastern United States (1836–1842) as well as the Mexican-American War (1846–1848).[14] As a result, from the end of the Mexican War to the outbreak of the American Civil War, the Marine Corps held fast and even increased its service ashore protecting American lives and property, principally in Latin America and the Pacific. Marines also participated in Admiral Matthew Perry's famous "opening" of Japan in the early 1850s.[15]

Archibald Henderson, the "grand old man of the Marine Corps," died suddenly in January 1859 and was replaced by John Harris. Harris led the Corps during the raid on Harpers Ferry, Virginia, during which Lieutenant Israel Greene and eighty-six marines, accompanied by Brevet Colonel Robert E. Lee, ended the insurrection led by abolitionist John Brown. Harris remained commandant for most of the Civil War. During that time, the marines' contribution as a land force was not particularly significant, but the marines who manned guns aboard US Navy warships were consistently cited for their bravery and performance. Of the "seventeen Marines awarded the new Medal of Honor during the Civil War, thirteen were sergeants and corporals serving as gun captains and gun division commanders."[16] By the end of the war, Harris had been replaced by Jacob Zeilin, the first marine to achieve the rank of brigadier general. He remained commandant until 1876, when he was replaced by Charles McCawley, who served until 1891.[17]

With the end of the Civil War, the navy demobilized rapidly, and by 1868 mostly modern steam frigates and sloops remained. For their part, the marines returned to their traditional duties as ships' guards, sentries at navy yards, and members of landing parties. It was in the latter role that the marines found their forte. Highly publicized landings occurred in Korea in 1871 and Panama in 1885. During the latter expedition, marine barracks and ships were stripped to form a brigade of nearly 700 officers and men to protect American lives and property during a secessionist insurgency waged against Colombia. In the end, the two battalions raised did not see combat, but the idea of using marines for "interventionary" purposes was born. It was also during McCawley's tenure that Marine Corps officers began to enter service from the US Naval Academy at Annapolis, Maryland. Among the graduates between 1882 and 1898 was John Lejeune (class of 1888), who was arguably the most important commandant in Marine Corps history.

During the 1880s the US Navy experienced changes that were felt not only in the fleet but also throughout the Marine Corps. Indeed, the first three decades of the twentieth century would be a period of crisis for the Corps, a crisis of identity and of purpose. In 1882 Congress authorized the construction of three steel cruisers: USS *Atlanta,* USS *Boston,* and USS *Chicago.* These ships were to be followed by world-class battleships to serve as a concentrated fighting force to defend against invasion of the United States as well as to protect commerce. Although Congress at first balked at the cost of the plan, appropriations were nonetheless approved to fund the construction of three battleships—the USS *Indiana,* USS *Massachusetts,* and USS *Oregon*—all of which were as good as any battleship then operated by European naval powers. The question was, would marines serve aboard these new battleships?

The new commandant, Charles Heywood, certainly believed marines belonged on battleships, but many navy officers disagreed. To these self-styled reformers, marines might have been necessary in the past to keep sailors in line, but the navy had adopted a new leadership style and dispensed with many of the tasks and punishments that had caused sailors to rebel. The most outspoken reformer and opponent of marines aboard ship was Lieutenant William Fullam, a Naval Academy graduate who would rise to the rank of rear admiral. Fullam believed marine guards on ships at sea were an anachronism that should be abolished. Although the assertion gained little traction at first, Commodore Frank Ramsay, chief of the Bureau of Navigation, ordered that all-marine gun crews on warships be discontinued. This action was followed by a request from Captain Robley "Fighting Bob" Evans, commanding the battleship USS *Indiana,* that all marines be removed from his ship. Evans was a Civil War hero who would later command the "Great White Fleet" on its worldwide cruise from the Atlantic Ocean through the Strait of Magellan to the Pacific Ocean in 1907.[18] As a highly regarded navy officer, Evans's request sent shock waves through both the US Navy and the Marine Corps.

With backing by such men as Ramsay and Evans, the "Fullamites" pressed for the Marine Corps to be transferred to the US Army, an idea that was at least tacitly supported by Assistant Secretary of the Navy Theodore Roosevelt.[19] Commandant Heywood strove to keep the Marine Corps intact within the Department of the Navy—if not aboard ships, then as an interventionary force of the sort sent to the Isthmus of Panama. Over time, Heywood succeeded in convincing Roosevelt and Secretary of the Navy Hilary Herbert to not only retain the Marine Corps but also expand its role. Fortunately for Heywood and the marines, the sinking of the battleship USS *Maine* in Havana harbor, Cuba, and the subsequent Spanish-American War worked to the marines' advantage.[20]

Believing the destruction of the *Maine* to be an act of sabotage committed by the Spanish, the United States declared war on Spain on April 1, 1898. Colonel Heywood was quickly authorized the end-strength he had long pressed for, and five days after the war formally began, new Secretary of the Navy John Long ordered Heywood to organize a battalion of marines for expeditionary duty with the Atlantic Squadron in the Caribbean Sea. The First Battalion, led by Lieutenant Colonel Robert Huntington, seized Guantanamo Bay, the first serious fighting on Cuban soil and an action that secured a necessary forward base for the navy. Afterward, newspaper reporters sang songs of high praise for the marines. Among them was Stephen Crane, one of the most innovative writers of his generation and author of *The Red Badge of Courage.* Crane wrote that the marines demonstrated great courage and professional skill at the Battle of Cuzco Well,[21] and other reporters "waxed rhapsodic" about the marines in combat.[22]

The Spanish-American War proved to be a watershed event for the marines. With the establishment of an American empire and the expansion of the navy to protect that empire, the US Navy and its Marine Corps became the first line of defense. Pressure mounted on Congress to enlarge the fleet and build bases overseas to protect the new possessions as well as the planned canal to be built across the Isthmus of Panama. The war also propelled Teddy Roosevelt to the presidency. Although Roosevelt had not been a stalwart supporter of the Marine Corps before the war, he did not resurrect Fullam's ideas when the war concluded. In fact, Heywood was promoted to major general, and Colonel George Reid, USMC, was given a seat on the General Board. The chairman of the board was Admiral of the Navy George Dewey, hero of the Battle of Manila Bay and a strong supporter of the Marine Corps.

In 1903 Colonel George Elliott succeeded Charles Heywood as commandant. Unfortunately, Elliott was not as politically or administratively astute as his predecessor. During his tenure, the Navy Department sought to reorganize the Marine Corps into permanent expeditionary battalions that could seize bases overseas and defend them for use by the US Battle Fleet. With this in mind, Fullamites who had achieved senior rank once again called for the marines' removal from navy warships, arguing that the ships' detachments would be needed to flesh out the Advance Base Force battalions. The request to remove marines from shipboard duty became official on October 16, 1908, when it was signed by Rear Admiral John Pillsbury, chief of the Bureau of Navigation. To the consternation of a great many marines, Elliott acquiesced to the proposal, and Secretary of the Navy Victor Metcalf recommended approval to the president.

On November 12, 1908, President Theodore Roosevelt issued Executive Order 969, removing marines from ships and assigning them to garrison navy yards and stations, to furnish a mobile force to defend bases at home and abroad, to garrison the Canal Zone in Panama, and to perform other expeditionary duties as required, including the seizure of advance bases. Alarmed at this development, friends of the Marine Corps in Congress set up a special investigating committee to review the removal order, chaired by Representative Thomas Butler (R-PA), father of marine captain Smedley Butler. The senior Butler's committee challenged the order and sought to refute every claim made by the Fullamites, and when Marine Corps representatives testified before the committee, they argued that it would be cheaper to build large landing parties from multiple ships brought together rather than embark whole battalions on navy transports.

The House of Representatives as a whole took up the matter and attached a rider to the Naval Appropriations Act that amounted to a threat to defund the Marine Corps unless marines were placed aboard battleships, armored cruisers, and other fighting ships at a strength no less than 8 percent of the ship's complement. The Senate likewise voted to return marines to shipboard duty, and the Appropriations Act went to Roosevelt with the rider intact.

Roosevelt was in no mood to fight Congress over the matter, given that he wished to expand the navy and wanted the marines to perform interventionary functions. He signed the bill with little hesitation. The navy complied with the legislation, immediately placing marines aboard twenty-eight ships of the line. The navy did try to prevent marines from manning heavy guns, but this limitation was overturned by newly elected president William Howard Taft, who ordered that the marines be restored to all their pre–Executive Order 969 duties.

President Taft acted on behalf of the marines because he adopted his predecessor's aggressive foreign policy, which had abandoned the old policy of nonintervention in the affairs of other nations. The new policy was rooted in commerce, finance, and missionary activities both secular and religious. With the Roosevelt corollary to the Monroe Doctrine, "interposition" had evolved to "intervention," and Taft sought to continue this policy. Interposition meant landing American troops in a crisis to protect American citizens and property, but once the immediate danger had passed, the troops were withdrawn. This occurred repeatedly in the latter half of the nineteenth century and into the first decade of the twentieth century. Intervention, however, meant that naval forces would be used not only to protect lives and property but also, and more importantly, to alter the political behavior and even the institutions of another country. Naval forces were ideal for intervention, for as Rear Admiral John Pillsbury noted, "You can land a Sailor or a Marine and it is not considered war; but if you land one section of the Army that is war."[23] But even if intervention was not state-versus-state warfare per se, it involved combat and therefore became widely known as a form of "small war."

The Nature of Small Wars

The late Harry Summers, author of *On Strategy: A Critical Analysis of the Vietnam War,* wrote: "Americans do not like war, do not like to think about war, and even in the midst of war prefer to call it something else."[24] Summers's complaint at the time was precipitated by the US military's use of the term "low-intensity conflict," defined as a limited politico-military struggle to achieve political, social, economic, or psychological objectives. Such struggles were regarded as protracted, generally confined to the developing world, and characterized by constraints on the weaponry, tactics, and level of violence. According to Summers, this was no definition—it was "a description masquerading as an explanation."[25] He therefore advocated using the archaic term "small wars." According to Summers, "Unlike low intensity conflict, 'small wars' is blunt, and in being blunt it truthfully and explicitly alerts the American people to the dangers they face. Not the least of its advantages is that it forces policymakers and decision-makers to . . . confront the messy military and political realities small wars entail and the military and political costs they exact."[26]

The term "small wars" itself can be traced to the Napoleonic Wars and the French occupation of Spain. Spanish resistance to the French occupation did not involve massed forces of "regulars" but instead "irregulars" in what became known as a small war—that is, *guerrilla,* the diminutive form of *guerra,* or "war," in Spanish. The French referred to such "irregular warfare" (that is, war waged outside of acknowledged conventions) as *petite guerre.*[27] The German-speaking peoples used the term *kleinkrieg,* the literal equivalent of *guerrilla* and *petite guerre.* But German-speaking writers also employed other terms that provided a clear analytical distinction between the "form of war"—for example, *kleinkrieg* (small war) and *volkskrieg* (people's war, a general uprising)—and the "form of the conduct of war"—for example, *partisanenkrieg* (partisan warfare), *bandenkrieg* (bandit warfare), and *bandenkämpferkriegsführung* (guerrilla warfare). Today Germans writers use *bandenkrieg, guerrillakrieg* (a modern term), and *partisanenkrieg* interchangeably, which is regrettable, for they do not mean the same thing. Bandits are criminals. Partisans support regular forces. And guerrilla warfare is a distinct form of the conduct of war. It is for this reason that the German word *kriegsbild* proves so useful. *Kriegsbild* literally means "war picture," that is, appreciating the nature of war. It is an important concept because the core idea of *kriegsbild* does not call for description but rather understanding ("Got the picture?"). Small wars as a form of war, as well as a form of the conduct of war, demand a clear understanding of the nature of the conflict. This is what the great Prussian military philosopher Carl von Clausewitz meant when he wrote that the politician and the commander must know what kind of war they are getting into.[28]

With regard to the nature of small wars (as opposed to their character), two works stand out as classics: British Major General Charles Callwell's book *Small Wars: Their Principles and Practice* (1896) and the US Marine Corps' *Small Wars Manual* of 1940. In many respects these seminal works are quite similar. Their differences lie primarily in the role of "popular support," and this in no small measure reflects the differences in British and American foreign policy at the beginning of the twentieth century.

An essential feature of the literature treating small wars is that the conduct of small wars is different from that of conventional warfare (war waged within the constraints of certain conventions).[29] In that regard, Callwell and the Marine Corps highlighted the many attributes of small wars that, generally speaking, contradict the rules of conventional or regular warfare. Chief among these attributes is the diverse character of small wars, each having a unique identity that affects nearly every aspect of military planning and operations. Every small war presents its own peculiar challenges to regular forces and demands that leaders carefully scrutinize the unique circumstances extant in developing a campaign plan (a thoroughly Clausewitzian idea). Small wars also seem to require greater initiative and independence of action than conventional wars in terms of the latitude of action of both senior and subordinate commanders. Finally, both the Marine Corps and Callwell understood that vigorous action and careful attention to the psychological element are vital to successfully waging a small war. Unlike the relative uniformity associated with conventional warfare tactics, techniques, and procedures, the peculiarities of each small war prevent a clean, categorical definition of the rules and roles for military forces conducting small war operations. The Marine Corps especially recognized that flexibility is critical to the successful conduct of small wars. Thus, the *Small Wars Manual* was not particularly theoretical or prescriptive; rather, it provided a framework for dealing with small wars based on practical experience. The transcendent message throughout is the need for flexibility.

Callwell warned the commander that, unlike in regular warfare, the origin of a small war must be taken thoroughly into account, "quite apart from the plan of [the] campaign which the commander of the regular forces may decide upon."[30] The traditional Western model of conventional warfare (that is, pitched battle between two disciplined regular armies) does not hold in small wars. Indeed, the unique conditions of "native" tactics, weaponry, culture, psychology, and numerical strength, as well as the origin of the small war itself, must be considered by the commander and his staff in their preparations. Thus, Callwell arrived at much the same conclusion as the Marine Corps: "in small wars all manner of opponents are met with, [and] in no two campaigns does the enemy fight in the same fashion."[31]

The importance of indigenous culture in small wars may appear out of place to the practitioner of conventional warfare. In major wars between professional armies, cultural considerations are often deemed of marginal importance from a tactical and even an operational point of view. In small wars, however, Callwell emphasized that "the habits, the customs, and the mode of action on the battlefield of the enemy should be studied in advance."[32] The Marine Corps agreed, noting that "the campaign plan and strategy must be adapted to the character of the people encountered."[33] Mirroring Callwell's advice, the *Small Wars Manual* urged officers and enlisted men alike to employ themselves in "a serious study of the people, their racial, political, religious, and mental development."[34]

Another feature of small wars that differs from conventional operations is the dispersion of forces and the concomitant need for initiative. Callwell observed, "in small wars separation in the field is often a necessary consequence of the conditions of the campaign."[35] This dispersion would usually prevent a commander from closely monitoring the needs, situations, and decisions of his far-flung subordinate commanders. Because of this reduced level of command and control, he argued, "a great deal of latitude must be left to subordinates, whose judgment should remain as far as possible unfettered."[36] The same conclusion was recorded in the *Small Wars Manual*: "In small wars, the units of the force are generally so widely distributed throughout the theater of operations that the commander may have difficulty in keeping abreast of the situations existing in the various elements. Operations orders should usually be phrased in general terms and the details of execution delegated to subordinate commanders."[37]

Yet another conclusion shared by Callwell and the Marine Corps was the importance of bold and vigorous action coupled with psychological operations. Again, this contrasts with the standard treatment of psychology in conventional warfare doctrine. The *Small Wars Manual* stated, "the application of the principles of psychology in small wars is quite different from their normal application in major warfare or even in troop leadership."[38] Callwell similarly observed that the effects of bold and vigorous action against the enemy in a small war is likely to produce a reaction quite different from that expected in a major war against a professional army. "A vigorous offensive," he wrote, "has the effect of keeping at home those who hesitate to take up arms and . . . thereby [diminishes] the fighting strength of the enemy."[39] Thus, in small wars the role of psychology is directly coupled to the numerical and moral strength of enemy forces to a much greater extent than when facing a conventional army.

The principle of the offensive, then, is of great significance in small wars, although not necessarily more than in conventional warfare (we'll leave aside

Clausewitz's discussion of defense as the stronger form of war). Callwell wrote: "The regular army must force its way into the enemy's country and seek him out. It must be ready to fight him wherever he may be found."[40] While this may be considered reckless advice in a major war against a disciplined army, the nature of small wars allows that "moral force is even more potent than physical force. . . . A happy appreciation of this great principle has from time to time enabled soldiers of decision and resource to achieve most signal results, and has led to their gaining startling triumphs with relatively insignificant forces."[41] The Marine Corps likewise recognized this principle: "So long as there is armed opposition to the occupation, the intervening force must maintain the principle of the offensive."[42] In fact, the *Small Wars Manual* warned that a defensive or positional attitude would allow guerrilla forces to multiply rapidly, isolating government outposts and convincing the populace of the weakness of the central government and intervening forces. (If the reader is a science fiction fan, think of the failed Harkonnen strategy in Frank Herbert's classic *Dune,* itself something of a study in insurgency and failed counterinsurgency.)[43]

There were certain aspects, however, in which the Marine Corps did not agree with Callwell and British small wars theory and practice. British forces of the nineteenth and early twentieth centuries were used to police the empire within a clear framework of direct imperial administration of those areas in which small wars took place. American policy, in contrast, was generally opposed to the idea of direct imperial administration. However, to prevent European powers from establishing a strategically threatening foothold in the Americas, it was deemed in the United States' national interest to intervene commercially, diplomatically, and at times militarily to ward off European designs in the region. This fundamental distinction in motivation resulted in conceptual and practical variations between the British army and the US Marine Corps, the principal instrument of American intervention. Because the British Empire dealt with the problem directly, Callwell's book promoted an almost exclusively military solution in small wars, especially regarding so-called punitive expeditions.

In contrast, the Marine Corps' *Small Wars Manual* consistently emphasized that marines were both soldiers and diplomats in small wars, and they were often referred to as "State Department Troops in small wars."[44] For the marines, intervention was an extension of diplomacy, and it was "undertaken only as a last resort after all diplomatic means of adjusting differences have failed."[45] Thus, the character of US interventionist policy accounts for nearly all the primary differences between the American and British approaches to small wars before World War II. Consequently, the Marine Corps' small wars "doctrine" (in this case, informal), by necessity, confronted issues that Callwell never dealt with in his treatise. Issues such as conducting elections, establishing and training an apolitical native constabulary force, dealing fairly with local political leaders, and encouraging an altruistic and democratic mind-set among the local populace took center stage in the *Small Wars Manual.* Indeed, according to the manual, the less violence used to accomplish the mission, the better. In a manner that Sun Tzu would have appreciated, the manual stressed, "Instead of employing force, one strives to accomplish the purpose by diplomacy. A Force Commander who gains his objective in a small war without firing a shot has attained far greater success than one who resorted to the use of arms."[46]

The issue of punitive measures in small wars also reflects the differences between the British and American approaches. Callwell believed that "the adoption of guerrilla methods by the enemy almost necessarily forces the regular troops to resort to punitive measures directed against the possessions of their antagonists."[47] Such measures included "destroying villages, carrying off livestock and trampling down crops and so on."[48] In contrast, the *Small Wars Manual* reflected a more "enlightened" attitude that the common people must be distinguished from guerrilla fighters. The idea that punitive measures would simply encourage more people to join the guerrillas was a cornerstone of early Marine Corps "pacification" theory. Thus, according to the manual, "National policy and the precepts of civilized procedure demand that our dealings with other peoples be maintained on a high-moral plan[e]," and the manual stressed the careful regulation of the marines' attitude and behavior in their dealings with civilians.[49]

In the end, one can think of Callwell and the Marine Corps authors of the *Small Wars Manual* as the Jomini and Clausewitz of small wars.[50] In that regard, Clausewitz and Jomini were both well aware of irregular warfare and small wars. They each devoted only one chapter of their famous books to the subject, but what they had to say is important because they articulated the basic problems of small wars in terms of the military challenges they present. In fact, small wars today raise many of the same issues first raised in print by Clausewitz, such as the problems posed by a "people in arms" and the difficulty of achieving rapid results when faced with "wars in the interior."

Clausewitz described the effect of such conflict as not unlike the evaporation of water, meaning that the will of the extant power (whether indigenous or occupying) may gradually diminish and ultimately vanish. And clearly this kind of "people's war" was unfamiliar and unwelcome to Jomini, who recognized it as something new and disturbing.[51]

Of course, both men were reflecting on the French experience in Spain, as described earlier. The difficulty encountered by the French armies was that the *guerrillos* (or *banditti,* whatever term is de rigueur) ran away from direct confrontation with the massed firepower of the French troops, yet they also harried the French, ambushed them, committed atrocities against captured French soldiers, and then melted into the civilian populace when the French arrived in force to deal with the situation. In an attempt to dominate the human as well as the physical terrain, the French dispersed their troops, but these small garrisons were vulnerable and often overwhelmed by large bands of *guerrillos.* In their frustration, French forces resorted to atrocities of their own to subdue the Spanish population. But the more the French brutalized civilians, the fiercer the resistance became. Large-scale sweeps by the French netted only a few *guerrillos,* and dispersed operations by the *guerrillos* negated the disciplined firepower that was the great strength of the French army. Two centuries later these same problems remain. Thus, unconventional war, irregular war, or small war is real war. It has structure and a theoretical underpinning, and it is a phenomenon that manifests specific, peculiar characteristics. And as with any field of study, terms and their meanings become a key part of the analysis.

Terms of Art

Callwell defined small wars as any instance in which "regulars" fight "irregulars."[52] The authors of the Marine Corps' *Small Wars Manual* agreed, but they also offered a more nuanced and American-specific definition: small wars are "operations undertaken under executive authority [meaning the president, without action from Congress], wherein military force is combined with diplomatic pressure in the internal or external affairs of another state whose government is unstable, inadequate, or unsatisfactory for the preservation of life and of such interests as are determined by the foreign policy of the United States."[53] Note that national interest is not an explicitly expressed overriding concern; the extant conditions in another state are simply unsatisfactory.

The manual goes on to state that, in such small wars of intervention, "it can be expected that hostile forces in occupied territory will employ guerrilla warfare as a means of gaining their end."[54] This seems quite straightforward, but to the layman, guerrilla warfare can have multiple meanings; even professional military officers often conflate insurgency and guerrilla warfare as meaning the same thing. But as the authors of the *Small Wars Manual* understood, guerrilla warfare is a form of the conduct of war, a means to an end, not an end in itself or a form of war.

With the above in mind, guerrilla warfare is a tactic. As Mao Tse-tung admonished his followers: "In guerrilla warfare, select the tactic of seeming to come from the east and attacking from the west; avoid the solid, attack the hollow; attack; withdraw; deliver a lightning blow; seek a lightning decision. When guerrillas engage a stronger enemy, they withdraw when he advances; harass him when he stops; strike him when he is weary; pursue him when he withdraws. . . . Fight when you can win, move away when you can't."[55] Historically, guerrilla warfare has been the preferred mode of warfare to suit basically two purposes: as a means for an unquestionably inferior force to resist a superior opponent (as in the case of small wars), or as an adjunct to larger regular forces (such as the relationship between John Singleton Mosby's Rangers and Robert E. Lee's Army of Northern Virginia during the American Civil War). For the guerrilla, pitched battle is avoided unless the outcome is certain to be in his favor. Guerrilla warfare is a legal form of combat if certain conventions are followed, such as wearing a uniform and abiding by international law regarding what is and is not permitted in war.[56] In contrast, terrorism is, by definition, a criminal act and therefore always illegal. Guerrillas often use terror, but they are not "terrorists" except in the broadest sense of the term.

Regrettably, the term "guerrilla warfare" is often used interchangeably with "rebellion," "resistance," and "insurgency." But these terms do not mean the same thing. As already noted, guerrilla warfare is a tactic and can be employed by regular and irregular forces alike. Rebellion is a behavior. Robin Hood did not seek to overthrow the English Crown; he was simply in rebellion against Prince John and the Sherriff of Nottingham. Teenagers often rebel against their parents, and peasants rebel against their landlords and constituted authority. But as Mao understood, rebellions usually fail owing to the absence of a unifying political goal, poor organization, inadequate leadership, and a lack of human and material resources. Resistance is an act against an outsider, such as the Hebrews' resistance to Roman occupation. The Jewish people did not seek to overthrow the Roman Empire; they simply wanted to expel the Romans from their lands. The same can be said about Native Americans, whose goal was not the overthrow of the US government but the extirpation of white settlers. They both employed guerrilla warfare, but neither example constituted insurgency, which is armed political violence. At the core of insurgency is a political motive (the acquisition of political power) and the use of a variety of tools (terror, guerrilla warfare, political and labor organizations) to achieve a change in the status quo, whether to overthrow the status quo (an "offensive" insurgency) or to separate from the status quo (a "defensive" insurgency in the sense of irredentism). Insurgency manifests the mobilization of a mass base of popular support with which to establish a counterstate (or "shadow government") to challenge the state for political power. The American Revolution is therefore more accurately described as a war for independence, a defensive insurgency, whereas the French Revolution was an offensive insurgency. Likewise, the Communist Party of the Philippines and its armed wing, the New People's Army, is an offensive insurgency with the intent to overthrow the Filipino government. In contrast, the Moro National Liberation Front pursued (for a time) a defensive insurgency with the intent to remove the island of Mindanao (and others) from the Republic of the Philippines. It was a secessionist movement not unlike the Confederate States of America (another defensive insurgency).

"Revolution" is the fundamental overturning of something, whether it be a revolution in military affairs or a political revolution. What marks a political revolution is the role of ideology. As the *Small Wars Manual* notes, "The outward events of revolutions are always a consequence of changes, often unobserved, which have gone slowly forward in men's minds. Any profound understanding of a revolution necessitates a knowledge of the mental soil in which the ideas that direct its course have to germinate."[57] With this in mind, the American War of Independence was arguably not revolutionary at all, given that the colonists sought to retain their existing social, economic, and political structures while separating from the British Empire. However, the French Revolution was intended to result, and did result, in profound social, economic, and political changes. Thus, "revolutionary warfare" is insurgency with the intent to achieve a revolution.

An important point to keep in mind when considering the above terms (and others not covered here, such as the distinction between "terror" and "terrorism," the former being a tool and the latter being a form of armed political communication in which substate actors attack the innocent to make political demands) is the relationship between the leaders and followers of a "movement" (insurgency, resistance, and so forth). As James Scott brilliantly pointed out in his 1979 essay "Revolution in the Revolution," one "cannot necessarily assume a consensus of beliefs merely from the joint participation of elites and nonelites in the same movement. . . . The project of revolutionaries may have very little or nothing to do with why men rebel."[58] Scott goes on to say: "It is by no means clear that all or even most of the participants in vast popular movements share the ideas which motivate their erstwhile leaders. . . . Within most rebellions . . . one will find both the ideas which may justify the label 'nationalist' or 'communist' *and* a popular revolt with quite divergent visions of order and justice which threatens to usurp the rebellion for its parochial ends."[59]

The key point is that although we may refer to "revolution" in Haiti, the Dominican Republic, or Nicaragua at the beginning of the twentieth century, the leaders and followers may not have had the same goals as the rank and file. As Scott writes:

> At the level of ideas it may be reflected in local demands for subsistence, land, and autonomy versus elite demands for nationalist rule or a planned socialist economy. . . . At the level of organization it may be reflected in the classic peasant forms of struggle—banditry, secret societies, and millennial movements—versus elite efforts to create a secular, centralized, disciplined party bureaucracy. . . . At the level of tactics it may be reflected in peasant desires for immediate justice through attacks on landlords, moneylenders and officials versus elite attempts to develop a long-term strategy bringing together a winning team at the national level.[60]

In short, when we speak of the Haitian revolution or the Sandino rebellion, we are describing, in shorthand fashion, something that is more complex than the term implies and ascribing to it a certain coherence of ideas and unity of organization that do not exist.

Thus, the extant government or occupier must understand what motivates guerrillas (rebels, bandits, what have you)—both the leaders and the followers. The leaders may wish for fundamental political transformation (say, from monarchy to communism), but the followers may simply wish to be rid of a foreign presence, especially a foreign military presence, which is resistance. As noted earlier, simple rebellion becomes insurgency when it takes on certain characteristics, including mass mobilization and the creation of a counterstate.[61] Sometimes a conflict can exhibit characteristics of rebellion, resistance, and insurgency all at once. Even so, the conduct of war usually takes the form of guerrilla warfare, at least until the forces opposing the status quo believe themselves powerful enough to stand toe-to-toe with government or occupying forces.

Aviation in Small Wars

So where does aviation fit in? That is what the marines were trying to figure out following World War I, and that is the subject of this book. Notably, the *Small Wars Manual* included a full chapter on aviation, something the current Marine Corps doctrinal publication on counterinsurgency does not do (and perhaps for good reason, given that aviation is but one piece of the modern Marine Air Ground Task Force). Suffice it to say here that the Marine Corps concluded, "In order to secure the fullest measure of cooperation between the air and ground forces, it is necessary that each understands the problems of the other,"[62] which is a philosophy that has carried over to today's Marine Corps, in which every marine (including aviators) is a "rifleman."

In the end, as Callwell noted and the Marine Corps understood, it is not the scope or scale of a small war that matters. "The essence of a small war is its purpose and the circumstances surrounding its inception and conduct, the character of either one or all of the opposing forces, and the nature of the operations themselves."[63] In short, the manner of pacification—that is, the design of the campaign—depends on the political objective, and "the military strategy of the campaign and the tactics employed . . . must be adapted to the situation."[64] This proved especially true with aviation. In that regard, "after a study has been made of the people who will oppose the intervention, the strategical plan [that is, the campaign plan] is evolved."[65] According to the *Small Wars Manual,* the campaign goal, in simplest terms, "should always be to restore normal government or give the people better government than they had before."[66] Aviation played a significant role in this mission, and the marines employed their airplanes to that end in a variety of nontraditional ways. And we can learn from that experience.

With all this in mind, the future undoubtedly holds many more instances of rebellion, insurgency, and revolution, along with terrorism, insurrection, civil war, and other forms of internal conflict.[67] The experience of the Marine Corps described in this book provides useful lessons to guide the employment of aviation (indeed, air power) against irregular opponents in small wars. Political and military decision makers need not be experts in the history of small wars to appreciate its distinctive nature and distinguishing characteristics; they need only to counter their ignorance by seeking out and heeding the lessons learned by those with experience in the field, especially the experience of the US Marine Corps between the world wars.

Ignorance is excusable, but failure to seek out wisdom is not.

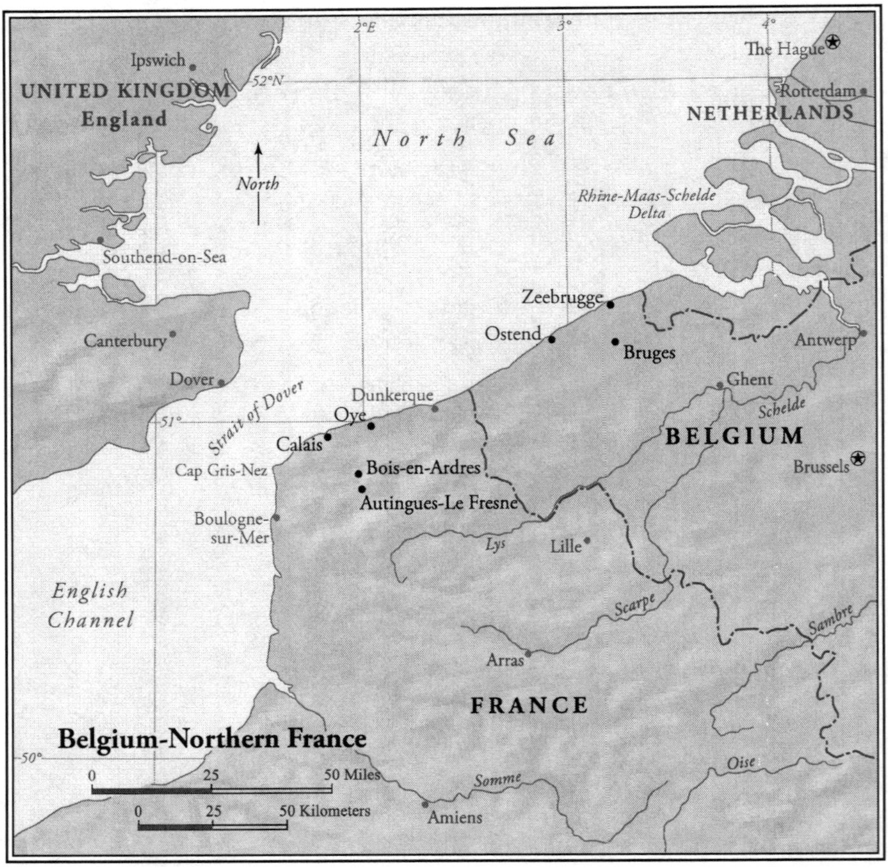

Belgium–northern France. The operational area of the First Marine Aviation Force during World War I. Most air operations took place in the Zeebrugge-Bruges-Ostend triangle. The main flying field was at Autingues–Le Fresne, southeast of Calais.

1

Origins of Marine Corps Aviation

> I was asked if I was willing to try it alone, and said I was. I took off safely and felt confident in the air.
>
> A. A. Cunningham, Marine Aviator No. 1

The first marine to fly solo under official orders was Lieutenant Alfred Austel Cunningham on August 20, 1912, after a little more than two hours of instruction at the Burgess Company and Curtiss aircraft factory in Marblehead, Massachusetts.[1] Six days earlier, Major Smedley Butler (son of Congressman Thomas Butler of Pennsylvania) led marines ashore in Nicaragua in yet another of the seemingly interminable American interventions in Latin America. A few weeks following Cunningham's solo flight, the First Balkan War broke out in Europe, pitting the Balkan League against the Ottoman Empire. Among the members of the league was Greece, which had purchased four French Farman Aviation Works MF-7 airplanes, one of which was converted to a "hydroaeroplane" called the Nautilus, an aircraft we would refer to today as a seaplane. These airplanes performed reconnaissance and bombing missions during the war, the most notable sortie being an attack by the Nautilus on the Ottoman fleet anchored in the Dardanelles—the first naval-air combat mission in history.[2]

The invention of the airplane occurred at an awkward time for the US military because the nation was just beginning to emerge from a long period of public apathy regarding military matters. The Spanish-American War had been but a brief interruption of more than thirty years of peace, discounting efforts to keep the Plains Indians in check. In military circles the most promising technological development of 1903—the year the Wright brothers first flew a motor-driven, heavier-than-air flying machine—was the Springfield rifle.[3] In Europe, however, the situation was far different. European designers quickly took what the Wright brothers had wrought and added innovations of their own, introducing such devices as ailerons for turning.[4] Thus, when Louis Blériot flew across the English Channel in July 1909, the British were made well aware that their "splendid isolation" was over. Three years later the French Deperdussin company constructed a racing plane that featured a "monocoque" wooden fuselage and a rotary piston engine, rendering the Wright planes primitive toys by comparison.[5] By 1913 the French were spending more than $7 million per year on aviation, the Germans some $5 million, Great Britain $3 million, and Italy $2 million. Even Mexico spent more than the United States on aviation.[6]

In the United States, the Wrights first approached the War Department in 1905 but were rebuffed. However, President Theodore Roosevelt took note of the brothers' accomplishment in 1906 when foreign governments expressed serious interest in their machine. The Wrights offered the US government the use of a similar aircraft and instructions on how to fly it for $100,000, which they later reduced to $25,000. The chief of the US Army Signal Corps, Brigadier General James Allen, subsequently issued specifications for a military heavier-than-air craft and solicited additional bids. Forty-one bids were received, but only three complied with the army's specifications; the Wright brothers secured the contract after the other two bidders failed to deliver a machine on the date specified in the solicitation. The Wright army airplane was delivered at Fort Meyer, Virginia, on August 20, 1908. On September 9 US Army Lieutenant Frank Lahm became the first military passenger in an airplane, lifting off from the parade ground at Fort Meyer. Eight days later, Lieutenant Thomas Selfridge, an army officer who had himself designed and flown an experimental aircraft for the Aerial Experiment Association, became the first military aviation fatality when the Wright airplane crashed with Orville Wright at the controls (Wright survived).

In 1909 the Wright brothers delivered an improved machine to the army, the Wright A. Trials continued until the final test flight was conducted on July 30 with Orville Wright at the controls and Lieutenant Benjamin Foulois (a future commander of the Army Air Corps) as an observer and navigator on what has been billed as the first cross-country flight, although they flew only from Fort Meyer to Alexandria, Virginia, a distance of 10 miles. Afterward,

Lieutenants Lahm and Foulois were selected by General Allen to be trained as the first army pilots at the civilian airfield at College Park, Maryland. Foulois, however, was detailed as a delegate to the International Congress of Aeronautics in Nancy, France, and was replaced by Lieutenant Fredric Humphreys of the US Army Corps of Engineers. Humphreys would make the first military solo flight on October 26, 1909.[7]

In 1911 Robert Collier, publisher of *Collier's* magazine, purchased a new Wright Type B airplane and "leased" it to the army for $1 per month so that army aviation would not pass into oblivion. Embarrassed, Congress passed its first appropriation for army aviation that same year: $125,000, a third of what Mexico had spent during its civil war. In December 1913 General Orders 79 designated the facility at North Island near San Diego, California, as the Signal Corps Aviation School, placing it among the army's service schools. At the same time, Congress appropriated $25,000 for the US Navy to purchase airplanes. Thus, US naval aviation was officially born on May 8, 1911, when the navy ordered two Curtiss biplanes.[8] Autonomous Marine Corps aviation would emerge several years later.

The Birth of Marine Corps Aviation

Born in Atlanta, Georgia, on March 8, 1882, A. A. Cunningham became enthralled with the idea of flying when he took a ride in a gas balloon in 1903, the same year Orville and Wilbur Wright made their historic flight at Kitty Hawk, North Carolina. When war broke out with Spain in 1898, sixteen-year-old Cunningham enlisted as a corporal in Company A, Second Georgia Volunteer Infantry. He later transferred to the Third Georgia Infantry, first organized in April 1861 as part of Confederate General Robert E. Lee's Army of Northern Virginia. Cunningham served Stateside during the Spanish-American War and was later sent to Cuba as part of the occupation forces.[9] Mustered out in April 1899, he spent the next ten years selling real estate, during which time he made his balloon ascent and became a "confirmed aeronautical enthusiast."[10] At twenty-seven years of age, Cunningham joined the US Marine Corps, where he hoped to learn to fly, and was appointed a second lieutenant on January 16, 1909.[11] Trained as an infantryman, Cunningham nonetheless visualized the military possibilities of heavier-than-air flight and, in an essay published in 1916, extolled the virtues of aviation, which had "revolutionized tactics in land fighting."[12]

After serving aboard the Delaware-class battleship USS *North Dakota* and several other ships, Cunningham was promoted to first lieutenant on September 29, 1911, and was assigned to Company E of the Advance Base Battalion at the Marine Barracks at the League Island Naval Shipyard in Philadelphia, Pennsylvania. In Philadelphia he found an active community of like-minded aviation enthusiasts, both military and civilian, and began to cultivate an idea regarding aviation in the Marine Corps. But he needed an airplane, so he rented one from a down-on-his-luck pilot for $25 per month (deducted from his monthly pay of $166) and joined the Aero Club of Philadelphia, one of the earliest flying clubs in the United States.[13] He then secured permission from Rear Admiral Albert Grant to use a half-mile strip of land at the north end of the shipyard to fly his airplane and test his ideas. His airplane, nicknamed "Noisy Nan," never actually flew more than a few feet.[14] Nevertheless, Cunningham used his Aero Club connections to advocate for Marine Corps aviation among officials in Washington, including Major General William Biddle, commandant of the Marine Corps and scion of a prominent Philadelphia family. During this time Cunningham volunteered for flight training, and on May 22, 1912—regarded as the birth date of Marine Corps aviation—he was assigned to aviation duty by General Biddle and reported to the US Navy's new flying school near the Naval Academy at Annapolis, Maryland.

The US Navy (USN) first investigated the possibilities of heavier-than-air powered flight when Lieutenant George Sweet, USN, and naval constructor William McIntee were detailed to observe the test of the Wright Flyer for the US Army at Fort Meyer in September 1908. Sweet was scheduled to fly as a passenger that day but yielded to Thomas Selfridge, the earliest US Army flier and an experienced airman. As noted earlier, Selfridge was killed when the propellers fouled the control wires leading to the rudder and the plane crashed. Undeterred, Lieutenant Sweet went on to become the first navy officer in the United States to fly in a heavier-than-air machine. Backed by Rear Admiral William Cowles, brother-in-law of Theodore Roosevelt and chief of the navy's Bureau of Equipment, Sweet convinced the secretary of the navy to acquire, test, and develop airplanes for naval purposes.

In 1910 Captain Washington Irving Chambers, USN, of the Bureau of Equipment attempted to enlist the Wright brothers in a demonstration of their aircraft launching from a US Navy man-of-war.[15] The Wrights declined, whereupon aviation pioneer Glenn Curtiss took up the challenge.[16] On

November 14, 1910, civilian Eugene Ely successfully flew a 50-horsepower (hp) landplane from a specially constructed platform on the bow of the Chester-class scout cruiser USS *Birmingham* at Hampton Roads, Virginia.[17] Convinced of the future of aviation, the navy asked Curtiss to instruct other officers how to fly. At first this was done free of charge, given that no money had been appropriated by Congress for this purpose.[18]

On January 18, 1911, while performing at an air show in San Francisco, California, Ely landed his plane on the armored cruiser USS *Pennsylvania* (the first of its class), and after an overnight stay on the ship, he flew back to shore. That same month, Curtiss and Navy Lieutenant Theodore "Spuds" Ellyson designed and constructed a hydroaeroplane attachment for ships.[19] On January 26 Curtiss landed his personal hydroaeroplane alongside the *Pennsylvania* and was successfully hoisted aboard using the device.[20] Now firmly convinced of the war-fighting possibilities of aviation, the US Navy ordered Lieutenants John Rodgers and John Towers, as well as Ensign Victor Herbster, to undergo flight training.[21] The navy purchased two Curtiss aircraft and one Wright airplane, and in the summer of 1911 the first naval aviation unit was organized at Greenburg Point near the Naval Academy at Annapolis. Although the Aviation Camp was briefly transferred to San Diego, it soon moved back to Annapolis, where tent hangars were constructed fronting the Severn River.[22]

Having secured a place at the US Navy's Aviation Camp, Cunningham, to his undoubted dismay, was promptly sent to sea for temporary duty on the Virginia-class battleship USS *Georgia*. He also served with the Second Regiment, First Provisional Brigade, in the Caribbean. When the *Georgia* returned to Hampton Roads, Cunningham made his way to Maryland and reported to Lieutenant Rodgers. Upon graduation from the Aviation Camp, Cunningham was designated Naval Aviator No. 5 (and, ultimately, Marine Aviator No. 1).[23] The next four marines to attend flight school at the Aviation Camp were Bernard "Barney" Smith (Naval Aviator No. 6),[24] William "Mac" McIlvain (Naval Aviator No. 12),[25] Francis "Cocky" Evans (Naval Aviator No. 26),[26] and Roy "Jiggs" Geiger (Naval Aviator No. 49). Geiger would become one of the most famous Marine Corps aviators in history, perhaps second only to Cunningham.[27]

When Cunningham arrived at the Aviation Camp, all the aircraft used for training had been wrecked the previous winter, and repairs were not yet complete. Thus, his actual in-flight instruction occurred at Marblehead, where he flew a Curtiss pusher-type C-3 F-Boat seaplane.[28] With the pusher configuration, the engine is mounted in the rear of the aircraft with the propellers facing rearward, so the airplane is pushed rather than pulled by an engine in front (known as a "tractor"). Although seemingly relegated to airplanes of an earlier era, many modern types, including the Rutan Long-EZ and several unmanned types such as the MQ-9 Reaper and the Israel Aerospace Industries Heron, are pusher aircraft. In the Curtiss F-Boat, the student and instructor sat side by side in a single cockpit ahead of the wings. The first five navy F-Boats were labeled C-1 through C-5, but in March 1914 they were redesignated AB-1 through AB-5, the letter A designating the manufacturer (Curtiss) and the letter B identifying the airplane as a "flying boat."

Several ABs accompanied the US expedition to Veracruz, Mexico, in 1914, along with an A-3 hydroaeroplane.[29] Carried aboard the battleship USS *Mississippi* (the lead ship of its class), the AB-3 was flown by Navy Lieutenant (Junior Grade) P. N. L. "Pat" Bellinger, who made a twenty-eight-minute reconnaissance flight over Veracruz on April 25.[30] A second, photographic mission was flown on April 28. As a lieutenant commander, Bellinger would later command the famous NC-1 flying boat (N for navy and C for Curtiss) during the navy's first transatlantic flight in 1919. Forced down in fog west of the Azores, Bellinger, Lieutenant Marc "Pete" Mitscher, and the rest of the crew were picked up by a Greek merchant ship before the airplane sank in heavy seas. Bellinger retired as a vice admiral in 1949 and died in May 1962. Lieutenant Mitscher rose to the rank of vice admiral by the end of World War II, commanding the Fast Carrier Task Force during the war. After the war he was promoted to admiral and was serving as commander in chief, US Atlantic Fleet, when he died in Norfolk, Virginia, in 1946.

In January 1913 the schooner-rigged collier USS *Sterling* deposited members of the Aviation Camp at Fisherman's Point in Guantanamo Bay, Cuba, for maneuvers with the fleet. The objective was to demonstrate the utility of aviation in supporting the fleet, thereby stimulating interest among its officers. The pilots had at their disposal a Burgess Company and Curtiss Model K D-1 (D designating Burgess) flying boat, pusher-type Curtiss hydroaeroplanes, and a modified Wright B-1 equipped with a Burgess pontoon and a new Sturtevant engine.[31] Arriving aboard the Florida-class battleship USS *Utah*, Cunningham reported for duty along with fellow pilots Towers, Bellinger, and Herbster. Despite poor weather, the fliers demonstrated several capabilities, including aerial photography, wireless telegraphy, and the dropping of "missiles" from as high as 1,000 feet. Interestingly, the aviators divided themselves according to their machines, with Cunningham and his mechanic known as the Marine Camp, Herbster and Ensign William Billingsley referred to as the Wright Camp, and Marine Lieutenant Bernard Smith as the Curtiss Camp. By February, Lieutenant Towers was reporting to his superiors that he and the aviators had achieved many converts among the sailors.[32] Among the distinguished persons taken aloft for orientation flights were Congressman Lemuel Padgett, chairman of the House Committee on Naval Affairs, and future commandant of the Marine Corps John LeJeune.[33]

The aviators broke camp at Guantanamo Bay in mid-March and had arrived back in Annapolis by the end of the month. Upon his return to Maryland, Cunningham completed the requirements for a certificate as a hydroaeroplane pilot with the Féderation Aéronautique Internationale (FAI) and was awarded FAI Certificate No. 2 by the Aero Club of America. But, having completed his flight instruction, Cunningham requested detachment from flying duty to soothe the fears of his fiancée, Josephine Jefferies, who refused to marry him unless he gave up flying. Cunningham therefore asked to be assigned to the Marine Barracks at the Washington Navy Yard as the post quartermaster. His request approved, it appeared that Cunningham's career as a flier had ended.

In October 1913 Cunningham assumed his duties as post quartermaster at the Navy Yard. However, he continued to advocate for aviation in the Marine Corps, and a month later he received orders to participate on a board chaired by Captain Chambers and "convened for the purpose of drawing up a comprehensive plan for the organization of a naval aeronautics service."[34] Lieutenant Towers was the board's recorder. The Chambers Board met for six days and produced a document that laid the foundation for the expansion of naval aviation, concluding that "adequate sea power cannot be maintained . . . unless adequate superiority is maintained over the whole of aerial development."[35] Based on the recommendations of the board, a Naval Aeronautical Station (later, Naval Air Station) was established at Pensacola, Florida, in 1914. After serving on the Chambers Board, Cunningham returned to his duties as post quartermaster.

But, unwilling to remain permanently grounded, Cunningham soon returned to flying. First, he obtained authorization from the commandant to participate in experiments with a new Burgess Company and Curtiss D-2 flying boat then undergoing alterations at the Navy Yard. Then, apparently with the consent of his bride, Cunningham campaigned to return to flying full-time. In doing so, he secured the assistance of a number of friends, including the politically powerful Congressman Oscar Underwood of Alabama.[36] In April 1915 Cunningham's return to aviation duty was approved, and he was ordered to Pensacola to requalify as a pilot.[37] In the meantime, other developments heralded the emergence of an independent Marine Corps air arm.

In the aftermath of the Spanish-American War, the General Board of the Navy (initially chaired by Admiral George Dewey) concluded that an "advance base force" would be needed to secure and defend navy bases overseas,[38] and in 1901 a four-company battalion of marines was formed at Annapolis and at Newport, Rhode Island. The mission of the Advance Base Force was to secure and defend mobile and fixed bases in support of US Navy operations, and in the beginning the force was to be divided between Philadelphia and Olongapo in the Philippines. A school was created in New London, Connecticut, but was later moved to Philadelphia. At roughly the same time, a Marine Corps recruitment depot was established at Parris Island, South Carolina. The depot at San Diego, California, was opened in 1916, and the facilities at Mare Island, California, were expanded. A 300-man Advance Base Battalion was formed in 1911 at the Marine Barracks in Philadelphia, colocated with the school. The 1,600-man Advance Base Force was organized in 1913. It consisted of the First Advance Base Brigade with the First Regiment (Fixed Defense) and Second Regiment (Mobile Defense), the forebears of Marine Corps regiments today. An aviation section of two officers and ten enlisted men was attached to the headquarters.

When war broke out in Europe in 1914, the Marine Corps concluded that the facilities on the West Coast were adequate, but when the United States declared war on Germany in April 1917, the inadequacy of the Navy Yard in Philadelphia became all too clear. Less than two weeks later, a committee charged by the commandant to find suitable land for quartering, training, and storage recommended a plot of land along the Potomac River near Dumfries, Virginia, known as Quantico.[39] As the camp at Quantico grew, the Marine Corps school in Philadelphia moved there, and since 1917, virtually every Marine Corps officer and many enlisted personnel have received at least part of their education and training at Quantico, known as the "crossroads of the Marine Corps."

As the facility at Quantico was being developed, Mac McIlvain, eleven enlisted men, and a single airplane were organized into the Marine Section,

Navy Flying School, at Pensacola.[40] Cunningham arrived there in May 1915, began his refresher training, and received his navy air pilot certificate in September. It was during his time at Pensacola that Cunningham famously piloted a Curtiss flying boat launched from the quarterdeck (facing aft) of the Tennessee-class armored cruiser USS *North Carolina* while the ship was under way.[41] Unfortunately for Cunningham, the engine failed at takeoff, and the airplane dived off the catapult into the water (some sources claim the catapult itself failed). Because the *North Carolina* was under way at the time, both Cunningham and the airplane were run over by the ship. Cunningham survived but suffered a back injury.[42] The airplane was a total loss.

During the summer of 1915, Secretary of the Navy Josephus Daniels concluded that the advance base concept would require Marine Corps aviators to fly landplanes as well as seaplanes. Consequently, he worked out an agreement with the US Army Signal Corps to train Marine Corps pilots at the Signal Corps Aviation School on North Island. Cunningham applied for training there, reported for flight school in June 1916, and soloed shortly thereafter. That same year he wrote an article for the *Marine Corps Gazette,* arguing for the expansion of naval aviation.[43] Then, on January 30, 1917, the chief of naval operations, Admiral William Benson, wrote to the commandant, Major General George Barnett, requesting that Cunningham "be ordered to proceed to Philadelphia . . . for temporary duty in connection with the establishment of an Aeronautic Advance Base unit at that place."[44]

Upon his arrival, Cunningham quickly set about organizing the unit and recruiting pilots and other personnel. He began with the first wartime class of the Marine Officers School in August 1917. According to twenty-one-year-old college graduate and future lieutenant general Karl Day, Cunningham's speech was not auspicious, but the result was spectacular:

> Major Rixley assembled the battalion and said Captain Cunningham [from] headquarters had a message for us, and introduced Captain Cunningham. Cunningham said, "Uh, uh, gentlemen, the Secretary of the Navy has a.a.a.a.authorized t.t.t.t.the [that's how he got the nickname of Mutter (Mother) Cunningham]. . . ." Anyway, he told us that we were going to have an aviation section, that we would go to France, and that he was down there to talk to anybody who was interested in becoming a pilot. He said, "Anybody who's interested please take two steps forward." And as I say, he might just as well

> have said, "Forward, March!" I think that maybe with the exception of 15 or 20 the whole bloody outfit volunteered.[45]

First Steps: Marine Corps Aviation in World War I

By 1916 the war in Europe had been raging for two years, and many observers, including Cunningham, were certain the United States would become embroiled in the conflict—which occurred formally on April 6, 1917. Yet by that late date, the entire Marine Corps section of naval aviation consisted of only a handful of airplanes, five officers, and thirty enlisted men.[46]

The first airplane acquired by the Marine Corps was a modified Curtiss pusher, a Model E floatplane designated the A-2, then the E-1, and finally the AX-1, delivered to the navy in 1911 and handed over to the marines in 1913.[47] The Model E was a two-seat, open-framed biplane, a waterborne version of the basic Curtiss pusher that had been around since 1909. As a landplane, the airplane had a tricycle undercarriage; as a seaplane, it had a large central pontoon and outriggers under the wings.[48] The navy purchased the seaplane variant, the A-1, and Spuds Ellyson first flew it off Lake Keuka near Hammondsport, New York, on June 30, 1911.[49] As more aircraft were acquired, they were numbered AH-1 through AH-18. The aircraft originally designated A-2 was purchased as a landplane in July 1911; it was converted into a floatplane less than a year later and was then rebuilt as flying boat—the navy's first. It was modified again with retractable landing gear, making it "amphibian,"[50] and redesignated AX-1, whereupon it was handed over to the Marine Corps.[51]

By 1917 there were four seaplanes of the Curtiss type at Pensacola. But with the American declaration of war on the Central Powers, Secretary Daniels realized that if the Advance Base Force deployed to Europe, the Marine Corps would require landplanes in addition to seaplanes. Thus Cunningham was ordered back to the Navy Yard in Philadelphia to form the Marine Aeronautic Company with 34 officers and 330 enlisted men. The company was officially created on April 27, 1917.[52] The pilots and mechanics came from Pensacola, and four other officers arrived from the Marine Corps Reserve Flying Corps, which had been established by Congress alongside the Navy Reserve Flying Corps in 1916. The reserve officers were Lieutenants Allen Boynton (Naval Aviator No. 856), Brock Davey (Naval Aviator No. 534), W. H. Batts (Naval Aviator No. 599), and Edmund Chamberlain (Naval Aviator No. 96½).[53]

The history of the Marine Corps Reserve Flying Corps begins with the establishment of the Marine Corps Reserve, which can trace its roots to the American Civil War. Officially, it came into existence in March 1915, when the Sixty-Third Congress created a Navy Reserve and thus a Marine Corps Reserve. The latter consisted of five classes of personnel: Fleet Marine Corps Reserve, Marine Corps Reserve A, Marine Corps Reserve B, Volunteer Marine Reserve, and Marine Corps Flying Corps.[54] In the absence of sufficient "active-duty" marines and reservists volunteering for flight school (there were only three officers and thirty-two enlisted reservists when war was declared), Cunningham turned to the US Navy for trainees, most of whom agreed to transfer to the Marine Corps because "they could expect to get action sooner."[55]

The precursor to modern Marine Corps tactical air units, the Aeronautic Company at Philadelphia had at its disposal an old Farman trainer, three JN-4 landplanes, two floatplane versions of the JN-4 (the N-9), and two Curtiss R-6 seaplanes.[56] The Curtiss R series was a tractor-type aircraft used as both a landplane and a seaplane and widely employed for scouting, observation, and training. The early navy models were two-seat, twin-float airplanes powered by a 150 hp Curtiss V-X engine. The R-6 used by the marines was an improved version with a 200 hp V-X-X engine, essentially a water-cooled V-8. The final version, the R-6 (L), had a Liberty V-12 engine that could produce between 360 and 400 hp. The R-6 was the first US-built aircraft to serve overseas in World War I, and the Liberty engine was America's most significant technological contribution to the Allied war effort. Conceived by two engineers from the Packard and Hall-Scott Motor Companies, the Liberty was designed with mass manufacture in mind. The eight-cylinder version first appeared in August 1917 and was rated at 270 hp, but the engine had significant teething problems and only fifteen were built. The air-cooled 400 hp V-12 that followed was one of the most powerful engines of the war, and some 20,000 were produced before the armistice.[57]

Once the United States was formally involved in the war in Europe, the Marine Corps rapidly expanded from a little over 500 officers and 13,000 enlisted men in April 1917 to more than 2,000 officers and some 70,000 enlisted personnel by November 1918.[58] Major General Barnett moved quickly to organize a brigade of marines to send to France and launched an aggressive effort to build up Marine Corps aviation to support the brigade.[59] Although lacking an official title, now-Captain Cunningham became the de facto head of Marine Corps aviation, charged with recruiting pilots, skilled mechanics, and other important specialists. Reflecting later on this period of rapid growth, Major General Ford O. "Tex" Rogers declared: "Cunningham was the father of [Marine Corps] aviation. . . . Without him, there never would have been any aviation."[60]

On October 12, 1917, the Aeronautic Company at Philadelphia was divided into the First Aviation Squadron, consisting of 24 officers and 237 enlisted men, and the First Aeronautic Company, consisting of 10 officers and 73 enlisted men. The First Aeronautic Company would fly seaplanes, and the First Aviation Squadron would fly landplanes. At the same time, to make room for the newly approved Naval Aircraft Factory at Philadelphia,[61] the First Aeronautic Company, now commanded by Captain Cocky Evans, was moved to Cape May, New Jersey. By then the unit had acquired two R-6 seaplanes, converted for use as a torpedo bomber in addition to training and scouting. The First Aviation Squadron, under the command of now-Captain McIlvain, moved to Hazelhurst Field in Mineola, Long Island, New York (renamed Roosevelt Field after the war).[62] But owing to poor weather there (described as "howling winds and rain which swept in from the ocean"), the squadron soon moved to the US Army's Gerstner Field near Lake Charles, Louisiana.[63]

As Marine Corps aviation expanded, a vigorous effort was launched to find the right men to pilot the airplanes as well as maintain them on the ground. Cunningham traveled to Quantico to seek good candidates for flight training from among the freshly minted second lieutenants arriving there. He found plenty of volunteers, many of whom would become icons of Marine Corps aviation. Some were drawn to the challenge and glamour of flying; others, like Lieutenant Lawson "Sandy" Sanderson, had other motives: "Well, hell," he recalled later, "I thought I can ride better than I can walk. So I volunteered for aviation. . . . I had only seen about two airplanes in my life, but I'd rather ride than walk."[64] Out of dozens of volunteers who came forward during that first visit, only eighteen were selected, and only six were sent to Miami, Florida, for flight school.

On December 7 the First Aeronautic Company was ordered to Naval Base 13, Ponta Delgada, on the island of Sao Miguel in the Azores, some 930 miles west of Lisbon, Portugal. The company deployed aboard the transport USS *Hancock* with a full complement of seaplanes: ten R-6 floatplanes, two N-9 floatplanes, and six HS-1 flying boats.[65]

The R-6 has already been described. The Curtiss N-9 was a primary and advanced seaplane trainer originally powered by a 100 hp Curtiss O-X-X-6 engine, an early water-cooled V-8. A derivative of the famous Jenny landplane, the N-9 had a longer wingspan to compensate for the added weight of its large centerline float. It was widely believed at the time that a seaplane like the N-9 could not be looped.[66] But on February 13, 1918, Cocky Evans looped his Pensacola-based N-9 from 3,000 feet and then safely recovered the airplane.[67] Before World War I the N-9 had proved to be a satisfactory trainer, but greater performance was required once the United States entered the war. Consequently, the Curtiss engine was replaced with a Spanish-designed 150 hp Hispano-Suiza Model A engine, which was then being manufactured in the United States under license to the Wright-Martin Company. The improved model was designated the N-9H. The HS-1, another Curtiss aircraft, was a single-engine pusher-type flying boat, a smaller version of the earlier twin-engine H model (HS stood for H, single engine). The original power plant was a 200 hp Curtiss V-X-X water-cooled V-8, but in late 1917 the HS-1 was married to the new Liberty V-12. The HS-1L (L for Liberty) became the navy's standard coastal patrol flying boat during the war.

Arriving in the Azores in January 1918, the First Aeronautic Company has the distinction of being the first fully fledged American aviation unit of any branch to deploy overseas during World War I. However, despite its auspicious beginnings, the First Aeronautic Company spent the war patrolling the mostly empty waters around the Azores, and its only official combat action occurred in September. An R-6 piloted by Lieutenant Walter Poague sighted a German U-boat on the surface and dropped a single bomb, which missed the submarine and failed to explode. Lieutenant Poague and his observer then watched helplessly as the submarine leisurely submerged, disappearing from sight.[68] Less than a year later, Poague would drown when his airplane crashed into the ocean while on patrol.[69] Poague's death highlighted the danger of over-water flight even in the absence of combat. According to one veteran's account: "Those who served in the Azores remember towing back to the base a few ships that were forced to land at sea because of gasoline shortage or mechanical trouble [and recalled] the thrill of guessing whether the gasoline in the ship was sufficient to get back to the base."[70] In July 1918 half the company was withdrawn from the Azores to train new pilots in the United States, at which point Cocky Evans was succeeded by Captain David "Ditty Box" Brewster (Naval Aviator No. 99).

When the First Aeronautic Company began operations in the Azores, Captain Cunningham was sent to France aboard the transport and former passenger liner USS *Saint Paul* to inspect the front and make recommendations regarding the employment of Marine Corps aviation in support of the Allied effort.[71] Although the voyage was uneventful, Cunningham stood lookout for submarines and spotted for two of the ship's forward defense guns. During his time in France, Cunningham strove to convince the staff of the American Expeditionary Force to attach aircraft to the Marine Corps brigade raised for duty there. But army officials denied his request, stating that if the squadron ever got to France, it would be used for training purposes.[72] Thus, upon his return to the United States, Cunningham reported to the General Board of the Navy, which included Admiral George Dewey, the hero of Manila Bay and a strong proponent of aviation, that the Marine Corps should perform a special antisubmarine mission. Cunningham described this mission in a 1920 *Marine Corps Gazette* article as daylight attacks launched from Dunkirk, France, against German submarine bases at Ostend, Zeebruge, and Bruges, all along the Belgian coast.[73] The board approved the idea, and Captain Roy Geiger was selected to organize and prepare a force for this mission.

In February 1918 Geiger, some forty officers and enlisted men, two R-6 seaplanes, and a single Farman trainer were loaded aboard a special train with "Forty and Eight parlor cars" and transported to Miami, where they initially set up shop at the Naval Air Station at Dinner Key, then under the command of Navy Lieutenant Commander Albert "Pee-Wee" Read.[74] Flying operations began at a Curtiss school on the outskirts of Miami, on the edge of the Everglades. The marines took over the Curtiss facilities and acquired several "stick-controlled" and "Deperdussin system–controlled" JN-4 Jennies from the former Curtiss school. In the Jenny's original design, a wheel worked the rudder, a shoulder yoke operated the ailerons, and the elevators were controlled by moving the control column fore and aft. The JN-3 replaced the original controls with the Deperdussin control system, in which a wheel operated the ailerons and a rudder bar operated the rudder. JN-3s built in Canada, however, replaced the Deperdussin system with a stick control, known as the JN-4C Canuck. At Mineola, the marines had learned to fly wheel-controlled JN-4Bs, but they encountered Canuck Jennies at Gerstner Field in Louisiana. In June 1917 the Curtiss Company offered a new design in the United States, the JN-4D, which replaced the Deperdussin controls with stick controls. This is the aircraft most often thought of as the "true" Jenny. Serving unofficially as the first "director" of Marine Corps aviation in Washington, Cunningham was able to acquire twenty almost new JN-4H Jennies from the US Army for the Miami-based marines, each equipped with the more powerful 150 hp Hispano-Suiza engine.[75]

The Curtiss Jenny is one of the most famous airplanes in aviation history. In addition to being the most widely used trainer in the US and Canadian armed forces during World War I, the Jenny became well known after the war as a barnstorming airplane. Barnstorming was a popular form of entertainment in the 1920s in which pilots performed various aerial stunts, either individually or in groups known as "flying circuses." Lone pilots also traveled around the country selling airplane rides, usually from some farmer's field. The design of the Jenny originated with a British engineer hired by Glenn Curtiss to produce a tractor-type trainer to succeed his pusher aircraft, which were becoming obsolete. The first design was the Model J, built in Hammondsport. The Model N soon followed; this was later developed into the N-9 seaplane described earlier. The Model J was discontinued, but the Curtiss Company combined the best features of the J and N into a single airplane, the JN, hence the name Jenny.

The development of the Jenny progressed from the JN-1 to the JN-4. Only eleven of the earliest models, the JN-1 and JN-2, were built. The first JN-3s were purchased by the British. The US Army also purchased eight JN-3s in 1916, and these were assigned to the First Aero Squadron at Fort Sam Houston in San Antonio, Texas. The 90 hp JN-3 had a top speed of less than 80 miles per hour and, with a crew of two, could reach a maximum altitude of only 10,000 feet. The airplane was a good trainer but proved woefully inadequate as a combat platform when the First Aero Squadron deployed in the spring of 1916 to support Brigadier General John Pershing's punitive expedition against the Mexican revolutionary guerrilla Francisco "Pancho" Villa. The JN-3 was modified in 1916 to improve its performance and was redesignated the JN-4, but the improvement was only marginal. The Jennies acquired by Cunningham, however, were the much improved JN-4H with Hispano-Suiza engines built by the Wright-Martin Company. In addition to flying faster, higher, and farther, these aircraft were equipped with machine guns and bomb racks for advanced training, having earlier been assigned to various specialized training units in the US Army.

On April 1, 1918, the First Aviation Squadron moved to Miami from Louisiana. Awaiting them at Coconut Grove outside Miami was a tiny detachment of flying marines under the command of Captain Geiger. Geiger and his men had broken away from the Naval Air Station, then commanded by Lieutenant Pete Mitscher, who would fly the Curtiss-built NC-1 on an ill-fated transatlantic flight in 1919.[76] The Marine Corps detachment initially consisted of Geiger and Lieutenants Douglas Roben and Arthur Page Jr., but they were soon augmented by more than a dozen recently commissioned second lieutenants. Upon the arrival of the First Aviation Squadron, the two units merged and, along with the First Aeronautic Company, became the First Marine Aviation Force on April 15, 1918. Captain Cunningham arrived from Washington to take command, after which four squadrons and a headquarters company were established, and the Coconut Grove facility officially became the Marine Flying Field, the first in Marine Corps history. By June 1918 the Marine Flying Field would boast seven JN-4s, six JN-4Bs, thirty JN-4Hs, twenty-two JN-4HGs, four DH-4s, and ten S-4Bs.[77]

The First Marine Aviation Force can be considered the forerunner of today's Marine Aircraft Group, the equivalent of a regiment, given that it contained multiple subordinate elements. At first the squadrons were designated First through Fourth, but for reasons that remain obscure, these designations were changed to A through D. As the senior Marine Corps officer present, second only to Cunningham, Captain Geiger took command of Squadron A. Captain McIlvain assumed command of Squadron B, and Squadrons C and D were commanded by now-Captain Douglas Roben and First Lieutenant Russell Presley, respectively.[78] Rounding out the First Marine Aviation Force was a Balloon Company, formed at Quantico in late June 1918 and commanded by Captain Page, the first Naval Academy graduate to volunteer for aviation duty with the Marine Corps. Later known as the Balloon Detachment, this unique outfit began with two kite balloons and two *caquot* ("free") balloons and was tasked with supporting the Marine Heavy Artillery Force (Tenth Regiment) then at Quantico by providing aerial observation and "spotting" for marine gunners.[79] The permanent presence of Marine Corps aviation at Quantico dates from the activation of the Balloon Company there.[80]

By this time, the marines had fully taken over the Curtiss facilities in Miami and commissioned the civilian instructors into the Marine Corps Reserve. Leaving Geiger in charge there, Cunningham returned to Quantico, where he recruited six more new lieutenants. According to one account, Captain Cunningham asked but one question during the interview: "Why do you want to fly?"[81] He then toured the naval air stations in southern and northwestern Florida, where he recruited qualified navy officers to transfer to the marines. Of 135 Marine Corps aviators who flew in France during World War I, 70 were former navy officers.[82] Skilled mechanics, carpenters, electricians, and other enlisted specialists also swelled the ranks, and an aggressive schedule of training got under way, including aerobatics, formation flying, gunnery, bombing, and reconnaissance.[83]

Some of the student pilots had never been in an airplane, and the ground school was rudimentary at best. According to Lieutenant Kenneth Collings (Naval Aviator No. 776), a writer and soldier of fortune in the best tradition of the fictional character Indiana Jones,[84] his entire introduction to flying before he took to the air was the following:

> "All of you mugs listen and get this the first time," said Burly. Words rolled off his tongue: "You push this stick forward to lower the nose. You pull it back to raise it. You shove it to the right to drop your right wing, to the left to drop your left wing. That bar down there is your rudder. You can't get balled up on *that* because it works just like steering a sled or the handlebar on a bicycle—only backward.
>
> "This gadget here is the throttle, and that's all you need to know about your motor. If you[r] motor is OK, when you crack your throttle, it will run; if it doesn't, get a mechanic to fix it—*if* you are on the ground, that is. If you are in the air, you can't fix it until you land anyway. If you get down alive, there'll be plenty of grease balls to fix it; if you don't get down alive, you won't care whether it's ever fixed."
>
> I was puzzled. "Sir," I said to Lieutenant Davey, "do-don't we get any ground school *at all*?"
>
> Davey flicked his cigarette butt away and froze me with a glance. "Ground school? Ground school? Weren't you listening to Lieutenant Burlingame, man? You've just finished ground school."[85]

To accommodate the possibility of "pursuit" flying in France—that is, flying fighter aircraft—marine pilots at Miami also trained at army airfields in the army's E-1 pursuit trainer, powered by a 100 hp Gnome rotary engine and built by the Standard Aircraft Company of Elizabeth, New Jersey. Some of these US Army–trained Marine Corps pilots flew with the army in France and wore army wings before joining their brother marines upon their arrival.

They were not qualified for naval aviator wings, however, because they lacked the required three hours of flight time piloting a seaplane.[86] In addition to training in the E-1, the marines acquired several 80 hp Le Rhône–engined S4-B Thomas-Morse Scouts (more commonly known as the Tommy or Tommy-Morse), built in Bath, New York.[87] Although slated to be a landplane unit, the marine fliers at Miami also trained in a variety of seaplanes to qualify as naval aviators.[88] As training ramped up, the Marine Flying Field was described as a "madhouse," with the marines working from dawn to dark.[89] Accidents were common. Before the squadrons departed for France, four officers and three enlisted men were killed in crashes, and one student pilot flew an old F-Boat into a seawall.[90]

On July 13, 1918, the men of the First Marine Aviation Force, less Squadron D, left New York City aboard the transport USS *Dekalb,* a former German mail ship and auxiliary cruiser interned upon US entry into the war. The *Dekalb* arrived off Brest, France, on July 30, and three days later Cunningham procured a French freight train to transport the marines to Calais, detraining on August 5. Twenty-three days later Cunningham was promoted to the temporary rank of major. During that time the marines constructed "aerodromes" at Oye, a small seaside town about 4 miles east of Calais, for Squadrons A and B and at Le Fresne (Fresnes-lès-Montauban), about 7 miles southwest of Calais in the Hauts-de-France region, for Squadron C. Cunningham located his headquarters at the small hamlet of Bois en Ardes, some 12 miles southeast of Calais, where the town's mayor presented the new wing's colors to its commander.[91] Two supply bases were established at Paulliac and Eastleigh in southern England. Squadron D left the United States in September and arrived at Le Fresne on October 5.[92] Strangely, during transit, the squadrons' designations were changed back to First, Second, Third, and Fourth Squadrons, but by the time they settled in at their airfields in France, they had become the Seventh, Eighth, Ninth, and Tenth Squadrons, the first six numbers being reserved for US Navy squadrons.[93] The Seventh and Eighth Squadrons were based at Oye, and the Ninth and Tenth Squadrons at Le Fresne. The four Marine Corps squadrons were now officially part of the Day Wing, Northern Bombing Group, US Naval Forces Operating in European Waters, British Expeditionary Forces.[94]

Before their departure for France, there had been considerable debate about the exact nature of the marine squadrons' mission, from aerial fighting to bombing German U-boats in the shallow waters off the coast of Belgium.[95]

Ultimately, bombardment became the mission, and the plan was to link a force of six Marine Corps squadrons with six US Navy squadrons in France to bomb the submarine pens in the Ostend-Zeebruge-Bruges triangle. This joint force became known as the Northern Bombing Group.[96] The Day Wing comprised the Marine Corps squadrons, equipped with British-designed DH-4 bombers. The six US Navy squadrons constituted the Night Wing and would operate Italian-built multiengine Caproni Ca 5 bombers. Unfortunately, there simply were not enough men and machines for six marine squadrons, and production of Caproni bombers was insufficient to equip six navy squadrons. Moreover, the Capronis that were delivered had poorly designed Fiat engines and were mostly unserviceable. Of the seventeen that set out from Italy to the base in Saint Inglevert, France, only eight survived the ferry flight, and the Night Wing conducted only one raid with one airplane.[97]

Prior to deployment, Cunningham procured seventy-two American-built DH-4 bombers from the US Army and had them shipped to France. The airplanes arrived at about the same time as the first three squadrons, but owing to delays in assembly and possible sabotage, the first airplane did not reach the squadrons until September 7.[98] For a variety of reasons, including warped wings, most of the airplanes had to be shipped to Paulliac and Eastleigh in the United Kingdom to be rebuilt. Eager to get in the fight, Cunningham struck a deal with the British, who had a surplus of airframes for the new DH-9 (an improved DH-4), sans engines. Serendipitously, the Americans had a surplus of the new Liberty V-12 engines. With Navy Department approval, Cunningham agreed to deliver three engines to the British in exchange for one complete aircraft. By this bargain, Cunningham was able to build a force of thirty-eight aircraft, a little more than half the original planned strength. Of these, twenty were British DH-9s with American Liberty engines, and the remainder were army-supplied DH-4s.[99]

The two-seat De Havilland (DH)-4 was designed by Geoffrey de Havilland for the British Aircraft Manufacturing Company, or Airco, established in 1912. It first flew in August 1916 and entered service with the British Army Royal Flying Corps in March 1917. Several different engines were tried, the best of which was arguably the 380 hp Rolls-Royce Eagle VIII. The DH-4 was an open-cockpit, all-wood, tractor-type biplane that could carry 460 pounds of bombs fitted to external racks. A single synchronized Vickers machine gun was installed in the nose of the airplane, and the observer-gunner behind the pilot was armed with one or two .303-inch Lewis machine guns mounted in a Scarff ring.[100] The design's biggest drawback was the placement of the fuel tank between the pilot's and observer's cockpits; this solved center-of-gravity issues for the designer, but even in a minor crash, the pilot would be crushed by the fuel tank. Moreover, the widely separated cockpits made communication between the pilot and observer very difficult. Worse, the pressurized fuel tank had a tendency to explode when hit by enemy bullets, and a rubber fuel line under the exhaust manifold produced in-flight fires. For this reason, the DH-4 was known as the "Flaming Coffin."[101] Nevertheless, the DH-4 was a reliable airplane and served with distinction throughout the war.

The DH-4 Liberty was an American-made adaptation of the British design. Instead of the Rolls-Royce engine, the DH-4 Liberty was equipped with the 400 hp Liberty V-12, which was only slightly inferior in performance compared with the Rolls-Royce. Early problems resulting from the marriage of the Liberty engine to the DH-4 airframe were ultimately overcome, and more than 4,000 American-made DH-4s were produced, mainly by the Dayton-Wright Company, which had been formed in 1917 upon the declaration of war against Germany. These were the airplanes Cunningham procured before the squadrons in Miami shipped out. Depending on the variant, the DH-4 had a ceiling between 14,000 and 20,000 feet, a top speed at sea level of greater than 120 miles per hour, and a range between 250 and 550 statute miles. One particular model, the DH-4B, was completely covered with plywood rather than the fabric used on early machines, and the DH-4B-1 had an enlarged fuel tank. Of significance to the marines following World War I, the DH-4M (M for "modernized") had a welded steel-tubed fuselage. The navy purchased thirty of these aircraft for the marines, and they were manufactured by the Boeing Airplane Company using a new arc-welding process. The Boeing aircraft were designated DH-4M1 to distinguish them from later Atlantic-Fokker DH-4M2s, manufactured with a gas-welded fuselage. Many of the DH-4M1s saw service in the small conflicts between the world wars and were given a new designation, 02B-1, to identify them as observation aircraft manufactured by Boeing. Nevertheless, the 02B-1 was virtually indistinguishable from the DH-4B.

As noted earlier, the DH-4 was a dangerous airplane to crash-land—an all-too-frequent occurrence—owing to the location of its fuel tank. Therefore, Airco produced the DH-9 to replace the DH-4. The DH-9 used the wings and tail of the DH-4 but had a redesigned fuselage, relocating the fuel tank aft of the engine and incorporating a wind-driven fuel pump. This arrangement made the DH-9 a much safer airplane to land; it also enabled the pilot and the observer to sit closer to each other. Externally the DH-9 resembled the DH-4, but the DH-9 was powered by the Beardmore-Halford-Pullinger / Galloway-Adriatic six-cylinder engine, which could be mass produced and, the British hoped, would enable the DH-9 to hold its own against German fighters. However, the engine failed to produce the expected horsepower, and the DH-9's performance was actually worse than that of the airplane it was designed to replace. The DH-9 also featured a radiator slung beneath the fuselage that could be lowered into the airstream to cool the engine. This proved unwise, as German fighters attacking from below often holed the radiator, causing the engine to seize.[102] Unfortunately, these and other shortcomings did not become obvious until the airplane was already in full-scale production.

The DH-9s fitted with Liberty V-12 engines were designated the DH-9A, dubbed by the British the "Ninak." The DH-4s acquired from the US Army were numbered D-1 through D-17, and the British-built DH-9As were numbered E-1 through E-21.[103] The latter flew with American roundels painted over the British markings on the wings, and the fuselage roundel was painted over and replaced by station markings. The DH-4s would become the mainstay of Marine Corps aviation following World War I, and many would see service in Haiti, the Dominican Republic, and Nicaragua. Late in 1918 the US Army and US Navy ordered an American-built version of the DH-9A, the USD-9A, but only a handful of prototypes were produced, and the order was canceled at the war's end.

In the short time the First Marine Aviation Force served in France, it carved out a commendable record and a number of firsts. After being brought up to its full strength of 149 officers and 842 enlisted men, the original plan to bomb the submarine pens was shelved when the Germans abandoned the area. Therefore, the Day Wing of the Northern Bombing Group operated alongside its British counterpart in support of British and Belgian ground forces. Now under the command of a US Navy officer, Captain David Hanrahan, the marine crews were assigned to fly with No. 218 Squadron and No. 217 Squadron of the newly independent Royal Air Force.[104] Upon completion of their combat training, the marines were supposed to return to their own units, but the arrangement was so successful that the marine aviators continued to fly combat missions with the two British squadrons. During a bombing mission on September 28, 1918, Lieutenant Everett Brewster and Gunnery Sergeant Harry Wersheiner scored the marines' first aerial victory. Although both men were badly wounded when attacked by German fighters over Courtemarke, Belgium, they managed to shoot down a German Albatross fighter. The next day Captain Francis "Pat" Mulcahy and his observer, Corporal Thomas McCullough, shot down a German Fokker D.VII fighter over Courtemarke. Unfortunately, that same day Second Lieutenant Chapin Barr died of wounds he had received on the twenty-eighth.

One week later, three marine aircrews participated in a dramatic aerial resupply operation. Second Lieutenant Frank Nelms Jr. and his observer, Gunnery Sergeant Archie Paschal; Captain Robert Lytle and his observer, Gunnery Sergeant Amil Winman; and Captain Mulcahy and his observer, Corporal McCullough, dropped more than 2,600 pounds of food and other supplies to a besieged French regiment near Stadenburg, Belgium, that had been cut off. The three pilots received the Navy Distinguished Service Medal, and the enlisted men were awarded the Navy Cross.[105] Nelms would later be interned by the Dutch when the engine of his airplane failed and he drifted across the frontier and crash-landed. Mulcahy would continue to make a name for himself following the war, flying missions over Haiti, commanding aircraft squadrons in Nicaragua from 1931 to 1933, and commanding the "Cactus Air Force" and the Second Marine Air Wing on Guadalcanal during World War II.[106]

By October 1918 the marine squadrons of the Day Wing had received sufficient DH-4s and DH-9As to start flying their own missions independent of the British. On October 14 perhaps the war's most famous action involving marine aviators occurred when five DH-4s and three DH-9As of the Ninth Squadron, led by Captain Lytle, raided a German-held rail yard at Thielt, Belgium. Homeward bound, they were attacked by twelve German fighters: eight Fokker D.VIIs and four Pfalz D.IIIs. The Germans, following their usual tactic, singled out one of the DH-4s and separated it from the others. The observer, Gunnery Sergeant Robert Robinson, managed to shoot down one of the German airplanes before being wounded in the elbow. Despite his injury, Robinson was able to clear a jammed machine gun and fight off the other Germans while his pilot, Lieutenant Ralph Talbot (a former navy officer and Naval Aviator No. 456), maneuvered furiously. Robinson was hit twice more, taking one bullet in the stomach and another in a thigh, and lapsed into unconsciousness. By this time, however, Talbot had gained an advantage over one of the German aircraft and shot it down with his fixed, forward-firing machine guns (American DH-4s had two forward-firing guns), after which he entered into a steep dive to escape the remaining Germans. Leveling off somewhere around 50 feet, Talbot crossed over Allied lines and landed safely at Hondschoote on the French side of the Franco-Belgian frontier, just inland from the North Sea. Robinson recovered, and both he and Talbot received the Medal of Honor. Regrettably, Lieutenant Talbot was killed a few days later while carrying out an engine test on another DH-4. The engine failed on takeoff, and the airplane plunged into an embankment, bursting into flames when it hit the ground. Talbot's observer, Lieutenant Colgate Darden Jr., was thrown clear of the airplane and survived; he later became the governor of Virginia and president of the University of Virginia in the 1940s.[107]

As Talbot and Robinson fought for their lives, Captain Lytle sought to come to their aid. Maneuvering to intervene in the fight, Lytle's engine suddenly quit. In a long, sloping descent, Lytle was able to land his DH-4B in the midst of heavy German antiaircraft fire in front of the Yser defensive line near Pervijze, West Flanders, Belgium. Captain Lytle and his observer quickly scrambled out of the airplane and, with the help of a group of Belgian soldiers, managed to manhandle the airplane tail first into a shell crater, out of the line of sight of German positions. Then they ran to a dugout in the Belgian lines as German artillery took aim at them. Lytle used a field phone to call his squadron and request that mechanics be sent to retrieve the disabled DH-4. A motor convoy arrived on the morning of October 15, and the mechanics made their way to the crater and disassembled the airplane, returning it to friendly lines piece by piece. Belgian soldiers assisted with the largest portion, the fuselage, employing a section of narrow-gauge railway used to haul supplies to the front.[108] The disassembled airplane was then loaded onto a truck and trailer, at which point German artillery fire started again (surprisingly, the Germans had not shot at the marines all day). Under cover of darkness the convoy managed to escape to Pervijze and then returned to Le Fresne without incident. In the end, however, the airplane was not repaired; its parts were cannibalized for other airplanes.[109]

For the next several weeks, flying without escort, Marine Corps DH-4s and DH-9As bombed German targets at Bruges, in the Flemish region of Belgium, as well as at Eecloo, Ghent, Lokeren, and Deinze in East Flanders. Between their arrival in France in August and their departure in November 1918, marine aircrews took part in forty-three combat missions with the British and carried out fourteen raids of their own. The tonnage of bombs they dropped is difficult to determine, but depending on the source and the means of measurement, it was somewhere between 27,000 and 52,000 pounds of bombs.[110] The number of enemy aircraft the marines shot down is equally difficult to pinpoint, ranging from a low of four to a high of twelve.[111] Only one Marine Corps aircraft was shot down during the war. This occurred on October 22, when seven German fighters separated Lieutenant Harvey Norman and his observer, Lieutenant Caleb Taylor, from the rest of the formation. Their DH-9A was promptly shot down over the Bruges-Ghent canal. According to one account, the Germans circled and machine-gunned the wreckage, which infuriated the marines.[112] In toto, four pilots were killed in combat or died of their wounds, in addition to Lieutenant Talbot, who was killed during a test flight. At least three other officers and thirteen enlisted men died of Spanish influenza, including the highly esteemed commander of Ninth Squadron, Major Roben.[113] On a more positive note, members of the First Marine Aviation Force received thirty awards and decorations, including four Distinguished Service Medals and the Medals of Honor awarded to Talbot and Robinson. More broadly, Marine Corps aviation had expanded from 4 officers, 1 warrant officer, and some 30 enlisted men in April 1917 to 250 officers, 32 warrant officers, and more than 2,000 enlisted men in November 1918.[114]

Marine aviators had proved their worth in war. Now they would have to prove their worth in peace. And yet the Marine Corps had not really been at peace since the turn of the century, intervening in Nicaragua in 1912 and becoming embroiled in two nasty small wars on the island of Hispaniola in the Caribbean. These "savage wars of peace"[115] did not involve marine aviation units until after World War I, but once the First Marine Aviation Force returned home, it was only a matter of time before some of the veterans of France and the Azores would be dispatched to these hot spots. Marine aviators of Squadrons D and E (redesignated as such upon their return to the United States) first deployed to the Dominican Republic. Six Jennies arrived in San Pedro de Macoris in February 1919. At the end of March six more Jennies, six HS-2L flying boats, and a single N-9 floatplane began operations at Port-au-Prince, Haiti. The experience in Haiti would represent the most important proving ground for Marine Corps aviation in the early small-wars era.

Alfred Austel Cunningham, Marine Corps Aviator No. 1 and the father of Marine Corps aviation. He first became enamored with the idea of flight when he took a ride in a gas balloon in 1903, the same year Orville and Wilbur Wright inaugurated motor-driven heavier-than-air flight at Kitty Hawk, North Carolina.

An N-9, the floatplane version of the venerable JN Jenny landplane. Two N-9s, three JN-4s, two Curtiss R-6 seaplanes, and an old Farman trainer constituted the initial complement of the Aeronautic Company at Philadelphia.

The Curtiss R-6 was used by the Marine Corps for training and scouting and as a torpedo bomber. It had a 200-horsepower V-X-X engine, a water-cooled V-8. A later version was equipped with the more powerful Liberty V-12 engine. The R-6 was the first US-built aircraft to serve overseas during World War I.

The flight line at Miami, Florida, including a variety of JN aircraft and tent hangars. As training ramped up during World War I, the Flying Field at Miami was described as a "madhouse," with the marines working from dawn to dark.

Aeronautic Company floatplanes being prepared for reassembly at Naval Base 13, Ponta Delgada, on the island of Sao Miguel in the Azores. The company deployed with ten R-6 floatplanes, two N-9 floatplanes, and six HS-1 flying boats. It was the first full-fledged US military aviation unit to deploy to the war in Europe.

Two R-6 floatplanes at Naval Base 13. The Aeronautic Company spent the war patrolling the mostly empty waters around the Azores. Its only official combat action occurred when an R-6 piloted by Lieutenant Walter Poague dropped a single bomb that missed a German U-boat and failed to explode.

DH-4s at Le Fresne, France. The First Marine Aviation Force can be considered the forerunner of today's Marine Aircraft Group, the equivalent of a regiment, given that it contained multiple subordinate elements.

Marine ground crew servicing a DH-4 in France. Note the Scarff ring surrounding the rear cockpit, which mounted one or two Lewis machine guns. Maintenance of the aircraft by "ship keepers" (also called "mechanicians") was crucial to keep the machines in the air and in the fight.

Bernard "Barney" Smith, Naval Aviator No. 6. Smith flew combat missions with the French air force before US entry into the war, when he was appointed assistant to the US naval attaché. He resigned in 1920 but served in the reserves and was called to active duty during World War II.

William "Mac" McIlvain, Naval Aviator No. 12, commanded Squadron B in France. He was the first marine to receive landplane training at the US Army flying school on North Island near San Diego, California. He resigned from active service in 1921 but served in the reserves until 1948.

Francis "Cocky" Evans, Naval Aviator No. 26, commanded the First Aeronautic Company before World War I and again in China. Following two crashes in 1935, he was grounded and then medically retired in 1937. He was later recalled to active duty in World War II and served until 1944.

Roy Geiger at the controls of a "pusher" seaplane at Pensacola, Florida. Despite crashing an airplane at Pensacola, Geiger came into his own at Miami and commanded Squadron A in France during World War I. Geiger eventually became one of the most famous marine aviators in history, second only to A. A. Cunningham.

A very young looking Ralph Talbot standing before a JN Jenny trainer. Talbot began his military service in the US Navy but transferred to the Marine Corps and received the Medal of Honor for action on October 14, 1918. He later died in a crash while performing an engine check on a DH-4B.

"Gunny" Robert Robinson posing for a formal photo. Robinson was wounded thirteen times while fending off German fighters after the raid on Thielt, Belgium, on October 14, 1918. He received the Medal of Honor and survived the war, serving as a lieutenant in the reserves until 1936.

Captain Robert Lytle crash-landed his aircraft forward of Belgian lines on October 14, 1918, during the same fight in which Ralph Talbot and Gunny Robinson shot down two German fighters. The plane was disassembled and returned to the aerodrome, where it became a "hangar queen," providing spare parts for other aircraft.

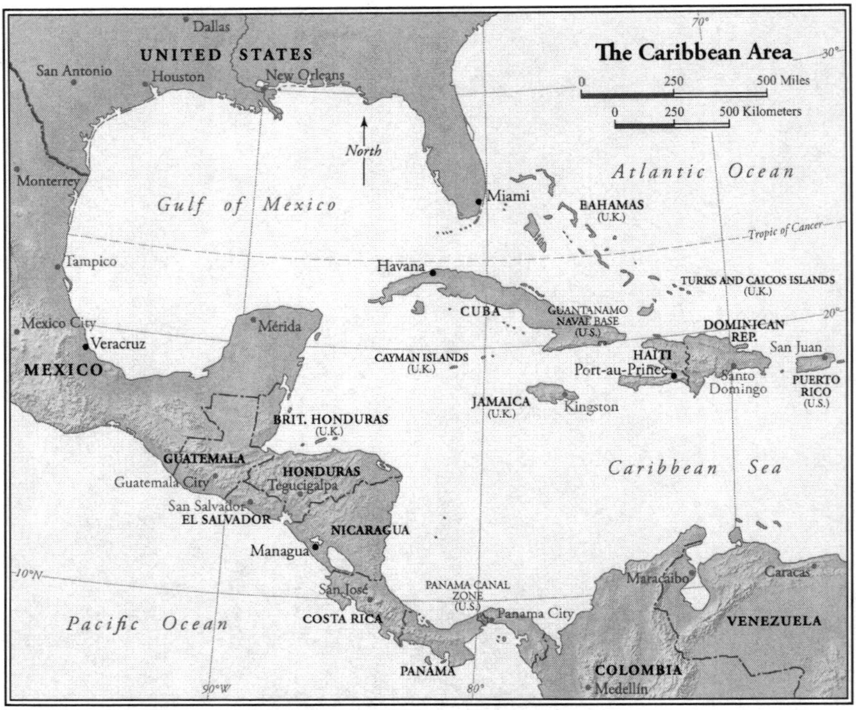

The Caribbean. From the Marine Flying Field in Miami, Florida, the marines deployed to Haiti on the island of Hispaniola, east of the US Naval Base at Guantanamo Bay, Cuba, sitting astride the Windward Passage.

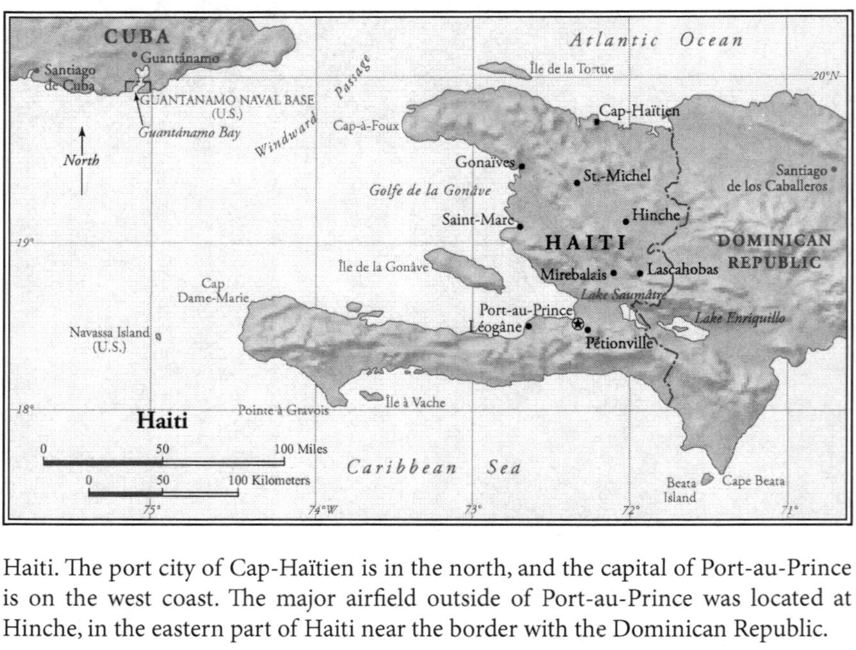

Haiti. The port city of Cap-Haïtien is in the north, and the capital of Port-au-Prince is on the west coast. The major airfield outside of Port-au-Prince was located at Hinche, in the eastern part of Haiti near the border with the Dominican Republic.

2

Proving Ground

Haiti, 1915–1934

> So perverse is mankind that every nationality prefers to be misgoverned by its own people than to be well ruled by another.
>
> General Sir Charles Napier, Knight Grand Cross, Order of the Bath

The Spanish-American War in 1898 marked the emergence of the victorious United States as a major world power and an imperial power in its own right.[1] As such, the US government made it quite clear that the internal affairs of other states, especially in Latin America and the Caribbean, were of considerable national interest to the United States and that military intervention was probable if instability in these states threatened American lives or other interests. Indeed, US involvement in Caribbean affairs increased dramatically with the American assumption of the construction of the Panama Canal in 1904. From that point forward, "successive administrations in Washington committed the United States to a policy of maintaining political stability in the Caribbean as a means of preventing foreign encroachment that might threaten the developing American military, political, and economic hegemony in the area."[2] The Panama Canal, which would be completed in 1914, made the Windward Passage between Cuba and the island of Hispaniola, comprising the Dominican Republic and Haiti, of peculiar strategic interest.[3] In the end, if economic motives provided the incentive for interfering in the internal affairs of Caribbean states, securing the Panama Canal provided strategic justification.

Perpetual disorder and insolvency in the Caribbean increasingly attracted the attention of the US government in the early 1900s, and the Monroe Doctrine, which identified the Western Hemisphere as being of particular

American interest, was found wanting. As Secretary of State Elihu Root wrote, "The inevitable effect of our building the Canal must be to require us to police the surrounding premises."[4] It was this assumed need to police disorderly Caribbean societies that prompted Congress to pass the Platt Amendment in 1901, giving the United States a free hand in the internal affairs of Cuba to prevent intervention by European powers.[5] Moreover, President Theodore Roosevelt asserted a moral mandate to ensure the stability of Latin American countries and to compel them to pay their bills. Under this policy, known as the Roosevelt corollary to the Monroe Doctrine, even short-term intervention by European powers would no longer be tolerated. To prevent them from doing so, the United States itself would assume the task of intervention.[6]

President William Howard Taft added a new dimension to Roosevelt's "big stick" policy by encouraging American investment in Latin America to foster stable economies. "Dollar diplomacy" sought to control the finances of strategically important yet unstable Latin American countries, primarily through guarantees of protection by the US government. In 1905 an agreement was reached with the Dominican Republic whereby the United States would take over customs collections, after which 45 percent of the revenues would fund the operating expenses of the Dominican government and the remaining 55 percent would be turned over to creditors on a pro rata basis. Four years later, the State Department negotiated a treaty with Honduras that sought to consolidate and re-fund Honduran debt by American bankers and set up an American receivership.[7] A similar agreement was reached in Nicaragua in 1912 after US marines landed there and, for all intents and purposes, installed a pro-American government.[8]

Matters came to a head in Haiti in July 1915. US marines and navy "bluejackets"[9] from the USS *Eagle,* a gunboat[10] and former yacht built in 1890, and the USS *Washington,* a Tennessee-class armored cruiser and flagship of Rear Admiral William Caperton, commanding the Atlantic Cruiser Squadron, landed at Cap Haïtian with the mission to protect the lives and property of Americans and other foreign nationals from marauding political factions. When the Haitian government fell later that same month, the *Washington* moved quickly to the capital city, Port-au-Prince, and landed troops there for the same purpose. Thus began an almost twenty-year occupation of Haiti by the United States.

The burden of security and administration in Haiti fell mostly to the marines, who performed a variety of tasks not normally expected of occupying military forces at that time. This later became the foundation for Marine Corps doctrine related to counterinsurgency ("pacification"). But as Keith Bickel notes in his incisive study *Mars Learning*, "the Marines in Haiti did not take long to learn what worked."[11] And that included the coordinated employment of air and ground forces. Although Marine Corps aircraft first alighted in the Dominican Republic (then known as Santo Domingo), it was the marines' experience in Haiti from 1915 to 1934 that shaped the development of Marine Corps aviation in relation to small wars and indeed to war in general.

Background to Intervention

The Republic of Haiti occupies the western third of the Antillean island of Hispaniola and lies some 60 miles across the Windward Passage from the Oriente province of Cuba. Roughly the size of Maryland, it is traversed by three mountain ranges running approximately east to west, with the tallest peak reaching above 9,000 feet. Among the mountains are alluvial plains of rich soil with many streams and rivers, the most prominent of which is the Artibonite, originating in the Dominican Republic and emptying into the Gulf of Gonâve. There are two rainy and two dry seasons, with winter ordinarily being the driest. The island has historically been rife with disease, primarily malaria.

Haiti is the second oldest independent state (after the United States) in the Western Hemisphere. First seen by European eyes in December 1492, Haiti was known as Saint Domingue during the mercantilist era of the eighteenth century. With the arrival of the Spanish, the indigenous population was virtually exterminated, and African slaves were brought in to replace them.[12] English, French, and Dutch pirates later settled on the island and, with French assistance, drove out the Spanish. Genuine French domination began with the Treaty of Ryswick (1697), ending the War of the Palatine Succession fought between Louis XIV of France and a coalition of other European powers. Under French suzerainty, plantations on the island were steadily enlarged, and with the loss of "New France" (Canada) to Great Britain during the Seven Years' War (1756–1763), Saint Domingue became the most lucrative colonial outpost of the French empire.

Haiti achieved independence during the French Revolution (1789–1799), a consequence of a slave insurrection[13] led by Tousaint L'Ouverture and Jean Jacques Dessalines, the latter becoming the first postindependence leader and, by his own declaration, Emperor Jacques I of Haiti (the French colonial name being discarded in favor of the aboriginal word *Haïti,* meaning "land of mountains"). France initially refused to recognize Haitian independence but acceded in 1824 in return for extensive commercial concessions and the payment of a large indemnity. Unfortunately for the new nation, the great wealth of the former colony was destroyed during the protracted war for independence, and the indemnity was only the beginning of years of foreign indebtedness.[14]

Unlike the United States, the Republic of Haiti did not emerge from its war for independence with stable political institutions, a sound economy, or any sense of national unity. In the northern half of the country, military strongmen held sway; in the southern half and in the major cities, a small, educated elite came to dominate. Indeed, the inhabitants of Haiti divided themselves into virtual castes according to color, education, and cultural values.[15] Before independence, the free *gens de couleur* (predominantly mulattoes) of Saint Domingue adopted the language and mores of their colonial masters and subjected their more dark-skinned brethren to the same vicious race prejudice they had both experienced at the hands of white colonists. Moreover, the elite were almost exclusively Roman Catholic, whereas the majority of black peasants practiced *vodoun,* or voodoo, brought to Hispaniola by West African slaves. Thus, the segregation of the elite (approximately 3 percent of the total population) from the masses was defined by language, culture, religion, and somatic norms. That is not to say, however, that the elite class was denied to blacks entirely. *Noirs,* especially those with military backgrounds, could become part of the elite, and on occasion they even ruled Haiti. Nevertheless, "as in colonial Saint Domingue, where the *gens de couleur* and black slaves hated each other, racial antagonism persisted between the *élite* and the black peasantry of Haiti."[16]

Though Haiti was nominally a republic with legislative, judicial, and executive branches of government, as established by the Constitution of 1806, the reality was altogether different. Haitian politics was dominated by the minority elite and by a succession of military strongmen. The result was a seemingly endless series of "revolutions."[17]

Insurgency in Haiti followed a fairly predictable pattern. A military strongman would form a *caco* army, consisting mostly of semiprofessional soldiers and peasants.[18] The *caco* army would seize the capital of Port-au-Prince, surround the legislature, and oversee the "election" of the strongman as the new president. A period of relative tranquility sometimes followed, but stability came at a price: state use of force against political opponents and the general population was common, as was the adoption of compulsory labor modeled on the corvée system.[19]

Political power in Haiti was simply the power to make money. According to a Marine Corps history written in 1934, politicians aspired to office—in particular, the presidency—to make enough money through graft to "retire to Paris, there to end their days in comfort."[20] Patronage was the norm, and appointments to customs collection houses were especially sought after. According to the same report, "Several months was all the time required for a collector of customs to become rich, particularly during the coffee season."[21] Corruption was endemic, and with constant looting of the treasury, public debt increased from $4.4 million in 1891 to over $25 million in 1895.[22] By the early 1900s, Haiti was debt ridden and completely dependent on foreign imports.

The US government's interest in Haiti was long standing, with strategic and economic factors figuring most prominently in American policy. Before independence, France imposed a system on Saint Domingue known as the *exclusif*, requiring the colony to sell its exports to and purchase its imports from France alone.[23] It was virtually the same mercantilist system imposed by the British on their own North American colonies. But a contraband trade emerged with British colonists in Jamaica and North America: the American colonists purchased molasses to make rum, and the Saint Dominguans imported dried fish to feed the slaves. Following the American Revolution, Americans were divided over whether to support the Haitians in their own struggle for independence. Southerners in the United States feared the precedent set by a successful slave insurrection, whereas merchants in New England were intrigued by the commercial possibilities of a newly independent state in the Caribbean. Most American politicians were pragmatic when it came to Haitian affairs, but during the years between Haitian independence and the American Civil War, pro-slavery sentiment in the South was sufficient to deny Haiti the recognition its independence would otherwise warrant.[24] In the 1880s the US government sought to obtain the Môle Saint-Nicolas in Haiti as a naval base, but Guantanamo Bay, Cuba, was substituted, based on the recommendation of Admiral Alfred Thayer Mahan. Thus, if Haiti figured at all in American foreign policy before World War I, it was in connection with the Monroe Doctrine.[25] On four occasions between 1884 and 1891, European powers were warned to stay out of Haiti.[26]

American commercial interests in Haiti increased following the Spanish-American War. By 1910, US imports accounted for some 60 percent of the Haitian economy.[27] More important than trade, however, was banking. For decades, foreign bankers had pressured the Haitian treasury to take out loans, followed by thinly veiled threats of intervention if the loans were not repaid promptly. In the end, the National City Bank of New York outmaneuvered European banks and dominated financial matters in Haiti, creating a new Banque Nationale de la République d'Haiti. Even so, commercial and financial interests became secondary with the completion of the Panama Canal, which gave Haiti a strategic importance for the United States that far outweighed its financial value.[28] Thus, by the time President Woodrow Wilson took office, observers in Washington were watching events in Haiti with grave concern.

On January 27, 1914, Haitian president Michel Oreste was deposed by two brothers, Oreste and Charles Zamor.[29] As European warships waited offshore, a landing party consisting of two officers and fifty-four men was put ashore at Port-au-Prince by the Tennessee-class cruiser USS *Montana,* followed by the remainder of the marine detachment on January 29. Seven days later, the French cruiser *Conde* and the British Monmouth-class cruiser HMS *Lancaster* landed troops of their own.[30] These "international" forces remained ashore until February 9 when, by mutual agreement, they returned to their respective vessels.

The year 1914 would prove pivotal for the tiny republic. Threatened by a *caco* army led by Joseph Davilmar Théodore and his ally Dr. Rosalvo Bobo, Oreste Zamor requested US assistance, in return for which he agreed to American proposals regarding a customs receivership. President Wilson acted quickly, sending the Connecticut-class battleship USS *Kansas* and the transport USS *Hancock,* with some 800 marines, to Haiti. But it was too late; Zamor fled the country in a Dutch ship before the marines arrived, and they returned to the United States.[31] Théodore took office as the president of Haiti. On October 30, acting secretary of state Robert Lansing instructed the American minister to Haiti, Arthur Bailly-Blanchard, to impress on the new president that the United States "might be compelled to take necessary steps to prevent a period of disorder or anarchy which would harm the rights and property of Americans and other foreigners."[32] In other words, if necessary, American warships and the marines would return.

And within a few months, the navy and the marines did return, this time to move some $500,000 in gold bullion from the Haitian treasury (half its holdings) to the National City Bank of New York aboard the gunboat USS *Machias*. Upon arrival, a squad of eight marines went ashore and, "armed with stout canes and concealed revolvers," escorted the gold to the gunboat, where it was loaded without incident.[33] Ostensibly, the gold was moved to prevent the reintroduction of European troops seeking to enforce existing claims against the Banque Nationale. Not surprisingly, the Haitian government protested this unilateral act, but Secretary of State William Jennings Bryan replied that the United States had acted within its powers and assured the Haitians that the gold would be available for redemption. In fact, the gold was returned to the Haitian treasury in 1919, with 2 percent interest.

Regarding the Théodore administration with growing disapproval, President Wilson became convinced that a more active American role in Haiti was required. Giving point to the president's anxiety, on February 22, 1915, after only three and a half months in office, Théodore was overthrown by *caco* forces led by General Jean Vilbrun Guillaume Sam, son of Tirésias Simon Sam, Haiti's president from 1896 to 1902. The following month, President Wilson sent a three-member commission to inform the new Haitian government that the United States would provide assistance if it had genuine popular support, not simply the protection of the *cacos*. Sam rebuffed the commission. Accordingly, the commissioners departed Haiti, and Wilson refused to recognize the new government. However, on March 24, much to the consternation of Wilson, Italy and Germany recognized the Sam government, and France followed suit a month later. Wilson quickly sent Paul Fuller Jr., a prominent New Yorker, to Haiti to sort things out.[34]

Fuller arrived in May, carrying credentials as presidential envoy extraordinary and minister plenipotentiary and with instructions to seek an agreement whereby the United States would provide military support to Sam if he would accept American direction in financial matters. Negotiations broke down, and Fuller returned to Washington in June, recommending that a military occupation would be necessary to stabilize the country. In the meantime, new revolutionary forces were at work, headed this time by Rosalvo Bobo, former minister of the interior under Théodore. By the middle of June, Bobo had raised a *caco* army of his own, occupied Cap Haïtian, and looted the customhouse.

Intervention

Rear Admiral Caperton had taken command of the Cruiser Squadron of the US Atlantic Fleet in January 1915, flying his flag on the cruiser *Washington.*[35] With war raging in Europe and the Caribbean being harassed by German raiders, the Cruiser Squadron was responsible for monitoring events in the region. Admiral Caperton's first visit to Haiti was uneventful, but soon after departing he was recalled owing to Sam's bid to seize power. He met with Sam in Cap Haïtian and informed him that US forces would not interfere so long as he kept his *cacos* under control. The squadron then shadowed Sam and his army down the coast to Port-au-Prince, where Sam took control of the Haitian government. Shortly afterward, Caperton's squadron steamed to Mexican waters to keep an eye on things there.[36] During Caperton's absence, Bobo raised an army of his own and occupied Cap Haïtian, whereupon American consul Lemuel Livingston reported witnessing "the worst savagery in all his seventeen years at the Cap."[37]

On June 19 the French cruiser *Descartes* landed troops at Cap Haïtian. Admiral Caperton was ordered back to Haiti to "thank the French commander and take the necessary steps to protect property and preserve order."[38] Caperton's squadron arrived off Cap Haïtian on July 1, after which the French warship embarked its troops and withdrew. Determined to avoid fighting in the city, Caperton ordered his ships, including the newly arrived gunboat USS *Eagle,* to lay off the Cap and await developments. Sam's army marched north from the capital and drove out Bobo's forces. When Sam's forces moved into the countryside to pursue the remnants, Caperton landed sailors and marines to secure the town and then steamed under forced draft to Port-au-Prince.[39]

Meanwhile, in the capital city, Sam had arrested somewhere between 150 and 200 political opponents, many of them from Haiti's *mulâtre élite.* As a result, prominent men crowded all the foreign legations (with the exception of the American), fearing their own arrest. These men began to hatch schemes to overthrow President Sam. Anticipating this, Sam moved *cacos* into the city for his own protection. However, when the presidential palace was attacked on the night of July 26, Sam's *cacos* failed him and took to the hills surrounding the city. Sam took refuge in the nearby French legation. He then ordered his chief of police, Charles-Oscar Etienne, to execute the political prisoners at the police arrondissement in the lower city.[40] All but five were slaughtered.[41] According to one observer, it was "one of the most horrid and inexcusable crimes ever recorded against government agents in the history of Haiti."[42]

Later that same day, the prison was opened so that families could recover the bodies of their loved ones. Shortly afterward, a mob surrounded the French legation but did not enter the grounds. The next morning, however, seeing the smoke of Admiral Caperton's flagship on the horizon and fearing that Sam would escape, several men entered the legation, seized Sam, and murdered him; they then threw his body over the fence, whereupon the mob dismembered him and paraded the body parts through the streets of Port-au-Prince.[43] At the same time, an equally enraged mob invaded the legation of the Dominican Republic, seized Etienne, and shot him to death. The mob then demolished his house, "literally pulling it apart, brick by brick."[44]

The American chargé in the capital, Robert Davis, cabled an account of these and other events to Washington and sent word to Caperton aboard his flagship. Davis claimed that no government then existed in Haiti and that *cacos* in the countryside were preparing to attack the defenseless city, presumably on behalf of Bobo. Admiral Caperton quickly assessed the situation and, on his own initiative, decided to send troops ashore to restore order. While preparing the landing force, Caperton received a message from the State Department expressing the secretary's desire that troops be landed.[45]

Occupation

The occupation of Haiti unfolded in four phases, roughly linked to the development of an indigenous constabulary force, first known as the Gendarmerie d'Haiti and later the Garde d'Haiti,[46] and the passage of administration from a US military government to the Haitians themselves. The first phase, 1915–1920, involved active military operations against the *cacos,* the creation of a "popular" government, the establishment of the gendarmerie, and the introduction of Marine Corps aviation. The second phase, 1921–1925, concentrated on the professionalization of the gendarmerie as well as social, political, and economic development. Real progress came with the creation of the Garde d'Haiti between 1926 and 1929, a period of relative tranquility until strikes and riots broke out in 1929. Finally, 1930–1934 is regarded as the Haitianization period, a time during which domestic economic and political concerns in the United States forced the withdrawal of US forces.

With Sam dead, no one was officially in charge of the country, save for a self-appointed Committee of Safety. After informing the foreign legations,

Admiral Caperton landed marines and bluejackets under the command of Captain George Van Orden, USMC, on the evening of July 28, 1915, at the dilapidated Haitian navy yard at Bizoton, just outside Port-au-Prince. The following day, another company of marines commanded by Captain William Fay Jr. arrived from Cuba aboard the collier USS *Jason*.[47] Resistance was negligible, and order was restored to the city. Nevertheless, Caperton cabled the Navy Department and requested that a regiment of marines be sent to Haiti. On July 30 Secretary of the Navy Daniels ordered the Second Regiment, First Brigade, under the command of Colonel Eli Cole, to embark the battleship USS *Connecticut* for duty in Haiti.[48] The First Regiment, under the command of Colonel Theodore Kane, would follow shortly aboard the armored cruiser USS *Tennessee*. Also on board the *Tennessee* was Colonel Littleton "Tony" Waller, who would assume command of the brigade upon his arrival in Haiti.[49]

As events unfolded, Bobo saw an opportunity, revived his *caco* army, and laid siege to Cap Haïtian, which was promptly abandoned by government forces under the command of General Probus Blot. Concerned about what would follow, Admiral Caperton dispatched the 1,300-ton gunboat USS *Nashville* (another converted yacht) to Cap Haïtian to assist the *Eagle*, landing marines there on August 1. Bobo's forces subsequently withdrew and moved south. Marines and bluejackets now controlled the two largest cities in Haiti. Moreover, on August 4 the Second Regiment arrived in Port-au-Prince, and with the arrival of the remainder of the First Brigade over the next several days, the *caco* problem was, in theory, under control.[50]

Realizing that genuine and lasting order could not be attained so long as the *cacos* were the principal mechanism by which presidents were elevated to office, Admiral Caperton consented to allow the Haitian legislature to elect a new president—but without *caco* interference. There were two outstanding candidates: Rosalvo Bobo and Philippe Sudre Dartiguenave, president of the Haitian Senate. Caperton cabled Washington on August 5 that Dartiguenave was the preferred candidate, given that Bobo appeared to be mentally unstable. Caperton met with both men on August 8 and, working through his French-speaking chief of staff Captain Edward Beach, USN, the admiral asked each man what he would do if the other succeeded to the presidency. Dartiguenave replied that he would offer Bobo his "most loyal, earnest support."[51] Bobo declined to reciprocate and failed the interview. Recognizing which way the wind was blowing, the Haitian legislature elected Dartiguenave as president on August 12, 1915.[52] The United States formally recognized the Dartiguenave government six days later.[53] Bobo left Haiti aboard a French ship. He died in Paris in 1929.

A little more than a month after the election, the United States and Haiti signed a treaty giving the United States legal justification for occupation for a period of ten years, renewable on demand by either party for an additional ten years. The treaty provided for a Haitian constabulary organized and officered by Americans, customs receivership under American control, and public works related to agriculture and sanitation. The United States agreed to "lend all official aid for the preservation of Haitian independence and to the maintenance of a government adequate for the protection of life, property, and individual liberty."[54] Such was the price of recognition.

On August 15 the First Regiment arrived in Port-au-Prince, along with Colonel Waller and his brigade headquarters. Thus reinforced, Admiral Caperton decided to extend the American presence across the depth and breadth of Haiti. In short order, the gunboat USS *Castine* delivered a marine detachment to the port town of Saint Marc in the northwest; other detachments were sent west to Léogâne, east to the mountain village of Pétionville, and south to the coastal town of Jacmel. Additional marines were dispatched to smaller villages around the country, and American ships began patrolling the coastline from Cap Haïtian to the southernmost tip of Haiti. In this manner, towns where trouble had occurred and all the major seacoast towns came under American control. By August 31, with the arrival of the brigade artillery battalion, there were 88 officers and just under 2,000 enlisted marines ashore in Haiti.[55]

With no prospect of income from another insurgency, the *cacos* resorted to thievery. *Caco* leaders in the north were especially hostile to the American presence, and the situation soon became critical. In early September the seacoast town of Gonaïves was surrounded by *cacos* and cut off from the outside world. Admiral Caperton cabled the Navy Department that conditions there were intolerable, and he ordered the marines to open access to the beleaguered town. When the *cacos* learned of this, they began destroying railroad tracks outside Gonaïves and engaged a marine patrol in a firefight. Six *cacos* were reportedly killed.[56] On September 20 Major Smedley Butler, son of Congressman Thomas S. Butler and commander of the First Battalion, First Regiment, took charge of the detachment at Gonaïves and immediately went to work dispersing the *cacos*.[57] During an encounter on September 21 with *caco* chief Pierre Benoît Rameau, Butler literally yanked the "general" from his saddle and admonished him for his behavior and that of his men.[58] Even so, the *cacos* attacked the marines the next day, prompting Butler to scatter them and recapture Rameau, who finally agreed to withdraw and send his men home.[59]

As they had done at Gonaïves, *cacos* surrounding Cap Haïtian began to interfere with the food supply. Colonel Cole, the commander in the area, realized that more vigorous campaigning would be required, and on September 27 he led five companies to Quartier Morin to destroy *caco* headquarters. Once this mission was accomplished, he sent patrols to disperse the remaining *cacos* in the area, which resulted in the first marine killed in Haiti, Sergeant John Platt.[60] Colonel Waller followed up by meeting with the principal *caco* chieftains and negotiating an agreement by which the *cacos* would, for a sum of money, disarm and cease interfering with communications and commerce. Some *cacos* did disarm, but a large number refused.[61] These men had to be rounded up or destroyed, and the mission fell to the doughty Major Butler. He marched on Fort Capois, the mountain stronghold of the *cacos*. En route, the small detachment of marines was attacked crossing a stream on the night of October 24. During the firefight, a horse carrying the only machine gun was killed midstream, but the weapon was recovered by Gunnery Sergeant Dan Daly, for which he received the Medal of Honor—his second, having earned the first during the Boxer Rebellion in China in 1900. The next day Butler and his men assaulted the fort in converging columns, routing the *cacos*.[62]

Despite their defeat at Fort Capois, many *cacos* remained troublesome, and Colonel Waller took personal command of the northern area. Waller's strategy was to force the *cacos* off the productive plains and into the mountains, where their trepidations would be less damaging. To do so, he had to secure several other old forts; the most prestigious was Fort Riviere, which the *cacos* believed to be impregnable. By November 16, the last diehards had been pushed into Fort Riviere, and Major Butler was again selected for the task of reducing the redoubt. Waller and Cole planned another converging attack, employing detachments from the Fifth, Thirteenth, Fifteenth, and Twenty-Third Companies, as well as a contingent from the battleship *Connecticut*. Leading the main assault force, Major Butler attacked from the west. His objective was a small opening in the western wall that the *cacos* used as a gate, as the original gate in the north wall had become overgrown with vegetation and was unusable. The assault occurred on November 17, taking the *cacos* by surprise. Marines from the Fifteenth Company reached the wall first, and despite heavy fire, Sergeant Ross Iams, Private Samuel Gross, and Major Butler rushed through, in that order. All three survived, thanks to poor *caco* marksmanship. Twenty other marines poured through the opening, and the *cacos* fled, most of them cut down as they scaled the walls to escape. Butler, Iams, and Gross received the Medal of Honor for their actions. For Butler, it was his second, having been awarded the first for action at Veracruz in 1914. Thoroughly demoralized, the remaining *cacos* melted into the countryside, and the majority turned to petty crime to support themselves.

Thus the First *Caco* Campaign, lasting from September to November 1915, came to an end. The marines had lost two killed and several wounded. *Caco* dead were estimated at 200, with many more wounded. The suppression of the *cacos* brought relative peace to Haiti, but it did not bring stability. To that end, Admiral Caperton attempted to reform the financial system, taking over the customhouses and installing navy paymasters as collectors.[63] At first ill prepared for the assignment, the sailors adapted quickly and established a reputation for efficiency and scrupulous honesty.[64] The Haitian elite, however, were stunned: "American assumption of customs control . . . for the first time brought home to the elite (which in this context is to say all politicians) some hard practicalities of foreign intervention. For that entire class, whose livelihood after all had been the public treasury, the blow, square in the pocketbook, was disastrous."[65] To add insult to injury, Caperton pushed for constitutional and juridical reform in Haiti. Although sympathetic to Caperton's goals, President Dartiguenave was unsure he could deliver, especially given the "American insistence on eliminating graft, reducing palace patronage . . . and ending fraud and kickbacks on government contracts."[66]

To facilitate the reforms he envisioned, Admiral Caperton declared martial law throughout the country. The next step was to rewrite the constitution—Haiti's seventeenth since independence. The draft was passed to Washington for comment, and the recommended changes were delivered to the Haitian legislature as an American *dictat*. The Haitian Assembly balked, but the newly created gendarmerie, headed by Major Butler, was called in and closed the legislature (it did not reopen until 1930). The amended constitution was then presented as an all-Haitian referendum in early 1918, which duly passed.[67]

The gendarmerie had been organized informally in September 1915 to provide local police services. It quickly became evident, however, that the paramilitary force would have to expand, given that the First Brigade had begun a steady reduction in force in Haiti. An insurgency had developed in the neighboring Dominican Republic, and Admiral Caperton moved his flagship to the capital, Santo Domingo City, to oversee American intervention there. In addition, from May to July 1916, the brigade's artillery battalion, three companies of the First Regiment, and the headquarters and Fourteenth Company of the Second Regiment relocated to the other side of Hispaniola. Afterward, for reasons that remain unclear, the regiments exchanged numbers. In December 1915 there were 90 officers and more than 1,800 enlisted marines in Haiti; by the end of 1916, marine forces in Haiti had been reduced to 73 officers and 841 enlisted men, including one company offshore aboard the Connecticut-class battleship USS *Vermont*.[68] The troops ashore were organized into a brigade headquarters, a signal company, a constabulary detachment to man the emerging gendarmerie, a depot detachment, and the regiment. Offsetting the reduction, the gendarmerie swelled to 112 officers (100 from the Marine Corps, and 12 from the US Navy) and 2,500 gendarmes.[69]

On December 3, 1915, Colonel Waller formally tasked Major Butler with organizing the gendarmerie and appointed him its first commander. The central idea was to create a small, efficient force that was free from politics. When the marines arrived in Haiti in 1915, there had been five different police forces: communal, or city, police; arrondissement, or state, police; administrative police in the larger cities; the palace police, under the Ministry of War; and the secret police. "In addition to the above forces, there was also the army, an undisciplined, untrained mob."[70] Rather than trying to reform the police and the army, the marines decided to start from scratch and from the bottom up. Administratively, the gendarmerie answered to the Haitian government; therefore, marines officering the gendarmerie held Haitian commissions while retaining their Marine Corps rank and pay. The newly promoted Lieutenant Colonel Butler held the rank of major general in the gendarmerie.[71] Throughout the initial development of the gendarmerie, the brigade headquarters acted more as an administrative than a tactical command, and command of the brigade changed hands several times.[72]

When Butler formally took command, many of the gendarmes were former soldiers, and some were former *cacos*. But most came from the landless and unskilled peasantry. No member of the *mulâtres* would join. The physical condition of the recruits was uniformly poor, and Butler testified to Congress that "95 percent of them had blood disease and 85 percent had intestinal worms."[73] The recruits were also illiterate and spoke patois, a French-derived indigenous dialect understood by few Americans. Not surprisingly, then, all commands were given in English. The first gendarmes were armed with .45-70-caliber rifles left over from the Haitian army, but these were soon replaced with .30-40-caliber Krag-Jorgensen rifles, the standard rifle of the US Army and Marine Corps from 1900 to 1906. Before the marines departed in 1934, the gendarmes would receive the 1903 model .30-caliber Springfield rifle.

As the gendarmerie grew, most marines were withdrawn from the interior and posted to major coastal towns, where they became a training cadre for the larger gendarmerie units as well as a quick-reaction force.[74] Under Haitian administration, the country was divided into departments, arrondissements, communes, and sections, but the marines organized the gendarmerie along geographic lines. There were three departments: Cap Haïtian, the northern peninsula; Port-au-Prince; and Les Cayes, a seacoast town in southwestern Haiti. Each department was commanded by a gendarmerie colonel. The departments were divided into districts, with gendarmerie captains commanding the garrisons. The larger districts were divided into subdistricts, each commanded by a gendarmerie lieutenant, usually a Marine Corps noncommissioned officer.[75]

For marines in the major towns, living conditions were Spartan, but for those manning remote outposts, living conditions were primitive. Food, water, and other supplies were brought in by pack trains and bull carts that had to navigate narrow mountain trails that offered ideal ambush sites for the still defiant *cacos.* Communication between the outposts and headquarters was by land wire, or telegraph. Although unused to the rigorous discipline meted out by their marine mentors, the gendarmes adjusted, and "it did not take long for [them] to make better soldiers than their instructors had hoped for."[76] Thus, whereas the preoccupation Haitian army and police had routinely been beaten by the *cacos,* the American-led gendarmes were soon able to defeat the *cacos* in a series of engagements, often against superior numbers.[77]

The Haitian-American Treaty of 1915 specifically provided for improved sanitation and other public works, and American military personnel and civilians oversaw various projects across Haiti. According to Keith Bickel, there were three principal reasons for the marines' willingness to participate in public works. The first was intellectual: the marines believed there was an economic "underpinning" to Haitian instability, and better roads would improve the economy by permitting the easy transport of crops and other goods to market. The second was utilitarian: there was military utility in the reformation of the Haitian government, the implementation of new services in the country, and the construction of roads to facilitate the rapid movement of troops about the countryside. That brings us to the third reason: inadequate manpower. The marines never had enough troops, and the ability to move forces rapidly from one place to another was a key component of their strategy. Thus, the marines engaged "in a pattern of civil activities that they hoped would induce the populace to cease supporting the Caco insurgents" and at the same time enable the marines to dominate the human and physical terrain.[78]

In the beginning, public works were welcomed by the *noirs,* if not the elite and the *cacos.* In testimony to Congress, Colonel Waller told of one project in which he obtained more volunteer labor than he could employ.[79] But such volunteerism soon evaporated, and labor costs soared. Lacking sufficient funds, Butler discovered in the rural code the long-forgotten corvée provision instituted after the revolution. According to Butler's testimony to Congress in 1921, he was able to reduce the cost of building a road from $51,000 per mile to just over $200 per mile. To his credit, Butler took pains to provide shelter, food, and entertainment for the laborers, but they resented the impressment nonetheless. Moreover, the corvée lent itself to abuse by Haitians and marines alike. Butler's successor, Major Alexander Williams, officially abolished the practice on October 1, 1918.[80] Unfortunately, it persisted. In one particularly notorious example, Major Clarke Wells, a district commander in northern Haiti, defied official guidance while denying as much in his reports to brigade headquarters.[81]

As resistance to the corvée grew, it manifested most strongly in the northern and mountainous east-central parts of Haiti. Seizing the opportunity, politicians in those regions, many of whom were still loyal to Rosalvo Bobo, contrived to transform resistance into insurgency. One particularly ambitious insurgent was Charlemagne Massena Péralte, a French-educated lawyer and former soldier from a respected elite family in the east-central town of Hinche, near the Dominican border. Péralte, most often referred to by his first name, Charlemagne, was the brother-in-law of the late president Oreste Zamor and a supporter of Bobo.

In October 1917 Charlemagne and his two brothers attacked the home of the Hinche district commander, Captain John Doxey. Thwarted,

Charlemagne was arrested, tried, and sentenced to five years of hard labor. He was put to work sweeping streets and other distasteful tasks. Nine months later, he induced his guard to help him escape and took to the hills, where he soon organized a *caco* army and shadow government. His chief subordinate, Benoît Batraville, a former police chief and Bobo admirer, commanded insurgent elements in central Haiti while Charlemagne directed operations in the north. At its peak, Charlemagne's insurgency controlled a quarter of the country, and it soon became obvious that the gendarmerie was not up to the job of pacification.

Thus began the marines' Second *Caco* Campaign, which lasted until 1920. It was during this campaign that a detachment of airplanes arrived in Haiti and, according to the annual report of Marine Corps commandant Major General George Barnett, these aircraft "proved very efficient in locating and, with the assistance of the land forces, in dispersing bands of outlaws by machine-gun fire and the dropping of bombs."[82]

Setting the Stage

Within months of the armistice that ended World War I, the manufacturing of airplanes in the United States was crushed by across-the-board cancellations of federal contracts worth $100 million. Production of new aircraft nose-dived from more than 4,000 airplanes in the last quarter of 1918 to 26 for the same period a year later. Ninety percent of production facilities constructed during the war were liquidated. On top of that, the stock market would take a tumble in 1920 as part of a worldwide recession.[83] Not surprisingly, Congress and the US Navy were in no mood to entertain the expansion of Marine Corps aviation.[84] A few months after the war, the Marine Corps' regular force was sharply reduced in size, and reservists were demobilized at an accelerating rate (by 1922, 87 percent of reserve officers and 90 percent of enlisted reservists had been discharged).[85]

The Flying Field at the old Curtiss school in Miami did not lay fallow after the departure of Squadron D in 1918 (redesignated Tenth Squadron upon its arrival in France); instead, the field was abuzz with activity, continuing its training mission as well as serving as a base for aerial patrols off the coast of south Florida. And while Captain A. A. Cunningham was away in France (where he was promoted to temporary major), Lieutenant Harvey Mims, a former corporal, replaced him as the very junior officer in charge of aviation in Washington.[86] Mims's biggest challenge, and that of his successors, was to expand the pool of qualified aviators, especially pilots. To that end, Marine Corps Headquarters formally authorized the training of enlisted pilots, several of whom would fly missions during the small wars era.[87]

The first enlisted man of any service to be recognized as a pilot was arguably Sergeant William Ivy, US Army, who flew a balloon (with an officer observer) over the Spanish fleet at Santiago, Cuba, during the Spanish-American War.[88] The first enlisted pilot of a heavier-than-air machine was Corporal Vernon Burge, US Army, in 1912.[89] The first enlisted pilot in the US Navy was probably Harold "Kiddy" Karr, who also learned to fly a heavier-than-air machine in 1912 and was employed by the navy as an aviator (but was not officially recognized as a naval aviation pilot until 1920).[90]

Enlisted marines were first assigned to aviation in 1914, when First Sergeants Jacob Makohin and Victor Czegka,[91] along with Corporal Walter McCaughtry, were detailed for "extra duty" as aviation mechanics aboard the pre-dreadnought battleship USS *Mississippi,* "at the rate of fifty cents per diem for each day so employed."[92] The three enlisted men maintained AB F-Boat number C-3, flown by marine Lieutenant Bernard Smith, and participated in the occupation of Veracruz. According to one source, Sergeant Makohin was the first to be given the opportunity to fly the F-Boat, followed by the others.[93] Another other source claims it was McCaughtry who first took flight.[94] Yet another source claims that Sergeant James Maguire was the first enlisted marine assigned to aviation duty and possibly the first enlisted man to fly when he was detailed to the Aviation Camp at Annapolis, following training as a mechanic at the Burgess Company and Curtiss aircraft factory at Marblehead. According to a Marine Corps Aviation Association document, "While on duty there, Maguire may well have been the first Marine enlisted man to pilot an aircraft."[95]

Officially, Benjamin Belcher was the Marine Corps' first enlisted pilot. He enlisted in 1917 and was transferred to aviation in 1920 as a mechanic. Unofficial oral histories claimed he had been a flier before joining the Corps and had logged more than 300 hours of flight time as an aircraft mechanic, usually testing airplanes he had worked on. In 1921 he deployed to Haiti, where he was praised for his mechanical skills working with Liberty engines. In 1923 he was designated a pilot, and that same year he flew on a record-breaking flight from the Dominican Republic to San Francisco, California.[96] Regardless of who was the first enlisted pilot, Corporal McCaughtry would become the first warrant officer pilot in the Marine Corps, and as a commissioned officer he would command the squadron deployed to the Dominican Republic in 1919.

In 1915 Captain Mark Bristol, USN, then the navy's head of aeronautics, ordered the commanding officer at the Pensacola Naval Air Station "to detail eight chiefs or petty officers and two Marine Corps first sergeants or sergeant majors from the *North Carolina* or the aeronautic station" to see "if they will answer as pilots as well as mechanicians."[97] Upon leaving his post, Bristol reported to the secretary of the navy that the men selected were making "excellent progress" and recommended that ten enlisted men attend such training every three months. In early 1919 "preliminary flight training and ground school instruction to suitable enlisted men" began at Naval Air Station San Diego using N-9 floatplanes.[98] At the same time, the term "naval aviation pilot" was coined to describe enlisted navy and marine pilots (known informally as "nappies"), in contrast to commissioned officers, who were designated "naval aviators."[99] But it was not until 1924 that the navy's Bureau of Navigation codified the enlisted terminology as a basic rating, and it was not until 1926 that the term received legal definition in legislation.[100]

As rapid as military expansion had been during World War I, demobilization following the war was equally rapid. The First Marine Aviation Force formed during the war was not spared this process and was disbanded at Miami in February 1919. Over a period of five months, the headquarters, squadrons, First Marine Aeronautic Company, balloon detachment, and marine detachment remaining at the Miami Flying Field all ceased to exist.[101] But before the Flying Field at Miami closed, the First Division, Squadron D, was created in February 1919 for expeditionary duty with the Second Brigade in the Dominican Republic. Two weeks later, the First Division, Squadron E, was formed for similar expeditionary duty with the First Brigade in Haiti. Use of the term "division" was an innovation in the immediate postwar period; it would soon end but would later be resurrected at the insistence of the navy.[102] Once the two divisions from Squadrons D and E were deployed to the Caribbean, what remained was dispersed to Parris Island, South Carolina, and Quantico. Squadrons A and C were then re-formed at Quantico for duty with a revived Advance Base Force, and a "new" Squadron B, consisting of two Jennies and their crews, was formed on the West Wing parade ground at Parris Island (later, a flying field was constructed at an old rifle range at the receiving station for recruits).[103] In September 1919 the Flying Field at Miami was closed for good.

With the closing of the Flying Field and the arrival of Squadrons C and A at Quantico from France (in June and September 1919, respectively), a piece of land was leased south of the Chopawasmic Creek along the Potomac River for flying operations. The aviators would have preferred to establish the flying field at Belmont Farms near Woodbridge, but Marine Corps Headquarters wanted it closer to the Marine Barracks at Quantico. Two airstrips were constructed: Field No. 1 was 2,000 feet long on a strip of land running northeast to southwest, and Field No. 2 was 2,500 feet long running north to south.[104] Barracks were built using prefabricated buildings known as "Dixie huts," shipped from Miami. The airfields were connected to the Marine Barracks by a railroad trestle across the creek. But automobiles and trucks from the flying field had to travel by dirt road to Highway 1 (also dirt), then north for several miles, then several miles along another dirt road toward the Potomac River to reach the Marine Barracks area.

Deployment of the two divisions to Hispaniola was a matter of survival for Marine Corps aviation. As General Vernon Megee, USMC, a veteran of the intervention in Nicaragua and later World War II, recalled, aviators in the Marine Corps were not taken seriously:

> They were looked upon as daredevil circus performers, whose sartorial eccentricities and off-duty exuberances did not endear them to the stiff-backed disciplinarians of the *Old Establishment.* Nor did their studied flair for military unconventionality add to the prestige of airmen as credible counselors on the trends of future warfare. . . . This appraisal of the embryonic air arm carried over into the postwar era, and much of it rubbed off on the Marine Corps. . . . Marine Aviation was still searching for a mission and a valid reason for survival; it must be admitted that in those days our air arm appeared to be less a military organization and more a gentlemen's flying club.[105]

To make matters worse (and through no fault of its own), the First Marine Aviation Force had not supported marines on the ground in France during World War I. As Cunningham noted in 1920, "During the war we were unfortunately not allowed to serve with the Fourth Brigade, but were placed in a sector containing only British, French, and Belgian troops."[106] As a result, he wrote, "One of the greatest handicaps which Marine Corps aviation has to overcome is a combination of doubt as to usefulness, lack of sympathy, and a feeling on the part of some line officers that aviators and aviation enlisted men are not real Marines."[107] In the absence of common battle experience, it almost seemed that ground combat officers and aviators were from different planets. In some ways, marine aviators brought this notion of "separateness" upon themselves. According to General Megee, "In those days aviators of company rank were entitled, for some obscure reason, to wear riding boots (less spurs), an article of uniform otherwise sacrosanct to officers of field grade. Certain of the crustier field officers felt aggrieved at this flaunted intrusion into their fringe benefits; this sense of outrage was further aggravated by other peculiarities of aviation dress, such as the leather flight jacket and the forerunner of the 'fifty mission cap.'"[108]

The marine aviators in the Azores and France had operated under a navy umbrella and therefore had little contact with senior marine officers; in addition, most of the young aviators had not served in the Marine Corps before World War I and were not indoctrinated in the traditions of the "old establishment." But at least the marines in the Azores had supported the fleet doing antisubmarine work; the Marine Day Wing of the Northern Bombing Group had not supported the fleet or the marines in France, instead performing long-range bombardment missions against rail yards and similar targets. Flying antisubmarine missions was a navy job, and long-range bombing supported marines on the ground only indirectly. Consequently, after the war, marine aviators had to demonstrate their worth not only to the public and Congress but also to the Marine Corps.

Following World War I, the Marine Corps desperately sought to convince Congress to at least maintain its prewar manning level. Within this context, Major Cunningham fought for permanent status for Marine Corps aviation. But to his frustration, senior marine officers seemed at odds with the new weapon. As World War I veteran Kenneth Collings noted:

> Having learned to soldier without airplanes, air power had played them a mean trick by sneaking up on them in the evening of their careers. Starting from nothing, in four short years aviation had changed warfare into a thing of three dimensions instead of two, thus knocking a good half of the accumulated military lore of the ages into a cocked hat. The change presented a fair challenge to young officers: they had ample time to learn. But all it offered a senior officer was the opportunity to mar, at its very end, a long and

> honorable career by the mishandling of a weapon with which he was not acquainted.[109]

Aviation might be important for the Marine Corps of the future, but no one was sure how or why. And senior navy officers were opposed to letting the marines continue to fly seaplanes, since overwater missions were clearly the purview of the navy.

By the end of 1919, many of the young aviators and most of the "duration" officers taken in during the war had been dismissed, and by the end of 1920, only two aviators held the rank of major: Cunningham and Geiger.[110] Moreover, the airfields created during World War I had all been temporary, and they began to close as soon as the armistice was signed, leaving only those at Quantico and Parris Island. Most important, there was no prewar precedent for the peacetime organization or manning of the air arm, which explains, in part, the constant redesignation of air units during and after the war. It was all ad hoc and improvised. There was no clear mission statement during the war, and now there was no clear mission after the war. Thus, in an appearance before the General Board of the Navy in April 1919, Cunningham sought to convince the board members as well as the leadership of the Marine Corps that, as he wrote in 1920: "It is fully realized that the only excuse for aviation in any service is its usefulness in assisting the troops on the ground to successfully carry out their operations."[111] The involvement of Marine Corps aviation in the small war in Haiti would provide the opportunity to prove his point.

The Second *Caco* Campaign: Adaptation and Innovation

By the time six Jennies, six HS-2L flying boats, and a single N-9 floatplane of the First Division, Squadron E, under the command of Captain Harvey Mims, arrived in Haiti in late March 1919, the insurgency led by Charlemagne Péralte was in full bloom. Having rallied former followers of Bobo and exploiting Haitian resistance to the corvée, Charlemagne organized formidable *caco* armies in northern and central Haiti, the latter commanded by Benoît Batraville, nicknamed *Ti Benoît* ("Little Ben") because of his small stature. Charlemagne had at his disposal some 5,000 hard-core *cacos* and at least 15,000 part-time fighters. The latter were loosely organized under local chiefs and lacked firearms, usually fighting with machetes and sharpened bamboo sticks. Charlemagne's greatest asset was his intelligence network, which forewarned him of virtually every move made by the marines and the gendarmerie. Women known as *marchandes* were especially valuable, circulating freely in the markets. Charlemagne also corresponded with family members and supporters in Port-au-Prince and the larger towns.

An intelligent man of the *mulâtre élite* with a military background, Charlemagne evolved a campaign of rural insurgency, starting with attacks on small gendarmerie outposts in the countryside. Aside from acquiring weapons, ammunition, and other supplies, the destruction of these three- to six-man detachments eliminated state presence, permitting Charlemagne to establish local control as part of the development of a counterstate. In October 1918 Charlemagne executed a major attack on Hinche, believing the time had come to take on the government more directly. About 100 poorly armed *cacos* assaulted the town but were driven off by the gendarmerie, leaving some 35 dead behind.[112] The next major attack came on November 10, 1918, at the town of Maissade, west of Hinche. Roughly 60 *cacos* attacked a small gendarmerie detachment of 10 men commanded by a Haitian sergeant. The *cacos* succeeded in driving out the small detachment and burned a number of buildings. However, Charlemagne's brother, Paul Péralte, was killed, and a former gendarme who had escaped with Charlemagne earlier was captured, court-martialed, and executed. Nevertheless, for the next several months, the guerrilla attacks continued.

Roving bands of *cacos* made regular contact with gendarmerie patrols, and there were considerable losses on both sides. On February 3, 1919, a gendarmerie patrol fought a major engagement against some 200 *cacos* near Mirebalais, some 37 miles northeast of Port-au-Prince. The following day, the town of Cerca-la-Source, northeast of Mirebalais, was attacked by another large *caco* band, which was driven off only after a fierce firefight. Operations reports for February and March are littered with small-unit actions against large formations of determined *cacos* in places such as Lobas Canton Ravine, Grand-Bois, Lascahobas, Ranquitte, and Dufailly, where, on March 21, marine First Lieutenant Nicholas Moskoff was mortally wounded.

On March 16, 1919, the new commandant of the gendarmerie, Lieutenant Colonel Alexander Williams, informed Brigadier General Albertus Catlin, the new brigade commander in Port-au-Prince, that the insurgency had reached a stage that required the active assistance of the brigade. Yet by this time, the brigade had dwindled to a headquarters and a seven-company regiment with a total of 64 officers and fewer than 900 marines. This was insufficient to pacify the whole country, even with the assistance of the gendarmerie. Nevertheless, the marines once more took to the field: six companies were thinly divided among Hinche, Lascahobas, Mirebalais, and Saint-Michel-de-l'Atalaye, an area encompassing the main concentration of *caco* forces in north-central Haiti. The seventh company remained in Port-au-Prince. Fortunately, the brigade was soon reinforced with four companies from Guantanamo Bay, as well as First Division, Squadron E, from Miami.

The newly arrived aviation component comprised 11 officers and 138 enlisted men, along with the six Jennies, six HS-2L flying boats, and one N-9 floatplane.[113] The dispatch of Jennies and flying boats to Haiti illuminates the confusion about the roles and missions of Marine Corps aviation after the war, including what role aviation would play in interventionary expeditionary missions. The Jennies were worn-out "cast-offs" from the Flying Field in Miami. Moreover, they were trainers, not combat platforms, as had been well proved by the experience of the army's First Aero Squadron during the punitive expedition against Pancho Villa in 1916.[114] Flying boats were useful for coastal patrolling and antisubmarine work, not bombardment or strafing targets on land. The role these aircraft would perform in Haiti was still unknown, but they were the only aircraft available, and as marine Major General Ford O. "Tex" Rogers would later recall, "We were there and they used us, and they used us to their advantage, and consequently we became a useful and integral part of the Marine Corps."[115]

HS-1 flying boats had deployed with the First Aeronautic Company to the Azores in January 1918. The HS-1 was a single-engine pusher with a 200 hp Curtiss V-X-X water-cooled engine. Following the successful marriage of the HS-1 and the Liberty V-12 (resulting in the HS-1L), the navy ordered the flying boat into large-scale production, and additional manufacturers were asked to produce HS-1Ls under license. By the end of production, the Curtiss Aeroplane and Motor Company had built 664 machines; Standard Aircraft Corporation of Elizabeth, New Jersey, manufactured 200; Lowe, Willard, and Fowler of Long Island produced another 200; Gallaudet Aircraft Corporation of East Greenwich, Connecticut, produced 60; Boeing Airplane Company of Seattle, Washington, built 25; and Loughead Aircraft Corporation of Santa Barbara, California (now known as Lockheed), rolled out 2 more. But even with the Liberty engine, the HS-1L could carry only a standard load of two

180-pound depth bombs, which proved ineffective against submerged submarines and were of little use against targets on the ground. It was therefore decided to increase the wingspan of the airplane, adding a 6-foot panel between the center section and the outer wing panels, increasing the overall span from 62 to 74 feet. This modification increased the standard load to two 230-pound depth bombs and resulted in the new designation HS-2L, which the marines acquired in the Azores by the end of World War I and deployed to Haiti after the war.

Haiti's climate and topography were not well suited for air operations. The only viable airfield at the time was located at Port-au-Prince, and it was leased to the marines. The airfield was located northeast of the Gare du Nord railroad station on Avenue Dessalines (an extension of the Grande Rue). The marines set about improving the airfield, and before long it was roughly 1,800 feet wide by 2,200 feet long. The runway was level sod with good drainage. The same could not be said for other airfields, which literally had to be carved out of the jungle in some places.

By the end of the occupation, the marines had established airfields at Anse-à-Galets on the island of Gonâve, Anse-à-Pitres, Cap Haïtian, Gonaïves, Hinche, Jérémie, Môle-Saint-Nicolas, Quanaminthe, Pignon, and Port-de-Paix. "Tentative" landing strips were located at Cerca-la-Source and Saint-Michel-de-l'Atalaye, the latter described as a "plot of ground, 1,800 by 600 feet, located on the plantation of the West Indies Corporation . . . authorized to be used by the government, free of charge, for an aviation landing field." Its upkeep was charged to the gendarmerie and later to the Garde d'Haiti.[116] With the exception of the one at Anse-à-Galets, the airfields had single runways anywhere from 250 to 1,800 feet wide and 900 to 2,700 feet long. The surface of the runways ran the gamut from sod to clay to sand, and in many cases the drainage was poor. In fact, many were unusable after rainfall, and others were characterized as "very soft" when wet. Indeed, the airfield at Quanaminthe was reportedly covered with water for days after a heavy downpour. Obstructions were common, ranging from trees to high-tension wires and holes in the runway. Few airfields had lighting. Only the airfield at Port-au-Prince (later named Bowen Field for a marine aviator who died in a crash and today known as Toussaint Louverture International Airport) had hangars that were not made of canvas.[117] Most airfields had no hangars at all. The tentative landing fields were for emergency purposes, with the airstrip at Cerca-la-Source laid out on a "plateau about 30 feet above the river bed which surrounds over half the field."[118] On the bright side, the airfield at Cerca-la-Source was hard clay, so landings could be made at any time. But in truth, the marines landed anywhere they could find an open field.

According to Gunnery Sergeant Faustin Wirkus, USMC, who was posted to the island of Gonâve (off Port-au-Prince) as a gendarme lieutenant, aircraft from the mainland overflew Anse-à-Galets to drop off supplies, which he requested by carrier pigeon. But over time, he learned what the aviators needed to land on the island, and with forty men he cleared a runway 3,000 feet long and 800 feet wide. It took two months, given that the area was covered by trees with deep roots and "full of stumps," and "there were a great many stones." When it was completed, Wirkus sent a pigeon to Port-au-Prince with an invitation for the aviators to visit his new landing field. Within an hour and a half, a "big DH" piloted by Captain Harold "Hal" Major (Marine Aviator No. 71) landed. According to Wirkus, "There were hundreds of landings on the saline after that," and "a number of officers from the Gendarmerie and Marine Headquarters" visited the island.[119]

Aside from the airfield at Port-au-Prince, the principal airfield was located west of the small town of Hinche.[120] It measured 1,880 by 300 feet of hard, grassy turf. Drainage was good, and unlike many airfields, it had barracks and private quarters on the south side.[121] That said, it was described as a miserable place: "It was a wild and forbidding district, its very name bespeaking its sinister history. In the old days this had been a sort of No-Man's Land between the Spanish and the French colonies, a refuge for runaway slaves, brigands, outlaws; famous for wars, raids, reprisals. Here nature was at her worst and man at his cruelest. So it had been named *Hancha* in old Spanish, meaning 'hateful,' 'accursed.' Time has Frenchified the name to Hinche, pronounced nasally 'anch,' but still the countryside bore ample evidence of the primal blight that prompted its ancient name."[122]

On one occasion, Ken Collings was detailed to locate suitable plots of land near Hinche for possible use during a smallpox outbreak. Flying an antiquated Jenny, he flew to Mirebalais for fuel and then to Quanaminthe. From there, he intended to scout out two small villages near the Dominican border, Belledère and Lascahobas. Other pilots regarded both of them as wholly unsuitable, and Collings had been warned that it would be impossible to land at Lascahobas. Flying first to Belledère, Collings noticed a small clearing west of the tiny village and landed safely—but just barely. It was the first time an airplane had landed anywhere near the village, and Collings and his observer were instant celebrities. Collings then flew back to Mirebalais for fuel and started for Lascahobas the next day. "Except for [a] ridge," he wrote, "there was not a cleared space as big as a handkerchief. It was the ridge or nothing."[123] The grass was high and the slopes were steep, but Collings headed for it anyway, landing lengthwise along an upward sloping crest in a crosswind. Collings's optimism that the crest could be used as a landing field was quickly dashed, however, when his observer jumped out of the airplane and fell into a hole next to the fuselage. In fact, the ridge was "pock-marked with hundreds more, four or five feet in diameter" and waist deep. The Jenny had missed several holes by inches. At first, the two marines thought they might have to walk to Lascahobas and send for mechanics to disassemble the airplane and carry it down the mountain piece by piece. But, undaunted, Lieutenant Collings and Sergeant Mack laid out a takeoff strip free of holes and flew away. Collings wrote: "[No] one ever landed at Las Cahobas again."[124]

Despite Hinche's important role in aerial operations, Collings described it as the "worst flying field in Haiti—and that came close to qualifying it as the worst flying field in the world."[125] During the early years, before improvements were made, the airfield at Hinche had been merely a strip of grass roughly 30 yards wide at the narrowest point, "smack up against the foot of a mountain." The runway sloped uphill along the crest of a "hog-back," and the approach was over a river and the village. The mountain produced strange air currents with a constant downdraft that "churned into countless individual volcanoes of heated air by the cooking fires of the village. A few feet farther on, it was suddenly sucked down again by the cool waters of the river. The whole was a seething inferno of criss-crossing drafts and bumps through which we must stagger to a precision landing. . . . Hinche was always like that except on the rare occasions when the wind blew toward the mountain. Then it was worse."[126]

The main airfield at Port-au-Prince had been used to a limited extent before the marines' arrival by various aerial freight-hauling companies. Over the years, the marines established a fully functioning airfield, and Pan American Airlines was given special permission to use the facilities without charge.[127] The runway was long, with floodlights and an illuminated wind sock. The airfield was accessible in all weather conditions but had several obstructions, the most notable being a 185-foot smokestack to the north, 30-foot-tall high-tension wires to the west, and a 400-foot radio tower and telephone lines to the south.[128] By the 1930s, Pan American would be the only commercial air operation in Haiti, with Clipper-type flying boats arriving from Miami, staying overnight, and departing the next day for San Juan, Puerto Rico, and San Pedro de Macoris in the Dominican Republic. Others would stop in Haiti en route to Rio de Janeiro, Brazil, and Buenos Aires, Argentina. Some aircraft would arrive from Jamaica on their way to Santiago, Cuba. Pan American Clippers carried passengers, mail, and freight.

Flying boats like the Clipper dominated the international airline business in the 1920s and 1930s. Although inefficient from an aerodynamic standpoint, these aircraft could operate from any sheltered harbor, which made them ideal at a time when runways capable of handling large multiengine aircraft were scarce. The first aircraft to be called a Clipper was the Sikorsky four-engine S-40 amphibious flying boat, christened the "American Clipper" by First Lady Lou Hoover. A primitive airplane, the S-40 was nevertheless the largest aircraft built in the United States at the time. Before being replaced in 1936 by the Boeing B-314, a large flying boat with an astonishing range of 3,500 statute miles, Pan American's S-40s flew more than 10 million miles, and during World War II the US Navy used them as trainers for four-engine flight instruction. All were scrapped in 1943.[129]

Of course, the marines were not in Haiti to advance the financial interests of Pan American or any other airline; they were there to support the brigade. And in that regard, they soon proved their worth. A report dated July 15, 1921 (covering activities from July 1, 1920, to June 30, 1921), emphasized that the demands placed on the marines in "infected areas" were arduous, with an average of 225 "searching" patrols; they also guarded important villages and towns. According to the report, "In conjunction with the searching patrols as above referred to, excellent results were obtained by the hitherto untried employment of airplanes, in the searching out of bandit camps remotely situated in the dense mountainous regions."[130]

The report went on to describe an action in which two aircraft were operating with the gendarmerie in the Department of the North. On August 4, 1920, these aircraft participated in an attack on a "bandit" camp. According to Lieutenant General Merwin Silverthorn, who arrived in Haiti in 1923, "during the so-called banana wars, any group of dissidents who weren't for the government were called bandits. They might be very honorable people with a different political feeling. Nevertheless, they were bandits, and they were chased around the hills and shot at and killed whenever you could catch them." As for the *cacos*, however, Silverthorn called them "out-and-out outlaws." He based this opinion largely on his "contact with many marines who served [in Haiti] and chased them."[131]

During the air attack in August, the planes fired some 1,200 rounds of machine gun ammunition in support of the ground assault. A radiogram sent to headquarters by Major James "Jimmy" Meade, commanding the attack, stated that the aircraft "manoeuvered excellently and directed their fire with apparent good effect, starting the bandits from their hiding places, and having the desired moral effect."[132] In a later report, Major Meade posited that "this operation demonstrates that airplanes are a success in such affairs." Indeed, "the bandits were in carefully selected places, one that they thought would safeguard them from pursuit or attack. They soon found out that there was no place that would protect them."[133] As a result of the combined land-air attack, the *cacos* suffered heavy losses and were driven from their camp. According to the report, this particular group, which was the largest guerrilla band in the region, was so demoralized by the air attack that it split up into smaller bands, and they "were reached by the *Gendarmes* who soon cleared the region of bandits."[134] Major Cunningham now had proof that Marine Corps aviation was of significant value, especially with regard to "close air support."[135]

In May 1920 the First Division, Squadron E, became simply Squadron E (the unit's designator would change several more times before it was withdrawn in 1934), the first squadron in the Marine Corps to fly both land and water machines.[136] But the most important change came with the advent of better airplanes. As noted earlier, the First Division had arrived with worn-out Jennies from Miami and HS-2L flying boats. In time, the Jennies were upgraded to the JN-6HG, a gunnery trainer.[137] Developed from the JN-5H, an advanced trainer, the JN-6H had improved ailerons and provided stick and rudder controls in both cockpits (which permitted instructors to teach enlisted men how to fly the airplane). The airframe did not differ substantially from the JN-5H, but the JN-6HG-I was fitted with the 150 hp Wright-Hispano Model I V-8 engine, which delivered greatly improved performance. The new Jenny landplanes joined the First Division, and by the end of June 1920, there were eight HS-2L seaplanes, one N-9 seaplane, five JN-4HGs, and five DH-4Bs.

The most significant addition to the squadron was the arrival of the venerable DH-4B and, later, its Boeing look-alike the 02B-1 (the metal-fuselaged derivative). In 1919 the marines had received an assortment of surplus aircraft from the US Army, including fifteen DH-4Bs, six of the rightly famous German Fokker D.VII fighters, three two-place Fokker D.VII trainers (redesignated the C-1),[138] and eleven Thomas-Morse Scouts (redesignated the MB-3). As noted in chapter 1, the DH-4B was an improved version of the DH-4 Liberty used by the marines during World War I; it borrowed many features from the British DH-9, most notably the relocation of the pilot's cockpit and the main fuel tank. Forty-two DH-4Bs were transferred from the army to the navy after the war, and an additional eighty Liberty planes were remanufactured by the Naval Aircraft Factory in Philadelphia. The DH-4B proved to be a sturdy, maneuverable, and versatile airplane during the early small wars era, serving as an observation platform, a light transport, a bomber, and even an ambulance. The "DH," as it was affectionately known, would remain in service with the marines until 1929, and the last army models were not retired until 1932.[139]

As the insurgency in Haiti deepened, the brigade took to the field once again, but this time with enhanced air support. This was fortuitous, for what the *cacos* lacked in arms and equipment they made up for in mobility, physical endurance, and an ability to live off the land. They also greatly benefited from their intelligence network spread over the entire republic. Colonel Frederick "Dopey" Wise, who had arrived from France and taken over command of the gendarmerie in July 1919, summarized the situation:

> There was literally no beginning or end to Charlemagne's forces. A squad of [his] men would creep down from the mountains into one native village after another. The men in that village would join them and go with them to make the attack on which they were bent, or they were killed as American sympathizers, and their homes burned. So, all over the island, there were thousands of Haitians who were good citizens most of the year and bad Cacos every now and then.
>
> They lived off the country. Mangoes, alligator pears, yams, bananas, stolen cattle or pigs—these gave them all the food they needed. . . . They knew the country the way they knew the palms of their own hands. They needed no map or compass. Instantly they could disband, hide their weapons, and become peaceful inhabitants.
>
> Word would come in that a large Caco force was gathering somewhere in the interior. By the time the Marines . . . reached their spot, they found nothing. Then, that night, miles away, Charlemagne's men would raid some defenseless town.

> It was a combination of Blind Man's Bluff and trying to find a needle in a haystack.[140]

It was therefore in scouting and reconnaissance roles that Squadron E would first demonstrate its usefulness in supporting the brigade and the gendarmerie. Though seemingly routine, such missions were in fact quite dangerous, and aviators whose engines quit knew they probably faced a fate worse than death if captured by the *cacos*. According to Collings, "Mirebaalis was the place where the Cacos had caught Sergeant Muth, cut off his head, cleaned him like a beef-steer, pinned his arms behind his back with skewers, then tossed him into camp."[141] Like all the aviators of Squadron E, Lieutenant Collings understood the dangers he faced, and every marine in Haiti was familiar with the horrible death of Private Clarence "Mike" Morris, who was killed on November 4, 1919. According to a report submitted by the brigade commander on November 7:

> Lieutenant McFayden and Private Clarence E. Morris made a forced landing last night north of Maissade. Lieutenant McFayden left Morris in charge of [the] plane and walked to Hinche, arriving there at 7:00 a.m. this morning and reporting the landing of the plane. Patrols and another plane were sent to look for the disabled plane. The patrols first failed to find it but the disabled plane was located by another plane about 4:00 p.m. On landing it was discovered that Private Morris had left his plane taking with him the Lewis Air Machine Gun and three drums of ammunition. Patrols were sent out in every direction. Natives living in the vicinity and market women in the neighboring towns [were] questioned about Private Morris but to no avail.[142]

A subsequent report provided additional details: "It appears that Private Morris left his plane. . . . He obtained three natives to guide him and later gave the machine gun to one of the natives to carry. Becoming tired he sat down and while in this position one of the three natives came behind and struck him with a machete, killing him. The natives then took the machine gun, his clothes and ammunition and started out to join the bandits. The above information was given by a bandit chief who recently surrendered."[143] But an unofficial and more lurid tale was told among the marines. According to Lieutenant Collings:

> It was Benoit's gang [Benoît Batraville, Charlemagne's chief subordinate] and they intended murder from the first. They did not, however, act immediately because they suspected a trap. They could not picture a white man being so careless. They led Morris in circles for two days, just to test him. When he did not catch on, they were positive that he was really lost. Then they tied him to a tree and skinned him alive—a half strip at a time.
>
> And that was not the end. They ate Morris' heart to give them courage; then Benoit made a speech.
>
> "The white man," he told his followers, "has brains. That is why his bullets go straight. We have no brains so our bullets miss. Therefore we will grease our bullets in the white man's brains. They will then be endowed with the white man's ability to hit the mark." Placing Morris' brains in a bowl, they filed past, dipping their bullets. The Marines suspected most of that when they found Morris' horribly mutilated body. The gruesome details came out when Captain Cy Perkins killed Benoit and captured some of his fellows.[144]

The veracity of Collings's account cannot be confirmed (there is no such account in the official records), but it was a common tale.[145] Nevertheless, and regardless of the accuracy of the tale, marine aviators in Haiti were quite convinced that a similar fate awaited them if they were forced down. And they were all familiar with how Haitian president Guillaume Sam had been murdered and mutilated, his head paraded about Port-au-Prince on a staff.

By mid-March 1919, six companies of the Second Regiment were deployed to the interior: two at Lascahobas, two at Hinche, one to Mirebalais, and another to Saint-Michel. Later that same month, four additional companies arrived from the Seventh Regiment at Guantanamo Bay. Over the next six months, the brigade and the gendarmerie fought more than 130 actions, from skirmishes to company-sized pitched battles. As noted earlier, Squadron E's aircraft initially proved most useful in indirect roles, such as scouting and reconnaissance, ferrying personnel and supplies to remote posts, carrying dispatches and the mail, other communications missions, and aerial mapping. But with the arrival of the DH-4B and a new commander—Captain Roy Geiger—the squadron's mission soon took on a new complexion. It was just prior to Geiger's assumption of command that the marine aviators in

Haiti developed a tactic that became fundamental to their principal role of close air support: dive-bombing.

It is difficult to pinpoint the origin of dive-bombing—or, more accurately, glide-bombing—since World War I aviators on both sides used steep bomb delivery on occasion, and US Army fliers are said to have experimented with the technique as early as 1917.[146] But it was the marines who embraced dive-bombing and advanced the technique after the war, incorporating it into their tactical doctrine.[147] Until the intervention in Haiti, however, the marines had followed the standard technique developed in World War I of allowing the observer in the rear of the aircraft to release bombs from horizontal flight using a crude British-designed Wimpers bombsight.[148] But dropping bombs on railway marshaling yards was one thing; dropping them accurately on *cacos* in close proximity to marines on the ground was quite another.[149]

Arguably, dive-bombing as a technique dates back at least to the Mexican Civil War, when French mercenary Didier Masson dropped homemade dynamite bombs consisting of 15-inch pieces of iron pipe packed with sticks of dynamite and scrap metal onto the gunboat *Guerrero* in Guaymas harbor.[150] Early in World War I, a French pilot on a scouting mission lost his engine at 8,000 feet, volplaned,[151] and dropped his bombs on the German airship hangars at Metz, causing considerable damage. In 1914 a British Royal Naval Air Service pilot flying a Sopwith Tabloid destroyed the Zeppelin ZIX in its hangar at Düsseldorf, diving to some 600 feet before releasing his bombs. By the close of the year, a British journalist argued that, "when gliding from a height, with the aircraft under power, the tangent to the trajectory and the axis of the machine would gradually become parallel and therefore the accuracy of aim would be increased."[152] He concluded that, for best results, the bomb should be released at the end of a dive to 500 feet, when the axis of the aircraft was pointing at the target. By the end of the war, all the air forces of the major combatants were using diving or "plunging" attacks, although "strafing"[153] and horizontal bombing remained the preferred methods.

Following World War I, ground attack remained an integral part of every air force's repertoire, and the emphasis placed on dive-bombing depended on the nation and the air force. During the interwar years, the new German Luftwaffe emphasized long-range aerial interdiction over close air support, despite the close association between the Luftwaffe and the German army and the considerable infamy gained by the Ju-87 Stuka dive-bomber at the outset of World War II.[154] France built more warplanes between the world wars than any other country, but the early emphasis was on "level" bombers such as the Lioré et Olivier 20 and the Lioré et Olivier 451, the fastest medium bomber in the world at the outbreak of World War II (outpacing the German *Schnellbomber* types—the Dornier Do-17K, Heinkel He-111E, and Junkers Ju-88A). Japan's air arms (army and navy) followed the general European trend, conducting no dive-bombing experiments until the late 1920s. Of the few nations experimenting with dive-bombing, Great Britain took the early lead, but the Royal Air Force soon dispensed with the idea in favor of long-range heavy bombers.[155]

Surprisingly, it was the US Army that kept the dive-bomber concept alive between the world wars. Although the United States was a latecomer to World War I, many American aviators had served with French and British units, and the employment of heavily armed aircraft for ground support gained considerable favor. Consequently, during the early 1920s, a number of experimental "strafers" were developed, but the substantial reduction in performance occasioned by the weight of the armament and armor lessened their promise. Nevertheless, a number of aircraft entered into the new "attack" category, including the Curtiss A-12, the first US aircraft designed specifically for ground-attack purposes. The earliest US Army plunging experiment probably occurred in late 1919 at Aberdeen Proving Ground in Maryland. US Army Air Service Lieutenant Lester Sweeley dove his DH-4B from some 5,000 feet to within 1,000 feet of the ground before releasing a 300-pound bomb from a Mark XVI bomb rack. Although the bomb struck the undercarriage and veered slightly from its course, it continued on to the target and exploded.[156]

Around the same time that Sweeley was experimenting with plunging attacks at Aberdeen, Marine Corps lieutenants Sandy Sanderson and Vernon Brown, then stationed at Gonaïves, discussed the idea of pointing the nose of the aircraft at a target on the ground, gliding at an angle of no more than 45 degrees to the horizontal, and releasing a bomb at low level. As discussed in chapter 1, Sanderson had enlisted in the Marine Corps in September 1917. He completed flight school and was commissioned as a second lieutenant in January 1919, whereupon he deployed to Haiti with the First Division, Squadron E, in March. According to Sanderson, "The dive bombing idea was more or less forced on us. We were required to bomb the hostile forces in the immediate vicinity of our Marines. Fifty to 100 yards in front of friendly troops. We could not do this with safety to our troops when employing horizontal bombing."[157]

A few days after his conversation with Brown, Sanderson jerry-rigged a bomb rack consisting of a canvas mail sack attached to the underside of the airplane and tied at the opening with sash cords leading to the pilot's cockpit. To aim the bomb, Sanderson added a rifle barrel with a cross-hair peep sight above the engine cowling. He dropped several 20-pound practice bombs at Mirebalais and later recalled that the accuracy was "astonishing." Not long afterward, he and his observer, Lieutenant Lewis "Chesty" Puller of the gendarmerie, used the technique in combat operations against the *cacos,* with "excellent results."[158] Thereafter, other crews of Squadron E adopted the practice, and when Captain Geiger took command in December, he ordered that all pilots be trained in the technique.[159]

From April through September 1919, the marines and the gendarmerie averaged twenty contacts with *cacos* per month. Squadron E flew regularly, providing logistical and close air support. During this time, marine aircraft were holed on numerous occasions, and for their own protection, the aviators resorted to using the lids from their Buzzacott wood-burning stoves as armored seats.[160] Operating in close coordination with mobile ground forces, Squadron E rendered yeoman service during the pursuit of Charlemagne and the mopping-up operations that followed. In addition to flying ground-attack missions, squadron crews conducted aerial mapping, flew photographic and communication sorties, delivered mail, transported and air-dropped supplies to troops in the field, evacuated sick and wounded marines, and performed observation, scouting, and reconnaissance missions.

The absence of cavalry or other means of scouting and reconnaissance other than patrolling on foot placed a premium on aerial missions. As one marine put it, "The lack of good roads and means of transportation to overcome the hardships of fighting bandits in the high mountains and many valleys has brought our squadron of 'eyes' to Haiti."[161] The eyes of the squadron were the observers, both officer and enlisted. Commissioned aerial observers were required to be qualified infantry officers with good judgment, capable of determining the strength, disposition, activities, and probable intentions of enemy forces, as well as able to distinguish *bons habitants,* or peaceful inhabitants, from *mauvais habitants,* that is, *cacos* and other ne'er-do-wells among the *ajoupas* (thatched huts).[162] But as the occupation wore on into the late 1920s and early 1930s, enlisted men (sometimes clerical or other support personnel) took over the role of observers, and the pilots often used the opportunity to teach promising enlisted men how to fly. Moreover, the marine aviators took to mapping the countryside during routine missions to support operations on the ground.

Previously, maps of Haiti dated back to those created by French civil engineers before the American Revolution. According to marine aviator Hayne "Cuckoo" Boyden, "In all the valleys and plains, the Artibonite, the Cul de Sac, the Northern Plain all the way from Port Margot to Ounaminthe, the Plain of Goaives, L'Arcahaie, and out to the Aux Cayes plain are the parallel roadways and section lines, long and straight."[163] The French surveyors had done a fine job, and the marines used the old French lines as a secondary control from the air to complement primary control on the ground. Along with his observer Sergeant Herbert Dugan, Lieutenant Boyden mapped the whole of Haiti from 10,000 feet. This was no mean feat, given the treacherous air currents over the mountains and plains and the primitive equipment at Boyden's disposal. As he explained: "It is next to impossible to hold a plane at a given altitude in [such conditions], for it will gain or lose several hundred feet. The conventional altimeter furnished in a plane to indicate height is calibrated in hundreds of feet, and is comparatively sluggish in registering a change. By the time it shows the loss or gain, it is too late. The harm is done. The pictures will be too much out of scale while going down or up, and in regaining the correct altitude."[164]

To overcome this challenge, Boyden secured a balloon statoscope to be used in conjunction with the altimeter.[165] The device proved invaluable: "When the desired altitude was once picked on the altimeter, then all that was necessary was to watch the drop of red fluid in the glass tube of the statoscope, and the moment it showed a loss or gain in altitude, nose the plane more up or down till it read zero. I could thus hold the plane within fifty feet of ten thousand feet. The combination of the French Colonial surveying and the statoscope, with care in putting together the pictures, made accurate mosaic maps possible."[166]

In light of today's technology, the employment of airplanes to deliver the mail and to provide communication between forces on the ground might seem especially inefficient. However, the roads in Haiti were primitive at best, described as "numberless trails, winding and climbing up the mountain slopes, and varying in character from poor dirt roads to tortuous rock-strewn donkey-paths."[167] And although primitive radios existed, they were scarce and unreliable. Even less reliable was the telephone system, as described by Captain John Craige: "Our telephone at Hinche was connected with

Headquarters at Port au Prince by a single strand of bare wire, most of it iron wire, at that. Under the best circumstances we could barely understand what the person on the other end was talking about. Most of the time one couldn't quite do that. A voice buzzed and mumbled from the receiver. Occasionally it would rise to shriek incoherences."[168] Thus, if a message was truly important, it was carried by airplane: "At about noon, when the rain stopped, an airplane zoomed into camp. The pilot tossed out an oilcloth case of dispatches labeled 'urgent.' They were from Gendarmerie Headquarters and quoted a message from Lieutenant South stating that there had been an uprising in St. Michel, that the gendarmes had revolted and the lieutenant was besieged in his house. South's message ended in a frantic appeal for help, and Headquarters instructed me to go to his aid with all possible dispatch."[169]

In addition to oilcloth dispatch cases, the marines used pigeons to communicate with their brothers in arms on the ground. Although almost completely forgotten today, homing (or carrier) pigeons were widely used for communication purposes and were often carried in airplanes in the early 1900s. Training with pigeons was a routine but very important matter in Haiti, as indicated by an operations report dated October 25, 1930, that stated, "pigeon training consisting of one flight and two hundred and forty (240) miles were covered in training."[170] The operations officer went on to note that pigeons were carried on all mail trips by Marine Corps aircraft.

Pigeons had been used for communication purposes as far back as ancient Greece, and during World War I several birds on the Allied side became famous for their heroic exploits, including "Spike," "Cher Ami," and "The Mocker." At the outbreak of World War I, the Germans had a well-established pigeon service, as did the British army, and in 1917 the US Army Signal Corps created a Pigeon Section. The US Army had first attempted to use pigeons in the 1870s during the Plains Wars, but the experiment failed when the birds fell prey to hawks. Nevertheless, the army resumed using pigeons during World War I and employed them again in World War II. The Pigeon Service at Fort Monmouth, New Jersey, was closed in 1957.[171]

In the late 1800s the US Naval Academy sent one of its professors, Francis Marion, to Belgium to learn about the care and training of carrier pigeons. The result was a manual on the subject published in 1899. The manual required that a record be kept for each bird, noting the number of flights and other pertinent information. "Pigeoneers" received a quartermaster rating—Quartermaster (Pigeon), or QM (P)—from the Bureau of Navigation, as reflected in the enlisted code book of 1919. As late as 1926, the navy still had twelve pigeon lofts and approximately 800 birds. However, by 1930, owing to advancements in wireless radio technology, the navy closed the majority of its lofts, retaining only those at Lakehurst, New Jersey, and Guam, with some 400 birds between them. But during their heyday in the navy, the marines used pigeons, especially in Haiti.

The marines understood that the care and training of these birds required a particular expertise: "The physical condition of the bird is all-important, and a homer, no matter how carefully bred, must have a course of training before it will function efficiently."[172] Indeed, the director of naval communications for the Bureau of Navigation informed navy and marine commanders in 1921, "It has been brought to the attention of this office that occasionally men who have been made expert pigeon trainers have been transferred by commanding officers to other duties, and the work and care of training the birds is left to inexperienced hands." To prevent this, the bureau issued Circular Letter No. 88 on March 10, 1921, which stated: "All men who have qualified as expert pigeon trainers will be immediately assigned to such duty and will not be transferred to other details without reference to the Bureau of Navigation. In case expert pigeon trainers are now attached to air stations on which there are no pigeon lofts, please report to the Bureau."[173]

Although it might seem odd, pigeons were used extensively as a means of communication between aircraft and the ground both during and after World War I. The pilot or observer would write a message on a piece of paper and insert it into a small capsule attached to the bird's leg. The pigeon would then be released to fly to its home loft with the message. When the bird arrived at its coop, a buzzer sounded, indicating that a new message had arrived. The drawback, of course, was that no responses could be sent by the same means. But this was true whether the bird was released from a ground station, in the air, or at sea.

During the early years of the occupation, transporting supplies was a consistent challenge for the marines in Haiti. Numerous early reports rated supply as "unsatisfactory." This was mainly due "to insufficient receipt of supply from the United States," but the inadequate roads in Haiti also played a role. Consequently, marines in the field often had to rely on reserve rations until food and other supplies were delivered. Even when motor vehicles such as "quad" tractors[174] were introduced (the first automobile arrived in Haiti in 1917), parts problems handicapped motorized transportation efforts. Thus, in a report filed in April 1921, the brigade requested "cargo airplanes . . . for emergencies and economy." Unfortunately, at the time, the marines lacked aircraft designed for or well suited to handling cargo. Therefore, supplies had to be transported by whatever aircraft were available, which is to say DHs, flying boats, and even Jennies. But even without specialized cargo aircraft, air transportation of personnel and material was described as "faultless."[175]

The same was true for medical evacuation. Medical evacuation by air was not a novel idea. During the siege of Paris in 1870, the French had used a balloon to evacuate several soldiers who had fallen ill. As a result, at the outbreak of World War I, the French *l'avion sanitaire* was established. Moreover, one of the most important innovations of the French air service in Morocco following World War I was the use of aircraft as flying ambulances. The French developed special models of Farman and Bréguet bombers for exclusive use as air ambulances. These aircraft could land on rough fields close to the front lines and remove wounded and sick soldiers quickly to well-equipped hospitals in the rear.[176] By the major campaigns of 1925, the French had established a large-scale aerial "medevac" system employing specially modified Bloch 81, Potez 29, and Hanriot 431 airplanes.[177] Collection points at forward landing fields were established, and the French flew a regular schedule of flights to transport casualties from the front lines to military hospitals in an hour or less. During the heavy fighting against Rif troops in 1925, the French evacuated just under 1,000 wounded and sick soldiers by air.[178] Unfortunately, neither the US Army nor the US Navy expressed much interest in air ambulances, and the *Baltimore Sun* newspaper went so far as to argue against the development of such a capability, claiming that "the hazard of being severely wounded is sufficient without the additional hazard of transportation by airplane."[179]

Transporting sick or slightly injured soldiers by air, with the patient riding in the observer's cockpit, was fairly routine for the marines, but transporting seriously ill or badly injured persons by air had not been considered before the arrival of Squadron E in Haiti. And in the absence of a specially configured airplane, the only way to accomplish such a mission was to strap the patient to the wing of the aircraft. This occurred on at least one occasion in Haiti before a modified DH was dispatched to the squadron from Quantico.[180]

On that occasion, Lieutenant Collings received a radio call from Maissade, requesting that he fly his DH to the town to deliver a propeller for another aircraft and pick up a local man who had been badly hurt. While attempting to crank the aircraft's engine in preparation for takeoff, the man had been struck by the propeller, resulting in damage to both. The man's body was rigidly splinted "from head to foot," so he was unable to sit in the observer's cockpit. Collings therefore elected to tie the patient to the wing of his airplane. With assistance from the local doctor and others, Collings crafted a wooden stretcher measuring 15 inches wide by 6 feet long. The injured man was sedated and then lashed to the plank of wood, complete with helmet and goggles. The contraption was then tied to the lower left wing of the DH, close alongside the fuselage. The doctor climbed into the observer's cockpit.

The landing strip at Maissade was crude, short, and curved, with high trees at the end. Marines from the local detachment held the wings and lifted the tail into a level flying position until the engine reached full power, letting go when given the signal by Collings. The DH lifted off quickly, and Collings nosed the airplane down to gain speed. After clearing the trees at the end of the runway, he headed for Cap Haïtian over the Masif du Nord mountain range. Despite the need for altitude and speed, Collings had to throttle back the engine because the airflow over the wing was forcing his semiconscious passenger backward. Fortunately, as Collings recounted, he had long experience flying in Haiti:

> I had flown that course a hundred times; I knew every foot of it. The knowledge came in handy now as I started flying through the defiles in the mountains, picking my way from valley to valley, twisting, zigzagging and not caring so long as the general course was north. Every foot of the way I had to watch the mountains skating by my wing-tips to guard against collision and I had to watch the man on my wing for fear he would slip again—and never for a second did I forget that this was still bandit country. A forced landing would be just too bad.[181]

Collings's exploit was written up in *Popular Science* magazine,[182] but such derring-do was neither safe nor efficient, and the marines set about creating a purpose-built flying ambulance of their own. Very little information is available, but in 1922 "Cocky" Evans apparently designed a flying ambulance based on the DH-4, "with a turtle-back fuselage" and a "Stokes" stretcher. Two were built at the Naval Aircraft Factory in Philadelphia, each able to accommodate one reclining and one sitting passenger. "They could cut evacuation time from three days by muleback, cart, and truck to two hours' round trip."[183] DH-4B A-5811 was assigned to Haiti, and A-5883 was assigned to the Dominican Republic.[184]

The End of the Second *Caco* Campaign

In order to deal with the insurgency more effectively, the new brigade commander, Colonel John "Pug" Russell, reorganized his command, "gridding" the whole country and assigning troops to areas of responsibility.[185] He then created an improved intelligence organization and stressed offensive combat operations to the commander of the gendarmerie, Colonel Wise. "Decapitation"—that is, capturing or killing Charlemagne, the animating spirit of the *cacos*—was deemed the most efficient way to crush the insurgency. The result was one of the most dramatic exploits in Marine Corps history.

Gendarmerie captain Herman Hanneken (a marine first sergeant) persuaded an influential local citizen, Jean-Baptiste Conze, to set a trap by declaring his opposition to the occupation and establishing himself as a loyal follower of Charlemagne at Fort Capois, the former *caco* stronghold taken by Major Butler in 1915. Conze's outspoken support soon attracted the *caco* leader's attention. To solidify Conze's new reputation as a dedicated insurgent, the gendarmes staged a mock attack on the fort, in which Hanneken was wounded. Following the "failed" attack, Charlemagne, his brother, assorted *caco* chiefs, and some 1,200 *cacos* arrived at Fort Capois with plans to capture the town of Grande Riviere du Nord. Alerted by Conze, the marines reinforced the garrison and awaited the *cacos.* Then, Hanneken and First Lieutenant William Button blackened their faces to resemble Haitians and, leading a force of eighteen gendarmes dressed as civilians, stole their way into Charlemagne's camp bearing the false news that Grande Riviere had been taken. When he found Charlemagne, Hanneken killed the insurgent leader with two shots from his .45-caliber semiautomatic pistol. Button opened fire with a .30-06-caliber Browning automatic rifle that he had managed to conceal beneath his clothing. By the end of the firefight, nine of Charlemagne's bodyguards lay dead alongside him. At daybreak, Hanneken and his men made their way down the mountain with Charlemagne's body. Meanwhile, the *caco* attack on Grande Riviere had failed.

Charlemagne's body was taken to Cap Haïtian, where a Roman Catholic bishop positively identified the body. Following an unwise public display of the body meant to warn his followers of their own fate should they continue the fight, Charlemagne was buried in a concrete vault to prevent any voodoo "shenanigans."[186] Hanneken and Button both received the Medal of Honor for their actions, and Conze returned to his former life, substantially rewarded for his efforts. Hanneken was subsequently commissioned a second lieutenant and would go on to other exploits, retiring as a brigadier general.[187]

The death of Charlemagne brought relative calm to northern Haiti, but *cacos* led by Benoît Batraville continued their depredations in the central region. In preparation for a final offensive to deal with Batraville, Colonel Russell again reorganized the brigade, splitting the Second Regiment, which had been reinforced with two companies, into two regiments: the Second and Eighth. Lieutenant Colonel Louis McCarty Little, recently arrived from the United States, commanded the Eighth Regiment, responsible for central and southern Haiti, while the Second Regiment, under the command of Lieutenant Colonel Randolph Berkeley, was responsible for the northern department. Berkeley was a Medal of Honor recipient who had served at Veracruz.[188] Central Haiti was declared the focus of the brigade's counterguerrilla efforts, and Russell instituted a system of mounted, foot, and air patrols to keep the *cacos* off balance and on the run.

At the height of his power, Batraville had roughly 2,500 *cacos* under his command and perhaps another 5,000 active sympathizers among the peasantry. On New Year's Day 1920, Russell launched his offensive.[189] Batraville's reaction was to attack Port-au-Prince with some 300 *cacos* in the early-morning hours of January 15. The attack was beaten off, and gendarmerie patrols were sent out of the city in pursuit. During one of these patrols, a small group of marines led by Sergeant Lawrence Muth was ambushed while ascending a steep mountain trail. Muth was hit in the head and stomach when the *cacos* opened fire. The patrol was forced to abandon the sergeant, but once the men returned to base they were reorganized and led back by Lieutenant Colonel Little. At the site of the ambush they discovered Muth's decapitated body. On a more positive note, the failed *caco* assault on Port-au-Prince signaled the end of Batraville's power in the region. In February alone, some 3,000 *cacos* surrendered. On February 21, Dominique, a powerful *caco* leader in central Haiti, surrendered at Lascahobas; Papillon, Charlemagne's so-called minister of war, surrendered as well.[190] Batraville's demise would soon follow—and Marine Corps aviation would help seal his fate.

On March 31, in a manner not unlike his earlier killing of Charlemagne, Hanneken stole into the camp of Osiris Joseph, a major *caco* chief in the north, and shot him dead. With Joseph's death, the marines and gendarmes then concentrated on Batraville's group. Several aircraft from Squadron E were moved to small airstrips in *caco* country to support the ground forces. From these unimproved landing fields, marine aviators flew reconnaissance missions and bombed and strafed *caco* camps and bands of *cacos* moving about the area. It was during this time that Captain Edward Ostermann, a Medal of Honor recipient during Butler's march to Fort Dipitie and now in command of a unit near Mirebalais, requested two aircraft to help him break up a *caco bamboche,* an all-night drinking party staged for Batraville. The air raid scattered the partygoers, and Ostermann later reported: "We had no more trouble from Batraville in my area."[191]

On May 18, 1920, Batraville and a force of some 200 *cacos* were located near Lascahobas. A thirty-man patrol led by Captain Jesse Perkins was sent to make contact. A firefight broke out, and Batraville was killed.[192] With the deaths of Charlemagne, Batraville, Joseph, and other *caco* leaders, Louis Nord and his brother became the most important *caco* chiefs in Haiti. The two brothers were soon located on Mount Nappe, east of Cap Haïtian. Major Jimmy Meade, commander of gendarmerie operations in the north, requested two aircraft to support a ground attack on the *caco* hideout. Ken Collings flew one of the aircraft. He and Captain Hal Major were briefed by Geiger and departed for Cap Haïtian from Hinche. Upon their arrival, they learned that Louis Nord had left his hiding place on Mount Nappe but was expected to settle somewhere nearby. "Then we would strike, on the ground and in the air," Collings later wrote, "in a simultaneous effort to wipe out his entire force."[193]

After six days of waiting, Collings and Major received word to meet with Hanneken in Perches, a tiny village nearby. Hanneken informed the two aviators that Louis Nord was hiding in a gap in the crest of twin-peaked Mount Salnave. The plan was to attack the camp from the air and on the ground at daybreak. Hanneken informed Collings that "there isn't a 'bon inhabitant' on the whole mountain, so riddle every hut with machine gun bullets and pour them into the thickets besides."[194] Collings and Major retraced their steps to Cap Haïtian, arriving just in time to start up the engines of their DH airplanes and join the attack. Captain Major's Liberty engine started without difficulty, but after six days idle, Collings's engine balked. Once Collings's engine started, Major's quit, so Collings took off without him.

Lieutenant Collings spotted Hanneken and his gendarmes in a clearing just below the crest of the mountain. Sergeant Guy Smith, Collings's observer-gunner, began firing his Lewis machine gun, mixing ball and tracer and shooting at "everything which looked like a bandit shelter." No *cacos* broke from the buildings, so Smith turned his attention to the nearby woods. It was then that Collings's Liberty engine "*quit cold!*" No more than 30 feet from crashing into the ground, Collings was preparing to "pancake" his airplane into a stand of trees when the engine restarted. He and Smith then flew back to Cap Haïtian. Only four *cacos* were killed by the air attack, but according to Collings, the engagement "marked the first time in all their long history of bandit fighting [in Haiti] that the Marines used a concerted land and air attack."[195]

Marine Corps Aviation Settles in for the Long Haul

By the end of 1921, there were six Jennies, seven DHs, and six HS-2Ls in Haiti. That same year, Captain Arthur Page Jr. (Marine Aviator No. 41), commander of the Fourth Air Squadron (Flights G and H—formerly Squadron E—effective January 1, 1921), wrote a letter to the commandant in Washington, stating that pilots should not be detailed to Haiti for more than one year.[196] It was his experience and that of his predecessor, Major Geiger (promoted back to that grade during his tour in Haiti), that the nature of operations in Haiti was such that pilots rapidly lost "their value for formation work, gunnery, bombing etc." The reason was straightforward enough, according to Captain Page: "Continued straight flying from point to point" offered no development of a pilot's skills. In addition, the climate had an adverse effect on aviators, and "continual manual work" in such an environment produced "mental strain." In that regard, there was "no opportunity to relax by stunting" (that is, aerobatic or stunt flying). Finally, Page wrote, "Pilots on this kind of work [were] very apt to become overcautious if kept at it too long thereby losing the most necessary qualification of an excellent pilot."[197]

Two points must be made. First, flying in Haiti after the Second *Caco* Campaign was routine, but that routine could quickly become deadly, as Lieutenant Collings's descriptions amply demonstrate. Indeed, on June 1, 1921, while en route from Maissade to Port-au-Prince in a DH, Lieutenant Guy Hall flew into a massive thunderstorm at 6,000 feet. He increased his altitude to 7,000 feet but was unable to fly over the storm. For some thirty-plus minutes, he was unable to see past his wingtips, and although he managed to rise to 10,000 feet, he was still unable to get over the storm. Seeing a break in the clouds, he spiraled down to about 3,000 feet and, recognizing the central plain of Saint-Michel, dropped close to the ground and flew safely to his destination. According to a *Marine Corps Gazette* essay written by the chief of aviation, Major Thomas Turner:

> During the time he was in the storm, Lieutenant Hall had at times practically no control over the plane. The way the compass continually twisted and spun indicated that the plane was being turned about in a manner which defied the pilot's effort to maintain direction. At one time the plane dropped down in a straight line more than a thousand feet. To all these difficulties . . . Lieutenant Hall did not know whether he was over the mountains or the plains, and therefore after descending below 600 feet there was a danger of crashing into a mountain. Upon landing he found that the propeller had been chewed by the rain and ruined beyond repair.[198]

On the same day, Collings flew from Port-au-Prince to Jérémie to deliver vaccines. He too encountered a "wind and rain storm so dense that after four attempts to pass around and over the storm he was forced to return to Port-au-Prince." The next day, Collings and Page both set out for Jérémie in separate DH-4Bs, each with a package of vaccines. Page intended to fly along the north coast, and Collings was to fly along the south coast. "By flying just off the water both planes kept track of the shore line and got through to Jeremie and dropped the vaccine." But during their return trip the storm increased in intensity, and they were forced back to Jérémie. From there, Page and Collings both took the northern coastal route back to Port-au-Prince, again flying just offshore.[199]

The second point is that the issue of mental strain in the tropics was real—at least to the marines. Although one might be inclined to dismiss Captain Page's letter as the whining of a bored pilot, the brigade commander forwarded the recommendation, with his concurrence, to the commandant.[200] And recall the case of Lieutenant South, whose plea for help resulted in Captain Craige being directed to go to his aid after an uprising of the local gendarmes. South was the sole marine posted to Saint-Michel and was in charge of the gendarmerie detachment there. When Craige arrived, he learned there had been no mutiny; South's mental state had simply degenerated to the point that he had pulled a gun on his subordinates. South's actions were symptomatic of the mental and emotional strain that afflicted North American (that is, white) troops in the tropics: "To white men who stay south too long," wrote Craige, "something happens. The stolid slow up; the nervous blow up."[201] Craige described a "mysterious terrible psychological disorder" that produced strange behaviors. "If he is transferred at this stage . . . all may yet be well. Otherwise he passes swiftly to a condition of nervous hysteria," and "his messmates say: 'The tropics have got him.'"[202] Being posted to an airfield was undoubtedly less of a strain than being alone in an isolated mountain village surrounded by *cacos* and the indigenous population, but the stress of flying had a physiological and emotional impact all its own.

Moreover, the marines' mission in Haiti became more complicated beginning in 1920 than it had been during the early years of the occupation. Major Harold Utley, who had served in World War I and in both *caco* campaigns and would later serve in Nicaragua from 1928 to 1929, wrote in 1931:

> When Uncle Sam occupies the territory of a small nation he wants to enforce his will, but he does not want any trouble, that is, anything that will cause undue comment among his own or foreign people. Such comments may not only cause countless "investigations" at a more or less later date (there have been seven in Haiti in the fourteen years of occupation), but what is more important from our point of view, such comments in the Halls of Congress and in the press of our own and nearby countries are interpreted by the natives as having far greater weight than they really possess, are taken indeed as an indication of strong support for the forces arrayed against us, and thus serve to intensify and prolong the opposition we must overcome. Of course the leaders know better, but they are skilled in the use of propaganda for their own ends, and there will always be found so-called Americans who under one pretext or another will assist in originating and spreading tales of alleged "atrocities" said to have been committed by our troops. If we were at war, if the Laws of War applied, we could justly charge them—the originators and the publishers—with giving aid and comfort to the enemy. But in Small Wars we are at peace no matter how thickly the bullets are flying.[203]

As Utley alludes, interventions of the sort taking place in Haiti were not peaceful, but they were not war either. And as any modern veteran of Iraq and Afghanistan will corroborate, the mental strain of counterinsurgency is considerable, especially when the rules of engagement impose serious constraints on the employment of violence by soldiers, "no matter how thickly the bullets are flying."[204] In that regard, the occupation of Haiti occurred during a pivotal time of transition for the Marine Corps, from an earlier "roughneck" era associated with minor punitive expeditions or those involving interposition to the more complex requirements of intervention and "pacification," that is, counterinsurgency. The former goal of "teaching the *cacos* a lesson" had been in keeping with the "punitive" tradition of Marine Corps operations in the Caribbean and Central America. "There were good Haitians, and there were bad, and punitive discipline placed the latter at the wrong end of [a] Springfield rifle."[205] But counterinsurgency is not law enforcement; nor is it merely counterguerrilla warfare. This is not an artificial distinction. It arises from the practical reality that the counterinsurgent's task is precisely the opposite of the insurgent's.

With the policy in Washington being to uphold the central government of Haiti as well as to "uplift" the Haitian people, the use of force had to be constrained. If the use of force did not lead to bad publicity, it was deemed appropriate. If bad publicity and investigations resulted, it was deemed "excessive." This applied to both the employment of aviation and the use of force on the ground. Fortunately for marine aviators, "The Haitians had a great awe for the planes and the aviators." Indeed, as Captain Craige wrote: "They thought the planes were big birds trained by the *blancs* [whites] and that the whites who rode them were all-powerful *bocours* [also, *bokor*], a species of God."[206] Merely the appearance of Marine Corps aircraft overhead often caused the *cacos* to scatter. This was fortuitous, for as Craige claimed, "We didn't want to kill a lot of those poor devils, so the planes never did any bombing [following the collapse of Charlemagne's insurgency]. They would go up a couple of times a day to spot large bands of *cacos*. When they found a big band, they would take a dive at it. The noise of the motor would nearly scare the *cacos* to death, and they would take it on the run for the tall timbers."[207]

As aviation became more integrated with the marines on the ground,[208] the pacification campaign against the *cacos* in the northern and central valley areas was carried out aggressively, but arguably with less success. During the initial landings, the *cacos* were generally not supported by the peasantry.

However, during the insurgency led by Charlemagne, the peasants supported the *cacos* both passively and actively. Thus, the marines had to adjust their approach during the insurgency itself and after the death of Charlemagne. In garnering popular support, Charlemagne had called on a long tradition of peasant rebellion and hatred of whites. To make matters worse, the marines continued to use the terms *caco* and "bandit," and it was during the revolution that the term *caco* was first applied to slaves who had fought against the French. With the eruption of the insurgency led by Charlemagne, the *cacos* were now set squarely against not only the central government in Port-au-Prince but the occupation as well. Rebellion and resistance merged into insurgency. In other words, the desire to rid themselves of an oppressive "puppet" government was wedded to an emergent sense of nationalism alongside a long-held xenophobia, combining to make the peasants more amenable to supporting the *cacos.* Even if the peasants did not actively fight alongside the *cacos,* they provided help in the form of logistics and intelligence. Thus, non-*cacos* and *cacos* joined forces, blurring the line between peasant and insurgent and between *bons habitants* and *mauvais habitants.*

In retrospect, the Second *Caco* Campaign and what followed did not constitute a "punitive expedition" in the earlier roughneck tradition of the Marine Corps. Marines who served during the campaign later understood this. One of them was General Lemuel Shepherd, who served in the Garde d'Haiti, as the commander of Caserne Dartiguenave from 1930 to 1932, and then as the chief of police of Port-au-Prince until 1933, and who later became the twentieth commandant of the Marine Corps. In an oral history interview many years later, Shepherd likened the experience to "frontier fighting" in the American West (counterguerrilla warfare), as well as to the counterinsurgency effort then ongoing in South Vietnam. According to Shepherd, "You've got to fight [the] kind of war in the way that they're waging it on you," that is, counterinsurgency and counterguerrilla warfare.[209] But at the time, the marines were still learning the rudiments of counterinsurgency, and their early mistakes enabled Charlemagne's movement to prosper until his death. Afterward, the structural conditions remained, and resistance to the occupation now included a broad swath of the general population.

Nevertheless, from 1920 to 1929, Haiti remained relatively tranquil. During this period, the number and types of aircraft deployed to Haiti fluctuated. For example, the total number of Jennies dropped, but those remaining were improved versions such as the JN-4HG. In 1927 all the Jennies were withdrawn. Thereafter, the DH-4B was the principal steed of the aviators in Haiti, including the DH-4B-1 and 02B-1.[210] In 1924 three Vought VE-7 Bluebird navy fighters arrived, used by the marines for training and observation purposes.[211] In 1926 the marines in Haiti received an OL-2 amphibian. First flown in 1923, the Loening OL was a high-performance aircraft with a large single hull and stabilizing floats fitted underneath each lower wing.[212] The airplane had a tandem cockpit with dual controls (a wheel in the forward cockpit and a removable stick in the rear). Its principal drawback was that although the airplane could be flown from either cockpit, only the front cockpit had navigation and engine instruments. The hull of the OL had five watertight compartments and a bilge pump operated from the rear cockpit. The US Army was the first to express interest in the airplane, and the prototype XCOA-1 was powered by a 400 hp Liberty V-1650-1 engine; the engine was mounted in an inverted position to provide clearance for the three-bladed variable-pitch steel propeller. The fuel tanks were mounted in the hull, on which was built the fuselage. A number of variants were manufactured, and the navy acquired five OL-2s that were virtually identical to the army's COA-1, the production version of the XCOA-1.

In 1928 four modern Vought 02U Corsairs were deployed to Haiti as part of the overall modernization of Marine Corps aviation.[213] By 1929, there were seven. In 1930 an OL-8 amphibian arrived. As the OL series evolved, increasingly powerful engines were fitted to the airplane. The OL-3 had a 475 hp Packard 1A-1500 engine and three cockpits in tandem. The next three versions also had three cockpits and were equipped with the Packard 400 hp V-1650-2 engine. When the OL-6 was fitted with a 450 -hp Pratt & Whitney R-1340-4 engine, it became the OL-8, which returned to two cockpits. Twenty of these aircraft were manufactured. Another twenty OL-8As were produced; these were identical to the original OL-8 but equipped with an arrestor hook for aircraft carrier operations.

In 1931 the OL-8 was withdrawn from Haiti. It was replaced in 1932 with an RS-1, the navy designation for the Sikorsky S-41, an amphibious flying boat and a scaled-up monoplane version of the Sikorsky S-38 biplane. One author described it as "shaped like a shoe with the pilot at the top of the laces."[214] The S-41 had a parasol wing configuration with two radial engines mounted on struts between the fuselage and the wing. The hull was metal, and the cabin was completely enclosed, accommodating fifteen passengers. The navy purchased three of these aircraft, and one was involved in a tragic accident involving Lieutenant Colonel Thomas Turner, the chief of Marine Corps aviation. On October 26, 1931, Turner was flying as a passenger to Gonaïves. Upon arrival, the airplane taxied ashore and became stuck in a soft spot on the beach. When Turner pushed aside the pilot and looked out the window to assess the problem, he was struck in the head by a propeller. He died two days later, after managing to walk to the hospital under his own power.[215]

The RS-1 remained in Haiti and was joined in 1933 by one OL-9, seven SU-2s, and seven SU-3s (improved Corsairs). Depending on the variant, the SU series (numbered 1–4) was equipped with either the 600 or 690 hp Pratt & Whitney R-1690-42 Hornet engine and was employed by the US Navy and Marine Corps as a "scout." Pan American Airlines also operated the S-41 on Haiti and throughout the Caribbean and South America, as well as between Boston, Massachusetts, and Halifax, Nova Scotia.[216] The marines on Haiti used the S-41 (RS-1) to ferry important personnel, as well as for various communication purposes.[217]

The Final Phase of Occupation: Haitianization

Although Marine Corps aviation was on the upswing as the 1920s unfolded, the occupation in Haiti was receiving unrelentingly bad press, and the presidential election in 1920 focused the American public's attention on the tiny republic. Much to the displeasure of the Wilson administration, the Republicans used the Haitian occupation as a political weapon against the Democrats, and a series of investigations were undertaken.[218] Republican presidential candidate Warren G. Harding criticized Wilson's penchant for intervention abroad, and when Franklin D. Roosevelt, the Democratic vice presidential candidate, claimed that he had authored the Haitian constitution (a claim he later recanted), Harding replied: "If I should be elected president . . . I will not empower an assistant secretary of the Navy to draft a constitution for hapless neighbors in the West Indies and jam it down their throats at the point of bayonets borne by the United States Marines."[219]

Nevertheless, once he was elected, President Harding continued the occupation, and subsequent investigations added little to the American understanding of events in Haiti. The only major change was the appointment of a high commissioner to oversee the administrative machinery of the occupation. To that end, former brigade commander John Russell was named high commissioner just prior to the Haitian elections that replaced Dartiguenave with Louis Borno. Russell proved to be a skilled diplomat and administrator, and he was generally well liked by the Haitian people. In addition, Haiti's public debt was steadily reduced, and for the first time in the country's history, the public treasury had a cash surplus.

The marines and gendarmes had defeated Charlemagne's insurgency by employing a counterinsurgency plan that emphasized national reforms as well as small-unit patrols that saturated the countryside and methodically tracked down the remaining *cacos* in their haunts. Though greatly outnumbered, the marines and gendarmes prevailed at the tactical level owing to their training, discipline, and superior weaponry, and aviation added greatly to the marines' tactical success. However, at the strategic level, the Haitian people's desire to be rid of the occupation simmered. In truth, the Haitians never embraced the occupation, and resentment lingers to this day.

Following the death of Charlemagne, the number of marines in Haiti steadily declined, reflecting reduced operations in the field. By July 1924, the brigade was organized into a headquarters, a constabulary detachment, the Second and Eighth Regiments, and the aircraft squadron. Flights G and H, Fourth Air Squadron, were combined on August 29, 1922, into VO-2, part of a broader reorganization of Marine Corps aviation. In July 1927, VO-2 became VO-9M, a part of Aircraft One, Fleet Marine Force, Quantico. This dizzying change of nomenclature reflected the dynamics of navy and marine aviation at the time and is addressed in some detail in the next chapter. That said, beginning in 1920, navy squadrons were designated according to their principal mission: the first letter indicated whether the squadron operated heavier-than-air machines (V) or airships (Z); the following letter denoted the mission, such as fighter (F) or observation (O). In 1927 marine squadrons were distinguished by the addition of an "M." Thus, in Haiti, VO-9M designated Marine Observation Squadron Nine. From 1923 to 1929, most of the brigade was concentrated at Port-au-Prince or at Camp John Russell in Pont Beudet, just outside the capital. While the marines on the ground concentrated on training and drill, VO-2 (later VO-9M) marines delivered the mail, transported passengers, and performed medical evacuations, as well as continuing to fly scout, observation, and reconnaissance missions.

As the marines settled in for the long haul, political opposition to American occupation increased, and the loudest opposition came from the Haitian elite. Despite enormous investment by the US government and the American private sector in the development of Haitian infrastructure and education (such as the Service Technique de l'Agriculture et l'Ensignment Professional, a system of agricultural and vocational schools), as well as sanitation (the Service d'Hygiène) and other improvements, the vast majority of Haitians still looked forward to *désoccupation.* As the decade unfolded, members of the *mulâtre* class in particular complained about racial discrimination, press censorship, and the constitution, which they claimed had been forced on them against their will in 1918.

There was much truth to the Haitians' charges. As historian Mary Renda has argued, the American occupation was paternalistic:

> The white US marines who arrived in Haiti in and after 1915 were armed—if inadequately—with a nationalism that posited the inherent stability and racial basis of US American identity. Yet, these marines were probably the first to experience the challenge to American identity that the occupation, and its paternalistic rhetoric, would pose. Thrust into a foreign context to carry out an intervention justified by, and organized according to, a notion of benevolent paternalism, marines—particularly those stationed in the Haitian countryside—were encouraged to take up the role of father to what was considered a child nation. We have seen that this paternalist injunction had contradictory implications. On the one hand, it degraded Haitians and justified violence committed under the guise of necessary discipline; on the other hand, it suggested the efficacy of learning Creole and inserting oneself into "native" society.[220]

Indeed, in his testimony to the Senate Select Committee investigating the occupation, Smedley Butler asserted: "We were all embued with the fact that we were the trustees of a huge estate that belonged to minors. That was the viewpoint that I personally took, that the Haitians were our wards and that we were endeavoring to make for them a rich and productive property, to be turned over to them at such time as our government saw fit."[221] But regardless of their good intentions, the marines had, among other things, dissolved the legislature and installed a puppet president in 1915, installed a new Haitian constitution written in Washington, seized customhouses, taken control of Haitian finances, revived the corvée (at least temporarily), and censored the Haitian press.

Thus, by the latter half of the 1920s, the Haitian pot began to boil over, and American officials' optimism regarding the future of Haiti was replaced by an awareness that, with limited potential for economic development, Haiti seemed doomed. The agricultural and vocational schools had made some progress, but not enough to move Haiti toward a self-sustaining level of development. And while the defeat of the *cacos* had restored relative peace to Haiti, in its wake, peasant resentment and political controversy simmered. Claims of atrocities committed by marines and gendarmes were investigated by multiple entities. Most of the claims of brutality involved the Hinche district in central Haiti, where Major Wells had illegally continued the corvée. These widely publicized charges tarnished the image of a benevolent occupation, and many prominent Americans back in the United States called for an end to it. Although immediate withdrawal was rejected by President Harding and by his successors Calvin Coolidge and Herbert Hoover, the Senate Select Committee's recommendation that the marines' role be reduced was implemented. Thus, when Russell became high commissioner in March 1922, administrative supremacy passed from the Marine Corps to the Department of State. Even the gendarmerie, renamed the Garde d'Haiti in 1928, was placed under the control of the State Department and the high commissioner.[222]

But these actions were not enough. In the fall of 1929 the relative quiet was broken by a series of student strikes. The spark that lit the flame was a change in scholarship policies at the agricultural college in Damien. Students at the medical and legal colleges followed suit. With the threat of a general strike, President Borno announced that he would not seek reelection in 1930. Unrest spread, and newly promoted Brigadier General Russell advised the State Department on December 3, 1929, that reinforcement by an additional 500 marines would be necessary. On December 4 a strike by customs employees in Port-au-Prince led to mob violence, and Russell reluctantly invoked martial law and placed the Garde d'Haiti under the supervision of the brigade.

However, newly elected president Franklin D. Roosevelt had campaigned on a "good neighbor policy"[223] toward Latin America and the Caribbean in 1932. And although deeply troubled by developments in Haiti, he was committed to withdrawal—the sooner the better. Moreover, in his reply to General Russell regarding reinforcements, President Hoover's Secretary of State, Henry Stimson, had flatly told the high commissioner that no reinforcements would be forthcoming and that he would be wise to further reduce the marines' profile throughout the Haitian republic.

The Marines Withdraw from Haiti

On December 6, 1929, a large body of peasants descended on the small town of Aux Cayes on the southern coast of Haiti, intending to air their grievances and lend support to striking stevedores. Marines rushed to the town, and when they found themselves surrounded by a mob, they opened fire. At least twelve Haitians were killed and another twenty-three were wounded. The Haitian press claimed that the "massacre at Aux Cayes" resulted in twenty-four dead and fifty-one wounded.[224] The incident at Aux Cayes set in motion a process that would lead to the Marine Corps' withdrawal and Haitian self-government. As news of the "massacre" spread, international condemnation followed. The French paper *Liberte* trumpeted the right of self-determination, and Argentina's *La Prensa* called for an immediate end to the occupation.[225] The editors of the influential American magazine the *Nation* similarly called for immediate withdrawal of the marines, claiming, "Our every act in Haiti has been a denial of American principles and ideals."[226]

Everyone saw it coming. Even President Hoover had seen the handwriting on the wall and had appointed a commission headed by William Forbes (an investment banker and diplomat) to assess the situation in Haiti, with an eye toward withdrawal. Hoover also appointed Robert Moton, principal of the Tuskegee Institute, to lead another investigative body and to recommend improvements to the education system to facilitate Haitianization and an end to the occupation.[227] The Forbes Commission held several hearings, and President Hoover subsequently announced that the United States would be withdrawing from Haiti. He left office before he could put that decision into effect, but the riots of 1929, the violence at Aux Cayes, and political developments in 1930 hastened the transfer of political control to Haitian politicians.

In 1930 Louis Borno stood down as president, and the Council of State elected Eugène Roy to replace him. Roy took office in May, but his administration was short-lived. Reflecting the ongoing bitter struggles between the *mulâtres* and nationalistic *noirs,* Sténio Vincent, a light-skinned *noir,* was elected to the presidency in November. The following year, the United States signed an agreement for an accelerated transfer of power to the Haitians. A final agreement for the withdrawal of the marines was signed in Port-au-Prince on August 7, 1933, with complete withdrawal scheduled for October 1, 1934. However, following President Roosevelt's visit to Haiti and talks with President Vincent, the date was moved up to August 15.[228]

Dana Munro, a long-serving Foreign Service officer, was sent to replace General Russell and preside over the departure of the marines and other personnel.[229] The thorniest problem facing Munro was defining the Haitian government's postoccupation financial obligations. Since the crash of the stock market in New York in 1929, precipitating the Great Depression, the US government had reduced and restricted its assistance to American businesses operating in Haiti under the "good neighbor" policy. As a result, National City Bank of New York offered to sell Banque Nationale to the Haitian government. The sale was not completed until 1935, but the offer demonstrated the haste with which American commercial and financial interests wished to extricate themselves from the Caribbean republic.

The actual withdrawal of the marines was rather anticlimactic. By the time President Roosevelt arrived in Haiti and gave his speech (partially in French), few marines were still present, and almost all of those who remained were in Port-au-Prince. The First Brigade consisted of headquarters, transport and signal companies, headquarters companies of the Second Marine Regiment and First Battalion, and two rifle companies, one of which was at Cap Haïtian. On August 1, 1934, the American flag was lowered with honors at brigade headquarters, and an elaborate ceremony marked the Garde d'Haiti's transfer to Haitian control. On August 6 the rifle company at Cap Haïtian moved to Port-au-Prince, and it departed with the ground element on August 15. Aircraft of VO-9M had departed the day prior.

Marine Corps Aviation Leaves Haiti

In a memorandum to the brigade commander dated June 29, 1934, the commander of VO-9M, Major James Moore, presented his "plan of evacuation" from Haiti. The memo recommended that fifteen days prior to final withdrawal, all air-mail sorties be discontinued except to Cap Haïtian and that no sorties be made anywhere in Haiti except to "localities where Marine Corps personnel may be stationed."[230] Major Moore considered fifteen days the minimum time necessary to prepare the squadron's airplanes to be ferried (flown) to the United States. Other missions, such as aerial photographic work, were to end some forty days prior to departure. Over this forty-day period, the squadron would work from dawn to dusk (lighting would be inadequate after dark) dismantling four large hangars and two smaller buildings at the airfield, as well as preparing supplies and equipment for loading aboard ship.

To facilitate these activities, motor transportation would be retained until "D-day," when the entire rump brigade would depart Port-au-Prince.[231]

Although certain supplies, equipment, and household effects of squadron members would be shipped home, other materials would be left behind. A board was convened in November 1933 to determine which US Navy and Marine Corps property belonging to VO-9M was to be shipped, sold, or simply handed over to the Haitians. The inventory was quite specific, ranging from crockery and tableware to carrier pigeons, vehicles, ordnance, and weapons. Among the items recommended for destruction were aerial bombs and fuses, as well as the pigeons. All told, the squadron expected to ship 436,505 pounds of material, some 28,823 cubic feet requiring 1,272 square feet of deck space.[232]

In May 1934, VO-9M sent a more detailed description of salvageable "station buildings" and recommended that several other buildings, including "two cement block bomb magazines," be sold "as is" in Haiti.[233] The squadron commander also recommended that two obsolete generators be sold. However, the navy's Bureau of Aeronautics determined that the hangars and shops should be dismantled and shipped to Parris Island, and an order was issued.[234] The Bureau of Ordnance instructed the squadron to dump into the ocean fifty-seven 17-pound fragmentation bombs, fifty-eight 25-pound fragmentation bombs, and one hundred Mk 11 B primers. Shipment orders were issued for ninety-six 30-pound bombs, along with the fuses, as well as thirty-four Mk 11 wingtip flares, sixteen Mk 111 aircraft flares, one hundred yellow smoke signal cartridges, and one hundred green signal cartridges.[235]

All the aircraft stationed in Haiti were to be flown back to the United States—specifically, to Quantico, where the crews would report to the commander of Aircraft One, Fleet Marine Force. Major Moore submitted a list of planes and crews (seven officers and nineteen enlisted men) to the brigade commander, as well as a proposed itinerary from Port-au-Prince to Quantico.[236] The first day, the aircraft would fly to Guantanamo Bay and then to Moron, Cuba, where they would remain overnight. The next day, the marines would fly from Moron to Miami for a two-night stay at the Naval Reserve Air Station there. From Miami, the marines would continue their flight to Jacksonville, Florida, and then on to Charleston, South Carolina, for a two-night stop. On the sixth and final day, the marines would ferry their aircraft to Fayetteville, North Carolina, and then to Quantico.[237]

The flight would be divided into three sections of seven SU-2 and two SU-3 airplanes, with two aircraft in each section equipped with radios.

Another "independent section" comprised the RS-1 and the OL-9, both of which carried radios. According to Major Moore, "Inter-Squadron communication between SU's will be on same frequency as designated for plane to shore communications. Between OL-9, RS-1, and SU's on 5690 Kcs [kilocycles per second]. Communication between squadron and Naval Radio Stations will be on frequency designated by Navy Department. Communication will be maintained with Pan American Airways stations via the RS-1 on 5690 Kcs."[238]

Before the aviators departed Haiti with their airplanes, a recommissioned Wickes-class destroyer of the Special Service Squadron, USS *Jacob Jones,* was directed to take up a position off Dog Rocks Cay, Sal Bank, the Bahamas, on August 13 to act as a "plane guard."[239] With planning completed, VO-9M left Haiti the day prior to the departure of the main body of the brigade, and all the aircraft made it safely to Quantico.

Epilogue

Reflecting on the occupation and its aftermath, it is not difficult to find commentators who denounce the intervention as a racist exercise in imperialism by the United States. Hans Schmidt writes: "The belief that Haitians were inherently inferior, coupled with the dictates of State Department diplomacy in the Caribbean, led to [a] grotesque perversion of the declared missionary ideal of spreading liberal democracy."[240] An essay in the *Marine Corps Gazette* offered a more positive analysis, claiming the occupation "lent itself to the expeditious reformation of the country and the government."[241] Most of the mainstream American press was simply pleased to be rid of Haiti and its problems. The *Denver News* editorialized: "It is good to see the marines leaving. The island's situation was very tangled indeed when they first landed, and they did a lot of very excellent work; but in the end the Haitians must work out their own salvation as an independent state, and they can't do that until the last American marine has gone."[242]

In retrospect, it is probably closer to the truth to posit that all the arguments about the occupation of Haiti contain a grain of truth and that the marines fell victim to "mission creep."[243] The original justification for intervention (rather than simple interposition, which had been done before) was for strategic purposes—safeguarding the Panama Canal. But once the marines were ensconced, the purpose was no longer to safeguard the passages to the canal but rather "nation building." And with that, a paternalistic mind-set took hold. Smedley Butler's use of the term "wards" certainly betrayed a paternalistic, Progressive Era outlook whereby the assertion of authority and control was masked as benevolent fatherly intent. Regardless, the country fell into chaos not long after the Americans departed, and sadly, Haiti has failed to overcome its tragic past.

According to Haiti veteran John Craige, the French called Haiti *Pays des Revenants,* "the country to which you are bound to come back."[244] Indeed, the US military would return several times, most notably in 1994 to impose stability and install a "preferred" president as part of Operation Uphold Democracy.[245] But in 1994 there would be a "new cast of rogues and star-spangled cowboys," including US Army Special Forces soldiers, operatives of the Central Intelligence Agency, the US Navy and US Air Force, and a host of others.[246] For its part, the Marine Corps would send the Special Purpose Marine Air Ground Task Force Caribbean (SPMAGTF Carib), built around Second Regiment headquarters, commanded by Colonel Thomas Jones.[247] The 1,900 marines and sailors of the SPMAGTF included the Second Infantry Battalion, which formed the basis of a "battalion landing team." This team was reinforced by a provisional rifle company provided by Battery B, First Battalion, Tenth Marine Regiment (minus howitzers), as well the Second Light Armored Reconnaissance Battalion and Combat Service Support Detachment 29. The SPMAGTF also included an air combat element (ACE) built around a marine medium helicopter squadron, HMM-264, with its complement of Boeing Vertol CH-46E Sea Knight medium-lift helicopters. Rounding out the ACE were Sikorsky CH-53E Super Stallion heavy-lift helicopters, Bell UH-1 Huey utility helicopters, and Bell AH-1 Cobra attack helicopters.[248]

For a short time, at least, Marine Corps aviation had returned to Haiti.

A JN-4 being serviced at Miami. Note that the propeller is missing, as well as part of the right wing. Perhaps the aircraft was being disassembled for shipment to Haiti.

A JN-4 gunnery trainer with several aviators (probably pilots and gunners) at Miami. The man second from the left appears to be "Cocky" Evans, and the man standing behind the propeller without helmet and goggles appears to be "Tex" Rogers.

A JN-6H over Miami. The JN-6H had improved ailerons and stick and rudder controls in both cockpits. The JN-6HG-1 was fitted with a 150-horsepower Wright-Hispano V-8 engine, which delivered greatly improved performance. Several Jennies were sent to Haiti, and by the end of June 1920, there were five JN-4HGs there.

Servicing an engine in Miami on what appears to be a locally crafted engine test stand (note that the propeller is turning). Engine technology developed rapidly from the four-cylinder engine of A. A. Cunningham's "Noisy Nan" to V-12 engines with outputs exceeding 400 horsepower.

HS-2L flying boats on the ramp at Port-au-Prince, Haiti. The HS-2L was first acquired for duty in the Azores during World War I. Although useful for patrolling offshore, the airplane was not well suited to supporting marines on the ground in the interior.

A weathered and worn-out HS-2L at Port-au-Prince. HS-1 flying boats were deployed to the Azores in 1918, where they were upgraded with Liberty engines (HS-1L). The HS-1L was then modified with longer wings, producing the HS-2L, which became the mainstay of US Navy and Marine Corps flying boats for many years.

An HS-2L enters the water from the wooden ramp at Port-au-Prince. Operated by a three-man crew (pilot, copilot, and observer), the HS-2L could carry two 230-pound depth bombs but normally did not carry a machine gun.

The first DH-4B to take flight in Haiti, piloted by Lieutenant Harold "Hal" Major, Naval Aviator No. 71. With the arrival of the DH planes, the aerial mission in Haiti took on a new complexion, including the employment of dive-bombing to support marines engaged with *cacos* on the ground.

"Cocky" Evans designed a flying ambulance based on the DH-4B with a turtle-back fuselage. Two were built at the Naval Aircraft Factory in Philadelphia, each accommodating one reclining and one sitting passenger. DH-4B A-5811 was assigned to Haiti, and A-5883 was assigned to the Dominican Republic.

Arthur Page Jr., Naval Aviator No. 41, on the lower right wing of an R-6 floatplane. Captain Page commanded the balloon detachment at Quantico and then the squadron in the Dominican Republic, but he was ordered to Haiti when A. A. Cunningham arrived to take command of the First Squadron in Santo Domingo.

Arthur Page Jr. standing in front of a racing plane. Captain Page commanded the Fourth Squadron in Haiti, and later in China he "cracked up" an airplane carrying Brigadier General Smedley Butler. He died in a crash while racing an experimental XF6C-6 monoplane during the 1930 Curtiss Marine Race.

Hal Major seated in the pilot's cockpit of a JN gunnery trainer. Captain Major was the first to land a DH-4B on the island of Gonâve, off Port-au-Prince, where Gunnery Sergeant Faustin Wirkus, the so-called white king of La Gonâve, served as resident commander of a gendarmerie unit.

Lawson "Sandy" Sanderson. While stationed at Gonaïves, Sanderson hit upon the idea of pointing the nose of his DH-4B at a 45-degree angle to the ground, allowing the more precise delivery of bombs in support of the marines engaged in combat with the *cacos*. When Geiger took command, he ordered all pilots to learn the tactic.

Enlisted pilots Elmo "Socko" Reagan (left) and Benjamin Belcher (right) with Hayne "Cuckoo" Boyden, who mapped Haiti from 10,000 feet using a balloon statoscope. According to one source, Reagan pioneered dive-bombing at Quantico, well before Sanderson initiated the practice in Haiti.

A group photo of Marine Corps aviation pioneers in Port-au-Prince. Seated (left to right) are Basil Bradley, Arthur Page, A. A. Cunningham, Francis Evans, and Francis Mulcahy. Standing (left to right) are Kenneth Collings, Leo Sullivan, Lawson Sanderson, Guy Hall, Hayne Boyden, Harmon Norton, and Harold Major.

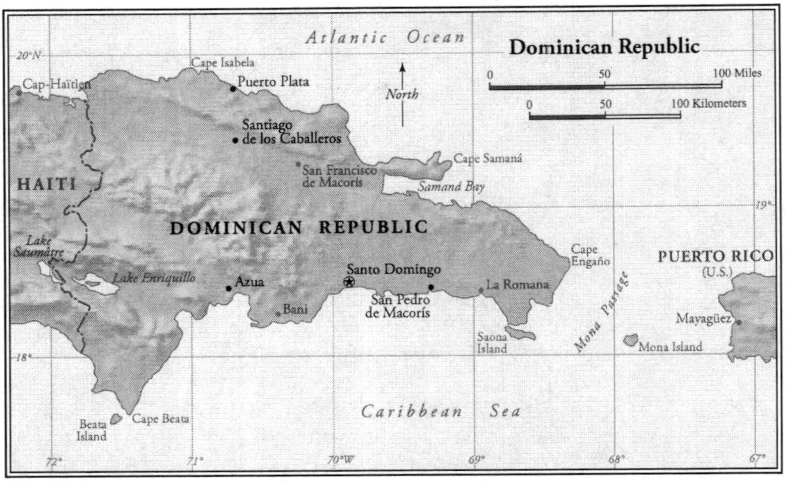

The Dominican Republic. The first airfield in the Dominican Republic was located at San Pedro de Macorís on the south coast. Later the airfield was moved nearer the capital city of Santo Domingo, west of San Pedro de Macorís.

Northern China. The marine brigade and its flying units were located at Tientsin (Tianjin), southeast of Peking (Beijing).

3

Advance to Maturity, 1919–1935

> Marine Corps Aviation . . . is an integral part of Naval Aviation, and its mission is to furnish the air forces necessary for expeditionary duty, advanced base operations and the defense of naval bases outside the continental limits of the United States.
>
> Major Edwin Brainard, USMC, Officer in Charge, Aviation (1925–1929)

Marine Corps aviation won its battle for survival in the 1920s. After a long legislative struggle following World War I, Congress authorized 1,200 marines for aviation, and permanent bases were established at Quantico, Parris Island, and San Diego. Once Congress established a national policy for aviation, a policy for naval aviation emerged soon afterward, detailed in General Order No. 132 issued on July 7, 1924. In short, naval (US Navy and Marine Corps) aircraft would operate from mobile platforms or from the shore in support of the battle fleet for purposes of scouting, reconnaissance, observation, adjusting naval gunfire, and patrolling, as well as attacking enemy shore installations. In addition, Marine Corps aircraft would perform functions not unlike those of US Army aircraft, such as attacking inland targets.

Major Cunningham's position as the head of Marine Corps aviation was officially recognized in January 1919, and an Aviation Section was established in the newly formed Division of Operations and Training in December 1920. That same month, Cunningham handed over the reins to Major Thomas Turner (Marine Aviator No. 73). Turner had enlisted in the Marine Corps in 1901, and a year later he was commissioned a second lieutenant. He served in the Philippines and Puerto Rico and was with the First Brigade at Veracruz in 1914. In 1916 he commanded the marine detachment aboard the New York–class battleship USS *Texas.*[1] From there he went to San Diego, where he volunteered for aviation duty. He attended flight school at the US Army Signal Corps Aviation School at North Island, San Diego, and was assigned to fly with the army at Ellington Field, Texas, built in 1917 on 1,280 acres of land east of Houston (now Pasadena). At one point, he commanded the airfield at Ellington, a bomber training base. Returning to the Marine Corps in 1919, Turner served in Haiti as an infantry officer with the First Regiment until 1920, receiving the Haitian equivalent of the Medal of Honor. That same year, he requested to return to flying, and the commandant, Major General John Lejeune, made him the head of aviation. Cunningham departed to take command of the squadron deployed to the Dominican Republic (First Division, Squadron D; later, First Air Squadron, Flights A and B), replacing Captain Arthur Page Jr., who reported to Port-au-Prince to take command of the Fourth Squadron.

There is some controversy surrounding Turner's ascension and Cunningham's departure. Although Turner was senior to Cunningham in rank (having been promoted to major prior to Cunningham), it has been argued that Turner was chosen to head aviation owing to his close personal friendship with Lejeune. Supporting this contention is the fact that it was customary to assign air commanders on the basis of their naval aviator numbers, regardless of rank. In that sense, Cunningham was certainly senior to Turner. Later, Roy Geiger would be named director on the basis of his aviator number, even though he was junior to another marine aviator, Ross Rowell. Some have speculated that Lejeune preferred Turner because he had proved himself as an infantry officer and was more politically shrewd and less fanatical about aviation than Cunningham. In any case, in a letter to Geiger following his relief by Turner, Cunningham stated that he would help the new head of aviation any way he could.[2]

In October 1920 the Advance Base Force headquartered in Philadelphia was moved to Quantico. Prewar facilities and a variety of aircraft were already there, including the DH-4, JN-4, JN-6, N-9, and a few balloons. The airfield comprised three steel hangars, two seaplane hangars, fourteen Dixie hut temporary barracks, a recreation hall, shops, and numerous storage buildings. That same month, Lejeune approved an air table of organization that provided for Marine Corps "wings" composed of squadrons, which in turn were made up of "flights." Reorganization produced four squadrons, each with two flights. The First Squadron, consisting of Flights A and B, was in the Dominican Republic. The Second and Third Squadrons (Flights C, D, E, and F) were at Quantico. The Fourth Squadron, comprising Flights G and H, was based in Haiti. The small detachment at Parris Island was designated Flight L. But to bring the marine squadrons in line with the navy's extant aviation organization, the flights were soon redesignated "divisions."[3]

In 1921 aviators from Quantico participated in the bombing of the former German Helgoland-class battleship SMS *Ostfriesland* (widely considered unsinkable) as part of joint US Army Air Service and US Navy bombing tests.[4] Tragically, while returning from a practice run leading five DH-4Bs, Lieutenant Walter Brown was killed when he became disoriented in fog over the Potomac and crashed into the river, the first pilot fatality at Quantico. In May 1922 the Quantico airstrips (Nos. 1 and 2) were named Brown Field in his honor.[5] That same year, Quantico received new Martin MB-1 heavy bombers manufactured by the Glenn L. Martin Company of Cleveland, Ohio. An advanced design produced for the US Army in 1918, the MB-1 (or GMB, for "Glenn Martin Bomber") was powered by two 400 hp Liberty 12-A engines driving two-bladed, fixed-pitch wooden propellers. The airplane was intended to replace the British Handley-Page 0/400 bombers acquired during World War I, as well as Caproni bombers of Italian design. The MB-1 had a top speed at sea level of 109 miles per hour (mph), a ceiling of 9,000 feet, and a combat range of 400 statute miles. The navy bought two of these aircraft in 1920 as torpedo bombers (MBT, for "Martin Bomber-Torpedo").[6] Eight improved versions with longer wings were also acquired and designated MT (for "Martin Torpedo"); the MT had an MB-1 fuselage and improved wings. Six of these aircraft were provided to the Marine Corps (those remaining with the navy were redesignated TM-1). In April 1923 four of the MTs were flown from San Diego to Quantico in eleven days, completing what was then the longest and largest aerial delivery of aircraft in Marine Corps history.[7] The last Martin bomber flown by the marines retired in 1928.[8]

In July 1920 Brigadier General Smedley Butler succeeded Major General Lejuene as the commander at Quantico. Butler's tenure was one of the most colorful in Quantico's history, and aviators played a major role.[9] In the summer of 1921 Butler instituted the first of a series of maneuvers open to the public at famous Civil War battlefields. In June and July, for example, Butler led a reinforced brigade with aviation support in refighting the Battle of the

Wilderness outside Fredericksburg, Virginia. The following summer he refought the Battle of Gettysburg in Pennsylvania. For the Gettysburg maneuver, the aviators at Quantico contributed three Martin bombers, six DH-4Bs, six Vought VE-7s, and a Type-F kite balloon. Although the nominal purpose was to create positive publicity for the Marine Corps,[10] refighting Civil War battles also permitted the employment of emergent tactics over a variety of terrain and taught the marines valuable lessons regarding staff work and coordination between ground forces and supporting aviation.

In late 1922 the designation Advance Base Force was dropped in favor of Marine Corps Expeditionary Force, a less restrictive title and a more accurate reflection of what the Corps had been doing since the end of the Spanish-American War. As a result, Quantico became the East Coast Expeditionary Force. The West Coast Expeditionary Force was formed at San Diego. The aviation units were then reorganized along functional lines (observation, pursuit, and lighter-than-air), and the Quantico units were collectively designated the First Aviation Group. Its two subordinate units were Observation Squadron Three (VO-3) and Fighting Squadron One (VF-1), redesignated from the Second and Third Squadrons, respectively. By 1924, two more squadrons were added at Quantico: Service Squadron One, a nonflying unit with mechanics ("ship keepers") and other specialists, and Kite Balloon Squadron One (ZK-1).[11] By 1927, a "utility" squadron was also established, VJ-6M (the "M" designation for Marine Corps aircraft squadrons was added in 1927).[12] All the squadrons at Quantico emphasized the ability to deploy quickly as part of the Marine Corps' expeditionary mission.

Following the establishment of the First Aviation Group on the East Coast, the marines activated a similar echelon on the West Coast. When Observation Squadron One (VO-1, formerly the First Squadron) returned from the Dominican Republic in 1924, it became the nucleus for the Second Aviation Group at San Diego. VO-1 was joined by Fighting Squadron Two (VF-2) in 1925. A year later, and at the navy's insistence, Marine Corps aviation was reorganized again, and the First and Second Aviation Groups became Aircraft Squadrons, East Coast Expeditionary Force and West Coast Expeditionary Force, respectively.[13] In 1934, in conjunction with the creation of the Fleet Marine Force, the air expeditionary forces became Aircraft One (Quantico) and Aircraft Two (San Diego).[14] Then things settled down a bit until the echelon in San Diego became the First Marine Aircraft Group and the Quantico unit became the Second Marine Aircraft Group.[15]

As noted in chapter 2, the reserves were gutted following World War I; however, in February 1925 Congress passed a bill that revived the Marine Corps Reserve and its aviation component. Effective July 1, the reserves comprised two "classes": the Fleet Marine Corps Reserve and the Volunteer Marine Corps Reserve. Four reserve areas corresponding to existing recruiting boundaries were established. Many veterans of World War I returned to the Marine Corps as reservists, and two regular officers were assigned to each reserve regiment—one as the commander, and the other as an administrative assistant.[16] In addition, a Reserve Section was created in the Office of the Commandant,[17] and many distinguished officers served there, including Captain Oliver "OP" Smith (also known as "The Professor," Smith would achieve iconic status commanding the First Marine Division during the Battle of Chosin Reservoir during the Korean War).[18] Over time, the reserve component grew and added aviation units.

Demobilization after World War I resulted in the virtual elimination of the Marine Corps Reserve Flying Corps.[19] Indeed, the commandant made no mention of it in his annual reports to Congress from 1919 to 1925. By the end of March 1919, only eleven first lieutenants and sixty-three second lieutenants remained on the rolls, one of whom was Lawson "Sandy" Sanderson, who had volunteered for aviation because he preferred flying over walking.[20] As discussed in chapter 2, the Marine Flying Field at Miami was closed and its personnel and airplanes were distributed to Quantico and Parris Island. The new chief of aviation, Major Turner, tried to strengthen the air reserve before he departed, but to little avail. It was Brigadier General Smedley Butler's "march" to Gettysburg, supported by the aircraft squadrons at Quantico, that brought aviation to the forefront of public consciousness and thus to the attention of Congress, resulting in the legislation in 1925 that not only revived the reserves but also provided funding for reserve aviation. It was also after the Gettysburg maneuvers that Lejeune issued the new table of organization for aviation, effective August 3, 1922, which created the First and Second Aviation Groups.

The Naval Reserve Act of 1925 established several reserve aviation units in the Marine Corps: the Eastern Reserve Area–Observation Squadron, 6-M, Division 2; the Central Reserve Area–Observation Squadron, 6-M, Division 3; the Southern Reserve Area–Fighting Squadron, 5-M, Division 2; and the Western Reserve Area–Observation Squadron, 8-M, Division 2. When Major Edwin Brainard took over as head of aviation at Marine Corps Headquarters, he brought in Captain Thomas Shearer to oversee these units. In 1927, when the aviation groups were redesignated Aircraft Squadrons, East and West Coast Expeditionary Forces, a modern Marine Corps air reserve was born (that is, for each active squadron allowed by the table of organization, one or more inactive squadrons was allowed). These "skeleton" formations would be filled by reservists who "could be quickly integrated into the Regular Establishment."[21]

Flight training for reservists entailed enlistment as a private and assignment to inactive aviation duty, followed by primary and advanced flight school, a one- to two-year stint with an active squadron, and then attachment to an inactive squadron. Primary flight instruction included ten hours with an instructor pilot and thirty hours of "regulated solo flight in a primary type plane."[22] This occurred at one of four naval reserve aviation squadrons located at Squantum, Massachusetts; Rockaway Beach, Long Island, New York; Great Lakes, Illinois; and Sand Point, Seattle, Washington.[23] One marine officer pilot (an "inspector-instructor") and three enlisted mechanics were assigned to each station. Advanced training occurred at Pensacola Naval Air Station in Florida. This included 100 hours of flight time in seaplanes so that the pilots could be designated as naval aviators. Graduates were commissioned into the Volunteer Marine Corps Reserve and ordered to active duty with an active squadron. Upon completion of this tour, the officer returned to inactive status and was attached to a reserve squadron. Over a five-year period, this program produced more than 250 qualified pilots.[24]

Lieutenant Colonel Roy Geiger took over as head of Marine Corps aviation in November 1931 and served in that capacity until May 1935, when Lieutenant Colonel Ross "Rusty" Rowell assumed the reins. Geiger was instrumental in encouraging the entire aviation community, both regular and reserve, to attend lectures on air-ground integration and demonstrations of close air support tactics at Quantico. During Geiger's tenure, the Fleet Marine Force was established (1933), which greatly affected aviation. The immediate effect, as discussed earlier, was the redesignation of the East and West Coast Expeditionary Force squadrons as Aircraft One and Aircraft Two. From these active units (and the inactive units created in 1931 and 1932), Marine Corps aviation would explode to around 10,000 pilots during World War II, practically all of whom held reserve commissions.[25] But before that occurred, the marines continued to refine air operations during their nonage in the Dominican Republic, followed by an expedition to China that, along with the second Nicaraguan campaign (1927–1933), brought Marine Corps aviation into the modern age.

Operations in the Dominican Republic

As noted in chapter 1, the first Marine Corps aviators to deploy for expeditionary duty in support of interventionary forces (outside of Veracruz in 1914) were elements of Squadrons D and E (so redesignated upon their return from France) sent to the Dominican Republic (at the time, more commonly known as Santo Domingo, after the capital city). Nine officers and 131 men arrived at San Pedro de Macorís on February 25, 1919, under the command of Captain Walter McCaughtry. A month later, the cargo ship USS *Lake Superior* delivered 175 tons of aviation materials and six Jennies.[26] As part of Cunningham's effort to demonstrate the utility of aviation in support of marines on the ground, the First Division, Squadron D, performed many of the same functions in Santo Domingo as the aviators in Haiti (First Division, Squadron E, which arrived in that country a month later under the command of Captain Harvey Mims).

Marines first set foot in the Dominican Republic during the closing stages of the quasi-war between the United States and France that lasted from 1798 to1800. To fight what amounted to a naval conflict, Congress authorized funds for new frigates and a marine guard for each. One of the new frigates was the USS *Constitution,* which conducted escort duty for merchantmen and patrolled the waters along the East Coast and in the Caribbean. The highlight of the *Constitution*'s service during the quasi-war came in May 1799, when Lieutenant Isaac Hull, USN, led the ship's marine detachment and several sailors to seize the French privateer and former British packet ship *Sandwich* near Port-au-Platte (Puerto Plata) in the French colony of Saint Domingue—"the first deed in the history of the landings of the United States Marines recorded."[27] More landings would follow, including that of the Sixth and Ninth Companies aboard the former J. P. Morgan transatlantic ocean liner USS *Prairie* on May 5, 1916, securing the American legation in Santo Domingo de Guzmán, the capital and largest city in the Dominican Republic. Some thirty-three months later, the six Jennies would arrive at San Pedro de Macorís.

The Dominican Republic occupies the eastern two-thirds of the island of Hispaniola (*La Isla Española*), which it shares with Haiti. The island is part of the Greater Antilles archipelago, which includes Cuba, Puerto Rico, and Jamaica. For some 5,000 years before Columbus's arrival, the island had been occupied by a blend of immigrants from other parts of Latin America known collectively as the Taíno people. Columbus referred to them as Indians, and later ethnologists called them Arawaks. By the end of the fifteenth century, there were several million Taíno living on the island, and they were organized into five political regions known as *kacikazgos.* On Christmas Eve 1492 Columbus's flagship the *Santa Maria* ran aground, and he was forced to abandon it. But before departing for Spain, he ordered that a small fortress be built from the timbers of the ship, and he left behind some forty crewmen to man *Fortalesa La Navidad.* Owing to their bad behavior—which included rape and plunder—these men were killed by the otherwise peaceful inhabitants.

Upon their return in 1493, the Spanish established Isabella, the first permanent European settlement, not far from where San Felipe de Puerto Plata is located today. The Spaniards quickly conquered the Taíno people in the area and subjected them to forced labor. In 1496 the city of Santo Domingo was established. The Spanish then decided to conquer the whole island and waged a ruthless military campaign to eliminate the Taíno *kacikes* (chieftains). Unlike the European invaders and the African slaves they brought with them, the Taíno had no resistance to the diseases brought by the Spanish, including smallpox in 1518. After twenty-five years of Spanish occupation, only 50,000 to 60,000 aboriginal inhabitants remained, and most of them fled to inhospitable regions on the island, forming runaway or *cimarrón* (maroon) communities. But within a generation, these people had mixed with Spaniards and African slaves, forming the "tripartite" people known today as Dominicans.

By 1515, the Spanish had concluded that the colony was no longer lucrative as a source of gold, particularly after Hernándo Cortés made his astonishing conquest of Mexico. Seemingly overnight, the Spanish abandoned Santo Domingo. What few settlers remained continued to intermarry with the Taíno and concentrated on raising cattle and pigs to sell to Spanish ships that stopped at the island en route to other destinations in Latin America. On New Year's Day 1586 the English pirate Sir Francis Drake attacked and plundered Santo Domingo City, extorting a ransom from the Spanish government. Seventy years later, Santo Domingo City was attacked again by the English, this time by a fleet sent by Oliver Cromwell to seize Jamaica. The Spanish reaction was to remove the population from coastal towns and villages, which then permitted smugglers and buccaneers to move in.[28] Most of the pirates settled on the west coast of the island, which had been practically deserted by the Spanish. By the middle of the seventeenth century, the island of Tortuga (Catalan for "turtle" or "tortoise"), located west of Cap Haïtian, was a pirate stronghold.

Envious of Spanish possessions in the Americas, the French sent their own colonists to settle in Tortuga and the northwestern coast of Hispaniola (as described in chapter 2). In addition, the French brought in prostitutes and other female criminals to domesticate the pirates. In time, these French colonists spread across the western third of the island, and the colony of Saint Domingue was formed. In 1795 the Spanish ceded Santo Domingo to the French by the Treaty of Basilea. Following the Haitian revolution, Santo Domingo was occupied by forces led by Haitian revolutionary Toussaint L'Ouverture. An island-wide constitution was written, which provoked Napoleon to dispatch forces under the command of his brother-in-law, General Charles Leclerc, to recover the island. Leclerc made some headway in the beginning but was ultimately defeated by Haitian Jean-Jacques Dessalines, who then attacked Santo Domingo but failed to conquer that portion of the island. Thus, although an independent Haiti was declared in the west, the French still controlled the east, until they were driven out by the Spanish in 1809.

In 1821 Santo Domingo's lieutenant governor, José Núñez de Cáceres, declared the colony's independence as "Spanish Haiti" and requested that the new country be admitted into Simón Bolívar's Republic of Gran Colombia. But Haitian forces led by Jean-Pierre Boyer, a free *gens de couleur* who had fought alongside L'Ouverture and Dessalines and later became president of Haiti (1818–1843), invaded and occupied the former Spanish colony in February 1822. Boyer abolished slavery, but the occupation imposed a heavy toll on the people, forcing many to flee to Cuba, Puerto Rico, and Venezuela, all three of which remained under Spanish rule. Over time, the economy collapsed, and anti-Haitian resistance movements emerged and coalesced around Juan Pablo Duarte, contributing to Boyer's overthrow in 1843 and the departure of the Haitian occupation force.

On February 27, 1844, Duarte declared independence from Haiti, and the *República Dominicana* (Dominican Republic) was born. The republic's first constitution was adopted on November 6, 1844, modeled on the US Constitution. But the new leaders faced almost immediate political opposition, and six months later they were ousted from power. From this point onward, Santo Domingo was almost constantly ruled by military strongmen known as *caudillos*.[29] And over the next seventy years, the republic was wracked by a series of civil wars that produced economic ruin. During the first twenty-five years, power swung back and forth between General Pedro Santana, a native of Hinche, and General Buenaventura Báez, a freed slave. Santana believed the new nation could not survive without being reincorporated into the Spanish empire. He therefore seized power and exiled Duarte, the founding father of the new state. Santana held office until the Spanish returned and annexed the country. For his part, Báez wanted France to resume control, but the French refused. He then tried to convince the United States to annex the country. He almost succeeded in 1872, when the Spanish were forced out again and President Ulysses S. Grant attempted to incorporate Santo Domingo into the United States. But this was thwarted by the US Senate.[30]

Before the Grant administration, US policy had been one of noninvolvement owing to the confused situation in Santo Domingo. American concerns focused primarily on ongoing attempts by France, Spain, and England to dominate Dominican affairs. Uncertain of its status, the United States did not formally recognize the Dominican Republic until 1865. Nevertheless, and not unlike in neighboring Haiti, American commercial interests were established in Santo Domingo long before formal recognition by the US government. As early as 1849, President Zachary Taylor offered to guarantee Dominican independence in return for commercial access to Samaná Bay. Later, President Franklin Pierce appointed General William Cazneau as a special agent to the republic, seeking a treaty of amity and commerce along with the establishment of a coaling station at Samaná Bay. Dominican president Santana agreed to these terms, believing the United States would protect the new state from another Haitian invasion as well as European predations. But bitter opposition arose in the United States, led by Massachusetts senator Charles Sumner, a member of the Free-Soil Party, who denounced the treaty as a scheme to expand the influence of the southern slave states. On the day Santana was supposed to sign the treaty and deliver it to the Dominican Senate, a British warship appeared in the harbor at Santo Domingo City, and the treaty was never signed.

The American Civil War quickly eliminated any concerns about Santo Domingo, at least for a time, and it was during this period that Spain resumed suzerainty over its former colony. A degree of relative peace and stability followed until 1882, when General Ulysses Heureux, known as "Lilis," came to power and expelled the Spanish. But by 1903, the Dominican government could not repay its foreign debts.[31] Most of the debt was owed to European creditors, but the United States also had a large stake in the country by way of the American-owned San Domingo Improvement Company. The company had purchased a number of bonds held by European firms, and by the turn of the century, it was at odds with the Dominican government over mining and construction concessions. The US government entered into negotiations with the Dominican government on behalf of the Improvement Company, and they reached a settlement that included acquisition of the company's bonds by a New York bank. These new bonds were secured by customhouse receipts, the most important of which were at Puerto Plata.

As financial matters came to a head in Santo Domingo, the Panama Canal project became the prime consideration in US strategic thinking. Security of the canal would require control of the approaches to it, and Hispaniola was the linchpin in the arc of islands extending from Venezuela to the Yucatán Peninsula. As noted in chapter 2, the Windward Passage was the key waterway, but the Mona Passage, east of Hispaniola, was also important. Control of these sea lines of communication by an unfriendly power would seriously interfere with if not interdict the movement of US naval forces from the Atlantic Ocean to the Pacific, where the growing power of Japan threatened US interests in Asia.[32] Thus, keeping the island chain free of foreign (that is, European) control became a fundamental tenet of US national security strategy. With the conclusion of the Spanish-American War, Cuba became a US protectorate and Puerto Rico an American possession, but the Lesser Antilles remained under the control of the British, French, Danes, and Dutch, and both Haiti and Santo Domingo were stumbling from one major crisis to another. A financial crisis in Santo Domingo provided the conditions for a European power to regain a foothold on the island, the very scenario American strategists feared.

In 1904 President Theodore Roosevelt promulgated his corollary to the Monroe Doctrine. In doing so, he warned Congress in his annual message that the Dominican Republic was in "imminent danger" of European intervention, and only American assurance of assistance would prevent it.[33] Negotiations between the State Department and the Dominican government resulted in a treaty in February 1905 authorizing the United States to assume the collection of customs revenue by a receiver general of Dominican customs appointed by the US president. But the Senate failed to ratify the treaty before adjournment, so Roosevelt and Dominican president Carlos Morales entered into an executive agreement (modus vivendi) that implemented the terms of the treaty anyway. According to one distinguished historian, Roosevelt "felt that the establishment of a customs receivership . . . was the only means by which European intervention could be avoided."[34] Two years later, the executive agreement was replaced by a Senate-ratified treaty incorporating the same terms.

The six years that followed were halcyon days compared with what had transpired since the 1840s, and American receivership was ably assisted by the honest administration of Dominican president Ramón Arturo Cáceres Vasquez, who assumed office in 1906. But it all came crashing down in 1911 when Cáceres was assassinated. Many different factions capitalized on the political chaos that followed, and a new regime headed by Eladio Victoria y Victoria spawned several rebellions supported by the Haitian government. Consequently, President William Howard Taft sent two commissioners to Santo Domingo City, accompanied by 750 marines, to calm the situation. President Victoria resigned in late 1912, and Archbishop Alfredo Alejandro Nouel was installed as the very reluctant head of government. He resigned in March 1913, the same month President Woodrow Wilson took office in the United States. A new provisional president, José Bordas Valdés, took control in Santo Domingo, but he was no more successful than the archbishop when local *caudillos* rose up in open rebellion.

Whereas Roosevelt's policies were driven primarily by political expediency and Taft's approach was motivated by economic self-interest, Wilson was moved by idealism. Wilson was a missionary for democracy, but his missionary zeal did not exclude—as we have already learned—the use of force. Wilson's solution for Santo Domingo was "constitutional democracy" (even though the Dominican Republic had produced several constitutions over the years, including a virtual copy of the US Constitution). But in Wilson's mind, once a new, democratically elected government took office, no further "revolutions" would be countenanced by the Dominican people. Two candidates, Juan Isidro Jiménez and Horacio Vásquez, represented the strongest political factions in the country. The aged Jiménez was elected in December 1914, but he won only by agreeing to name an infamous *caudillo,* Desiderio Arias, as minister of war.

Wilson's initial policy toward the Jiménez government was one of full support, and the president dispatched James Sullivan to Santo Domingo City as US minister, replacing longtime diplomat William Russell. Sullivan had no experience in the region and did not speak Spanish, but he was politically well connected and was aligned with New York financiers who controlled the National Bank of Santo Domingo. As tensions increased in early 1915, Wilson insisted that Santo Domingo agree to an American financial comptroller who would draw up a budget and approve the disbursement of funds. He also pushed for a national constabulary officered by Americans. Such arrangements were not provided for in the treaty of 1907, and Jiménez refused. Negotiations dragged on until the Domincan government collapsed in 1916. Sullivan then requested American military intervention to protect lives and property, and on May 5 a provisional battalion (Fifth and Sixth Companies) of marines from the auxiliary cruiser USS *Prairie* landed at Santo Domingo City under the command of Captain Frederic "Dopey" Wise. He and his marines soon found themselves in the midst of a civil war.[35]

On May 12, 1916, Admiral Caperton of the Atlantic Cruiser Squadron arrived at Santo Domingo City aboard his flagship, the gunboat USS *Dolphin*. More marines followed, including two companies from Haiti and another from Guantanamo Bay. On May 23 Colonel Theodore Kane and the headquarters of the Second Regiment arrived aboard the auxiliary cruiser USS *Panther* (the former SS *Venezuela*). It was clear to Colonel Kane that occupation of the whole country would be necessary to end the violence. Admiral Caperton therefore requested more marines, and the Fourth Regiment under the command of Colonel Joseph "Uncle Joe" Pendleton was dispatched from San Diego to New Orleans. There, they boarded the transport USS *Hancock* for Monte Cristi, arriving on June 21.[36] They were joined by marine detachments from the Virginia-class battleships USS *Rhode Island* and USS *New Jersey*. That same month, major operations got under way to pacify the country, with two "flying columns" converging on Santiago.[37]

The Dominican army was small and poorly trained and equipped. Nevertheless, as was the case elsewhere in Latin America, the army was "inevitably the means through which, by corruption or promise of corruption, revolutions were engineered."[38] The leaders of the army generally answered to the *caudillos*. Thus, the marines' first task was to destroy the Dominican army. The engagement at *Las Trencheras* (fortifications dug into two hillsides blocking the way to Santiago) set the pattern for the remainder of the campaign. "Against Marine superiority in artillery, machine guns, small-unit maneuver, and individual training and marksmanship, no Dominican force could hold its ground."[39] The marines pushed through to Navarette, and along the railroad line at Alta Mira, Lieutenant Douglas Roben, who would later become a marine aviator (Naval Aviator No. 535), was wounded during the engagement.[40] The Dominican army collapsed, and the marines entered Santiago on July 6, ending large-scale organized resistance. Consequently, elements of the First Regiment, which had arrived before the march to Santiago, returned to the United States, followed by the Second Regiment. However, the First Regiment left behind its headquarters and staff as the Third Provisional Regiment. Together, the Third and Fourth Regiments became the Second Provisional Brigade.

With organized resistance overcome, the marines took up the task of running down any remaining "bandits" and establishing a new Dominican government (Jiménez had resigned when the marines first arrived). A provisional government was created by the Dominican congress on July 25, with Dr. Franciso Henríquez y Carvajal as president. But the new government immediately clashed with the American leadership, and on November 29 Captain (later Rear Admiral) Harry Knapp, who had succeeded Admiral Caperton, declared the Dominican Republic under the military jurisdiction of the United States. Legal justification for this action was provided by the financial provisions of the 1907 treaty. The American military government ruled by decree, and its first decree suspended the Dominican congress.[41] Most Dominicans quietly acquiesced, but a resistance movement emerged in the province of San Francisco de Macorís. Colonel Pendleton therefore divided the country into northern, southern, and eastern districts. The eastern district, which was the center of armed resistance, was the responsibility of the recently arrived Fifteenth Regiment, commanded by Colonel James Breckenridge.[42] Accompanying the regiment was Captain McCaughtry and his Jennies.

Like the *cacos* in Haiti, Dominican bandits (more precisely, *gavilleros*) usually coalesced around a charismatic local leader, and bands rarely numbered more than 50 men; a very large band, however, might have as many as 200 men.[43] Most *gavilleros* were armed with only machetes or the occasional pistol or revolver. A few had black-powder rifles, and even fewer had Krags or Springfield rifles. Despite their weakness in firepower, the insurgents were difficult to locate, and they usually initiated engagements with the marines. Therefore, as was the case in Haiti, the marines employed a combination of civil and military measures to pacify the populace and defeat the guerrillas, including the establishment of a constabulary, the Guardia Nacional Dominicana, officered by marines.[44] Small-unit patrols by the marines and the Guardia were accompanied by educational reforms, improved sanitation, agricultural and commercial development, and a wide variety of public works, including new roads.[45]

During the occupation, the Second Brigade was initially commanded by Pendleton. He was succeeded by Brigadier General Ben Hebard "Uncle Ben" Fuller, who would later become the fifteenth commandant of the Marine Corps. A Naval Academy graduate, Fuller had a distinguished career prior to his arrival in the Dominican Republic, including service aboard the protected cruiser USS *Columbia* during the Spanish-American War and combat service in the Philippines.[46] As military governor, Admiral Knapp was succeeded by Rear Admiral Thomas Snowden. Fuller was replaced by Brigadier General Logan Feland, who would later take command of the marines in Nicaragua in the late 1920s.[47] On August 1, 1921, the Third and Fifteenth Regiments were redesignated the First and Fourth Regiments, after which the two brigades in Haiti and the Dominican Republic exchanged numbers. General Feland was followed by Brigadier Generals Charles Long and Harry Lee; the latter oversaw the withdrawal of the marines in 1924.[48]

General Lee perhaps best understood the counterinsurgency mission he had been given, writing:

> There are records where civilized powers, whose armed forces were engaged in the suppression of banditry, countenanced the most drastic methods. These . . . included the destruction of stocks and crops . . . the burning of homes and villages, the laying waste of entire sections, where the inhabitants harbored brigands. However, such drastic measures were never employed in Santo Domingo, because there exists one great disadvantage of their use: the moral effect upon the peaceful inhabitants, who become so exasperated as to forfeit their friendship for generations. That the friendship of the people of an occupied state should be sacrificed by any unnecessary measure was avowedly contrary to the policy of the United States.[49]

Even so, and not unlike in Haiti and later Nicaragua, "overshadowing all other factors was that of personal hatred and fear of the Marines and the Marine-created and controlled *Guardia Nacional Dominicana* (National Guard)."[50]

The marines and other American officials arrived in Santo Domingo culturally and otherwise unprepared for what awaited them. To the Dominican peasants, the marines might as well have been Martians. They looked different, dressed strangely, spoke an unintelligible language, and were rude, at least by Dominican standards. The peasants were frightened by the marines, and well-publicized examples of marines abusing and even killing Dominicans who were not irrefutably guerrillas served to foster the resistance.[51] In the east, where a number of displaced and bitter peasants resided, men from the sugar *bateys* (company-owned villages) and those who had lost their lands to the sugar companies became ready-made "grievance guerrillas."

As already noted, the eastern district was the most troubled, which explains why a detachment of airplanes was sent there with the Fifteenth Regiment. The First Division, Squadron D, hacked out an airstrip from the jungle near Consuelo, 12 miles from San Pedro de Macorís, the third largest city in the country. But in 1920 the detachment moved to a more suitable airstrip near the large sugar mills of San Isidro, a short distance from Santo Domingo City. There, they were reequipped with DH-4Bs delivered by the cargo ship and former German passenger liner USS *Kittery*. Major Russell Presley, then commanding, was the first to take a DH-4B aloft in the Dominican Republic, flying to Santiago and back.[52] Six more DH planes were delivered by another former German ship, USS *Gulfport*. And with the arrival of Major A. A. Cunningham aboard the transport USS *Hancock*, the First Division, Squadron D, became the First Air Squadron, Flights A and B.[53]

To promote esprit de corps, the squadron adopted the ace of spades as the unit's emblem. In the upper left-hand corner of the emblem, the letter *A* stood for "air," and in the bottom right-hand corner, the letter *S* stood for "squadron."[54] The two flights were commanded by Captains "Ditty Box" Brewster and Presley, respectively. There was one steel hangar and three canvas hangars, in addition to machine shops, living quarters, and storage buildings. A "hangar detail" consisting of twenty-five men supervised by Gunnery Sergeant Bill Hennemen was responsible for maintenance of the aircraft. According to a *Popular Aviation* article:

> While the Marines can boast of the finest pilots in the world, they can also take pride in the mechanics that keep those pilots in the air. The men on the ground are too frequently overlooked, yet they deserve 60 per cent of the credit for the success of any air unit. . . . The

> First Air Squadron had "mechanics." Such men as Gunnery Sergeants Codding and Stroba and Sergeants Priebe, McEnery and Sheppard with their crews were the back-bone of the organization. Sergeant Gilliam had direct charge of the test block which he constructed himself, where all motors were tested after overhaul before being mounted in the ships.[55]

Sergeant Gilliam and another sergeant, Charles Hanst, were former US Army Air Service pilots who enlisted in the Marine Corps after World War I to continue their aviation adventures.[56]

As was the case in Haiti, the aviators in the Dominican Republic carried out their mission in the face of considerable difficulties and often great danger.[57] The mountainous terrain posed significant challenges in terms of wind and updrafts, and the weather might turn bad at the worst possible moment. Therefore, landing fields were established at the important towns: Santo Domingo City, Santiago, and San Pedro de Macorís. Other airstrips were available at Azua, Hato Mayor del Rey, San Francisco de Macorís, Puerta Plata, El Seibo, San Juan, and Barahona.[58] However, these latter landing fields were quite small, and even the best pilots found it challenging to land there. The landing field at Santiago was not even constructed for that purpose; it was actually a rifle range measuring 600 yards long and 30 yards wide. At Azua, pilots immediately flew over a cemetery after lifting off, complete with white headstones and other distractions.[59] Crashes were common. One report noted:

> On Wednesday the Commanding General of the Second Brigade, with the Commanding Officer of the First Division, Squadron D, were transported by airplane to San Pedro de Macoris for an inspection of marine posts in the Eastern District. On Saturday the two planes flew to San Pedro de Macoris. On the return, the plane transporting General Feland successfully cleared the small field, but the other was wrecked while taking off. The field was covered with a heavy growth of tall grass, and this in addition to the heavy weight which the plane was carrying, and the strong gusty cross wind slowed the plane down so that it was impossible to clear the trees at the end of the runway. The pilot attempted to turn, but lacking room, hit the ground. The motor was salvaged, but the plane was a total wreck. This squadron now has two planes of the J N type in operation.[60]

Fortunaly, the marine mechanics worked wonders. And they sometimes went to extraordinary lengths to keep the airplanes flying. For example, in early 1919:

> A plane was badly damaged in landing at a point fourteen miles distant by air line. Early the following morning a rescue party of fifteen men arrived. The entire plane was torn down and loaded onto an ox cart, the only available means of transportation. It was hauled in this manner to the end of a narrow gauge railway. By rail it was hauled to the docks of a sugar company, loaded on a barge, towed for a distance of eight miles down one river and up another to the Consuelo docks, and again hauled by railway to the flying field, arriving there a 6 o'clock the same evening. The following afternoon the plane was again ready for service.[61]

The marine aviators occasionally engaged in direct combat operations. The first occurred on July 22, 1919, when Lieutenant Manson Carpenter and his observer, Lieutenant Nathan Noble, responded to a report that marines had become involved in a firefight with bandits near Guaybo Dulce, northwest of Mata de la Palma. Arriving over the marines' reported position, the two aviators surprised some thirty mounted guerrillas fleeing across an open meadow (*sabana*). At 800 feet, Carpenter "could easily see through the telescopic sight, small puffs of smoke coming from their pistols." He charged his "Marlin automatic,"[62] firing as he dove to within 100 feet of the ground. He then banked sharply to allow Lieutenant Noble to open fire with his Lewis machine gun. Having lost altitude and traveling at a high rate of speed, Lieutenant Carpenter returned to a higher altitude "in the hopes of locating another group." Unsuccessful, he made another pass over the meadow, where the two marines counted six bodies. The next day he flew the officer commanding the marine patrol to the scene, where he confirmed the body count.[63]

The greatest difficulty for the aviators in the Dominican Republic was coordinating air and ground operations from the air. Radio communication had not been sufficiently developed, and other means of communication between airplanes and marines on the ground had yet to be worked out. Thus, air support to ground forces was usually serendipitous. For example, in June 1919 Lieutenant H. N. Miller departed La Paja on a patrol with twenty marines on horseback. Entering the Matapalacio section by way of Los Ranchos, Miller noticed several airplanes circling low over some "heavy underbrush." At that point, the marine patrol came under fire. One of the planes flew very low and motioned to Miller, indicating the whereabouts of the bandits. The mounted marines then galloped in that direction and surprised three guerrillas, who ran toward the brush. Miller's marines dismounted and opened fire, killing two of the men. As the marines on the ground advanced, the airplanes dropped several bombs. The remnants of the guerrilla band quickly abandoned their position and dispersed into the countryside.[64]

But combat actions like those experienced by Lieutenant Carpenter and the anonymous aviators encountered by Lieutenant Miller were rare. Thus, the squadron's greatest contributions lay in support services, such as carrying the mail and personnel rapidly from one place to another, as well as dropping messages to far-ranging patrols. But unlike in France during World War I, the aviators in Santo Domingo were completely devoted to providing services to the marines on the ground, mostly the Fifteenth Regiment under the command of Colonel Breckenridge (later Lieutenant Colonel William Harlee). The eastern part of the country, where the regiment was located, was mountainous and heavily forested, with winding trails "so narrow in places that mounted troops cannot ride two abreast."[65] Therefore, the Jennies were quickly put to work scouting and reconnoitering for the marines on the ground, as well as delivering "strictly confidential or secret messages" between commanders.[66] Later, the DH planes performed the same services and were better suited to close air support. According to one account:

> Their work is entirely in co-operation with the troops. Officers in command of foot or horse-Marines have been taken in airplane flights over the districts in which they operate and allowed to observe the contour of the land, the larger trails, the most favorable places for bandit camps and the best means of reaching them.
>
> The aviators, in their patrols, fly low over the mountains, searching for bandit camps, mapping new trails and all points of military interest.
>
> When bandits have been located by troops in dense, inaccessible areas, the aviators fly over and drop a few bombs in their midst. As they come out of the jungles they are seized by the ever ready Marines on foot.

> Though the bombs used thus far have been constructed of gas-pipe and loaded with black powder, they have had a decided effect on the bandits. . . . They speak of the airplanes as "birds of evil" and the bombs as the bird's "eggs."[67]

In truth, most of the squadron's missions were of the nonlethal variety. Regular mail flights were made between Santiago and San Pedro de Macorís, and mail was carried elsewhere as necessary. Airplanes often carried special dispatches from the commanding general, and passengers often accompanied these flights. On one occasion, Lieutenant Christian Schilt ferried three physicians to Santiago from Santo Domingo City. During a second trip, he delivered two more. On his second return trip, Schilt made a forced landing in his DH-4B when the electrical system failed. Fortunately, "he landed his machine without wrecking it."[68] On another occasion, Sergeant Hanst (the former Army Air Service officer) ferried an intelligence officer and the wife of well-known guerrilla leader Ramon Natera from San Pedro de Macorís to Santo Domingo City in a DH-4B. Natera's wife sat in the lap of the intelligence officer for the entire flight. Upon arrival, the captain's legs were so numb that he had to be lifted from the airplane.[69] Special flights of this sort were not unusual. Lieutenant Schilt flew several sorties in a DH-4B with a "regulation Fairchild K-1 camera" rigged in the rear cockpit and pointed down through the floor to make an aerial survey and mosaic map of the island's entire coastline. As discussed in chapter 2, a colleague of Schilt's in the First Squadron, Hayne "Cuckoo" Boyden, flew the same kind of mission and became a highly regarded expert on aerial mapping and aerial photography. Boyden got his nickname in the Dominican Republic because of his erratic flying technique and odd manner.[70]

Boyden wrote several essays for *Leatherneck* magazine and the *Marine Corps Gazette* that provide useful insight into what it was like to fly in the Dominican Republic. On his first cross-country flight after arriving in the country, Boyden and Lieutenant "Rove" Rovegno had departed Consuelo and were heading for Santo Domingo City when the engine quit and they were forced to land in a savanna. They were immediately surrounded by curious locals, and Boyden "remembered the story of lieutenant McFayden's sergeant-observer in Haiti, whom the Cacos killed and, it was reported, ate." Lieutenant Rovegno "didn't like the prospects very much himself, so he gave her [the airplane] the gun." They managed to take off, but the engine quit again, the airplane stalled, and they crashed, flipping the plane on its back. Boyden quickly scrambled out, followed by Rovegno. They were once more surrounded, but the local residents turned out to be quite friendly and offered to help. Provided with horses, the two marine aviators returned to Consuelo, gathered some tools, and made their way back to the airplane. With the assistance of several local men, they disassembled the airplane and proceeded to haul it back to base. Sixteen local men carried the engine using wooden poles, and thirty men brought up the rear carrying the fuselage. The arduous trip was made worse by pouring rain. But Boyden and Rovegno purchased some bread and rum at a Dominican "country store," and "after this they went along with much more pep." The marine aviators finally met up with a special train that had been sent to retrieve them and their airplane, which took them to the coast. The two marines and their wrecked aircraft were loaded aboard the former *Norddeutscher* Lloyd liner, USS *Huron,* and sailed to San Pedro de Macorís.[71]

In all, "Cuckoo" Boyden experienced five forced landings while flying in the Dominican Republic. On another occasion, he had to land when his Jenny overheated, and then he had to find his way back to the base. He returned to the plane, got it flying again, and returned home "uneventfully."[72] But that forced landing and others paled in comparison to a flight Boyden made from Santiago to Santo Domingo City. He had flown to Santiago in a DH-4B to drop off a navy officer and was returning with a corporal used for "ballast."[73] The weather turned very bad very quickly, and Boyden dropped from 6,000 feet to 2,500 feet through a hole in the clouds in an attempt to turn around and return to Santiago. But at the lower altitude he found himself in the midst of a powerful rainstorm and decided to climb in a spiral to avoid the 3,000-foot-plus mountains on either side of him. As he rose through the storm, his airplane stalled and spun several times, until "suddenly my stick came back to my stomach [and] the nose fell over to the right . . . into a right spin." This time he spun down for 1,000 feet, all the while recalling several friends who had crashed and died in similar circumstances. Boyden kicked his rudder hard left and stopped the spin, but now he found himself in a steep nosedive. Once more he fell into a spin, but this time "the lights went out." He had crashed into the side of a mountain.[74]

Boyden was unconscious for an hour and a half. The corporal, who had regained consciousness first, dug himself out and then Boyden. The engine had broken free, the wings and stabilizers had been ripped off, and the fuselage had come to rest on its back against the mountainside. Once they had recovered sufficiently, the two men started down the mountain. "It was so steep [they] had to hold on to bushes to keep from falling." They found the engine 30 feet below the wreck. Dazed and exhausted, they slept overnight on the mountainside. The next day they worked their way down to a valley, where they found a Dominican family and were treated to fried eggs. They continued down an unfinished road until they found an American civil engineer, who telephoned the airfield at Santiago. A doctor retrieved Boyden and took him to Santiago, first by horseback and then by Ford truck, a total of some 30 miles. Boyden seemed to recover quickly, but following a flight to locate his downed aircraft, he experienced facial paralysis and deafness on his left side. Christian Schilt flew him to Santo Domingo City, where X-rays revealed that he had a fractured skull. He was hospitalized for three months, during which time the corporal who had served as ballast set out with a mounted detachment to find the airplane. They failed. Later, Boyden and "Ditty Box" Brewster tried again, riding burros. They too failed, turning back when they ran out of food. Boyden concluded his essay, "So I am looking forward some day, when I return to that Island-land of palms, sea, mountains and white clouds—to going again up into those Maimon mountains" to find the wreck.[75] He never did.

On July 1, 1922, the First Squadron was redesignated Observation Squadron One (VO-1). That same year, Alfred Cunningham was succeeded as squadron commander by Major Edwin Brainard, a future head of Marine Corps aviation.[76] Brainard would command the squadron until its departure in 1924. From 1919 to 1924 the number of aircraft in the Dominican Republic fluctuated, from a low of two JNs in 1919 to five JN-6HG-Is, two DH-4Bs, and five JN-6HGs in June 1920. The most modern airplane deployed to Santo Domingo was the VE-7G, one of which arrived in 1924. The squadron's chief difficulty was obtaining spare parts, which took anywhere from three to six months to arrive.[77]

Most of the aircraft that deployed to Santo Domingo were disassembled in the United States and shipped in pieces, but on April 22, 1922, Major Turner led a two-plane flight of DH-4Bs from Washington, DC, to Santo Domingo City. At the time, this was the longest "unguarded" flight over land and water by landplanes. Turner flew in the rear cockpit of the first airplane, piloted by Lieutenant Basil Bradley. "Sandy" Sanderson flew the second plane, accompanied by Gunnery Sergeant Charles Rucker.[78] As described by Turner, the worst part of the flight was over the Windward Passage, where the airplanes were buffeted by "baffling, heavy gusts of wind."[79] Turner intended to fly on to Saint Thomas in the Virgin Islands, but "because of the quarantine at Porto Rico [*sic*], due to the presence of Bubonic Plague, the planes did not go beyond Santo Domingo City, D. R."[80]

That same year (1922), Brigadier General Lee was instructed to withdraw marines from the interior, concentrate at three places in preparation for withdrawal from the Dominican Republic, and turn security duties over to the Guardia, which was redesignated the Policia Nacional Dominicana. President Wilson had wanted to withdraw the marines as early as 1920, and his successor, Warren G. Harding, had made withdrarwal a campaign platform. But the Dominican government refused to cooperate with the terms of withdrawal, and it was not until the Americans threatened to remain indefinitely that the Dominicans agreed to the Hughes-Peynado plan, named after Secretary of State Charles Evans Hughes and the lead Dominican negotiator, Francisco Peynado. On October 21, 1922, a new Dominican government came into being, headed by Juan Batista Vicini Burgos. Allied with American high commissioner Sumner Welles, Burgos facilitated elections, which took place on March 15, 1924. General Horacio Vasquez was elected president, and his Alianza party gained a majority in both houses of a restored Dominican congress. Both results were satisfactory to the US government, and immediately after Vasquez's inauguration, elements of the brigade began leaving Santo Domingo. Among the first to go was VO-1, which departed for Quantico on July 18.[81] Only a few years later, many of these marines found themselves in northern China.

Operations in China

Western interest in China dates back at least to the Crusades, but it was Marco Polo's extensive travel in China, which he referred to as Cathay, that awakened real interest. In 1498 Portuguese explorer Vasco da Gama, the First Count of Vidigueira, became the first European to sail around the southern tip of Africa and then on to India, where, for a short time, he was the viceroy of Portuguese India. Soon, this principal route of international trade connected China, India, and Europe. Portugal and Great Britain were the first European states to exploit the riches of China, with Portuguese traders arriving in the mid-1500s. They settled in Macao, on the western side of the Pearl

River Delta across from modern-day Hong Kong, near the ancient capital city of Pun Yue. British traders arrived around 1627, at which time Canton (Guangzhou) was the only Chinese port open to European commercial interests. By the 1800s, European powers had built vast colonial empires in Asia, and in 1839 Great Britain declared war on the Qing Dynasty, the first of the so-called Opium Wars (1839–1842 and 1856–1860) fought to force the Chinese to allow the expansion of British trade. With the signing of the Treaty of Nanking in 1842, Britain gained access to several ports and acquired Hong Kong as a colony.

Two years after the Treaty of Nanking was signed, an American trader became embroiled in a local dispute on Whampoa Island, off Canton. The sloop USS *St. Louis,* the flagship of the East India Squadron, arrived with a contingent of marines, who helped the US consul settle the dispute. This resulted in the Treaty of Whampoa, which permitted the United States to trade freely in China. With the close of the Spanish-American War and the acquisition of the Philippines from Spain, the United States promulgated an Open Door policy toward China, an attempt to forestall its partition by the Europeans and Japanese. Secretary of State John Hays sent a letter to the major powers (including Russia) requesting that they formally recognize the territorial and administrative integrity of China and allow free use of treaty ports by all concerned. By 1900, each respondent had agreed in principle to the policy, although fierce competition for special concessions from the Chinese continued.

Their participation in arbitrating the Whampoa Island dispute was the marines' first time in China, but it would not be their last. Although US policy was to avoid entanglements in European activities in China owing to the Open Door policy, the US government was committed to protecting US interests there, including Christian missionary activities. Marines landed in Shanghai in 1854, Shanghai and Hong Kong in 1855, Canton in 1855, Shanghai again in 1859, and Newchwang (Yingkou), Tung Chow Foo (Tongzhou, Nantong), and Shanghai in 1866. But it was not until 1895 that marines went ashore in northern China.

Following a brief war in 1858 involving the British and French against the Chinese, the Treaty of Tientsin (Tianjin) permitted foreigners almost unlimited access to China. However, Chinese resistance to penetration by outsiders and foreign religions provoked years of civil and political unrest. During the

Sino-Japanese War in 1894, Japanese forces advanced on Beijing (Peking), and antiforeigner riots broke out. The American minister, Colonel Charles Denby, a Union officer during the Civil War, requested marines to guard the legation. Rear Admiral Charles Carpenter, commander of the Asiatic Squadron, dispatched the protected cruiser USS *Baltimore* to Chefoo (Yantai) with orders to put the ship's marines at the minister's disposal. In January 1895 Captain George Elliott and his marines arrived at the American legation, where they would remain for six months.

Civil unrest continued after the marines' departure, and they returned in 1898 and again in force during the Boxer Rebellion of 1900. The *I Ho Ch'uan,* or "Fist of Righteous Harmony"—more commonly known as the Boxers (or *Yihetuan* movement)—was a semireligious and protonationalist movement opposed to foreign influence and Christian missionary activity in China. Chinese from all walks of life, from aristocrats to the dregs of society, were involved. Foreigners called them Boxers owing to the martial arts and calisthenics they practiced. As the movement spread from the south to the north toward Beijing, its adherents attacked European missionaries and Chinese Christians. By late spring, they were active in Beijing itself. American minister Edwin Conger, who had replaced Colonel Denby, telegraphed the State Department and requested marines once again to secure the legation. The protected cruiser USS *Newark,* with marines under the command of Captain Newt Hall, was the first American ship to arrive. It was soon joined by the Indiana-class battleship USS *Oregon,* with its detachment of twenty-five marines and their commander, Captain John "Handsome Jack" Myers. Combined under the command of Captain Myers, the marines of the two ships marched to Tientsin.

Tientsin is located some 85 miles southeast of Beijing near the mouth of the Pei-Ho River (today the Hai or Bai He River), which empties into the Yellow Sea at the Bohai Gulf. In June 1900 much of the town was seized by the Boxers. It was retaken by the so-called Eight-Nation Alliance (Austria-Hungary, France, Germany, Great Britain, Italy, Japan, Russia, and the United States), and a provisional government was established. Shortly thereafter a multinational column under the command of Vice Admiral Sir Edmund Seymour of the British Royal Navy set out to reinforce the legation guards in Beijing. The column met stiff resistance and attempted to return to Tientsin, which had been overrun once more by the Boxers, this time joined by Chinese Imperial Army troops.

Rear Admiral George Remy, commander of the American Asiatic Squadron, ordered a contingent of marines under the command of Major Littleton Waller to proceed from the Philippines to China. Among Waller's officers was Smedley Butler. The hospital ship USS *Solace* landed Waller and his marines at the Taku Bar in the Pei-Ho estuary. They were joined by marines from the gunboat USS *Nashville.* Combined with a Russian battalion of infantry and British marines, the US marines rescued the foreign settlement (known as "concessions") and were greeted by Colonel Denby, who placed a barrel full of beer in the street. Each marine helped himself to a bottle, some of them using their bayonets to remove the bottle caps. A relief column was then quickly dispatched to rescue troops under the command of Vice Admiral Seymour. The remainder of the Boxers in the walled city were defeated not long after elements of the US Army's Ninth Infantry Regiment (First and Second Battalions) arrived. They were commanded by Colonel Emerson Liscum, a Civil War veteran who was mortally wounded during the battle. The Ninth Infantry was supported by marines under the command of Colonel Robert Meade, who arrived aboard the armored cruiser USS *Brooklyn.* With Tientsin secured, the multinational force set out for Beijing to rescue the legations there.

On August 5 some 18,000 troops (including 2,500 marines) defeated the Imperial Army at the Battle of Beicang, and the next day they achieved another victory at the Battle of Yangcun (Yangstun). The international force then assaulted Beijing on August 14. The British arrived in the legation quarter first, followed by the Americans. Marine casualties were few, but they included Smedley Butler, who had also been wounded during the assault on Tientsin. Chinese opposition melted away, and on the following day the Alliance troops occupied the Imperial City. On August 28 Alliance soldiers marched through the "Forbidden City" to demonstrate their complete control of Beijing. Dowager Empress Cixi signed a treaty on January 7, 1902, and the Boxer Rebellion was at an end. But the marines were not done with China, and during the next intervention, they would bring airplanes.

Modernization had come slowly to China, and the army, which had been humiliated by the Japanese conquest of Korea in 1895, turned to its erstwhile foes—the Europeans and the Japanese—for assistance in developing a modern military. Among the officers trained in Japan was a young Chiang Kai-shek. In addition to military modernization, new political ideas were adopted, and by the time two-year-old Puyi (or Pu Yi) ascended to the Dragon Throne in 1908, several political parties existed. As these parties contested for dominance, the imperial court lost control, resulting in a series of rebellions collectively known as the 1911 Revolution. Puyi abdicated in 1912 and was replaced by a provisional government under longtime revolutionist Sun Yat-sen. But his control over the country was no better than the monarchy's, and he resigned in favor of Yuan Shikai, commander of the army. Yuan intended to seize total control and unify the country, leading to a second, abortive revolution in 1913 by Sun. Defeated, Sun went into exile. Thus, China's two-millennia-long imperial era ended in 1912. Nearly four decades of civil war would follow, with the principal factions being the Chinese Communists and the Chinese Nationalists, the Kuomintang. Maneuvering for power between these two antagonists were various "warlords," former imperial retainers. Looking on with aggressive intent was Japan.

Following the defeat of Sun Yat-sen and the Kuomintang, Yuan sought to restore the monarchy—with himself as emperor. He ruled until 1916 but never achieved formal ascension. He renounced the throne and died in June. His death provoked renewed civil war as former regional military governors effectively established independent states. The Japanese promptly took advantage of the situation, returning Sun to China. He raised an army and set about defeating the warlords one by one. By 1919, his control was sufficient to establish a capital at Canton and declare the re-formation of the Kuomintang. Two years later, he helped establish the Chinese Communist Party to assist him in subduing the remaining warlords. In 1923 the Communists agreed to a "united front" with the Kuomintang, which proved useful in mobilizing leftist elements in the cities. They also brought in Soviet assistance, including the funding necessary to establish a military academy at Whampoa (Huangpu, a district of Canton) led by Chiang Kai-shek.

The revived Kuomintang and its Communist allies made slow progress and suffered several defeats at the hands of the warlords. The situation changed dramatically, however, when Sun died in early 1925. The Kuomintang split into factions, and Chiang emerged as a major player, taking command of his own army in 1926. He proposed to carry Sun's campaign against the warlords into northern China. By 1927, his forces were gaining momentum. Alarmed, the Communists sought to undermine his progress, but Chiang reacted quickly. He moved his capital to Nanjing and purged Communists from the Kuomintang, bringing the united front to a bloody end. Weakened but not down for the count, the Communists reorganized and attacked

Kuomintang (Nationalist) forces. Nevertheless, by the fall of 1926, the Nationalist army had reached the Yangtze River Valley in central China and was poised to strike Hankow (Hankou) and Shanghai, which contained large foreign settlements. Urgent appeals for protection were sent out, recalling the dark days of 1900.

The Nationalist conquest of Beijing in June 1928 lent an air of legitimacy to Kuomintang rule, capitalizing on the traditional Chinese acquiescence to the "mandate of heaven." But Chiang's hold on the country remained tenuous. Many warlords remained in power, the Communists had survived, and the Japanese had conluded that a united China was not in their interest. In 1930 three warlords joined to defeat Chiang during the so-called Central Plains War. However, Chiang emerged victorious and turned his attention to the Communists. But before Chiang could act, the Japanese manufactured two "incidents" justifying direct military intervention.[82]

As China reeled during the 1920s, the United States still had a force of some 500 marines in Beijing, as well as the US Army's Fifteenth Regiment garrisoned at Tientsin. The first unit to deploy to reinforce these troops was the Fourth Marine Regiment, which sailed from San Diego in late January 1927. More marines followed, and the Third Provisional Brigade was formed under the command of Brigadier General Smedley Butler, veteran of the Boxer Rebellion. The Third Brigade comprised three infantry regiments, part of an artillery regiment, an engineer company, a tank detachment, and, for the first time, a dedicated aviation unit. The latter comprised elements from the Aircraft Squadrons, West Coast Expeditionary Force. Together, the aviation and ground units formed an early version of today's Marine Air Ground Task Force (MAGTF).

Interestingly, the idea to send airplanes to China with the ground units was not entirely the marines'. John MacMurray, the US minister to China, urged the deployment of a "substantial detachment" of aircraft because the "Chinese are ignorant of the effectiveness of this weapon and are apt to disparage it."[83] Regardless of whose idea it was, on April 7, 1927, the headquarters detachment of the Aircraft Squadrons, West Coast Expeditionary Force, commanded by Major Cocky Evans, and Fighting Squadron Three (VF-3M, the lineal forerunner of VMFA-232, an F/A-18 Hornet squadron known as the "Red Devils," based at Marine Corps Air Station Miramar, California), commanded by Lieutenant William Wallace, set out from San Diego aboard the transport USS *Henderson*. Four days later, the cargo ship USS *Gold Star* (the former *Arcturus*) departed Orote Field, Apra Harbor Naval Station, Guam, with Captain Walter McCaughtry and 102 men from Scouting Squadron One (VS-1M).[84]

VS-1M began life as an unnumbered aviation detachment at Parris Island immediately after World War I and became Flight L, Fourth Squadron, during Lejeune's reorganization of flying units in 1920. In 1921 Flight L was sent to Guam, the first Marine Corps flying unit posted to the Pacific. VS-1M was redesignated as a patrol squadron in late 1927 (VP-3M) and remained on Guam until February 1931, when it was decommissioned. While at Parris Island, the unit comprised twelve DH-4s, two JN-4HGs, four JN-4HG-Is, two N-9s, and five Standard E-1s.[85] The Standards were withdrawn from Parris Island in 1921, and by the time the unit moved to Guam, it comprised two N-9 floatplanes, two HS-2L flying boats, and four F5-Ls.

The twin-engine F5-L was a British Felixstowe F series seaplane designed by John Cyril Porte at the Royal Naval Air Service seaplane experimental station. Squadron Leader Porte became head of the station in 1915 and persuaded the Admiralty to acquire flying boats designed by Glenn Curtiss. Although originally designed for commercial use, the Curtiss boats were adapted for use by the Royal Navy with a new hull designed by Porte, designated the Felixstowe F1. The F1 was found to be inadequate for North Sea patrols, and Curtiss was asked to build a larger aircraft (the Curtiss H8, or "Large America"). Once again, the hull was found to be unsuitable for North Sea operations and was redesigned by Porte. In addition, the American engines were replaced by more powerful 250 hp Rolls-Royce Eagles. This aircraft was designated the F2, and with additional modifications it became the F2A, which served until the end of World War I. At that time, a new version appeared, the F3, which could carry a heavier load owing to extended wings and a longer fuselage, but it employed the same engine. As a result, the F3 was not popular with crews because it was slower and less maneuverable than the F2.

The prototype Felixstowe F5 first appeared in 1918, with the major improvement being the use of veneer for the hull instead of doped linen. The F5 was also powered by an improved 400 hp Liberty 12A engine. The prototype was built in England, but the production models were manufactured by the Naval Aircraft Factory in Philadelphia, which produced 137. The F5 was too late to see operational service during World War I, but it became the standard postwar flying boat for the Royal Air Force (which had absorbed the Royal

Naval Air Service). Curtiss manufactured sixty F5s, and some of these were converted to civilian use as the Aeromarine 75 by the Aeromarine Plane and Motor Company in 1919. The F5 was designated the F5-L by the US Navy (owing to the Liberty engines) and became the navy's standard flying boat until the late 1920s. The marines acquired four, one of which crashed on a night patrol off Guam on February 21, 1922.

With the transfer of Flight L to Guam, the marine aviation detachment at Parris Island was officially abandoned on September 25, 1922. A year later, Flight L became Scouting Squadron One (VS-1). The squadron lost one N-9 but gained two more HS-2Ls, in addition to the four F5-Ls. The number of aircraft and types remained constant in 1924, but the F5-Ls were withdrawn in 1925 and the number of N-9s increased to two. In 1926 the N-9s were withdrawn, but the contingent of HS-2Ls was increased to six, and they were joined by two VE-7H Bluebirds, a two-seat trainer built for the US Army but also acquired by the navy.

The VE-7 was a product of the Lewis and Vought Corporation, which was created in 1918 after the Aircraft Production Board urged American industry to turn out new designs for wartime employment. Vought was asked to produce an advanced trainer using the 150 hp water-cooled V-8 Hispano-Suiza Model A engine. The Vought design resembled the DH-4 in some ways but had the nose of the famous French "Spad" fighter.[86] Although the airplane did not go into full-scale production before the war ended, the navy expressed continued interest in it, requesting a 180 hp Wright-Hispano E-1 engine. More than 120 machines were built by Vought and the Naval Aircraft Factory. In 1922 the VE-7 became the first airplane to take off from an American aircraft carrier.[87] It was so successful as a trainer that it was put to work in a variety of other ways, including the VE-7G, which was armed with a forward-firing Lewis machine gun and a flexible Lewis gun mounted on a scarf ring in the rear cockpit. The VE-7H, provided to the marines of VS-1, was the seaplane variant. Later, the VE-7S, a single-seat fighter with one synchronized Vickers machine gun in the nose, was also acquired by the marines. Another version, the VE-7SF, was the same airplane outfitted with flotation gear for emergency landings on water. With the addition of the 180 hp Wright-Hispano engine and a larger tail fin, the VE-7 became the VE-9.[88] The VE-9 typically carried no armament but could be outfitted as a landplane or a floatplane. Both the VE-7 and the VE-9 passed out of service in the US Navy before 1927, but a couple remained operational with the marines until

1928. In retrospect, the VE-7 began a relationship between Vought and the navy and marines that would last more than sixty years.[89]

As the marines flowed into northern China in the spring of 1927, a portion of VS-1M accompanied them, leaving behind the two Bluebirds. By May 3, the detachment from VS-1M and nine Boeing FB-1 fighters from VF-3M (later redesignated VF-10M to avoid confusion with a navy squadron) were in Shanghai harbor, crated aboard ships. They remained in storage for some time because no firm decision had been reached about their employment. That decision rested with Admiral Clarence Williams, commander in chief of the Asiatic Fleet.[90] General Butler arrived in late March aboard the armored cruiser USS *Pittsburgh,* the fleet's flagship. Butler and Williams were at odds over the use of the marine aircraft. Butler wrote to Lejeune that the admiral did not want to put them ashore because of possible diplomatic repercussions, even though the British had offered the marines the use of their airstrip. But in truth, Admiral Williams was uncomfortable employing combat aircraft over China because he had virtually no experience with them.

Combat aircraft were not entirely novel in China, however. In 1913 two German naval aviators, Lieutenants Gunther Plüschow and Friedrich Muellerskowski, traveled to the port of Tsingtao (Green Island) accompanied by two Rumpler *Taube* (Dove) aircraft.[91] In 1898 the Manchu government had signed a treaty with Imperial Germany allowing a settlement for the resupply and repair of German ships and the building of fortifications. With Tsingtao as headquarters, German mining companies, banks, merchants, and other businessmen spread throughout China to the Russian border. Upon the aviators' arrival, a hangar was constructed at the northern end of a racetrack to house the two airplanes as well as two captive balloons. Plüschow was the first to go aloft. Muellerskowski followed and crashed his airplane—the day before Germany declared war on Russia (August 1, 1914). Lieutenant Plüschow's *Taube* therefore became the only German heavier-than-air craft employed in the defense of Tsingtao against Japanese and British forces. His story, though barely known, stands as a remarkable achievement in the annals of combat aviation history.

With Japan's declaration of war on Germany, a three-place Japanese Farman pusher seaplane (Type Fu) from the seaplane carrier *Wakamiyo Maru* dropped a small bomb near the Bismarck Battery at the heart of the German fortifications. It caused no damage but was the first aerial bomb dropped over Tsingtao during the war.[92] Afterward, the four Farmans aboard the *Wakamiyo Maru* overflew the city to locate and bomb the German aircraft hangar.[93] Although they found their target, they failed to hit it. Plüschow then moved his airplane to a camouflaged location and constructed a decoy that was moved around the airfield, which proved very effective. On September 13 Plüschow took off and discovered a Japanese infantry column near Wo-ko Tschuang Bay. His superiors were delighted by this intelligence and quickly became believers in the value of aviation.[94]

The Germans endured a long Anglo-Japanese air-land-naval siege, and Plüschow continued to fly missions in support of the defense. After the captive balloons were lost, his Rumpler was the only means of aerial reconnaissance and observation. Consequently, Japanese aircrews intent on removing the *Taube* from the fight fired pistols at Plüschow and attempted to drop bombs on his airplane in flight, but they never succeeded in bringing him down. For his part, Plüschow managed to shoot down one Japanese airplane with his 9mm Parabellum Mauser handgun, but he was later ordered to steer clear of Japanese airplanes because his Rumpler was so valuable to the defense.[95] In the end, the German defenses collapsed, and Plüschow escaped in his *Taube* down the coast to Haichow, where he burned the airplane.[96]

Although the German commander in Tsingtao during World War I was convinced of the utility of airplanes, Admiral Williams was not, and he feared they might antagonize the Chinese. Fortunately, General Butler managed to persuade the admiral to send the marine aviators and their aircraft to the Philippines to be held in reserve.[97] Additional planes joined them at Olongapo Naval Base on May 9, and within the month they had received their full complement of aircraft: nine FB-1s, six Boeing 02B-1s (DH planes), and five Loening OL-6 amphibians. They remained in their crates, however, much to the exasperation of Butler and the pilots.[98] One reason was that a substantial amount of aviation supplies and equipment remained in San Diego awaiting shipment. This error was later used as evidence that the marines needed their own aircraft carrier. In testimony to Congress, the head of Marine Corps aviation, Major Brainard, claimed that the aircraft squadrons were of "no use" to General Butler because of the lack of suitable landing fields, as well as the shortage of spare parts and other supplies. Had the marines owned their own aircraft carrier, he argued, the embarked aircraft could have gone into action "at a moment's notice [and] go to any point required."[99] The FB-1s were especially missed, owing to the perceived threat from Japanese aircraft.

The FB-1 was the US Navy's version of the Boeing PW-9 biplane fighter built for the US Army as a private venture, the Model 15. Boeing engineers were impressed by the German Fokker D.VII from World War I, particularly its mixed metal and wood construction and the semicantilevered wings that eliminated some of the drag-inducing wires. The Model 15 owed much to the D.VII, and three prototypes were produced, powered by a 435 hp Curtiss D-12 in-line engine. Although the army was not in the market for a fighter at the time, Boeing's gamble paid off. The army agreed to test the aircraft, which was given an Army Air Service designation of XPW-9, and it was delivered for trials at McCook Field, Dayton, Ohio, in 1924. The navy soon became interested in the fighter as an alternative to the Fokker XPW-7 and conducted its own trials, subsequently ordering fourteen planes in 1925, designated the FB-1 (Boeing Fighter Type 1).[100] The FB-1 was almost identical to the army version (PW-1), with the same split-axle undercarriage and no provision for carrier operations. They were handed off to the Marine Corps and sent to Olongapo.[101]

The aircraft squadrons at Olongapo were finally deployed to Tientsin when the fighting among the Chinese factions intensified and Admiral Williams decided to fortify the town and bring in reinforcements. The squadrons sailed to China aboard the transport USS *Chaumont,* unloading the men and twenty-four airplanes at Taku Bar on the Gulf of Chihli, downriver from Tientsin. The airfield was constructed at Hsin Ho (Camp MacMurray, so named in honor of the American minister), some 5 miles from the mouth of the Hai River. The arrival of these reinforcements calmed matters considerably, and Butler divided his time between negotiating with the Japanese, who were becoming increasingly aggressive toward the Chinese, and negotiating with the other military forces in the area, including the local US Army commanders, who wanted the marines integrated into the "protocol defense system."[102] For their part, the marine aviators confined their flights to Tientsin and a 2-mile-wide communication line following the rail line from Tientsin to Beijing. If the line of communication were blocked, Butler envisioned using the airplanes to support his ground forces as they reopened the line. To that end, the aircraft were equipped to carry 163-pound and 25-pound fragmentation bombs to augment their machine guns.[103]

Flight operations in China were fairly routine, if flying in the 1920s could ever be described as routine. For example, General Butler wished to personally inspect Camp MacMurray, and Captain Arthur Page Jr. was sent in a 02B-1 to retrieve Butler from his headquarters and fly him to the airfield. Upon landing at Camp MacMurray, Page overshot the runway, and the airplane came to an ignominious halt in a Chinese laundry. Annoyed, Butler reportedly remarked: "A little close wasn't it? You'll kill yourself some day, Page! Do it when I'm not with you!"[104] Undaunted, Butler expanded the airspace in which marine aircraft could fly and scheduled another flight from the airfield to Tientsin with Minister MacMurray and a member of his staff (future commandant, Major Alexander Vandegrift) as passengers. The aircraft was met by an exuberant crowd of Chinese, most of whom had never seen an airplane before.[105]

Cocky Evans, commander of the aircraft squadrons, was never a favorite of General Butler's owing to his independent streak. When Evans was replaced by the newly promoted Lieutenant Colonel Thomas Turner, Butler was pleased. Always the showman, the general embarked on a series of air shows to impress the Chinese. The aerial demonstrations were a huge success, and on one occasion Captain James "Nuts" Moore made a low pass over the crowd of spectators, then went into a climbing roll and lost the wings of his airplane in the process. Moore bailed out and parachuted safely to the ground. But the mainly Chinese crowd was delighted with the stunt, unaware that it had not been planned that way.[106]

As the winter of 1927–1928 approached, consideration was given to greatly reducing flying activities. For one thing, the marine aviators had little to no experience flying in harsh winter weather. But Lieutenant Colonel Turner pressed his fliers to continue their patrols, which prompted Butler to describe Turner as a "first class commander." Butler likewise praised the men who flew the airplanes and the marines who kept them in flying condition. This was well deserved, for the mechanics had to devise innovative methods to keep the airplanes running and airborne in the often subfreezing conditions. One trick was to drain all the fluids (fuel, oil, and water) from the airplanes, place them in drums, and light small fires under the drums to keep the fluids warm overnight. The next day the fluids were returned to the aircraft, which would then start without difficulty.[107]

At their peak, the marine forces in Tientsin reached 3,372 men.[108] Admiral Williams was replaced by Admiral Mark Bristol, who wanted to begin a withdrawal of the marines, beginning with the aircraft squadrons. The State Department balked, believing the marines' presence restrained the Japanese and encouraged the Chinese to respect their treaty obligations. Butler objected specifically to the withdrawal of the aircraft squadrons; he believed they had a deterrent effect on the Japanese and would be needed if fighting broke out. Minister MacMurray agreed, and navy headquarters in Washington declined to approve Admiral Bristol's recommendation. Nevertheless, the aviation contingent was nominally reduced when Marine Corps Headquarters decided to deactivate VS-1M's expeditionary detachment and its unit personnel and aircraft were transferred to VF-10M (formerly VF-3M). Even so, by the middle of 1928, the aircraft squadrons fielded ten FB-1s, one OC-1, eight OC-2s, five 02B-1s, and six OL-6s.[109] The Curtiss OC Falcons were a particularly welcome addition.

The Curtiss Falcon XO-1 prototype was one of twelve prototypes evaluated by the US Army Air Service in 1924, with the Douglas XO-2 declared the winner.[110] Curtiss then gave the Falcon a Packard 1A-1500 engine for the 1925 trials, which won the event. But the production version (O-1) ordered by the army failed to live up to expectations and was refitted with a 435 hp Curtiss V-1150 engine. The new airplane was delivered in October 1927, designated the A-3 under the new "Attack" designation (that is, for close air support of ground forces). The navy also adopted the Falcon in 1927 as the F8C-1 and later the F8C-3, a shipboard fighter. The Falcons delivered to the Marine Corps were designated OC-1 and OC-2. The OC-1 (F8C-1) Helldiver was powered by a 420 hp Pratt & Whitney R-1340 Wasp radial engine. Four were provided to the marines in 1928. The OC-2 (F8C-3) was no different from the OC-1; it was merely the second delivery of the airplane to the marines. The Falcon was highly successful, and civilian and export versions were manufactured. One was sold to Charles Lindbergh as the "Lindbergh Special." Variants of the export version saw combat during the Brazilian Constitutionalist Revolution of 1932, in fighting between Colombia and Peru from 1932 to 1933, and during the so-called Chaco War fought between Bolivia and Paraguay from 1932 to 1935. With the addition of the OCs to the aircraft squadrons in China, the marines had an airplane well suited to refining air-ground operations with the infantry. Indeed, during field exercises in China, the marines experimented with radio sets in some aircraft and Morse code devices in others. The results were reportedly "excellent up to a distance of 15 miles." Thus, in addition to becoming the eyes of the infantry, marine aviators could "furnish effective air support at the time needed."[111]

In April 1928 Nationalist forces of the Kuomintang renewed their operations. By June, they had secured Beijing and began moving toward Tientsin on the coast. For the next two weeks, the aircraft squadrons of the Third Brigade patrolled daily, reporting Chinese troop movements. During the fighting between the Nationalist forces and troops of the local warlord, marine aircraft were struck seven times by ground fire, but none were lost, and the marine aviators did not return fire. Officers were sent to discuss the matter with Chinese commanders and were assured that the aircraft had been shot at by mistake (the Chinese believed them to be Japanese). The Chinese commanders promised there would be no further shooting at American planes, and this proved to be true.

On June 17 the city of Tientsin was abandoned to the Nationalists, and with Chiang Kai-shek's forces firmly in control, a relative peace was established in northern China.[112] Admiral Bristol once again recommended that the marines be withdrawn, as he believed the Fifteenth Infantry was sufficient to deter any attack on American citizens. This time, the State Department concurred, and the bulk of the marines were withdrawn to the Philippines, leaving only the Fourth Regiment in Shanghai and the Legation Guard in Beijing. Of the aircraft squadrons, VF-6M departed first, followed by VO-10M, which by mid-November was the last marine aviation unit still in China. On November 22 what remained of the Third Brigade was loaded aboard the *Chaumont* and sailed to Shanghai and then to San Diego.[113]

The Third Brigade disbanded in January 1929. But the China expedition had left General Butler with a very positive impression of what aviation could provide to the Marine Corps, especially in terms of close air support to marines on the ground. He therefore determined that marine aviation squadrons "should be part of the brigade, 'body and soul,' and not a separate arm directed by and under the control of some officer in Washington."[114] Later he claimed, "The air force was of more value to me than a regiment."[115] His conclusions regarding the utility of air-ground cooperation were reinforced by the experience of the Second Brigade, which provided outstanding air support to marine operations in Nicaragua from 1926 to –1933, the subject of chapter 4. Serendipitously, the aviation industry in the United States began producing state-of-the art aircraft and engines, and Marine Corps aviation would be among the beneficiaries.

Modernization of Marine Corps Aviation

Although, on paper, Marine Corps aviation appeared to be growing during the so-called Roaring Twenties, this was not the case. In 1920 the US economy experienced a deep deflationary recession, viewed by some as a necessary market correction and by others as a bona fide depression. With funding cut by Congress and the navy, the marine squadrons had to stretch manpower and equipment to meet mission requirements. Thus, only one or two divisions in each squadron were on active status, and the number of available aircraft was limited.[116] Fortunately, for the remainder of the decade, the authorized end-strength of Marine Corps aviation remained fairly constant.[117] Although the commissioned strength of the Marine Corps was fixed at 1,093 in toto, the marines were able to offset the pilot shortage with enlisted fliers, as discussed in chapter 2. This was possible because the Naval Appropriations Act of 1920 limited *officer* end-strength, not *pilots.* Flight training for qualified enlisted men was stepped up, and the informal training of enlisted personnel in the squadrons was officially sanctioned. The idea was that, in wartime, these men could quickly be commissioned and assume command billets as required.

Whereas personnel matters would continue to plague the Marine Corps for years, the good news was that newer and better airplanes were being acquired, especially in the second half of the 1920s. As discussed in chapter 2, First Division, Squadron E, arrived in Haiti in 1919 with worn-out Jennies and HS2-L flying boats of little utility beyond observation and coastal patrolling. That same year, the squadron received DeHavilland DH-4Bs from those turned over to the Marine Corps from the US Army during World War I. But in early 1921 the marines began to receive the new Vought VE-7 Bluebird and the Naval Aircraft Factory version, the VE-7SF. In addition to the Vought airplanes, the marines received the Curtiss F5-L, which they used as a bomber. The airplane was manufactured by Curtiss, which built 60; the Naval Aircraft Factory, which produced 137; and Canadian Aeroplanes Limited, which built 30. The F5-L was a major advance for Curtiss, incorporating ailerons with parallel leading and trailing edges instead of the typical tapered trailing edges of earlier Curtiss flying boats. However, the F5-L was a very heavy airplane and difficult to get out of the water on takeoff. Once in the air, it maneuvered sluggishly. In 1921, when the navy adopted a new designation system, the F5-L became the PN-5, but it was still routinely referred to as the

F5-L until its retirement in 1928. Despite its weight and some other annoying issues, the F5-L was the most modern patrol plane in the Marine Corps' inventory.

By 1925, Marine Corps aviation was a hodgepodge of very old and some new aircraft, ranging from Jennies and DH-4s in Haiti to the VE-7, VE-9, and MT-1 at Quantico.[118] But the marines would soon receive state-of-the-art aircraft as a result of congressional action. In 1923 the secretary of war appointed a board headed by Major General William Lassiter to evaluate the US Army's posture with respect to aviation. The Lassiter Board found the Air Service to be in "critical condition" and recommended legislation to remedy the situation. A House committee headed by Florian Lampert (R-WI) took up where the Lassiter Board left off, noting that the United States could "have no adequate national defense without an adequate air force." The Lampert Committee recommended a five-year acquisition plan for the War and Navy Departments, with each receiving $10 million per year to purchase new aircraft. At roughly the same time, President Calvin Coolidge appointed Dwight Morrow, a New York banker and chief civilian aide to General John Pershing during the war (as well as Charles Lindbergh's father-in-law), to study the role of aviation in national defense. The Morrow Board supported the expansion of army and navy aviation and corroborated the Lampert Committee's findings.[119]

As a result of congressional action in the second half of the 1920s, the US Navy—and, by extension, the US Marine Corps—received new aircraft of superior, modern design. These aircraft included a new generation of fighters, such as the Boeing FB series and the Curtiss F6 series. As discussed earlier, Boeing had converted the Thomas-Morse MB-3 for US Army use and also studied the German Fokker D.VII, regarded as the best fighter of World War I.[120] The first Boeing aircraft, the Model 15, incorporated many of the Fokker's features, and its success launched Boeing's production of the FB series. Boeing FB-1s went to the Marine Corps; nine served with the Third Brigade in China, and the others were assigned to Stateside squadrons.[121] An improved and more powerful FB-5 (Model 67) equipped Navy Squadrons VF-1B and VF-6B aboard the aircraft carrier USS *Langley* and later the fast carrier USS *Lexington.*[122] Several of these aircraft were then passed on to the marines, including VF-6M at San Diego. As already discussed, the early Boeing fighters were landplanes, but two FB-2s (Boeing Model 53) were modified for carrier operations, including a beefed-up fuselage and cross-axle undercarriage. The later FB-3s had 510 hp Packard 1A-1500 twelve-cylinder liquid-cooled in-line engines, as opposed to the original Curtiss D-12 (V-1150) in-line power plant.[123] What transformed the FB series, however, was the advent of the air-cooled radial engine, initially produced by the Curtiss-Wright Aeronautical Corporation but later by Pratt & Whitney.

In-line engines facilitate a more streamlined fuselage shape and result in less drag, theoretically offering greater speed. Moreover, because of the liquid cooling, in-line engines produce more power from less displacement, which also (again, theoretically) produces more speed. In contrast, radial engines are lighter because they dispense with the engine block and the liquid cooling system. Because these engines are lighter, designers were able to achieve greater power output simply by producing larger engines. The US Navy was quick to realize that the radial engine excelled in terms of takeoff and landing speed, which is crucial to carrier operations. As a result, the navy came to prefer radial engines and used them almost exclusively. By the same token, the US Army employed radial engines on its multiengine aircraft such as bombers (the B-17 Flying Fortress) because they allowed large aircraft to lift heavy loads quickly and permitted lower landing speeds without stalling. Over time, radial engines developed a well-deserved reputation for ruggedness and reliability.

Although the Liberty engine is rightly famous for its role in World War I, the first truly great American-designed and -built engine was the Curtiss D-12 in-line engine, introduced in 1922. In-line engines for airplanes are very similar to most automobile engines. There is a cast block of metal with cylinders that move up and down, driven by the detonation of some kind of flammable fuel. There is a drive shaft that delivers power to the wheels or, in the case of an airplane, to the propeller. Curtiss racers equipped with the D-12 were the first to break the 200 mph mark, and Curtiss engines traded speed records with airplanes powered by Hispano-Suiza engines. The British Royal Air Force was quite impressed by the D-12 and enjoined the Rolls-Royce and Napier companies to produce a domestic equivalent. The result was the outstanding Rolls-Royce Kestrel engine. The success of the Kestrel placed the British firmly in the in-line camp for bombers as well as fighters. Given the success of the Kestrel, Rolls-Royce went on to produce the superb Merlin engine (the Kestrel could produce 470 hp, whereas the Merlin leaped to 1,050 hp). During World War II, Merlin engines powered the Supermarine Spitfire, Hawker Hurricane, and DeHavilland Mosquito fighters, as well as the Avro Lancaster four-engine bomber. The Merlin also powered the American Curtiss P-40F Kittyhawk Mk II and the North American P-51 Mustang fighter.[124]

In addition to paving the way for the Rolls-Royce Kestrel and Merlin engines, the Curtiss D-12 encouraged fellow American manufacturers to produce their own in-line engines. The Allison Engine Company's first contribution was a standard V-configuration and resembled the German Jumo Motoren 210 and 213 engines produced in the mid-1930s. The large-displacement Jumo 211 powered the JU-87 Stuka dive-bomber and most of the German twin-engined bombers. The Jumo 213A powered the superb Focke-Wulf 190D-9 Dora fighter in late World War II. Although not particularly powerful, the liquid-cooled Allison V-1710 twelve-cylinder engine was arguably the toughest in-line engine manufactured before and during World War II, powering the Bell P-39 Airacobra, early versions of the Curtiss P-40 Warhawk, and, with a turbo-supercharger, the highly successful Lockheed P-38 Lightning.[125]

Although American designers first became known for their in-line engines such as the D-12 and V-1710, they made the radial engine the premier power plant of the era for high-performance piston-driven aircraft. And although the radial engine was at first hampered by its complexity (multiple cylinders connected to a single shaft and extremely narrow tolerances for cooling), mastering the challenge played to American strengths, including a large university system and the American propensity for invention and "tinkering." Moreover, the demand for radial engines from commercial carriers provided incentive for development of the radial design. The results changed aviation almost overnight. For the US Navy, lower landing speeds promised greater safety. And the ability to get off a carrier deck quickly with a heavy bomb load made radial-engined aircraft ideal for dive-bombers, torpedo bombers, and fighters, as the Japanese would also conclude. Indeed, the Japanese licensed a Gnome radial engine from France that became the Nakajima Sakae, the power plant of the famous Mitsubishi Navy Type 0 Carrier Fighter, the A6M Reisen or Zero. During World War II, virtually all the fighters and bombers of the Imperial Japanese Navy and Army were powered by radial engines. Unlike an in-line engine, a radial engine has no engine block; instead, cylinders are arranged around the drive shaft in a circle (ergo, radial). Like the in-line, however, the radial engine is an internal combustion engine that generates considerable heat. But rather than using a liquid cooling system, the radial engine is air cooled. The cylinders are in direct contact with the airflow, and considerable effort is made to catch, direct, and retain the cooling effects of inflowing air.

Modern radial engines got their start when a small company owned by Charles Lawrence was purchased by the Wright Aeronautical Company, which then persuaded British aeronautical pioneer Samuel Heron to team up with Lawrence. Together they designed the Wright J-5 Whirlwind, a nine-cylinder engine rated at 200 hp. The J-5 was an immediate success and was used on numerous US Navy aircraft. As the engine was improved, the US Army purchased the J-5. Perhaps more important, civil aviation companies acquired the J-5 in large numbers. Indeed, the earliest Fokker and Ford tri-motor airplanes used the J-5, and Charles Lindbergh's solo flight across the Atlantic was accomplished in the J-5C-equipped *Spirit of St. Louis*. Later, Clarence Chamberlin and Bert Acosta flew record-breaking long-duration flights in aircraft powered by the J-5, including the famous fifty-plus-hour flight over New York City in a single-engine Wright-Bellanca WB-2, accomplished in 1927. The first successful flight from the US mainland to Hawaii was made by Albert Hegenberger and Lester Maitland in a Fokker F.VII powered by three Wright J-5 engines. And the first flight across the Pacific was made by Sir Charles Kingsford Smith in another Fokker trimotor powered by Wright engines, flyng from Oakland, California, to Brisbane, Australia, in 1928. Finally, it was a Wright-engined US Army Fokker C-2 (the military designation for the F.VII), known as the Question Mark, that established an endurance record of 150 hours, 40 minutes, and 14 seconds over Southern California in January 1929.[126] Not surprisingly, Charles Lawrence won the Collier Trophy in 1927 for his work on air-cooled radial aircraft engines.

With the success of the Whirlwind, other manufacturers leaped into the business of manufacturing radial engines. Although the Wright J-5 was the heavyweight of its day, Wright Aeronautical Company was a small enterprise that manufactured virtually handmade engines for a very small aviation community. Quietly encouraged by the navy, Wright president Frederick Rentschler[127] left the company with half the design team and founded Pratt & Whitney Aircraft Company, arguably the greatest builder of radial and turboprop engines in history.[128] Rentschler immediately began work on the 22-L Wasp, a remarkably efficient and reliable 450 hp radial engine. It was a splendid success and provoked Wright to produce its own equally good Cyclone engine. With these two engines as baseline, radial engine development exploded in the 1930s. And perhaps because of Americans' love for baseball statistics at the time, engine manufacturers in the 1920s and 1930s used displacement figures in the names of their products. For example, the Grumman F4F Wildcat fighter, made famous early in World War II, was powered by a Pratt & Whitney Double Wasp R-1830 (R for radial), with a 1,830–cubic centimeter displacement.

A major advance in radial engines was to double the number of cylinders by aligning them in two banks. Better cooling techniques permitted this arrangement, and it was even possible to enlarge the cylinder size. The first engine to use this design came in 1932, when the marines were leaving Nicaragua and two years before they departed Haiti. That engine was the Pratt & Whitney Double Wasp R-1830 with 825 hp, later increased to 1,200 hp. In multiengine service, the R-1830 was mounted on the Douglas Command semi-monocoque DC-3 (and its military variant the C-47),[129] the Consolidated Aircraft Company's four-engine B-24 Liberator bomber, and the Consolidated PBY Catalina twin-engine flying boat. The Double Wasp also powered the P-47 Thunderbolt, the US Army's sole World War II fighter powered by a radial engine. In addition, the Double Wasp powered the marines' Vought F-4U Corsair fighter during World War II (and later during the Korean War), as well as the Douglas SBD (Scout Bomber Douglas) Dauntless dive-bomber (an army version, the A-24 Banshee, was not successful). Curtiss-Wright subsequently beefed up its Cyclone engine; the R-1820, introduced in 1933 at 600 hp, was putting out 1,200 hp by the time it was mounted on the upgraded B-17G. The Curtiss-Wright R-1820 was the last big-cylinder single-row radial to be manufactured.

Wright's first double-row radial engine was the R-2600, pumping out 1,700 hp and mounted on the North American B-25 Mitchell medium bomber, the navy's Curtiss SB2C Helldiver dive-bomber, and the Grumman Avenger torpedo bomber, all of which served in World War II. The Pratt & Whitney R-2800 followed, leading to the twin-bank R-3350 rated at 2,800 hp; the infamous R-3350 powered the B-29 Superfortress (infamous because the engine was highly complex and prone to catch fire). The Curtiss-Wright R-3350 was the end of the line for wartime radials. Like the Pratt & Whitney engine, it was overly complicated and bedeviled by reliability issues, and fires routinely broke out on takeoff. That said, the postwar twenty-eight-cylinder quadruple-bank R-4360 Wasp Major was a fine engine, producing 3,000 hp and making its way onto the early Cold War B-36 bomber the Peacemaker, manufactured by Convair.[130]

Into the Modern Age

By the end of the 1920s, Boeing was producing one of the most famous aircraft in aviation history: the F4B single-seat fighter. The series began as a private venture intended to replace the F2B / F3B navy fighters and the PW-9 (the same airplane) used by the army. Two nearly identical prototypes were built (Models 83 and 89), with the first flights taking place in June and August 1928, during which time the navy designated both models the XF4B-1. Following additional tests, the navy ordered twenty-seven production models. The F4B-1 (Model 99) officially debuted in May 1929, powered by the R-1340-8 Wasp engine. Over time, the airplane underwent several changes in configuration (the F4B-2 being the first to employ a distinctive ring cowling around the engine), ending with the F4B-4 powered by a 550 hp R-1340-16 Wasp engine. At least one F3B served with the marines as a command plane (flown by a senior officer not attached to a squadron). A number of F4B-3s and F4B-4s also flew with the marines, the latter equipping two marine squadrons. The F4B-4 remained in service with the navy until 1937 and with the marines until 1938. Almost two dozen former army planes (P-12Es) were obtained by the navy in 1940 as F4B-4As, used as radio-controlled target drones.[131]

But in the beginning, the FB-1 was assigned to the marines to flesh out their newly formed fighter squadrons, and since the first of the series was not rigged for carrier operations, that made sense. Six FB-1s went to VF-1 at Quantico. On July 1, 1925, VF-2 was added at Quantico, and two months later, VF-3 was formed at San Diego, both equipped with the FB-1. On July 1, 1927, the three fighting squadrons were redesignated VF-8M, VF-9M, and VF-10M, eliminating any possibility of confusing them with navy squadrons. Nine of the FB-1s went with VF-3 (VF-10M) to China, while the tenth remained at San Diego with VO-1M. When the FB-1s returned to the States, they were assigned to VF-6M, but by the mid-1930s, they were all condemned and destroyed.[132]

While the Army Air Service was purchasing the navy version of a Boeing biplane fighter, Curtiss succeeded in selling its landplane, the single-seat F6C Hawk, to the US Navy. The first of the famous Hawk fighters was the P-1, which the navy modified as a floatplane: the F6C-1. Three of these aircraft were delivered to the Marine Corps in 1927 and were flown by VF-9M at Quantico. The F6C-1 had a 400 hp Curtiss D-12 in-line engine. Two aircraft were delivered as F6C-2s, with tail hooks and strengthened landing gear for operation from aircraft carriers. These same features were incorporated into the F6C-3. A number of these aircraft were employed by VF-8M at Quantico. When the Pratt & Whitney R-1340 Wasp radial engine was married to the same airframe, it became the F6C-4. Several of these aircraft were passed along to the marines, including VF-10M at San Diego.[133]

It was the F6C that inaugurated dive-bombing for the US Navy in 1926, when Fighter Squadron Two launched a mock attack on the Pacific Fleet using the new maneuver. "Capable of making almost vertical dives, planes of the Curtiss F6C series gave [navy] and Marine aviators for the first time a craft which could execute effectively their new tactic of dive bombing."[134] Moreover, a demonstration of the Hawk's capability at the Cleveland air races "profoundly impressed Ernst Udet, who later fostered the idea of the 'Stuka' and was appointed Inspector of Fighters and Dive Bombers to the *Luftwaffe* in 1936."[135] The F6C-1 was the first fighter to be ordered in quantity by the navy. The F6C-2 had a strengthened rear fuselage and a modified undercarriage, allowing it to "hook" the transverse deck lines of the USS *Langley.* The first production navy fighter to be fitted with the Pratt & Whitney Wasp engine was the F6C-4, thirty-one of which were manufactured and eight of which were assigned to VF-10M. Navy and marine pilots alike gave high marks to the Hawk, whether powered by the in-line or radial engine. They were easy to fly and very maneuverable.

Another radial-engined machine operated by the Marine Corps was the F7C Sea Hawk, designed by Rex Biesel of the Curtiss Company. The F7C's swept-back upper wings were its primary difference from the F6C-4. The navy acquired eighteen production versions, and all were eventually passed to the marines, serving with VF-5M (later VF-9M) at Quantico. The F8C series Hell Diver, an improvement of the F7C and another Rex Biesel design, was flown by the marines in Nicaragua. The Hell Diver was a product of the Marine Corps' need for a multirole aircraft capable of performing as a fighter, a dive-bomber, and an observation platform. The Curtiss Company altered its O-2 / A-3 Falcon design, replacing the water-cooled V-12 with a Pratt & Whitney R-1340-4 Wasp nine-cylinder engine. Two prototypes (XF8C-1) were delivered to the marines in early 1928, followed by four production models.[136] A year later, the marines tested a nearly identical XF8C-3 and then took delivery of twenty-one production versions. As Marine Corps aircraft, the C-1 was designated the OC-1, and the C-3 was designated the OC-2, both of which served on the East and West Coasts of the United States as well as in China. These aircraft replaced the venerable but aging DH-4B and 02B-1 in several marine squadrons and saw combat with VO-7M in Nicaragua. An improved version, the F8-4C, arrived at the end of the decade, followed by the F8-5C, equipped with new superchargers. The marines designated the F8-5C the 02C-1, and it remained active with VO-6M and VO-7M as late as 1937. A handful continued in service after 1937 as "hacks," that is, for utility duties, but they were withdrawn from front-line service before the outbreak of World War II.[137]

Yet another radial-engined aircraft obtained by the marines in the 1920s, one that proved to be an outstanding combat aircraft in Nicaragua, was the Vought 02U Corsair, which, like the OC-1 and OC-2,[138] replaced the DH-4B. Powered by a 400 hp Pratt & Whitney R-1340 Wasp engine, the Corsair incorporated a steel-tube fuselage and wooden wings covered in fabric. A number of Corsairs were converted to seaplanes. The Corsair was so successful that more than 140 were still serving in the US Navy and Marine Corps at the beginning of World War II.[139] Moreover, variants of the Corsair were exported to Argentina, Peru, Brazil, Germany, and China. Mexico purchased twelve, which were used to put down a military coup. Mexico then built thirty-one more under license, designated the Corsairios Azcárate (02U-4A), and purchased ten more in 1937 (some of which may have made their way to Spain). The Peruvians and Chinese also used Corsairs in combat. However, the most famous "combat" operation was probably the use of Corsairs to shoot King Kong off the Empire State Building. The marines would use the Corsair with great effect in Nicaragua (discussed in chapter 4). In 1929 there were two 02U-1s with the East Coast Expeditionary Force at Quantico, eight 02U-1s in Haiti with VO-9M, and six in Nicaragua with VO-7M. By the following year, there were three Corsairs at Quantico, four in Nicaragua (augmented by three OC-1s and three OC-2s), and seven in Haiti.

In addition to using the Corsair as a landplane, the marines used it for carrier operations from November 1931 to November 1934. The carriers USS *Saratoga* and USS *Lexington* had been commissioned in 1927, and the first takeoff from the "Lady Lex" was by navy Lieutenant A. M. Pride in a Vought UO-1 on January 28, 1928. Six days later, Commander Marc Mitscher took off in a similar airplane from the *Saratoga*. From the beginning, marines regarded themselves as naval aviators, capable of flying not only land-based planes, seaplanes, and amphibians but also carrier-based aircraft. Indeed, as noted earlier, the Marine Corps had pressed for its own aircraft carrier. This did not occur, but in 1931 two Marine Corps squadrons were organized at San Diego for service with the navy's Aircraft Battle Force aboard carriers. Scouting Squadron Fourteen (VS-14M) was established on October 15, commanded by Captain William Wallace, and Scouting Squadron Fifteen (VS-15M), commanded by Lieutenant William Brice, was established on November 2.[140] VS-14M reported to the *Lexington* with a handful of 02U-2s; these were later replaced by improved SU-1s and SU-3s with 600 hp R-1690-C engines, upping their speed some 24 mph over the 02U's 147 mph. Pilots were rotated in and out of the scouting squadrons until 60 percent of Marine Corps pilots had experienced some carrier duty.[141] On July 2, 1934, the two squadrons were detached from the *Saratoga* and *Lexington* and assigned to the *Langley*. On November 15 they were disbanded, and their personnel and aircraft were assigned to VO-8M.[142]

In the Public Eye: Dive-Bombing and Air Races

As the marines acquired better aircraft with superior engine performance, the publicity-conscious Marine Corps found it useful to participate in a variety of spectacles similar to Smedley Butler's maneuvers in Virginia and Pennsylvania. Marine Corps aviators conducted scheduled exercises and demonstrations for public consumption, and dive-bombing was a big part of that showmanship. Ross Rowell, who would later command the aircraft squadrons in Nicaragua, first came into contact with dive-bombing at Kelly Field in San Antonio, Texas, where he was sent in 1923 for advanced flight training. At the time, the school was using DH-4Bs, which Rowell believed could not survive the wing strain. He was pleasantly surprised to learn that this was not true.

The instructors at the school were all veterans under the command of Major Lewis Brereton, US Army Air Service, who would later go on to command three numbered air forces (Third, Ninth, and Tenth) and the First Allied Airborne Army (paratroops and glider troops) in Europe during World War II. There were no training accidents, and the accuracy of the technique impressed Rowell, who visualized the tactic in use against ships and in counterguerrilla warfare. Upon completion of his training at Kelly Field, Rowell was posted briefly to the army's First Pursuit Group at Selfridge Field, Harrison Township, Michigan, commanded by Major Carl Spaatz. Spaatz would go on to command American strategic air forces during World War II and would become the first chief of staff of the newly independent US Air Force in 1947. Upon leaving the First Pursuit Group, Rowell took command of VO-1M following its withdrawal from the Dominican Republic. The squadron was equipped with the DH-4B, and Rowell took it upon himself to train his pilots in dive-bombing, which would later prove useful in Nicaragua. At first, the aircraft employed locally manufactured bomb racks, but Rowell later acquired US Army A-3 bomb racks. In 1925 Rowell's squadron took part in the opening of several West Coast airports and capitalized on the opportunity to demonstrate the dive-bombing technique, using smoke bombs.[143]

Such performances became routine for marine aviators in the late 1920s and early 1930s, and the pilots enjoyed great freedom to demonstrate their equipment and flying skills. As discussed earlier, marine aviators accomplished significant aerial feats, including record-breaking long-distance flights. Stunting and air races became part of the Marine Corps repertoire, from small-town races to major national competitions such as the Pulitzer Trophy Race. The air races provided the army and navy (and, by extension, the Marine Corps) with the opportunity to assess which combination of airframe design and engine provided the best performance. The races also kept the public informed about developments in aviation technology. One particularly famous airplane was the Curtiss R3C, a single-seat airplane configured as both a landplane and a seaplane. Flying the R3C-1, the landplane version, Cyrus Bettis won the Pulitzer Trophy Race in October 1925 with a speed slightly under 249 mph. The RC3-2 was a twin-float seaplane specifically constructed for the Schneider Cup Race. Army Air Service pilot James "Jimmy" Doolittle won the Schneider Cup in 1925, clocking in at over 232 mph. The next day he established a new world's record at 245.7 mph. In November 1926 Marine Corps aviator Christian Schilt flew a navy R3C-2 floatplane in the Schneider Cup Race and came in second at 231.364 mph.[144] Such accomplishments were very gratifying to the marines, even though the spectators did not know the pilots were marines. But following the death of Arthur Page Jr. in a crash in 1930, Marine Corps participation in air racing came to an end.[145]

Marine Corps Aviators and the US Army Air Corps Tactical School

Marine Corps air operations during the 1920s and early 1930s reflected the enhanced capability and sense of purpose of the aircraft squadrons. While the air races and demonstration flights captured the public's attention, the combat experience gained in Haiti, the Dominican Republic, China, and Nicaragua, as well as the emphasis on the newly created Fleet Marine Force and amphibious operations, prompted the Marine Corps to consider the role of its aviation arm more seriously and in greater depth. As a result, many veterans of the small wars period attended the US Army's Field Officers Course at Langley Field, Virginia, and later the Air Corps Tactical School at Maxwell Field near Montgomery, Alabama. At both schools they were able to compare their experiences and visions for the future of Marine Corps aviation with what was emerging theoretically and doctrinally in the army's air arm.

The US Army's Air Service (later Air Corps) Tactical School was the highest educational establishment within the army's air arm. Its basic mission was to train and educate air officers in the strategy, tactics, and techniques of air warfare. When the United States entered the First World War in 1917, there had been no time to develop a comprehensive educational system for Air Service officers. But after the war, and in keeping with the precedent of professional military education and advanced training for the other branches of the army, the Air Service formulated a plan for its own system. On February 25, 1920, the War Department authorized the establishment of eleven special service schools for the Air Service, including the Air Service School at Langley Field near Norfolk, more commonly known as the Field Officers Course and later the Air Service Tactical School. In 1926, with passage of the Air Corps Act by Congress, the school at Langley was redesignated the Air Corps Tactical School, which moved to Maxwell Field in the summer of 1931.

Instruction at the Tactical School was both theoretical and practical, and many of the instructors and graduates became general officers in World War II. These men included Oscar Westover, Lewis Brereton, George Kenney, Kenneth Walker, Claire Chennault, Haywood Hansell, Harold George, and Laurence Kuter, all of whom were both graduates of and instructors at the school. Other graduates included Ira Eaker, Elwood Quesada, Hoyt Vandenberg, George Stratemeyer, Nathan Twining, John Cannon, and Carl Spaatz. These airmen believed they were fighting an uphill battle against the hidebound interests of the ground-oriented army, and in 1921 the chief of the Air Service invited representatives from the other arms (infantry, artillery, cavalry, and so on) to the school, hoping to influence their thinking about air power and to disseminate Air Service doctrine throughout the army. The initial classes were small, and absent a coherent vision of the future, the instructors developed a close association with the infantry, the "Queen of Battle."

Indeed, "during this early period, school instructors expressed few advanced ideas on the employment of the air force. Air operations were closely related to surface strategy, with the air arm considered a vital element in winning the ground objective."[146] In that regard, Marine Corps aviator General Vernon Megee wrote that, during these early years, the army and the school were "developing a sound doctrine for close support of ground units, and we were able to absorb a considerable portion of the tactics and techniques used by their so-called 'Attack Aviation.'"[147] But after the school moved to Maxwell Field, the focus evolved to an emphasis on long-range "strategic" bombardment, especially "high altitude daylight precision bombing."[148]

From the start, the Tactical School included lessons on naval aviation taught by the assigned faculty. However, as the curriculum evolved, lectures on naval matters were delivered by guest speakers from the navy. For example, in February 1929 Commander John Towers delivered a lecture defining how the navy organized its aviation component. He then offered a scenario explaining how naval aviation would support the Battle Fleet in a major engagement with an enemy fleet. In short, naval aviation was deemed a fleet support function, not an autonomous capability and certainly not an independent war-winning capability. Navy aircraft would scout ahead to locate the enemy fleet and then participate in the engagement by spotting for the battleships (the "gun line"), as well as attacking the enemy fleet with bombs and torpedoes while the fighters defended the American fleet and gained command of the air over the battle space.[149] The following year, Captain Lewis Coxe, USN, opened his lecture with a quote from Thucydides and then went on to describe the organization of the navy and its fighting power, emphasizing the contribution of naval aviation. According to Coxe: "The importance that aircraft have assumed in naval operations in the brief period since the World War is shown by the fact that, today, more than one dollar in every seven spent on our Navy and approximately ten percent of the total commissioned and enlisted personnel are devoted to aeronautics."[150] Towers and Coxe (and presumably the other navy officers) steered clear of any discussion of the Marine Corps or the conflict between Brigadier General Billy Mitchell and the navy, even though Mitchell's influence at the school was considerable, and many of his works were unofficially part of the curriculum.[151]

The first marines to attend the Tactical School at Langley Field in 1925 were Louis Bourne, Charles Lutz, and Ford Rogers. Thomas Turner, Ralph

Mitchell, and another marine aviator attended the following year. Pat Mulcahy graduated in 1928, along with Cocky Evans and a third marine. Upon his return from Nicaragua in 1929, Rusty Rowell also attended the school. More marines would follow, including Christian Schilt, Lawson Sanderson, William Brice, Cuckoo Boyden, and Vernon Megee, the last graduating in 1936 when the school was devoted almost solely to long-range bombardment of "vital centers." The last marine to graduate before the Tactical School was closed was Thomas Walker in 1940. Over the years, these marines received instruction from such air-power icons as Westover, Kenney, Walker, Chennault, and George. They also studied alongside Hansell, Kuter, Stratemeyer, Vandenberg, and Quesada, as well as Frank Andrews, George Brett, Frank Tyndall, Ennis Whitehead, and Muir Fairchild. Anyone familiar with the US Army Air Force during World War II and the decade afterward will immediately recognize these names.

Although Marine Corps participation in air races and aboard the carriers *Lexington* and *Saratoga* has received some attention in the literature, marines' attendance at the Air Corps Tactical School and their contribution to the curriculum and the education of their fellow fliers from the army (the navy rarely sent students to the school) have been largely ignored. Yet Francis Mulcahy graduated first in his class in 1928, and Ross Rowell wrote what amounted to a textbook for "minor warfare" (an essay that he later published).[152] But as noted, Army Air Corps thinking evolved, and small wars and air support to ground forces took a backseat to long-range strategic attack. Thus, statements in the syllabus that declared an interdependent relationship between air and ground forces became secondary to the possibility of the independent employment of "strategic" air power.[153] Marines in attendance found such thinking beyond the capability and mission of Marine Corps aviation, leading Megee to declare: "Undeterred by any necessity for counter-air operations, and untempted by any 'wild blue yonder' schemes of semi-independent strategical forays, the Marines buckled down to their primary mission of supporting Marine ground forces."[154] Indeed, the manual entitled *Employment of Marine Corps Aviation,* written in 1935 and used in the Marine Corps schools, made it clear that aviation existed "for the purpose of furnishing ground units with aërial reconnaissance facilities, protection against hostile air attacks, and a means for delivering effective attacks against hostile forces."[155] This was, of course, perfectly in keeping with A. A. Cunningham's claim "that the only excuse for aviation in any service is its usefulness in assisting the troops on the ground to successfully carry out their operations."[156] This core belief regarding aviation would not be altered by Marine Corps aviators' attendance at the Air Corps Tactical School. Their belief in the proper role of aviation in the Corps was cemented by their experience in Nicaragua, the subject of the next chapter.

In 1922 Quantico received new Martin MB-1 heavy bombers, powered by two 400-horsepower Liberty 12-A engines. Six MB-1s were operated by the marines, and in April 1923 four were flown from San Diego to Quantico in eleven days, completing what was then the longest aerial delivery of aircraft in Marine Corps history.

Captain Walter McCaughtry, a former enlisted man, led the first detachment of Marine Corps aircraft (six Jennies of the First Division, Squadron D) to Consuelo, near San Pedro de Macorís in the Dominican Republic (Santo Domingo) in February 1919.

Major Russell Presley (left) was the first marine aviator to take a DH-4B aloft in Santo Domingo, flying the airplane to Santiago and back. As it did in Haiti, the DH transformed the aviation mission in Santo Domingo.

A DH-4B in the foreground with the distinctive "ace of spades" emblem of the First Air Squadron. Captain Arthur Page Jr. commanded the DH-equipped squadron, and the two flights making up the squadron were commanded by Captains Russell Presley and "Ditty Box" Brewster.

In January 1921 A. A. Cunningham arrived in Santo Domingo to take command of the First Air Squadron, replacing Captain Arthur Page Jr., who was sent to command the squadron in Haiti. Major Cunningham is seen here at the controls of a DH-4B.

Crashes and crack-ups were common in Santo Domingo. This DH-4B nosed over on takeoff or landing, breaking the left wheel of the landing gear. In all, Hayne "Cuckoo" Boyden experienced five forced landings while in Santo Domingo.

"Tex" Rogers and First Sergeant Benjamin Belcher preparing to take off from Santo Domingo in a DH-4B-1, on their way to the St. Louis Air Meet and then on to San Francisco for an American Legion convention. They flew some 11,000 miles and logged 127 hours of actual flying time.

The pilots who ferried US senators from Santo Domingo to Haiti to investigate the alleged abuse of Haitians. From left to right are Lieutenants Hayne Boyden and Harmon Norton, Captain Russell Presley, Major A. A. Cunningham, Lieutenants Duncan Lewis and Christian Schilt, and Sergeant Charles Hanst.

An HS-2L belonging to VS-1M being towed by a tractor on Guam. VS-1M (later VP-3M) began as an unnumbered detachment at Parris Island. It was sent to Guam as Flight L with two N-9 floatplanes, two HS-2L flying boats, and four F-5L flying boats.

An OL-6 from VS-1M, commanded by Captain Walter McCaughtry, being unloaded in northern China. Although the scouting squadron comprised seaplanes of various types over the years, in 1926 two VE-7H Bluebirds, a two-seat trainer, joined the unit. When VS-1M deployed to China, the Bluebirds remained in Guam.

The flight line, crew quarters, and maintenance facilities of the Aircraft Squadrons, Third Brigade, in China. A DH-4B is being pushed backward past an FB-1 to a service area. Marine Corps aircraft were fired on and holed seven times during operations over northern China.

Major Edwin Brainard (the head of aviation) standing beside his personal F6C-4 Hawk. The F6C series employed the 400-horsepower Curtiss D-12 in-line engine until the F6C-4 was designed, which married the Pratt & Whitney R-1340 Wasp radial engine to the airframe. Several of these planes were passed on to the Marine Corps, including VF-10M at San Diego.

A superb photograph of a Marine Corps F4B-3 fighter–dive-bomber (note the bomb rack beneath the fuselage). The F4B series is one of the most famous aircraft in aviation history, and it marked a major leap in capability. The F4B-4 remained in service with the Marine Corps until 1938.

A Loening OL-9 amphibian. First flown in 1923, the OL was designed to be a seaplane with the performance of a landplane. Early versions were fitted with the 400-horsepower Liberty V-1650-1 engine in an inverted position, but subsequent versions employed the Wasp radial engine, as seen here.

The Sikorsky RS-1, a civilian airliner converted for use by the marines. In 1931 Thomas Turner flew to Haiti as a passenger in an RS-1. When the airplane became stuck on the beach, Turner pushed his head out the pilot's window to try to determine the problem and was struck by a propeller. He died two days later.

Nicaragua. Most of the major actions during the marines' Second Nicaraguan Campaign took place in the far north, near the towns of Ocotal and Quilali. There was a major airfield at Puerto Cabezas on the east coast, and the primary flying field was at the capital, Managua, near the west coast.

4

Marine Corps Aviation Comes of Age

Nicaragua, 1926–1933

> I say, Frank . . . it's always been our contention that an aeroplane capable of invariable command by its operator would be of immense value in warfare.
>
> Captain Wilbur Lawton, *The Boy Aviators in Nicaragua; or, In League with the Insurgents,* 1910

As was the case with the interventions in Haiti and the Dominican Republic, the marines' interventions in Nicaragua in the early twentieth century have been described as both a strategically necessary example of well-intentioned and restrained counterinsurgency and capitalist imperialism at its worst. Most Marine Corps veterans' recollections are of a job well done, despite incredible hardships.[1] Others (at the time and later) were highly critical, with the late Neil Macaulay of the University of Florida describing the actions of marine aviators as "aerial terrorism."[2] Thus, in any review of the literature on intervention in Nicaragua, it seems that where one stands on the matter depends on where one sits.[3] Regardless, there is no question that, at the time, Nicaragua was deemed important to US commercial and strategic interests. Bluejackets and marines were repeatedly landed in Nicaragua for the purpose of protecting these interests. But ordinary Nicaraguans became incensed at these intrusions, and the intervention in 1926 in particular provoked great animosity in Nicaragua, elsewhere in Latin America, in the United States, and around the globe. Nevertheless, the marines did the job they were sent to do, and as was the case on Hispaniola and in China, this included Marine Corps aviation.

Background to Intervention

Nicaragua lies between the Caribbean Sea and the Pacific Ocean in Central America. It is the region's largest country and is slightly larger than the state of New York. Spanish explorer Alonzo Niño Gil González Dávila coined the name "Nicaragua," combining the word *nicarao* (the indigenous name for the capital city) and the Spanish word for water, *agua,* referring to the two large lakes in the western part of the country, Lake Nicaragua and Lake Managua. It is often noted that Nicaragua is two countries divided by topography, climate, culture, and wealth. Eastern Nicaragua (commonly referred to as Zelaya, and currently comprising the self-governing North Caribbean Coast Autonomous Region and South Caribbean Coast Autonomous Region) is a wilderness of heavy rainfall, dense mahogany forests, great humidity, extreme poverty, and very poor communication with the rest of the country, other than numerous rivers running from the interior to the Caribbean. On the northeast coast is the small port town of Puerto Cabezas. Farther south along the east coast is another port town, Bluefields, at one time a virtual British colony. And in the far south is San Juan del Norte (formerly Greytown). Western Nicaragua is a well-drained, rolling plateau of fertile soil with a more temperate climate and wet and dry seasons. Not surprisingly, most of the people and wealth of Nicaragua reside in the west. At the time of the marines' Second Nicaraguan Campaign (1927–1933), roads were few and primitive, and there was no road from coast to coast. The only "real" road was from Managua (the current capital) to Tipitapa, northeast of Managua, between the lakes.[4] Léon was the largest city, some 150 miles north of Managua. Farther north and west was the principal port city of Corinto, on the Pacific coast south of the Gulf of Fonseca. Some 70 miles southeast of Managua was Granada (a former capital), on the shore of Lake Nicaragua. All three major towns were connected by rail (with a branch line extending northeastward from Léon to El Sauce).

Nicaragua was first seen by European eyes in 1522, when Alonzo González discovered Fonseca Bay on the far northwestern coast. Having just emerged from ten bloody years of war against the Moors, the Spanish *conquistadores* who sailed to Nicaragua were inured to human suffering, and the consequences for Nicaragua were tragic. According to José Dolores Gámez's *Historia de Nicaragua*, Central America "had the bad luck to receive the worst part of the Spanish emigration . . . a brutal and superstitious soldiery, collected from gambling houses, taverns, and, often, penitentiaries."[5] As a result, some 200,000 Amerindians (about a third of the total population) were rounded up and sent to Panama and Peru as slaves, making Nicaragua the principal source of the Central American slave trade.[6] During the Spanish colonial period, Nicaragua was part of the captaincy general of Guatemala (part of the viceroyalty of New Spain, or Mexico). As the slave-based *encomienda* system evolved into the *hacienda* system (alongside the *caudillo* system), the slave trade ended in 1542.[7] That said, the lives of indigenous peoples and African slaves brought to Nicaragua were scarcely improved with the end of chattel slavery.

In the latter half of the sixteenth century, English and other pirates raided the Atlantic coast of Nicaragua, that is, the eastern part of the country on the Caribbean Sea.[8] These raids increased in the next century and moved inland. The towns of Léon and Granada were plundered repeatedly, and both were occupied by pirates in 1685. Interestingly, pirate activity brought English settlers to Nicaragua, and they developed close relations with the indigenous peoples, especially along the northeastern coast. The British negotiated a "treaty of friendship and alliance" with the Miskito people in 1740, and some historians claim they went so far as to claim the Miskito Coast as a protectorate during the War of Jenkins' Ear (1739–1748).[9] British settlements were concentrated in the Black River area, Cape Gracias a Dios (where the Coco River flows into the Caribbean), and Bluefields. The Miskitos delivered other indigenous peoples to the British as slaves, helped secure British holdings in British Honduras (Belize), provided security against slave uprisings, captured runaway slaves, and even helped the British hunt down "maroon" guerrilla fighters in Jamaica (see chapter 2, note 13).

In 1821 Nicaragua declared its independence from Spain and joined the Mexican Empire.[10] In 1823 Nicaragua joined the United Provinces of Central America,[11] but a long civil war resulted in the collapse of the union in 1838, at which point Nicaragua became fully sovereign. But an independent Nicaragua was no less troubled. There had been considerable friction in the previous century between the *peninsulares* (those who were born in Spain) and the *criollos* (those of Spanish descent born in the New World), as well as with those of mixed blood. Although the first elected chief of state, Dionisio

Herrera, proved to be a capable leader, enmity among *peninsulares, criollos,* people of mixed race, and indigenous peoples (as well as between the rich and the poor) persisted. To survive in such an "incipient society, anarchic and lacking in political morality, [the government] had to seek the support of the military."[12] Consequently, a form of social militarism became the norm, and armed fighting among various factions spread, fed by the fierce competition between the cities of Granada and Léon, a rivalry that would dominate Nicaraguan politics for the next 100 years.

In 1848 a dispute erupted between Nicaragua and Great Britain when the British attempted to establish an independent Miskito Amerindian republic.[13] This garnered the attention of the United States, owing to its interest in digging a canal across Nicaragua from the Caribbean Sea to the Pacific. In keeping with the Monroe Doctrine, the United States opposed the British intent, which led to the Clayton-Bulwer Treaty of 1850. Under its terms, both countries were prohibited from seeking exclusive control over a canal in Nicaragua and from seeking "dominion" in Central America. Nevertheless, the United States intervened militarily in 1854 when civil war broke out between the *Partido Legitimista* (the Legitimist Party, also known as the Conservatives), based in Granada, and the *Partido Democrático* (the Democratic Party, also known as the Liberals), based in Léon.[14] The US Navy and Marine Corps also figured prominently in the Walker affair from 1855 to 1857.

During the civil war that began in 1854, the Liberals sought military assistance from Tennessean William Walker. Liberal leader Francisco Castellón signed a contract with Walker to bring up to 300 armed "colonists" to Nicaragua. Walker arrived in May 1855 with 60 men, and with an additional 100 local residents, he formed an army. On September 4 Walker's forces defeated the Conservatives at the Battle of La Virgen, and he took control of the Conservative capital of Granada. Walker governed through a provisional president, Patricio Rivas, and US president Franklin Pierce recognized the regime in May 1856. However, Walker and his "filibusters" were driven out by a coalition of Central American armies in 1857.[15] In 1860 Walker sailed to Honduras and prepared to reenter Nicaragua. But he was captured by a British warship, handed over to Honduran authorities, and executed at Trujilla, Honduras, on September 11.[16]

Thus, US interests in Nicaragua did not arise suddenly with the disturbances of the 1920s. Indeed, two years after Nicaragua gained its independence from Spain, Dewitt Clinton, a onetime Republican presidential candidate, governor of New York, and the promotional genius behind the Erie Canal, expressed an interest in building a canal across Nicaragua. Ultimately, the canal was constructed in Panama as a result of the Hay-Pauncefote Treaty of 1901, but economic penetration of Nicaragua began in anticipation of building a canal there. American diplomats quickly secured transit rights across Nicaragua, and American businessmen promptly organized an interoceanic company to transport freight and passengers from San Juan del Norte (Greytown) on the coast of the Caribbean Sea in southeastern Nicaragua to San Juan del Sur on the southwestern Pacific coast. When the anti-American Liberal dictator José Santos Zelaya (1893–1909) started courting Great Britain and Japan (to build a canal) and revoked earlier concessions granted to American businessmen, President William Howard Taft began to consider more pronounced intervention in Nicaragua's internal affairs.[17]

Marines landed twice during Zelaya's regime to protect American lives and property: first at Corinto in 1896, and again at Bluefields in 1899.[18] But Zelaya's downfall came in 1909 when another Liberal, Juan José Estrada, rebelled against the Zelaya regime, and the Conservatives seized the opportunity to rise up as well. President Taft openly supported the Conservatives, and when Zelaya ordered the execution of two captured American engineers employed by Estrada as explosives experts, the Nicaraguan chargé in Washington was expelled. Having pushed the Americans too far, Zelaya's power quickly faded, and he resigned. He was replaced by Dr. José Madriz, another Liberal leader.

Although American investment in Nicaragua climbed with the installation of Madriz as president, political conditions remained fraught with conflict and violence. The country was close to anarchy and collapse in 1910 when the US Navy began to concentrate ships in Nicaraguan waters. Colonel James Mahoney, USMC, and elements of the First Regiment from Panama lay off Corinto aboard the auxiliary cruiser USS *Buffalo.* Among the marine officers under Colonel Mahoney's command was Major Smedley Butler, whose battalion had come up from Camp Elliott in the Panama Canal Zone.[19] Butler made a reconnaissance of the western part of the country by rail and goat cart, and the *Buffalo* returned to Panama with this information, never landing the whole regiment. In May 1910 the gunboat USS *Dubuque* and another Dubuque-class gunboat, USS *Paducah,* anchored in Bluefields Harbor and landed bluejackets and marines in support of the Conservative rebels led by Estrada, who was ably assisted by Adolfo Díaz, an employee of an American mining concern. President Madriz sent government forces to Bluefields, and a blockade was declared (to be enforced by a single armed vessel purchased in New Orleans). But the blockade was ineffective because the Americans refused to honor it. Once the situation stabilized, the *Dubuque* steamed to Colón, Panama, took aboard two companies of the First Regiment under the overall command of Major Butler, and returned to Bluefields. By the middle of June, more reinforcements arrived in Bluefields aboard the USS *Prairie* and the Morgan ocean liner SS *El Sol.*[20] Nicaraguan government forces withdrew, and Butler and the marines returned to Panama. In August the Conservative army entered Managua, and Estrada became the new president, with Díaz as his vice president.

By the spring of 1911, the new Conservative government found itself in financial distress, as civil war had ruined industrial and agricultural production.[21] Protests turned into bloody demonstrations, and the US State Department sent Thomas Dawson, a Harvard lawyer and career diplomat, to study the situation and recommend actions to relieve the strife.[22] Financial reorganization followed, and Dawson managed to negotiate a loan from the United States to Nicaragua. Although economic conditions improved, the political state of affairs continued to deteriorate. The new ambassador to Nicaragua, Elliott Northcutt, pointedly noted that the majority of Nicaraguans remained hostile to American interests, especially in the mountainous backcountry. Thus, the atmosphere was ripe for yet another armed "revolution" and American intervention.

The First Nicaraguan Campaign

In the summer of 1912, impending civil war and the concomitant threat to American commercial interests prompted the first large-scale US intervention and what amounted to the marines' occupation of Nicaragua. Not long after taking office, Estrada's minister of war, General Luis Mena Vado, declared his desire to be president. Sensing his own vulnerability, President Estrada resigned in favor of Vice President Díaz. In July, Díaz replaced Mena with General Emiliano Chamorro Vargas, leader of the Conservatives. General Mena then launched an insurgency, and many of the Liberals who had supported the Zelaya regime joined him. The central government found itself all but impotent to protect foreign interests, and the Americans in Nicaragua appealed to Washington for protection.[23]

The US Navy and Marine Corps had been watching these events closely, and in early August the Denver-class protected cruiser USS *Tacoma* arrived in Corinto with its detachment of marines, who quickly moved by rail to Managua. This was a significant event, marking the first time marines had penetrated the interior of Nicaragua and entered the capital. In the meantime, General Mena bombarded the city, killing hundreds of people, including women and children. This action and his interference with the rail line from Corinto to Managua (and Granada) led to the dispatch of Smedley Butler and more than 300 marines from Panama to Nicaragua.[24] Butler and his Panama Battalion arrived in Corinto aboard a former schooner purchased for collier duty, USS *Justin*, on August 14.[25] He traveled to Managua and then back to Corinto (a more harrowing experience than can be related here) to pick up some 450 bluejackets from the Pennsylvania-class armored cruiser USS *California* and the protected cruiser USS *Denver*.

Late in August, President Taft ordered reinforcements to Nicaragua, and the First Provisional Regiment was formed in Philadelphia, commanded by Colonel Joseph Pendleton. The regiment sailed first to Cristobal in the Panama Canal Zone and then embarked aboard the *Prairie*, landing at Corinto with two battalions. Upon his arrival, Colonel Pendleton met with the new American ambassador to Nicaragua, George Weitzel, and determined that the marines and bluejackets in Managua should be reinforced by Butler's battalion. Major Butler was then directed to open the rail line south to Granada, which was controlled by General Mena. Mena's forces were not up for a fight and quickly surrendered the town. Mena was then allowed to go into exile in Panama. However, another rebel force, led by former lawyer Benjamin Zeledón, held the town of Masaya along the rail line, as well as the important and supposedly impregnable high ground of Barranca-Coyotepe. Butler's marines and government troops attacked the southeastern slopes of Coyotepe on October 2. Although the government soldiers faltered and withdrew, Butler and his marines overran Coyotepe in a bayonet charge. General Zeledón was captured, and he was later murdered by his own men for failing at Coyotepe.[26] Four marines and three sailors were killed, and three sailors and eight marines were wounded.

Zeledón was the last of the Liberal leaders in rebellion, and his death brought about a period of relative calm. Indeed, rebel forces across western Nicaragua surrendered, and by mid-November, most of the marines had departed. Remaining behind was a Legation Guard of four officers and some

100 enlisted men in Managua (even though, with the exception of the bombardment by Mena's forces, the legation had never been seriously threatened). The Legation Guard would remain in Managua in the Campo de Marte until 1925, a symbol of US power and the willingness of the US government to intervene in Nicaragua again should the need arise.[27] The large American presence provided a measure of tranquility, but it also made the central government complacent, secure in the knowledge that it could call on the marines at a moment's notice. Reports filed by the marines noted rampant corruption and graft throughout the government, including the military, which could fill its ranks only through forced conscription.[28]

World War I and the 1920s

The outbreak of World War I proved disastrous for Nicaragua, as the national economy simply disintegrated. In 1916 a Liberal, Dr. Julian Irias, was elected president, much to the dissatisfaction of the United States. But Irias's presidency was short-lived, and Conservative Emiliano Chamorro was elected unopposed in 1917.[29] The belief throughout Latin America was that the US government was pro-Conservative and had engineered Chamorro's election. Therefore, the State Department suggested in 1920 that the electoral process be revised to allow the opposition a greater opportunity to compete in national politics. To assist in rewriting the law, Dr. Harold Dodds, a professor at Case Western Reserve University, was dispatched to Nicaragua as a technical adviser.[30] A new law was drafted and adopted by the Nicaraguan congress, and registration for the 1924 elections was carried out.[31]

The United States had grown weary of its role in Nicaragua, and the State Department hoped the national elections in 1924 would create conditions favorable for the marines' withdrawal. Crucial to the American plan was the creation of an indigenous constabulary to keep the peace. US motives in encouraging the creation of the constabulary were not unlike those behind the creation of the gendarmerie in Haiti. Dana Munro, who oversaw the marines' withdrawal from Haiti in 1934, explains:

> The establishment of non-partisan constabularies in the Caribbean states was one of the chief objectives of our policy from the time it became clear that the customs collectorships wouldn't assure stability by them-selves. The old armies were or seemed to be one of the

> principal causes of disorder and financial disorganization. They consumed most of the government's revenue, chiefly in graft, and they gave nothing but disorder and repression in return. We thought that a disciplined force, trained by Americans, would do away with the petty local oppression that was responsible for much of the disorder that occurred and would be an important step toward better financial administration and economic progress generally.[32]

The constabulary would be organized and trained by "suitable instructors . . . with experience gained in other countries in organizing such [a] corps."[33] This, of course, meant officers and enlisted men of the US Marine Corps, who would be offered commissions in the new constabulary.

But even with the electoral machinery adjusted and a commitment to the creation of an apolitical constabulary, dissent emerged within the ranks of the Conservatives. In 1920 Emiliano Chamorro had supported his uncle, Diego Manuel Chamorro, for the presidency. Diego died in October 1923, and Vice President Bartolmé Martinez completed Chamorro's term of office. Emiliano, who had been his uncle's minister to the United States in Washington, returned to Nicaragua and stood for election to the presidency in 1924.[34] According to the new law, Martinez could not run for reelection, so he formed a coalition with the Liberals and supported a different Conservative candidate for president, Carlos Solórzano, as well as the Liberal candidate for vice president, Juan Sacasa. The election of Solórzano and Sacasa in October was legal, and the State Department declared it satisfactory to American interests.[35] Upon gaining the presidency, Solórzano requested that the Legation Guard remain until the constabulary could be fully organized. To that end, Major Calvin Carter, a retired US Army officer and former member of the Philippine constabulary, was contracted to organize the Guardia Nacional de Nicaragua.[36]

On August 3, 1925, the marines of the Legation Guard boarded the transport USS *Henderson* at Corinto and departed for the United States. The day was declared a national holiday in Nicaragua. But within the month, General Chamorro, who had fully consolidated his power over the national army, seized control of the government in what amounted to a coup d'état. Chamorro pressured Solórzano to purge the government of Liberals, take a "leave of absence" owing to purported health problems, and appoint Chamorro acting president. US Secretary of State Frank Kellogg refused to recognize this illegitimate government.[37] Civil war soon followed. The opposition was headed by former vice president Sacasa, who had been impeached by the Nicaraguan congress and fled to Mexico.[38] Having just emerged from its own revolution and being sympathetic to the Liberal cause, Mexico claimed that Sacasa was the rightful heir to the presidency and supplied arms and ammunition to his military forces in Nicaragua, led by General José Moncada. Without foreign aid, the Nicaraguan economy soon collapsed, and the treasury, which had been built up over the previous decade of relative peace, was emptied.[39]

Predictably, the Guardia Nacional became an auxiliary of the national army.[40] In May 1926 Guardia forces and government soldiers defeated rebel forces at Bluefields led by Liberal Bertram Sandoval, who had sailed from Mexico.[41] In June, Sacasa formed his own army in Guatemala, and by August, these forces had landed and taken control of most of the east coast of Nicaragua, with Conservative forces holding out in the port of Bluefields. Consequently, on August 27, 1926, more than 100 marines and bluejackets from the Denver-class protected cruiser USS *Galveston* landed at Bluefields to protect American lives and property, and a "neutral zone" was established.[42] Emboldened by the arrival of the Americans, Chamorro declared war on the Liberals and sent the national army to the east coast.

At first, the United States refused to take sides in the fight, and the Liberals began to gain the upper hand. Rear Admiral Julian Latimer, commanding the US Navy Special Service Squadron in the Caribbean, called for an armistice. With the treasury running dry, Chamorro agreed to the truce, and both sides met aboard the USS *Denver*, anchored off Corinto.[43] Sacasa, fearing for his safety, sent representatives to the conference. The conferees were unable to reach a settlement, but on the day the truce ended, Chamorro resigned the presidency and handed over the government to Senator Sebastián Uriza, appointed by the Nicaraguan congress.[44] Uriza's tenure did not last long, as the United States once again refused to recognize the new government. As a result, a new Nicaraguan congress convened and reinstated eighteen senators and deputies who had been removed by Chamorro. The conference at Corinto reconvened, and this time a settlement was reached. Shortly thereafter, the reconstituted Nicaraguan congress elected Conservative Adolfo Díaz as chief executive.[45] The United States recognized the new government under Díaz, but Mexico refused to do so, claiming that Sacasa remained the true president of Nicaragua. Consequently, Mexico continued to send arms and ammunition to Liberal forces. Thus, on November 15, Díaz requested American assistance in bringing peace to Nicaragua. Newly elected US president Calvin Coolidge initially ignored the request, but, disturbed by continued Mexican support of the Liberals, he allowed the Díaz government to purchase arms and ammunition from the United States on credit.[46]

On December 1, 1926, former vice president Sacasa and his followers landed at Puerto Cabezas, on the northeastern coast of Nicaragua, and Sacasa declared himself the "constitutional" president. Mexico immediately recognized Sacasa, and where the Liberals dominated the countryside, they quickly imposed taxes on American businesses and seized American property. This sent shock waves through Washington, and Undersecretary of State Robert Olds summed up the situation for the United States:

> There is no room for any outside influence other than ours in this region. We could not tolerate such a thing without incurring grave risks. . . . The action of Mexico in the Nicaraguan crisis is a direct challenge to the United States. . . . We must decide whether we shall tolerate the interference of any other power (i.e., Mexico) in Central American affairs or insist upon our own dominant position. If this Mexican maneuver succeeds it will take many years to recover the ground we shall have lost. . . . Until now Central America has always understood that the governments which we recognize and support stay in power, while those which we do not recognize and support fall. Nicaragua has become a test case. It is difficult to see how we can afford to be defeated.[47]

In short, the United States could not allow the Liberal insurgency, supported by Mexico, to take control of Nicaragua. Moreover, European governments and the Chinese were asking President Coolidge to intervene to protect their own citizens and property. American prestige was at stake, and the stage was set for another military intervention.

In truth, the United States did not wish to intervene a second time. When the marines left in 1925, the United States had hoped it was for good. But a bond had emerged between Nicaraguans opposed to the Díaz government and Mexican Marxists, and the US government wanted to contain any potential "revolutionary wave" in Central America.[48] Unfortunately, Nicaraguan government forces were routinely beaten by Liberal forces, and President

Díaz was moved to provide a legal justification for American military intervention. On the west coast, US marines and sailors were already enforcing a neutral zone around Corinto and had sent a detachment to Managua, but this was not enough. On December 22, 1926, a landing force from the New York–class armored cruiser USS *Rochester* arrived at the small village of Barra de Rio Grande on the Caribbean coast, establishing another neutral zone. That same month, bluejackets and marines from the USS *Denver* and the Denver-class protected cruiser USS *Cleveland* established another neutral zone at Puerto Cabezas. Sailors and marines also established several smaller neutral zones along both coasts, and soon the Special Service Squadron became overextended, prompting the squadron commander to request reinforcements.[49]

Additional marines arrived in force at Bluefields with the Second Battalion, Fifth Regiment, aboard the transport USS *Argonne* on January 27, 1927.[50] They had embarked from Guantanamo Bay under the command of Haiti veteran Lieutenant Colonel Jimmy Meade. Upon their arrival in Bluefields, the marines reestablished the neutral zone along the Escondido River and posted a company to the town of Rama, not far from the coast. The remainder of the battalion then reboarded the *Argonne* and passed through the Panama Canal to Corinto. From there, they traveled to Managua, dropping off guards along the way to protect the rail line. Throughout the following weeks, more marines arrived,[51] including a provisional battalion from the Scouting Fleet composed of detachments from the battleship USS *Texas,* the USS *Florida* (the lead battleship of its class), and another dreadnought of the Wyoming class, USS *Arkansas.*[52] On February 26 VO-1M, under the command of Major Ross "Rusty" Rowell and consisting of eight officers, eighty-one enlisted men, and six DH-4B aircraft, arrived at Corinto alongside the First Provisional Company (Rifle).[53] Almost immediately upon their arrival, VO-1M aircraft began reconnaissance missions and were fired on, but none of them returned fire—at least at first.[54]

The Second Nicaraguan Campaign

The Second Nicaraguan Campaign officially lasted from August 27, 1926, to March 30, 1930. What distinguished this American intervention in Nicaragua from earlier interventions in the Dominican Republic and Haiti was the fact that US forces never occupied Nicaragua as a military government. Whereas in Port-au-Prince and Santo Domingo martial law had been declared and the marines had conducted operations as they saw fit to restore order, in Nicaragua the marines were dispatched to support the Díaz government (a mission that today would be termed foreign internal defense). On March 7, 1927, the Fifth Regiment (less the Second Battalion) and the staff of the Second Brigade, under the command of Brigadier General Logan Feland, arrived.[55] The situation in the major towns and cities, including Managua, improved considerably with the arrival of these troops, and the railway was protected all along the line.[56] However, the countryside was another matter altogether.

Despite his obvious weaknesses, the US government had decided to stick with President Díaz. In late March, President Calvin Coolidge sent former secretary of war Henry Stimson to Nicaragua to broker a deal between the warring Liberals and Conservatives.[57] Stimson, a veteran of tough negotiations with Filipino insurgents following the Spanish-American War, had successfully arbitrated a dispute between Peru and Chile in 1925. He arrived in Managua on April 17 and conferred with American and Nicaraguan authorities. President Díaz proposed that an American-controlled electoral commission be organized and that the Guardia be reconstituted and officered by American military personnel. He also proposed that, until the new Guardia was on its feet, the marines should remain in Nicaragua.[58] On April 22 Díaz offered terms to the Liberals, and one of the principal features was the simultaneous disarmament of both armies.

A truce was declared, opening the way for a peace conference at Tipitapa, the village along the river of the same name. The Tipitapa Agreement (also known as the Black Thorn [*Espino Negro*] Treaty) was concluded on May 4, and the so-called constitutionalist war came to an end. As part of the agreement, an Arms Commission was established, commanded by Captain Julian Brown, USMC.[59] Although the Liberal leadership agreed to the cease-fire and disarmament called for by the agreement, some units under General Moncada refused to comply, including a small band led by Augusto Nicolás Calderón Sandino, a pint-sized Nicaraguan nationalist who had once lived in Mexico and served under the *caudillo* and revolutionary guerrilla José Doroteo Arango Arámbula, better known as Francisco "Pancho" Villa.[60] When Sandino disobeyed Moncada's order to disarm and withdrew his men to the wilderness of northern Nicaragua to carry on the fight, President Díaz requested additional marines to disarm them.[61]

As Stimson prepared to depart Nicaragua, the Eleventh Marine Regiment was reactivated under the command of Lieutenant Colonel Arthur

O'Leary, who arrived at Corinto aboard the seaplane tender USS *Aroostock* on May 17, 1927.[62] Over the next six days, the Eleventh Regiment (less one battalion) arrived in Nicaragua, along with an additional observation squadron, VO-4M, comprising seven officers, seventy-eight enlisted marines, and six Boeing 02B-1s (the metal-fuselaged derivative of the DH-4B). VO-4M was also placed under Major Rowell's command, and combined, the two units were designated Aircraft Squadrons, Second Brigade.[63] The arrival of these additional forces gave the brigade a total strength of 178 officers and 2,725 enlisted men.[64]

The Sandino Rebellion

The Sandino rebellion combined insurgency and resistance. It was the local expression of an anti-imperialist sentiment emerging throughout Latin America and culminating in a January 1928 proclamation by the All-American Anti-Imperialist League meeting in Mexico City. The proclamation complained that "pan-Americanism means submission to the yoke of Wall Street."[65] But Sandino was simply a nationalist who refused to submit to the terms of the Tipitapa Agreement, even declining an offer to become governor of Jinotega.[66] He was also a "spiritist" who believed that he had been "called to protest the betrayal of the Fatherland."[67] Thus, with 200 of his followers, he formed the Ejército Defensor de la Soberanía Nacional de Nicaragua (Army Defending Nicaraguan National Sovereignty) and marched toward the towns of San Rafael and Jinotega, well beyond the territory controlled by the marines.[68] Colonel Luis Gulick, commander of the Fifth Regiment, personally led a force that pursued Sandino in an attempt to persuade him to surrender his arms. Sandino proved adamant, although a handful of his followers did submit when the marines, called *Machos* by the Sandinistas, arrived in Jinotega.[69] Sandino dispersed the remainder of his men and retired to Yali with fewer than fifty followers. Thereafter, not unlike the guerrillas in the Dominican Republic and Haiti, Sandino and his men were called bandits.

The term "bandits" was in some ways both appropriate and unfortunate. Banditry was common in Nicaragua at the time, and the northern part of the country was especially prone to banditry.[70] Antibandit operations were occasionally launched by the central government but invariably failed to make much headway. In many cases those sent to quell banditry became bandits themselves, and the local inhabitants regretted they had ever come. According to one marine author, "Public safety has never been a fact very far north and east of the railroad line and big cities, and smuggling, robbery and murder has been the recourse of the peasant."[71] Indeed, banditry was in some ways an industry in itself. As the same author noted:

> People imagine from reading the papers during the occupation that there was a bandit army; but the fact is there was no such army, but rather were bandit chiefs and bandit gangs. Sometimes they might [join] temporarily for a purpose, but usually they operated independently or semi independently. They had existed before . . . some of them smuggle but all of them would be willing to resort to a little honest murder to get money. It was easier to live that way than to try to farm, because if a man really tried to farm he probably would be robbed by bandits. It would not be far from the truth to say that practically every person, male or female in Nueva Segovia was either a bandit, or had actual bandit affiliations.[72]

But calling Sandino's followers bandits may have had the opposite effect of the one intended.[73] In short, far northern Nicaragua was fertile ground for the ideological indoctrination of a xenophobic people with deep roots in what amounted to commercially motivated guerrilla warfare. Nevertheless, and irrespective of whether the peasants were ideologically inspired, Sandino and many (if not most) of his subordinate leaders (jefes) were certainly motivated by ideology, and the people of Nueva Segovia were ready-made guerrilla fighters who could move quickly, live off the land, and blend into the small communities dotting the countryside.

While the marines of the Fifth Regiment set out to subdue Sandino, the Eleventh Regiment, under the command of another Haiti veteran, Colonel Randolph Berkeley, took up the job of policing other parts of Nicaragua. For the men of both regiments, constant patrolling was the rule, both on foot and on horseback.[74] Mounted detachments soon played an essential role in pacifying the countryside, and although automobiles and trucks were available, their use was severely hampered by road conditions. Even so, pacification of the country seemed to be well in hand by late spring, and the decision was made to reduce the number of marines in Nicaragua. By late June, marines of the Eleventh Regiment began to depart; the Second Battalion left Corinto aboard the *Argonne,* and the First Battalion set sail from the east coast. By the end of July, the Eleventh Regiment had ceased operations in Nicaragua.[75] But before his departure with the Eleventh Regiment, General Feland ordered that Sandino be brought to heel and that the operation be executed mainly by the Guardia Nacional.[76]

At this point, simple rebellion evolved to insurgency. Sandino raided the San Albino gold mine, where he had once been employed. Soon afterward, he declared himself sovereign in Nueva Segovia and established a shadow government.[77] At the time, there were only about 40 marines in Nueva Segovia, mostly in the town of Ocotal, under the command of Captain Gilbert Hatfield. The marines' plan was to occupy the main towns in the north and send out patrols to make contact with Sandino's forces. Major Oliver Floyd was appointed commander of a combined force of some 75 marines and 150 members of the Guardia, tasked with running Sandino to ground.[78] As the operation got under way, Major Floyd received word that the garrison at Ocotal had been attacked. He sent forward a mounted detachment of 50 marines to reinforce the garrison. The bulk of the expedition—that is, the supply train of oxcarts and mules—followed, arriving a day after the "horse marines."[79] Running down Sandino would be more challenging than expected. As one marine veteran recalled later, "This was quite a different matter from operations conducted a few miles inland from coast towns, which usually distinguished the West Indian expeditions."[80] Regardless, the Second Nicaraguan Campaign had begun in earnest.

Early Aviation Efforts

As described earlier, two squadrons of aircraft arrived in Nicaragua to support the Second Brigade, both falling under the command of Rusty Rowell. From February until the end of May 1927, VO-1M and VO-4M flew patrols in support of the ground forces, but owing to the perceived lessening of the threat, most of VO-1M returned to San Diego in June. Before its departure, VO-1M handed over two airplanes to VO-4M, which was redesignated VO-7M on July 1, 1927. Major Rowell remained in Nicaragua to command VO-7M.[81]

A third squadron, VO-6M, arrived at Corinto on February 16, 1928, aboard the Lexington-class aircraft carrier USS *Saratoga*.[82] The squadrons' mission was dedicated support of the brigade's ground forces "by providing observation aviation, ground attack aviation, and transport service."[83] When VO-6M arrived at Managua from Corinto, Rowell wrote: "When the train pulled into the station . . . the heads sticking out of the coach windows were a sight for sore eyes. 'Pop' Stewart, Archie Paschal, Tommie Whitman, 'Skinny'

Leeper, Joe Kittle, and many others of the old guard of Quantico."[84] The initial complement of aircraft for VO-6M in Nicaragua consisted of three Curtiss F8C-1 Falcons and six 02B-1s. Later, Atlantic-Fokker TA-1 and Ford RR trimotors would join the squadron, which would then be redesignated VJ-6M. As described later, these large transports enabled the marines to conduct military air transportation on a new scale.

VO-1M had actually arrived ten days ahead of the main body of the Second Brigade, at which time US forces were expected to remain neutral with respect to the contesting factions. Upon arriving in Managua, the squadron constructed an airdrome in a pasture near an old baseball field that was being used by the two Hisso (Laird) Swallow aircraft that constituted the entire Nicaraguan air force.[85] The Swallows had been purchased by a Nicaraguan businessman from the Checkered Cab Company of San Francisco. Two Americans, Lee Mason and William Brooks, had flown the planes to Nicaragua and had promptly been impressed into Nicaraguan government service. The former barnstormers were commissioned as officers in the constabulary and were soon dropping crude homemade bombs—made of iron pipes containing sticks of dynamite lit by the pilots' cigars—on Liberal forces.[86]

In mid-January 1927 a large Liberal force under the command of General Francisco Parajón attacked government forces commanded by General Alfredo Noguera Gómez near Chinandega and surrounded the city, taking it in February.[87] The Swallows were quickly dispatched to bomb Liberal forces in the city. The use of these airplanes was so novel that, during the battle, the Liberals stampeded from the field.[88] As Brooks wrote for the *New York Times*, "That homemade bomb made more dust than a 100-pound missile would in a wetter country. The whole landscape seemed to rise. When the dust settled, I saw Liberal troopers running in every direction."[89] But once they recovered from their initial shock, these same forces largely ignored the efforts of Mason and Brooks during the Battle of Muy Muy, driving off government forces despite their air support.[90] The net effect was to convince Liberal troops that airplanes invariably belonged to the enemy, but they were of little consequence. This attitude would change when Marine Corps aircraft struck their first concerted blow at former Liberal troops led by Sandino.

Although the marines were ostensibly neutral at the outset of the intervention, and General Moncada had instructed his forces to refrain from shooting at Americans, Marine Corps aircraft were routinely fired on and holed on almost every flight.[91] According to Major Rowell: "We carried only front machine guns; we had no rear guns or bombs. We had authority to return hostile fire, but the American mission was to stop the war—not to become involved in it. I appealed to all pilots to avoid hostilities and to return fire only when necessary to save their own lives. During the period of observation our planes were hit twenty-three times."[92]

Fortunately, none of Rowell's aircraft were badly damaged, and none of his aviators were wounded or killed. Moreover, during this period of American neutrality, Rowell and his crews observed the tactical methods of Liberal troops, noting where they placed their command posts, how they deployed, how they dug in, and so forth. As Rowell later wrote, "It was splendid training for the campaign which followed."[93] But neutrality soon gave way to active combat operations when, unlike in China, the Liberals continued to fire on Marine Corps aircraft and Sandino deliberately attacked marine patrols and garrisons, as well as other Americans and their property. Major Floyd's Nueva Segovia expedition would mark the first offensive effort by the marines, and as the American role in Nicaragua became wider and deeper, operational constraints on marine aviators were loosened (but never approximating the freedom the marines enjoyed in the Caribbean).

Major Floyd's Nueva Segovia Expedition

Sandino's base of operations was in the remote northern province of Nueva Segovia. The nearest railroad was more than 100 miles away, and the roads were barely passable by oxcart. Regardless, on May 31, 1927, Major Harold Pierce got the ball rolling when he left Managua for Nueva Segovia to establish control of the department under a new Liberal governor, Arnoldo Ramierez, as per the Tipitapa Agreement. Accompanying Pierce were Lieutenant Lawrence Norman and Captain Hatfield. On June 8 Lieutenant Frank Lamson-Scribner and an enlisted pilot, Corporal Lawrence Pabst, took off with their observers in DH-4Bs to reconnoiter ahead of Peirce's column, but they found nothing to report.[94] Arriving in Ocotal on June 9, Pierce left Hatfield and ten marines there alongside a forty-seven-man platoon of the Guardia.[95] On June 11 Lamson-Scribner and his observer, along with Captain Robert Archibald and his observer, flew to Ocotal and surveyed the surrounding area but again found nothing significant to report.[96] A later reconnaissance patrol consisting of two aircraft led by Lieutenant Cuckoo Boyden likewise found nothing to report. Sandino had gone to ground, and his men knew how to hide in the thick forest.

While at Ocotal, Pierce communicated with headquarters in Managua employing a novel technique that made good use of the regular airplane patrols to the town. The marines on the ground would lay out panels alerting pilots that a handwritten message was available for pickup.[97] The marines would then erect two poles some 75 feet apart in an open field, placing the message in a bag strung between them. The pilot would descend close to the ground and, using a weighted line, snag the string between the poles and haul the bag into the airplane. This technique was not particularly efficient (or safe), and a landing strip was soon constructed near the town. Nevertheless, this method continued to be employed where no landing strips were available, and new crews were trained in the "message pickup" technique.[98]

Aware of the presence of Hatfield and his troops in Ocotal, Sandino wrote to him, initiating a remarkable exchange of letters. Sandino's letters were vitriolic, full of threats and revolutionary jargon, whereas Hatfield's replies (he could read, write, and speak Spanish) were generally tongue-in-cheek. The captain's missives enraged the revolutionist,[99] and the straw that broke the camel's back was apparently a letter Hatfield closed by stating: "If words were bullets and phrases were soldiers, you would be king of the mountains, as you call yourself, instead of being the ignorant cattle thief that you are."[100] Upon reading this note, Sandino decided to attack Ocotal and do away with the annoying marine officer.

Fortunately, Captain Hatfield had anticipated such an attack and planned accordingly. He placed his command post inside City Hall, a sturdy building. On the other side of the plaza were Captains Darnell and Bleasdale, the latter described as "a man who literally ate cold steel and fire, and enjoyed it."[101] On July 15, 1927, more than 400 guerrillas led by Sandino attacked the garrison at first light.[102] Sandino's men first infiltrated the town, hoping to take the marines and Guardia troops by surprise, but they were soon discovered, and fighting broke out at around 1:15 a.m. Though outnumbered, Hatfield's troops stood fast and managed to force the guerrillas to retreat and reorganize at around 3:00 a.m. Fighting then broke out anew. During the lull in the fighting, Sandino offered Hatfield the opportunity to surrender, but the captain famously replied that marines do not know how to surrender. Fighting continued at close quarters, and during the second attack, one marine was killed. The fight continued for hours, but Marine Corps aviation would soon make an appearance and turn the tables on the Sandinistas.

Shortly after dawn, a regular two-plane patrol discovered that something was wrong in Ocotal. The airplanes were piloted by Cuckoo Boyden and Chief Warrant Officer Michael Wodarczyk, the "Polish Warhorse."[103] Lieutenant Boyden could not hear the rifle fire owing to the noise of his engine. He landed on the airfield outside of town to find out what was happening in the village, which appeared to be deserted.[104] A friendly peasant ran to the airplane and informed Boyden that Sandino was attacking, so he quickly took off under a hail of gunfire, several bullets piercing his wings. Boyden and Wodarczyk then formed up and attacked the guerrillas. Once they had exhausted their ammunition, they returned to Managua and reported that the marines and Guardia troops at Ocotal were under attack by strong bandit forces. Unfortunately, the nearest friendly ground forces were some six days away by overland march. VO-7M was the only unit capable of providing immediate assistance to the beleaguered garrison, and Major Rowell was ordered to provide whatever support he could.[105] At the time, the squadron had a mix of DH-4Bs and 02B-1s that were long in the tooth. Nonetheless, Rowell had trained his pilots in dive-bombing (see chapter 3), and he decided to attack the guerrillas using this maneuver.

Ocotal was more than 100 miles from Managua, with no emergency landing strips in between, and the weather was bad. But within an hour after first receiving news of the battle, all five of the VO-7M's aircraft took off for Ocotal, with Rowell in the lead. Each of the airplanes carried 600 rounds of .30-caliber ammunition for their Lewis guns but only a partial load of small bombs, as the long flight required a heavy load of fuel.[106] Navigating between thunderstorms, the formation of old biplanes arrived over Ocotal at around 3:00 p.m. After making one pass to reconnoiter the situation, Rowell attacked. He described what happened next:

> On our second approach we went at them. It was our first engagement but it was the most dramatic fight we ever fought. The setting was theatrical in the extreme. On the ground our men were fighting for their lives, and they had been fighting for sixteen hours without sleep or food. They did not know how much assistance we could give them, and we ourselves were none too sure. I went in first, leading the attack. As I went down I could see enemy troops firing in groups. They were absolutely unconcerned. Just before I dropped the first bomb I saw a puff of smoke come from a man sitting on a horse and

> smoking a cigar. After the first bomb dropped the whole picture changed. We could see enemy groups milling around. Then they seemed to hesitate as if they were too surprised to know what to do. Complete panic followed the second and third attacks. Men threw away their rifles, jumped over fences and raced wildly through the streets. Everywhere they went planes were diving at them. After we finished our bombing my men became so interested in chasing enemy groups out of town and down the road that I could hardly assemble them to return before our gas was exhausted. It was a complete rout for Sandino.[107]

According to Rowell, "Accustomed as they were to the aerial attacks of Mason and Brooks . . . the Sandinistas had never dreamed we could do so much damage. . . . Now the Nicaraguans saw for the first time just how destructive planes could be."[108]

At first, the marines began their dives at 1,500 feet, pulling out at 600 feet. After a while, however, they started their dives at 1,000 feet and pulled up at 300 feet. During each dive, after the bomb was released and the aircraft began to climb, the observer suppressed the area with machine gun fire.[109] The air attack lasted forty-five minutes. At about the same time the marine aviators' bombs and ammunition were expended and their fuel began to run low, the storms they had managed to skirt on the way to Ocotal closed in. The marines decided to fly west toward Fonseca Bay, hoping to avoid the storms, but they "were bucked by the blinding rain." Two planes were forced down at Léon, without mishap, and the next day they flew safely to Managua.[110] For the Ocotal action, Rowell became the first marine aviator in Nicaragua to receive the Distinguished Flying Cross.[111] More importantly, officially and for the first time, the marines had proved the efficacy of dive-bombing in the role of close air support.

Sandino and his men suffered a devastating setback with significant casualties (though they later denied it, claiming they had calmly evacuated their position down the mountainside).[112] Marine casualties were one dead and one wounded. The Guardia troops suffered three wounded. After the fight was over, the marines discovered that many inhabitants of the town had joined the guerrillas, resulting in fourteen killed and twenty wounded. Many other civilians died as well, and newspapers around the world voiced their outrage, denouncing the air attack as a "massacre" and "mass murder."[113] But according to the marines, most of the civilians who died were Conservatives who had been murdered by Sandino's men when their homes and businesses were looted and burned.[114]

Sandino never attacked Ocotal again, but he was not finished. And as one Marine Corps document attested, "There was no precedent in our experience of bandit warfare in Haiti and San Domingo or in what we knew of it from other similar affairs for a leader to keep his prestige and his force together after such humiliations as the Ocotal repulse and the march of Floyd through his territory."[115] As Major Floyd's column continued its trek to San Albino, it was ambushed near San Fernando, and one marine was wounded. The same day a patrol plane overhead was fired on and returned fire, but apparently with no effect. Over the next several days, more planes were fired on. Floyd found San Fernando empty, and upon leaving, the marines were ambushed once again by a force that was mounted and well armed. On July 27 two marine aircraft spotted a large group of guerrillas just south of the Honduran border, and Floyd's column made for it. On July 29 the column reached Jicaro, commonly referred to as Sandino City, not far from the Honduran border. It was becoming clear, as Bernard Nalty's semiofficial monograph noted later, that "Sandino had a great deal of popular support" in the area. The marines "persisted in calling him a bandit, [but] they recognized that he was a rebel [in fact, an insurgent] determined to overthrow the coalition government."[116]

The marines lost track of Sandino (he most likely moved into Honduras), but intelligence reports mentioned a secret impregnable fortress constructed by Sandino known as El Chipote.[117] Colonel Gulick ordered Floyd to find and reduce the fortress and then proceed to Quilali. On August 1 the column and its train reached San Albino without incident. There, residents told Major Floyd that the El Chipote redoubt was a myth, a bit of insurgent propaganda. He informed his superiors and requested permission to drop the quest for El Chipote, which was denied. Floyd also learned that Sandino had been in San Albino and had carried off some $5,000 worth of gold from the mine. Thus, although the rainy season was fast approaching, Floyd's search for Sandino and El Chipote continued, and he arrived in Quilali on August 5. He then returned to Ocotal and handed over his command to Captain Victor Bleasdale (who would later command the Guardia Nacional after Colonel Robert Rhea served a short stint as jefe director). It was the end of the Floyd expedition.

At this point, large-scale operations by the marines and the Guardia ceased for a time. For one thing, the bulk of American forces were in the western and north-central towns (only one company was at Rama on the east coast), not in Nueva Segovia. Larger towns such as Managua, Granada, Léon, and Corinto were occupied by substantial garrisons, and there were garrisons at smaller towns such as Matagalpa, Jinotega, Ocotal, and Masaya. Even villages too small to appear on a map had garrisons, but these were usually Guardia troops. There was simply not enough manpower for large-scale sweeps in the far north. Thus, from the occupied towns and villages, marine and Guardia patrols ranged the countryside, frequently making contact with small groups of men who were lightly armed. But this was not always the case. In early October 1927 a patrol led by Lieutenant George O'Shea unexpectedly engaged a large and well-armed guerrilla force.[118] His patrol had been sent out to rescue the crew of a DH that had gone down while on patrol near Quilali.

On October 8 two DeHavillands, one piloted by Lieutenant Earl Thomas with Sergeant Frank Dowdell as his observer, spotted a guerrilla pack train and immediately attacked it with fragmentation bombs and machine gun fire, routing the train. Turning toward Ocotal, Thomas's DH suddenly went down ("conked out"). Presumably, some vital part of the airplane, such as the fuel tank or the fuel line, had been hit by ground fire.[119] The airplane crashed on a ridgeline of Montaña el Zapatillo, a mountain roughly 7 miles northwest of Quilali.[120] Thomas waggled the wings furiously as he descended (a sign of distress) and then put the airplane down in the jungle. Chief Warrant Officer Wodarczyk and his observer saw Thomas and Dowdell jump from the plane upon crashing. Wodarczyk flew low over the crash site and dropped a map to the downed aviators. He then flew to a marine outpost in Jicaro and dropped a message there, reporting the crash and requesting a rescue party.

All the men under Rowell's command had been warned about "the customs of the enemy as to torturing prisoners and mutilating the dead." According to a letter sent to General Feland in 1930, Rowell and his men had decided among themselves that, should anyone be brought down, he "would not be taken alive in order that the enemy might not be afforded the opportunity of inflicting humiliation on an officer or man wearing the American uniform."[121] The bodies of Thomas and Dowdell were never found, but various details emerged, based on interrogations of prisoners and local residents, as well as interviews of Sandino and other guerrillas. Major Rowell conducted his own investigation, claiming later:

> It so happened that the scene of the crash was only about 500 yards from a Sandinista outpost. Thomas and Dowdell proceeded toward our outpost at Jicaro and almost immediately encountered a party of about twelve men. The two Marines fled down a ravine hotly pursued by the bandits. Finding themselves overtaken, they took cover . . . and opened fire at short range. . . . [T]he enemy fled in disorder leaving behind several of their number who had fallen. The two aviators pushed on [and] a short time later on a small trail, they were met by two natives armed with machetes. The Marines captured the two natives and ordered them to precede them and clear the trail toward Jicaro.[122]

After a short time on the trail, Thomas concluded that they were being led astray by their new guides. When he accosted the Nicaraguan man in the lead, the other man attacked Thomas with his machete, nearly severing the lieutenant's arm.[123] Sergeant Dowdell quickly shot and killed the machete-wielding man with his .45-caliber semiautomatic pistol. The other man, though wounded by Dowdell, managed to escape. This man found the guerrilla outpost and reported the location of the marine aviators. Finding them was easy, for Lieutenant Thomas was leaving a trail of blood. Rowell continued: "Upon reaching a small stream Thomas became weak from loss of blood and stopped while Dowdell bathed and attempted to bandage the wound. At this time they were overtaken by about twenty-five bandits armed with rifles. The two flyers took shelter behind a small fold in the ground and fought against the overwhelming odds until they were both killed. . . . It was stated that they killed three more of the enemy before they finally fell."[124]

Carleton Beals, a popular left-wing journalist at the time, interviewed Sandino sometime after the event, confirming many of Major Rowell's details but differing on others. From the Club de Corresponsales Estranjeros en México in San Juan, Beals also wrote a letter to General Feland, corroborating that the two Nicaraguan peasant guides had attacked Thomas and Dowdell. But according to Beals, Dowdell was killed in the fight, Thomas managed to defend himself, and both guides fled, unharmed. Thomas later "barricaded himself behind rocks or in a cave on the mountain side, where he defended himself for a number of hours and killed four Sandinistas before being shot himself."[125] The one important point that both Rowell and Beals agreed on was that Sandino had been impressed by the courage of the marine officer.

Beals quotes Sandino as stating: "The Yankee was a very brave man, he killed four of our men before we got him."[126] Regardless of his courage, Lieutenant Thomas was hung from a tree and photographed, and the photo was sent to the marine flying field in Managua, where it was posted on a bulletin board for all to see.[127]

Meanwhile, the rescue party—Lieutenant O'Shea's column of eight marines, ten Guardia, and a navy surgeon brought along to attend to the downed aviators (if necessary)—was ambushed on the way to the crash site. Six of the marines had just recovered from malaria and were still weak. The large guerrilla force surrounded the patrol and was on the verge of overpowering them when O'Shea decided to attack to his own rear, which succeeded. Having lost his compass and his local guides (who had fled at the first shots), O'Shea pressed on, taking a direction he thought was correct and fighting the guerrillas along the way. The young officer's sense of direction was good, and they ended up in Jicaro. There were no marine casualties, but four Guardia were killed.

In addition to O'Shea's column, two others had been sent out to locate the downed aviators, one led by Lieutenant Moses Gould and the other by Lieutenant Clarence Chappell. The two columns were supposed to converge at the crash site, extract the downed aviators, and make for Jicaro. Chappell arrived first, on October 26, and was immediately attacked. His small unit held out along Zapotillo Ridge until Gould's forces showed up and, along with several aircraft overhead, put the guerrillas to flight. After the enemy fled, Captain Robert Hogaboom (who would be awarded the Legion of Merit twice in World War II and later chaired the famous Hogaboom Board) climbed a tree and spotted the downed airplane.[128] The marines found no traces of the two aviators but noted that the Lewis machine guns were gone (Thomas and Dowdell had removed them but apparently discarded them at some point). The combined column then ran into another guerrilla force outside of Jicaro, and one marine and one Guardia were killed in the firefight. All in all, there were some twenty clashes with Sandino's forces during the rescue attempt, anticipating in some ways the remarkable fight to recover "Bat 21 Bravo" during the Vietnam War.[129]

Headquarters in Managua was now certain that the secret fortress must be real. Indeed, having reconstituted his forces, Sandino entrenched a portion of them in the strong mountain redoubt he called El Chipote.[130] In November the marines were busy observing the national elections and patrolling the towns that contained polling sites when, on November 23, Major Rowell discovered El Chipote some 26 miles from the Honduran border and 7 miles from Zapotillo Ridge.[131] He later described El Chipote as "a well-fortified mountain, with a great many trenches, and they had machine guns there. They had fields of fire cleared, and they had constructed shacks at each defensive position for the shelter of their men, and on top of the mountain were quite a number of these shacks they had built, some for storehouses, apparently, and some for dwelling places."[132] From the day of its discovery, marine aviators pummeled the fortress with machine gun fire and 17-pound fragmentation bombs carried by the DeHavillands and look-alike Boeings. On one occasion, Sergeant Albert Munsch in his DH engaged in a long-running duel with a Sandinista machine gunner on the ground, leaving his airplane "shot full of holes." When Rowell dived in his plane to call off Munsch's personal vendetta, one of Rowell's tires was shredded, resulting in a none-too-graceful landing at Ocotal.[133]

The air attacks were not having the desired effect, so Colonel Gulick decided to execute a joint air-ground operation against the stronghold, with two columns of marines and Guardia converging on El Chipote. Captain Richard Livingston, a forty-two-year-old former enlisted man, led a column of 114 marines and Guardia plus 213 animals in the pack train. He departed Jinotega on December 19 to meet up with Lieutenant Merton Richal's 40 Guardia from Telpaneca and Lieutenant Thomas Bruce's 20 Guardia, plus 117 animals, from Quilali. Concurrently, smaller patrols filtered north toward Ocotal.[134] When the columns were in place and ready to attack, the airplanes would be sent to support them.

Lieutenant Richal's patrol was attacked almost immediately, but it continued its trek, covered by Rowell's aviators. Captain Livingston's column—stretched out single file along the Camino Real, a narrow trail running along the Jicaro River—was also ambushed, but with the assistance of other marine aircraft, it managed to drive off the guerrillas. That said, it was an expertly laid ambush that killed five marines and wounded another eight, including Livingston.[135] Lieutenant Gould took over command of Livingston's column, and on January 1, 1928, he and his men were ambushed 6 miles northwest of Quilali. On point was Guardia Lieutenant Bruce, who was killed instantly. The guerrillas pushed back the advance guard of the patrol and rushed down the hill, looting and then mutilating Bruce's body with machetes.[136] Lieutenant Richal and his men came up immediately and were preparing to attack when Richal was shot in the face. Gunnery Sergeant Edward Brown took command, and the guerrillas were driven off. Fortunately, another patrol arrived, along with marine aircraft bombing and strafing likely ambush positions ahead of them.[137]

The next morning the columns combined and moved toward Quilali with airplanes overhead. The marines and Guardia entered the town with thirty-one wounded and were promptly surrounded by guerrillas. If the wounded were to be extracted, it would have to be accomplished by aerial evacuation. Richal made a desperate plea for air support. He wrote: "A full concentration of planes, with a thorough searching of all trails and a thorough bombing of Chipote . . . is most *urgently* recommended." He added: "If humanly possible, I recommend that a Corsair land here to evacuate the wounded."[138] The marines and Guardia then set about constructing a crude airstrip down the middle of Quilali.

Quilali was located in a deep valley surrounded by high mountains. The only level ground was the narrow grass-covered main road with a 3-foot drainage ditch running down the middle. As alluded to in Lieutenant Richal's request for help, the DH-4Bs and 02B-1s had been augmented by the recently arrived Vought 02U-1 Corsair, an airplane that would prove invaluable to air-ground operations for the remainder of the campaign.[139] A Corsair flown by thirty-two-year-old Lieutenant Christian Schilt and a second airplane dropped picks and shovels to the desperate marines on the ground, who promptly demolished houses on one side of the road, making a rough runway 70 feet wide and 300 feet long. The landing strip was completed on January 6, 1928.[140]

While a plan was being developed to relieve Richal's besieged defense, Lieutenant Schilt volunteered to bring out the wounded. He first replaced the Corsair's factory undercarriage with much larger wheels and tires from a DH-4B.[141] This would provide a smoother landing on the rugged airstrip, but the airplane would have no brakes. Schilt departed Managua in poor weather—heavy rain, fog, and low clouds. After a failed first attempt, he "dropped" his unarmed airplane through withering enemy small-arms fire onto the improvised runway, bouncing into the air before being brought to a stop by several marines who grabbed on to the wings. He recalled:

> On my next attempt, I decided to drop the plane onto the "field." The first drop was about 10 feet. I rolled a short distance and bounced

> thirty feet. Then the plane hit the ground again, bounced 10 feet, and rolled up to the deep ditch at the end of the "field." I got out of the plane, expecting to find half of it spread out on the ground. But I was surprised to find it intact. The first to greet me upon landing was Lieutenant Gould. His first words were: "My God, Schilt, an angel from heaven would be no more welcome than you."[142]

After loading the wounded Lieutenant Richal, Schilt took off under the covering fire of an escort plane flown by Lieutenant Lamson-Scribner. Captain Livingston was the next marine to be evacuated, "shot through the elbow with a dumdum bullet."[143] Over the course of three days, Schilt made a total of ten trips, retrieving the two officers plus sixteen wounded enlisted men, sometimes two at a time.[144] In addition, Schilt delivered a relief commander, Captain Roger Peard, and 1,400 pounds of provisions and medical supplies.[145] Schilt highly praised the Wasp engine–equipped Corsair, which took a considerable beating. For his heroism, Schilt was awarded the Medal of Honor, only the third such medal earned by a marine aviator and the first awarded to a "living airplane pilot for heroism 'above and beyond the call of duty.'"[146] With the wounded evacuated and a new commander in place, the battered column withdrew from Quilali under continuous air escort. Observation planes identified three guerrilla ambushes, and in each case the air escort drove them off; the column incurred no further casualties.[147] Thereafter, such "infantry missions" became routine.[148]

The Eleventh Marines Return to Nicaragua

The same month Captain Livingston's column was ambushed by Sandino's forces near Quilali, the Eleventh Regiment was reactivated under the command of Colonel Robert Dunlap, an artillery officer. Some 65 percent of the enlisted men of the regiment had just graduated from recruit training at Parris Island, and many had joined the Marine Corps to be musicians.[149] Nonetheless, the First Battalion sailed for Corinto from Norfolk, Virginia, and Parris Island aboard the Omaha-class light cruisers USS *Milwaukee*, USS *Trenton*, and USS *Raleigh*. They were joined in Nicaragua by the Second Battalion, which had sailed aboard the ammunition ship USS *Nitro* from San Diego. A third battalion was formed and traveled to Nicaragua on the stores ship USS *Bridge* and the former passenger steamer USS *Oglala*, a seaplane tender and minelayer.[150] The arrival of the Eleventh Regiment added well over 1,000 officers and men to the 1,145 marines already serving in Nicaragua.[151] Its arrival also restored Brigadier General Feland to command of the Second Brigade, returning Colonel Gulick to command of the Fifth Regiment.[152] With a force this size, it seemed only a matter of time before Sandino would be defeated.

But Sandino's stronghold at El Chipote remained intact. The guerrillas were dug in and well armed with rifles and machine guns, plus so-called *chula* weapons. Rowell claimed:

> Sandino, to bolster up the courage of his followers, had told them that he had a weapon absolutely deadly to airplanes. It was supposed to be the invention of an Indian genius and was known as "the Chula gun." The gun was really a small trough through which rockets, with sticks of dynamite attached, were shot in the air. . . . As we zoomed down on them with motors roaring, they began shooting their "Chula guns." The pyrotechnical display was wonderful and although the air waves caused by the dynamite explosions in the air rocked our planes, we were unhurt.[153]

Air patrols had continued to harass the fortress since its discovery, and they had encountered considerable ground fire, including from what appeared to be tripod-mounted heavy weapons. Captain Roger Peard, now at San Albino, was directed to march on El Chipote, and marine aircraft maintained continuous patrols over the column to protect it from ambush. On January 12 one of these air patrols spotted an ambush and attacked the guerrillas with bombs and machine gun fire. Less than three hours later, a second guerrilla force on the trail was broken up by air attack. Although the Peard expedition was reinforced with an additional 200 men, General Feland considered a ground assault on El Chipote too risky (the mountain peak was at 3,000 feet, and the only approaches were through steep ravines). He therefore ordered Rowell to attack the stronghold from the air alone. The timing was propitious, for all the DH-type airplanes had been replaced with four modern 02U-1 Corsairs. In addition, there were a handful of Curtiss Falcons (OC-1). With the Corsair, VO-7M could fly much farther on a single tank of fuel and deliver heavier bomb loads. Heralded as the "first independent and unsupported air attack ever made against a fortified position held by ground troops,"[154] Rowell's airplanes bombarded El Chipote on January 14 using

17-pound fragmentation bombs, 50-pound demolition bombs, machine guns, and white phosphorous hand grenades, the latter burning down wooden buildings and shacks constructed by the guerrillas.[155] According to Rowell:

> A swift approach was made from an unexpected direction, attacking in two columns without reconnoitering. The attack was met by a barrage of incendiary sky rockets [*chula* weapons]. We came down with the front guns wide open and opened up with light bombs at 600 feet. The rifle and machine gun fire was heavy and most of the planes stopped some bullets. The following ships came in with heavier bombs. After the second dive, the enemy broke cover and there was a wild stampede. . . . On the following day the mountain was devoid of bandits. According to Sandino's own statement, his entire army deserted him except about 150 of his old reliables.[156]

Despite Sandino's *chula* guns and several heavy machine guns, the Sandinistas were routed on El Chipote, as they had been at Ocotal (Sandino again claimed they had merely withdrawn from the mountain). Rowell had quite a scare, however, when his engine threatened to quit in the midst of the attack. As it "coughed and sputtered," he turned his Corsair toward Ocotal "and began working a hand pump [for fuel] desperately." Three times the engine was on the verge of failing, but Rowell managed to nurse the sick airplane to the airstrip at Ocotal. Upon landing and checking the engine, the lucky marine aviator discovered that "a horse-fly had become lodged under the needle valve in the carburetor. Just a common horse-fly, but he had almost brought the commander of the Nicaraguan air force down, and at a time and place where a forced landing would have meant certain death."[157]

Meanwhile, Peard's column received word that the air attack had succeeded and Sandino's forces in the area were dispersing. Marine patrols between San Albino and the Coco River reported numerous contacts with small guerrilla bands from Quilali to Telpaneca. A large marine force was then assembled to take El Chipote, under the command of Major Archibald Young. It took the marines six days to climb their way to Sandino's camp, and when they arrived, it was deserted.

Because it was Sandino's main base, many of the guerrillas had brought their families with them to El Chipote, and unfortunately, many women and children were killed and wounded in the air strike. As Michael Schroeder of Lebanon Valley College has definitively shown, many Nicaraguans at the time reacted to Marine Corps aircraft with fear and horror, and elderly Nicaraguans in the 1980s recalled numerous aerial "atrocities," including those at Ocotal and El Chipote.[158] Some claim that Marine Corps airplanes attacked villages haphazardly. Marine Corps veterans seemed to confirm that this was at least partly true. According to Major Harold Campbell, writing in the early 1930s: "While the ideal objective is the destruction of the enemy's main force . . . this objective is frequently difficult to obtain." Consequently, "an attack on something of importance to the rebels, such as their villages, crops, or herds, may force them to surrender or to give battle and so lay themselves open to defeat."[159] And it goes without saying that buildings, crops, and animals are easily targeted from the air.

That is not to say that the marine aviators deliberately targeted civilians. But as is the case in almost every small war, it was nearly impossible to distinguish between civilians and guerillas from the air. Thus, the marine aviators devised elaborate procedures to distinguish the civilians they were in Nicaragua to protect from the Sandinistas, just as the aviators in Haiti had sought to distinguish *bons habitants* from *mauvais habitants.* The main objective, as Rowell put it, was to distinguish the "normal" from the "abnormal."[160] When something on the ground seemed out of the ordinary, marine pilots would swoop down to investigate. Towns that appeared to be abandoned were especially suspicious. He wrote: "If the enemy is hiding there, some member of the party will probably decide to find a better place and make a dash for it. This may be induced by the patrol making a feint to attack. Under some circumstances, it will be possible to develop the situation by use of a few bursts from the front or rear guns. Occasionally a bomb may be expended for the same purpose."[161]

Major Rowell instructed his pilots to fly no higher than 2,000 feet and generally to remain at 1,500 feet or lower—well within small-arms range—to allow them to distinguish between men and women and to identify horses, cattle, and the like. He also stressed that his pilots and their observers should become "expert" in the "organization, equipment, and habits of the enemy" through careful study.[162] But as Major Campbell observed: "On diving to the attack, should the leader find that the hostile column has transfigured itself into a woman, with a highly tanned baby in each arm, he must let his conscience be his guide, and use his own judgment."[163]

The marines' judgment can be questioned. On April 4, 1928, Christian Schilt flew over a village southwest of Matagalpa, where he observed "about twenty-five men standing in the doorways of the houses. Three men were standing on the road, one armed with a rifle and the other two with machetes. Upon the close approach of the planes, these men ran inside one of the houses. This house was strafed with machine-gun fire but no one appeared. . . . The reason that the houses were not bombed [was that] approximately fifteen women and ten or twelve children were present."[164] Owning a rifle was not uncommon in Nueva Segovia, and most rural Nicaraguans owned machetes. The men had run, but Schilt had no way of knowing whether they were guerrillas because most peasants ran from airplanes—at least in the beginning. Over time, they realized that in order to appear "normal," they had to remain in the open. Ironically, appearing too unconcerned was also deemed suspicious.

Nevertheless, the marines tried to identify suspicious persons and often went to extraordinary lengths to avoid harming noncombatants. In his annual report dated June 20, 1928, Major Rowell recounted that marine aircraft would approach suspicious locales "from behind hills or mountains, the planes gliding in with throttled engines," whereupon the pilots would fly low enough to the ground so the observer in the rear of the aircraft could "look into windows and doors." As a counter to this extraordinary tactic, the guerrillas included women and children among their parties, "secure in the knowledge that the women [would] not be attacked." This is not surprising, given that Rowell and his crews were often (though not always) under standing orders not to attack towns and villages at all, even if the presence of guerrillas was indisputable. In February 1928, for example, Rowell discovered Sandino and his main column in the town of San Rafael del Norte. His fully armed patrol flew within a few feet of the building where Sandino was being interviewed by American journalist Carleton Beals, at a level "where the pilots and observers looked into the muzzles of the enemy rifles." But Rowell did not attack. He later wrote, "This rare opportunity was passed by because it was the policy of the Commanding General to avoid the possibility of injury to the lives and property of innocent persons by refraining from attacks on towns."[165]

In April, Rowell flew over Jocomico, where he observed a large number of horses near a ranch house. "Two men were in the yard but paid no attention to the planes. A woman with a baby and two children came out and stood in front of the house. . . . Several bursts were fired into the yard of the house, but no one paid any attention. . . . The actions of the persons there appeared abnormal under the circumstances [but] they were not attacked on account of the women and children."[166] Thus, there is no question that civilians were killed and injured by air attack, but it is also clear that the marines tried to avoid harming civilians, whereas European air forces attacked civilians with little if any compunction.[167] Even so, as is the case in every counterinsurgency in which civilians are harmed, the effect was to elicit hatred for the marines and their machines.

Nicaraguans were not the only ones who regarded the employment of airplanes in their country with disgust. Newspapers around the globe were highly critical of the tactics employed by the Marine Corps aviators. For example, "In Buenos Aires, [the newspaper] *Crítica* decried 'the American airplanes' offense against the Nicaraguan heavens, throwing hand bombs against the defenseless population.'"[168] Politicians in the United States, such as Senator Burton Wheeler (D-MT), "thundered that, while [President] Coolidge promoted pan-American friendship . . . 'the newsboys were selling extras telling about American bombing planes scattering death and terror over defenseless Nicaraguan villages.'"[169] This criticism angered Rowell, who wrote: "We are required to conform to all of the rules of civilized warfare, while the enemy will torture prisoners, murder the wounded and mutilate the dead."[170] Rowell had a point. The marines at least took some precautions to avoid civilian casualties, while European air forces routinely bombed and even gassed civilian populations in their colonies and protectorates.[171] Thus, although the scope of this study does not permit an in-depth examination, one can point out one of the peculiarities of air power history: proponents have often claimed that air power is a more humane instrument of war, whereas critics claim that bombs dropped from the air are somehow more immoral than artillery fire or economic sanctions—even if the latter results in a greater number of civilian deaths, which was the case in World War I.[172]

Continuing the Pursuit of Sandino

Sandino never again contested the American marines or the Guardia Nacional in positional warfare. In fact, Rowell noted that "the loss of [his] much vaunted stronghold was a severe blow to the prestige of Sandino," and afterward he "never occupied a position of any sort."[173] Thereafter, fearing the firepower of the Marine Corps' *lanzabombas* (as the Sandinistas called the airplanes), Sandino and his men resorted to traditional guerrilla tactics.[174] They moved mostly at night, camouflaged their encampments and stables, and confined their operations to terrain that offered cover from aerial observation and protection from aerial attack.[175] Consequently, the marine aviators no longer enjoyed the spectacular ground-attack successes experienced at Ocotal and El Chipote, whereas observation, reconnaissance, infantry missions (air escort, scouting, and liaison), aerial resupply, and air transport gained in importance.

Following his defeat at El Chipote, Sandino largely abandoned Nueva Segovia and withdrew to the even more rugged interior of the Prinzapolca department.[176] The Eleventh Regiment sent forces into the area, and some 200 "horse marines" were garrisoned at Matagalpa under the command of Major Keller Rockey. Mounted patrols sent out from Matagalpa were routinely escorted by airplanes to provide cover as well as to scout ahead for guerrillas lying in ambush. For example, on March 19 air patrols uncovered guerrillas with high-powered rifles and machine guns near Muy Muy.[177] As the ground patrols pushed deeper into the countryside, VO-7M aircraft maintained communications between the base camps and the patrols, and they also delivered supplies to far-flung units.

One especially famous example of the aerial delivery of supplies occurred when Captain Merritt "Red Mike" Edson led a series of patrols 350 miles up the Coco River, along the border between Nicaragua and Honduras. When Sandino's guerrillas fled Nueva Segovia, most of them moved east toward the coast. As a result, Major Harold Utley was placed in command of a garrison at Puerto Cabezas, which sent out patrols looking for guerrilla bands. At the time, Edson was in command of the marine detachment aboard the USS *Denver*, and fifty-six of his men followed him ashore to serve under Major Utley.[178] Captain Edson was convinced that the Coco River was the key to reaching Sandino, or at least to blocking his forces from reaching the east coast. The longest river in Central America, the Coco River runs 400 miles from its source in western Nicaragua to the Caribbean Sea. Edson believed that a waterborne patrol up the river, in conjunction with patrols on land, could catch Sandino in a pincer. He intended to use Miskito Indians as guides, as the Miskitos had no love for Sandino or other Hispanic Nicaraguans.

The first patrol, a reconnaissance ordered by Utley, departed on March 8, 1928. Edson took five marines up the river for three weeks in the *Zambita*, a 16-foot flat-bottomed launch powered by a motor salvaged from a

Model T Ford automobile and leased from an American living in Cape Gracias á Dios, at the mouth of the Coco. After returning to Puerto Cabezas, Edson fell ill with malaria, the first of four such spells. But Edson's reconnaissance was deemed a success, and Major Utley established a series of small garrisons in the Coco delta from which patrols were sent up other rivers. Edson's next task was to retrace his journey to the small village of Huaspuc (also known as Waspuc) to establish a blocking position. Accompanying him was Lieutenant Jesse Cook and thirty-seven marines, as well as a navy corpsman from Bluefields. The marines boarded the USS *Galveston,* which delivered them to the mouth of the Coco River to begin their movement upriver. The trip was arduous, but by April 14 they had reached Huaspuc. It was at this point that the aircraft squadrons would prove their worth in supporting the river patrol.

Late in April, Major Rowell dispatched three officers and thirty enlisted men to Puerto Cabezas, operating five Loening OL-8 amphibian observation aircraft.[179] The intent was for the amphibians to search for guerrillas and ensure that the patrols were never surprised by ambuscade. The Loenings were soon joined by Corsairs. In addition to the scouting and ground-attack missions, the planes were supposed to make deliveries—the amphibians landing on quiet stretches of the river, and the Corsairs touching down on sandbars to off-load supplies. If this was not possible, the aircraft would drop messages, supplies, and weapons from the air.[180] On April 28 two Corsairs flown by Lieutenants Christian Schilt and Vernon Guymon flew up the river and located Edson and his men. Schilt dropped a message requesting to land on a sandbar near Sansang, the most important village on the river and the site of a small garrison. Edson signaled that the surface of the sandbar was suitable for landing, and Schilt delivered a message from Major Rowell: Utley had been informed that Edson's force was "defeated" in a firefight and Edson killed; Utley was therefore sending additional troops with a radio set. Edson later wrote: "Beyond dispelling one good rumor of an outlaw victory and my own recent decease and burial, I [was] able to give them very little information."[181]

The reinforcements were led by Lieutenant Milo Carroll, who arrived at Huaspuc with the radio set on May 1. It was then that Edson learned that a patrol of marines from the Asheville-class gunboat USS *Tulsa,* under the command of Captain John Tebbs, had struck out from Puerto Cabezas inland toward the mines at San Pedro Pis Pis in an attempt to trap the guerrillas between his force and Edson's. But, unable to locate the guerrillas and push them toward Edson, Captain Tebbs had returned to Puerto Cabezas. Major Utley then sent two patrols toward the mines and ordered Edson to block the guerrillas' escape into Honduras. Edson pushed upriver along the Musawas Trail to Great Falls to lay his ambush.

After being informed by radio that two amphibians would fly from Puerto Cabezas to the village of Kuabul to establish liaison and obtain information about the guerrillas, Edson made for the village. The flight arrived on time and dropped a message: "Where are the bandits?" Because Edson and his men had no signal panels to communicate with the aircraft, they had to resort to spreading their undershirts along a sandbar to give the aviators the information requested. To the frustration of all concerned, however, the thick jungle canopy screened the pertinent trails from aerial observation, and neither Edson nor the aviators learned anything of value. The ambush had failed. In the meantime, Utley had sent three more patrols into the interior toward Bocay. Therefore, on his own initiative, Edson pushed on to Bocay and linked up with two of the patrols on May 31. Unfortunately, Sandino and his troops had already passed through the town and moved on, so Edson returned to Puerto Cabezas. The first Coco patrol was a failure.

Nevertheless, while inspecting the garrison at Puerto Cabezas, General Feland and Major Utley discussed the possibility of giving it a second try. A patrol of eighty-nine men (eighty-seven marines and two navy corpsmen from the cruisers USS *Denver* and USS *Galveston*) and two officers (besides Edson) would assemble at Bocay and start upstream on July 23. The objective was a concentration of guerrillas at Poteca, along the eastern edge of Nueva Segovia but protected from the marines in the northern area by impenetrable jungle. On June 15 Marine Corps aircraft bombed the guerrillas at Poteca, but it soon became clear they could be pushed out only by ground forces. General Feland promised better air support for the second patrol, mainly because none of the portable radios could transmit over such a great distance, and aerial resupply would enable the patrol to move more swiftly upriver.

The second Coco patrol went wrong from the start. They were not able to depart until July 29, and instead of eighty-nine men, Edson left Puerto Cabezas with only forty-six, owing to transportation problems. The remainder were to follow, led by Lieutenant Jesse Cook. Edson organized his force into two platoons of five squads each, plus a headquarters section. They moved out in native *pitpans* measuring about 35 feet long and 3 feet wide, each capable of carrying a squad plus the three Miskito boatmen hired for the job.

Each squad carried three rifles, a Browning automatic rifle, and the new Thompson .45-caliber submachine gun.[182] The officers carried Colt Model 1911 .45-caliber semiautomatic pistols. The marines carried no packs or haversacks, nor did they carry any tents. They had only enough food to last until August 4, when they were supposed to be resupplied by air. For the first five days out of Bocay it rained, and the Coco River became a raging torrent, slowing Edson's advance. Near Mastawas, the marines traded shots with some guerrillas and uncovered a cache of arms and letters from various guerrilla jefes. On August 4, as planned, two OL-8 amphibians flew low over the patrol at around noon, dropping mail and sixteen sacks of rations.[183]

During the airdrop,[184] one of the pilots saw signs of a guerrilla camp some 2 miles ahead of the patrol, and the two amphibians proceeded to bomb and strafe the area. Edson then took about half his men and headed toward the guerrilla position through the jungle. By doing so, he took them by surprise. Summoned by a messenger, the remainder of the marines moved up from the drop zone along the opposite bank. The firefight that followed was short and sharp. One marine was killed and three wounded. Sandino had been nearby, but he fled with some of his men when the OL-8s dropped their bombs. Nonetheless, ten guerrillas were killed, many were wounded, and the ambush was completely broken up. The Loenings returned that night to remove the body of the dead marine and evacuate the wounded. All were flown to Puerto Cabezas, and the three wounded marines were treated and survived.

The second Coco River patrol reached Poteca on August 17, following another firefight on the fourteenth that resulted in the capture of a high-ranking Sandinista jefe, Abram Rivera, the chief of Sandino's transportation service. On another occasion, an airplane "caught two raft-loads of bandits in the middle of the stream and dropped bombs right in the center of their rafts and did a lot of good."[185] Still, Sandino escaped again, and Edson headed downriver, back to where he started.

With the end of the second Coco patrol, the Northern Area Command, principally the marines of the Eleventh Regiment, now assumed greater responsibility for keeping Sandino and his followers on the move and off balance. Adding to the marines' burden was the fact that members of the electoral commission were arriving at their stations in towns and villages to supervise the national election in November, and the marines were tasked with escorting and guarding them.[186] But with Sandino temporarily subdued, prospects for a successful election had never been brighter. From a military standpoint, the Sandinistas had taken a beating. And although Sandino had not been captured and had not lost his magnetism, the constant pressure applied by ground and aerial patrols prevented the guerrillas from disrupting the election. Moreover, aviation would play a role in the election that contributed not only to counterguerrilla warfare but also to counterinsurgency.

The 1928 Election

As the hard fighting of 1927 and 1928 slackened, the marine squadrons in Nicaragua concentrated on observation, communications, and logistical support.[187] The aircraft squadrons proved very useful in these roles, but they proved even more useful in supporting the political process crucial to counterinsurgency. First, marine aircraft conducted psychological operations by dropping leaflets to peasants and Sandinistas alike. Thousands of propaganda circulars were dropped by aircraft, often directly over enemy encampments. According to Major Rowell, "They were really effective."[188] But more important than simply conveying propaganda, the aircraft squadrons played a crucial role in the democratic process itself: "It was necessary to ferry by plane most of the American personnel to outlying districts, to supply them there, to maintain communication with them, to patrol the towns and mesas on registration and election days, and, finally, to bring to Managua the ballots. In order to accomplish this work, flying time generally reached its peak during the weeks immediately before and after the election periods. . . . [O]n election day 237 cantons were visited by airplanes."[189]

The electoral commission was headed by a tough and uncompromising US Army officer, Brigadier General Frank McCoy.[190] Each of Nicaragua's thirteen election departments was supervised by an American officer, mostly marines but also navy and army officers. There were 432 polling places to guard, and the marines and Guardia were stretched thin. Despite Sandino's declared commitment to causing as much mayhem as possible during the election, it was conducted in a legal and orderly fashion in November 1928. Former Liberal general José Maria Moncada won the election by some 20,000 votes.[191] Both the Liberals and the Conservatives conceded the election had been fair, and the marines considered it their first "decisive" victory. And aviation played a crucial role. But the success of the election and the ascension of a Liberal to the presidency did not persuade Sandino to return to a normal existence. Instead of insurgency, he would now focus on resistance—that is, expelling the *Yanquis*.

Settling in for the Long Haul

Following the 1928 election, the marines continued motorboat patrols up and down the Coco River between Poteca and Santa Cruz, but the guerrillas declined to engage them. The main effort remained in Nueva Segovia. Meanwhile, the US Navy's Special Service Squadron, now under the command of Admiral David Sellers, continued to ply the waters off both Nicaraguan coasts.[192] By the end of the year, there were almost 5,000 marines and sailors in Nicaragua, including the two aircraft squadrons of the Second Brigade. But Republican Herbert Hoover was elected president at roughly the same time as Moncada, and he made it clear during his campaign that the marines would not stay in Nicaragua forever.

In the third year of intervention, a stalemate developed between the forces of Augusto Sandino and the marines. Many Nicaraguans refused to help the marines—some for nationalistic reasons, others for fear of reprisal from Sandino's troops. The marines could not force the people to support them, so the only solution seemed to be to place the Guardia Nacional in the forefront of counterguerrilla operations. From 1929 until their departure in 1933, the marines would act primarily as trainers of the Guardia, but also as leaders and advisers. However, in any situation in which the Guardia was overmatched, the senior marine officer in the area would assume command of combined marine-Guardia forces until order was restored. This would be the norm for the next three years. Thus, combat operations did not end, and marines continued to fight and die in Nicaragua.

In April 1932 an encounter between Guardia Nacional troops led by marines and Sandino's guerrillas was particularly deadly. Lieutenant Laurin Covington and eleven Guardia soldiers departed Apali with a pack train to supply the garrison at Jalapa. They were attacked by a large force of guerrillas near Las Puertas, where the road ran between two hills. Guerrillas on both hills opened with withering rifle and machine gun fire, and several Guardia were killed. Lieutenant Covington and four of his soldiers then charged one of the hills and dispersed the guerrillas. In the meantime, a column was launched from Apali, led by several marine officers and a navy medical officer, Lieutenant Whitehead, to rescue the pack train. They met up with Covington, and one marine officer and Lieutenant Whitehead headed back to Apali with the dead. They were attacked by guerrillas, and both officers and three Guardia were killed. The remaining officer, Lieutenant Johnson, heard the sound of gunfire and hurried to the firefight, routing the guerrillas. He later discovered that the two officers had been horribly mutilated; as a result, Lieutenant Johnson "lost his reason" and had to be transported to Managua by plane for treatment.[193] Such contacts remained common, and the intervention of Marine Corps aircraft saved many marines and Guardia.

Beginning in 1928 the marines established outposts throughout the interior of Nicaragua, most of which could be resupplied only by aircraft, and it was in support of these forward operating bases that aviation proved to be of immense worth. At the beginning of the campaign, supplies and personnel were transported by the light observation biplanes then operated by the squadrons under Rowell's command. But with the arrival of the first TA-1 Atlantic-Fokker trimotor transport in January 1928, flown by Major Louis Bourne, Lieutenant Jacob Platcha, and Master Sergeant Benjamin Belcher, the air transport mission evolved to a new level.[194] During its first six weeks of operation, this one airplane ferried 27,000 pounds of freight and 204 passengers. The trip between Managua and Ocotal normally required ten days to three weeks by oxcart and mule train, but the TA-1 could accomplish the same mission in less than two hours.[195] Indeed, according to Major Edwin Brainard, then with the navy's Bureau of Aeronautics, during the dry season it took "from three to five weeks" by "bull train" to get rations and other supplies to remote outposts, "and in the wet season it is impossible to get rations there at all. With the Fokker, the trip can be made in one hour and twenty minutes, carrying a ton of stores, including medical supplies, ammunition, clothing, etc., or eight men can be carried with their equipment and ammunition. The plane can make two round trips a day and if necessary, three, which means that three tons of stores can be moved daily."[196] Additional trimotors were immediately requested, and two more TA-1s arrived, one nonstop from Miami in March 1928.[197] These airplanes were subsequently reinforced by the more easily maintained all-metal Ford RR-2 trimotor transport, and VO-6M became a utility squadron, VJ-6M, which pioneered almost all the "air mobility" missions that are common today.

The Advent of Air Mobility

Military air mobility can trace its roots to World War I, but early aircraft did not have the power, range, or capacity to be genuinely useful in the air mobility role.[198] That said, for the United States, the first official air mobility mission occurred on September 7, 1918, when several US Army airplanes transported soldiers from Chanute Field, Illinois, to nearby Champaign.[199] The most famous effort was the largely ineffectual attempt to sustain the "Lost Battalion" (some 500 soldiers from the US Seventy-Seventh Division) by the Fiftieth Aero Squadron during World War I.[200] In short, air mobility did not play much of a role during the war. But that did not prevent air leaders from envisioning greater possibilities. For example, Brigadier General William "Billy" Mitchell conceived a bold plan to air-drop the US Army's First Division behind German lines using sixty squadrons of British-built Handley Page bombers. According to Mitchell's plan, the division would be wholly sustained by air once it was on the ground. Although the commander of the American Expeditionary Force, General John Pershing, found merit in the proposal, there were not enough bombers available, and the war ended before the plan could be implemented.[201]

Following the war, the US Army Air Service took no real interest in the "power projection" possibilities of air mobility because of the country's isolationist attitude, as well as Air Service officers' emphasis on bombers, pursuit aviation, and ground-attack aircraft. The subject of transportation aviation was not even taught at the Air Service Tactical School. Air mobility advanced primarily because of commercial aviation, which focused on moving people rather than cargo, and the airplanes designed for that purpose were not ideal for the long-range movement of material.

Nevertheless, the 1920s witnessed considerable advances in civil aviation technology, and the Air Corps (established in 1926) took advantage of the situation. The air staff in Washington argued that, to defend a country as large as the United States, air forces would have to concentrate wherever the enemy presented himself, and this would require their rapid movement. Air Corps maneuvers in 1927 validated this thinking, and by the end of the decade, the Air Corps sought to acquire commercially manufactured cargo aircraft to move combat air forces and their ground support. As a result, the First Air Transport Group (Provisional) was created in 1932, with one air transport squadron located at each of four strategically located air depots for the purpose of moving aircraft engines and other spare parts and related equipment to operational bases as required. But critical resource shortfalls persisted. The Air Corps claimed it needed 200-plus cargo aircraft to do the job, but only a handful were purchased. Thus, the Air Corps was forced to use bombers to accomplish the air mobility mission until the outbreak of World War II.

For the navy's part, single-engine amphibians (such as the Grumman JF Duck and the improved version, the J2F) functioned as ship-to-shore utility aircraft, carrying personnel and small cargo loads. Twin-engine amphibians (Sikorsky RS and JRS [S-43], Douglas RD Dolphin, and Grumman JRF Goose) carried heavier loads to and from coastal bases as well as to island bases. The navy also used a small number of off-the-shelf civilian land planes (Kinner RK Envoy and Beech Model 17 Staggerwing [GB]) as fast couriers. Since transport ships at sea adequately served the logistical needs of the Battle Fleet and forces ashore overseas, the few commercial airliner types procured (Fokker and Ford trimotor airplanes, Douglas DC-2 [R2D], and Lockheed Model 18 Lodestar) were used primarily for transporting very important personnel. The first true US Navy transport squadrons were not created until the latter part of 1941. The marines, however, quickly adapted the few Fokkers delivered to them by the navy for missions never envisioned by either the army or the navy.

The first Fokker F.VII / 3m trimotor acquired by the navy was identical to those acquired by the army in 1926 (and designated the C-2).[202] The navy purchased three of them (designated the TA-1). All three were assigned to VO-6M in Nicaragua in 1927. In 1928 VO-6M received two of the improved versions, the TA-2, which had a longer wingspan. The all-metal Ford RR trimotor acquired by the marines originated with Henry Ford's acquisition of the Stout Metal Airplane Company. Using methods developed in Germany by Hugo Junkers, William Stout pioneered the use of cantilevered, all-metal airframes skinned with corrugated "duraluminum." The army acquired and tested Ford's first trimotor, the 4-AT-A, powered by three Wright J-4 engines. It subsequently ordered seven aircraft with upgraded engines, designated the C-3A. In March 1927 the navy purchased the fourth 4-AT-A, under construction as the XJR-1. Two improved versions were then purchased, equipped with the 300 hp Wright J-6-9 radial engine. These were designated JR-2, and both were assigned to VJ-6M (formerly VO-6M) in 1929.[203] In 1930 the three TA-1s and two TA-2s were modified to accept the 300 hp Wright R-975 engine, and all of them were returned to service as the TA-3. When the navy adopted the designation "R" for transport in 1931, the TA-3s became RA-3s, and the two Ford JR-2s operated by the marines in Nicaragua became RR-2s. The RA-3s do not appear in Marine Corps records after 1932, and presumably they were withdrawn from service. The RR-2s continued in service until 1934.[204]

The transports were apparently flown mostly by enlisted pilots, although officers initially flew the airplanes to Nicaragua. For example, in his nomination for the Navy Cross, Master Technical Sergeant Archie Paschal was described as the "non-commissioned officer in charge of transport type airplanes."[205] In that capacity and as a line pilot, he had logged 1,040 hours, "flying over mountainous and partly unexplored jungle," often in bad weather, for "the purpose of locating and supporting ground patrols." During his time in Nicaragua, Paschal carried, "without mishap," 840,000 pounds of freight.[206] This was a remarkable record, for mishaps did occur. On August 4, 1930, a Ford RR plane flown by an enlisted pilot crashed upon landing at the Ocotal airfield when the ailerons locked. A fuel tank caught fire, but the aircraft did not burn. Even so, Staff Sergeant Robert Burns, the crew chief, was recommended for the Distinguished Flying Cross for his heroism that day, prying open the damaged cargo door so that he and two passengers could escape. He then returned to the airplane and "dragged Lieutenant [Roy] Gulick, who had been knocked unconscious, to safety."[207]

Because they were able to fly six tons of supplies per day, Rowell called the contributions of the Fokker and Ford trimotors to the brigade's mission "immeasurable." In his annual report submitted in 1928, Rowell wrote: "The list of serious emergencies that have been met by these airplanes is too long to include in this report. Entire garrisons in the most remote localities depend wholly upon the transports for supply, an entire regimental headquarters was transported to the front, minor troop movements are effected, the sick and wounded evacuated, casual officers and enlisted men are carried, the mail is delivered and emergency articles and materials of every conceivable nature are delivered with the greatest speed and efficiency." Although the transports operated only during the latter part of the period covered by this report, it is worth noting that they carried approximately 900,000 pounds of material and 1,500 passengers.[208]

In addition to carrying supplies, delivering the mail, and distributing payroll to marines at various crude airstrips around the country, the transports air-dropped weapons, ammunition, medical supplies, and rations to the deep-penetration patrols and conducted aerial spraying for mosquito control.[209] More importantly, they provided air mobility to concentrate ground combat forces. In November and December 1931 a large group of guerrillas operating in the Chinandega, Léon, and Esteli provinces threatened to overwhelm local Guardia troops. The prompt movement of additional Guardia soldiers by air and their rapid concentration at key points kept the guerrillas constantly on the move and off balance. The guerrillas ultimately quit the area.[210]

Innovation in Nicaragua

In an effort to explore the possibilities of vertical takeoff and landing, the marines sent an unusual airplane to Nicaragua in 1932: the Pitcairn PCA-2 Autogyro. The Autogyro derived its lift from an overhead rotor, in much the same way as a helicopter. "A single [Wasp] engine powered both the rotor and a front propeller. In taking off, the pilot first used a clutch to connect the engine to the overhead rotor. After bringing it up to takeoff speed, he switched power to the front propeller, leaving the rotor turning freely. The machine then was supposed to lift into the air after a short takeoff run and fly with the spinning rotor and stubby wings providing air lift. The autogyro could take off and land almost vertically, but it could not hover as can a helicopter."[211]

The PCA-2 was the first rotary-wing aircraft to achieve type certification in the United States. The airplane was the brainchild of Harold Pitcairn, who first ventured into flying in 1924 with the Pitcairn Flying School and Passenger Service, forerunner of the now defunct Eastern Airlines. In 1926 Pitcairn started the Pitcairn Aircraft Company to build his own airplanes for his growing passenger and cargo service. He then purchased an airfield in Montgomery Country, Pennsylvania, and began flying the PA-1 Fleetwing as a mail plane, as well as an improved version powered by a Wright Whirlwind, the PA-5. In 1927 he brought aboard friend and fellow designer Agnew Larsen, who at the time was working for the Thomas-Morse Company. Together the two men purchased a Cierva C.8W Autogiro and the manufacturing rights for the airplane, leading to the creation of the Pitcairn-Cierva Autogiro Company (later renamed the Autogiro Company of America).[212] In 1929 the company demonstrated the PCA-1 at the Cleveland air races, and in 1931 the *Detroit News* purchased a PCA-2 for aerial photography. That same year, Pitcairn landed a PCA-2 on the White House lawn. The airplane was also flown by Amelia Earhart, reaching over 18,000 feet on her second flight. She toured the country in a bright green PCA-2 as advertisement for the Beech-Nut Packaging Company. She crashed twice during the tour.[213]

Despite its limitations—it was difficult to fly and could carry only fifty pounds in addition to the pilot—the navy evaluated a PCA-2 in 1931 aboard the USS *Langley*, designated the Pitcairn OP-1.[214] It was the first rotary-wing aircraft to land aboard a US Navy ship.[215] The marines evaluated the machine as a possible search-and-rescue aircraft, recalling the crash and deaths of Thomas and Dowdell years earlier. The arrival of the Autogyro (nicknamed the Turkey Hen)[216] caused quite a stir in Managua, and the marines used it for publicity purposes as well as testing. On July 4, 1932, the Autogyro took part in air maneuvers celebrating American independence. Twelve aircraft participated, "from the little Corsair to the gigantic Fokker." The Autogyro took off and landed several times "with marvelous rapidity" at the Campo de Marte. Prior to one of the landings, a marine "made an intrepid descent in a parachute."[217] On the occasion of Nicaraguan president Moncada's visit to the marine airfield on July 29, Dr. Flores Vega, one of his ministers, went up in the Turkey Hen, the first Nicaraguan to do so. Apparently, the other minister accompanying the president, Anastasio Somoza García, declined.[218] Despite its success as a publicity venture, the Autogyro's limitations prompted the marines to conclude that, at best, it could be used only for reconnaissance purposes. Reconnaissance was a priority mission for the aircraft squadrons, and fortunately, Rowell had state-of-the-art aircraft available for that purpose.

The "Long War" in Nicaragua

Sandino's resistance activities decreased after the 1928 election, and during the lull, the Guardia Nacional took the lead in fighting the Sandinistas. The Aircraft Squadrons, Second Brigade, provided air support. The Guardia units first took to the field with strong marine elements maneuvering alongside them, but over time, fewer marines and more Nicaraguans fleshed out the patrols. By 1930, the Guardia was sending out independent patrols led by Nicaraguan officers. Although mutinies were a problem (there were ten in all), and seven marines lost their lives as a result, all but one occurred at remote outposts.[219] More troubling to the marines was President Moncada's decision to raise a paramilitary force known as the *voluntarios.*

The idea behind the *voluntarios* was not unlike that of the Guardia: putting a Nicaraguan face on operations in the field. The marines reluctantly agreed to the proposal, acknowledging that locally recruited volunteers might be better at interacting with their neighbors and kin.[220] The first "army" of *voluntarios* was formed in January 1929. Each army had a headquarters and four companies of twenty-five men each. The men enlisted for four months and were paid a dollar a day by the Nicaraguan government. The commanding generals of the armies, two from Mexico and one from El Salvador (all three had served under Moncada during the civil war), were paid by the US government. One of the three armies comprised mostly rural policemen. Seven companies were drawn from troubled areas in the southwest, and the eighth company was composed of "hillmen" from the area surrounding Somoto in Nueva Segovia. Marines and Guardia usually accompanied the *voluntarios* in the field.[221]

It soon became evident that the hillmen were far superior *voluntarios* than the men recruited elsewhere. Many of the latter were "former bandits," and one had participated in the Battle of Octocal in 1927 as a minor bandit "chieftan."[222] The hillmen were described as "intelligent, aggressive, and accustomed to life in the open."[223] In the opinion of one marine officer, "If all the companies [had] been composed of hillmen . . . the *voluntarios* might have accomplished a great deal more than they did. As it was, the native troops were practically helpless in the field."[224] In the end, "they failed to win the confidence of their own countrymen" and had a tendency to execute anyone they declared to be a bandit, often settling old scores.[225] Thus, when the enlistment period ended, two armies were quickly disbanded and not re-formed (in truth, most of the *voluntarios* had already deserted). The third survived for a time, but the marines eventually persuaded President Moncada to disband it too.[226]

Despite the failure of the *voluntario* experiment, the Guardia performed well, and it was enlarged under the command of Lieutenant Colonel Calvin Matthews, USMC. Nevertheless, President Hoover's new secretary of state, Henry Stimson, pointedly informed Colonel Matthews that, being in the employ of the Nicaraguan government, the Guardia should expect no further assistance from the US government. In short, the new American strategy was to turn over security duties to the Guardia Nacional as soon as possible, enabling withdrawal from the country (much as Haitianization and Vietnamization were intended to facilitate American withdrawal from Haiti and South Vietnam). But until the marines withdrew, they would continue to lead Guardia units, and one marine officer in particular became famous for leading "native" troops: Guardia Captain Lewis "Chesty" Puller—known as *El Tigre* (the Tiger) of Nueva Segovia.[227]

Puller and his second in command, Guardia Lieutenant William "Ironman" Lee, an enlisted marine, aggressively scoured the countryside for Sandinista guerrillas, leading two companies of approximately thirty men each. Puller and Lee were often in the bush country for weeks at a time, and Puller's Company M was especially effective. In fact, Sandino offered a bounty of 5,000 córdobas for Puller's head.[228] It was Puller and his men who fought the last official battle of marines versus Sandinistas on December 26, 1932, at El Sauce. The government had just finished a rail line to El Sauce, and a large group of guerrillas attacked a train from Léon carrying a contingent of Guardia headed to El Sauce for the opening ceremonies. Outnumbered and surprised, Puller and his Guardia soldiers nevertheless managed to fight off the guerrillas, capturing sixty-three horses and mules, as well as several rifles and ammunition. Three Guardia enlisted men and several railroad employees were killed.[229]

Toward the end of 1929, in anticipation of the Americans' evacuation, the arduous task of hauling stores of material from inland posts to Managua and Corinto began. In some cases, automotive transport was used, but the bulk was moved by oxcart, mules, and the trimotor transports. In August 1929 the Eleventh Regiment once again departed Nicaragua. On August 23, 725 enlisted men and 23 officers embarked on the USS *Henderson* at Corinto. This left only the Fifth Regiment. As a result, much of the reconnaissance mission, which included patrols over the desolate eastern region, was handed over to the aircraft squadrons. And it was a good thing they remained, for by the summer of 1930, Sandino had returned in force to take Jinotega. Once again, however, marine aviation thwarted his plans when a routine airplane patrol spotted Sandino's column and warned the Jinotega garrison.

For the next three years, the marines played a constantly diminishing role on the ground. Their primary role was to act as a reserve for the Guardia. Although Sandino's forces remained at large and well armed, the guerrillas avoided major contact following their failed assault on Jinotega. This was fortunate, for at this point the air patrols were the sole means of communication between field forces and headquarters. Telegraph lines were strung between the principal towns, but the guerrillas quickly cut them. Marines and Guardia were sent out to repair these lines, and one of these repair parties suffered the largest number of marine casualties during the Second Nicaragua Campaign. On December 31, 1930, a "line patrol" of ten men was ambushed near Las Cruces, northeast of Ocotal. Some 100 guerrillas surprised the patrol and managed to kill eight marines and wound two. Surprisingly, the guerrillas fled, and the bodies of the dead were taken to Ocotal.[230]

The next two years brought no peace, but major Marine Corps operations in Nicaragua were over. With the United States in the throes of the Great Depression, the Hoover administration was not interested in small wars like the one still raging in Nicaragua. Hence, even though the northern area remained infested with guerrillas, by May 1931, all marine units had been withdrawn to the southern area, in preparation to leave Nicaragua altogether. Having been withdrawn from the principal territory of guerrilla operations, the marines took up routine garrison duties. On the plus side, the campaign of attrition by the Guardia Nacional seemed to be bearing fruit. According to Marine Corps reports, most of the guerrillas originally inspired by "revolution" had died, surrendered, or returned to their former civilian lives. Those remaining with Sandino appeared to be genuine bandits, interested mostly in looting and pillaging. Even so, for the Guardia, the counterguerrilla effort remained as deadly as ever. And as before, the pilots and crews of the aircraft squadrons gave unstinting support to Guardia patrols on the ground, even those that were not officered or accompanied by marines.

The Earthquake of 1931

By the spring of 1931, US intervention was in its fifth year. On the last day of March, which marked the end of Holy Week, the most important festival on the Nicaraguan calendar, most of Managua's 60,000 residents were in the country visiting family or at the seashore. For those who remained in the city, there would be a procession of the Stations of the Cross on Good Friday, followed by the Easter Day celebration. By midmorning, the streets and the central market were crowded with people, mostly women and children. Colonel Robert Denig, chief of staff of the Guardia Nacional, was sitting outside the *Commandancia* (headquarters), being interviewed by an American journalist. Not far away, Captain Evans Carlson was writing his monthly report. He had recently captured a number of *ladrones*, guerrillas who posed as Guardia and raided large haciendas at night.

At 10:20 a.m. there was a tremor, followed almost immediately by violent shaking. Buildings began to collapse. Colonel Denig ran and fell, breaking his ankle. Carlson was thrown to the floor and stayed there until the quaking stopped. The Second Brigade commander, Colonel Frederic Bradman, wandered out of the *Commandancia* covered in dust and blood. Carlson led

Bradman to the brigade hospital, which was now just a pile of rubble. The navy doctors and corpsmen were trying to remove patients from the debris and place them in the courtyard. Sailors, marines, and Nicaraguans staggered about in shock. Only Carlson seemed cool-headed, directing others to take a head count and help the injured.

Managua was an old city, but it was built of solid adobe and roofed in red tile and was believed to be fireproof. But within the walls were wooden frames, and the tiles were overlaid with reed mats. Overturned cooking fires quickly turned the city into an inferno. The six-second earthquake had destroyed the central market, and men searched through the debris and the hundreds of bodies, looking for their wives and children. The 100-man police department was quickly overwhelmed and requested help from the commander of the Guardia, Major General Calvin Matthews. A command post was immediately set up at the base of the flagpole on the parade ground. General Matthews placed Colonel Walter Sheard in charge of sorting things out, replacing Denig as chief of staff. Within minutes, marine patrols were headed into the city with orders to shoot looters on sight.

The naval radio station, the link to the Special Service Squadron ships offshore, was flattened. Telephone and telegraph lines were down. But word had already gone out. A former marine operating the privately owned Tropical Radio Company, a subsidiary of United Fruit Company, had run to the radio station from his home and broadcast the following: "City of Managua, Nicaragua, destroyed by earthquake. On fire. Send help."[231] According to *Outlook and Independent Magazine*, "The earthquake and fire in Managua, capital of Nicaragua, showed the United States Marines at their best."[232] And this included the aviators and ground-support personnel of the Aircraft Squadrons, Second Brigade.

The day had begun with two routine patrols, one led by Major Ralph Mitchell in 02-U Corsairs and another in OC-2 Helldivers. Transport ships were in the harbor, waiting to be loaded with men and material arriving from Ocotal. "Aviation suddenly found itself without a mess hall, post exchange, sick bay, photographic laboratory, squadron offices, headquarters, operations office, telephone central, motor shop, machine shop, electrical shop, carpenter shop, fabric shop, metalsmith shop, quartermaster office, quartermaster storeroom, officers quarters, officers mess hall and kitchen, one half its enlisted barracks, water and electric lights, not to mention countless minor facilities. In fact it may be said that the only major facilities left standing and undamaged were the hangars and all planes, a galley, garage, test stand, armory, and two small store rooms."[233]

Despite the damage, the aviators and ground-support personnel immediately went to work. An emergency water system was built, drawing water from Lake Nicaragua. Emergency telephone lines were run into the city. Those who were not performing specific tasks were gathered together, armed, and dispatched to the city—some sixty men. Following the Tropical Radio broadcast, Pan American Airlines' radio station sent out its own shortwave message. With the brigade radio station out of action, these two private stations became the only means of communication with navy ships in the harbor and with the outside world.[234]

Patrols were immediately sent aloft to survey the damage to Managua and surrounding towns. Amazingly, only Managua had been damaged. Granada, Léon, and Corinto had experienced only minor tremors, which are common in Nicaragua. The fires in Managua, however, continued to rage, and by midnight, the American Legation had been destroyed. The next morning, an Isthmanian Airways plane from Panama landed with a journalist, and a United Fruit Company airplane arrived shortly thereafter with radio supplies and food. Two Pan American Ford trimotors also arrived, carrying medical supplies.[235] Meanwhile, a Marine Corps photographic airplane took aerial views of the city for planning purposes.

At 1:30 p.m. a US Navy airplane from Panama brought more medical supplies and a doctor. Thirty minutes later, additional supplies arrived aboard a navy Sikorsky transport. At 4:00 p.m. two OL-type planes and three Martin T4M-1s[236] arrived from the aircraft carrier USS *Lexington* with more supplies and four more doctors. Given that the marine squadrons were mostly combat aircraft, their first efforts were mainly emergency relief missions and aerial photography. However, the trimotors of VJ-6M would soon play a major role.

The Thursday after the earthquake, Pan American began running regular relief flights into Managua from various airfields around Central America. The marines of the aviation squadrons assisted Pan American employees "in every possible way."[237] The original airplanes from the *Lexington,* now off the east coast near San Juan del Norte, returned to the ship, but five T4M-1s and one OL-8 arrived with cots and blankets. Enlisted marine Archie Paschal piloted a Pan American transport to San Salvador, El Salvador, to obtain bread, and at 4:30 p.m. a Fokker Universal owned by the Tela Railroad Company in

Honduras arrived with fruit and radio parts.[238] Six more planes from the *Lexington* arrived the next morning.

On Friday, VJ-6M's trimotor transports and several from Pan American evacuated more than 180 civilians, mostly "foreign" women and children, from Managua to Corinto (the rail line was blocked by landslides).[239] They were then ferried to the auxiliary transport USS *Chaumont.*[240] That same day, "two Waco planes from San Salvador" arrived with more medical supplies.[241] At 10:30 a.m. the commander of the Special Service Squadron, Admiral Arthur Smith, stationed aboard the cruiser USS *Rochester* (accompanied by the hospital ship USS *Relief*), arrived by marine aircraft from Corinto. Two hours later, Ernest Swift from the American Red Cross arrived, sent to Managua by President Hoover to oversee relief efforts. Swift had traveled by train from Washington to Miami and then flew to Managua via Pan American Clipper. He later wrote: "One can not too highly commend the work of the Marine Corps." With the assistance of the Guardia, they "brought order out of chaos."[242] According to Ralph Mitchell, then commanding the aircraft squadrons:

> Aviation's biggest part in the relief work was its evacuation in conjunction with Pan American Airways . . . all being families of officers and enlisted men and civilian residents of Managua. . . . Excellent too was all the reconstruction and repair work and commendable was the work of the guards who walked the streets day and night to the point of exhaustion, and who then returned to carry on their aviation duties. Not a man quibbled, not a man complained, but all turned to whole heartedly and tirelessly for the common good. Worn out, exhausted and depressed pilots continued to fly their ships until the work was done. The showing was truly magnificent and every officer and man is deserving of highest commendations.[243]

Relief efforts continued long after Holy Week, with Marine Corps transports flying missions from the United States to Managua to deliver supplies. On April 4, for example, Major Roy Geiger flew from Philadelphia to Miami to Managua, hauling "500 cubic centimeters of anti-serum, 8,000 units of smallpox vaccine, 20,000 tubes of chloride of lime," and other assorted medical supplies.[244] Today, disaster relief and humanitarian assistance by air are routine for the US military, but the marines' efforts in Nicaragua were in many ways unprecedented, and the contributions of the aircraft squadrons were pioneering.

Marine Corps Aviation Leaves Nicaragua

Hauling relief supplies to Nicaragua in the aftermath of the 1931 earthquake and supporting the Guardia Nacional were not the only missions carried out by the aircraft squadrons of the Second Brigade. One mission in particular—supporting the democratic electoral process—set the conditions that allowed the marines to leave Nicaragua. As a result of negotiations between the two governments, the United States agreed to oversee Nicaraguan national elections once again in 1932, as it had in 1928. The assistance provided by marine aviators during the 1932 election proved invaluable and was described as the most extensive use of aviation in a political support role during the entire intervention in Nicaragua.[245] The result was an overwhelming Liberal victory, with the Liberals taking seventeen of twenty-four seats in the Nicaraguan senate and twenty-eight of forty-three seats in the chamber of deputies.[246] With the political situation reasonably stable, the marines began to leave in earnest, but aerial patrols continued and remained as dangerous as they had ever been.

On August 24, 1932, Lieutenant Raymond Rutledge was killed while coming to the aid of an amphibian that had gone down in a storm near Muelle de Los Bueyes in eastern Nicaragua. The OL's three-man crew of one officer and two enlisted marines had parachuted safely from the airplane.[247] Over several days, Rutledge maintained contact with the downed crew, dropping tools and supplies and also directing a ground patrol to their location. According to the citation for Rutledge's Distinguished Flying Cross,[248] his airplane simply crashed in the jungle. However, a Nicaraguan newspaper claimed he had been shot in the stomach by ground fire: "Rutledge, gravely wounded, threw the rudder over hurridly [*sic*], diving the plane at the ground at full speed. His flying companion, [Sergeant Orville] Simmons, who was still alive, broke his neck upon crashing, catapulted from the plane."[249] Regardless of what caused the crash, the bodies of the two aviators were recovered, returned to Managua, and sent by train to Corinto for shipment to the United States. The funeral procession from the airfield to the train station in Managua was accompanied by the Fifth Regiment band and two companies of infantry; it was overflown by four Corsairs, which leveled off and dropped roses over the station. The Corsairs continued to drop flowers over the train as it departed.[250] Happily, the amphibian's crew was rescued the same day by Guardia troops pushing up the Chilamate River, with covering aircraft overhead.[251]

In the fall of 1932 the White House ordered the marines' complete withdrawal from Nicaragua. November and December were spent moving tons of stores to Managua for loading aboard US Navy ships, and during the last days of December, the marines began departing from Corinto. On December 22 the Naval Transportation Service cargo ship USS *Sirius* left the port with several marine officers and 180 tons of cargo.[252] It was followed by another cargo ship, USS *Antares,* and the *Henderson.* By the end of the month, marine officers and men of the Guardia Nacional had resigned their positions and handed over complete responsibility for the constabulary to the Nicaraguans.[253] The *Henderson* had the honor of taking aboard the last remaining marines of the Second Brigade, which then disbanded after six years as a major unit of the Marine Corps.[254]

By late 1932, activity on the airfield at Managua signaled that something was afoot. Major Rowell had left Nicaragua in 1928, replaced in succession by Major Louis Bourne Jr., Major Ralph Mitchell, and Captain Francis "Pat" Mulcahy.[255] Not unlike the marines' departure from Haiti, Mulcahy concluded that the easiest and cheapest way to return the airplanes to the United States was to fly them there.[256] Accordingly, preparations were made, and the newspaper *El Comercio* reported that a hangar dismantled in late October had been reconstructed. According to the article, "This act has been the subject of much comment among the public, it being supposed the fleet of American planes has received order not to leave Managua. Still, the American Legation has made definite statements to the effect that not a single Marine will be left in Managua after 2 January."[257] Marine Corps records do not show why the hangar was taken apart and put back together, but the writer was correct: the marines were leaving, and that included the aircraft squadrons.

In a press release from the Navy Department on December 27, 1932, Secretary of the Navy Charles Adams announced that the Aircraft Squadrons, Second Brigade, would depart Nicaragua on January 1and 2, 1933, in accordance with the general plan to withdraw US Navy and Marine Corps personnel from the country.[258] According to Captain Mulcahy, the landplanes would depart in two groups—one traveling to Brownsville, Texas, by way of Central America and Mexico, and the other by way of Belize, British Honduras, to Havana and then on to Miami. Both groups would then fly to Quantico, with multiple stops along the way to refuel and rest.

The first group of seven officers and sixteen enlisted men, under the command of Cuckoo Boyden (Flight C), left Managua on January 1 with five Vought Corsairs and two Ford trimotors.[259] The second group of ten officers and fifteen men, under the command of Pat Mulcahy (Flight A), departed on January 2 in nine Curtiss Helldivers and one Ford trimotor.[260] Two groups of amphibians flying together (Flight B), comprising one Sikorsky and four Loenings, departed on January 1 with five officers and eight enlisted men, under the command of Major Harold Major. They flew to Miami, with stops in Honduras, Belize, and Cuba along the way.[261] After resting in Miami, they flew on to Quantico.

Once all the aircraft were in the United States, they flew to Quantico without mishap over several days. In February all the aircraft of the Aircraft Squadrons, Second Brigade, flew in a mass formation from Quantico to the Naval Air Station at Anacostia, Washington, DC, where they were met by the secretary of the navy; the Nicaraguan chargé, Luis Manuel Debayle; the commandant of the Marine Corps, Major General Ben Fuller; the chief of the navy's Bureau of Aeronautics, Rear Admiral William Moffett; and Major Roy Geiger, head of Marine Corps aviation. After circling briefly overhead, all the airplanes landed at Anacostia and were greeted by the distinguished visitors and others. Then they mounted their aircraft and returned to Quantico.[262]

In his privately published classic about American intervention in Nicaragua between 1912 and 1934, *Quijote on a Burro,* Lejeune Cummins wrote: "Perhaps the only subject regarding the American intervention . . . upon which all authorities are able to agree is the efficacy with which the marines employed the air power at their disposal."[263] Indeed, in his annual report for 1929, Secretary of the Navy Curtis Wilbur declared that Marine Corps aviation in Nicaragua had been "of inestimable value."[264] Thus, Cummins was moved to note: "It is probably not an exaggeration to say that the marine occupation . . . could not have been accomplished" without Marine Corps aviation.[265]

In the end, marine aviators could look back on this period as one of significant achievement. They had developed and refined their organization and tactics to fulfill their primary role of supporting their fellow marines on the ground, and this would prove equally valuable during World War II. Likewise, the marines had set the standard for the employment of aviation in small wars of the future. Major Rowell later wrote: "Probably no broader experience has been gained, or greater success achieved through the employment of aircraft in minor warfare, than that which attended the operations of our own Marines during the Nicaraguan campaign of 1927 and 1928."[266] Indeed, Marine Corps aviator and Nicaragua veteran General Vernon Megee wrote:

> It may be said that Marine aviation came of age during the Nicaraguan campaign. The lessons learned were incorporated in the training manuals later concocted for the guidance of a younger generation; the officers and men who flew in Nicaragua were destined to be leaders in the great Pacific war; the doctrine of close air support was refined to an exact science through the medium of instant and reliable radio communications; new and far more effective aircraft were made available under the impetus of all-out war to meet the conditions of major amphibious operations. All this spilled over, of course, into the subsequent Korean hostilities.[267]

MeGee and his fellow marines, aviators included, gave high marks to Sandino for his performance as a guerrilla commander. Megee wrote of Sandino:

> [He] planned his forays to avoid concentrations of strength on the part of his opponents. After the first year, he confined his troop movements to overgrown jungle trails, or to periods of darkness or inclement weather—thus countering the Marines' one advantage of supporting air. Furthermore, Sandino was able to control the civilian population within his zone of operations, either through political adherence or well-founded fear of savage reprisal. He lived off the country, necessarily, either through voluntary contributions or requisition. . . . He operated adjacent to a zone of refuge [Honduras]—into which his pursuers were politically forbidden to follow.[268]

As a retired general during the Vietnam War, Megee saw direct parallels between Nicaragua and what was happening in South Vietnam, and he urged a thorough study of the marines' employment of aviation in the Second Nicaraguan Campaign.[269]

Most important, the marines understood that there was a new kind of guerrilla in the offing, not the *cacos* and bandits of the past, but nationalists and ideologically inspired insurgents. As the *Small Wars Manual* warned, "If marines have become accustomed to easy victories over irregulars in the past, they must now prepare themselves for the increased effort which will be necessary to insure victory in the future."[270] In that regard, "There is no service which calls for greater exercise of judgment, persistency, patience, tact, and rigid military justice than in small wars."[271] And this includes the employment of aviation.

Epilogue

The Second Nicaraguan Campaign was the last time the marines would be employed in Latin America as a tool of the Roosevelt corollary to the Monroe Doctrine (although they would deploy years later to the Dominican Republic, Panama, and Haiti). From a strictly military standpoint, the marines learned a great deal in Nicaragua, and as General Megee noted, many icons of Marine Corps history who would go on to become famous if not legendary in World War II cut their teeth in Nicaragua as small-unit leaders—men like Merritt Edson, Evans Carlson, and Chesty Puller. The aviators in Nicaragua also learned a great deal, not only about leadership but also about air-ground operations and air mobility operations—men like Rusty Rowell, Francis Mulchay, and Christian Schilt, all of whom rose to general officer rank during World War II. While it cannot be said that the marines were victorious in Nicaragua, they did not lose. They were withdrawn as the United States turned its attention to domestic issues and the US Navy and Marine Corps turned their attention to the burgeoning threat posed by Japan in the Pacific. During World War II the marines would carve out a record of courage and war-fighting ability that remains their principal reputation today.

With the departure of the marines, Sandino ended his resistance movement (he had ended his insurgency earlier), but he continued to rail against his old antagonists in the government, and many of them feared he might return to his guerrilla ways. Even the election of his old mentor Sacasa did not mollify him. Nicaragua remained a troubled nation after the marines departed, and it was not long before President Moncada tampered with the Guardia Nacional and installed his cronies in its highest ranks. He placed Liberal Anastasio "Tacho" Somoza in the director's position; then Moncada named Somoza to be war minister. Thus, it was not long before plans were implemented to get rid of Sandino once and for all. Gathering secretly in February 1934, Tacho Somoza and other senior Guardia officers signed a resolution entitled *La muerte de césar* (the death of Caesar), a death warrant for Sandino. On the evening of February 21, Guardia soldiers rounded up Sandino, his brother, and some of Sandino's followers after a dinner hosted by newly elected president Sacasa. They were all shot to death near the old flying field that had once been occupied by the Aircraft Squadrons, Second Brigade. Two years later, Somoza overthrew the Nicaraguan government in a military coup and instituted an authoritarian regime that would last until the Frente Sandinista de Liberación Nacional (FSLN), or Sandinista National Liberation Front, overthrew his son, Anastasio "Tachito" Somoza, in 1979.

Americans Lee Mason and William Brooks in a Laird Swallow preparing to attack Liberal forces, perhaps during the battle for Chinandega. The effect of the air attack was to stampede the Liberals from the town. Note the crude homemade bombs being used. Two Swallows constituted the entire Nicaraguan air force.

The original airfield at Managua, Nicaragua, with DH planes in view. Later the marines would construct a new airfield with barracks, hangars, and maintenance facilities. The marines also built other airfields around the country, including the principal airstrips at Ocotal in the north and Puerto Cabezas on the east coast.

Ross "Rusty" Rowell served as a recruiter and an artillery officer before learning to fly in Haiti. At age thirty-nine he became a naval aviator, took advanced flight training (including dive-bombing) at Kelly Field in San Antonio, Texas, and then took command of VO-1 at San Diego.

A DH plane belonging to VO-1M (one of six) being unloaded at Corinto on the west coast of Nicaragua. The Second Nicaraguan Campaign officially began on August 27, 1926, and lasted until March 30, 1930. The marines remained in Nicaragua, however, until 1933.

Message pickup by a DH-4B. Francis Pierce and Arthur Page first came up with this idea at Quantico. As seen in the photograph, the pilot flies low over the message, which is contained in a bag strung between two poles. The pilot snags the bag with a weighted line, and the observer hauls it into the airplane.

An O2U-1 Corsair being reassembled after shipment to Nicaragua. The Corsair was in such demand owing to its performance that the entire November 1928 production of the airplane was sent to the marines in Managua under urgent orders.

A Corsair fully armed with bombs under the wing. Flying a Corsair with DH-4B landing gear and no brakes, Christian Schilt made ten flights into Quilali to evacuate two officers and sixteen enlisted men while delivering a relief commander and supplies. Schilt praised the Wasp-engined Corsair, which took a beating.

Christian Schilt wearing the Medal of Honor (the Tiffany Cross design) awarded by President Calvin Coolidge on the White House lawn. Schilt's medal was only the third awarded to a Marine Corps aviator and the first to a living airplane pilot.

Merritt "Red Mike" Edson with his naval aviator wings pinned to his chest. Edson would lead a series of patrols up the Coco River between Nicaragua and Honduras, supported by aircraft from Puerto Cabezas.

An OL beached alongside a 30-foot *pitpan* at Huaspuc. The native boat was capable of carrying a squad of marines plus three Miskito boatmen. Marine aircraft searched for guerrillas, provided close air support, and resupplied the river patrols, often landing on sandbars or on the river itself.

Old and new: the standard Nicaraguan means of transport, a bull cart, alongside a Marine Corps trimotor transport. Enlisted pilot Archie Paschal is in the group to the right (front row, fourth from the left). Trimotors transformed the air mobility mission in Nicaragua and formed the basis of a new "utility" squadron, VJ-6M.

A Pitcairn OP-1 Autogiro in flight. In addition to being very adaptive to the circumstances they found themselves in throughout the small wars era, the marines embraced innovations such as the PCA-2 Autogyro, which employed a Wasp engine to power the overhead rotor and the front propeller.

A lone marine makes his way through the rubble after the earthquake in the spring of 1931. Marine Corps, navy, and civilian aircraft brought tons of relief supplies to Managua, and the trimotors evacuated marines' dependents to Corinto, where they boarded the auxiliary transport USS *Chaumont*.

Francis "Pat" Mulcahy was the last commander of the Aircraft Squadrons, Second Brigade. He concluded that the cheapest and easiest way to return the brigade's airplanes to Quantico was to fly them there. Mulcahy went on to command the "Cactus Air Force" during the battle for Guadalcanal in World War II.

A good view of the Marine Flying Field at Managua in 1933. Note the variety of aircraft: landplanes, seaplanes, trimotors, and the Pitcairn Autogyro (lower left corner, near the bend in the road). Note also that deconstruction of one of the hangars is under way. Lake Managua is visible in the distance.

Conclusion

> We cannot undo the past, but we are bound to pass it in review, in order to draw such lessons as may be applicable to the future.
>
> Winston Churchill

The late military historian John Keegan wrote that "continuities, particularly hidden continuities, form the principal subject of historical inquiry." It is the identification of "links between the past and present which most readily helps us to understand the world our ancestors lived in and, in so doing, to increase our comprehension of our own," to put our own actions in context.[1] Even so, B. H. Liddell Hart warned that history "has limitations as a guiding post . . . for although it can show us the right direction, it does not give detailed information about the road conditions."[2] Hart believed history's negative value as a warning sign is more definite (something with which Thucydides undoubtedly would have agreed). "History can show us what to avoid, even if it does not teach us what to do—by showing the most common mistakes that mankind is apt to make and to repeat."[3] Thus, although historians learn to beware the pitfalls of apparent continuities and warn their readers of these same dangers, continuities do exist.

One of the relevant martial lessons from the past that we seemingly have to relearn over and over again is the distinction between small wars and "conventional warfare." Conventional warfare is based on three essential elements: position, formation, and concentration. The idea behind position is that a conventional or regular army must be able to conquer, hold, and defend some kind of vital ground, be it an industrial region, a capital city, or a line of communication. Tactically, unfavorable ground can be traded for better ground, and space can be traded for time through the art of maneuver. Nevertheless, conventional armies generally must take and hold something. For this reason, conventional warfare is often rightfully called "positional warfare." Indeed, inasmuch as conventions are culturally relative, the word "positional" is a more objectively descriptive and meaningful term. Unfortunately, conventional warfare tends to train the mind that unconventional or irregular warfare is inferior, even *unfair,* and therefore unworthy of the soldier's professional attention. This is especially true for the aviator, who prefers easily identifiable targets. But guerrillas and other irregulars rarely take and hold ground, and they work hard not to expose themselves to air attack. Thus, as my coauthor James Corum and I concluded in our book *Airpower in Small Wars,* "The support role of airpower (e.g., reconnaissance, transport, etc.) is usually the most important and effective mission" for aviation in small wars.[4]

Small Wars

From the point of view of an established government or occupying power, dealing with irregular opponents (insurgents and others) can be likened to exterminating unwanted pests—cockroaches, killer bees, fire ants, rats, and the like. Like such vermin, guerrillas and resistance fighters tend to display certain common traits. Whether they constitute a mere irritant or present a serious threat to the stability of a nation depends on the level of infestation and the ability of the government or occupying force to deal with them in an appropriate and timely manner. Responses to rebellion, resistance, and insurgency also tend to follow certain patterns, although copying successful techniques from one situation to another is no guarantee of success (and is the principal drawback of the current counterinsurgency doctrine of the US armed forces). Thus, there is much that current armed forces can learn from the past, in terms of both how internal conflict manifests itself and the ways and means to bring about its end. Adaptation and innovation are the keys, and aviation can play a decisive (though not *the* decisive) role in that regard.

An insurgency (or resistance movement) gives rise to a corresponding counterinsurgency, creating what is, fundamentally, a contest of wills. On one side is the government or occupying power. While the government may exert a modicum of control, "Elite intransigence [and] reactionary policies . . . exacerbate rather than rectify a dissynchronized social structure . . . or violate the formal, envalued norms of the system" the elite is trying to preserve.[5] This was certainly true in Haiti and was arguably true in the Dominican Republic and Nicaragua as well. With regard to resisting an occupying power, history is replete with examples of peoples willing to fight to the death to expel the outsider, from the ancient Hebrews to the American Indians. Who emerges as the victor depends on a number of factors, but ultimately, it boils down to whose will holds out and whose does not. The struggle for motivation becomes decisive. As Friedrich Freiherr von der Heydte claimed, "Victory in irregular war does not signify . . . that the adversary has been militarily defeated, but it always signifies that he is exhausted and bled dry, that he is psychologically defeated."[6] In short, in big wars as well as small, the loser is the side whose will breaks first.

Surveying the literature of small wars, one concludes that the strengths and weaknesses of the irregulars, as well as their strategies and tactics, have remained fairly constant over time, regardless of place, cause, and even technology. In comparing regular forces with guerrillas and other irregulars, Callwell wrote:

> It is a singular feature of small wars that . . . regular forces are upon the whole at a distinct disadvantage as compared to their antagonists. . . . In great campaigns the opponent's system is understood; he is guided by like precedents, and is governed by the same code; it is only when some great reformer of the art of war springs up that it is otherwise. But each small war presents new features, and these features must if possible be foreseen or the regular troops will assuredly find themselves in difficulties and may meet with grievous misfortune.[7]

Among the advantages enjoyed by irregular forces are mobility, intelligence, limited logistical requirements, and fighting on home turf. Tactics common to all "movements," whether rebellious tribesmen or revolutionary insurgents, are hit-and-run attack, ambush, assassination, sabotage, and general harassment of government and military targets before fading back into the population or to remote bases.

Thus, another relevant martial lesson for any major state (including the United States) engaged in a small war at the dawn of the twenty-first century is to appreciate the distinction between the conventional style of warfare it prefers and the styles of warfare common in the developing world and largely feared and misunderstood in the West. This is important because such unconventional warfare is the type most likely to be encountered in the future. However, this is not the first generation to face such threats. The United States has had considerable experience with small wars of the type proliferating around the globe today. American history is littered with armed conflicts involving irregular warfare, and the US military has a veritable storehouse of information that can be used by analysts, planners, and commanders to construct a workable campaign design to counter unconventional types of war. Yet civilian and military decision makers tend to overlook these case studies in their attempts to craft strategies and plans. Thus, the late Bernard Fall, a remarkably astute student of irregular warfare and, in particular, of the war in Vietnam, aptly wrote in 1964: "American readers—particularly those who are concerned with today's operations in South Vietnam—will find to their surprise that their various seemingly 'new' counter-insurgency gambits, from strategic hamlets to large-scale pacification, are mere rehashes of old tactics to which helicopters, weed killers, and rapid-firing rifles merely add a new dimension of speed and bloodiness without basically changing the character of the struggle."[8] Although Fall would have been better served by remarking on the nature of the struggle rather than its character, his allusion to the role of air power was on point. As he noted elsewhere with regard to air power's contribution to counterinsurgency, the enemy "hardly offers conventional aerial targets."[9]

Unfortunately, the lessons of these earlier conflicts are too often recorded rather than learned (and are soon forgotten), and they have recently had to be relearned in places like Iraq and Afghanistan. The most basic lesson remains, however, that small wars cannot be fought using the conventional strategies and tactics of "major theater war." As Callwell famously wrote, the "conditions of small wars are so diversified, the enemy's mode of fighting is often so peculiar, and the theatres of operations present such singular features, that irregular warfare must generally be carried out on a method totally different from the stereotyped system." Indeed, "the conduct of small wars is . . . in certain respects an art by itself, diverging widely from what is adapted to the conditions of regular warfare."[10] The authors of the Marine Corps' *Small Wars Manual* were certainly cognizant of this fact when they wrote: "Small wars demand the highest type of leadership directed by intelligence, resourcefulness, and ingenuity."[11] As noted earlier, flexibility, adaptation, and innovation are the keys to success in small wars, so it seems axiomatic that aviation would play an important if not a decisive role in countering guerrilla tactics and suppressing insurgencies of different stripes. Thus, the best way to counter irregular warfare is by understanding it and responding to it in an appropriate manner. To paraphrase Sun Tzu, if you know yourself and know your enemy, you may fight a hundred battles without disaster.

That said, insurgency, terrorism, and even guerrilla warfare seem different today. The "bad guys" have access to weapons, communications technology, and other resources that the *cacos* and bandits faced by the marines did not. But in truth, it is a matter of degree, not kind. The Sandinistas were well armed with modern machine guns and other weapons. Consequently, the authors of the *Small Wars Manual* were moved to write:

> If marines have become accustomed to easy victories over irregulars in the past, they must now prepare themselves for the increased effort which will be necessary to ensure victory in the future. The future opponent may be as well armed as they are; he will be able to concentrate a numerical superiority against isolated detachments at the time and place he chooses; as in the past he will have a thorough knowledge of the trails, the country, and the inhabitants; and he will have the inherent ability to withstand all the natural obstacles, such as climate and disease.[12]

Any veteran of the wars in Iraq, Afghanistan, and South Vietnam can corroborate this salient point. Thus, "fifth-generation warfare" and "hyperechelon warfare" may be novel in some respects, but in other important ways, they are old wine in a new wineskin.[13]

Fortunately, states and conventional militaries have one major advantage over guerrillas: aviation. That said, small wars theory makes it clear that the employment of aviation must be adapted to the unique conditions of each small war. In conventional warfare, the most decisive use of aviation is rapid concentration of firepower against the enemy at some "decisive point." This is rarely possible in counterguerrilla warfare (the marines' air attack on El Chipote in Nicaragua being the exception that proves the rule). Any attempt to bring decisive, devastating firepower down on guerrillas is usually doomed to failure (and ultimately counterproductive if innocent civilians are killed in the process).

While aviation may not be as "decisive" as it purports to be in conventional warfare, it offers many significant advantages, as the marines learned between the world wars. Aviation can assist ground forces by providing indirect support in the form of operational mobility (to and from remote regions), tactical mobility (within regions), medical transportation, supply, command and control, intelligence, reconnaissance, surveillance, and target acquisition. Moreover, aviation is often the most efficient tool—sometimes the *only* tool—to support elections and other political activities in remote regions. As the marines ably demonstrated in Nicaragua, aviation can contribute significantly to free elections and other legitimate government functions. Aviation can also conduct psychological operations aimed at hostile elements, as well as deliver propaganda to the general population. That said, direct support can occasionally be significant as well, taking the form of close air support, driving off ambushes (infantry missions, now generally termed "armed overwatch"), and even the rare opportunity for tactically independent bombing missions.

The history of small wars during the interwar period reveals that aviation was used in many parallel roles by the United States and the major European powers. Each country employed aviation as a powerful tool to support its ground forces, which is as it should be. At the same time, there was a key difference between the European and the American approach to small wars: European states utilized some form of "air control" that emphasized the lethality of aviation, whereas the US Marine Corps used aviation according to a theory of restrained combined-arms operations. This difference in the use of aviation was derived from the traditional difference in outlook with respect to small wars in general. Europeans viewed small wars primarily as a military problem to be solved through punitive measures, while the United States viewed military intervention in broader political, psychological, economic, and cultural terms. There is no question that the marines often failed in that regard, but the point is that they made the leap from nineteenth-century punitive expeditions and interposition to intervention and counterinsurgency as we understand these concepts today.

Lessons Learned

The employment of aircraft to counter rebellion, resistance, and insurgency began almost immediately after World War I. Since that time, the advantages of aviation have belonged almost exclusively to the regular forces of the government or to intervening forces, not to the enemy. Properly employed, aircraft (manned and unmanned, fixed and rotary wing, civil and military, heavier and lighter than air) have the ability to eliminate or mitigate many of the inherent advantages of the guerrilla. However, the nature of the irregular enemy (small dispersed units, little to no infrastructure) provides little in the way of "strategic" targets for attack by aerial forces, so most air operations must be of the tactical variety, either in direct or indirect support of ground forces (military, paramilitary, police). And although technologies continue to evolve (often to the advantage of the irregular enemy), they have added little to the fundamental roles and missions allotted to aviation that were pioneered in some form by the Marine Corps between the world wars, some of which predated the invention of the airplane (reconnaissance, communication, and artillery spotting, to name a few).

One of the more significant advantages that aviation can offer to security forces is "leverage." Supported by airplanes, a small ground force can exert the military effectiveness of a much bigger unit or even several units. Following World War I, the British demonstrated this by "air policing" some of their colonies and protectorates. But during the heyday of air policing, the British were not terribly concerned about the "hearts and minds" of native peoples and vigorously subdued any sign of native rebellion. Thus, the Royal Air Force was used to punish rebellious tribesmen and others from the air.[14] This was accomplished much more rapidly than would be possible with ground forces alone. The British soon discovered that using airplanes with bombs and machine guns to inflict pain on rebels was more cost-effective than maintaining large numbers of British regulars in-country.[15] This was especially important given the expansion of the British Empire following the war. And despite some negative reports that reached Parliament detailing heavy-handedness against the "natives," many politicians claimed that the prompt use of aviation stopped tribal insubordination in its tracks. Such innovation became the hallmark of aviation between the wars, and the marines were quick to take note.

Adaptation and innovation were prominent features of the Marine Corps' experience during the so-called Banana Wars of the early twentieth century. As noted earlier in this book, the Marine Corps was credited with pioneering dive-bombing as a tactic in small wars, but whether the marines invented dive-bombing is not the point. Marine aviators embraced dive-bombing as an aerial tactic to precisely deliver ordnance close to their fellow marines on the ground. This led to other innovations employed by the marines: the use of signal panels to communicate with aircrews, as well as the novel method of suspending messages between two poles to be "snagged" by an airplane trailing a wire. The airplane also played a vital role in supplying remote garrisons and deep-penetration patrols in the field, and on more than one occasion, aircraft defended outposts from guerrilla attack. Of course, the marines were quick to claim that the air attack on Ocotal in Nicaragua was the first time an enemy had been driven from the battlefield by airplanes, independent of ground attack; however, the real innovation was air-ground coordination, communication, and cooperation. Indeed, air-ground coordination became the trademark of the Marine Corps in later years, and it remains so today.

Yet another innovation pioneered by the Marine Corps was the use of airplanes to support "civic action" and "civil affairs."[16] Marine Corps aircraft supported the elections in Nicaragua in 1928 and 1932, contributing to the democratic process. They also moved medical personnel and other specialists around Hispaniola and Nicaragua to serve local communities. Other civic actions included humanitarian assistance and disaster relief. The most notable occurred after the earthquake devastated Managua, Nicaragua, in 1931. Marine Corps airplanes were launched immediately to survey the damage and provide commanders and government officials with "situational awareness"—some idea of where help was needed most. Beginning the next day and for days afterward, Marine Corps airplanes brought in food, medicine, and other supplies from around the region and from the continental United States. In the end, Marine Corps aircraft flew scores of relief and evacuation sorties as part of a coordinated civil-military operation directed by a Red Cross official.

As part of the civil affairs mission, Marine Corps airplanes carried government officials, both American and local, from one place to another, anticipating the use of light planes for this purpose by President Ramon Magsaysay during anti-Huk operations in the Philippines during the 1950s. As secretary of defense and later as president, Magsaysay used the Filipino air force to conduct surprise inspections of government agencies such as post offices. He also visited military units to ensure that they were being properly led and were not being used to oppress the local population. Finally, he traveled to remote villages to meet with peasant leaders and ordinary citizens to hear their grievances. This kept military leaders and government employees on their toes, and it indicated to the people on Luzon and the other islands that the government cared about them. Taking its cue from Magsaysay, the United States deployed Detachment Three (a US Air Force special operations unit) to Howard Air Force Base, Panama, to conduct civic actions and train regional troops in counterguerrilla warfare in the 1960s. This robust civic action program provided assistance of all kinds, including a mobile medical unit that was flown to remote locations aboard a U-10 Helio Courier light utility plane.

Thus, the marines pioneered virtually every role and mission that is commonplace for today's air forces (including army and naval aviation), as witnessed in Iraq and Afghanistan. These roles and missions can be divided into three categories: logistical support, intelligence support, and combat support. Although this general classification is subjective, it is useful in describing how aviation was employed by the Marine Corps during the interwar period. Logistical support covers a great variety of missions, including aerial supply and resupply, airlift of personnel, medical transportation, communications, and support of long-range ground operations, including riverine operations. The intelligence support role includes scouting, reconnaissance, observation, surveillance, and mapping missions. Combat support missions fulfill the immediate needs of the ground forces through close air support and armed overwatch.

From a logistical perspective, the marines pioneered the use of state-of-the-art transport aircraft to provide an operational and tactical advantage, that is, rapidly transporting supplies between locations or dropping them directly to fielded forces, including far-flung patrols and deep-penetration "hunter-killer" teams. This reduced the dependence of scattered outposts and patrols on land-based supply lines and pack trains, and it reduced the financial and manpower burden of operating and protecting supply depots. Moving supply lines into the sky also reduced their vulnerability to guerrilla attack. In addition to delivering supplies, marine aircraft proved useful for transporting troops within the theater, enabling commanders to decisively concentrate their forces against guerrilla formations.[17] The marines developed this "combat multiplier" during the latter stages of their time in Nicaragua, when the Guardia Nacional had taken over the burden of security for the country.

Another logistical contribution to small wars operations adopted if not entirely pioneered by the marines was the use of airplanes for medical evacuation. Care and transport of the sick and wounded had long been a considerable burden on patrols and flying columns in small wars. Unless they were evacuated, the wounded, sick, or otherwise disabled were an encumbrance to a patrol's mobility, effectiveness, and even survivability. Moreover, the patients' medical needs could rarely be satisfactorily met in the field. Therefore, the advent of the "air ambulance" had the dual effect of increasing the combat effectiveness of the patrols and increasing the survival rate of the sick and wounded. Both these factors, in turn, greatly improved morale. In Haiti and the Dominican Republic the marines recognized the utility of the air ambulance and ultimately modified two DH airplanes to serve that purpose. In Nicaragua the marines fulfilled the medical evacuation mission with the large Fokker and Ford trimotor transports. Even so, the marines continued to use combat aircraft that were not specifically designed for casualty evacuation as the need arose, usually to evacuate personnel from emergency landing fields.

Besides logistical support, Marine Corps aircraft fielded during the small wars era provided intelligence support such as scouting, reconnaissance, observation, and aerial mapping and photography. For the marines, airplanes assumed the role of cavalry in the reconnaissance mission. Aerial mapping and photography provided commanders with situational awareness, both locally and theater wide. The marines expended considerable time and resources conducting these missions, and marine commanders extolled their contributions in their reports, which made their way to Marine Corps Headquarters in Washington. Anticipating modern intelligence, surveillance, and reconnaissance (ISR) missions, the marines pioneered the employment of the airplane as an ISR platform, just as they pioneered the use of transport aircraft for air mobility missions not then envisioned by the army or navy. Logistical and intelligence-gathering missions enhanced the performance of Marine Corps aviation in its more heralded form: combat support.

Every major power involved in small wars has used aviation in the role of combat support. Two specific missions generally make up the combat support role: armed overwatch and close air support.[18] The job of Marine Corps aircraft performing the armed overwatch mission (then called infantry missions) was to prevent ambushes, provide warning of guerrilla attacks, and provide fire support to marines patrolling on the ground. Scouting and infantry missions were inextricably linked, for even as airplanes scouted ahead, they remained immediately available to support marines on the ground should the need arise. Although not centrally controlled, this was an efficient use of a limited asset, given that the same aircraft often performed both missions in a single sortie.[19] In fact, close air support largely grew out of the scouting mission as first conducted in Haiti. Marine pilots began to experiment with various ways to provide aerial-delivered firepower to ground forces in close contact with the enemy. By the time the marines arrived in Nicaragua in 1927, dive-bombing as a close air support technique had become a standard tactic. Even amphibians were used for close air support. They were outfitted with small bombs, and although they did not mount machine guns, the observers carried Thompson .45-caliber submachine guns, which they used to fire on guerrillas.

As described earlier, the British used their aircraft in a similar manner as part of the concept of air control. The theory of air control arose after World War I due to a confluence of considerations. First, the financially strapped imperial powers of Europe were faced with the task of maintaining order in their various colonial holdings in a postwar, demobilized economy and thus with greatly reduced military resources. In Britain's case, the leaders of the Royal Air Force, especially marshal of the Royal Air Force Sir Hugh Trenchard, needed to justify the continued existence of the independent air arm to Parliament, in light of demobilization and the weakened state of the British Empire. The result was a punishment-based air control doctrine that advocated using aviation as the primary means of controlling indigenous peoples under imperial dominion. The idea was that air power could keep rebellious tribes in check with fewer men, fewer casualties, and less cost to the treasury. But as already noted, the central premise of air control was that it treated colonial policing as a purely military problem that could be solved with a purely military solution.

In contrast to the British approach to air control, the Marine Corps implemented restrained combined-arms operations. While the European theory regarded small wars as a purely military problem, the marines emphasized the political, psychological, economic, and cultural dimensions, in addition to the military dimension of intervention. This resulted in an informal doctrine of limited operations in which the marines strove to separate the population from the guerrilla forces, both physically and psychologically. Propaganda missions, support of a democratic-constitutional political process, and civic action played a major part in the marines' repertoire during the interwar years. In that regard, Marine Corps aviation made a significant contribution to each of these missions, especially in Nicaragua. The same cannot be said of the European air forces at the time or even the US Army Air Service or later the Air Corps. In contrast to using explosives and poison gas to wipe out whole villages, Marine Corps aircraft bombed villages and enemy encampments with thousands of propaganda circulars; they dropped bombs or fired their machine guns only when the pilot believed he had armed guerrillas in his sights.[20] During the 1928 and 1932 national elections in Nicaragua, Marine Corps aviation proved instrumental in ferrying election personnel around the country, supplying them, and maintaining communications with them, as well as transporting ballots to and from Managua. Similar operations took place in Haiti and the Dominican Republic, though on a reduced scale.

As noted above, a key element of emerging Marine Corps doctrine for counterinsurgency (formerly pacification) was the idea of restraint—that is, using the least force required to accomplish the mission. As the *Small Wars Manual* noted, "In small wars, caution must be exercised, and instead of striving to generate the maximum power with forces available, the goal is to gain decisive results with the least application of force and the consequent minimum loss of life."[21] Moreover, the marines understood that the campaign goal was not simply to destroy or defeat the enemy in the field. Instead, "the purpose should always be to restore normal government, or give the people a better government than they had before, and to establish peace, order, and security on as permanent a basis as practicable. Gradually, there must be instilled in the inhabitants' minds the leading ideas of civilization, the security and sanctity of life and property, and individual liberty. In doing so, one should endeavor to make self-sufficient native agencies responsible for these matters. With all this accomplished, one should be able to leave the country with the lasting friendship and respect of native population."[22] Thus, when briefing his pilots in Nicaragua during the early period of American neutrality, Major Rowell "appealed to all pilots to avoid hostilities and to return fire only when necessary to save their own lives."[23] Marine commanders at the time recognized that inflicting casualties on the general populace was counterproductive, and restraint is a core feature of counterinsurgency today.[24] That said, distinguishing guerrillas from the general population was an ever-present problem, and from the air, the task was (and remains today) even more difficult. As such, Rowell "instructed his pilots to fly no higher than 2,000 feet and generally 1,500 feet or lower—well within small-arms range—in order to distinguish between men and women, horses and cattle, and so forth."[25]

A brief comparison of the two methods reveals that air control doctrine was not nearly as effective as the restrained combined-arms approach. Despite years of brutal punishment inflicted on Rif warriors and their families by both the Spanish and French air forces, the Rif rebellion continued until the forces of Abd el Krim were overwhelmed by sheer mass and firepower during the combined Spanish and French offensive of 1925–1926. Likewise, in spite of heavy bombing, the French effort in Syria against the Druze was concluded only with massive ground intervention. In Iraq, Palestine, and Afghanistan, the Royal Air Force never came close to controlling the population with air power alone, and large numbers of ground troops were still deployed to those regions. In short, punishment bombing was strategically ineffective. The Marine Corps, however, integrated aviation into the ground scheme of maneuver, and the two in combination operated within the fundamental tenets of modern counterinsurgency warfare. Marine aircraft made significant and often vital contributions to the interventions in Haiti, the Dominican Republic, China, and Nicaragua. That the marines were withdrawn from each place for political reasons should not detract from what the Marine Corps accomplished with regard to the employment of aviation in small wars. Despite protestations to the contrary from some zealots, air power cannot win small wars on its own, and even with all it brings to the fight, aviation cannot substitute for a flawed strategy or the decision of a higher political authority to quit the fight. Although aviation technology has proved to be a decisive element in war fighting, it will never be *the* decisive capability in small wars.

The topic of appropriate technology for a given counterinsurgency situation cannot be adequately covered here, but it remains an ongoing concern, especially in terms of the employment of aviation, which is more sophisticated and expensive than a mortar tube. Under the category of "the old is new again," not long ago the US Air Force examined requirements for a low-cost counterinsurgency aircraft. The principal candidates were turboprop airplanes: an attack version of the Beechcraft T-6 Texan II trainer (the AT-6 Wolverine) and the Embraer EMB 314 Super Tucano (A-29), the latter capable of carrying two 500-pound guided bombs, a pair of air-to-ground missiles such as the Hellfire, and a fixed, forward-firing machine gun. Whether the air force needs such an aircraft is open to debate (the propeller versus jet controversy has been rendered moot by the advent of precision weapons such as the joint direct attack munition, or JDAM), but smaller air forces, especially in developing countries that have to deal with insurgents, narcotics trafficking, and so forth, can make excellent use of such aircraft.[26] Even so, while technology and tactics can minimize many of the guerrilla's advantages, it cannot eliminate them altogether, or at least not for long.

As to the future, the United States will continue to strive for near godlike dominance of the battle space in small wars as well as big ones. Although unmanned aerial systems were not available at the time, there seems no doubt that the marines of the small wars era would have embraced the use of unmanned systems of all types. With different platforms (manned and unmanned), new sensor technologies, and improved data link capabilities, counterguerrilla forces now have access to persistent observation in a way that makes aviation almost omnipresent. Equipped with precision weapons such as the JDAM, aviators (in the air and in control facilities on the ground) can unleash a "bolt from the blue" that (most of the time) will eliminate only confirmed guerrillas, even when they are among noncombatants. Unfortunately, the history of warfare shows that technological advantages are fleeting. The enemy has a nasty habit of developing countertactics or acquiring similar technology. This will surely be the case with current technological advantages, so we had best enjoy it while we can, anticipate the counter, and work on developing the "counter-counter."

Although it did not present a distinct challenge to the marines during the interwar period, one of the challenges we face today is responding to terrorism. In that regard, the Middle East has been the focal point for a shift from traditional guerrilla warfare to terrorism. Although guerrilla tactics and terrorism frequently overlap, there is a distinction. Guerrillas operate more openly against security forces, while terrorists operate underground and target the civilian population. Admittedly, this distinction is fuzzy, so it is probably best to think of guerrillas and terrorists as part of a spectrum rather than as two diametrically different groups. Both rely on stealth and camouflage for survival. Both require some degree of popular support or external sponsorship to finance their activities. But the primary difference remains target selection. Guerrillas attack primarily military and other government targets, although they occasionally conduct "terror" attacks on civilians. Terrorists target civilians. Guerrilla warfare can be legal in some circumstances and within certain internationally recognized norms, but terrorism (where terror is the only tool employed and it is used against civilian targets) is always illegal. How aviation can be employed against terrorists is a tricky question, but everything from precision munitions to "dumb bombs" dropped by B-52 bombers is open to use, depending on the target.[27]

Perhaps the greatest challenge to the employment of aviation in small wars is the proliferation of surface-to-air missiles, especially so-called man-portable weapons. Until the 1970s, air forces were able to operate with relative impunity against guerrillas and other irregulars. Although antiaircraft heavy weapons have been available since World War I, their threat level did not approach that of man-portable antiaircraft missiles. Sandino had the right idea with his *chula* weapons, but the technology was simply not available to him. Things are different today. In the 1960s the United States and the Soviet Union improved their guided missile technology to the point that they developed shoulder-fired surface-to-air missiles, and the use of American Stinger missiles by the Afghan mujahideen played a major role in the withdrawal of Soviet forces from Afghanistan. At the same time, Soviet antiaircraft artillery and man-portable antiaircraft missiles began to show up in the hands of various insurgent movements around the globe. One of the earliest Soviet designs, the SA-7, was used against British aircraft in Oman as well as against the Portuguese in Guinea and Mozambique.[28] Whether of Russian or American design (or some other origin), the appearance of surface-to-air missiles in small wars will be a major challenge to any air force and a real threat to "alternative technology platforms" such as the Wolverine and Super Tucano. As a whole, the last few decades have witnessed significant changes in the dynamics of small wars. Nevertheless, many of the principles of counterinsurgency and counterguerrilla warfare remain valid and have withstood the test of time. And although emergent technology has enhanced the capability of irregulars, very few have been able to contest the skies, and none have secured command of the air.

Final Thoughts

The twenty-odd years of the small wars era are not even a flyspeck in the mind of God and are only a small portion of Marine Corps history (as evidenced by the rather superficial treatment Marine Corps aviation during this period receives in most histories). But the marines got it right, and we can benefit from their experience today. As British air chief marshal Sir Brian Burridge noted: "I have a prejudice: My prejudice is that airmen do not like thinking: Airmen are obsessed with bombs, fuses, cockpits and screens and are actually rather uncomfortable exploring the underpinning logic and doctrine: So producing a thinking air force is a strategic requirement."[29] Air power—that is, the employment of aviation in its broadest sense—can be and often is decisive in war, large and small. But the role of air power in small wars is different from that in conventional or big wars. Aviation plays a supporting role, which the marines understood and quickly acceded to. But that supporting role is not a subordinate role. As General Norton "Norty" Schwartz, former chief of staff of the air force, wrote in a letter to *Air Force Magazine*, "In the end, our ultimate focus must recognize that jointness isn't a pejorative term, nor is it a notion that diminishes our Air Force."[30] Are aviators (or airmen) diminished in some way if soldiers on the ground depend on them? Of course not. The relationship between air and ground forces is not unlike the two blades of a pair of scissors. Can one cut a piece of paper with a single blade? Yes. But it is immensely more efficient and productive if both blades work in concert.

In the opening line of his most famous work, *Winged Defense*, Brigadier General William "Billy" Mitchell claimed, "The world stands on the threshold of the 'aeronautical era.' During this epoch the destinies of all people will be controlled through the air."[31] With all due respect to General Mitchell, an airpower icon and a genuine visionary with sufficient backbone to stir up the status quo, history has proved otherwise. Many people have controlled their destinies without employing airplanes, even when confronted with the significant coercive capacity of an enemy's air power. Ho Chi Minh and his followers bested the French and the Americans, and the mujahideen ousted the Soviets from Afghanistan. Neither "Uncle Ho" nor the Taliban employed airplanes, and both operated in an environment where their adversaries had complete control of the air. These and scores of other people either did not read Mitchell or decided to ignore him. He and the other original air power enthusiasts were right in many respects. Air power did change the face of conventional war. Winning command of the air and taking advantage of the same have proved decisive in many cases. But history has also shown that the decisive potential of air power varies greatly with the character of the conflict. War is complex, and its complexity tends to increase as war takes on an unconventional character. Aviation has been a useful tool in small wars of the past and will continue to play a major role in small wars of the future. But aviation's future role will invariably be a supporting one, and the marines of the interwar years intuitively understood this most salient of points. In small wars of the future, aviation will never be a stand-alone game winner; in fact, it may only buy time unless there is a sustained national will to do what needs to be done to win. Thus, aviation (whether wielded by a superpower or a small country) must continue to adapt to its multiple roles in wars big and small.

In closing, aviation technology promises to offer even greater advantages in small wars of the future, provided practitioners understand the character of the conflict they are involved in. Current trends in aviation technology promise improved precision, selectable and controllable lethality, and improved urban combat performance. Improvements in real-time intelligence technology, joint coordination, and net-centric command and control capabilities will undoubtedly reduce response times between the request for close air support and its provision. Coupled with emergent unmanned technology, this could lead to strike platforms with extremely long loiter times and near-instantaneous precision strike capabilities. These advances will significantly aid future counterguerrilla and counterterrorist operations. In addition, greater tactical mobility afforded by aircraft such as the Marine Corps' MV-22 Osprey (arguably the lineal descendant of the Pitcairn OP-1 Autogiro) will greatly improve all-around air mobility capabilities. Similar advances will enhance the role of platforms dedicated to intelligence, surveillance, and reconnaissance missions.

Thus, political and military leaders need not be experts in irregular warfare to appreciate its distinguishing characteristics. Nor do they need to be aviators to properly understand the role of aviation in small wars. They need only counter their ignorance by reading the historical record of small wars. With regard to the role of aviation in small wars, there is no better place to begin than the experience of the US Marine Corps from 1915 to 1934.

Appendix A

First 100 Marine Corps Aviators by Naval Aviator Number

Fractions resulted whenever it was discovered that aviators had erroneously been given the same number. Aviators who transferred from the US Navy to the Marine Corps received a second naval aviator number, given in parentheses.

Name	Naval Aviator No.
Alfred A. Cunningham	5
Bernard L. Lewis	6
William M. McIlvain	12
Francis T. Evans	26
Roy S. Geiger	49
David L. S. Brewster	55
Edmund G. Chamberlain	96½ (768)
Russell A. Presley	100¾ (769)
Doyle Bradford	111½
Clifford L. Webster	112½
Arthur H. Wright	148 (803)
Herman A. Peterson	163½
George Mc. Laughlin III	165 (790)
Charles B. Ames	193
John H. Weaver	251 (794)

Alvin L. Prichard	279
George C. Willman	299 (795)
Herbert D. Elvidge	424
Hazen C. Pratt	426
Sidney E. Clark	442 (800)
Frederick C. Schley	443 (801)
Charles A. Needham	444
John B. Bates	449
Ralph Talbot	456
Thomas C. Comstock	473 (789)
Francis O. Clarkson	474 (788)
Guy M. Williamson	477
Grover C. Alder	479
Edward Kenealy	480
Donald N. Whiting	503
Howard A. Strong	505
John P. McMurran	508 (791)
James K. Noble	510 (792)
Vincent C. Young	519
Province L. Pogue	522 (782)
Duncan H. Cameron	527 (787)
George F. Donovan	532 (798)
William H. Derbyshire	533 (770)
Frederick B. Davy	534 (771)
Douglas B. Roben	535 (774)
Arthur H. Page Jr.	536 (775)
Gove Compton	537 (773)
Thomas J. Butler	541 (786)
Thomas R. Shearer	559
Ford O. Rogers	560
Homer C. Bennett	562 (797)
John E. Powell	563
William M. Barr	567 (799)
Harry E. Stovall	568
Harvery B. Mimns	576
Winfield S. Shannon	583
Everett R. Brewer	585

John G. E. Kipp	586
Frederick L. Kolb	587
George F. Kremm	588
Jesse A. Nelson	589
Hermann J. Jesse	590
William W. Head	591
Gustav H. Kaemmerling	592
Jesse F. Dunlap	593
Trevor G. Williams	594
Clyde N. Bates	595
Melville E. I. Sulivan	596
Francis P. Mulcahy	597
Benjamin L. Harper	598
Walter H. Batts	599
Henry T. Young	600
Karl S. Day	601
Fred S. Robillard	602
Melchior B. Trelfall	603
Harold C. Major	604
Robert S. Lytle	605
Thomas C. Turner	772
Kenneth B. Collings	776
Donald B. Cowles	777
Maco Stewart Jr.	778
Henry S. Ehret Jr.	779
Raymond J. Kirwan	780
Frank Nelms Jr.	781
Harvey C. Norman	783
Delmar Leighton	784
John T. Brecton	785
William W. Torrey	793
Joseph W. Austin	796
Bunn G. Barnwell	804
Walter J. Willoughby	805
Chester J. Peters	806
Roswell E. Davis	807
Horace W. Leeper	808

Byron B. Freeland	809
Robert J. Paisley	810
Charles T. Holloway II	811
Frank H. Fleer	812
Maurice K. Heartfield	813
Robert J. Archibald	814
Arthur J. Sherman	815
Philip W. Blood	816
Albert A. Kuhlen	817
Earl F. War	818
August Koerbling	819

Appendix B

Marine Corps Aircraft Acquired 1913–1934

Designation	**Type**	**Year Assigned**	**Manufacturer/ Type**	**Engine**
AX-1	Biplane, boat, 2 crew	1913	Curtiss	Curtiss 90 hp
JN-4B	Biplane, trainer, 2 crew	1917	Curtiss Jenny	Curtiss 100 hp
H-12	Biplane, boat patrol, 2 crew	1918	Curtiss, others	2X Liberty 300 hp
H-16	Biplane, boat patrol, 2 crew	1918	Curtiss, others	2X Liberty 300 hp
HS-2	Biplane, boat patrol, 2 crew	1918	Curtiss, others	Liberty 330 hp
HS-2L	Biplane, boat patrol, 2 crew	1918	Curtiss, others	Liberty 360 hp
Kirkham Fighter	Experimental, triplane, 2 crew	1918	Curtiss	Kirkham 400 hp
N-9	Biplane, float, 2 crew	1918	Curtiss, Burgess	Curtiss 90 hp
R-6	Biplane, float, 2 crew	1918	Curtiss	Curtiss 200 hp
DH-4	Biplane, observation, 2 crew	1920	Dayton-Wright	Liberty 360 hp

Designation	Type	Year Assigned	Manufacturer / Type	Engine
DH-4B	Biplane, observation, 2 crew	1920	US Army	Liberty 400 hp
E-1 (M)	Biplane, fighter	1920	Standard	Le Rhône 80 hp
HS-1	Biplane, boat patrol, 2 crew	1920	Curtiss	Liberty 360 hp
JN-4	Biplane, trainer, 2 crew	1920	Curtiss Jenny	Curtiss 100 hp
JN-6-HG-1	Biplane, trainer, 2 crew	1920	Curtiss Jenny	Hispano 150 hp
VE-7	Biplane, trainer	1920	Lewis & Vought	Hispano 180 hp
Fokker C-1	Biplane, fighter, 2 crew	1921	Netherlands Aircraft Co.	BMW 243 hp
Fokker D. VII	Biplane, fighter	1921	Fokker	Packard 350 hp
VE-7G	Biplane, trainer, 2 crew	1921	Naval Aircraft Factory	Hispano 180 hp
VE-7SF	Biplane, trainer	1921	Vought	Hispano 180 hp
DH-4B-1	Biplane, observation, 2 crew	1922	US Army	Liberty 400 hp
F5-L	Biplane, boat patrol, 2 crew	1922	Naval Aircraft Factory	2X Liberty 360 hp
MB-3	Biplane, fighter	1922	Thomas-Morse	Hispano 300 hp
MBT	Biplane, torpedo bomber, 3 crew	1922	Martin	2X Liberty 400 hp
MT	Biplane, torpedo bomber, 3 crew	1922	Martin	2X Liberty 400 hp
DT-2	Biplane, torpedo bomber	1923	Douglas, others	Liberty 450 hp
JN-4H	Biplane, trainer, 2 crew	1923	Curtiss Jenny	Hispano 150 hp
T3M-1	Biplane, torpedo bomber, 3 crew	1923	Martin	Wright 575 hp
VE-9	Biplane, observation, 2 crew	1923	Vought	Wright 180 hp

DH-4B-2	Biplane, observation, 2 crew	1925	Naval Aircraft Factory	Liberty 400 hp
JN-6H	Biplane, trainer, 2 crew	1925	Curtiss Jenny	Hispano 180 hp
JN-6H-B	Biplane, trainer, 2 crew	1925	Curtiss	Hispano 180 hp
02B-1	Biplane, observation, 2 crew	1925	Boeing	Liberty 400 hp
TW-3	Biplane, float, trainer, 2 crew	1925	Dayton-Wright	Wright 180 hp
VE-7H	Biplane, float, trainer, 2 crew	1925	Vought	Wright 180 hp
F6C-3	Biplane, float, fighter	1926	Curtiss Hawk	Curtiss 400 hp
FB-1	Biplane, fighter	1926	Boeing	Curtiss 400 hp
NB-1	Biplane, float, trainer, 2 crew	1926	Boeing	Wright 200 hp
NB-2	Biplane, float, trainer, 2 crew	1926	Consolidated	Wright 200 hp
NY-1	Biplane, float, trainer, 2 crew	1926	Douglas	Packard 500 hp
OD-1	Biplane, observation, 2 crew	1926	Douglas	Packard 500 hp
OL-2	Biplane, observation, 2 crew	1926	Loening	Liberty 400 hp
XS-1	Experimental, biplane, float	1926	Cox-Klemin	Kinner 84 hp
F6C-1	Biplane, fighter, 2 crew	1927	Curtiss Hawk	Curtiss 400 hp
F6C-4	Biplane, fighter, float, 2 crew	1927	Curtiss Hawk	Pratt & Whitney 410 hp
O2U-1	Biplane, float, observation, 2 crew	1927	Vought Corsair	Pratt & Whitney 425 hp

Designation	Type	Year Assigned	Manufacturer / Type	Engine
OL-4	Biplane, amphibian, 3 crew	1927	Loening	Liberty 400 hp
OL-6	Biplane, amphibian, 3 crew	1927	Loening	Packard 475 hp
TA-1	Monoplane, transport, 3 crew	1927	Atlantic-Fokker	3X Wright 220 hp
XF6C-5	Experimental, biplane	1927	Curtiss Hawk	Pratt & Whitney 525 hp
F7C-1	Biplane, float, fighter	1928	Curtiss Sea Hawk	Pratt & Whitney 450 hp
F8C-1	Biplane, fighter, 2 crew	1928	Curtiss Helldiver	Pratt & Whitney 450 hp
F8C-3	Biplane, fighter, 2 crew	1928	Curtiss	Pratt & Whitney 450 hp
NY-1B	Biplane, float, trainer, 2 crew	1928	Consolidated	Wright 220 hp
O2B-2	Biplane, observation, 2 crew	1928	Naval Aircraft Factory	Liberty 400 hp
OC-1	Biplane, observation, 2 crew	1928	Curtiss Falcon	Pratt & Whitney 410 hp
OC-2	Biplane, observation, 2 crew	1928	Curtiss	Pratt & Whitney 410 hp
OL-8	Biplane, amphibian, 2 crew	1928	Loening	Pratt & Whitney 425 hp
TA-2	Monoplane, transport, 2 crew	1928	Atlantic-Fokker	3X Wright 450 hp
UO-1	Biplane, float, observation, 2 crew	1928	Vought Corsair	Udet 250 hp

UO-5	Biplane, observation, 2 crew	1928	Vought Corsair	Wright 220 hp
XOL-8	Experimental, biplane, amphibian, 3 crew	1928	Loening	Pratt & Whitney 425 hp
FB-5	Biplane, fighter	1929	Boeing	Packard 475 hp
JR-2	Monoplane, transport, 2 crew	1929	Ford	3X Wright 300 hp
OL-3	Biplane, amphibian, 3 crew	1929	Loening	Packard 475 hp
XHL-1	Experimental, amphibian, 2 crew	1929	Loening	Pratt & Whitney 525 hp
F8C-5	Biplane, fighter, 2 crew	1930	Curtiss Helldiver	Pratt & Whitney 450 hp
O2U-4	Biplane, float, observation, 2 crew	1930	Vought Corsair	Pratt & Whitney 450 hp
TA-3	Monoplane, transport, 2 crew	1930	Atlantic-Fokker	3X Wright 300 hp
XN2B-1	Experimental, biplane, 2 crew	1930	Boeing	Wright 165 hp
XOC-3	Experimental, biplane, 2 crew	1930	Curtiss Falcon	Pratt & Whitney 450 hp
NT-1	Biplane, trainer, 2 crew	1931	New Standard	Kinner 115 hp
O2C-1	Biplane, fighter, 2 crew	1931	Curtiss	Pratt & Whitney 450 hp
O3U-2	Biplane, observation, 2 crew	1931	Vought Corsair	Pratt & Whitney 525 hp
OL-9	Biplane, amphibian, 2 crew	1931	Loening	Pratt & Whitney 450 hp

Designation	Type	Year Assigned	Manufacturer / Type	Engine
OP-1	Autogiro, 2 crew	1931	Pitcairn	Wright 300 hp
RA-3	Monoplane, transport, 2 crew	1931	Atlantic-Fokker	3X Wright 300 hp
RC-1	Monoplane, transport, 2 crew	1931	Curtiss-Wright	2X Wright 300 hp
RR-2	Monoplane, transport, 2 crew	1931	Ford	3X Wright 300 hp
RR-3	Monoplane, transport, 2 crew	1931	Ford	3X Pratt & Whitney 300 hp
RS-1	Parasol wing, amphibian, 2 crew	1931	Sikorsky	2X Pratt & Whitney 575 hp
RS-3	Biplane, amphibian, 2 crew	1931	Martin	Pratt & Whitney 525 hp
T4M-1	Biplane, torpedo bomber, 3 crew	1931	Martin	Pratt & Whitney 525 hp
F4B-4	Biplane, fighter	1931	Boeing	Pratt & Whitney 500 hp
RR-5	Monoplane, transport, 2 crew	1931	Ford	3X Pratt & Whitney 450 hp
SU-2	Biplane, scout, 2 crew	1932	Vought Corsair	Pratt & Whitney 600 hp
F3B-1	Biplane, float	1933	Boeing	Pratt & Whitney 450 hp
N2C-3	Biplane, trainer, 2 crew	1933	Curtiss	Wright 240 hp
RE-3	Monoplane, transport, 2 crew	1933	Bellanca	Pratt & Whitney 450 hp
SU-3	Biplane, scout, 2 crew	1933	Vought Corsair	Pratt & Whitney 600 hp

F4B-3	Biplane, fighter	1934	Boeing	Pratt & Whitney 500 hp
JF-1	Biplane, utility, amphibian, 2 crew	1934	Grumman Duck	Pratt & Whitney 700 hp
R2D-1	Monoplane, transport, 2 crew	1934	Douglas	2X Wright 725 hp
R4C-1	Biplane, transport, 2 crew	1934	Curtiss-Wright	2X Wright 725 hp
RR-4	Monoplane, transport, 2 crew	1934	Ford	3X Pratt & Whitney 450 hp
SU-1	Biplane, scout, 2 crew	1934	Vought Corsair	Pratt & Whitney 600 hp

Appendix C

Squadron Designations and Redesignations, 1920–1936

1920–1922	29 May 1922	1 July 1927	1 July 1930	1930–1936
1st Squadron	VO-4	VO-7M	VO-7M	VO-7M
2d Squadron	VF-2	VF-9M	Decommissioned	
	VF-1*	VF-8M	Decommissioned	
3d Squadron	VO-3	VO-6M	VO-6M	Decommissioned
4th Squadron	VO-2	VO-9M	VO-9M	VO-9M
Flight L	VS-1	VP-3M	VP-3M	Decommissioned
	VO-1*	VO-8M	VO-8M	VO-8M
	VF-3*	VF-6M	VF-10M	VB-4M*
				VB-6M†
	VJ-6*	VJ-6M	VJ-6M	VJ-6M
	VO-10*	VO-10M	VO-10M	Decommissioned
			VF-4M*	VF-8M‡
			VF-5M*	VF-9M
			VF-6M*	Decommissioned
			VJ-7M*	VJ-7M
				VS-14§
				VS-15§

Note: "V" designates fixed-wing aircraft, and "M" designates Marine Corps. The types of squadrons are as follows:

VB = Bombing Squadron
VF = Fighter Squadron
VJ = Utility Squadron
VO = Observation Squadron
VP = Patrol Squadron
VS = Scouting Squadron

* Newly commissioned.
† Commissioned 1932–1933; recommissioned 1935.
‡ Decommissioned 1933; recommissioned 1936.
§ Commissioned 1931 for carrier duty; decommissioned 1934.

Notes

Abbreviations

GPO	Government Printing Office
MCHD	Marine Corps History Division
MCHRC	Marine Corps Historical Research Center
RG	Record Group

Introduction

1. British marines (seagoing soldiers) were assigned specific duties aboard ship; these involved mainly protecting the officers from a mutinous crew, but also engaging the enemy with musket fire, repelling boarders, and serving as gunners when needed. They were not, however, expected to work the sails or perform other duties of sailors. Indeed, during the American War of Independence, the British commander, General William Howe, issued a standing order specifically stating that marines were "not to be forced to go aloft." Later, Parliament extended the order, declaring that marines should not be beaten or otherwise punished for any disinclination to go aloft, "provided they do their duty on deck." That said, officers were not to prevent British marines "from rendering themselves expert in a seaman's duty, at proper opportunities agreeable to the standing instructions." Julian Corbett, *Signals and Instructions, 1776–1794: Publications of the Navy Records Society,* vol. 35 (London: Navy Records Society, 1908), 89.

2. The tall wooden masts of large sailing ships were not single spars; rather, they were constructed of separate sections, each with its own rigging. On a square-rigged ship of the sort common in the eighteenth century, the "top" was a platform near the upper end of the lower or main mast. The fighting top was an enlarged platform, sometimes with swivel guns, manned by marines to fire down on the decks of enemy ships. British Vice Admiral Horatio Nelson was killed at the Battle of Trafalgar by a marksman from a top on the *Redoubtable,* a seventy-four-gun ship of the line of the French navy.

3. "Letter from the Secretary of the Navy, Transmitting Rules and Regulations for the Government of the Navy of the United States; Prepared in Obedience to a Resolution of May 24, 1842," 27th Cong., 3d sess., in *House Documents, Otherwise Published as Executive Documents,* vol. 4 (Delhi, India: S. N. [Reink] Books, 2017), 71, document no. 148.

4. Today, US marines commonly refer to the floor or the ground as the "deck," a holdover from the days when marines routinely served aboard ships.

5. James Allen, Chief Signal Officer of the Army, Signal Corps Specification No. 486, "Advertisement and Specification for a Heavier-than-Air Flying Machine," December 23, 1907, https://www.libraries.wright.edu/special/wrightbrothers/packet/signal, accessed March 24, 2017. It reads in part: "Sealed proposals, in duplicate, will be received at this office until 12 o'clock noon on February 1, 1908, on behalf of the Board of Ordnance and Fortification for furnishing the Signal Corps with a heavier-than-air flying machine. All proposals received will be turned over to the Board of Ordnance and Fortification at its first meeting after February 1 for its official action." Of note, Major James Squier, serving under Brigadier General Allen at the time, actually wrote the solicitation for bids and later flew as a passenger on the Wright Flyer.

6. The French word *aéroplane* is derived from the Greek *aēr* (air) and probably the Latin *planus* (level), referring to the action of an airplane's wing as it moves through the air. Over time the term came to be used for the entire aircraft. The English word "aeroplane" is still used in Great Britain and Commonwealth countries with the exception of Canada, which has adopted the American word "airplane" for technical and other publications.

7. Prior to declaring independence from the British Empire, the Second Continental Congress of the American colonies convened in the spring of 1775 to plan the coming war with Britain. Among other decisions, the Continental Congress ordered the creation of a Continental Navy and the Continental Marines (November 10, 1775). By December, five companies of 300 marines were raised (albeit without uniforms). Over the course of the war, the Continental Marines served ashore and at sea; their last combat action was seizing the British merchant ship *Baille* in the West Indies in January 1783. The Continental Marines' last official act was to escort silver coins from Boston to Philadelphia; King Louis XVI of France had loaned the coins to the Americans to facilitate the opening of the Bank of North America, chartered on May 26, 1781, and opened in Philadelphia on January 7, 1782. For all intents and purposes, this marked the end of the Continental Marines, but they were not officially disbanded until June 1785.

8. At the outbreak of the Civil War, the USS *United States* was in port in Norfolk, Virginia, where it was seized by the Confederacy and renamed CSS *United States* (although it was usually called *Confederate States*). Being very old, the ship was used solely for harbor defense until being scuttled in 1862 to block Union access to the Elizabeth River. When the US Navy retook Norfolk, the *United States* was raised, towed to the navy yard, and broken up in December 1864. *Dictionary of American Naval Fighting Ships*, NH 1016 USS *United States* (1797–1861), Naval History and Heritage Command (online), accessed March 24, 2017.

9. Charles Neimeyer, "First United States Marine Officer Killed in Combat: 'Shall I Board Her, Sir?'" *Leatherneck* 95, no. 11 (November 2012): 48.

10. A good resource on America's war against the Barbary pirates is Joseph Wheelan, *Jefferson's War: America's First War on Terror, 1801–1805* (New York: Carroll & Graf, 2003).

11. Allan Millett, *Semper Fi: The History of the United States Marine Corps* (New York: Macmillan, 1980), 55–56.

12. Ibid., 59–60.

13. Ibid., 60.

14. At the end of the Mexican-American War, Henderson was presented with a sword inscribed, "From the Halls of Montezuma, to the Shores of Tripoli," providing the opening words to the Marine Corps hymn. The latter phrase refers to Lieutenant O'Bannon's

adventures on the Barbary Coast, and the former refers to the Battle of Chapultepec Castle during the Mexican War. The author of the Marine Corps hymn is unknown, although legend has it that a marine penned it in Mexico using commonly known nineteenth-century lyrics and adding the euphonic phrase inscribed on the sword as the opening verse.

15. See George Feifer, *Breaking Open Japan: Commodore Perry, Lord Abe, and American Imperialism in 1853* (Washington, DC: Smithsonian Institution Scholarly Press, 2006).

16. Millett, *Semper Fi,* 97.

17. Zeilin approved the design of the eagle, globe, and anchor as the official emblem of the US Marine Corps.

18. "Great White Fleet" was the popular nickname for the US Battle Fleet that sailed around the globe from December 1907 to February 1909. President Theodore Roosevelt ordered the fleet to undertake the journey to demonstrate the United States' growing power. The fleet started out with ninety ships, many of them older wooden vessels, but by the end of the expedition, the fleet included many modern steel ships, all of which were painted a stark white. See James Reckner, *Teddy Roosevelt's Great White Fleet* (Annapolis, MD: Naval Institute Press, 2001).

19. See Jack Shulimson and Graham Cosmas, "Teddy Roosevelt and the Corps' Sea-Going Mission," *Marine Corps Gazette* 65, no. 11 (November 1981).

20. Twenty-eight marines perished on the *Maine,* and it was Captain Charles Sigsbee's marine orderly, William Anthony, who led the captain to safety through the smoke and flames. All who died aboard the *Maine,* sailor and marine alike, were declared martyrs by the American press.

21. Following a short, sharp naval battle off Guantanamo Bay, the First Battalion of Marines, consisting of six companies, landed unopposed from the auxiliary cruiser USS *Panther.* Joined by Cuban guerrillas, the marines attacked Cuzco, about 2 miles from Fisherman's Point and the only source of potable water for the Spanish forces in the area. Seizing the well at Cuzco would force the Spanish to retreat to Ciudad Guantánamo (Guantanamo City). Two companies under the command of Captain George Elliott, a future commandant of the Marine Corps, accompanied by roughly fifty Cuban guerrillas, assaulted the Spanish garrison with fire support from the gunboat USS *Dolphin.* The marines took the town and its well but were unable to cut off the Spanish retreat. Even so, the marines laid down heavy fire on the retreating Spanish, who broke and scattered. John Clifford, "History of the First Battalion of US Marines," 1930, MCHRC, Cochrane Collection, PC 1, box 15.

22. Millett, *Semper Fi,* 134. Crane wrote: "The Marines made their strong faces businesslike and soldierly. Contrary to the Cubans, the bronze faces of the Americans were not stolid at all. One could note the prevalence of a curious expression—something dreamy, the symbol of minds striving to tear aside the screen of the future and perhaps expose the ambush of death. It was not fear in the least. It was simply a moment in the lives of men who have staked themselves and have come to wonder which wins—red or black?" R. R. Keene, "The Battle for Cuzco Well," *Leatherneck* 81, no. 9 (September 1998): 48. For additional information, see these other articles by Keene: "Battle of Cuzco Well, Guantanamo Bay, Cuba," *Leatherneck* 91, no. 9 (September 2008); "Guantanamo and the 1st Marine Battalion, 25 June 1898," *Marine Corps Gazette* 82, no. 7 (July 1998); "Giants of the Corps: John H. Quick," *Leatherneck* 58, no. 5 (May 1975).

23. Edwin McClellan, "American Marines in Nicaragua," *Marine Corps Gazette* 6, no. 1 (March 1921): 51.

24. Harry Summers, "Small Wars (and Operations Other than War)," Marine Corps Command and Staff College, course card, overview, May 2005, 5.

25. Ibid.

26. Ibid.

27. One can easily become bogged down in definitional debates regarding "regular" and "irregular." In its simplest terms, an irregular is defined as "a soldier who is not a member of a regular force." *Webster's Ninth New Collegiate Dictionary* (Springfield, MA: Merriam-Webster, 1985), 640. According to Friedrich Freiherr von der Heydte, a German *Fallschirmjäger* (paratroop) officer during World War II and a lawyer and judge after the war, irregular warfare is "usually . . . conceived to be an armed conflict, in which the parties are not large units, but small and very small action-groups, and in which the outcome is not decided in a few large battles, but the decision is sought, and ultimately achieved, in a very large number of small, individual operations." Friedrich Freiherr von der Heydte, *Modern Irregular Warfare, in Defense Policy as a Military Phenomenon,* trans. George Gregory (New York: New Benjamin Franklin House, 1986), 3.

28. Or, as Clausewitz put it, "The first, the supreme, the most far-reaching act of judgment that the statesman and commander have to make is to establish . . . the kind of war on which they are embarking." Carl von Clausewitz, *On War,* ed. and trans. Michael Howard and Peter Paret (Princeton, NJ: Princeton University Press, 1976), 88.

29. The author is indebted to Professor von der Heydte for this insight. To this day, military professionals, scholars, and laypeople alike think of tanks, airplanes, and artillery as defining "conventional" warfare, when in fact, conventional warfare is defined by international law and custom, that is, agreed-on rules and norms for waging war. Irregular warfare does not follow the rules. As von der Heydte wrote: "Irregular warfare . . . is unconventional by nature. It is war waged outside of the 'conventions,' on which the 'laws and norms' created for conventional war do not apply." Freiherr von der Heydte, *Modern Irregular Warfare,* 8.

30. C. E. Callwell, *Small Wars: Their Principles and Practice,* 3d ed. (1906; reprint, Lincoln: University of Nebraska Press, 1996), 29.

31. Ibid.

32. Ibid., 3.

33. *Small Wars Manual* (1940; reprint, Washington, DC: Department of the Navy, 1987), 1-8-13. The *Small Wars Manual* was originally separately issued pamphlets that were compiled and became chapters within the self-contained manual. The chapters are divided into sections, paragraphs, and subparagraphs. For example, chapter 1 (Introduction), section 1 (General Characteristics), paragraph 1-1 (Small Wars Defined), appears on page 1 of chapter 1, cited as 1-1-1. Chapter 1, section 2 (Strategy), paragraph 1-7 (The Basis of Strategy), appears on page 11, cited as 1-7-11. It is necessary to cite the page numbers in this manner because the numbering starts over in each chapter. This is confusing to the modern reader, but one must recall that the manual was not issued as a single text; it was issued pamphlet by pamphlet (in effect, chapter by chapter).

34. Ibid., 1-10-18.

35. Callwell, *Small Wars,* 108.

36. Ibid., 142. According to Marine Corps doctrine, command and control is dynamic: "command is the exercise of authority and control [is] feedback about the effects of the action taken." *Command and Control,* Marine Corps Doctrine Publication 6 (Washington, DC: Headquarters, US Marine Corps, 1996), 40.

37. *Small Wars Manual,* 2-16-33.

38. Ibid., 1-10-18.

39. Callwell, *Small Wars,* 76.

40. Ibid., 75.

41. Ibid., 80.

42. *Small Wars Manual,* 6-3-2.

43. Frank Herbert, *Dune* (New York: G. P. Putnam's Sons, 1965).

44. *Small Wars Manual,* 1-7-11.

45. Ibid.

46. Ibid., 1-10-18.

47. Callwell, *Small Wars,* 22.

48. Ibid., 84. Callwell admitted, however, that the "wholesale destruction of the property of the enemy may sometimes do more harm than good." Ibid., 149.

49. *Small Wars Manual,* 1-8-13.

50. Baron Antoine Henri Jomini was one of the foremost military thinkers. He, along with Clausewitz, articulated, interpreted, and systematized Napoleon's method and theory of war.

51. Jomini regarded "intestine"—that is, internal—war as particularly brutal and recommended that outside powers avoid such conflicts if possible. Indeed, he wrote: "As a soldier . . . I acknowledge that my prejudices are in favor of the good old times when the French and English Guards courteously invited each other to fire first . . . preferring them to the frightful epoch when priests, women, and children throughout Spain plotted the murder of isolated soldiers." To Jomini, internal wars were "cruel," and intervention was tantamount to attempting to "restrain the explosion of a mine when the powder has already been ignited; it is far better to await the explosion and afterward fill up the crater than to try to prevent it and to perish in the attempt." Baron de Jomini, *The Art of War,* trans. G. H. Mendell and W. P. Craighill (Philadelphia: J. B. Lippincott, 1862), 31, 22, 23. The marines had no choice in the matter, being sent to fight small wars regardless of whether they believed such wars to be "winnable." Thus, where Jomini posited that "no army, however disciplined, can contend successfully against such a system . . . unless it be strong enough to hold all the essential points of the country, cover its communications, and at the same time furnish an active force to beat the enemy wherever he may present himself" (ibid., 29), the Marine Corps wrote: "The occupying force must be strong enough to hold all the strategical points of the country, protect its communications, and at the same time furnish an operating force sufficient to overcome the opposition wherever it appears" (*Small Wars Manual,* 1-9-15). Setting aside the obvious plagiarism, the marines took Jomini's warning and turned it on its head.

52. The author is indebted to Dr. Thomas A. Marks of the College of International Security Affairs, National Defense University, for his insights into distinguishing the different manifestations of small wars, from rebellion to revolution.

53. *Small Wars Manual,* 1-1-1.

54. Ibid., 1-9-14.

55. Mao Tse-tung, "Yu Chi Chan [Guerrilla Warfare]," in *Mao Tse-tung on Guerrilla Warfare,* trans. Samuel Griffith (New York: Frederick A. Praeger, 1961), 46; *Selected Works of Mao Tse-tung,* 5 vols. (Peking: Foreign Language Press, 1963), 1:241.

56. Guerrillas operating in accordance with international law must therefore be treated according to the laws of war when captured.

57. *Small Wars Manual,* 1-13-21.

58. James Scott, "Revolution in the Revolution: Peasants and Commissars," *Theory and Society* 7 (January–May 1979): 99.

59. Ibid., 97 (emphasis in original).

60. Ibid., 102–3.

61. The marines recognized that the "application of purely military measures may not . . . restore peace and orderly government because the fundamental causes of the condition of unrest may be economic, political, or social." Consequently, "the solution of such problems being basically a political adjustment, the military measures to be applied must be of secondary importance." This is a remarkable statement for that era, as it emphasized nonmilitary solutions to what had hitherto been viewed as an exclusively military problem. Indeed, an entire section of the manual addressed the issue of "revolutionary tendencies" under the general heading of "psychology." Of particular interest was the characterization of revolution as having a potentially legitimate causation. Whether this contention was an outgrowth of the marines' experience between 1915 and 1935 is unclear; nevertheless, the manual was explicit regarding the relationship between revolution and insurgency: "Abuses by the officials in power and their oppression of followers of the party not in power, are often the seeds of revolution." *Small Wars Manual,* 1-9-15, 1-9-16, 1-11-19, 1-13-20, 1-13-21.

62. Ibid., 9-1-1.

63. Ibid., 1-1-1.

64. Ibid., 1-8-13. What made the *Small Wars Manual* unique at the time was its in-depth exploration of revolutionary guerrilla warfare. Although it was informed by Callwell's work and others, the marines paid considerably greater attention to the roots of conflict as well as to the character of the enemy, and they realized that emergent small wars in the twentieth century were different from those of previous centuries. Consequently, the authors of the *Small Wars Manual* gave special consideration to the socioeconomic and political grievances that give rise to insurgency and thus defined the theory of victory in such situations as relying on an accurate assessment of the root causes of internal war.

65. Ibid. When the *Small Wars Manual* was written, there was no concept of an "operational" level of war connecting the strategic and tactical levels. Thus, in some cases the writers meant the strategic level as we understand it today, but in most cases they meant the operational level of war, where the campaign plan is written and executed. For the marines of the small wars era, the "strategical plan" meant the campaign plan. Policy and strategy was set in Washington—that is, the Monroe Doctrine and the strategy of intervention to uphold the doctrine. Campaign design and execution—that is, "operational art"—rested with the marine force commander on the ground in obedience to the intent

and guidance provided by the senior officer in overall command of the intervention, usually a navy officer.

66. Ibid., 1-17-32.

67. For an in-depth examination of the analytical distinction among terror, terrorism, and insurgency, see Wray Johnson, "Terror Groups Are Not Invincible," *Marine Corps Gazette* 95, no. 10 (October 2011).

1. Origins of Marine Corps Aviation

1. Edwin McClellan, "The Birth and Infancy of Marine Aviation," *Marine Corps Gazette* 15, no. 5 (May 1931): 13.

2. Zisis Fotakis, *Greek Naval Strategy and Policy, 1910–1919,* Cass Series: Naval Policy and History (London: Routledge, 2005), 75. See also Walter Boyne, ed., *Air Warfare: An International Encyclopedia,* vol. 1 (Santa Barbara, CA: ABC-CLIO, 2002), 66, 268. There is some dispute as to whether the Greek airplane was called the Nautilus or the Daedalus.

3. Formally the US Rifle, Caliber .30-06, Model 1903, the Springfield was a bolt-action rifle with a five-round magazine; it remained in service into World War II, although officially it was replaced by the semiautomatic, eight-round M1 Garand rifle. A copy of the famous German Mauser, the Springfield rifle was highly accurate and very popular. Ernest Hemingway used the rifle with "iron sights" to hunt big game, including lions, as related in *Green Hills of Africa.*

4. In French, *aileron* means "little wing." An aileron is a hinged flight-control surface on the outboard portion of a fixed-wing aircraft's wing. Ailerons are used to bank the aircraft to the right or left by working in opposition; that is, as the right aileron is deflected upward, the left is deflected downward (and vice versa), causing the wing tip to move up or down, which results in a curved flight path. Although this is the norm for lateral control today (in addition to the rudder), early powered aircraft such as the Wright brothers' original Flyer employed "wing warping," which used cables and pulleys to twist the trailing edges of the wings in opposite directions.

5. *Monocoque* literally means "single shell" (in Greek and French). Early aircraft were constructed with internal frames covered in fabric. The fabric "skin" was tightened using aircraft "dope" to reduce drag. But the skin contributed nothing to the structural integrity of the aircraft. The Deperdussin designers used three layers of laminated strips of glued poplar veneer, which not only added to the structural integrity of the fuselage but also streamlined the shape, making the Deperdussin machine very fast. It won many races, leading to numerous copies. For additional details, see T. H. G. Megson, *Aircraft Structures for Engineering Students* (London: Edward Arnold, 1972).

6. During the "Great Revolution" that broke out in 1910, the secretary of war and navy, General Manuel Mondragón, approved the creation of the Escuadrilla Aérea de la Milicia Auxiliar del Ejército, an air auxiliary to the Mexican army. In 1915 Venustiano Carranza, who had assumed the presidency the previous year, founded the Arma de Aviación Militar, regarded as the precursor to the current Mexican air force. Although weak in the beginning, the Mexican air arm steadily grew stronger until the late 1920s, during which time the United States deemed it necessary to post a strong air force of its own along the

border. For a useful treatment of this topic, see Kenneth Ragsdale, *Wings over the Border: Pioneer Military Aviation in the Big Bend* (Austin: University of Texas Press, 1984).

7. Lieutenant Lahm was the first American military flier to receive an airplane pilot certificate from the Féderation Aéronautique Internationale.

8. Roy Grossnick, ed., *Kite Balloons to Airships . . . the Navy's Lighter-than-Air Experience* (Washington, DC: Deputy Chief of Naval Operations, Air Warfare, n.d.), 3. See also Sandy Russell, ed., *Naval Aviation, 1911–1986: A Pictorial Study* (Washington, DC: Deputy Chief of Naval Operations, Air Warfare, 1986), 2.

9. Carlton Thaxton et al., eds., *A Roster of Spanish American War Soldiers from Georgia* (Americus, GA: Thaxton, 1984).

10. Gerald Astor, *Semper Fi in the Sky: The Marine Air Battles of World War II* (New York: Random House, 2005), 3.

11. "Official Commendatory Remarks About and Career Information Regarding Select Early Marine Corps Aviators," n.d., MCHD, Aviation: Aviators (Early).

12. Alfred Cunningham, "Aviation in the Navy," *Marine Corps Gazette* 1, no. 4 (December 1916): 333. Apparently, the essay had little to no impact on Marine Corps thinking at the time. As Marine Corps General Vernon Megee wrote during the Vietnam War, "Then as now, the unsolicited opinion of a mere winged lieutenant could not weigh overly heavy in the upper councils. Nothing in the way of an organized Marine Aviation unit materialized until suddenly we found ourselves catapulted into the First World War." Vernon Megee, "The Evolution of Marine Aviation," *Marine Corps Gazette* 49, no. 8 (August 1965): 21.

13. The Aero Club of America was founded in 1905 by Charles Jasper Glidden, an automotive pioneer, and Augustus Post, another automobile enthusiast, to promote aviation in the United States. As part of its charter, the club issued certificates of qualification to aviators; at the time, no such certification was issued by any US government entity. The certificate was required for US Army aviators until 1914 and was highly sought after, given that any American aviator who wished to participate in an international flying event required Aero Club certification. In 1923 the Aero Club became the National Aeronautic Association, which still exists today as a nonprofit 501(c)(3) organization. See Bill Robie, *For the Greatest Achievement: A History of the Aero Club of America and the National Aeronautic Association* (Washington, DC: Smithsonian Institution, 1993).

14. Cunningham later wrote of his first airplane, "I called her everything in God's name to go up. . . . I pleaded with her, I caressed her. I prayed to her, and I cursed that flighty Old Maid to lift her skirts and hike but she never would. Though I will say this, that beyond that she never threw me down. I learned of air things from that Old Girl." James Jacobs, "Alfred Austell Cunningham, 1882–1939," 8, MCHRC, Cunningham Papers, PC 49, Personal Papers Collection.

15. Chambers was born in Kingsport, New York, in 1856 and graduated from the Naval Academy in 1876. He served in a variety of billets at sea and ashore. In 1907 he was named assistant chief of the Bureau of Ordnance. Secretary of the Navy George von L. Meyer appointed Chambers to oversee aviation matters as assistant to the aide for material in the Bureau of Navigation. He later became the first officer in charge of aviation, reporting to the General Board. Although Chambers initially had little interest in aviation—even after witnessing the Wrights fly up the Hudson River to Grant's Tomb in 1909—he was fascinated by the mechanics of flight and, encouraged by Curtiss, quickly converted to the idea

of airplanes aboard ships. Chambers Field in Norfolk, Virginia, was named in his honor in 1938. See Stephen Stein, *From Torpedoes to Aviation: Washington Irving Chambers and Technological Innovation in the New Navy, 1876–1913* (Tuscaloosa: University of Alabama Press, 2007).

16. Whereas Orville and Wilbur Wright "were finical Ohio shopkeepers whose orderly approach to building the first flying machine can be interpreted either as scientific method or a natural manifestation of straightlaced fussiness," Glenn Curtiss "was a roughneck who raced motorcycles in the farming village of Hammondsport, New York," and was "a gifted technician" with a "more pragmatic intuition for aeronautics." Wayne Biddle, *Barons of the Sky: From Early Flight to Strategic Warfare; the Story of the American Aerospace Industry* (New York: Simon & Schuster, 1991), 27.

17. Iowan Eugene Ely moved to California and took up auto racing. He later moved to Nevada and then Oregon, where he worked as a salesman for E. Henry Wemme, a wealthy businessman who had purchased one of Glenn Curtiss's first biplanes. Ely flew Wemme's plane and crashed it, whereupon he bought the wreckage, repaired the plane, and flew it several more times. At an aircraft exhibition in Minneapolis, Ely met Curtiss and began flying for him. When Ely launched from the *Birmingham,* his plane grazed the surface of the water. Shaken, he flew to the beach rather than circle the harbor as originally intended. When he later flew to the *Pennsylvania,* his airplane included a tail-hook system designed and built by aviator, inventor, and daredevil circus performer Hugh Robinson. Ely never joined the navy, although he tried (naval aviation had not yet been organized when he applied for a commission). He continued to fly exhibitions until he was killed in a crash in Georgia in October 1911. In 1933 Congress posthumously awarded him the Distinguished Flying Cross "for extraordinary achievement as a pioneer civilian aviator and for his significant contribution to the development of aviation in the United States Navy." *US Air Services* 18, no. 3 (March 1933): 14.

18. See George Van Deurs, *Wings for the Fleet: A Narrative of Naval Aviation's Early Development, 1910–1916* (Annapolis, MD: Naval Institute Press, 1966), 13–16.

19. The Virginia-born Ellyson graduated from the Naval Academy in 1905. He first served aboard the Maine-class battleship USS *Missouri* and later on the armored cruisers *Pennsylvania* and *Colorado.* He then volunteered for submarine duty and was assigned to the Holland A-class submarine USS *Shark.* In 1910, while commanding the submarine USS *Tarantula,* Ellyson volunteered to attend Glenn Curtiss's flying school in San Diego, California, when instruction was offered free of charge. Ellyson became the first US Navy officer assigned to aviation. He returned to sea duty in 1913, serving on battleships until 1915. After a stint at the Naval Academy as an instructor, he served as assistant for operations, Submarine Chaser Detachment 1, during World War I, for which he received the Navy Cross. After the war he commanded two destroyers, USS *Little* and USS *Brooks.* In 1921 he became chief of plans for the new Bureau of Aviation in Washington. In July 1925 he took command of Torpedo and Bombing Plane Squadron One. Commander Ellysson died in an airplane crash on February 27, 1928. See Ross Grossnick et al., "A Few Pioneers, 1898–1916," in *United States Naval Aviation, 1910–1995,* 4th ed., ed. Roy Grossnick (Washington, DC: GPO, 1997).

20. John Fry, "The First Seaplane: Glenn Curtiss' Arrival at North Island," Association of Naval Aviation, San Diego Squadron Newsletter, April 2010, 1–5.

21. Rodgers was the grandson of two famous commodores: John Rodgers and Matthew Perry. He died in 1926 when the airplane he was piloting crashed into the Delaware River. John Towers is widely recognized for his contributions to aviation and was chief of the Bureau of Aeronautics from 1939 to 1942. In October 1942 he became commander, Air Force, Pacific Fleet, and in 1945 he took command of the Second Carrier Task Force and Task Force 38. In late 1945 he commanded Fifth Fleet. Following World War II he chaired the US Navy General Board and retired in 1947. He died in 1955 and is buried in Arlington National Cemetery. Victor Herbster served continuously in aviation from November 1911 to his retirement in July 1936. He returned to active duty in August 1940 and again served in aviation until his final retirement in 1946. He died in New York in December of that year. For Rodgers, see http://www.arlingtoncemetery.net/johnrodg.htm, accessed June 17, 2017. For Herbster, see http://www.earlyaviators.com/eherbste.htm, accessed June 17, 2017.

22. The first four naval aviators were, in order, Spuds Ellyson, John Rodgers, John Towers, and Victor Herbster. W. H. Sitz, "A History of US Naval Aviation," Technical Note 160, typescript, US Department of the Navy, Bureau of Aeronautics, April 1925, 6–7. See also Douglas Smith, *One Hundred Years of US Navy Air Power* (Annapolis, MD: Naval Institute Press, 2010); Grossnick, *United States Naval Aviation,* 403–4.

23. Owing to his brief hiatus from flying, Cunningham's name was omitted from the first list of pilots receiving certificates. As a result, Bernard Smith was initially designated Naval Aviator No. 5 and Marine Aviator No. 1. This was later corrected, and Cunningham became Naval Aviator No. 5 (Smith moving to No. 6) and Marine Aviator No. 1.

24. Barney Smith was born in Richmond, Virginia, in 1886 and studied mechanical engineering at Virginia Polytechnic Institute. He was commissioned into the Marine Corps in 1909 and served at sea for a time before being ordered to the Aviation Camp at Annapolis. Early in World War I he was posted to Paris, France, as assistant to the naval attaché. While in France he flew combat missions with the French Armée de l'Air. Upon American entry into the war, he was assigned to the aviation section of the Office of Naval Operations. While in this billet he frequently consulted with the Naval Aircraft Factory in Philadelphia, Pennsylvania. Like Cunningham, Smith joined the Aero Club chapter in Philadelphia and received a certificate for hydroaeroplanes as well as an "expert aviator" designation, the latter requiring the completion of demanding distance and altitude tests. Smith resigned from the Marine Corps in 1920 but returned to service as a lieutenant commander in the Naval Reserve in 1931. He joined the Marine Corps Reserve as a major in 1937. When the United States declared war on the Axis powers, Smith was called to active duty; he served in Central America and established the Marine Corps' barrage balloon program. He left the Marine Corps in 1946 to become superintendent and chief engineer of Aeromarine Airways in Key West, Florida. Smith was killed in an automobile accident in Coral Gables, Florida, in 1947. See http://vpiworldwarone.lib.vt.edu/items/show/406, accessed July 17, 2017.

25. William McIlvain was born in Bethesda, Maryland, in 1885. He entered the Marine Corps in 1909 and served aboard the battleships USS *Connecticut* and USS *North Dakota.* In November 1913 he reported to Annapolis for flight school. Upon completion of training he reported to Pensacola, Florida, where he briefly served aboard the battleship USS *Mississippi* and the armored cruiser USS *North Carolina.* When Bernard Smith was sent to

Paris as an assistant naval attaché and Cunningham was posted to Washington, DC, McIlvain was the sole marine aviator at Pensacola. Of note, McIlvain was the first marine to receive landplane training at the US Army's flying school on North Island near San Diego, California. He left active service in 1921 and joined the reserves, retiring in 1948. He died in 1963 at Camp Pendleton, California. See http://www.earlyaviators.com/emcilvan.htm and https://www.findagrave.com/cgi-bin/fg.cgi?page=gr&GRid=35833012, accessed July 17, 2017.

26. Cocky Evans was born in Delaware, Ohio, in June 1886. He attended Ohio Wesleyan University and was a member of the Ohio National Guard until joining the Marine Corps in 1909. Evans was grounded following two crashes in 1935 and was medically retired in 1937. However, he was recalled to active duty when the United States entered World War II and served until December 1944. He had two sons, both of whom flew in World War II as part of the US Army Air Force and, after 1947, in the newly independent US Air Force. The older son died in a plane crash while trying to avoid a playground full of children in Forestville, Maryland. An elementary school in Clinton, Maryland, is named in his honor. The younger son took his father for his first and only jet ride in a T-33 "Shooting Star" in 1947. Cocky Evans died in March 1974 and is buried in Arlington National Cemetery. See Walter Knapp, "The Marines Take Wing," *Aviation History,* May 2012, 51.

27. See Roger Willock, *Unaccustomed to Fear: A Biography of the Late General Roy S. Geiger* (1968; reprint, Quantico, VA: Marine Corps Association, 1983). A Florida native, Geiger obtained a law degree from John B. Stetson University in 1907 and practiced law for a time but soon decided that was not the life he desired. He enlisted in the Marine Corps and was commissioned a little over a year later. He went ashore in Nicaragua in 1912 with Company E, Second Battalion, First Provisional Regiment, and participated in the attack on Coyotepe Hill (see chapter 4). He remained in Nicaragua with the Legation Guard but soon transferred to Camp Elliott in the Panama Canal Zone. He then volunteered for flying duty and served in France during World War I. After the war he was posted to Haiti as commander of Fourth Squadron (see chapter 2). He returned to the United States and took command of the First Aviation Group at Quantico, Virginia, then went back to Haiti in 1925, once again as squadron commander. Following graduation from the US Army War College in Washington, he became head of aviation at Marine Corps Headquarters. When war broke out in Europe in 1939, Geiger was ordered to London as the naval attaché for air. Upon his return home he was promoted to brigadier general and commanded the First Marine Aircraft Wing before heading to Guadalcanal in 1942 to lead the "Cactus Air Force" during the Solomons campaign. He then became deputy commanding general and later commanding general of the First Marine Amphibious Corps. His corps was redesignated Third Amphibious Corps just prior to taking Guam during the Marianas campaign. In the fall of 1944 he led Third Corps in seizing Peleliu in the Palau island group. Geiger's final campaign was the conquest of Okinawa, when he again led Third Corps. He also assumed the role of assistant commander of Tenth Army and, upon the death of the commander, Lieutenant General Simon Boliver Buckner, US Army, briefly commanded Tenth Army. Following World War II Geiger's health declined rapidly, and he died in January 1947. He was advanced to the rank of general and is buried in Arlington National Cemetery. Also see George Clark, *United States Marine Corps Generals of World War II: A Biographical Dictionary* (Jefferson, NC: McFarland, 2008), 53–56.

28. Thomas Craven, "History of Aviation in the United States Navy: From Its Beginning until the Spring of 1920," 1977, Thomas T. Craven Papers, File ZGU, Subject File, 1911–1927, RG 45, Library of Congress, Washington, DC. It should be noted that Cunningham's instruction at Marblehead was at no expense to the US Navy; Captain Chambers alluded to potential aircraft purchases in the future as recompense.

29. The US occupation of Veracruz was prompted by the so-called Tampico affair, an incident involving US Navy sailors and Mexican troops on April 9, 1914. The occupation lasted six months. For a detailed account, see Jack Sweetman, *The Landing at Veracruz, 1914* (Annapolis, MD: Naval Institute Press, 1968). Also see Thomas Davis, "With No Thought of Aggression," *Military History Quarterly* (2007): 34–43.

30. "Aviators Pick out Federal Positions," *New York Times*, April 30, 1914.

31. The Model B was the Wright brothers' first airplane to be produced in quantity. It was also the first Wright airplane to boast a true elevator at the tail rather than at the front, and it was the last Wright machine to have an open-frame tail. The Model B carried two people, the pilot and a passenger, sitting side by side on the leading edge of the lower wing. The B-1 was a seaplane variant with two steel and aluminum pontoons.

32. The sources for the discussion of the Aviation Camp at Guantanamo Bay are several letters from Lieutenant John Towers to, among others, Captain Chambers and Lieutenant Ellyson, found in Washington Irving Chambers Papers, box 11, "Aviation Camp Guantanamo Bay, 1910–1919," Naval Historical Foundation Collection, Manuscripts Division, Library of Congress, Washington, DC; hereafter cited as Chambers Papers.

33. Ibid. John "Gabe" Lejeune (also known affectionately as "Old Indian") was the thirteenth commandant of the Marine Corps and is one of the most distinguished officers in Marine Corps history. During his tenure he led dramatic changes in organization, education, and training. He left the post of commandant in 1929 and became superintendent of Virginia Military Institute, serving in that capacity for eight years. In February 1942 he was advanced to the rank of lieutenant general on the retired list. He died the following November and is buried in Arlington National Cemetery. See Glenn Harned, *Marine Corps Generals, 1899–1936: A Biographical Encyclopedia* (Jefferson, NC: McFarland, 2015), 59–66.

34. United States Navy Board on Aeronautics Report, appendix B, Minutes of the Proceedings of the Board of Naval Aeronautics, November 19, 1913, Chambers Papers, box 19, "Naval Aviation Progress, 1910–1919."

35. Ibid.

36. Oscar Underwood of Alabama was the only Democrat to lead his party in both the House of Representatives and the Senate and was the first formally designated floor leader in the Senate. He ran for president in 1912 and 1924. Although he failed on both occasions, he remained one of the most powerful men in Congress until his anti–Ku Klux Klan stance made him unpopular in his own party, so he retired. Afterward he wrote a book, *Drifting Sands of Party Politics*. See James Fleming, "Oscar W. Underwood: The First Modern House Leader, 1911–1915," in *Masters of the House: Congressional Leadership over Two Centuries*, ed. Raymond Smock and Susan Hammond (New York: Westview Press, 1998), 91–118.

37. With regard to terminology, a "pilot" is someone who controls the flight of an aircraft, whether fixed wing or rotary wing (that is, a helicopter), or an airship such as a

balloon or dirigible. In the early days of powered flight, pilots were simply known as "aviators," derived from *aviateur* in French and from the Latin *avis,* meaning "bird." The term for a female aviator was "aviatrix," from the French *aviatrice.* Today, such a gender distinction is regarded as archaic (if not insulting). While other crew members aboard an aircraft (such as the navigator or engineer) are generally regarded as aviators, they do not manipulate the aircraft's flight controls. Thus, the term "pilot" came into common usage to identify the person who operates the flight controls and is ultimately responsible for the safe completion of the flight.

38. The concept of an "advance base" had its origins in the Spanish-American War and was the reason for the establishment of the First Battalion of Marines. Formed from East Coast barracks companies, the First Battalion comprised five infantry companies and a 3-inch landing gun company. Because of the battalion's success during the war, the commandant, Colonel Charles Heywood (ninth commandant of the Marine Corps), proposed that a 2,000-man force be raised. There is inconsistency in the General Board's correspondence regarding use of the term "Advanced" or "Advance," but the original intent seems to have been to designate the unit the "Advance Base Force," so that term is used in this work.

39. *Quantico* is an Algonquin term translated as "by the long stream" or, alternatively, "place of dancing." Charles Fleming et al., *Quantico: Crossroads of the Marine Corps* (Washington, DC: Headquarters, US Marine Corps, History and Museums Division, 1978), iii, 1.

40. Van Deurs, *Wings for the Fleet,* 123–30.

41. Cunningham was preceded in this feat in November 1915 when Henry Mustin, USN (Naval Aviator No. 3), then commandant of the Naval Aeronautic Station at Pensacola, piloted a Curtiss AB-2 launched by catapult from the *North Carolina* while at anchor. Following Cunningham's failed attempt to launch while under way, Lieutenant Godfrey de Courcelles Chevalier, USN, was catapulted off the *North Carolina* in the more powerful AB-3, becoming the first aviator to successfully launch from a ship while under way. In 1919 Mustin led a record-breaking flight of a dozen airplanes from San Diego to Balboa, Panama Canal Zone. He was promoted to captain in 1922 and died in 1923.

42. Some sources claim that Cunningham suffered no injury at all. See, for example, "Marine Corps Aviation: Enough of Its History to Appreciate Its Accomplishments," *Headquarters Bulletin* 239 (September 1945).

43. Cunningham, "Aviation in the Navy," 333–42. In this essay, Cunningham described the work being done by US Navy and Marine Corps aviators at Pensacola and pointed to the advancements made by the belligerents in the ongoing war in Europe. In particular, he described how the German naval air service had helped avert disaster at the Battle of Jutland. In conclusion, Cunningham sought to dispel some of the "myths" surrounding aviation, especially the notion that aviators needed more bravado than brains.

44. William Benson to George Barnett, January 30, 1917, Cunningham Papers, Orders File.

45. Lieutenant General Karl Day, USMC, Ret., oral history transcript, August 5, 1968, Oral History Collection, Headquarters, US Marine Corps, History and Museums Division, Washington, DC. General Day began his flying career with the First Aeronautic Company in Philadelphia. He was sent to France with Squadron C, First Marine Aviation Force, Northern Bombing Group, but flew almost exclusively with No. 218 Squadron,

Royal Air Force, flying the DH-9. He left active service and spent the next decade in a variety of flying jobs before joining American Airlines. Day is credited with pioneering instrument flying and radio navigation and wrote a book on the subject in 1938. He remained in the reserves until he returned to active duty in 1940, when he was assigned to Admiral "Bull" Halsey's staff. On September 15, 1944, he went ashore on Peleliu, where he oversaw reconstruction of the Japanese airfield on the island to support the invasion of the Philippines. After World War II he returned to the reserves and American Airlines and retired in June 1962. He died in 1973 and is buried in Arlington National Cemetery. See "Gen. Karl Day, 76, a Marine Aviator," *New York Times*, January 22, 1973.

46. "By early 1917, the Army's Aviation Section had a grand total of seven 'combat' squadrons—four in the US, two in Panama, and one in the Philippines. Compared to Europe's active air units, they were strictly recreational." Biddle, *Barons of the Sky*, 79.

47. US Marine Corps, *Marine Corps Aircraft: 1913–1965* (Washington, DC: Headquarters, US Marine Corps, Historical Branch, 1967), 5.

48. *World Aircraft Information Files* (London: Bright Star Publishing, 2002), file 891, sheets 42–43.

49. Some sources claim the flight occurred on July 1. The A-1 was a Curtiss Model E and was the US Navy's first aircraft. The A-1 was called the "Triad" because it could operate on land, on water, and in the air.

50. Technically, a seaplane is any airplane that can land on water. Therefore, a seaplane can be either a flying boat or a floatplane. If the airplane can also operate from land, it is an amphibian; amphibians can be either floatplanes or flying boats. A flying boat is based on a single boat-like hull that, in addition to permitting the airplane to maneuver on water, serves as its fuselage. A floatplane is an ordinary landplane equipped with streamlined floats instead of wheels. Gordon Swanborough and Peter Bowers, *United States Navy Aircraft since 1911* (New York: Funk & Wagnalls, 1968), 93–94, 104–5.

51. The amphibian was known as the OWL, or "Over Water and Land." The airplane was destroyed in November 1915. Michael Taylor, *Jane's Encyclopedia of Aviation* (London: Studio Editions, 1989), 276–78. See also Swanborough and Bowers, *United States Navy Aircraft since 1911*, 86–89. In July 1914 the US Army Signal Corps banned the use of all pusher aircraft because they stalled too easily and the pilot would be crushed to death by the engine in the event of a crash.

52. Officially, the Aeronautic Company was the first Marine Corps aviation unit designated as an organization separate and apart from the US Navy. However, in 1914 Lieutenants Bernard Smith and Mac McIlvain were detached from Pensacola to Culebra, Cuba, to participate in an exercise with Navy Flying Boat C-3. One could argue that this two-man detachment was the first autonomous Marine Corps aviation unit. See Robert Sherrod, "Marine Corps Aviation: The Early Days," part 1, *Marine Corps Gazette* 36, no. 5 (May 1952): 54–55.

53. Ibid., 55, n. 4.

54. Reserve Officers of Public Affairs Unit 4-1, *The Marine Corps Reserve: A History* (Washington, DC: Headquarters, US Marine Corps, Division of Reserve, 1966), 4.

55. Ibid., 11, quoting reserve Brigadier General and Marine Corps aviator Karl Day.

56. Roger Emmons, *First Marine Aviation Force, 1917–1918*, ed. George Clark (Pike, NH: Brass Hat, 1964), 5. Marine Corps records do not indicate the specific model of

Farman aircraft in use at this time. This is not surprising, given that Farman Aviation Works, founded by brothers Richard, Henri, and Maurice Farman in France, produced more than 200 types between 1908 and 1941. One can speculate from the period and photographs, however, that the trainer sent to Miami was a Farman III pusher-type biplane.

57. Swanborough and Bowers, *United States Navy Aircraft since 1911*, 98–99.

58. Edward Johnson, *Marine Corps Aviation: The Early Years, 1912–1940* (Washington, DC: Headquarters, US Marine Corps, History and Museums Division, 1977), 11.

59. The Advance Base Force was dissolved at the outset of World War I when the Fourth and Fifth Brigades, comprising the Fifth, Sixth, Eleventh, and Thirteenth Regiments, as well as the Fourth and Fifth Machine Gun Battalions, were raised and sent to France. As discussed in chapter 2, the Second Regiment deployed to Haiti in 1915, and the Third and Fourth Regiments occupied the Dominican Republic. However, the Advance Base Force was reconstituted in 1917 with the Eighth and Ninth Regiments serving in Texas and Cuba, respectively, to counter any German intervention in the Caribbean as well as to protect Mexican oil fields around Tampico. The Ninth Regiment moved to Texas in 1918 and, along with the Eighth Regiment, became the Third Brigade. The First Regiment was reactivated in Philadelphia as the Fixed Defense Force. The Advance Base Force was redesignated the First Advance Base Force on October 1, 1919, and the Second Advance Base Force was activated the same day in San Diego. The US Navy's "Train" (fleet support) was established the following year, and the marines of the Advance Base Forces were tied directly to the Navy Base Force. The Quantico-based First Advance Base Force was redesignated the Marine Corps Expeditionary Force (MCEF) in 1921, built around the Fifth Regiment. At the same time, the San Diego–based Second Advance Base Force was reorganized as the Fifth Marine Brigade, formed around the Fourth Regiment. The MCEF was renamed the East Coast Expeditionary Force in 1922, comprising the Fifth and Sixth Regiments of the Fourth Brigade, and the Fifth Brigade (Fourth Regiment) at San Diego became the basis of the West Coast Expeditionary Force in 1925.

60. Major General Ford O. Rogers, USMC, Ret., oral history transcript, December 3, 1970, 25, Oral History Collection, Headquarters, US Marine Corps, History and Museums Division, Washington, DC. Born in Waco, Texas, Rogers attended the Naval Academy for three years before enlisting in the Marine Corps. He was commissioned in 1917 and sent to Miami for flight training, after which he was ordered overseas as part of the Northern Bombing Group with Squadron 8 at Oye, France, flying DH-4s. He returned to the United States after the war and in 1922 was sent to the Dominican Republic, where he flew with the First Squadron, part of the Second Brigade. He left there in 1923 and in 1925 attended the US Army Air Service Tactical School at Langley Field near Norfolk, Virginia. In 1929 he was sent to Haiti, where he remained until 1931. Rogers served in a variety of roles until World War II, during which time he was chief of the Naval Aviation Mission to Peru from 1942 to 1944. He took command of the Third Marine Aircraft Wing in 1945. He retired in 1946 as a major general and died in 1972. He is buried in Arlington National Cemetery. Clark, *United States Marine Corps Generals of World War II*, 124–25.

61. The Naval Aircraft Factory was approved in 1917, and construction was completed at the Philadelphia Navy Yard in early 1918. Its first wartime role was to manufacture Curtiss H-16 flying boats, followed by N-1 pusher seaplanes and F-5L flying boats. The factory continued to manufacture commercial designs until 1922. Thereafter the factory

designed and flew several prototype aircraft of its own, and successful types were manufactured by civilian corporations. The factory also engaged in overhaul and modification work until World War II, including the conversion of army DH-4 Liberty planes to DH-4Bs. The factory returned to manufacturing airplanes in the 1930s, when Congress decreed that the US Navy would build 10 percent of its own aircraft as a means of keeping abreast of developments in the civilian industry. In fact, the factory was a major producer of navy aircraft during World War II. To distinguish Naval Aircraft Factory–made aircraft from civilian-manufactured types, the designator "N" was appended. For example, the N3N-3 was the last original design produced by the factory and the last biplane to see service with the navy (often referred to as the "Yellow Peril," owing to its bright yellow paint scheme). At the end of World War II the Naval Aircraft Factory was redesignated the Naval Air Material Unit, and the production of aircraft was discontinued. See Swanborough and Bowers, *United States Navy Aircraft since 1911*, 306–7. The Naval Aircraft Factory ended production for good in 1945 and was disestablished, its functions passing to the Naval Air Test Center at Naval Air Station Patuxent River, Maryland. Some of the buildings were converted for use by the Naval Surface Warfare Center, Caderock Division, as a research and development facility. See William Trimble, *Wings for the Navy: A History of the Naval Aircraft Factory, 1917–1956* (Annapolis, MD: Naval Institute Press, 1990).

62. Hazelhurst Field was renamed Roosevelt Field after World War I in honor of President Theodore Roosevelt's youngest and favorite son, Quentin, a US Army pursuit pilot who was killed in aerial combat over France. Roosevelt Field hosted many famous aviators, including Amelia Earhart and Wiley Post, and it was the launching point for Charles Lindbergh's solo transatlantic flight in 1927. The airfield closed in 1951 and is now the site of a shopping mall. Cunningham arranged for the marines to train at Mineola through Henry "Hap" Arnold, US Army, whom he had met at the Burgess factory in Marblehead while undergoing flight training there. Arnold had been at the factory to investigate a new tractor design that Burgess was trying to sell to the army. Jacobs, "Cunningham," 14–15.

63. Reserve Officers, *Marine Corps Reserve,* 12. According to an account written by Quartermaster Sergeant Lee Austin, the winter in Mineola was marked by snow, severe cold, and wind that was continually blowing over tents "about as fast as the ever-present morning, noon, and night detail could 'put 'em up again.'" Living conditions in Louisiana were not much better, as the army was unprepared for the marines' arrival; the men had to live on the train that delivered them for three days until living quarters were found in the cadet schoolhouse. That said, the flying weather was much better in Louisiana, and the marines "were instructing the Army boys where and how to 'oil and gas up' the Curtis Jennys in use there, and how to wait out on the field when the sudden sandstorms hit and get a good hold on the 'Jennys' wings to keep them from turning over." Lee Austin, *Marine Aviation: World War I* (Quantico, VA: First Marine Aviation Force Veterans Association, 1945), as quoted in ibid. See also Johnson, *Marine Corps Aviation,* 20.

64. Major General Lawson H. M. Sanderson, USMC, Ret., oral history transcript, December 3, 1970, 3, Oral History Collection, Headquarters, US Marine Corps, History and Museums Division, Washington, DC. Born in Washington State, Sanderson graduated from the University of Montana in Missoula in 1917 and promptly enlisted in the Marine Corps. He received his reserve commission and wings in 1919 and deployed to Haiti, where he joined Squadron E, attached to the First Brigade. But first he helped another

aviator, Walter Brown, establish a first-rate collegiate-level full-contact football program at Quantico. It was during his tour in Haiti that Sanderson began experimenting with dive-bombing (see chapter 2), a tactic that was quickly adopted throughout Marine Corps aviation. He returned to the United States in 1920 but went back to Haiti by way of the Dominican Republic along with another pilot, Lieutenant Basil Bradley, in a second airplane. At the time, this was the longest flight of a landplane over water. Both pilots and their observers were awarded the Distinguished Flying Cross. After a brief assignment in Washington, DC, Sanderson went to Nicaragua in December 1928, where he remained until 1930. In 1934 he attended the US Army Air Corps Tactical School at Maxwell Field in Montgomery, Alabama. In 1937 he took command of a fighter squadron on the West Coast and then commanded another squadron on the East Coast. When the United States entered World War II, he was ordered to Guadalcanal, where he was the operations officer for the "Cactus Air Force." He later took command of Marine Aircraft Group 2 on New Hebrides. Back in the United States, he assumed command of the Fourth Marine Aircraft Wing in 1945. In this capacity he accepted the Japanese surrender on Wake Island, the site of a heroic but futile stand by marines early in the war. After the war Sanderson served on Guam and in China and then served in a variety of roles in the United States before retiring as a major general in 1951. He died in June 1979. Clark, *United States Marine Corps Generals of World War II*, 132–34.

65. Terry Treadwell, *America's First Air War: The United States Army, Naval, and Marine Air Services in the First World War* (Osceola, WI: MBI Publishing, 2000), 46. See also Emmons, *First Marine Aviation Force*, 6.

66. A "loop" is begun from level flight. While keeping the wings level, the pilot pulls the nose of the airplane up and flies through a complete circle. A properly flown loop begins and ends at the same altitude and on the same heading. Although it is now considered a basic aerobatic maneuver, the loop was regarded as a difficult technique at the time, and because of the added weight and configuration of the centerline float and outboard "pontoons," it was thought that a floatplane such as the N-9 could not be looped.

67. For this feat Evans was awarded the Distinguished Flying Cross (DFC) in June 1936. Sherrod, "Marine Corps Aviation: The Early Days," part 1, 55. In truth, Evans was not successful until his fourth try, and there were no witnesses to his accomplishment, so he flew back to the Naval Air Station and performed the loop again close to shore. Ironically, the DFC was awarded less for his derring-do than for the stall and spin recovery techniques he developed that day. During his first three attempts, the N-9 "stalled." Stalls in fixed-wing flight occur when the pilot increases the wing's "angle of attack" beyond the "critical" angle, at which point there is a sudden reduction in airflow over the wing. This produces less "lift," and the aircraft may experience buffeting and even a precipitous dive from level flight. As the aircraft drops nose first, it may also enter into "autorotation" (that is, a "spin") because aileron control is lost. Evans discovered that by releasing back-pressure on the control stick and by applying the opposite rudder to the direction of the spin, he could level the wings and recover the airplane without difficulty. His stall and spin recovery techniques are still in use today.

68. Treadwell, *America's First Air War*, 46.

69. Lieutenant Poague died six days before the armistice was signed on November 11, 1918, bringing World War I to an end. He "was sealed in a copper-lined casket and

transported back to the United States by the protected cruiser, USS *Chicago*, on 21 November 1918." Antonio Godinho, "Marines in the Azores Islands in World War I: Diary of Walter S. Poague," *Fortitudine* 37, no. 1 (2012): 33.

70. Reserve Officers, *Marine Corps Reserve*, 14, quoting Austin, *Marine Aviation: World War I.*

71. Both Cunningham and Bernard Smith were sent to France to gather information, and they reported their findings to the navy's General Board. Transcripts are available in the Cunningham Papers and Smith Papers, MCHD and MCHRC.

72. Johnson, *Marine Corps Aviation*, 15. According to some accounts, the army staff in France under the command of General Pershing was still angry about newspaper reports that gave the marines almost exclusive credit for the victories at Château-Thierry and Belleau Wood. The reason for this was the army's edict forbidding the mention of regiments and other units by number in the press but permitting reference to general classifications such as infantry, artillery, and marines. Not surprisingly, given the marines' well-known exploits in various parts of the world prior to World War I, the newspapers reporting the two battles in France referred almost solely to "marines." Accordingly, in a fit of pique, Pershing's staff rejected any combat role for marine aviators in France. However, the British were more than willing to accept Marine Corps assistance, and Cunningham came up with the idea of assisting the British units fighting German U-boats operating from the coast of Belgium.

73. Alfred A. Cunningham, "Value of Aviation to the Marine Corps," *Marine Corps Gazette* 5, no. 3 (September 1920): 221–28. Following a demonstration of lighter-than-air flights at the St. Louis Exposition in 1904, Admiral Dewey reportedly told the fliers, "If you can fly higher than the crow's nest, we can use you." Van Deurs, *Wings for the Fleet*, 3.

74. Reserve Officers, *Marine Corps Reserve*, 12, quoting Austin, *Marine Aviation: World War I.* Lieutenant Commander Read (also known as "Putty") and a crew of six flew one of the famous Curtis "Nancy" flying boats, the NC-4, across the Atlantic from Naval Air Station Rockaway, New York, to Lisbon, Portugal, by way of the Azores. They departed New York on May 8, 1919, and arrived in Lisbon on May 27, flying from there to Plymouth, England, and arriving on May 31. Leo Murphy, *Flying Machines over Pensacola: An Early Aviation History from 1909 to 1929* (Gulf Breeze, FL: Pensacola Bay Flying Machine, 2003), 221.

75. Emmons, *First Marine Aviation Force*, 8. See also Gilles Auliard, "Maiden of the Skies," *Air Classics*, April 2009; Enzo Angelucci, *Great Aeroplanes of the World* (London: Hamlyn, 1973).

76. See Richard Smith, *First Across: The US Navy's Transatlantic Fight of 1919* (Annapolis, MD: Naval Institute Press, 1973).

77. The JN-4B was powered by an OX-2 engine. Seventy-six were built for the US Army and nine for the US Navy, six of which were used by the Marine Corps at Miami. The JN-4H employed ailerons and was powered by the license-built Hispano-Suiza 8 V-8 engine. The JN-4HG was a "gunnery" trainer. The DH-4 is discussed in detail later. The S-4B was a derivative of the Thomas-Morse S-4 "Scout," a compact single-seat biplane powered by a 100 hp Gnome rotary engine. The S-4 was designed by Benjamin Thomas, formerly with the British Sopwith Aviation Company; he also assisted with the design of the Curtiss JN-4. Twelve Scouts went to the US Navy. The S-4B used by the marines at

Miami had a 110 hp Gnome engine and proved more successful. The army purchased ninety-seven and the navy acquired ten. By 1918, the S-4B was being used by practically every "pursuit" flying school in the United States.

78. Emmons, *First Marine Aviation Force,* 10. Captain Roben had the distinction of leading the first night flight of Marine Corps aviators. During a training mission in April 1918, one of three JN-4s broke its propeller upon landing at Palm Beach, Florida. A new propeller was delivered from the Flying Field at Miami, but the airplane was not ready to go until after nightfall. Roben requested and received permission to lead the flight of planes back to Miami. Meanwhile, the marines at the Flying Field at Miami had outlined the airstrip with metal cans containing sand and gasoline, which they lit when they heard the airplanes overhead. All the airplanes landed safely. "Marine Corps Aviation," *Headquarters Bulletin* 239 (September 1945).

79. Tethered balloons allowed observers to see as far as 40 miles behind enemy lines. A kite balloon is stabilized in windy conditions by its streamlined envelope as well as by a harness (or yoke) connecting it to the main tether. In this manner, kite balloons are able to operate in conditions unsuitable for round balloons; for that reason, they were used extensively before and during World War I for observation and artillery spotting. The *caquot* balloon (more accurately, dirigible) was named after French engineer Albert Irénée Caquot, whose design was adopted by all the American armed services. The hydrogen-filled balloon could lift two passengers and their equipment to about 4,000 feet in good weather, although normal operations ranged between 1,000 and 4,000 feet. The *caquot* design was used again in limited numbers by the British during World War II. See Lennart Ege, *Balloons and Airships* (New York: Macmillan, 1974).

80. John Elliott and Clyde Gillespie, "MCAS Quantico," *Naval Aviation News,* May 1975, 9.

81. Kenneth Collings, *Just for the Hell of It* (New York: Dodd, Mead, 1938), 59.

82. Roger Emmons, "Navy Fliers Transferred to Marine Aviation, Marine Day Wing in France, 1918," First Marine Aviation Force Veterans Association Newsletter (Baltimore), 1971, 10.

83. In one month's time, marine aviators were required to complete seven hours of formation flying, four half-hour missions of low-level bombing, another four hours of bombing from 5,000 feet, thirty minutes of cross-country flying with a passenger, two hours of formation ground attack using four aircraft, thirty minutes of ground attack with six aircraft, and a final cross-country test in which the pilot had to use a map to navigate, find the target, attack, and return to base in forty-five minutes. "Outline of Bombing Training for Marine Corps Detachment at Miami, Florida," June 1918, 1–2, MCHD, Herman A. Peterson Papers, Accession no. 6B12, box 1.

84. Collings's *Just for the Hell of It* is an autobiographical adventure story and the best description of flying in Haiti between the world wars. Born in Nebraska and raised in Washington, DC, the young Collings witnessed Orville Wright demonstrate his flying machine at Fort Myer near DC on September 9, 1908. From that point forward, Collings wanted to fly. He joined the DC National Guard and, upon US entry into World War I, was commissioned into the Marine Corps, trained at Miami under the tutelage of Captain Roy Geiger, and deployed to France with Squadron A, First Marine Aviation Force, where he nearly died from Spanish flu. The war ended two days after he returned to flying duty.

After the war he went to Haiti with Squadron E and flew there for two years. A man who could not stay put, Collings resigned from the Marines Corps when he learned he was going to be posted to the Dominican Republic as an infantry officer, but he remained in the reserves until retiring in March 1940. After leaving active service he took up barnstorming with Gates Flying Circus and also flew for Pan American Airlines in the Caribbean. In 1928 he gained notoriety when he tore the roof off a truck with his airplane, retribution for the driver's spattering mud on it. At some point he became a salesman for National Life Insurance, where he became a top agent. During the 1930s he sold insurance for several months a year and pursued his love of adventure by traveling the rest. A prolific writer, he contributed to the pulp adventure magazine *Argosy* as well as *Liberty* magazine. Collings traveled to Ethiopia as a correspondent for *Liberty* during the Italian invasion of that country, fought against the Italian army, and was the only American to interview Emperor Haile Selassie. Later he traveled to Czechoslovakia to cover the German annexation. At one point he was taken prisoner by Russian soldiers; he was accused of spying and threatened with execution on three separate occasions but was ultimately released. Afterward he followed the Germans into Poland in 1939 and then returned to the United States in 1940. That same year he resigned from National Life and the Safair Flying School at Roosevelt Field, Long Island, New York, and volunteered his services to Canada as a ferry pilot, transferring bombers and other aircraft to North Africa from the United Kingdom. When he departed for Canada he told his wife and son he had taken a flying job in Chile; he did not tell them the truth until ten days later, when he and several other American fliers were notified that they were scheduled to travel to Britain aboard the armed Canadian troopship SS *Nerissa.* A week later the ship was torpedoed by the German submarine U-552, commanded by Lieutenant Erich Topp (who would serve in the postwar West German Bundesmarine, retiring as a rear admiral, and serve in the Pentagon as a naval representative for the West German government). Collings and more than 200 other passengers, including women and children and ten other American fliers, went down with the ship. Only 80 passengers survived. Collings's last act was to help a Canadian soldier climb aboard some floating debris before succumbing to hypothermia. Some weeks later, Collings's body washed ashore in Scotland; a special inscription on his wristwatch enabled his remains to be identified. He was buried at a nearby Royal Air Force cemetery. After the war his remains were returned to the United States and interred at Arlington National Cemetery. Collings wrote a number of articles and two books, *These Things I Saw* and *Just for the Hell of It.* He also coauthored "With Allenby in the Holy Land" with his close friend and fellow adventurer Lowell Thomas. "Kenneth B. Collings," https://www.nationallife.com/public/histarchive/military_collings.asp, accessed March 20, 2017. Also see "Collings Defied Death often in Flying Career," *New York Herald Tribune,* May 7, 1941; "Sea Gives up Lost Writer," *Long Island Daily Press,* August 13, 1943.

85. Collings, *Just for the Hell of It,* 64. "Brock" Davey was a reserve officer. In the early days of Marine Corps aviation, reserve officers were not identified as such in subsequent histories. According to Brigadier General Karl Day, a reserve officer himself, "Nobody gave a damn and few, if any, knew who were regulars, temporaries, duration reserves, or what have you." However, Day recalled that at Hazelhurst Field, "Pat Mulchay and I were Regulars—and maybe Kipp—though I am not sure, and the balance were Reserves." The identity of the first reserve naval aviator has not been firmly established, although

Robert Sherrod claimed it was Allen Boynton. Nevertheless, reserve pilots compiled a distinguished combat record, including Ralph Talbot (a former navy officer), who received the Medal of Honor in France. Some reserve pilots went on to become test pilots, a dangerous business. Gwen Newman died after the war when his Loening amphibian fell apart in the air during landing. Other reserve pilots left the Marine Corps and became barnstormers, mail pilots, and airline pilots. Edwin Musick, for example, became a senior captain for Pan American Airlines. Tragically, he was killed when his airplane "blew apart while he was exploring a route for Pan-American to Australia." Reserve Officers, *Marine Corps Reserve,* 12, 15.

86. Reserve Officers, *Marine Corps Reserve,* 14. Several marine aviators were killed in army service, including Lieutenant Kenneth Culbert, who died in the Toul sector of France on May 15, 1918. In addition, Marcus Jordan crashed and died in Italy while serving under the command of Captain Fiorello La Guardia of the Army Signal Corps. La Guardia later became a US congressman and mayor of New York City. Both aviators were reserve officers. Ibid., 14–15.

87. One source claims that the Thomas-Morse Scouts were late-production S-4Cs; see Johnson, *Marine Corps Aviation,* 17. The S-4C replaced the Gnome B-9 engine with the more reliable 80 hp Le Rhône 9C (beginning with the fifty-second production aircraft). More than 460 S-4Cs went to the US Army, and 4 went to the US Navy with floats. Thus, in all likelihood, the airplanes operated by the marines at Miami were S-4Bs.

88. Collings, *Just for the Hell of It,* 70.

89. Ibid., 85.

90. Johnson, *Marine Corps Aviation,* 19; Collings, *Just for the Hell of It,* 75.

91. "Marine Corps Aviation," *Headquarters Bulletin* 239 (September 1945).

92. By the end of the war, the marines of the Northern Bombing Group were still operating at Oye, Le Fresne, and Saint-Pol-sur-Ternoise in France, as well as at Hoondschoote, Ghietelles, Varsennaire, and Knesselaere in Belgium, the latter four owing to the Allied advance following the collapse of the German offensive in 1918.

93. During World War I the terms "group" and "wing" were first used in US naval aviation history. The Northern Bombing Group was subordinate to the commander, US Naval Forces in Europe, but under the tactical control of the Dover Air Patrol, a British command.

94. Collings, *Just for the Hell of It,* 87.

95. Johnson, *Marine Corps Aviation,* 16.

96. See Ralph Paine, "Naval Aviation Overseas," *Cross and Cockade Journal* 4, no. 1 (Spring 1963): 66; Robert Daley, *An American Saga: Juan Trippe and His Pan Am Empire* (New York: Random House, 1980), 6–14. The designation of the American force as the Northern Bombing Group may confuse some readers. During World War I the Americans conformed to the British system, in which a group was superior to a wing. The British retained this hierarchy during World War II, but the US Army Air Force reversed the system—that is, a wing became superior to a group. This superior-subordinate relationship between wing and group still applies to the US Air Force today, as well as to the US Navy and Marine Corps—that is, a Marine Aircraft Group is subordinate to a Marine Aircraft Wing.

97. For an in-depth examination of the Northern Bombing Group, see Adrian Van Wyen, *Naval Aviation in World War I* (1969; reprint, Honolulu, HI: University Press of the

Pacific, 2005); Archibald Turnbull and Clifford Lee Lord, *History of United States Naval Aviation* (Manchester, NH: Ayer, 1971). Also see Emmons, *First Marine Aviation Force,* in its entirety. For the failure of the Night Wing, see Noel Shirley, "La Guardia, Caproni Bombers, and the US Navy," *Cross and Cockade Journal* 25, no. 2 (1984); R. D. Layman, "Les Caproni Ca-5 de l'US Navy," *Avions* 4 (June 1993).

98. According to Collings, "Struts had been sawed almost in half—left so that they would break without warning; the cuts were filled with putty and painted over." In addition, "Aileron and flipper control horns had been bored with a series of almost adjoining holes, ready to give way under the least strain. The holes had been filled with lead and painted. The damage was invisible to the eye, but would very effectively kill anyone who tried to fly the planes." Collings, *Just for the Hell of It,* 91.

99. Johnson, *Marine Corps Aviation,* 16.

100. The American machines of the Northern Bombing Group employed two forward-firing Marlin .30-caliber machine guns in the nose and two Lewis guns mounted on the Scarff ring. The standard bomb load was two 50-pound and two 112-pound bombs. Emmons, *First Marine Aviation Force,* 18.

101. Of thirty-three DH-4s lost to enemy action by the US Army Air Service during World War I, fewer than ten went down in flames, "no worse than the average at the time." On November 12, 1918, the day after the armistice, the first DH-4 equipped with a self-sealing fuel tank arrived in France. W. M. Lamberton, *Reconnaissance and Bomber Aircraft of the 1914–1918 War* (Warwick, UK: Warwick Printing, 1962), 13.

102. J. M. Bruce, *The Aeroplanes of the Royal Flying Corps* (London: Putnam, 1982), 72; J. E. A. Baldwin, "Experiences of Bombing with the Independent Force in 1918," in *A Selection of Lectures and Essays from the Work of Officers Attending the First Course at the Royal Air Force Staff College, 1921–1923* (London: Her Majesty's Stationery Office, Air Ministry, 1923), 11.

103. Emmons, *First Marine Aviation Force,* 18.

104. The British Army Royal Flying Corps gained institutional independence as the Royal Air Force (RAF) on April 1, 1918, and is the oldest independent air force in the world. At its genesis, the RAF was an amalgamation of the former Flying Corps and the Royal Naval Air Service (RNAS). However, the RNAS achieved independence from the RAF when the Fleet Air Arm was turned over to the Admiralty in May 1939.

105. At the time of US entry into World War I, the Medal of Honor was the sole American award for valor. In contrast, European armies awarded a variety of medals for bravery. In 1918 the US Army created the Distinguished Service Cross and the Distinguished Service Medal. The US Navy followed suit in 1919, with the award retroactive to April 6, 1917. The Navy Distinguished Service Medal was originally superior to the Navy Cross; the former was awarded for heroism, and the latter was awarded for heroism and "other distinguished service." However, Congress reversed this precedence in August 1942, making the Navy Cross a combat-only medal, second only to the Medal of Honor.

106. Francis "Pat" Mulcahy was a Notre Dame graduate from New York who was commissioned into the Marine Corps in 1917, took flight instruction at Miami, and flew combat missions in France during World War I. A pioneer of close air support during the interwar years, he assumed command of the aircraft squadrons in Nicaragua at the tail end of Marine Corps operations there from 1927 to 1933 (see chapter 4). At the time of the Japanese attack

on Pearl Harbor, Mulcahy was serving as an observer with the Royal Air Force Western Desert Air Force in North Africa. He deployed to Guadalcanal, where he commanded the "Cactus Air Force." In September 1944 he succeeded Major General Ross Rowell as commanding general of aircraft, Fleet Marine Force. Rowell had also preceded Mulcahy as the first commander of marine aircraft deployed to Nicaragua in 1927. During the invasion of Okinawa, Mulcahy volunteered to command the US Army Air Force Tenth Tactical Air Force and went ashore to coordinate air support to Tenth Army during the bloody fight for the island. Owing to poor health, Mulcahy was relieved by Louis Woods, another marine aviator who had served in Haiti. Upon his retirement, Mulcahy was promoted to lieutenant general. He died in December 1973. Clark, *United States Marine Corps Generals of World War II,* 99–100.

107. The paragraphs summarizing the actions of the Day Wing are drawn from the following sources: Johnson, *Marine Corps Aviation,* 20–25; Treadwell, *America's First Air War,* 106–8; Emmons, *First Marine Aviation Force,* 20–28; Robert Sherrod, *History of Marine Corps Aviation in World War II* (Baltimore: Nautical & Aviation Publishing Company of America, 1987), 11–18. Also see Van Wyen, *Naval Aviation in World War I.*

108. Portable, narrow-gauge "field railways" were used by all sides during World War I to move supplies to the front lines from nearby railheads. For an in-depth examination, see Christian Wolmar, *Engines of War: How Wars Were Won and Lost on the Railways* (New York: Public Affairs, 2010), chap. 7.

109. Emmons, *First Marine Aviation Force,* 25–28.

110. Johnson, *Marine Corps Aviation,* 24, claims that the marines dropped 15,140 pounds of bombs in conjunction with the British and another 18,792 pounds independently, or 33,932 pounds. A 1925 study (Sitz, "History of US Naval Aviation," 42) claims a total of 52,000 pounds. Sherrod, *History of Marine Corps Aviation in World War II,* 16, arrives at a total of 126,302 pounds dropped by US Navy and US Marine Corps crews, with the latter accounting for 27,316 pounds.

111. W. H. Sitz claims the high of twelve, whereas Edward Johnson credits the marines with four kills. Sherrod acknowledges that only four downed enemy planes were confirmed in the official records of the Day Wing (one by Mulcahy and his observer, Corporal McCullough; the other three by Lieutenant Talbot and Gunnery Sergeant Robinson). However, Sherrod also points to a certificate signed by the commander of No. 218 Squadron, Royal Air Force, stating that Lieutenant Everett Brewer and Sergeant Harry Wersheiner downed one Fokker and probably another on September 28. Also, Captain Lytle received the Distinguished Service Medal for downing a German plane on October 14. Emmons claims that four enemy planes were shot down, "plus another possible eight enemy aircraft destroyed." Emmons, *First Marine Aviation Force,* 31.

112. Collings, *Just for the Hell of It,* 106.

113. Sherrod, *History of Marine Corps Aviation in World War II,* 18. According to Johnson, *Marine Corps Aviation,* 24, four officers and twenty-one enlisted men died from the Spanish flu. To appreciate the worldwide impact of Spanish influenza (which killed as many as 100 million people), see John Barry, *The Great Influenza: The Story of the Deadliest Pandemic in History* (London: Viking Penguin, 2005).

114. Sitz, "History of US Naval Aviation," 43.

115. The phrase "savage war of peace" was first popularized by British historian Sir Alistair Horne in his 1977 book of that title covering the Algerian revolution. Journalist Max Boot

gave his book a similar title: *The Savage Wars of Peace: Small Wars and the Rise of American Power* (New York: Basic Books, 2002). The origin of the phrase, however, can ultimately be traced to Rudyard Kipling's 1899 poem "The White Man's Burden," in which he writes: "Take up the White Man's burden / The savage wars of peace / Fill full the mouth of Famine / And bid the sickness cease / And when your goal is nearest / The end for others sought / Watch sloth and heathen Folly / Bring all your hopes to nought." The full poem is available at http://sourcebooks.fordham.edu/halsall/mod/kipling.asp, accessed March 20, 2017.

2. Proving Ground: Haiti, 1915–1934

1. Some Spanish holdings, notably Puerto Rico, Guam, and the Philippines, were openly seized by the United States, while others, such as Cuba, became in effect American protectorates. In either case, the United States was poorly prepared for the task of governing these ersatz colonies, having no formal colonial office to match the United Kingdom's professional corps of administrators.

2. Hans Schmidt, *The United States Occupation of Haiti, 1915–1934* (1971; reprint, New Brunswick, NJ: Rutgers University Press, 1995), 43.

3. Lying between the eastern tip of Cuba and the island of Hispaniola, the Windward Passage connects the Atlantic Ocean to the Caribbean Sea. It is the most direct path for ships heading from the Eastern Seaboard of the United States to the Panama Canal.

4. Philip Jessup, *Elihu Root* (New York: Dodd, Mead, 1938), 471.

5. In short, the Platt Amendment prevented Cuba from making any treaty with a foreign power that would infringe on Cuba's independence. The amendment also stated that Cuba could not acquire any public debt beyond its ability to pay, and it gave the United States the right to intervene to preserve order. See Samuel Bemis, *A Diplomatic History of the United States,* rev. ed. (New York: Holt, 1942).

6. As boldly declared by Teddy Roosevelt, "All that this country desires is to see the neighboring countries stable, orderly, and prosperous. Any country whose people conduct themselves well can count upon our hearty friendship. If a nation shows that it knows how to act with reasonable efficiency and decency in social and political matters, if it keeps order and pays its obligations, it need fear no interference from the United States. Chronic wrongdoing, or an impotence which results in a general loosening of the ties of civilized society, may in America, as elsewhere, ultimately require intervention by some civilized nation, and in the Western Hemisphere the adherence of the United States to the Monroe Doctrine may force the United States, however reluctantly, in flagrant cases of such wrongdoing or impotence, to the exercise of an international police power." See US Congress, *Congressional Record,* 1874, 19.

7. A receivership is a type of bankruptcy in which a government, a court, or a private enterprise appoints a "receiver" to oversee the financial matters of the entity in receivership. The receiver's responsibility is to recoup as much of the unpaid loans as possible. This is generally accomplished by giving the receiver the authority to dispose of the debtor's property, including tangible and intangible assets and rights.

8. Bemis, *Diplomatic History of the United States,* 526–28. See also Lester Langley, *The United States and the Caribbean, 1900–1970* (Athens: University of Georgia Press, 1980).

9. Following in the tradition of the British Royal Navy, early US Navy sailors—officers and enlisted seamen alike—wore dress blue uniform jackets (the service dress blue uniform remains in use today, although it looks nearly black). Thus, American sailors became known as "bluejackets."

10. In general, a gunboat is a warship weighing less than 2,000 tons and with a light battery, usually 4-inch rapid-fire guns, and a crew of 125 or fewer.

11. Keith Bickel, *Mars Learning: The Marine Corps' Development of Small Wars Doctrine, 1915–1940* (Boulder, CO: Westview Press, 2001), 91.

12. It was only at the behest of a Dominican priest, Bartolomé de Las Casas, that Charles V of Spain agreed to import African slaves to relieve the indigenous people still alive in the colony, thus beginning the African slave trade to the so-called New World.

13. A slave who had escaped to the mountains was known as a *maroon,* an archaic term derived from *cimarrón,* Spanish for livestock (such as sheep) that have gone wild. By the latter half of the eighteenth century, tens of thousands of maroons had organized themselves in the highlands, and they formed the basis of several unsuccessful slave revolts leading up to the Haitian revolution. Maroons were not unique to Haiti; escaped slaves throughout the Caribbean and Latin America were known as maroons. The most famous maroon community was in Palmares, Brazil, which withstood almost a century of Portuguese expeditions to wipe it out before being destroyed in the 1690s. Colonial governments sometimes signed treaties with maroons, most notably in Jamaica, Colombia, Ecuador, Cuba, Hispaniola, and Surinam. Only in Jamaica and the Guianas have descendants of the maroons continued as separate and distinct communities. For more information, see Barbara Kopytoff, "Guerrilla Warfare in Eighteenth Century Jamaica," *Expedition* 19, no. 2 (January 1977).

14. For a comprehensive general history of Haiti, see Robert Heinl and Nancy Heinl, *Written in Blood: The Story of the Haitian People, 1492–1971* (1978; reprint, Lanham, MD: University Press of America, 2005). Other useful works include H. P. Davis, *Black Democracy: The Story of Haiti* (New York: Dial Press, 1928); James Leyburn, *The Haitian People* (1941; reprint, New Haven, CT: Yale University Press, 1966).

15. Although describing the division of Haitian society as a "caste" system may be overstated, Yale sociologist James Leyburn argued as much in his benchmark work *The Haitian People.* Indeed, the white colonists in Saint Domingue "meticulously constructed a classification system to identify the offspring of blacks and whites based on 128 divisions of skin shade and ancestry," which would persist among mulattoes and blacks following independence. Bob Shacochis, *The Immaculate Invasion* (New York: Viking: 1999), 22. See also Schmidt, *United States Occupation of Haiti,* 21.

16. Schmidt, *United States Occupation of Haiti,* 21.

17. Ibid., 26–27. From 1806 to 1915, seventeen of twenty-four Haitian presidents were toppled by "revolution," and from 1888 to 1915, no Haitian president completed his full seven-year term. Most were murdered while in office, and seven of them died between 1911 and 1915. According to a history of the Garde d'Haiti written just prior to the marines' evacuation, "If a man from the South was President, the North rose in revolt. If a man from the North was President, the South took up arms." "The Formative Period, 1915–1920," typescript, n.d., 14, MCHD, Haiti: Histories.

18. *Caco* armies were generally raised in the rugged hills of northern Haiti. Mostly peasants, these mercenaries hired themselves out to presumptuous revolutionary leaders.

Indeed, in his colorful autobiographical account, Warrant Officer Faustin Wirkus, USMC, describes the *cacos* as "foraging revolutionists rather than brigands." Faustin Wirkus and Taney Dudley, *The White King of La Gonave: The True Story of the Sergeant of Marines Who Was Crowned King on a Voodoo Island* (Garden City, NY: Doubleday, Doran, 1931), 21. "Organized in bands under local chiefs, their hierarchy ran up in theory to a supposed 'Chief of the *cacos*,' or at least to a small group of top-level generals. This loosely hierarchical organization made it possible for the aspiring presidential candidate to secure the services of an entire *caco* army by striking an agreement with only a few men. The revolutionary leader normally promised a lump-sum payment in case of success, to be distributed by the *caco* chiefs to their followers according to rank. Everyone understood that a certain amount of looting would also swell the profits of the campaign. When the successful revolutionist was installed in the presidency, he paid off his army and it returned to its northern haunts, to await the bidding of the next plotters against the incumbent regime." David Healy, *Gunboat Diplomacy in the Wilson Era: The US Navy in Haiti, 1915–1916* (Madison: University of Wisconsin Press, 1976), 20–21. The term *caco* is a corruption of the Creole word for the taco, a bird of prey native to the island of Hispaniola. Horace Paulus-Sannon, *Histoire de Toussaint Louverture,* vol. 3, 2d ed. (Port-au-Prince, Haiti: Presses Nationals, 2003), 206 n. 15. See also Mary Renda, *Taking Haiti: Military Occupation and the Culture of US Imperialism* (Chapel Hill: University of North Carolina Press, 2001), 140; John Craige, "Development of the Republic of Haiti," n.d., 6, MCHD, Marines in Haiti. Craige's essay was published in June 1929 in *Military Engineer.*

19. Corvée is unpaid labor. Typically used in reference to medieval Europe, the corvée system entails the impressment of people of low social status by a feudal lord in lieu of paying tax. It differs from chattel slavery, in that the worker is not owned and is free in matters other than his or her labor. In the immediate aftermath of the Haitian revolution, former slave Henri Christophe established his own government in northern Haiti, styling himself king. To maintain the plantations, Christophe enforced the corvée in lieu of taxing the population. Although a despot, Christophe was able to maintain the economic viability of the north, whereas southern Haiti fell into poverty as the distribution of land to the masses ruined agricultural productivity. See "Corvées: valeur symbolique et poids économique," in *Pour une anthropologie du prélèvement seigneurial dans les campagnes médiévales (XIe–XIVe siècles): réalités et représentations paysannes,* ed. Monique Bourin (Paris: Publications de la Sorbonne, 2004), 271–381. Interestingly, Christophe purportedly served with French forces as a drummer boy in the Chasseurs-Volontaires de Saint-Domingue, a regiment composed of *gens de couleur,* during the 1779 siege of Savannah, Georgia, during the American Revolution. There is a statue commemorating the contribution of the Chasseurs-Volontaires in Franklin Square in downtown Savannah.

20. "History of the Garde d'Haiti 1492–1920," typescript, April 3–July 31, 1934, 13, MCHD, Haiti Garde.

21. Ibid.

22. Heinl and Heinl, *Written in Blood,* 321.

23. The French tried to overturn Haitian independence when Napoleon came to power. In 1801 he dispatched more than 30,000 troops under the command of his brother-in-law, General Charles Leclerc, to recover Haiti. Leclerc's army landed at Cap Français (Cap Haïtian) in 1802, and after three months of hard fighting, L'Ouverture

was defeated and sent to France, where he died in prison. However, Leclerc did not consolidate his victory, and over the next several months, he and most of his army succumbed to yellow fever. Leclerc was replaced by the Vicomte de Rochambeau, son of General Comte de Rochambeau, George Washington's famous ally during the American Revolution. Historians point to the younger Rochambeau's employment of terror against the populace as the catalyst for uniting mulattoes and blacks in another uprising. On November 18, 1803, an army headed by Jean Jacques Dessalines defeated the rump French forces at the Battle of Vertières. The French then evacuated Haiti, only to become prisoners of an English fleet. Dessalines proclaimed independence anew on New Year's Day 1804. For a more in-depth examination of this period, see C. L. R. James, *The Black Jacobins: Toussaint L'Ouverture and the San Domingo Revolution,* 2d ed. (New York: Vintage Books, 1989).

24. Ludwell Montague, *Haiti and the United States, 1714–1938* (Durham, NC: Duke University Press, 1940), 65.

25. Coming at the end of the Napoleonic Wars and after a Russian attempt to assert power in the Northwest in 1821, the Monroe Doctrine was first introduced in 1823. It declared that foreign (that is, European) meddling in the Western Hemisphere would be viewed by the US government as an act of aggression. See Ernest May, *The Making of the Monroe Doctrine* (Cambridge, MA: Harvard University Press, 1975).

26. Montague, *Haiti and the United States,* 175.

27. Ibid., 36.

28. Also figuring into American calculations was the previously mentioned Môle Saint-Nicolas, which lay astride the Windward Passage. Although the Môle was regarded as obsolete by Admiral Mahan and other US Navy officers, they did not want some other major power to possess it. With the outbreak of war in Europe in 1914, American officials were especially fearful of German adventurism in the Caribbean. In a letter to the Senate in 1922, Secretary of State Robert Lansing stated that the reason for intervention in Haiti in 1915 had been the threat of Môle Saint-Nicolas falling into German hands, particularly the prospect of German submarines operating from there. Lansing to Senator Medill McCormick, May 4, 1922, *Congressional Record* 62, pt. 6, 67th Cong., 2d sess., 1922, 685–88. Also see Robert Lansing, *War Memoirs of Robert Lansing: Secretary of State* (1935; reprint, Westport, CT: Greenwood Press, 1971).

29. Heinl and Heinl, *Written in Blood,* 372. Oreste fled to Jamaica.

30. US Department of the Navy, Office of Naval Intelligence, "A List of Expeditions Formed and Landings Effected by the US Naval Forces in Central America, Mexico and the West Indies, from 1901 to May 1, 1929," May 1, 1929, Naval Historical Center, Washington, DC.

31. The Special Service Squadron Battalion of Marines, comprising the Forty-Fourth, Forty-Fifth, and Forty-Sixth Companies, was detached from the First Brigade at Veracruz, Mexico, and steamed to Guantanamo Bay, Cuba, aboard the USS *Hancock.* The battalion disembarked to await the *Hancock*'s return from Philadelphia with the Thirty-Seventh, Forty-Seventh, and Forty-Eighth Companies. The combined command was designated the Fifth Regiment under the command of Colonel Charles Doyen. The regiment remained aboard the *Hancock* in Haitian waters until December 17, 1914, whereupon the ship returned to Philadelphia on December 23, 1914. Ibid.

32. Dana Munro, *Intervention and Dollar Diplomacy in the Caribbean, 1900–1921* (1964; reprint, Westport, CT: Greenwood Press, 1980), 342.

33. Ibid., 345.

34. "Paul Fuller Going to Haiti: Wilson Sending Him There to Report on Island's Affairs," *New York Times*, April 30, 1915.

35. An 1875 graduate of the US Naval Academy, Caperton served on the Wheeling-class gunboat USS *Marietta* during the Spanish-American War and was present at the shipboard signing of the peace protocol in August 1898. Upon completing the Naval War College, he was promoted to rear admiral, and in November 1914 he assumed command of the Cruiser Squadron. See Glenn Ameling, "Admiral and Diplomat: William Banks Caperton, Agent of United States Naval Policy in Latin America 1915–1919" (master's thesis, Brigham Young University, 1981).

36. US Congress, Senate Select Committee on Haiti and Santo Domingo, *Inquiry into Occupation and Administration of Haiti and Santo Domingo*, 67th Cong., 1st and 2d sess. (Washington, DC: GPO, 1922), 313. Hereafter cited as Senate Select Hearings.

37. Heinl and Heinl, *Written in Blood*, 393.

38. Senate Select Hearings, 299.

39. "The Formative Period, 1915–1920," 16.

40. Some sources claim Etienne ordered the murders on his own initiative.

41. "The Formative Period, 1915–1920," 17.

42. Davis, *Black Democracy*, 163.

43. Ibid., 167.

44. "The Formative Period, 1915–1920," 17.

45. Heinl and Heinl, *Written in Blood*, 394–400. Also see Senate Select Hearings, 307–8. It is important to note that Admiral Caperton intervened on his own authority, based on his understanding of American interests and his interpretation of his duty to safeguard American lives and property. After landing troops at Cap Haïtian, Caperton's legal officer drew up a memorandum regarding the legal basis for armed intervention, citing principally navy regulations. Even after the State Department signaled its desire for Caperton to intervene, minimal guidance followed, and throughout the early weeks of the occupation, Caperton was still acting based on his own interpretation of the situation and his own authority. In that regard, naval service and tradition had prepared him well for this responsibility. As Lester Langley has noted, "Naval officers were steeped in the nineteenth-century tradition of their role as diplomats and protectors of the sea lanes. . . . It was a tradition that carried over into the age of battleships and radio communications." Lester Langley, *The Banana Wars: United States Intervention in the Caribbean, 1898–1934* (Lexington: University Press of Kentucky, 1983), 7.

46. For details, see Richard Millett, *Searching for Stability: The US Development of Constabulary Forces in Latin America and the Philippines*, Occasional Paper no. 20 (Fort Leavenworth, KS: Combat Studies Institute Press, US Army Combined Arms Center, 2010), chap. 5.

47. US Department of the Navy, *Annual Report of the Secretary of the Navy, 1920* (Washington, DC: GPO, 1921), 249. Hereafter cited as *SECNAV Annual Report, 1920*. Also see Harry Ellsworth, *One Hundred Eighty Landings of the United States Marines, 1800–1934* (Washington, DC: GPO, 1974), 89–90.

48. Daily Diary, Commanding Officer (Colonel Eli K. Cole, USMC), First Marine Brigade, February 25, 1917, Naval Records of the Office of Naval Records and Library, RG 45, WA-7, box 632, National Archives, Washington, DC. By July 1915, the Marine Corps had managed to assemble the First Brigade, consisting of two regiments of some 2,000 officers and men, at Philadelphia. The brigade also had a three-company artillery battalion located at Annapolis. The primary mission of the First Brigade was the defense of advance bases during wartime, but it also acted as a rapid-reaction force for expeditionary missions and served in this capacity at Veracruz in 1914. Lacking adequate transports, the navy often used battleships and smaller warships to move the marines, an arrangement satisfactory to neither service.

49. Colonel Waller was a Virginian whose maternal grandfather was a congressman, a senator, and the twenty-sixth governor of the state. A career marine, Waller served in the Spanish-American War aboard the battleship USS *Indiana,* taking part in the Battle of Santiago on July 3, 1898. He later helped put down the Boxer Rebellion in China and then led marines in counterguerrilla operations during the Philippine Insurrection. He was court-martialed (and acquitted) for alleged war crimes on the island of Samar. After briefly returning to the United States, Waller commanded a provisional regiment in Panama and then a provisional brigade in Cuba. During the assault on Veracruz in 1914, Waller commanded the First Brigade. "Littleton Waller Tazewell Waller, Major General, United States Marine Corps." Arlington National Cemetery, http://www.arlingtoncemetery.net/lwwaller.htm, accessed March 20, 2017.

50. "The Formative Period, 1915–1920," 18.

51. Senate Select Hearings, 316.

52. Heinl and Heinl, *Written in Blood,* 417.

53. For details, see Senate Select Hearings, 315–21, 333.

54. Munro, *Intervention and Dollar Diplomacy in the Caribbean,* 158–59.

55. Brigadier General George Barnett, USMC, "Report on Affairs in the Republic of Haiti, June 1915 to June 30, 1920," October 11, 1920, 20, Office of Naval Records and Library, RG 45, Subject File, 1911–1927, WA-7, National Archives. Hereafter cited as Barnett Report.

56. Ibid., 24.

57. Major Smedley Butler, nicknamed the "Fighting Quaker" and "Old Gimlet Eye," is one of the most colorful figures in American military history. Over his thirty-four-year career in the Marine Corps, Butler saw action in the Philippines, China, Latin America, and Haiti. He also deployed to France during World War I but saw no action there. By the end of his career, Butler had received sixteen awards—five for heroism, including two Medals of Honor. Upon his retirement, Butler renounced war and imperialism and devoted his energies to dissident and leftist political causes. For a useful biography, see Hans Schmidt, *Maverick Marine: General Smedley D. Butler and the Contradictions of American Military History* (1987; reprint, Lexington: University Press of Kentucky, 1998).

58. Ibid., 76.

59. *SECNAV Annual Report, 1920,* 261.

60. Ibid., 262–64.

61. Barnett Report, 28–29.

62. Ibid., 30–31.

63. Senate Select Hearings, 333, 336.

64. Charles Conrad, "A Year in Haiti's Customs and Fiscal Service," *Proceedings,* April 1923, 605–24.

65. Heinl and Heinl, *Written in Blood,* 421.

66. Ibid., 437.

67. Ibid., 437–42.

68. In 1916 Admiral Caperton was replaced by Admiral Charles Pond.

69. Barnett Report, 39, 49; "Haiti: Historical Outline of the Military Occupation," n.d., 18, MCHD, Haiti: Occupation; "Annual Report of General George Barnett to the Secretary of the Navy, Fiscal Year 1916," October 5, 1916, 2–3, MCHD, Haiti, Occupation.

70. "The Formative Period, 1915–1920," 22. On paper, the Haitian army consisted of thirty-eight regiments of infantry, four of artillery, and an assortment of miscellaneous troops, including the Palace Guard. All these forces were led by some 300 generals and 50 colonels, as well as "honorary generals" appointed by the president. Robert Heinl, *Soldiers of the Sea: The United States Marine Corps, 1775–1962* (1962; reprint, Mount Pleasant, SC: Nautical & Aviation Publishing Company of America, 1991), 178.

71. Butler would be replaced as commandant of the gendarmerie in 1918 by Lieutenant Colonel Alexander Williams, who would in turn be replaced by Frederic Wise before the complete withdrawal of the marines in 1934.

72. Colonel Waller was provisionally promoted to brigadier general in November 1916 and relinquished command the same month to Brigadier General Eli Cole, who had first arrived in Haiti as commander of the Second Regiment. On November 28, 1917, Colonel John Henry "Pug" Russell took command; he was replaced in 1918 by Brigadier General Albertus Catlin—the "hero of Belleau Wood" in World War I. In 1919 Catlin was succeeded by Lieutenant Colonel Louis McCarty Little, who would return in 1931 as a brigadier general to oversee the withdrawal of the marines in 1934. Between Little's first and final posting to Haiti, there were twelve different brigade commanders, including Russell's second stint from October 1919 to January 1922.

73. Senate Select Hearings, 514.

74. Ibid., 695.

75. For example, Gunnery Sergeant Faustin Wirkus was commissioned a lieutenant in the gendarmerie in 1925; before that, he was a subdistrict commander at Arcahaie, a commune in the Ouest department. As a gendarmerie lieutenant, he was appointed "resident commander" on the island of Gonâve, northwest of Port-au-Prince. See Wirkus and Dudley, *White King of La Gonave;* Beth Crumley, "Warrant Officer Faustin Wirkus: From 'Breaker Boy' to King," http://www.mca-marines.org/mcaf-blog/2011/08/29/warrant-officer-faustin-wirkus-breaker-boy-king, accessed January 20, 2017.

76. "The Formative Period, 1915–1920," 29.

77. Barnet Report, 41–49. The most significant failure of the gendarmerie occurred in May 1916, when some 500 prisoners escaped from the national penitentiary. All but a handful were recaptured by government forces. See Clyde Metcalf, *A History of the United States Marine Corps* (New York: G. P. Putnam's Sons, 1939), 388–89.

78. Bickel, *Mars Learning,* 75–76.

79. Senate Select Hearings, 627.

80. Heinl and Heinl, *Written in Blood,* 450–51.

81. Senate Select Hearings, 649–59.

82. "Annual Report of General George Barnett to the Secretary of the Navy, Fiscal Year 1919," October 10, 1919, 4. MCHD, Haiti: Occupation.

83. Biddle, *Barons of the Sky,* 116.

84. In January 1919 an Aviation Section, Headquarters Marine Corps, was formally established. The Aviation Section reported to the commandant for administrative and operational purposes but was responsible to the head of naval aviation for purely aviation matters. The following year, Congress deemed that the Marine Corps' authorized strength would be one-fifth that of the US Navy. Likewise, marine aviation would be one-fifth of naval aviation.

85. Reserve Officers of Public Affairs Unit 4-1, *Marine Aviation: World War I* (Washington, DC: Headquarters, US Marine Corps, Division of Reserve, 1966), 23.

86. Mims's promotion to temporary second lieutenant from corporal can be found in *Official Bulletin* 1, no. 67 (July 28, 1917): 2.

87. Because congressional appropriations did not permit an excess of flying officers, the marines "attempted to remedy the pilot shortage by recruiting and training enlisted aviators. This was possible because [the legislation] limited only the officer strength—not the pilot strength." Johnson, *Marine Corps Aviation,* 35–37.

88. Juliette Hennessey, *The United States Army Air Arm: April 1861 to April 1917* (Washington, DC: Office of Air Force History, 1958), 11.

89. Vernon Burge enlisted in the US Army in 1907 and was assigned to the Signal Corps as a balloon handler and later as an airplane mechanic. In 1912 he was reassigned to the Philippines to assemble and maintain a new Wright Model C Scout, delivered to pioneer aviator Lieutenant Frank Lahm at Fort William McKinley. The Scout had a more powerful engine than its predecessors, as well as dual controls; it was sent to the Philippines to be a reconnaissance aircraft and trainer. Eight Scouts in all were produced, and seven were delivered to the army. However, the Scout had a short service life owing to a series of fatal crashes, destroying six of the eight aircraft manufactured. Although Lieutenant Lahm intended to train exclusively officer volunteers, only one stepped forward. Seizing the opportunity, Burge volunteered, and Lahm consented. Corporal Burge first flew as a student pilot on April 5, 1912. He went on to become the most celebrated enlisted pilot in the army, retiring as a full colonel in 1941. For an in-depth treatment of enlisted pilots in the US Army up to 1942, see Lee Arbon, *They Also Flew: The Enlisted Pilot Legacy, 1912–1942* (Washington, DC: Smithsonian Institution Press, 1992).

90. Ibid., xix.

91. Though virtually unknown today, Victor Czegka was a remarkable figure in Marine Corps history. He was born in 1880 in Hluchow, Austria, and served in the US Marine Corps from 1905 to 1916. He was a skilled marksman and a turret gun pointer aboard the armored cruiser USS *Maryland,* winning a bronze gunnery medal in 1908 when the *Maryland's* forward 8-inch main gun achieved the best score in the entire fleet, besting the guns of other cruisers and larger battleships. As a first sergeant, he won the Wimbleton Cup rifle match in 1909 (the first marine to do so), using a Marine Corps service rifle to which he had added a telescope of his own design. He won third place in the Leech match in 1910 and second place in an all–Marine Corps match in 1911. That

same year, he was a member of Marine Corps team that won the national team match. He served in Nicaragua in 1912 and during the occupation of Veracruz in 1914, at which time he was assigned to aviation duty. Upon leaving the Marine Corps in 1916, Czegka went to work for the Ordnance Engineering Corporation. He rejoined the Marine Corps and, as a master technical sergeant, accompanied the Byrd expedition twice to Antarctica, receiving the Navy Cross for each trip. He died in 1973 and is buried in Essex County, Massachusetts. See "An Ex Marine Who Has Made Good," *Recruiters' Bulletin* 4, no. 3 (January 1918): 20; Stephen Trask, "Scopes that Shoot through Day and Dark," *Arms and the Man* (*American Rifleman*) 64, no. 3 (April 13, 1918): 43.

92. "Memorandum, Major General Commandant [Barnett] to First Lieutenant Bernard L. Smith, MC, in charge Marine Detachment, Aeronautic Section, USS *Mississippi*," April 18, 1914, MCHD, Aviation: Enlisted Pilots.

93. Michael Belcher, "The Flying Sergeants," *Proceedings*, February 1982, 74.

94. Johnson, *Marine Corps Aviation*, 8.

95. Roger Emmons, "Enlisted Marine Aviation Pilots," Marine Corps Aviation Association Historian Memorandum, August 15, 1976, 1, MCHD, Aviation: Enlisted Pilots.

96. Over the years, Belcher worked at the Naval Aircraft Factory and flew in air races. In 1934 he achieved the highest score for dive-bombing during an annual fleet-wide competition for shore-based squadrons. He died in a plane crash in September 1938 while participating in a night training exercise at Quantico. Roxanne Kaufman, *1912–2012: 100 Years of Marine Corps Aviation; an Illustrated History* (Washington, DC: GPO, n.d.), 66–67.

97. Aviation History and Research (Op-504F), Office of the Chief of Naval Aviation, "Historical Sketch of the Naval Aviation Pilot Program," September 3, 1952, 1, MCHD, Aviation: Enlisted Pilots. The *North Carolina* later served as a tender for seaplanes, and A. A. Cunningham was catapulted from its deck in 1916.

98. Ibid., 2.

99. Prior to 1919, enlisted pilots in the navy were designated quartermaster (aviation), "on the theory that surface vessels had traditionally been steered by Quartermasters, and that therefore this was the preferable designation for airplane chauffeurs." Ibid. Marine Corps enlisted pilots received no such designation and were simply ordered to aviation duty without a title.

100. Ibid., 1–2, 5. In 1921 four enlisted aviator designations were established: naval aviation pilot (seaplane), naval aviation pilot (ship-plane), naval aviation pilot (airship), and balloon pilot. Naval aviation pilots were authorized to wear the insignia of an enlisted naval aviator, and balloon pilots wore the aviator's badge minus the right wing. Ibid., 3.

101. The Balloon Company at Quantico was deactivated in July 1919, and its equipment and personnel were absorbed into Squadron C upon its return from France. In 1930 the balloon hangar was disassembled and shipped to Sunnyvale, California. Elliott and Gillespie, "MCAS Quantico," 14.

102. In October 1920 a new organizational concept was approved for Marine Corps aviation. Lettered squadrons with divisions became numbered squadrons with flights, identified by sequential letters as indicated below:

1919–October 1920	October 1920–May 1922	Post-1920 Flights
Squadron A	1st Air Squadron	A, B
Squadron B	2d Air Squadron	C, D
Squadron C	3d Air Squadron	E, F
1st Division, Squadron E	4th Air Squadron	G, H
Parris Island Detachment	Flight L, 4th Squadron	

In August 1922 the First and Second Aviation Groups were organized at Quantico and San Diego, respectively. The Second Aviation Group would remain virtually unmanned for quite some time. In July 1922 the flights were redesignated divisions again to achieve uniformity with the navy's practice. The Marine Corps' first aviation ground-support unit was activated in 1924: Service Squadron One, attached to the First Aviation Group. Gordon Rottman, *US Marine Corps World War II Order of Battle: Ground and Air Units in the Pacific War, 1939–1945,* Military Book Club ed. (Westport, CT: Greenwood Press, 2002), 385. This reorganization is also discussed in chapter 3.

103. The constant redesignation of Marine Corps aviation units in the formative years is one of its most distinctive and bedeviling aspects. Not surprisingly, this has caused confusion among scholars and lay readers alike. The same is true for aircraft designations. In 1920 the secretary of the navy first directed the creation of a formal system of designation for navy aircraft and squadrons, including Marine Corps aviation. Before that time, squadrons had generally been numbered or lettered according to the order in which they were raised, and airplanes were assigned letters and numbers largely at random, which did not identify the type or the manufacturer. For example, the Marine Corps' HS-2L flying boat, which first deployed to the Azores with the First Aeronautic Company in World War I and then saw action in Haiti, was manufactured by Curtiss and several other manufacturers, but this was not reflected in the designation. By 1922, a lettering system would be adopted whereby the first letter designated the manufacturer and the second letter the type of aircraft; a number was appended to denote the modification. For example, a UO-1 was a Vought (U) observation airplane (O), first modification. A second number inserted between the manufacturer and the type indicated the order or model number of the designer's aircraft in the same class (beginning with number 2). Thus, a U2O-1 was a Vought observation airplane, second model of its class, first modification. In 1923 the system was revised again so that the manufacturer and type letters were reversed. US Marine Corps, *Marine Corps Aircraft,* 1–2. This system remained intact until the late 1960s, when the Department of Defense directed that one system be implemented across all the armed services be created to identify aircraft by type. Peter Mersky, *Marine Corps Aviation: 1912 to the Present,* 3d ed. (Baltimore: Nautical & Aviation Publishing Company of America, 1997), 16.

104. Elliott and Gillespie, "MCAS Quantico," 9.

105. Megee, "Evolution of Marine Aviation," 22, 24 (emphasis in original).

106. Cunningham, "Value of Aviation to the Marine Corps," 223.

107. Ibid., 222. The notion that Marine Corps aviators are somehow not "real" marines has persisted among infantry and other ground officers. A common slight is to say that a marine "swings with the wing."

108. Megee, "Evolution of Marine Aviation," 24.

109. Collings, *Just for the Hell of It,* 123–24.

110. Megee, "Evolution of Marine Aviation," 22.

111. Cunningham, "Value of Aviation to the Marine Corps," 222.

112. For his role in the fight, gendarmerie lieutenant (and marine first sergeant) Patrick Francis Kelley was promoted to captain in the gendarmerie and awarded the Haitian Médaille Militaire.

113. Some sources claim that seven HS-2L boats were part of the initial deployment. The only other seaplane was the float-equipped Jenny (N-9).

114. See James Corum and Wray Johnson, *Airpower in Small Wars: Fighting Insurgents and Terrorists* (Lawrence: University Press of Kansas, 2003), 12–21. Also see Roger Miller, *A Preliminary to War: The 1st Aero Squadron and the Mexican Punitive Expedition of 1916* (Washington, DC: Air Force History and Museums Program, 2003).

115. Major General Ford O. Rogers, USMC, Ret., oral history transcript, December 3, 1970, 25, Oral History Collection, Headquarters, US Marine Corps, History and Museums Division, Washington, DC.

116. "Army-Continued," n.d. (circa 1930s), MCHD, Other Reports.

117. Second Lieutenant James Bowen was killed in August 1920 when the engine of the airplane he kept at Mirebalais for the regimental commander "cut out on the take-off." He attempted to turn and "dump" the plane on its left wing to absorb the shock of the crash and save himself and his observer. Tragically, both men died in the crash. Collings, *Just for the Hell of It,* 145–46. Also see Willock, *Unaccustomed to Fear,* 112–13.

118. "Army Continued."

119. Wirkus wrote: "It was a great satisfaction to have them see for themselves how much could be accomplished by leaving a man alone to study the people and make up his mind how they were to be helped to help themselves, rather than driven into doing things according to the rules and regulations of outsiders who had no understanding of them at all." Wirkus and Dudley, *White King of La Gonave,* 239–40.

120. Eighty miles from Port-au-Prince, the airfield at Hinche was located nearly at the geographic center of Haiti.

121. "Army Continued."

122. John Craige, *Black Bagdad* (New York: Milton, Balch, 1933), 38. Craige wrote several articles while on active duty in the marines and two books about his experience in Haiti. In *Black Bagdad* he recalled being cursed by an old Haitian woman, which a newspaper account of his 1934 retirement called a "blessing in disguise" because his military career ended just before he shipped out to China. He retired as a captain after a car crash rendered him physically disqualified for military service. "A former newspaper man [he remained a member of the National Press Club after leaving the Marine Corps], University of Pennsylvania foot ball player, boxer and wrestler," Craige was commissioned in 1917. He served in France during World War I with the Eleventh Regiment and returned to the States in 1919. He served briefly as an aide to the commandant before being posted to Haiti, where he served in the gendarmerie and as chief of police in Port-au-Prince (1927–1928). He was slated for duty in China when the automobile accident occurred. "Haitian Curse Proves Blessing to Retiring Marine Traveler," *Washington Sunday Star,* October 28, 1934.

123. Collings, *Just for the Hell of It,* 187.

124. Ibid., 188–89.

125. Ibid., 139.

126. Ibid., 140.

127. The special arrangement to allow Pan American Airlines to use the marines' airfield at Port-au-Prince was not philanthropic. As one report noted, the aircraft employed by Pan American could "readily be transformed into military transport planes." "Army Continued."

128. Ibid.

129. Bill Yenne, *Seaplanes and Flying Boats: A Timeless Collection from Aviation's Golden Age* (New York: BCL Press, 2003), 72.

130. "Report of Operations, for Period July 1, 1920, to June 30, 1921 (Confidential)," MCHD, First Brigade Files.

131. Lieutenant General Merwin Silverthorn, USMC, Ret., oral history transcript, 1978, Oral History Collection, Headquarters, US Marine Corps, History and Museums Division, Washington, DC. See also Clark, *United States Marine Corps Generals of World War II,* 141–43.

132. Constabulary Detachment, USMC, Headquarters, Port-au-Prince, Republic of Haiti, "Report of Activities, July 1, 1920 to June 30, 1921," July 15, 1921, MCHD, Annual Reports.

133. Ibid.

134. Ibid.

135. According to the Joint Chiefs of Staff, close air support is officially defined as "air action by fixed-wing and rotary-wing aircraft against hostile targets that are **in close proximity to** friendly forces and **requires detailed integration** of each air mission with the fire and movement of those forces." *Close Air Support,* Joint Publication 3-3-09.3 (Washington, DC: Joint Chiefs of Staff, November 25, 2014), I-1 (emphasis in original). Notably, the US Air Force has always regarded close air support as a fixed-wing-only mission. In deference to the air force position, the marines and the army both used the term "close-in fire support" in the past for rotary-wing ground-attack missions, and today the army uses "close combat attack."

136. Newcomb Smith, "Watching Bandits in Haiti From the Air," *Recruiters' Bulletin* 5, no. 9 (October 1919): 17.

137. Ibid. The JN-6HG-I is often mistakenly referred to as the JN-6HG-I. Swanborough and Bowers, *United States Navy Aircraft since 1911,* 118.

138. Anthony Fokker founded his aircraft manufacturing company in 1912 in Schwerin, Germany, but moved it to his native Holland in 1919 following the end of World War I. Fokker managed to avoid the provisions of the Allied Armistice Commission regarding airplanes manufactured in Germany and shipped several D.VIIs and components to the Netherlands. European countries bought several D.VIIs, and some ended up in the United States. In addition to the single-seat and two-seat versions used by the marines, a three-seat version was produced for the commercial market. The two- and three-seat versions had a longer fuselage and wingspan, although a few standard D.VIIs were converted to two-seat aircraft. *World Aircraft Information Files,* file 894, sheet 33.

139. Swanborough and Bowers, *United States Navy Aircraft since 1911,* 156.

140. Frederic Wise and Meigs Frost, *A Marine Tells It to You* (1929; reprint, Quantico, VA: Marine Corps Association, 1981), 315.

141. Collings, *Just for the Hell of It,* 139.

142. Brigadier General George Barnett to Secretary of the Navy, "Report on Affairs in the Republic of Haiti, June 1915 to June 30, 1920," October 11, 1920, 73, MCHD, First Brigade Files.

143. Ibid.

144. Collings, *Just for the Hell of It,* 131.

145. According to Captain Craige, Private Morris "was a consistent idealist, and they ate him for it." A Quaker raised in Pennsylvania, Morris had joined the Marine Corps to fight the Germans in World War I, not to fight Haitians. In fact, according to Craige, Morris was opposed to the intervention and to imperialism in general, so he was put to work as a mechanic at the flying field. Although he flew as an observer on occasion, he did not participate in any bombing operations. Morris was known to fraternize with the local inhabitants in and around Hinche and "picked up enough Creole to get along." For this reason, Morris apparently believed he could leave the downed airplane and make his way back to the flying field. There was a standing order not to leave any machine guns when abandoning a plane, so he dismounted the Lewis gun and took it with him. A local *caco* leader, Papillon (French for "butterfly"), had seen the plane go down, and he and several followers intercepted Morris. Concerned that Morris was deceiving them, the *cacos* wandered in circles until they were convinced that Morris was alone. One evening when Morris had his back turned, Papillon struck him in the head with a *coco macaque,* a club believed to have magical powers (the official version is that he was murdered with a machete). Morris was then stripped and tied to a tree, after which he was skinned alive in "the *caco* fashion." Craige, *Black Bagdad,* 99–107.

146. Mersky, *Marine Corps Aviation,* 20. According to Kenneth Collings, the father of dive-bombing was an enlisted marine aviator, First Sergeant Elmo "Socko" Reagan of Overton, Texas. Reagan first conceived of the idea while in the Azores during World War I. This was corroborated in Quartermaster Sergeant Lee Austin's *Marine Aviation: World War I.* Reagan had enlisted during the war and rose through the ranks to become a warrant officer observer-gunner; he learned how to fly without permission. For this reason, he waited until after the war to promote his idea. At first, he tried to convince his commander at Quantico, Major W. P. T. Hill, to allow him to demonstrate his method of pointing the nose of the airplane at the target, but Hill refused, claiming the wings would be sheared off. After repeated denials of his request, Reagan loaded a "Hispano-motored Jenny" with two dummy bombs, flew to a nearby bombing range, and from 2,500 feet "nosed gently into a dive." As the dive steepened, several witnesses (including Collings) thought Reagan was going to crash, but instead he dropped his first bomb and achieved a bull's-eye on a 32-foot-square wooden target moored in the middle of a creek. Reagan did not make a second attempt because the first had damaged the airplane. Fearing disciplinary action, Reagan never informed Major Hill. Years later, he was killed in a crash in the waters off Pensacola. See Kenneth Collings, "The Man Who Invented Dive-Bombing, *Liberty* 19, no. 17 (April 25, 1942). In 1944 Colonel Lawson Sanderson noted, "In 1921 Marine Gunner Regan [*sic*] worked on an aiming device for dive bombing (Box and Pendulum affair) hoping to attain better results with his new sight than we were getting with our gun barrel

sight." Sanderson did not, however, corroborate Collings's claim that Reagan had actually employed the technique while piloting an airplane. Colonel L. H. M. Sanderson to Captain Waren H. Goodman, Historical Division, HQ USMC, subject: "Origin of Dive Bombing as I Know It," September 1, 1944, MCHD, Aviation: Dive Bombing.

147. David Mets, "Dive-Bombing between the Wars," *Airpower Historian,* July 1965, 86.

148. The Wimpers bombsight was attached to the outside of the fuselage. "This sight permitted the observer to aim at the target while standing, a position which kept him in readiness to fight off an attack by hostile aircraft." Bruce Hopper, "When the Air Was Young: American Day Bombardment, A.E.F., France, 1917–1918" unpublished manuscript, n.d., 13, Library of Congress.

149. Brigadier General L. H. M. Sanderson, USMC, to Chief of Naval Operations, subject: "Dive Bombing, History of," August 19, 1946, MCHD, Aviation: Dive Bombing. According to Sanderson, "Accurate bombing was necessary in order to obtain good results and to avoid hitting our own troops that were engaging the enemy at close quarters." Some of the aircraft deployed to Haiti at the time were DH-4B-2Bs, which had no bombsights; this accounts for the crude rifle-barrel sight employed by Sanderson. Peter Smith, *Dive Bomber: An Illustrated History* (Ashbourne, UK: Moorland, 1982), 20.

150. Masson's activities in Mexico can be constructed from reports in *New York Times,* May 8, 9, 20, 31 and June 22, 1913; *Los Angeles Times,* May 13, 1913; and other newspapers. See also Manuel Romero, *La aviacion durante la revolucion Mexicana* (Mexico City: Sporte Aeronautico, 1988); James Hinds, "Bombs over Mexico," *Aerospace Historian* 31, no. 2 (September 1984). Masson returned to France, joined the Lafayette Escadrille (winning the Croix de Guerre in 1916), and ultimately returned to Mexico, where he died in 1950.

151. "Volplaning" means to descend in a glide with the engine shut off.

152. Smith, *Dive Bomber,* 8–9.

153. The word "strafe" is derived from the German *bestrafen,* meaning "to punish."

154. John Buckley, *Air Power in the Age of Total War* (Bloomington: Indiana University Press, 1999), 126–27. Also see James Corum, *The Luftwaffe: Creating the Operational Air War, 1918–1940* (Lawrence: University Press of Kansas, 1997).

155. Smith, *Dive Bomber,* 17–18.

156. Ibid., 20.

157. Brigadier General Lawson Sanderson to David Mets, February 22, 1953, cited in Mets, "Dive-Bombing between the Wars," 86.

158. Willock, *Unaccustomed to Fear,* 110–11; Sanderson, "Dive Bombing, History of." Lewis Burwell "Chesty" Puller is the most decorated marine in US history and the only marine to be awarded the Navy Cross on five separate occasions. Over the course of his career, he fought in Haiti, Nicaragua, World War II, and the Korean War. He retired from the Marine Corps in 1955 and spent the remainder of his life in Virginia; he died in October 1971. For a complete biography, see Jon Hoffman, *Chesty: The Story and Life of Lieutenant General Lewis B. Puller, USMC* (New York: Random House, 2001).

159. Sanderson never claimed that he invented dive-bombing, and it remains a contentious subject today. In 1944, for example, in a letter written to Brigadier General Louis Woods, Captain Garrett Graham, USMC, vociferously denied that the marines could claim the honor of developing dive-bombing. As he put it, "All of this is patently absurd. The undersigned was an army bombing pilot in 1917–18. While stationed at Ellington

Field, Texas, for operational training, he, with several thousand other army pilots, practiced dive bombing in substantially the same form that it is used today." Captain Garrett H. Graham to Brigadier General Louis E. Woods, subject: "Origin of Dive Bombing," February 22, 1944, MCHD, Aviation: Dive Bombing. There are also multiple claims regarding the first combat use of dive-bombing. According to Colonel John Potts, USMC, officer in charge of the Historical Division, Headquarters, USMC, during World War II, "the first use of dive-bombing in actual combat . . . was in July, 1927, in Nicaragua" (this topic is addressed in some detail in chapter 4). Colonel John Potts to First Lieutenant John D. McElwey, Marine Aircraft Group Twelve, First Marine Aircraft Wing, subject: "Origin of Dive Bombing," September 8, 1944, MCHD, Aviation. See also Smith, *Dive Bomber,* chaps. 1–3.

160. Frank Buzzacott developed the stove used by the marines in Haiti in the late 1800s. It was made of wrought iron and weighed 160 pounds. The complete unit contained all the necessary pots, pans, and utensils necessary to prepare and serve a meal. Before leaving the army, Buzzacott was a field cook for the commanding general of the US Army, General Nelson Miles. "Cooking Outfits for an Army: A Chicago Inventor May Furnish Enough for 100,000 Men," *New York Times,* March 25, 1898.

161. Smith, "Watching Bandits in Haiti from the Air," 17.

162. *Manual of Military Occupation Specialties,* NAVMC 1006.PD (revised) (Washington, DC: Headquarters, US Marine Corps, Personnel Department, Classification Division Detail Branch, 1945).

163. Hayne Boyden, "Aerial Mapping in Haiti," 2, MCHD, Haiti: Air. Although the marines employed observers in World War I, there is no evidence that they took cameras into the air. That said, aerial photography was common in Haiti (and in the Dominican Republic). Boyden was the first marine aviator to attend the US Army School of Aerial Photography at Chanute Field, Illinois, in 1923. Before the outbreak of World War II, Boyden took more aerial photos than any other Marine Corps pilot (and survived several crashes in the process). After leaving Haiti, Boyden photographed the major landing exercises at Culebra, Puerto Rico (1924–1927), and in 1932 he mapped more than 500 square miles of northeastern Nicaragua. Marine Corps Aviation Reconnaissance Association, "USMC Photo Reconnaissance Pioneers," http://www.mcara.us/notables_photo_pioneers.html, accessed March 22, 2012.

164. Boyden, "Aerial Mapping in Haiti," 3.

165. The statoscope was developed before World War I (circa 1900) and soon became one of the most important instruments used on airships and balloons. The device is a simple aneroid barometer that is very sensitive to small changes in air pressure and responds immediately to any altitude gain or loss. "As used in ballooning, if the bubble 'breaks inward' the balloon is falling; if it 'breaks outward' the balloon is rising. The rate at which the bubbles break is a measure of the rate at which the balloon ascends or descends." "A Homemade Statoscope," *Popular Mechanics* 39, no. 6 (June 1923): 982.

166. Boyden, "Aerial Mapping in Haiti," 4.

167. Arthur Millspaugh, *Haiti under American Control, 1915–1930* (Boston: World Peace Foundation, 1931), 158–59.

168. Craige, *Black Bagdad,* 83–84.

169. Ibid., 84.

170. Headquarters, First Brigade, US Marine Corps, Port-au-Prince, Republic of Haiti, Major William Sullivan, Officer in Charge of Operations, subject: "Report of Operations from September 21, 1930, to October 20, 1930," October 25, 1930, 1, MCHD, First Brigade Files.

171. Pigeons were usually employed as a last resort when no other means of communication worked. According to one source, "ninety percent of the messages reached their destination after passing through every handicap imposed by battle conditions and unfair weather." James Miller, "The Passing of the Carrier Pigeon," *Popular Mechanics* 53, no. 2 (February 1930): 195. When the US Army disbanded the Pigeon Service, the last 1,000 birds at Fort Monmouth were offered for sale to the general public, and the more famous birds were donated to zoos.

172. Ibid., 196.

173. "Pigeons in the Navy," http://usmilitary.about.com/library/milinfo/blnavytrad-7.htm, accessed March 29, 2017.

174. The "quad" tractors were fully tracked Holt tractors used for towing artillery during World War I.

175. Headquarters (Operations), 1st Brigade, USMC, "Report of Operations," April 30, 1921, and "Report of Operations," May 31, 1921, MCHD, First Brigade Files.

176. Capitaine Plantey et le Médecin-Major Vincent, "Les Avions Sanitaires," *Aeronautique* 29 (October 1921): 398–400.

177. W. Breyton, "L'Aviation Sanitaire au Maroc en 1933," *Revue de L'Armée de L'Air* 56 (March 1934): 243–64. Descriptions of the aircraft can be found at ibid., 246–48.

178. Serge Lainé, "L'Aéronautique Militaire Française au Maroc (1911–1939)," *Revue Historique des Armées* 4 (1978): 107–20.

179. Quoted in Robert Futrell, "The Development of Aeromedical Evacuation in the United States Air Force, 1909–1939," *Journal of the American Aviation Historical Society* 23, no. 3 (Fall 1978): 214. See also Robert Futrell, "Development of Aeromedical Evacuation in the United States Air Force, 1904–1960," USAF Historical Study no. 23 (Maxwell Air Force Base, AL: Albert F. Simpson Historical Research Center, 1960).

180. The marines were aware that they needed a specially configured airplane for medical transportation. In a 1921 operations report, the brigade requested "an aero ambulance plane . . . to convey emergency cases from the field to base hospitals." Headquarters (Operations), 1st Brigade, USMC, "Report of Operations," May 31, 1921, MCHD, First Brigade Files.

181. Collings, *Just for the Hell of It,* 179.

182. "Injured Man Carried on Airplane Wing," *Popular Science Monthly* 100 (January–June 1922): 27.

183. Sherrod, *History of Marine Corps Aviation in World War II,* 22 n. 13. See also "Evacuation of Wounded—Marine Aviation 1922," MCHD, Miscellaneous. As noted in the commandant's annual report to the secretary of the navy in 1922, "An ambulance plane has been assigned to this squadron [Observation Squadron 2, Port-au-Prince, Haiti] and has proved of considerable service in transporting sick and wounded from [the] interior to the base hospital." Recall that Captain Evans commanded the First Aeronautic Company before American entry into World War I and was the first pilot to loop a seaplane, an N-9, at Pensacola. During the war he commanded that company in the Azores

until being replaced by Captain David Brewster. Evans was grounded after two serious crashes in 1935 and was retired for physical disability in July 1937. However, he was recalled to active duty in 1937 and served until December 1944, retiring from the Marine Corps as a colonel. He died in 1974.

184. William Larkins, *US Navy Aircraft, 1921–1941* [and] *US Marine Corps Aircraft, 1914–1959,* 1 vol. (1961 and 1959; reprint, Atglen, PA: Schiffer Military History/Aviation History, 1995), 9 (USMC Aviation section).

185. "Pug" Russell served as brigade commander from November 1917 to December 1918. He was replaced by Brigadier General Albertus Catlin and Lieutenant Colonel McCarty Little before returning in 1919 and remaining until 1922.

186. Charlemagne's body was laid on a door, arms outspread, and photographed. Prints were widely distributed, including drops by marine aircraft. But these photos fueled claims that Charlemagne had been crucified by the Americans, a story still told in Haiti today. With the departure of the marines in 1934, Charlemagne's body was disinterred, and he was given a state funeral.

187. After being commissioned, Hanneken served several more years in Haiti and was awarded the Navy Cross for killing another important *caco* leader, Osiris Joseph. He was awarded a second Navy Cross in Nicaragua for capturing José María Jirón Ruano, the Guatemalan chief of staff of Nicaraguan insurgent leader Augusto César Sandino. During World War II he commanded the Seventh Marine Regiment of the First Marine Division on Guadalcanal and was awarded the Silver Star for gallantry. He received the Bronze Star for his actions on Cape Gloucester in the Bismarcks during Operation Cartwheel, and he received the Legion of Merit for his actions during the battle for Peleliu. He retired in 1948 and was promoted to brigadier general. He died in 1986 and is buried at the Fort Rosecrans National Cemetery, San Diego.

188. A native of Virginia, Berkeley was commissioned during the Spanish-American War. Over a forty-year career he served in the Philippines, Cuba, Panama, China, Haiti, and Nicaragua. Arlington National Cemetery, http://www.arlingtoncemetery.net/berkeley.htm, accessed March 20, 2017.

189. John Russell, "Russell Report to US Military Representative in Haiti [Rear Admiral Thomas Snowden, USN], March 10, 1920, MCHD, Personal Papers Collection.

190. Barnett Report, para. 250.

191. Heinl, *Soldiers of the Sea,* 242.

192. Senate Select Hearings, 1719–20.

193. Collings, *Just for the Hell of It,* 146.

194. Ibid., 149.

195. Ibid., 151.

196. Captain Page previously commanded the balloon detachment at Quantico and then the squadron in the Dominican Republic. He was ordered to Haiti when A. A. Cunningham arrived from Washington to take command of the unit in Santo Domingo.

197. Commander, Headquarters, 4th Air Squadron, to Major General Commandant, Washington, DC, "Detail of Pilots for Aviation Duty in the Tropics," March 7, 1921, MCHD, Haiti: Other Reports.

198. Thomas Turner, "Aviation Notes," *Marine Corps Gazette* 6, no. 3 (September 1921): 297.

199. Ibid., 298. Combat pilots during World War I and postwar barnstormers flew only when the weather permitted. In a tropical rainstorm, single-engine aircraft were practically doomed. In addition to the buffeting, the engine would simply stop. If this occurred, the pilot's only option was to glide downward through the rain until he could see again and restart the engine or land the airplane. Multiengine aircraft flew longer only because the engines usually quit one at a time.

200. Headquarters, First Provisional Brigade, Brigade Commander, to Major General Commandant, US Marine Corps, Headquarters, Washington, DC, "Detail of Pilots for Aviation Duty in the Tropics," n.d., "Forwarded, Approved, Excepting [that Portion] which Contemplates Return to Finish Foreign Service," MCHD, First Brigade Files.

201. Craige, *Black Bagdad,* 193.

202. Ibid., 82–83.

203. Harold Utley, "An Introduction to the Tactics and Technique of Small Wars," *Marine Corps Gazette* 16, no. 1 (May 1931): 8.

204. Ibid.

205. Renda, *Taking Haiti,* 134–36.

206. Craige, *Black Bagdad,* 102.

207. Ibid., 101.

208. As Roy Geiger noted, "I think that every officer who serves on this island will return to the States a strong friend of Aviation. The planes have become an essential part of operations here." Captain Roy S. Geiger to Captain [Francis T.] Evans, August 10, 1920, MCHRC, box 1, folder 16, PC 312.

209. General Lemuel Shepherd, USMC, Ret., oral history transcript, September 19, 1978, 197–201, Oral History Collection, Headquarters, US Marine Corps, History and Museums Division, Washington, DC. Once again, it is important to recall that counterinsurgency and counterguerrilla warfare are often conflated to mean the same thing, but they are distinct. The former emphasizes political, economic, and other reforms aimed at dismantling the counterstate and detaching popular support from the insurgents, whereas the latter is simply operations in the field intended to find, fix, and destroy guerrilla formations.

210. In 1927 only DHs and 02B-1s remained in Haiti. The other aircraft were deployed elsewhere.

211. The VE-7 is described in greater detail in chapter 3.

212. The Loening OL was an unusual amphibian designed by Grover Loening, a talented aircraft engineer. Loening's intent was to design an amphibian with the performance of a landplane. As a result, the OL employed a boat hull carried under the fuselage. This configuration was used later on the Grumman JF and J2F Duck, which is not surprising, given that Leroy Grumman worked for Loening. The Grumman Company was founded to maintain Loening aircraft still in operation.

213. The 02U Corsair is described in detail in chapter 3. For general information on the Corsair and its scout variant, see Paul Eden and Soph Moeng, *The Complete Encyclopedia of World Aircraft* (London: Amber Books, 2002).

214. Daley, *American Saga,* 74.

215. John Elliott, "Early Marine Corps Aviators," *Naval Aviation News,* May 1977, 15.

216. Juan Trippe acquired seaplanes for Pan American Airlines because the Caribbean is not well suited for landplanes (there is very little level ground to land on). Moreover,

flying to South America required refueling every 200 to 300 miles, and the only way to do that was to establish refueling stations on the islands. Earlier, West Indian Aerial Express had tried and failed to provide service with landplanes. An Australian pilot for West Indian Aerial Express took off from Barahona, Dominican Republic, en route to Port-au-Prince in a Waco airplane. It disappeared, and the company contacted the marines in Haiti and asked for help finding its pilot and airplane. One of the marines' DH aircraft found them both near a lake, forced down by engine failure. After the marines helped the pilot repair his aircraft, the intrepid Australian took off again for Port-au-Prince, where he crashed. Daley, *American Saga*, 58.

217. See John Andrade, *US Military Aircraft Designations and Serials since 1979* (Leicestershire, UK: Midland Counties Publications, 1979), 218. For aircraft types and numbers from 1919 to 1934, see Larkins, *US Navy Aircraft* [and] *US Marine Corps Aircraft*, 15, 18, 20, 22, 27, 32, 37, 39, 48 (USMC Aviation section).

218. A Senate committee traveled to Haiti and conducted an investigation from August 5 to December 15, 1921. Chairman Joseph McCormick (R-IL) issued preliminary findings upon their return, calling for a continuation of the occupation and the appointment of a high commissioner. The final report noted the many accomplishments of the marines and found little fault in their military operations. However, the committee branded the adoption of the corvée a "blunder." Senate Select Hearings, 229–32.

219. Regarding Roosevelt's claim, see Frank Freidel, *Franklin D. Roosevelt: The Ordeal* (1954; reprint, Charleston, SC: Nabu Press [BiblioBazar], 2011), 81. Harding quoted in D. A. Graber, *Crisis Diplomacy: A History of U.S. Intervention, Policies and Practices* (Washington, DC: Public Affairs Press, 1959), 200.

220. Renda, *Taking Haiti*, 304.

221. Senate Select Hearings, 516.

222. The treaty the United States and Haiti signed in September 1915 called for "an efficient constabulary." The French phrase was *une gendarmerie efficace*. But according to *United States Daily*, July 12, 1929, the term *gendarmerie* was deemed no longer "properly descriptive in view of the expansion of its duties and its standing as the sole armed force of Haiti," especially given that a gendarmerie typically has purely police functions. Thus, by agreement between the Haitian government and the State Department, the name was changed to Garde d'Haiti.

223. The politically loaded phrase "good neighbor" dates back to at least the nineteenth century and Senator Henry Clay. President Wilson also invoked the phrase but then went on to send troops and warships to Veracruz in 1914. Franklin Roosevelt employed the phrase to convey a policy of noninterference and nonintervention. See Frederick Pike, *FDR's Good Neighbor Policy: Sixty Years of Generally Gentle Chaos* (Austin: University of Texas Press, 1995).

224. L. J. Debekker, "The Massacre at Aux Cayes," *Nation*, March 1930, 309–10. For a more objective examination, see R. A. Dodge, "Massacre in Haiti," *Proceedings*, November 1994, 60–64.

225. *New York Times*, December 10 and 11, 1929.

226. *New York Times*, March 14, 1929.

227. For a contemporary description of the mission, see John Rogers, "The Haitianization of the Garde d'Haiti," *Leatherneck*16, no. 10 (October 1933).

228. To cement the agreement for withdrawal, President Roosevelt decided to visit Haiti, the first time a sitting foreign chief of state had visited the country. In his speech, delivered partly in French, Roosevelt announced that the marines would be withdrawn no later than August 15.

229. By placing a civilian in charge of the occupation and bringing back the French-speaking Little as brigade commander, Washington hoped to foster a friendly parting of the ways.

230. Major James Moore, Commander, VO-9M, "Memorandum for the Commanding General [First Brigade]," June 29, 1934, MCHD, First Brigade Files.

231. Ibid.

232. Major James Moore (commanding), Captain Henry Carr (quartermaster), and First Lieutenant Ivan Miller, to Brigade Commander, "Recommendation for Disposition of Government Property, Navy and Marine Corps, in Hands of Observation Squadron 9-M, on Withdrawal from Haiti," December 18, 1933, MCHD, First Brigade Files. The board recommended against shipping the bombs and fuses because an ammunition ship or a ship with a magazine would be required.

233. Major James Moore, Commander, VO-9M, to Chief of the Bureau of Aeronautics, Navy Department, Washington, DC, "Disposition of Aeronautical Material on Evacuation from Haiti," May 31, 1934, MCHD, First Brigade Files.

234. Captain F. R. Murray, Assistant Chief, Bureau of Aeronautics, to Commanding Officer, Observation Squadron 9-M, Fleet Marine Force, First Brigade, USMC, Port-au-Prince, Haiti, "Disposition of Aeronautical Material on Evacuation from Haiti," June 11, 1934, MCHD, First Brigade Files. However, Marine Corps Headquarters sent a cable the following month directing the brigade to leave in place one hangar measuring 80 by 66 feet. US Marine Corps Radio Dispatch, July 12, 1934, ibid.

235. E. B. Larimer, Chief of Bureau of Ordnance (A. O. Stott, acting), to Commanding Officer, VO Squadron 9-M, Fleet Marine Force, First Brigade, US Marines, Port-au-Prince, Haiti, "Ammunition—Disposition of," June 13, 1934,. MCHD, First Brigade Files.

236. Major James Moore to Commanding General, First Brigade, "Evacuation," July 12, 1934, MCHD, First Brigade Files. The brigade commander, McCarty Little, forwarded the names of the officers and enlisted men to the commandant, along with a courtesy copy to the American legation in Port-au-Prince.

237. Major James Moore, Commanding, "Proposed Itinerary of VO Squadron 9-M, via Air, from Port au Prince, Haiti, to M. B., Quantico, Va.," n.d., MCHD, First Brigade Files.

238. Major James Moore, Commanding, "Crews and Planes of VO-9M, Traveling via Air from Port au Prince, Haiti, to M. B. Quantico, Va.," n.d., MCHD, First Brigade Files. Before 1960, frequencies were commonly referred to as "cycles per second" (cps) or related multiples, such as "kilocycles per second" (kcs). Both terms were replaced by "hertz" in the 1970s.

239. The Special Service Squadron of the US Fleet engaged in gunboat diplomacy in the Caribbean between the world wars and was headquartered at Balboa, Panama Canal Zone. A plane guard is a warship (or today, a helicopter) tasked to recover aircrews in the event an airplane is forced to "ditch" or crashes during flight operations.

240. Schmidt, *United States Occupation of Haiti,* 10.

241. J. C. Fegan, "After Nineteen Years We Leave Haiti," *Marine Corps Gazette* 19, no. 2 (August 1934): 23.

242. "Nation's Press Commends Marine Corps Withdrawal from Haiti," *Army and Navy Journal,* August 18, 1934, 1030.

243. The term "mission creep" first came into popular usage in association with the United Nations' peace enforcement mission in Somalia in the early 1990s. Mission creep is generally regarded as undesirable owing to the tendency to overreach, which often leads to catastrophic failure. See, for example, essays in the *Washington Post,* April 15, 1993, and *New York Times,* October 10, 1993.

244. Craige, *Black Bagdad,* 2.

245. Operation Uphold Democracy (September 19, 1994–March 31, 1995) removed a military regime installed by a 1991 coup d'état that overthrew elected president Jean-Bertrand Aristide. It was authorized by a United Nations Security Council resolution in July 1994. In 1959 a small contingent of marines and sailors commanded by Colonel Robert Debs Heinl Jr., USMC, was sent to Haiti as part of a training and advisory mission that grew out of contacts between the Haitian dictator Francois Duvalier and Marine Corps commandant General Lemuel Shepherd Jr., who had served in Haiti during the occupation. Shepherd and Heinl both believed that if the Haitian armed forces were professionalized, they could become the basis of a democratic Haiti in the future. This was not to be, as Duvalier simply wanted the window dressing of apparent American support. Upon his departure, Colonel Heinl upbraided the Haitian chief of staff for the Haitians' lack of genuine cooperation. Back home, Heinl fervently denied press reports that the marines had been in Haiti to prop up a despotic regime. Indeed, he claimed he had always intended to reinvent the armed forces of Haiti in the manner of the former gendarmerie, that is, to foster a professional, apolitical force. While in Haiti, he even went so far as to request that his marines be allowed to wear the old campaign hat still worn today by Marine Corps drill instructors. His thinking was that the Haitians would associate the campaign hat with the marines who had organized, trained, and led the gendarmerie. For more details, see Charles Williamson, *The US Naval Mission to Haiti: 1959–1963* (Annapolis, MD: Naval Institute Press, 1999).

246. Shacochis, *Immaculate Invasion,* 26.

247. It is no small irony that it was the Second Regiment that first landed in Haiti in 1915.

248. As of this writing, VMM-264 (the "Black Knights"), part of Marine Aircraft Group 26, Second Marine Aircraft Wing, stationed at Marine Corps Air Station New River, North Carolina, flies the MV-22 Osprey tilt-rotor aircraft (hence the squadron's redesignation). VMM-264 was the last East Coast squadron flying the CH-46 to transition to the Osprey.

3. Advance to Maturity, 1919–1935

1. In 1918 the battleship USS *Texas* acquired two "flying-off" platforms erected over its number-two turret forward and number-three turret aft. The installation of these platforms was copied from the British Royal Navy, and they were in fact constructed by a Royal Navy yard in Newcastle-upon-Tyne. The platforms enabled a pair of Sopwith Camels and a Sopwith 1½ Strutter to fly off the ship for observation purposes. Unfortunately, these wheeled aircraft could not be recovered at sea except by ditching alongside, so they

usually flew ashore. Nevertheless, they were more useful than the kite balloons sent aloft for observation purposes and towed behind the ship. The first flight from the *Texas* occurred on March 9, 1918, performed by Lieutenant Commander Edward McDonnell while the ship was anchored in Guantanamo Bay, Cuba. Observing the flight was a highly respected battleship captain, William Moffett, who became a quick convert to the potential of naval aviation and had a flying-off platform erected on his own ship, the USS *Mississippi.* Moffett would become a stalwart proponent of naval aviation and later headed the Bureau of Aeronautics. William Trimble, *Admiral William A. Moffett: Architect of Naval Aviation* (Washington, DC: Smithsonian Institution Press, 1994), 59–60.

2. James Ginther, "Marine Aviator Number One: Alfred Austell Cunningham and the Development of Early Marine Corps Aviation" (master's thesis, Abilene Christian University, 1993), 128–29 n. 14.

3. Johnson, *Marine Corps Aviation,* 31–32. As noted in the text, lettered squadrons with divisions became numbered squadrons with flights, identified by sequential letters, as indicated below:

1919–October 1920	October 1920–May 1922	Post-1920 Flights	Location
Squadron A	1st Air Squadron	A, B	Dominican Republic
Squadron B	2d Air Squadron	C, D	Quantico
Squadron C	3d Air Squadron	E, F	Quantico
1st Division, Squadron E	4th Air Squadron	G, H	Haiti
Parris Island Detachment	Flight L, 4th Squadron		Guam (1921)

In July 1922 the flights were redesignated divisions again to achieve uniformity with the navy's practice. As defined by the navy at the time, a division was composed of three two-airplane sections. On paper, a squadron comprised three divisions, but in the Marine Corps, this was the exception rather than the rule. See Rottman, *US Marine Corps World War II Order of Battle,* 385.

4. Although commonly thought of as a single event, the sinking of the *Ostfriesland* by the First Provisional Air Brigade of the US Army Air Service was in fact the culmination of a series of bombing tests conducted by the Air Service and the US Navy from May to July 1921. The sinking of the German battleship and other ships, including the obsolete American battleship *USS Iowa,* is regarded as a significant milestone in air power history. That said, the results remain controversial to this day.

5. Walter Brown enlisted in the Marine Corps in August 1917. After World War I he attended the Massachusetts Institute of Technology. He attended the Officer Training Camp at Quantico in 1920, and after flight training he assumed command of Flight F, Squadron C. Following his death, the enlisted marines of the squadron purchased a bronze plaque that was put on display and dedicated to Brown's memory on May 9, 1922. At the same time, a causeway across the Chopawamsic Creek was named in honor of Captain John Minnis, who died in a crash in September 1921 off Shipping Point, where marines

often embarked for overseas expeditionary duty. On November 1, 1940, Brown Field became the home of the Officer Training School. The plaque dedicated to Brown was removed to the Marine Corps museum at Quantico but was restored to a place of honor on the seventy-fifth anniversary of the school. The area crossed by the Minnis causeway was later filled in and is the site of the modern airfield in existence today. Elliott and Gillespie, "MCAS Quantico," 11.

6. "It was originally planned that these large land-based planes could be flown on a mission, land in the water and be hoisted aboard to be refurbished for another flight. However, flotation bags were installed in only one plane and the concept was dropped." Ibid.

7. Ibid., 12.

8. E. R. Johnson, *United States Naval Aviation, 1919–1941* (Jefferson, NC: McFarland, 2011), 13. Interestingly, the marines used the MT primarily as a transport.

9. It was under Butler's command that Marine Corps sports, especially football, grabbed the public's attention. Marine Corps football was born on the West Coast when the Mare Island team defeated college teams and athletic clubs and earned a spot in the Tournament of Roses game on New Year's Day 1918. Like the team in California, the Quantico team was formed with former college players from the Marine Corps. As many as 60,000 enthusiastic spectators watched the marines compete with opponents from the University of Southern California and the University of Michigan. Butler's enthusiasm for football resulted in the construction of a stadium at Quantico; it was built with donated and scavenged materials and marine labor (Butler and his officers pitched in). The secretary of the navy criticized the project as "damned foolishness," but Butler persisted. The stadium was not completed until after World War II. Fleming et al., *Quantico,* 42–44.

10. Thousands of spectators flocked to Butler's summer maneuvers, including high-ranking officials from Washington. En route to Gettysburg, Butler marched the marines past the White House, and President Harding made the trip to Gettysburg to witness a reenactment of Pickett's Charge.

11. The "Z" denoted a unit employing a self-propelled lighter-than-air craft, and "K" stood for "kite."

12. The creation of a utility squadron was intended to relieve the combat squadrons of those missions they were ill equipped to execute, such as transportation of people and cargo, rescue, ambulance and messenger service, and other tasks.

13. The designation "Group" had no administrative or tactical equivalent in the navy at the time. Lejuene therefore agreed with the navy's position on the matter, and aircraft groups were officially redesignated in September 1926. Years later, the "Group" designation would be restored.

14. See Gabrielle Neufeld and James Santelli, "1912–1941 Squadrons of the Corps," *Marine Corps Gazette* 57, no. 11 (November 1973).

15. In late 1940 Congress authorized a major expansion of naval aviation, and the marines subsequently organized two air wings with thirty-two squadrons. The First Marine Aircraft Wing (1st MAW) was formed at Quantico on July 7, 1941, with the First Marine Aircraft Group (which succeeded Aircraft One) as its initial component. Following the attack on Pearl Harbor, the 1st MAW transferred to San Diego and then deployed to Guadalcanal to support the First Marine Division during the battle for that island.

Today, the 1st MAW is part of the Third Marine Amphibious Force focused on the Pacific theater. The headquarters of the wing is located at Camp Foster, Okinawa. The Second Marine Aircraft Wing (2d MAW) was formed at San Diego three days after the 1st MAW, with the Second Marine Air Group (formerly Aircraft Two) at Ewa, Hawaii, as its initial component. The 2d MAW was badly damaged during the attack on Pearl Harbor but went on to carve out an impressive combat record during World War II. In 1946 the 2d MAW relocated to its present home at Marine Corps Air Station Cherry Point, North Carolina.

16. Reserve aviator Lieutenant Samuel Irwin, assigned to VO6-MR, Naval Reserve Air Base, Floyd Bennett Field, New York, was wounded at Belleau Wood during World War I. After the war, Irwin flew the mail for the Curtiss Company in Instanbul, Ankara, and Kaisarieh, Turkey. He was typical of many veterans who became reserve aviators and flew for civilian airlines and air freight-hauling companies. For example, Edwyn Schulz flew the largest Clipper for Pan American Airlines between Havana and Miami. Wallace Culberston flew for Pan American between Havana and the Panama Canal Zone. Parker Abbott became a test pilot for Lockheed. Donald Marshall signed on as a private pilot for the famous Hollywood producer Hal Roach. And the commander of VO6-MR, Stephen McClellan, was a pilot and assistant to the president of United Aircraft and Transport Corporation. "What Some of Our Reserve Officers Are Doing in Aviation," *Marine Corps Gazette* 19, no. 2 (August 1934): 56.

17. The first officer in charge of the reserve aviation section was Colonel Julius Turrill, a regular officer. "Marine Corps Reserve Notes," *Marine Corps Gazette* 14, no. 2 (June 1929): 134.

18. Reserve Officers, *Marine Corps Reserve,* 25. A fascinating aspect of the history of the Marine Corps Reserve is the fact that the Volunteer Marine Corps Reserve became the backbone of the reserve component, even though they drilled as volunteers, participated without pay, and usually had to buy their own uniforms, shoes, and equipment. "The period of 1925–1934 was one in which the reservists were, in effect, paying for the right to be reservists." They even had to organize themselves and do their own recruiting. Expansion of the reserve into regiments and later brigades created additional problems of administration and command. However, with the creation of the Platoon Leaders Course in 1935 and the assignment of navy ROTC graduates to the reserves, these forces were strengthened. By 1940, there were twenty-three organized reserve battalions and thirteen reserve aviation squadrons. In retrospect, the small office created in 1925 and employing three officers and six clerks was the "beginning of a machine that was to proliferate and provide for thousands of men and women from the civilian population who would rally to the Corps during the 1941–45 war years." Ibid., 35–61.

19. As late as 1927, there were only twenty-one aviator officers in the Marine Corps Reserve. "Marine Corps Reserve Aviation in the Department of the Pacific," *Marine Corps Gazette*19, no. 2 (August 1934): 52.

20. Reserve Officers, *Marine Corps Reserve,* 49–51.

21. Ibid., 52. The naval reserve began training aviators in 1925 and established bases with training aircraft and "ship-keepers to keep them in the air." The first Marine Corps Reserve squadrons were formed at five naval reserve air stations and operated under the supervision of both navy and marine reservists. In addition to learning how to fly, Marine Corps reservists were taught close-order drill and were required to qualify with the rifle

and pistol. "Marine Corps Reserve Aviation in the Department of the Pacific," 51–52. In time, the marines concluded that they wanted their own reserve air stations and established several in 1931 and 1932 (Reserve Officers, *Marine Corps Reserve,* 54):

Unit	Location	Date Organized
Service Squadron 7	Grosse Ile, MI	March 11, 1931
Service Squadron 4	Seattle, WA	March 12, 1931
Observation Squadron 7	Minneapolis, MN	March 15, 1931
Service Squadron 5	Squantum, MA	April 23, 1931
Fighting Squadron 6	Squantum, MA	April 23, 1931
Observation Squadron 8	Seattle, WA	June 12, 1931
Observation Squadron 6	Brooklyn, NY	June 13, 1931
Fighting Squadron 5	Detroit, MI	June 19, 1931
Scouting Squadron 3	Miami, FL	June 25, 1931
Fighting Squadron 4	Long Beach, CA	May 18, 1932
Observation Squadron 10	Oakland, CA	July 19, 1932
Utility Squadron 7	Washington, DC	October 4, 1932

22. By 1928, the course of instruction at the Marine Corps Reserve air stations consisted of forty-five hours of flying, including "dual, primary and secondary solo, recovery from unusual positions and elementary acrobatics." "Marine Corps Reserve Aviation in the Department of the Pacific," 52.

23. In 1931 a reserve flying squadron (VO-SMR) was established near Seattle, comprising two divisions. A Service Company (4MR) was also formed. This allowed 60 men for the squadron and 100 for the company, with 18 officers for one and 4 for the other. Two years later, an officer was detached from the squadron at Seattle and sent to Long Beach, California, to organize a new squadron, Fighting Squadron Four. An active-duty officer was also assigned to this unit to learn the intricacies of recruiting reservists, and once the authorized strength was reached, these two officers were posted to Oakland to raise another squadron. They were joined by another reserve officer to command the unit "and to act as Instructor-Inspector for the squadron." Ibid., 53.

24. Reserve Officers, *Marine Corps Reserve,* 53–54.

25. Ross Rowell succeeded Roy Geiger as head of Marine Corps aviation in May 1935 and would fill that billet until March 1939. During his tenure, Congress passed a bill providing for an aviation cadet program. This program provided much of the necessary manpower for World War II, including the Marine Corps. Gregory "Pappy" Boyington, the famous F4-U Corsair pilot who commanded the Black Sheep Squadron during the war, was an aviation cadet, along with other less renowned Marine Corps aviators who performed exceptionally well in combat. The aviation cadet program produced several Marine Corps general officers, including Richard Mangrum (Naval Aviator No. 4,477), who would become assistant commandant of the Marine Corps in 1965. Interestingly, Littleton Waller Jr., son of Littleton "Tony" Waller, was ordered to active duty as a reserve colonel in June 1941, heading the Target Practice Section and later the Gunnery Section in Plans and Policies, Headquarters, Marine Corps. He was appointed to head the Personnel Division

during World War II and was promoted to brigadier general, the first reserve general officer on active duty in the history of the Marine Corps. Like many of his compatriots, the younger Waller had served at Veracruz in 1914 and saw combat in World War I (where he commanded a machine gun battalion). He left active service in 1921 to care for his disabled father but remained in the reserves. In addition to heading the Personnel Division at headquarters, Waller served in the Pacific, commanding defense forces at Johnston and Midway atolls as well as in Hawaii. He retired in 1946 and was advanced to the rank of major general. He died in 1967. Clark, *United States Marine Corps Generals of World War II,* 167–68.

26. William Barr, "Tells How Marine Fliers Hunt Down Bandits," *Recruiters' Bulletin* 5, no. 5 (June 1919): 5. Five trips were made from the docks on Macorís Harbor to the landing field near Consuelo, partly by barge and partly by rail. Two days after the *Lake Superior* arrived, the first Jenny flew from the landing field; the next day, all six were "in commission and ready for service." Ibid.

27. Ellsworth, *One Hundred Eighty Landings of United States Marines.*

28. Although the word "buccaneer" is often used as a synonym for pirate, the original buccaneers were hunters on the islands of Tortuga and Hispaniola. They smoked the meat of wild boars and feral cattle in huts known as *boucanes,* and they sold it to pirates who preyed on shipping in the Caribbean Sea. Over time, the term buccaneer was applied to the local pirates and privateers. See P. K. Kemp [Christopher Lloyd], *Brethren of the Coast: Buccaneers of the South Seas* (New York: St. Martin's Press, 1961).

29. A *caudillo* is a military landowner (a strongman or warlord) who possesses oligarchic-plutocratic power by virtue of his charisma, political connections, and wealth. Military privilege (*fuero militar*) exempted the *caudillo* from paying certain taxes and often from criminal and civil prosecution. *Caudillos* usually commanded full-time armed militias to exert their authority and were very influential in the history of Hispanic America. See Hugh Hamill, ed., *Caudillos: Dictators in Spanish America* (Norman: University of Oklahoma Press, 1992).

30. See William Nelson, *Almost a Territory: America's Attempt to Annex the Dominican Republic* (Newark: University of Delaware Press, 1990). Also see Sumner Welles, *Naboth's Vineyard: The Dominican Republic, 1844–1924,* vol. 2 (New York: Payson & Clarke, 1928).

31. After Heureux was assassinated in 1899, several individuals came to power, only to be overthrown by their political opponents. From the establishment of the republic in 1865 until American intervention and occupation in 1916, there were thirty-five chief executives in Santo Domingo. The average term of office was less than a year. From 1910 to 1916 there were six presidents. Rufus Lane (brigadier general, adjutant and inspector, USMC), "Santo Domingo," n.d. (circa 1938), MCHD, Second Brigade Files.

32. The US Fleet was generally ported on the East Coast in the Chespeake Bay, and before completion of the Panama Canal it had to travel some 14,000 miles via the Atlantic and Indian Oceans or 19,700 miles by way of the Strait of Magellan. Even after the canal was completed, the fleet had to travel some 12,000 miles to reach the western Pacific Ocean. Nevertheless, the canal's importance was obvious to American strategic planners, as a "fleet's power was estimated to erode by 10 percent for each thousand miles it cruised from its base." Edward Miller, *War Plan Orange: The US Strategy to Defeat Japan, 1897–1945* (Annapolis, MD: Naval Institute Press, 1991), 32.

33. Dana Munro, *The United States and the Caribbean Area, 1921–1933* (1934; reprint, Princeton, NJ: Princeton University Press, 1974), 108.

34. Munro, *Intervention and Dollar Diplomacy in the Caribbean,* 107.

35. For a concise and useful treatment of the marines' occupation of the Dominican Republic, see Stephen Fuller and Graham Cosmas, *Marines in the Dominican Republic: 1916–1924* (Washington, DC: Headquarters, US Marine Corps, History and Museums Division, 1974). The term "civil war" was not one of those defined in the introduction to this book, but the meaning is fairly straightforward: a civil war is an internal war. As Friedrich Freiherr von der Heydte relates, "Civil war is the comprehensive employment of violence outside the arena in which the customary, contracted norms of international law are valid." In that sense, a civil war creates its own rules. But as von der Heydte also notes, "Every internal conflict is embedded in international power relationships such that the internal conflict inevitably has effects upon international relations, and the outcome of the conflict is inevitably influenced from the outside." Thus, a civil war becomes "an 'international' war in the sense of international law." When the marines arrived in the Dominican Republic, the civil war became an international war, with all the implications that entails. Freiherr von der Heydte, *Modern Irregular Warfare,* 20, 22.

36. Joseph Pendleton graduated from the Naval Academy and was commissioned into the Marine Corps in 1878. In 1916 he was sent to the Dominican Republic, was promoted to brigadier general, and took command of the Second Brigade. When he returned to the United States, he took command of the Second Advance Base Force at San Diego. Following several other command assignments, he was promoted to major general in 1923. After a short tour at Marine Corps Headquarters, he took command of the Fifth Brigade in San Diego. On June 2, 1924, he retired with more than forty years of service. He settled in Coronado, California, and was its mayor from 1928 to 1930. He died in February 1942. Harned, *Marine Corps Generals,* 52–58.

37. A "flying column" is a mobile, autonomous, combined-arms land force, often put together in an ad hoc fashion for a specific mission and period of time. Given that mobility is key, flying columns were usually lightly equipped and suitable for fast transport. See Hugh Chisholm, ed., "Flying Column," in *Encyclopædia Britannica,* 11th ed. (Cambridge: Cambridge University Press, 1911), 585. In the case of the marines' flying column in Santo Domingo, the main body comprised infantry and artillery, a hospital, and a supply train with twenty-four mule carts, seven trucks with trailers, two "motorized water carts," a horse-drawn water wagon, a "Holt tractor pulling four trailers," and eleven automobiles. The expectation was that the marines would "live and fight entirely on the supplies carried by this train." Fuller and Cosmas, *Marines in the Dominican Republic,* 14.

38. Welles, *Naboth's Vineyard,* 908.

39. Fuller and Cosmas, *Marines in the Dominican Republic,* 16.

40. Ibid., 20.

41. Marvin Goldwer, *The Constabulary in the Dominican Republic and Nicaragua: Progeny and Legacy of United States Intervention* (Gainesville: University of Florida Press, 1962), 7.

42. James Breckenridge was born into an important American family whose members had been politicians and military men stretching back to the American Revolution. He was commissioned into the Marine Corps in 1899 and saw service in the Philippines

during the Spanish-American War. In 1914 he participated in the occupation of Veracruz as commander of the marine detachment from the battleship USS *Utah.* Breckenridge served during World War I as a naval attaché in Petrograd, Russia, and also in Chistiania, Norway; Stockholm, Sweden; and Copenhagen, Denmark. Following the war he attended the Navy and Army War Colleges and was then sent to the Dominican Republic in command of the Fifteenth Regiment. He later commanded the Guardia Nacional Dominicana. He returned to the United States to command the Marine Barracks in Washington, DC, and then went back to sea. While serving aboard the battleship USS *Texas,* he wrote an article published by the *Annals of the American Academy of Political and Social Sciences* entitled "Land Ownership and Its Relation to National Stability," an outgrowth of his time spent in Santo Domingo. In 1930 Breckenridge was posted to China and was promoted to brigadier general. He returned to command the Marine Corps schools. During his second tour at the schoolhouse, he sought to implement the pedagogical ideas of Alexander Meiklejohn, a professor at the University of Wisconsin. He wrote: "Curiosity leads to investigation, which opens discussion, which gives rise to opinion, which breeds criticism, which results in improvement. All of this bespeaks a wide freedom in thought and an acute divergence from the arbitrary." He also oversaw the writing of the famous *Tentative Landing Forces Manual* and the first edition of the *Small Wars Manual.* He retired in October 1941, having reached the statutory retirement age of sixty-four. Mary Breckenridge, "Lieutenant General James Carson Breckinridge, USMC (September 1877–March 1942)," *Quarterly Bulletin of the Frontier Nursing Servive* 17, no. 4 (Spring 1942). See also James Carson Breckenridge Papers, MCHRC, file 11-H-4, Archives and Special Collections.

43. *Gavilleros* is Spanish slang, specific to the Dominican Republic, for gunmen or triggermen, originating from the word *gavilla,* meaning "gang." Elsewhere in Latin America, such men are usually called *banditos* ("outlaws" or "bandits"). *Gavilleros* were more than mere criminals; like the *cacos* in Haiti, there was a political dimension to their activities. Before the marines' occupation of Santo Domingo, the *gavilleros* were hired guerrillas. During the occupation, the populace regarded them as resistance fighters. See Humberto Müniz, "Sugar Land and Gavillero Warfare in Eastern Dominican Republic: The Case of Central Romana, 1910–1924," *Historia Y Sociedad* 12 (2000–2001): 3–47.

44. For details, see Millett, *Searching for Stability,* chap. 6.

45. Colonel Breckenridge believed that a close relationship existed between political strife and economic conditions in the Dominican Republic. The expansion of the predominantly foreign-owned sugar latifundia had converted large portions of the east from subsistence "multifundias" into large capital-intensive estates (*inmuebles*). This had a significant impact on independent peasants who had tilled the land for generations. Even those who farmed small gardens (*conucos*) found themselves pushed off their land. Landless and destitute, many peasants took up thievery and became bandits. But others became politically conscious and openly identified themselves as revolutionists. One of the more prominent leaders, Eustacio "Bullito" Reyes, called his band La Revolucíon. See US Military Government of Santo Domingo, *Santo Domingo: Its Past and Its Present Condition* (Santo Domingo City, Dominican Republic, 1920). See also Bruce Calder, "Some Aspects of the United States Occupation of the Dominican Republic" (PhD diss., University of Texas, 1974).

46. Ben Hebard Fuller graduated from the Naval Academy in 1889. He deployed to the Dominican Republic and afterward joined the faculty of the Naval War College. He

returned to Santo Domingo, where he was promoted to brigadier general. In 1930 he was named commandant. He retired in 1934 as a major general with more than forty-two years of service. He died in 1937 and was buried at the Naval Academy cemetery beside his son, Edward Fuller, who was killed during the Battle of Belleau Wood during World War I. Harned, *Marine Corps Generals,* 106–11.

47. Logan Feland attended South Kentucky College and the Massachusetts Institute of Technology, where he earned a degree in architecture. He joined the Kentucky State Guard and served on occupation duty in Cuba during the Spanish-American War. In July 1899 he was commissioned into the Marine Corps and served in the Philippines under Major Littleton Waller. During World War I he served as chief of staff of the US Army's Second Division, the first marine to hold such a position in an army division. Feland commanded marines at Bealleau Wood; after the war he was awarded the French Cross of War with Bronze Star and the Cross of War with Palm and was made an officer of the French Legion of Honor. He was cited multiple times in Second Division orders for gallantry, as well as for extraordinary heroism at Belleau Wood. At the end of the war he was awarded the army's Distinguished Service Cross. Harned, *Marine Corps Generals,* 148–57.

48. Charles Long was a Naval Academy graduate. During the Spanish-American War he served in the First Battalion and later served in the Canal Zone as part of the Advance Base Force mission. During the expedition to Vercruz in 1914, he commanded the First Regiment. He also served with the expedition sent to Haiti in 1915 and then served as the assistant to the commandant, Major General Barnett. Harry Lee was a descendant of Revolutionary War hero "Light Horse" Harry Lee, father of Confederate general Robert E. Lee. He joined the marines in 1898 but was mustered out after the Spanish-American War. Lee rejoined the Marine Corps and served aboard several ships as well as in the Philippines and China. He was part of the First Nicaraguan Campaign in 1912 and participated in the battle for Coyotepe Hill. He then participated in the occupation of Veracruz in 1914. He served briefly in Haiti in 1915 and served in France during World War I. In June 1918 he took command of the Sixth Marine Regiment at Belleau Wood when its commander, Albertus Catlin, was wounded. He returned to the States in July 1921 and was ordered to Santo Domingo to replace Brigadier General Long (who returned home owing to poor health). Dissatisfied with the pacification effort in the eastern district, General Lee relieved the commander and placed Colonel Charles Lyman in charge of pacification operations. Lyman organized "countergangs" that soon disrupted guerrilla operations in the district and led to the capture of notorious insurgent leader Ramon Nateras. Harned, *Marine Corps Generals,* 164–69.

49. Headquarters First Provisional Brigade, General Order 17, July 18, 1919, and Report, Military Governor of Santo Domingo, to the Secretary of the Navy, subject: Claim of Dugal McPhail, May 19, 1924, RG 38, E6, boxes 13 and 74, National Archives.

50. Bruce Calder, "Caudillos and Gavilleros versus the United States Marines: Guerrilla Insurgency during the Dominican Intervention, 1916–1924," *Hispanic American Historical Review* 58, no. 4 (November 1974): 662.

51. In one disputed but well-known case, a marine officer allegedly gunned down some thirty peasants working in a *cañaveral* (sugarcane field). In addition, Captain Charles Merkel, USMC, was accused of misreating peasants and prisoners on several occasions. In one case, he allegedly cut off the ears of a prisoner, cut the man across the chest, and then

rubbed salt in the wound. He withheld food and water from the man for three days. He also burned houses in Seibo province and committed various other crimes. Merkel committed suicide while awaiting court-martial. Lieutenant General Edward Craig, USMC, Ret., oral history transcript, June 8, 1968, 17, Oral History Collection, Headquarters, US Marine Corps, History and Museums Division, Washington, DC. Also see Horacio Fombona, *Crímenes del Imperialismo Norte-americano* (Mexico City: Ediciones Churubusco, 1927), 122; Major R. S. Kingsbury to Brigade Commander, subject: Report against Captain Charles F. Merkel, M.C., September 30, 1918, MCHD, Second Brigade Files. These and other activities (including alleged atrocities in Haiti) prompted several investigations by the US Senate.

52. Russell Presley, Commanding Officer, First Division, Squadron D, to Chief of Naval Operations, Washington, DC, subject: Weekly News Letter, for week ending November 27, 1920, December 3, 1920, MCHD, Second Brigade Files.

53. Cunningham arrived aboard the USS *Hancock* in January 1921, replacing Arthur Page Jr., who proceded to Port-au-Prince aboard the *Hancock* to take command of the Fourth Air Squadron. Commanding Officer [A. A. Cunningham] to Chief of Naval Operations, Washington, DC, subject: Weekly News Letter, for the week ending January 15, 1921, MCHD, Second Brigade Files.

54. The ace of spades emblem has become legendary in Marine Corps aviation and is today the unit symbol for Marine Attack Squadron 231 (VMA-231), Marine Aircraft Group 14, Second Marine Aircraft Wing, based at Marine Corps Air Station Cherry Point, North Carolina.

55. Charles Hanst, "Marine Aviation in Santo Domingo," *Popular Aviation,* October 1928, 26. Hanst's assertion about aviation mechanics is quite true. From the earliest days of military aviation in the United States, commanders have extolled the contributions of the "mechanicians." For example, following General John Pershing's unsuccessful pursuit of Mexican revolutionary Pancho Villa in 1917, Captain Benjamin Foulois, commander of the army's First Aero Squadron and later commander of the US Army Air Corps, commended his enlisted mechanics, writing that, without their "willing and efficient cooperation," the "flying service of the Punitive Expedition would have ended at [its starting point in] Columbus, New Mexico." Benjamin Foulois, "Report of the Operations of the First Aero Squadron, Signal Corps, with Punitive Expedition, USA, for Period March 15 to August 15, 1916," n.d., 11, Maxwell Air Force Base, AL, Historical Research Agency.

56. Hanst, "Marine Aviation in Santo Domingo," 26. Sergeant Hanst flew combat missions during World War I as an officer in the US Army Air Service. After the war he left the army, enlisted in the Marine Corps, and flew as an enlisted pilot in the Dominican Republic. He left the Marine Corps after servng in Santo Domingo and took up a variety of jobs, including state policeman, barnstorming pilot, airline pilot, and chief pilot for the Stinson School of Aviation in Detroit, Michigan. He wrote a book, *Eighty Plus,* that described his flying adventures.

57. Although the earliest marine aviators in the Dominican Republic survived the experience, several were killed later in accidents in the United States. Lieutenant Harmon Norton was killed when he crashed while testing an airplane for the Schneider Cup Race at Anacostia, a DC neighborhood on the Potomac River (and today the site of Joint Base Anacostia-Bolling). Lieutenant Duncan Lewis was killed in a collision between his VE-7

and a Fokker D.VII at Quantico in 1922. The pilot of the Fokker was also killed. Hanst, "Marine Aviation in Santo Domingo," 26.

58. "Report on First Air Squadron, Marine Aviation Force," n.d., 2, MCHD, Second Brigade Files. Air "routes" had to be established between all the airfields, and most of them involved flying "over mountain ranges with their accompanying winds, clouds, rainstorms, and absence of a possible forced landing place, long stretches of wooded jungle country where even small towns are far apart; while others led over waste stretches of hilly country where no water could be found under a day's hiking." Ibid. See also First Division, Squadron D, M.A.F., "Santo Domingo Aerial Pilot," 1st ed. (1920), MCHD, Second Brigade Files. "Santo Domingo Aerial Pilot" was an informal publication that provided aviators with specific information regarding air routes from Santo Domingo City to Port-au-Prince via Baní, Azua, Barahona, and San Juan.

59. Hanst, "Marine Aviation in Santo Domingo," 26.

60. Commanding Officer, First Division, Squadron D, to Chief of Naval Operations, Washington, DC, subject: Weekly News Letter, for week ending October 9, 1920, MCHD, Second Brigade Files.

61. Barr, "Tells How Marine Fliers Hunt Down Bandits," 5.

62. The "Marlin automatic" Lieutenant Carpenter referred to was the Colt-Browning Model 1895, nicknamed the "potato digger" because of its unusual operating mechanism. Based on a design by John and Matthew Browning, it was the first successful gas-operated machine gun to enter US service. It was considered obsolete by World War I and was used mostly for training. Colt ceased production in 1916 and sold the machinery and manufacturing rights to Marlin Rockwell and the Marlin Firearms Company in North Haven, Connecticut. Marlin manufactured an improved version of the M1895, designated the Colt-Browning M1895 / 14 and known as the "Marlin automatic," the "Marlin gun," and "Model 1917." The navy purchased the weapon, and a more radical version was introduced in 1917 for use on aircraft and in tanks, designated the M1918. Most of these machine guns saw service on aircraft as defensive weapons, but they were also used as fixed, forward-firing machine guns with synchronization gear for firing through the spinning propeller of the airplane. By the last month of the war, the US Army replaced the British Vickers machine gun on the Spad XIII with the Marlin automatic. In the United States, the Thomas-Morse Scout, used for advanced training, also employed the Marlin gun. See Roger Pauly, *Firearms: The Life Story of a Technology* (Santa Barbara, CA: Greenwood Press, 2004).

63. Second Lieutenant Manson C. Carpenter to Commanding Officer, First Division, Squadron D, subject: Contact with Bandits, July 28, 1919, MCHD, Second Brigade Files.

64. Second Lieutenant H. N. Miller to Commanding Officer, 44th Company, Third Provisional Regiment, subject: Report of Skirmish with Native Bandits on 10 June, 1919, June 11, 1919, MCHD, Second Brigade Files.

65. Barr, "Tells How Marine Fliers Hunt Down Bandits," 5.

66. As the commander for the eastern district noted, "During the operations, control and direction over the forces has been maintained by aeroplane communication and station and field radio service. Radio service being susceptible [to] being intercepted . . . strictly confidential or secret messsages are not sent by radio when aeroplane service is available. . . . Aeroplane service has enabled all companies of this regiment to move out

promptly and simultaneously for concerted action with complete and definite instructions for operations." District Commander [William Harlee] to Commanding General, Second Brigade, subject: Control of Field Forces by Regimental Headquarters, 15th Regiment, MCHD, Second Brigade Files.

67. Barr, "Tells How Marine Fliers Hunt Down Bandits," 5.

68. Commanding Officer, First Air Squadron, to Chief of Naval Operations, subject: Weekly News Letter, January 8, 1921, MCHD, Second Brigade Files.

69. Ibid. Some of the flights were of no particular military importance. For example, Sergeant Hanst recalled one flight made from Santo Domingo City to San Pedro de Macorís to purchase fresh fish for the commanding general. On another occasion he flew to San Francisco de Macorís with Cuckoo Boyden to purchase fresh eggs. Upon their return, Boyden made a hard landing ("pan-caked the old DH"), and all the eggs were smashed. However, other flights were quite important. A Senate committee traveled to Haiti and the Dominican Republic to investigate claims that the marines were using overly harsh measures in their pacification efforts. Committee members were transported by seven DH planes of the First Squadron from Cap Haïtian to Santo Domingo City. Major Cunningham led the flight, which included Sergeant Hanst, Captain Presley, and Lieutenants Schilt, Boyden, Norton, and Lewis. Hanst, "Marine Aviation in Santo Domingo," 120.

70. Ibid., 121.

71. Hayne Boyden, "Some Forced Plane Landings in Santo Domingo, *Marine Corps Gazette* 7, no. 2 (June 1922); Hayne Boyden, "Aerial Adventues in Hispaniola," *Leatherneck* 8, no. 31 (August 1925); Hayne Boyden, " . . . and Santo Domingo," *Marine Corps Gazette* 56, no. 11 (November 1972).

72. Boyden, "Some Forced Plane Landings."

73. Using nonaviators for "ballast" was not unusual, but it could be dangerous for the passenger if the pilot became incapacitated for some reason. For example, on March 22, 1932, Staff Sergeant Orlo Hoffer took off from San Diego for a routine test flight accompanied by Corporal Hilmer Torner in the rear cockpit. Torner had flown as a passenger on several earlier flights, but he was not a pilot and had never operated the controls of an airplane. During the flight, Staff Sergeant Hoffer fainted and fell forward onto the controls, causing the plane to go into a spin. Corporal Torner at first considered jumping out of the airplane with his parachute, but he noticed the pilot was unconscious and pulled him away from the controls. Torner then took control of the airplane, righted it, and succeeded in climbing to a safe altitude, where he practiced with the controls for some fifteen to twenty minutes before heading to North Island, where he "made a very creditable landing on the Rockwell Field." Upon landing he extracted the pilot, laid him under the wing, and was administering first aid when help arrived. He was awarded the Distinguished Flying Cross for his heroic action. See Senior Board Member of the Board for the Award of Medals of Honor, Distinguished-Service Medal, Navy Cross, Distinguished Flying Cross and Life Saving Medals, to the Secretary of the Navy, subject: Corporal Hilmer N. Torner, US Marine Corps—Extraordinary Achievement while in Aerial Flight—Award for, May 17, 1932, MCHD, Second Brigade Files. See also the citation accompanying the award of the Distinguished Flying Cross to Hilmer N. Torner, valor.militarytimes.com, accessed May 6, 2017.

74. Hayne Boyden, "Aerial Adventures in Hispaniola, Part II," *Leatherneck* 8, no. 37 (October 1925).

75. Ibid.

76. When Major Edwin Brainard took over as head of Marine Corps aviation, he was forty-nine years old. He had won his wings in 1920 at Pensacola. Before arriving in Washington, Brainard had flown landplanes and seaplanes of many types, openly admitting that he "pranged" a few. "On one occasion he took up a Loening *Amphibian* for the first time. After he got in the air, he drew in his wheels, played about for a while, and then came in to land on the ground. He landed on the ground, too, and then realized that he had forgotten to roll his wheels down. Slight damage resulted and the Major got out and stormed about the field demanding that he be elected president for life of the Navy's well-known 'Flying Jackass Club.'" See "Major Brainard, Chief of Marine Corps Aviation," *US Air Services* 12, no. 9 (September 1927): 49. Brainard resigned from the Marine Corps in 1929 to become vice president in charge of operations for the Curtiss Flying Service, a nationwide chain of airports and airfields. "Major Brainard Joins Curtiss," *US Air Services* 14, no. 6 (June 1929): 60.

77. "Report on First Air Squadron, Marine Aviation Force," n.d., 1, MCHD, Second Brigade Files.

78. A later fight made by Lieutenants Ford Rogers and Horace Palmer from Hispaniola to the US mainland also made aviation history, though not in the way originally planned. Two new DH-4B-1 airplanes were shipped from the Naval Aircraft Factory to Haiti, where they were reassembled and flown to Santo Domingo City, with the intent to fly them to the St. Louis air meet and back. Rogers and Palmer were accompanied by First Sergeant Benjamin Belcher, the first naval aviation pilot in the Marine Corps, and Sergeant Peter Tolusciak, a former Polish army pilot. After overcoming numerous difficulties, the intrepid marines made it to St. Louis on September 28, 1923, where they were met by Lieutenant Commander Marc Mitscher, USN. From there, they decided to fly to San Francisco for the American Legion convention. They took a route through Oklahoma, Texas, Arizona, and Southern California, arriving at San Francisco's Crissy Field on October 15. They departed on the twenty-second to return to Haiti. This time, they took a northern route to Bolling Field outside Washington, DC. From there, they flew to Quantico. On December 1 they took off from Brown Field at Quantico and headed south through the Carolinas to Florida. They arrived at Port-au-Prince on December 8. Lieutenant Rogers and Sergeant Tolusciak remained in Haiti. The following day, Lieutenant Palmer and Sergeant Belcher flew to Santo Domingo City, where they were greeted by Brigadier General Lee. The trip covered just under 11,000 miles in 127 hours of actual flying time, the second longest trip in the history of aviation at the time (the longest was a 1919 flight by a British twin-engine Vickers "Vimy" bomber from London to Darwin, Australia). For details of the historic marine flight, see John Eliott, "The Longest Flight: Early Marine Aviators Make History," *Leatherneck* 91, no. 5 (May 2008).

79. "Naval and Military Aeronautics," *Aerial Age Weekly* 13, no. 14 (June 13, 1921): 207.

80. Ibid.

81. Fuller and Cosmas, *Marines in the Dominican Republic,* 66.

82. At Mukden in September 1931, a bomb planted by the Japanese exploded along a Japanese-owned rail line. Blaming the Chinese, the Japanese invaded the northeast province of Manchuria, meeting little opposition. The territory seized was then turned into a puppet state, Manchukuo, and was exploited for the economic benefit of Japan. Embarrassed, Chiang Kai-shek resigned as head of the Kuomintang but retained his post as

military commander and head of the newly established National Military Council. In the second incident, the Japanese attempted to provoke an uprising by targeting Japanese businesses in Shanghai, one of the largest port cities in the world. The Japanese intended to seize the city and dominate Chinese trade. But this time, Chiang decided to fight and sent some of his best units to defend Shanghai. Chinese Nationalist forces were unsuccessful in defeating the Japanese, but international mediation resulted in the demilitarization of Shanghai. See Anthony Coogan, "Northeast China and the Origins of the Anti-Japanese United Front," *Modern China* 20, no. 3 (July 1994): 282–84; Yoshihisa Tak Matsusaka, *The Making of Japanese Manchuria, 1904–1932,* East Asian Mongraphs 196 (Boston: Harvard University Asia Center, 2003).

83. Telegram from John MacMurray to Secretary of State, April 6, 1927, in *Papers Relating to the Foreign Relations of the United States, 1927,* vol. 2 (Washington, DC: GPO, 1942), 104–5, cited in Gabrielle Neufeld and James Santelli, "Smedley Butler's Air Corps: The First Marine Aviators in China," *Proceedings,* April 1977, 50. MacMurray was a lawyer who served as assistant secreary of state from November 1924 to May 1925, during which time he became a leading China expert. He was appointed minister to China in 1925. He resigned from the Foreign Service in 1929 and spent several years in academia before returning to the Foreign Service in 1933, where he served as ambassador and special assistant to the secretary of state until his retirement in 1944. In 1935 he wrote a memorandum warning that the United States, China, and Great Britain were responsible for Japanese aggression and that unless Japanese grievances were addressed, there would be war. MacMurray's papers are at Princeton University and are available online. See also John MacMurray, *How the Peace Was Lost: The 1935 Memorandum; Developments Affecting American Policy in the Far East,* ed. Arthur Weldon (Stanford, CA: Stanford University Press, 1992).

84. Guam is the largest of the Mariana Islands in the western Pacific and the southernmost of fifteen islands of volcanic origin. The people of Guam (the Indo-Malayan Chamorro) did not intend for their island to become involved in international affairs, but because it lies directly along the route from Hawaii to the Philippines, it was of strategic value to whatever state possessed it. Spain incorporated the island chain into its empire in 1667, and for the next 200 years the islands were ruled by military governors. With the outbreak of war between Spain and the United States in 1898 and the spectacular defeat of the Spanish squadron in Manila Bay, the US Navy dispatched the protected cruiser USS *Charleston* and three chartered steamers to seize Guam. The *Charleston* received the Spanish surrender on June 21. Thus, the island of Guam, with its picturesque Spanish forts, civil government, and hapless population, passed into the hands of the United States. See Evelyn Nelson and Frederick Nelson, *The Island of Guam* (*Description and History from a 1934 Perspective*), ed. Mary McCutcheon (1934; reprint, Washington, DC: Ana Publications, 1992).

85. The E-1 was an open-cockpit tractor biplane built for the US Army by the Standard Aircraft Company. It was powered by an 80 hp Rhône or 100 hp Gnome engine. The airplane saw some action in World War I but proved unsuitable as a fighter and was converted to an advanced trainer. The marines first flew the E-1 while training at Gerstner, Louisiana. "Standard Aircraft," in *Encyclopedia of World Aircraft,* ed. David Donald (Etobicoke, ON: Prospero Books, 1997).

86. The S.XIII, manufactured by Société Pour L'Aviation et ses Dérivés (SPAD), is one of the most famous single-seat fighter aircraft of World War I and was flown by American aces Frank Luke (eighteen victories) and Eddie Rickenbacker (twenty-six victories), French aces George Guynemer and Rene Fonck, and Italian ace Francesco Baracca. See J. M. Bruce, Micahel Rolfe, and Richard Ward, *Aircam Aviation Series No. 9: Spad Scouts SVII–SXIII* (Canterbury, UK: Osprey, 1968).

87. VE-7s equipped the US Navy's first fighter squadrons, VF-1 and VF-2. A VE-7 flown by Lieutenant Virgil Griffin, USN, made history on October 17, 1922, when it took off from the newly commissioned aircraft carrier USS *Langley.* VE-7s remained the front-line fighter for the navy for several years, and three were still assigned to the *Langley* in 1927. All were retired the following year.

88. Two VE-7s were converted for the US Army and redesignated the VE-9. The speed and service ceiling of the new airplane were much improved. In 1927 twenty-two VE-9s were built for the army and another seventeen for the navy. That same year, four unarmed floatplane versions (VE-9H) were constructed for navy battleships. A final version, the VE-9W, was canceled.

89. Swanborough and Bowers, *United States Navy Aircraft since 1911,* 428–29.

90. At the height of the crisis, there were more than 170 warships of various nations anchored off Shanghai. The American force included four cruisers, four destroyers, an oiler, a minesweeper, and the transports carrying the aircraft from San Diego and Guam. The British Royal Navy had even more ships offshore.

91. Both Rumplers were powered by a 100 hp, six-cylinder, water-cooled, in-line Daimler-Mercedes engine. The airplane had a ceiling of 11,500 feet. Its top speed was officially 75 mph, and at cruising speed the airplane had a range of 250 statute miles. The *Taube*'s fuselage was steel tubing welded and bolted together and covered with "balloon cloth," sealed with dope. The wings were 21 feet long and resembled the wings of a bird. Each airplane had two cockpits. As senior aviator, Plüschow was assigned the newer of the two aircraft, Navy No. E-8. Robert Whittaker, *Dragon Master: The Kaiser's One-Man Air Force on Tsingtau, China, 1914* (Cleveland, WI: Compass Books–Video Films, 1994), 24–26.

92. The Japanese pilot who dropped the bomb on Bismarck Fort at Tsingtao was Lieutenant Hideho Wada, who survived the Tsingtao campaign in World War I as well as World War II, reaching the rank of admiral. Ibid., 72–73.

93. The *Wakamiyo Maru* was arguably the first aircraft carrier used in combat.

94. Whittaker, *Dragon Master,* 75–79.

95. Ibid., 103.

96. Ibid., 154. Lieutenant Plüschow managed to escape from China aboard the American passenger liner SS *Mongolia,* arriving in San Francisco on December 22. He then traveled to New York and sailed for Europe aboard an Italian steamer that made an unscheduled stop at Gibraltar, where he was detained by the British. He was transferred to England, but he escaped and made his way to Holland aboard a Dutch ship. From there, he traveled to Germany, where he received the Pour le Mérite (the famous "Blue Max") and a promotion. He commanded the German naval aviation force at Libau, near Riga, Latvia, until the end of the war. After the war he became a filmmaker and an explorer. On January 28, 1931, he died when he crashed his Heinkel HD-24 biplane into the Brazzo River near Ushuaia, Tierra del Fuego, Argentina. He was forty-four years old. Ibid., 176–88.

97. Neufeld and Santelli, "Smedley Butler's Air Corps," 51; Brigadier General Smedley Butler to Commandant of the Marine Corps, April 22, 1927, cited in ibid., 59, n. 3.

98. Ibid., 52; message, Headquarters Marine Corps to Commander in Chief, Asiatic Fleet, n.d., cited in ibid., 59, n. 4.

99. Ibid.; testimony before the subcommittee to the House Committee on Appropriations regarding the navy appropriations bill for 1929, 70th Cong. 1st sess., 703, cited in ibid., n. 5.

100. Paul Matt, *United States Navy and Marine Corps Fighters, 1918–1962,* ed. Bruce Robertson (Letchworth, UK: Harleyford Publications, 1962), 32–33.

101. The FB-2 was an FB-1 fitted with an arresting hook, hoist lugs, and a strengthened undercarriage, thus allowing the FB-2 to operate from an aircraft carrier. Two FB-2s were tested aboard the USS *Langley* and approved for fleet employment with minor modifications, which were incorporated into the FB-5. Ibid., 33.

102. Millett, *Semper Fi,* 227.

103. Neufeld and Santelli, "Smedley Butler's Air Corps," 53.

104. Ibid., 54. Tragically, General Butler proved prescient. Captain Page died in the crash of an experimental Curtiss Hawk during the 1930 Thompson Race at Chicago. Obituary of Arthur Page, *Capital Gazette,* July 30, 2009, www.legacy.com, accessed March 22, 2017.

105. Neufeld and Santelli, "Smedley Butler's Air Corps," 53–54.

106. Sherrod, *History of Marine Corps Aviation in World War II,* 28.

107. Neufeld and Santelli, "Smedley Butler's Air Corps," 54.

108. Millett, *Semper Fi,* 227.

109. While in China, two of the Third Brigade's aircraft squadrons were redesignated in accordance with ongoing efforts to achieve a coherent organization of Marine Corps aviation. Fighting Squadron Three (VF-3) became Fighting Squadron Six (VF-6M; redesignated VF-10M in 1930). Scouting Squadron One (VS-1M; formerly Flight L) became Patrol Squadron Three (VP-3M), although this did not take effect until its personnel and aircraft returned from China, where they had been folded into VO-10M (when the expeditionary detachment was deactivated). In 1929 VP-3M had three OL-3s and eight OL-6s. In 1930 the unit had one OL-6 and three OL-8s. In 1931 the squadron was decommissioned.

110. The XO-2 was a conventional biplane first powered by a 420 hp Liberty V-1650-1 in-line engine. The US Army ordered forty-five production models, designated O-2. The airplane proved to be very reliable, and an additional twenty-four aircraft were ordered—eighteen of which were dual-controlled O-2A machines equipped for night flying, and six of which were O-2Bs configured as command aircraft. Gordon Swanborough and Peter Bowers, *United States Military Aircraft since 1909* (Washington, DC: Smithsonian Institution Press, 1989).

111. Neufeld and Santelli, "Smedley Butler's Air Corps," 56.

112. Ibid., 57.

113. Ibid., 58. The Nationlist leadership clearly recognized the potential of aviation. In 1928 an Aviation Department was created within the Ministry of War, and in April 1929 a Nationalist air force was formally established. The Nationalist government immediately approved funding to acquire sixty-two airplanes. The first airplanes purchased were

Vought Corsairs, which arrived in Shanghai in early 1930. Within six months, the Nationalist air force had thirty-two Corsairs, and it acquired an additional thirty Douglas aircraft before 1932. These and other aircraft were organized into eight squadrons, seven composed of light bombing and observation aircraft; the remainder were pursuit aircraft. The new air force immediately set about aiding Nationalist ground forces in quelling rebellions led by several warlords in northern China and then turned its attention to the Communist Red Army in southern China. Guangqui Xu, "Americans and Nationalist Chinese Military Aviation, 1929–149," *Journal of the American Aviation Historical Society* 44, no. 1 (Spring 1999): 17–19.

114. Quoted in Neufeld and Santelli, "Smedley Butler's Air Corps," 58.

115. Ibid., quoting the final report of the Third Marine Brigade.

116. With regard to a squadron's wartime versus peacetime strength, Brainard noted, "In order to have an organization capable of expansion in time of emergency, the peacetime squadrons are only one-third their war strength, i.e., one division active and two inactive. A division consists of 75 enlisted men and 10 commissioned officers. This gives the nucleus around which to recruit the two inactive divisions, and the addition of a squadron commander and staff gives a war strength unit which should be fairly efficient and capable of shortly performing any task. A division consists of six planes active and three in reserve. Therefore, a full strength squadron has eighteen active planes and nine in reserve, and in addition two planes attached to squadron headquarters and one transport." Edwin Brainard, "Marine Aviation—A Lecture," *Marine Corps Gazette* 11, no. 3 (September 1926): 192.

117. Authorized end-strength was 100 flying officers and 1,020 enlisted men. However, in 1921 there were only 59 officers and fewer than 850 enlisted personnel. In 1923 the number dropped to 46 and just over 750, respectively. Johnson, *Marine Corps Aviation,* 35.

118. In 1925 the First Aviation Group had twenty-five operational aircraft: nine DH-4B-1s, six VE-7s, one VE-9, six Martin bombers, two trainers, and one 02B-1. The squadron at San Diego had six DH-4B-1s and one Jenny. The squadron at Port-au-Prince had two DH-4Bs and three DH-4B-1s. Three HS2-Ls were stationed on Guam. Johnson, *Marine Corps Aviation,* 42.

119. Mauer Mauer, *Aviation in the U.S. Army, 1919–1939* (Washington, DC: Office of Air Force History, 1987), 70–74.

120. In 1918 the US Army asked the Thomas-Morse Aircraft Company of Ithaca, New York, to produce a new fighter powered by a water-cooled 300 hp engine (the Wright-Hispano-Suiza V8) to replace the French-made Spad XIII. The result was the MB3, a single-seat biplane made of wood and fabric with fixed landing gear. Despite teething problems, the Air Service was sufficiently impressed to order the airplane into production in 1920, designated the MB-3. A modified version, the MB-3A, followed, which boasted stronger structural integrity. But to the consternation of Thomas-Morse, it was underbid by Boeing, which received a contract to produce 200 of the planes, reportedly rescuing the company from financial ruin after World War I. However, Thomas-Morse won a contract to produce twelve MB-3s for the Marine Corps. This order was later altered to substitute two MB-7 racers, an MB-3 with the biplane wings replaced by parasol wings. One of these aircraft crashed and was destroyed. In a similar vein, the army ordered three MB-6 racers with shorter wings and a more powerful engine. Regrettably, the MB-3s purchased by the Marine Corps were not popular with pilots and were withdrawn from service in July 1922;

they were sold to the army for use as MB-3M trainers. Alan Pelletier, "Made in America: Thomas Morse MB-3 and Boeing MB-3A," *Air Enthusiast* 131 (September–October 2007): 46–51.

121. As noted in the text, the FB-1 drew on studies of the German Fokker D.VII, 142 of which were brought back to the United States following World War I. The prototype Model 15 had a welded steel fuselage braced with piano wire and tapered, single-bay wings made of wood and covered in fabric. The US Army bought several versions, and when a navy version was developed, it was designated FB. The navy ordered sixteen planes, but they were not modified for carrier operations (addition of an arresting hook) and were handed over to the marines. Two FB-1s were tested aboard carriers, and as a result, the navy ordered twenty-seven FB-5s, which became its first fighter intended specifically for carrier duty. One FB-6 was built for testing, but a proposed FB-7 was never constructed. Peter Bowers, *Boeing Aircraft since 1916,* 2d ed. (London: Putnam Aeromautical Books, 1989).

122. The aircraft carrier USS *Lexington* was the lead ship of its class. Originally designed as a battle cruiser, the *Lexington* was converted to an aircraft carrier to comply with the Washington Naval Treaty of 1922, which ended all new construction of battleships and battle cruisers. The *Lexington* entered service in 1928 alongside the USS *Saratoga.* "Lady Lex" spent its entire career in the Pacific and was used to refine carrier tactics in a series of annual exercises before World War II, including the successful staging of a surprise attack on the largest US Navy base in the Pacific outside of California: Pearl Harbor, Hawaii. The *Lexington* and *Saratoga* both delivered relief supplies to Managua, Nicaragua, following an earthquake there in March 1931. The *Lexington* was at sea when the Japanese attacked Pearl Harbor on December 7, 1941. Shortly afterward, it fought at the Battle of the Coral Sea and was damaged by Japanese aircraft. Leaking aviation gasoline caused a series of explosions and fires that could not be controlled, and the *Lexington* was sunk by an American destroyer on May 8. See Robert Stern, *The Lexington Class Carriers* (Annapolis, MD: Naval Institute Press, 1993).

123. Six Boeing FB-3s operated by the Marine Corps took part in a record-breaking transcontinental flight in January 1927 when they were ferried from Quantico to San Diego, accompanied by six DH-4Bs. Ross Rowell led the flight, and Christian Schilt piloted one of the FBs. "Marine Corps Cross-Country Flight," *Aero Digest*10, no. 1 (January 1927): 30. The adventure began when Major Edwin Brainard led a flight of three DH airplanes, along with two other officers and three enlisted pilots, from San Diego to Quantico. Three of the pilots from San Diego mounted three of the Boeing fighters, and the other three Boeings were flown by Rowell and his men. The three enlisted pilots from San Diego and three enlisted pilots from Quantico accompanied the Boeings in the DH airplanes as a second flight. Upon arrival, the Boeing airplanes and three of the DH planes were handed over to the San Diego squadron. The six Quantico pilots returned to Virginia in the remaining DH planes. The whole complicated trip was undertaken to transfer the FB-3s to San Diego, saving the time and cost of moving them by rail or ship. The officer pilots were Rowell, Schilt, William Wallace, C. C. Jerome, and W. L. McKitterick. The enlisted pilots were Gunner Michael Wodarczyk, Gunnery Sergeant A. S. Munsch, Gunnery Sergeant C. V. Frith (all from San Diego), Master Technical Sergeant Archie Paschal, Gunnery Sergeant J. I. Hockman, and Sergeant J. H. Price (all from Quantico). Notably, this was "the

first transcontinental flight of a military squadron of observation planes [DHs] commanded entirely by enlisted men." Unfortunately, two of the DH aircraft never made it to San Diego. Sergeant Hockman's plane crashed near Fabens, Texas, and the DH flown by Gunner Wodarczyk, crashed near Tucson, Arizona. No one was hurt in either crash. The FBs and DHs lost to Quantico were replaced by twelve Curtiss Hawks, four of which were fitted with Wasp engines (replacing the Curtiss D-12). Frederick Neely, "As Usual, the Marines Had the Situation in Hand," *US Air Services* 12, no. 1 (January 1927): 23–24.

124. The P-51 Mustang was originally designed to use the Allison V-1710 in-line engine. However, early versions performed poorly with this engine, and the P-51 was relegated to dive-bombing duty as the A-36 Apache. Conversion to the Rolls-Royce Merlin transformed its performance at altitudes above 15,000 feet. The definitive version, the P-51D, was powered by the Packard V-1650-7, a license-built version of the Rolls-Royce Merlin 66 two-stage, two-speed supercharged engine.

125. Although not especially relevant to Marine Corps aircraft in the small wars era, the addition of superchargers completed the engine equation. An engine at 20,000 feet produces half the power of its sea-level rating, and this continues to fall at higher altitudes. Engineers invented the supercharger to compensate for this degradation of performance. Early versions set spectacular altitude records in the 1920s, and turbo-superchargers were used in a number of aircraft during World War II, including the P-38 Lightning and the Northrop P-61 Black Widow. Though an ungainly looking beast, the radial-engined P-47 had a turbo-supercharger and was one of the finest fighters in the world at high altitude and perhaps the best fighter above 25,000 feet. Before World War II, multiengine aircraft, even with crude superchargers, could fly higher and faster than existing pursuit aircraft. As a result, some observers doubted that the fighter plane could ever match the performance of high-flying multiengine bombers.

126. The previous June, the first aerial refueling had taken place when two US Army airplanes were linked by hose some 500 feet above Rockwell Field, North Island, San Diego. Three DH-4Bs performed the feat. The Belgian air force achieved the same thing weeks later with its own modified DHs. Inspired, Lieutenant Elwood "Pete" Quesada of the Army Air Corps discussed performing a similar feat with Marine Corps aviators at Anacostia Naval Air Station near Washington. But Captain Ira Eaker appropriated the idea from Quesada as an Army Air Corps project. This would be the celebrated and much-publicized Operation Question Mark, employing a Fokker C-2A as the "receiver" and two Douglas C-1 single-engine transports as "tankers."

127. The German American Rentschler had graduated from Princeton Univesity in 1909 and worked in the family business as a machinist. He was commissioned into the US Army during World War I and inspected Hispano-Suiza engines manufactured under license to the Wright-Martin factory in New Brunswick, New Jersey. Rentschler left the army convinced that a lighter engine with more power and reliability was the future of aviation. His proposed design for a radial engine was unconventional, and he was eager to pursue his vision when he became president of the new Wright Aeronautical Company. The company's investors were not supportive, however, and he resigned in 1924. Shortly thereafter he approached the Pratt & Whitney Machine Tool Company of Hartford, Connecticut, with his idea. That company agreed to provide funding as well as floor space to construct the prototype, and the result was the first Wasp engine. After World War II

Rentschler turned his attention to turbojet engines, and Pratt & Whitney produced its first, the J57, in 1953. The J57 powered the first Boeing B-52 Stratofortress in 1954. Rentschler died in 1956 in Boca Raton, Florida. He was posthumously awarded the Civilian Service Award for Exceptional Service by the US Air Force.

128. Pratt & Whitney's conversion from a machine tool company to a manufacturer of aircraft engines began when Frederick Rentschler joined the company (a subsidiary of Niles Bement Pond Corporation). Its first engine, the 425 hp R-1340 Wasp, was completed on Christmas Eve 1925. It was an immediate success, and many famous civilian aircraft mounted the new Wasp engine. The R-1340 was followed by another very successful radial engine, the R-985 Wasp Junior. Subsequently, a whole series of Wasp engines was manufactured. Many are still in use today (and replacement parts are still being manufactured). The next major step for Pratt & Whitney was the R-1690 Hornet—basically, a larger Wasp. In 1929 Rentschler ended his association with Pratt & Whitney Machine Tool Company (which had continued as a separate concern) and merged the Pratt & Whitney Aircraft Company with Boeing and several other companies to form United Aircraft and Transport Corporation. He was allowed to retain the Pratt & Whitney name.

129. Perhaps *the* transitional aircraft of the interwar period was the Boeing Model 200 Monomail, first flown in 1930. It incorporated an unprecedented number of cutting-edge features, ultimately leading to the production of the B-17 Flying Fortress. The Monomail designers sought to minimize "parasitic drag" to increase the airplane's speed. The Monomail's retractable landing gear added weight, but the payoff was less drag and greater speed. It also incorporated improved cowled engines, which enhanced cooling and also reduced drag. Finally, the Monomail had a semi-monocoque fuselage with stressed skin. This superior airframe permitted a cantilever wing without external bracing. The Monomail was a large but fast airplane, and the US Army acquired it as the YB-9 (Model 215), powered initially by the Pratt & Whitney R-1860-13 Hornet B (575 hp) and later by the Pratt & Whitney R-1860-11 Hornet B (600 hp). The civilian version, designated the Boeing 247, was the finest commercial airliner of its day. United Airlines purchased sixty of them. This prompted Trans World Airlines (TWA), operating old Ford trimotors, to seek a new aircraft of its own. The Douglas Aircraft Company, formed in 1921, came to the rescue. The prototype DC-1 was followed by the sensational DC-2, and Douglas was rewarded with a large contract from TWA. Douglas pressed ahead with an improved version, the DC-3, which went into service in 1936. The marines acquired a large number of "Gooney Birds" from the US Navy during World War II, designated the R4D. Interestingly, the marines also acquired an R3D-2 in 1940, powered by two Wright GR-1820-G102A Cyclone engines producing 1,100 hp. The civilian version of the R3D-2 was the DC-5, the least well known of the famous DC airliner series. The DC-5 was a twin-engine aircraft intended for short routes. It was not well received by the airline industry, and only five were built. One found its way into the Marine Corps.

130. Convair was formed in 1943 by the merger of Consolidated Aircraft and Vultee Aircraft Corporations, the former founded in 1923 by Reuben Fleet in Buffalo, New York, and the latter established in 1939 in Los Angeles, California. Consolidated was famous for its line of flying boats in the 1920s and 1930s, the most successful of which was the PBY Catalina built for the US Navy. Consolidated produced another famous aircraft during World War II, the B-24 Liberator, which, like the Catalina, saw action in both the Pacific and European theaters.

131. Johnson, *United States Naval Aviation,* 75.

132. Matt, *United States Navy and Marine Corps Fighters,* 33–34.

133. Swanborough and Bowers, *United States Navy Aircraft since 1911,* 145–46.

134. Johnson, *Marine Corps Aviation,* 42.

135. Matt, *United States Navy and Marine Corps Fighters,* 36.

136. Following US Army practice, the navy began using the "X" prefix to denote experimental aircraft beginning with an F6C-4 used as a test bed for the proposed F6C-5 (XF6C-5). Ibid., 39.

137. Johnson, *United States Naval Aviation,* 71–73.

138. Falcon biplanes were built by the Curtiss Aeroplane and Motor Company. Most saw service in the US Army as observation aircraft, designated O-1 and O-11, or as attack aircraft, designated A-3. The navy variants were initially used as fighter-bombers, designated F8C, and then as Marine Corps dive-bombers, dubbed the Hell Diver. They were introduced into the navy in 1925 and saw front-line service until 1934. The F8C-1 was powered by a 420 hp Pratt & Whitney R-1340 Wasp engine, and four were built for the marines as light bombers, fighters, and observation aircraft, redesignated OC-1. The OC-2 (F8C-3) had twin .30-caliber flexible machine guns in the rear cockpit and two fixed forward-firing .30-caliber machine guns in the lower wings. The airplane could carry ten 17-pound bombs. Several OCs were sent to Nicaragua (three in 1929, three in 1930, and two in 1931). The F8C-4 was designated the OC-3.

139. One advertisement for the Corsair described it as one of "the best *bullet firing* and *bullet evading* airplanes in production, owing to its maneuverability and controllability." See "Bullet-Evading Airplanes," *Aero Digest* 12, no. 6 (June 1928): 997 (emphasis in original).

140. William Wallace was commissioned into the Marine Corps in 1918. Following a short tour with the Tenth Regiment (artillery) at Quantico, he shipped out to Santo Domingo, where he remained until 1921. When he returned to the United States, he volunteered for flying duty and graduated from Pensacola in December, whereupon he was posted to Brown Field, Quantico. He went back to the Dominican Republic as an aviator in 1922 and returned to the States in 1924 with the rest of the squadron. He then attended the US Army Air Service Advanced Flying School, graduating in 1926. From there he went to China, serving as a squadron commander with the Aircraft Squadrons, Third Brigade. He returned to San Diego in 1929 and took command of VS-14M aboard the aircraft carrier USS *Saratoga* in 1931. With the dissolution of VS-14M, Wallace was sent to Maxwell Field, Alabama, to attend the army's Air Corps Tactical School, graduating in 1935. When Pearl Harbor was bombed in late 1941, Wallace was the executive officer of Marine Aircraft Group 21 in the Hawaiian Islands and participated in the defense of Ewa airfield. He was then appointed commander of the marine aviation detachment on Midway Island; from there he went to Guadalcanal. He returned to the United States in 1943 and was promoted to brigadier general the same year. He returned to the Pacific in 1944 and served on Okinawa, where he commanded the Air Defense Command and Fighter Command. He was promoted to major general in 1945, and after the war he served as director of Marine Corps aviation and assistant commandant. He retired in 1952 as a lieutenant general and died in 1977. Clark, *United States Marine Corps Generals of World War II,* 165–67.

141. Larkins, *US Navy Aircraft* [and] *US Marine Corps Aircraft,* 46.

142. "Marine Corps Aviation on Aircraft Carriers (Prior to World War II)," n.d., MCHD, Miscellaneous.

143. "Interview with Major General Ross E. Rowell, USMC, on the Origin and Early Use of Dive-Bombing Tactics, Held in the Aviation History Unit on 24 October 1946," n.d., 1–4, MCHD, Aviation.

144. Peter Bowers, *Curtiss Aircraft, 1907–1947* (London: Putnam, 1979). The RC3-2 piloted by Jimmy Doolittle in 1925 is preserved at the National Air and Space Museum's Steven F. Udvar-Hazy Center at Washington-Dulles International Airport, south of Washington, DC. It still bears the racing number 3.

145. In May 1928 Marine Corps aviator Major Charles Lutz took first place in the prestigious Curtiss Marine Trophy Race at Anacostia Naval Air Station, flying a pontoon-equipped Curtiss Hawk powered by a Pratt & Whitney engine. Captain Harold Major, USMC, also flying a Hawk, came in third. At the time, the forty-seven-year-old Lutz commanded Brown Field at Quantico. According to one report, Lutz "flew a remarkably consistent race. He finished with an elapsed time of 38 minutes 4.2 seconds." Major, then attached to the navy's Bureau of Aeronautics, clocked in with a speed in excess of 181 mph. See "Lutz Wins Curtiss Marine Trophy," *Aero Digest* 12, no. 6 (June 1928): 996. See also Johnson, *Marine Corps Aviation,* 49. Two years earlier, Secretary of the Navy Curtis Wilbur had expressed his desire that naval aviators stop flying in such exhibitions. Obviously, this "ban" was not enforced. Only after Marine Corps aviator Arthur Page Jr. died in a crash of the experimental XF6C-6 monoplane during the 1930 Curtiss Marine Race did the US Navy and Marine Corps withdraw from air racing altogether. Johnson, *United States Naval Aviation,* 312.

146. Robert Finney, *History of the Air Corps Tactical School, 1920–1940* (Washington, DC: Center for Air Force History, 1992), 61.

147. Vernon Megee, *Memoirs of a Marine: Old Corps–New Corps, 1919–1959* (Dallas, TX: Atriad Press, 2011), 67.

148. Langley Field was becoming too crowded as new units were formed there. Maxwell Field, an air depot, had plenty of space. Some historians also claim that the War Department wanted to get the airmen away from Washington, DC, hoping to dilute their influence on congressional thinking about air power's proper role in war. Indeed, by 1926, a concept of air warfare that differed from the traditional army doctrinal perspective had begun to take shape. Away from the army staff and in the virtual monastic environment of Maxwell Field, the primacy of the bomber became a firmly established concept, and by the mid-1930s, instruction focused on the so-called industrial web theory and the ability of long-range "strategic" bombardment to break an enemy's will.

149. John Towers, "Naval Aviation," lecture no. 4, February 28, 1929 (typescript, Maxwell Air Force Base, AL, US Air Force Historical Research Agency).

150. Lewis Coxe, "Types and Missions of Surface Vessels, Submarines and Aircraft," lecture at Langley Field, VA, March 4–5, 1930 (typescript, Maxwell Air Force Base, AL, US Air Force Historical Research Agency).

151. See, for example, Brigadier General William Mitchell, "Air Power vs. Sea Power," extract from *American Review of Reviews* (March 1921), and Brigadier General William Mitchell, "Aviation over the Water," extract from *American Review of Reviews* (October 1920), Maxwell Air Force Base, AL, US Air Force Historical Research Agency.

152. Ross Rowell, "Aircraft in Bush Warfare," January 1, 1931 (typescript, Maxwell Air Force Base, AL, US Air Force Historical Research Agency). See also Ross Rowell, "Aircraft in Bush Warfare," *Marine Corps Gazette* 14, no. 3 (September 1929). At the time, the Army Air Corps preferred the term "minor wars" to "small wars." However, the definition of a minor war was virtually identical to the definition of a small war in the work of British colonial officer Charles Callwell, with only a few words altered. In that regard, the reader is reminded that small wars have "no particular connection with the scale on which any campaign may be carried out; it is simply used to denote, in default of a better term, operations of regular armies against irregular, or comparatively speaking irregular, forces." Callwell, *Small Wars,* 21–22.

153. The 1929–1930 syllabus, "Air Force in Minor Wars," made it clear that "an air force will not be employed alone except, perhaps, to punish an offending tribe or bandit army, so the selection of the objective and the plan of campaign of the whole force will be the function of the commander of that force." This perspective on the relationship between air and ground fit quite nicely within the marines' existing worldview. However, in 1933 Lieutenant Harold George, Army Air Corps, a zealous advocate for bombardment, asked in a lecture, "Why, I beg, is it necessary to occupy in order to compel submission. . . . Do you believe that a nation which saw its industrial centers, its transportation system, its electrical power lines, its docks and terminals reduced to ruins would be long in hesitating about submitting its will to the power capable of continuing such devastation?" In another lecture the same year, the future lieutenant general asked, "Has the advent of Air Power brought into existence a method for the prosecution of war which has revolutionized that art and given to air forces a strategical objective of their own, independent of land or naval forces, the attainment of which might, in itself, accomplish the purpose of war?" See "Air Force in Minor Wars," May 1930 syllabus (typescript, Maxwell Air Force Base, AL, US Air Force Historical Research Agency). See also H. L. George, "Bombardment Aviation," lecture, n.d. (circa 1933) (Maxwell Air Force Base, AL, US Air Force Historical Research Agency); untitled lecture, n.d. (circa 1933) (typescript, Maxwell Air Force Base, AL, US Air Force Historical Research Agency).

154. Megee, "Evolution of Marine Aviation," 24. However, Roy Geiger's thinking on an independent air force and its attendant strategic mission evolved over time. In 1920, while stationed in Haiti as a captain, Geiger was contacted by Captain Thomas Craven, USN (see chapter 1, note 28), regarding his opinion on the establishment of a separate air force in the United States. Geiger's letter to Craven concluded: "Theoretically, I think a Separate Air Service is unsound; practically, I think it would be a failure and a source of friction and discord throughout both the Army and the Navy." Nine years later, Geiger's opinion remained unchanged. While attending the US Army War College, Geiger wrote a memorandum to the commandant explaining his views about a separate air force. In short, he wrote: "A search has failed to reveal any . . . logical grounds for a separate department." But in 1943 Admiral Harry Yarnell, a retired officer serving in the Department of the Navy during World War II, requested Geiger's viewpoint, noting that "the Navy Department has heretofore been consistently opposed to an Independent Air Force." At the time, Major General Geiger was serving at Marine Corps Headquarters. He replied to Yarnell: "There should be a Department of Air on an equal footing with the War and Navy Departments. . . . At times it will be necessary for the Air Force to operate with the Army, at times with the Navy, at

other times with both the Army and Navy, and at still other times it may function entirely independently. There appears to be no good reason why such an Air Force should belong to the Army any more than it should belong to the Navy. . . . The development of the Air Force should not be retarded by the prejudices of either of the older services." Obviously, much had occurred between 1920 and 1943 to change Geiger's views about an independent air force. See letter from Roy S. Geiger to Captain T. T. Craven, January 10, 1920; Memorandum for the Commandant, Army War College, Prepared by Major Roy S. Geiger, subject: Relation of the Army and the Navy Air Components in Joint Operations, April 29, 1929; letter from Major General Roy S. Geiger to Admiral H. E. Yarnell, Navy Department, September 11, 1943, all in MCHRC, Geiger Personal Papers, PC 311, box 1.

155. *A Text on the Employment of Marine Corps Aviation* (Quantico, VA: Marine Corps Schools, 1935), 16.

156. Cunningham, "Value of Aviation to the Marine Corps," 222.

4. Marine Corps Aviation Comes of Age

The epigraph is drawn from Wilbur Lawton, *The Boy Aviators of Nicaragua; or, In League with the Insurgents* (New York: Hurst, 1910), 10. Lawton ("a famous aviation instructor," according to the publisher) was one of the pseudonyms of journalist John Goldfrap, who wrote boys' adventure books. His teenaged characters Harry and Frank Chester took the "Golden Eagle," a remarkable motor-driven biplane, to Nicaragua to support the insurgency against dictator José Santos Zelaya. Goldfrap wrote eight books about the boy aviators from 1910 to 1914. He also wrote the Dreadnought Boys series (6 vols., 1911–1914) and the Ocean Wireless Boys series (6 vols., 1914–1917).

1. Not all marine veterans who served in Nicaragua recalled American intervention there as a philanthropic enterprise and a positive experience. Colman McCarthy of the *Washington Post* interviewed seventy-seven-year-old Bill Gandall, who remembered "taking part in rapes, burning huts, [and] cutting off genitals" (not unlike former secretary of state John Kerry's "Winter Soldier" testimony in April 1971 to the Fulbright hearings regarding possible war crimes during the Vietnam War). After leaving the marines, Gandall became a union organizer, and he claimed he "had nightmares for years." Colman McCarthy, "In Nicaragua, an Ex-Marine's Campaign of Conscience," *Washington Post*, March 2, 1986.

2. Neil Macaulay, *The Sandino Affair*, 3d ed. (1967; reprint, Micanopy, FL: Wacahoota Press, 1998), 115–16. One must take Macaulay's claims with a large grain of salt, for although he was an honor graduate of the Citadel and served in the US Army during the Korean War (where he managed a post exchange), he also served as a lieutenant in Fidel Castro's "26th of July Movement Army" during the Cuban revolution in 1958, where he trained firing squads. Macaulay was rewarded with a tomato farm but returned to the United States in 1961. He earned his PhD at the University of Texas and taught Latin American studies at the University of Florida. He returned once to Cuba in 1991 but resided in Micanopy, Florida, until his death in 2007. Obituary of Neil W. Macaulay Jr., *Gainesville (FL) Sun*, October 31, 2007.

3. The best study of Latin American reaction to the employment of Marine Corps aviation in Nicaragua during the Sandino rebellion is without question Michael Schroeder's

"Social Memory and Tactical Doctrine: The Air War in Nicaragua during the Sandino Rebellion, 1927–1932," *International History Review* 29, no. 3 (September 2007): 508–49. See also http://www.sandinorebellion.com/HomePages/air-docs.htm.

4. "Geography of Nicaragua," typescript, n.d., 1, MCHD, Secondary Literature. The roads were described as "two wheel ruts" and "seas of mud and clay" that were "impassable" in the wet season and "clouds of dust in the dry" season. According to the document, the roads "pass over impossible gradients and traverse deep swamps and dense tropical jungles that in the wet season become death traps for men and animals. They pass through arid regions and cross rivers that have no bridges and are unfordable in the wet season. . . . On the best road in the country, within twenty miles of the capital . . . a truck train bogged down for over three weeks in June 1927." Oxen pulling carts would often leave their hooves behind after struggling free of the deep mud. "Native" mules would go lame and have to be shot, and pack animals regularly fell to their deaths at the bottom of rocky canyons. Ibid.

5. As quoted in Lawrence Harrison, "Nicaraguan Anguish and Costa Rican Progress," *This World,* Fall 1983, 31.

6. Ibid., 32.

7. The *Encomienda* was the Spanish Crown's attempt to define the legal status of the indigenous peoples of the American colonies. It was an extension of the practice of exacting tribute from Muslims and Jews following the reconquest of Spain from the Moors (the *Reconquista*). Conquered peoples were considered vassals of the Spanish monarch, who could grant a particular individual a monopoly on the labor of those who had been conquered. The grants were usually given to *conquistadores,* but on occasion they went to ordinary Spaniards. The *hacienda* system amounted to landed estates. The *hacienda* was not tied directly to the early grants of indigenous labor, but they were linked. *Encomenderos* usually retained their wealth and power via the *hacienda.* In short, as the Crown moved to eliminate the *encomienda,* the *hacendados* consolidated their holdings and recruited free labor on a permanent or casual basis. See Robert Himmerich Valencia, *The Encomenderos of New Spain, 1521–1555* (Austin: University of Texas Press, 1991); James Lockhart, "Encomienda and Hacienda: The Evolution of the Great Estate in the Spanish Indies," *Hispanic American Historical Review,* 1969, 411–29.

8. Pirates routinely plundered Nicaragua along the coastline and in the interior. The Corn Islands, some 43 miles off the central east coast, were a favorite anchorage for raids. Many famous pirates ransacked Nicaragua, including Jean Davis, William Dampier, John Morris, and Sir Henry Morgan. In truth, Morgan (like Sir Francis Drake) was not a pirate but a privateer, a nonmilitary ship's captain given license (a commission) to wage maritime warfare on behalf of a government. Morgan had struck up a friendship with the governor of Jamaica, Sir Thomas Modyford, during a low point in relations between England and Spain, and in 1667 Modyford gave Morgan a letter of marque to attack and seize Spanish vessels and to raid towns and other settlements. From his base at Port Royal, Jamaica, Morgan sortied throughout the Spanish Main, becoming quite wealthy in the process and later becoming lieutenant governor. He was awarded numerous honors for his exploits by the British government and was knighted by Charles II. He died in August 1688. For a general examination, see Mark Hanna, *Pirate Nests and the Rise of the British Empire, 1570–1740* (Chapel Hill: University of North Carolina Press, 2015).

9. The War of Jenkins' Ear (coined by Thomas Carlyle in 1858 and known in Spain as *Guerra del Asiento*) was a conflict between Great Britain and Spain lasting from 1739 to 1748. In 1731, off the coast of Florida, the British brig *Rebeccca*, commanded by Robert Jenkins, was boarded by Spanish privateers from the *Guarda Costa* ship *La Isabella*, commanded by Juan de León Fandiño, who allegedly sliced off one of Jenkins's ears as punishment for smuggling. British trading companies and opportunist politicians seized on the act to provoke a war with Spain in order to expand British trading opportunities in the Caribbean Sea. The conflict became part of the wider War of the Austrian Succession, which ended with the Treaty of Aix-la-Chapelle in 1748. Richard Harding, *The Emergence of Britain's Global Naval Supremacy: The War of 1739–1748* (Suffolk, UK: Boydell & Brewer, 2010).

10. Lasting only two years, the short-lived Imperio Mexicano, ruled by Agustín de Iturbide, was the first independent postcolonial polity, followed by the empire of Brazil. See Guillermo del Castillo, *América Hispánica, 1492–1898* (Barcelona: Labor, 1985).

11. Following the abdication of Agustín de Iturbide in 1823, members of the Creole upper class from the Central American provinces assembled at Guatemala City to declare a federal republic independent of the Spanish empire, known as *Provincias Unidas De Centro-américa*, comprising the modern states of Guatemala, Honduras, El Salvador, Costa Rica, and Nicaragua.

12. Gámez, quoted in Harrison, "Nicaraguan Anguish and Costa Rican Progress," 33.

13. During the nineteenth century, the very existence of the indigenous Miskito "kingdom" (*Mosquitia*) and its borders became a serious diplomatic issue among the United States, the United Kingdom, Nicaragua, and Honduras. In 1860 the British and Nicaraguans negotiated a treaty that, among other things, reduced the Miskito territory but also made it an autonomous region. The area remained semi-independent until 1894, when the president of Nicaragua, José Santos Zelaya, negotiated its annexation. Even so, English is still widely spoken around Bluefields, and the town resembles other former and current British possessions in the Caribbean.

14. Ideology was not at the heart of the rivalry; rather, the issue was who would have the power to rule Nicaragua.

15. "Filibuster" is derived from the Spanish *filibustero*, as well as the early modern English term for "pirate" or "freebooter." In early American history the term was commonly applied to someone attempting to take over another country by means of a privately financed military expedition. The practice reached its peak in the 1850s with William Walker's attempt to take over Nicaragua. See Charles Brown, *Agents of Manifest Destiny: The Lives and Times of the Filibusters* (Chapel Hill: University of North Carolina Press, 1980).

16. "General William Walker: The King of the Filibusters," chap. 5 of Richard Davis, *Real Soldiers of Fortune* (1906; reprint, Ithaca, NY: Cornell University Library, 2009).

17. It was the insurgency against Zelaya that brought the "boy aviators" and their remarkable Golden Eagle to Nicaragua (see note to epigraph, above). Their father, Señor Don Alfredo Chester, a wealthy American businessman, "was heartily in sympathy" with the insurgents, for if it succeeded, "it meant fair treatment and equitable taxes for the American planters and businessmen of the republic." Lawton, *Boy Aviators of Nicaragua*, 26. Despite being a dictator, Zelaya instituted a number of reforms during his sixteen-year reign,

especially with regard to agriculture, separation of church and state, education, and transportation. For that reason, and because he was overthrown with the support of the United States, Zelaya is regarded as a folk hero by many Nicaraguans, and even a precursor to the coming of Augusto Sandino. Harrison, "Nicaraguan Anguish and Costa Rican Progress," 35.

18. The proximate cause for the landings was President Zelaya's declaration that, contrary to the Nicaraguan constitution, he would serve another term in office. Bluejackets and marines were landed at Corinto by the screw steamer (gunboat) USS *Alert,* and two years later the *Alert* would send another landing party ashore at Bluefields.

19. Marines had been stationed in Panama before the construction of the canal, and in 1903 they confronted the Colombian army, which had been fighting insurgents on the south side of the French "dig."

20. The SS *El Sol* was a cargo ship built in 1910 for the Morgan Line, a subsidiary of the Southern Pacific Company. In 1917 the US Army acquired the *El Sol* to transport horses and mules to France. It was subsequently transferred to the US Navy as the USS *El Sol* but was returned to the Morgan Line in 1919. In 1927 it collided with another ship in New York Harbor and sank; it was salvaged and then scrapped. Naval History and Heritage Command, *Dictionary of American Naval Fighting Ships,* (online, accessed May 1, 2017).

21. Dana Munro, *The Five Republics of Central America* (New York: Oxford University Press, 1918), 227–32.

22. Dawson was regarded as an expert on Latin America, having served several times in the region, as well as authoring a two-volume work entitled *The South American Republics,* published in 1903 and 1904.

23. Graham Stuart, *Latin America and the United States* (New York: D. Appleton-Century, 1938), 350–51.

24. Among the contingent this time was a future commandant of the Marine Corps, Second Lieutenant Alexander Vandegrift, commissioned in 1887. Vandegrift was a favorite of Butler, who nicknamed him "Sunny Jim," after a smiling cartoon character. After seeing action in the First Nicaraguan Campaign in 1912, he served at Veracruz and in 1915 saw action at Fort Capois in Haiti. He returned to Haiti in 1919 and participated in the Second *Caco* Campaign, remaining in Haiti until 1923. In 1927 he sailed for China and served under Butler once again as the operations and training officer of the Third Brigade. He returned to the United States a year later but sailed once more for China in 1935, where he was promoted to colonel. In 1937 Vandegrift reported to Marine Corps Headquarters, and in April 1940 he was promoted to brigadier general. He was detached to the First Marine Division in November 1941 as the assistant division commander. With American entry into World War II, he was promoted to major general and took command of the First Division. He commanded the division during the battle for Guadalcanal and was awarded the Medal of Honor. On January 1, 1944, he was sworn in as the eighteenth commandant. He was appointed a full general in March 1945, the first Marine Corps officer on active duty to achieve that rank. He left active service in December 1947. He died after a long illness in 1973 and is buried in Arlington National Cemetery. Clark, *United States Marine Corps Generals of World War II,* 160–62.

25. A collier is a bulk cargo ship designed to carry coal for use by coal-fired warships. The speed of transfer at sea was an important measure of naval efficiency and explains

why specially designed ships were produced. But as often as not, older vessels were simply refitted for coaling duty and usually serviced shore bases (coaling stations). In addition, older wooden-hulled sailing ships such as the *Justin* gained fame in the exploration of the South Pacific owing to their sturdy, flat-bottomed hulls, which were well suited to shallow waters. Perhaps the most famous American collier was the USS *Jupiter,* rechristened the USS *Langley* after its conversion to an aircraft carrier—the first in the US Navy.

26. According to some sources, Butler wrote to Admiral William Southerland, in command of all US forces in Nicaragua, for instructions as to what to do with Zeledón, stating in an aside that "he would personally suggest that through some inaction on our part someone might hang him." The day after Butler penned his note, General Zeledón met his demise. Richard Millett, *Guardians of the Dynasty: A History of the US Created Guardia Nacional de Nicaragua and the Somoza Family* (Maryknoll, NY: Orbis Books, 1977), 27.

27. From 1913 to 1921 the marines in Managua faced little trouble, but in early 1922 they were reinforced by the marine detachments aboard the cruisers USS *Denver* and USS *Galveston,* as well as the USS *Nitro,* an ammunition ship commissioned the previous year. Most of the marines returned to their ships by the middle of February.

28. Butler was openly derisive with regard to the combat performance of government forces during the 1912 campaign. A major problem was desertion. The Nicaraguan army impressed recruits, fully aware that many if not most would desert. It was therefore not unusual to see lines of men tied by ropes being marched under armed guard to army training camps. Such men were not highly motivated to fight and die in battle.

29. Floyd Cramer, *Our Neighbor Nicaragua* (New York: Frederick A. Stokes, 1929), 163–66.

30. As a member of the National Municipal League, Dodds was introduced to the electoral problems in Nicaragua and elsewhere in Latin America by league president and secretary of state (1921–1925) Charles Evans Hughes, the former governor of New York (1907–1910) and a former associate justice of the US Supreme Court (1910–1916). M. A. Farber, "Harold W. Dodds, 91, Former Princeton President," *New York Times,* October 26, 1980.

31. Stuart, *Latin America and the United States,* 367.

32. Millett, *Guardians of the Dynasty,* 41. Dana Munro received his PhD in economics from the University of Pennsylvania and spent two years in Central America studying economic and political conditions for the Carnegie Peace Foundation. After serving as an aviator during World War I, he worked for the State Department as an economist. He joined the diplomatic corps in 1922 and, as noted in chapter 2, oversaw the withdrawal of the marines from Haiti as a special envoy. He later served as the chargé d'affairs in Nicaragua and was subsequently named minister. He left the Foreign Service in 1932 to join the faculty at Princeton University and became chairman of its History Department in 1936. In 1939 he was named director of the Woodrow Wilson School of Public and International Affairs. He retired in 1961 and died in 1990. Alfonzo Navarez, "Dana G. Munro, 97, a Retired Professor and Ex-Diplomat," *New York Times,* June 19, 1990.

33. Ivan Musicant, *The Banana Wars: A History of the United States Military Intervention in Latin America from the Spanish-American War to the Invasion of Panama* (New York: Macmillan, 1990), 287.

34. Cramer, *Our Neighbor Nicaragua,* 185, 190–92.

35. Charles Chapman, *Republican Hispanic America: A History* (New York: Macmillan, 1937), 268. See also Mary Williams, *The People and Politics of Latin America* (New York: Ginn, 1945), 443.

36. Millett, *Semper Fi,* 241. See also Millett, *Searching for Stability,* chap. 7; Julian Smith et al., *A Review of the Organizations and Operations of the Guardia Nacional de Nicaragua, 1927–1933,* 2 vols. (Washington, DC: Headquarters, US Marine Corps, n.d. [circa 1934]). The Texas-born Carter later wrote an essay describing his experience organizing the new Guardia. Upon arriving in Bluefields, he was introduced to the governor "in his private office," where he was "lying in a hammock with a machine gun close behind him, three rifles leaning against the wall, and two bottles of brandy on the floor, all within easy reach," clearly ready for "friend or foe." Carter traveled by boat up the San Juan River and thence by a British-built steamer across Lake Nicaragua to Managua. He described politics in Nicaragua as "an old-fashioned feud," wherein large families that had competed with one another for generations aligned with either the Liberals or the Conservatives, according to family tradition. For this reason, volunteers were sworn to obey orders and to uphold the constitution. Nevertheless, Major Carter soon learned that an apolitical Guardia was not welcome, the commandant in San Carlos averring, "What would we do if we had a president we didn't like?" C. B. Carter, "The Kentucky Feud in Nicaragua: Why Civil War Has Become Her National Sport," typescript, n.d., 1, 3, 4, MCHD, Nicaragua: Guardia Nacional. The essay retained by the Historical Division is a typewritten file copy of Carter's essay published in *World's Work,* July 1927, 312–21. See Van Lieu Minor, "A Brief Classified Bibliography Relating to United States Intervention in Nicaragua," *Hispanic American Historical Review* 11, no. 2 (May 1931): 261–77, http://www.jstor.org/stable/2506291, accessed March 20, 2017.

37. Samuel Bemis, *The Latin American Policy of the United States* (New York: Harcourt, Brace, 1943), 210.

38. Having left the country, Sacasa was ineligible to challenge Chamorro, so the Nicaraguan congress confirmed Chamorro as president in January 1926. Chapman, *Republican Hispanic America,* 268–69. See also US Department of State, *A Brief History of the Relations between the United States and Nicaragua, 1909–1928* (Washington, DC: GPO, 1928), 29–30; hereafter cited as *US-Nicaragua Relations.*

39. Henry Stimson, *American Policy in Nicaragua* (New York: Charles Scribner's Sons, 1927), 23.

40. As the Guardia became corrupted by Chamorro, American minister Charles Eberhardt observed: "It is very apparent that the time has not yet come, if it ever will, when a nonpartisan constabulary or National Guard, organized and maintained under American ideals, will be a success in Nicaragua. *It is not wanted.*" Quoted in Millett, *Semper Fi,* 47 (emphasis in original). Major Carter tried his best but seemed blind to Chamorro's machinations.

41. Cramer, *Our Neighbor Nicaragua,* 202–3. Also see Robert Scheina, *Latin America's Wars,* vol. 2, *The Age of the Professional Soldier, 1900–2001* (Sterling, VA: Potomac Books, 2003). Major Carter claimed that some of the captured officers from the Liberal forces were Mexican army officers given "leave of absence" and delivered by the *Tropical,* "a boat under Mexican registry," from Salina Cruz, Mexico (Puerto Escondido), to Cosiguina Point on the west coast of Nicaragua. Arms and ammunition captured from the rebels

were marked "F. N. C.," the company that made cartridges for the Mexican army, and the rifles "bore the coat of arms" of Russia. The rifles had been manufactured in the United States, but the lot had been rejected by the Russian government and made their way to Nicaragua by way of the filibusters. Carter, "Kentucky Feud in Nicaragua."

42. Cramer, *Our Neighbor Nicaragua,* 203.

43. Harold Denny, *Dollars for Bullets: The Story of American Rule in Nicaragua* (1929; reprint, Westport, CT: Greenwood Press, 1980), 231. Although Denny was highly critical of American "gunboat diplomacy" in Nicaragua, he had high praise for Admiral Latimer, whom he described as a "sea-going diplomat" respected by Conservatives and Liberals alike. According to Denny, Latimer was "a jaunty and impeccable officer with a gift for being liked and an ability to hide profound thoughts behind his good-natured countenance which had won him the title 'Rosie Poker Face' among his friends." Ibid., 259–60.

44. According to Major Carter, the Liberal revolt "assumed nation-wide proportions," and "Chamorro realized that without American support he could never bring about a peaceful settlement. He called a meeting of his party leaders, and after they had agreed upon a successor he resigned." Carter, "Kentucky Feud in Nicaragua."

45. Stimson, *American Policy in Nicaragua,* 25–27.

46. Bemis, *Latin American Policy of the United States,* 210–11. President Coolidge authorized the shipment of 3,000 Krag-Jorgensen rifles, 200 machine guns, and 3 million rounds of ammunition to the Díaz government. Ibid.

47. Millett, *Guardians of the Dynasty,* 52.

48. The idea of a "revolutionary wave" suggests that a revolution in one place and time may inspire revolutions elsewhere, either at the same time or later. Moreover, a revolution in one place may inspire "affiliate revolutions" with similar aims in other places. So it is not surprising that, following the success of the Mexican revolution, US officials were concerned that Liberal success in Nicaragua, aided and abetted by Mexican Marxists, might inspire revolutionary movements elsewhere in Central America, threatening the Panama Canal and other interests. For a useful discussion of the concept, see Mark Katz, *Revolution and Revolutionary Waves* (New York: Macmillan–St. Martin's Press, 1997).

49. Metcalf, *History of the United States Marine Corps,* 418–19.

50. The *Argonne* was initially built for the US Army Transport Service but was almost immediately loaned to the navy in 1921. Selected for conversion to a submarine tender, the *Argonne* was permanently transferred to the navy in 1924. After dropping the marines at Corinto, it passed back through the Panama Canal and joined Submarine Division 20 in the Caribbean. Naval History and Heritage Command, *Dictionary of American Naval Fighting Ships.*

51. In February 1927 marines from Quantico embarked for Nicaragua on the USS *Henderson,* picking up additional forces from Parris Island along the way and landing at Corinto. Accompanying these forces was Brigadier General Logan Feland, commander of the Second Brigade, who reported to Admiral Latimer of the Special Service Squadron aboard the Omaha-class light cruiser USS *Milwaukee.* During World War II the *Milwaukee* served in both the Atlantic and Pacific Oceans and was at one point temporarily transferred to the Soviet fleet as the *Murmansk.* The *Milwaukee* returned to the United States in 1949 and was scrapped. See Norman Friedman, *US Cruisers: An Illustrated Design History* (Annapolis, MD: Naval Institute Press, 1984), 469.

52. "Protection of American Interests," *Marine Corps Gazette* 12, no. 3 (September 1927): 176–77.

53. Johnson, *Marine Corps Aviation,* 55. "Rusty" Rowell was born in Iowa and graduated from Iowa State College. He worked for two years as a topographer and draftsman for the US Geological Survey before joining the Marine Corps. After his initial training he was ordered to Cuba in 1906. From there he went to the Philippines and then to San Francisco as a recruiter. In 1914 he was posted to the Legation Guard in Managua. He was then assigned to New York City as the officer in charge of the Publicity Bureau, during which time he posed for the famous recruiting poster "Be a US Marine" by James Flagg (see Edwin Simmons, "Ross Rowell: Aviator with a Flair," *Marine Corps Gazette* 69, no. 5 [1985]). In the late summer of 1917 he found himself in an artillery battery at Quantico, and in 1918 he sailed for Haiti. From there he was ordered to France but arrived too late to see any combat. In 1919 he returned to Quantico and took command of an artillery battalion. He then went to Haiti as the brigade quartermaster, where he learned to fly with the Fourth Air Squadron. The thirty-nine-year-old marine with seventeen years of service then petitioned the commandant to become a full-fledged naval aviator, which was approved. With wings on his chest, Rowell took a course at the US Army's Advanced Flying School at Kelly Field, San Antonio, Texas, where he qualified as a pursuit pilot. In July 1924 he took command of VO-1 at San Diego, whereupon he led his squadron (VO-1M) to Nicaragua in 1927. Rowell left Nicaragua in August 1928, reporting to the Army Air Corps Tactical School. In 1935 he became director of Marine Corps aviation and was promoted to colonel. In 1939 he was promoted to brigadier general, the first marine aviator to achieve that rank, and he arrived in Cuba as the naval attaché for air. In 1940 he was ordered to San Diego as the force air officer. When war broke out in Europe, the Office of Naval Intelligence sent him to London as an observer. Returning in 1941, he assumed command of the Second Marine Aircraft Wing. He was promoted to major general when the United States went to war with Japan and took command of the newly created Marine Air Wing Pacific. His command was responsible for four aircraft wings. In 1944 he was replaced by Major General "Pat" Mulcahy and was directed to Lima, Peru, as the air attaché, having quarreled with Admiral Nimitz over the employment of Marine Corps squadrons in support of the fleet rather than in support of marines on the ground. He retired as a lieutenant general when the war ended. He died in September 1947 in San Diego. Clark, *United States Marine Corps Generals of World War II,* 126–29.

54. George Clark, *With the Old Corps in Nicaragua* (Novato, CA: Presidio Press, 2001), 32.

55. "Protection of American Interests," 177. Having fallen ill, General Feland departed Nicaragua with the Eleventh Regiment in 1927, returning to the United States via Port-au-Prince. He returned to Nicaragua in 1928 when the decision was made to go on the offensive against Sandino. The commandant, Major General Lejeune, accompanied Feland on the trip to Corinto aboard the Omaha-class cruiser USS *Trenton* in order to inspect the brigade before sailing to San Diego.

56. With the three battalions of the Fifth Regiment ashore, companies were sent to Managua, Granada, Masaya, and Matagalpa. Marines were posted along the railway to deter any fighting within 2,000 yards of it. "Report from the Commanding General to the Major General Commandant," March 12, 1927, Naval Forces Ashore in Nicaragua, MCHD, Second Brigade Files. See also Field Order No. 1, March 9, 1927, ibid.

57. Henry Lewis Stimson was a lawyer and Republican politician who became one of the most successful statesmen in American history. President Taft appointed him secretary of war in 1911, and he continued the reorganization of the US Army begun by his mentor, Elihu Root, laying the groundwork for the army's expansion during World War I. He left office in 1913 when Woodrow Wilson became president and joined a volunteer infantry division established by former president Teddy Roosevelt. Wilson refused to employ the volunteer division, and it was disbanded. However, Stimson joined the US Army and served in France as an artillery officer, rising to the rank of colonel. He continued his military service in the reserves and achieved the rank of brigadier general in 1922. He was appointed governor-general of the Philippines in 1927, after negotiating the agreement between the Liberals and Conservatives to end the civil war in Nicaragua He returned to Washington in 1929, and President Herbert Hoover appointed him secretary of state. Upon leaving that post, he became an outspoken opponent of Japanese aggression and Adolf Hitler in Europe. When war broke out in Europe, President Franklin Roosevelt appointed him secretary of war. After the war ended, Stimson insisted on proper judicial proceedings against captured Nazi leaders and those accused of war crimes, which led to the Nuremburg Trials of 1945–1946. He retired from public service in 1945 and wrote his memoirs with the assistance of McGeorge Bundy. He succumbed to a heart attack (his second) in 1950. He is buried in Cold Spring Harbor, New York, in the cemetery of St. John's Church. See David Schmitz, *Henry L. Stimson: The First Wise Man* (Lanham, MD: Rowman & Littlefield, 2000). Also see Henry Stimson and McGeorge Bundy, *On Active Service in Peace and War* (1948; reprint, New York: Hippocrene Books, 1971).

58. *US-Nicaragua Relations*, 46–47.

59. There was no formal written pact; nevertheless, both sides agreed to disarm and hand over their weapons to the marines. They also agreed to the creation of a nonpartisan constabulary and for elections to be held in 1928, supervised by the United States. American forces would remain in Nicaragua until a new president was installed. Executive memorandum no. 2, American Electoral Mission in Nicaragua, November 22, 1928, MCHD, Second Brigade Files. Government forces handed over 10,945 rifles, 308 machine guns, and roughly 4 million rounds of ammunition. The Liberal army "ransomed" 3,704 rifles, 31 machine guns, and approximately 1.5 million rounds of ammunition. "Final Report of Arms Commission from Captain Julian P. Brown to Commanding General," June 10, 1927, MCHD, Second Brigade Files. The village of Tipitapa was renamed Villa Stimson in 1929, in honor of Stimson's role in bringing the conflict to an end, but the Nicaraguan government restored the name Tipitapa in 1961.

60. The five-foot-tall Augusto Sandino was born in 1895, the illegitimate son of Gregorío Sandino, a wealthy Liberal landowner of Spanish descent, and Margarita Calderón, an indigenous servant. As a teenager, Sandino witnessed the American military intervention of 1912. Nine years later he fled the country after attacking the son of a prominent Conservative politician. He first traveled to Honduras and then Guatemala, eventually arriving in Tampico, Mexico. Having worked for several American-owned companies in Nicaragua, he was able to secure a job at a Standard Oil refinery in Tampico. At the time, Tampico was a hotbed of radical sentiment ranging from communism to syndicalism, the transfer of ownership and control of the means of production and distribution to workers' unions. He also became involved with the Seventh-Day Adventist Church, anarchist

politics, and spiritism, and he was imbued with "anti-*Yanqui*" Latin American nationalism (*Indigenismo*). When the statute of limitations ran out on the charges against him in 1926, Sandino returned to Nicaragua and found work at the San Albino gold mine in the Segovias Mountains, near the border with Honduras. See Macaulay, *Sandino Affair.* Regarding Sandino's apparent messiah complex, see Marco Navarro-Génie, *August "César" Sandino: Messiah of Light and Truth* (Syracuse, NY: Syracuse University Press, 2002).

61. Bernard Nalty, *The United States Marines in Nicaragua* (Washington, DC: Headquarters, US Marine Corps, History and Museums Division, 1968), 15. A marine aviator and veteran of Nicaragua, General Vernon Megee, would later write: "Sandino has been referred to as a bandit, an insurgent, and a guerrilla leader. He was all these things, and more, to the lawfully constituted government of his native land, and to the Marines who supported that government. He was also characterized in liberal circles as a patriot, a George Washington, a Bolivar, a liberator, an intellectual, a political idealist, and a socialist. To some contemporaneous writers and their befuddled disciples, Sandino was surrounded by an aura of romantic mysticism—the lone wolf howling his protest against hopeless odds, the patriotic underdog snapping at the heels of the invading Colossus. Sandino cleverly exploited this image to gain foreign support for his crusade against the Marines." Vernon Megee, "Guerrilla Lessons from Nicaragua," *Marine Corps Gazette* 49, no. 6 (June 1965): 40.

62. The Eleventh Regiment was one of two established in 1918 as part of the Fifth Brigade for service in France during World War I. For the deployment to Nicaragua, marines were drawn from Quantico and Haiti for the First Battalion; the Second Battalion was made up of marines available at Quantico. See Clark, *With the Old Corps in Nicaragua,* 31, The *Aroostock* was originally the SS *Bunker Hill,* a steam passenger ship that was converted to a minelayer during World War I. After the war the *Aroostock* was refitted as a seaplane tender to support the famous transatlantic flight by Curtiss NC floatplanes. The *Aroostock* serviced the Nancys at the port of Trepassey, Newfoundland, and later rendezvoused in England with NC-4, the only airplane to complete the flight. NC-4 was disassembled and returned to the United States aboard the *Aroostock.* Serving as both a minelayer and a seaplane tender, the *Aroostock* sailed in the Pacific and Atlantic Oceans during the 1920s. Although laid up for a time on reserve, the *Aroostock* was reactivated as a cargo ship in World War II. It was scrapped in 1947. See Naval History and Heritage Command, *Dictionary of American Naval Fighting Ships.*

63. Johnson, *Marine Corps Aviation,* 55–56.

64. "Protection of American Interests," 178. The additional company at Rama, not part of the Second Brigade, included three officers and seventy-five men. Nalty, *United States Marines in Nicaragua,* 15.

65. *Daily Worker,* January 10, 1928. Indeed, a leaflet distributed to marines at Hampton Roads, Virginia, made a similar claim and also stated that only the politicians had accepted the "Stimson Agreement"; the Nicaraguan people had not. The leaflet went on to equate Sandino's insurgency with the American Revolution, stating: "In 1776, George Washington was also termed a bandit because he defied British rule, and the first army of the United States was a small, poorly equipped one compared to the larger, better equipped British force. But the strength of [Washington's] army lay in the fact that it had the support of the entire American people, and no matter where the battles, in every farm house,

behind every tree, was a friend." See Workers Party of America and the Young Workers League of America, leaflet, March 23, 1928, MCHD, Nicaragua: Adversaries. Of course, the notion that every American colonist along the East Coast supported the rebellion and later the insurgency in 1776 is historical nonsense.

66. Although the Communist Sandinistas of the 1980s were the lineal descendants of Sandino and his followers, Sandino was more of a nationalist than a Communist. As one veteran recalled: "He was a self-made patriot and he disagreed with many of the things we did down there. . . . Sandino was a real native of the country . . . and just a few steps ahead of the cutthroat robbers. Just slightly ahead of being a mule thief." That said, "Sandino would not embrace communism. Regardless of what we say about him, or what we think about him, or what he did, he was not a communist." William "Ironman" Lee quoted in Tom Bartlett, "The Ironman," pt. 2 *Leatherneck* 67, no. 8 (August 1984): 27. Though less well known than Chesty Puller and other marines of the era, Ironman Lee was an iconic figure owing to his exploits in Nicaragua and later as a prisoner of the Japanese during World War II. He was born in Massachusetts and enlisted in the marines in 1918, seeing service in France before the end of the war. Lee was an expert rifleman and a skilled knife fighter. Puller gave him his nickname when their Guardia company was ambushed and Lee was wounded. Still, he managed to pin down the guerrillas with a Lewis machine gun while Puller maneuvered to a position of advantage, sending the guerrillas fleeing. Lee received his third Navy Cross for valor for this action. Puller wrote in his recommendation for the medal: "In the days of wooden ships, Lee would have been an iron man." Lee was sent to China in 1939, where he was made a warrant officer (and the last chief marine gunner) in 1941. On the day the Japanese attacked Pearl Harbor, he was captured by the Japanese and remained a prisoner of war for forty-four months. Lee was commissioned an officer during his captivity, and after the war he quickly rose to the rank of lieutenant colonel, retiring in 1950 as a full colonel. He died on December 29, 1998, in Fredericksburg, Virginia. See Eric Pace, "William A. Lee Is Dead at 98; Marines' Acclaimed 'Ironman,'" *New York Times,* January 2, 1999. See also Louie Estrada, "Marine Col. William A. 'Ironman' Lee Dies at 98," *Washington Post,* January 2, 1999. For Lee's exploits, see Bartlett, "The Ironman," 3 parts, *Leatherneck* 67, nos. 7–9 (July, August, September 1984).

67. Boot, *Savage Wars of Peace,* 236. Spiritism is a nineteenth-century philosophy begun by French educator Hippolyte Léon Denizard Rivail, who used the pseudonym Allan Kardec. The philosophy spread to other countries in the twentieth century and was influential in the development of Caodaism in Vietnam. Spiritism postulates that immortal spirits temporarily inhabit physical bodies (human beings) to further their moral development and serve as the prototype for universal fraternity. In this regard, spiritism embraces reincarnation, which distinguishes it from spiritualism, which holds that the spirits of the dead have the ability and the inclination to communicate with the living but cannot be reincarnated. While in Mexico, Sandino became an active member of the Escuela Magnético-Espiritual de la Comuna Univeral (Magnetic-Spiritual School of the Universal Commune), a spiritist group established in Argentina in 1911.

68. The Sandino army's flag "was a vertical bicolor, red at the hoist and black in the fly, the latter charged in white with a death's head over a crossed machete and rifle." Philip Reisman, "Sandinista Flags," pt. 1, *Flag Bulletin* 22, no. 5 (September–October 1983): 227. The Sandinistas actually carried many flags, usually manufactured locally and varying in

size and workmanship. The colors and emblems were borrowed from the syndicalist flags of the Mexican revolution. Although occasionally used to mark command posts, the flags' value was mostly psychological, the *bandera rojinegra* serving to "rally anti-government sentiment." According to the *New York Times,* however, "The grisly skull and crossbones device . . . resembling the conventional Jolly Roger [was] proof that the insurgents were not patriots at all, but self-proclaimed criminals." Ibid., 228.

69. Some sources claim that *Machos* was slang for "bull" or "tough guys." However, Max Boot claims it was slang for "blonds." Boot, *Savage Wars of Peace,* 396, n. 242, citing Sergío Ramierez and Robert Conrad, ed. and trans., *Sandino: The Testimony of a Nicaraguan Patriot, 1921–1934* (Princeton, NJ: Princeton University Press, 1990), 69.

70. One bandit leader, Pedro Altamirano, proudly told an American journalist that virtually every man in his family had embraced banditry as a "profession," and two of his sons had been killed while "trying to outwit the law." Bart Milton, "How Uncle Sam Hunts Bandits," *Popular Aviation* 11, no. 4 (October 1932): 227. Altamirano was described as a gentleman bandit, fastidiously dressed, tall and swaggering, "built like a football player, yet well over 60 years old." Especially fond of gold chains, Altamirano always carried a "high-priced 45 caliber revolver." Ibid.

71. "Geography of Nicaragua," 2.

72. Ibid. The author goes on to claim that "Sandino was not a bandit before the revolution; but . . . most of his jefes and sub jefes were, and most of his men. The revolution simply gave them a chance and a slogan."

73. In most cases, use of the term "bandits" has been an ill-considered (if understandable) decision in the history of counterinsurgency. For example, during the early part of the Malayan emergency (1948–1960), the British called the insurgents bandits, which was the same term used by the Japanese for the anti-Japanese resistance during World War II. Later the British coined the term "communist terrorists," which had a more productive psychological impact on the citizenry. See Richard Stubbs, *Hearts and Minds in Guerrilla Warfare: The Malayan Emergency, 1948–1960,* East Asian Historical Monographs (Oxford: Oxford University Press, 1990).

74. "Horse Marines," *Leatherneck* 5, no. 27 (May 1922). See also Louis Metzger, "The Horse Marines," *Marine Corps Gazette* 87, no. 4 (April 2003).

75. Operations Reports, Eleventh Regiment, June 29 to July 30, 1927, MCHD, Second Brigade Files.

76. General Feland departed with the Eleventh Regiment. Given that one regiment did not constitute a brigade, Colonel Gulick took command of all marine forces in Nicaragua.

77. Nueva Segovia is a department (currently one of fifteen) in Nicaragua. Its borders were first defined in 1543 and affirmed as an administrative part of the Spanish captaincy general of Guatemala in 1570.

78. Most of the marines came from the Matagalpa garrison of the Third Battalion. Operations Order no. 37, July 3, 1927, MCHD, Second Brigade Files.

79. "Summary of Operations and Final Report of Commanding Officer, Nuevo Segovia Expedition," August 21, 1927, MCHD, Second Brigade Files.

80. John Gray, "The Second Nicaraguan Campaign," *Marine Corps Gazette* 17, no. 4 (February 1933): 36.

81. Johnson, *Marine Corps Aviation,* 56.

82. The USS *Saratoga* was originally intended to be a battle cruiser, but it was converted into one of the US Navy's first "fast carriers" to comply with the Washington Naval Treaty of 1922. It entered service in January 1928, a month ahead of its sister ship, USS *Lexington.* The two ships were virtually identical, so *Saratoga*'s large funnel was painted with a black vertical stripe to help pilots recognize it from the air. On January 27 the *Saratoga* sailed from Camden, New Jersey, for the Pacific through the Panama Canal. It briefly diverted to Corinto to deliver VO-6M and then joined the Battle Fleet at San Pedro, California, on February 21. The *Saratoga* (nicknamed "Sister Sara" and "Sara Maru") was one of three US fleet carriers, along with USS *Enterprise* and USS *Ranger,* to see service throughout World War II. See John Fry, *USS* Saratoga, *CV-3: An Illustrated History of the Legendary Aircraft Carrier, 1927–1946* (Atglen, PA: Schiffer Publishing, 1996).

83. Francis Mulcahy, "Marine Corps Aviation in the Second Nicaraguan Campaign," *Proceedings,* August 1933, 122.

84. Quoted in Gary Parker and Frank Batha, *A History of Marine Observation Squadron Six* (Washington, DC: Headquarters, US Marine Corps, History and Museums Division, 1977), 3.

85. Smith, *Dive Bomber,* 27. Emil Laird partnered with the Wichita Airplane Company in 1920 to manufacture the Swallow TP, a simple and rugged biplane with tandem cockpits that was used to train many pilots in the 1920s and early 1930s. The fuselage was constructed of welded steel tubing with a fabric covering; the fabric-covered wings were made of spruce and plywood. The Swallow TP was easy to fly and very popular. It was powered by an OX-5 water-cooled engine, but later purchasers could choose among the OX-5, Siemens-Halske Sh-14, Kinner K-5, and Warner Scarab engines. Over the years, even more powerful engines were fitted to the Swallow. Nevertheless, most buyers opted for the ubiquitous OX-5, which was cheap and easy to maintain. The New Swallow (designed by Lloyd Stearman), a three-seat biplane with a cowled OX-5 engine, was manufactured in 1924 after Laird sold his first company (which became the Swallow Airplane Manufacturing Company) and formed a new one. In 1926 the E. M. Laird Airplane Company improved on the original Swallow design, dubbed simply the Swallow OX-5. About 250 of these were produced. Other variants included the Hisso Swallow, powered by a 150 hp Hispano-Suiza A engine. An unknown number of these were constructed in 1928. Marine Corps commentary notes the use of Swallows by Mason and Brooks but offers no details about the variant flown by the American mercenaries. However, in a *New York Times* essay, William Brooks described one of the aircraft as a "new swallow plane" with a Hispano-Suiza engine, and the other as an "older Swallow with the OXX motor." The aircraft must have been upgraded with new engines at some point, because the Checkered Cab Company, from which the aircraft were purchased, first acquired the Swallows in 1925, and Swallows manufactured that year were fitted with the OX-5 engine. See National Association of Manufacturers, *American Industries,* 6. For Emil Laird and the history of the Swallow, see Donald Patillo, *A History in the Making: 80 Turbulent Years in the American General Aviation Industry* (New York: McGraw-Hill Professional, 1998).

86. The Swallows were originally purchased by Humberto Pasos Díaz to start an air transport company. The airplanes were seized by the government, and Díaz was named technical adviser. Another American, a former US Navy pilot named Irvine Rutledge,

joined Díaz, Brooks, and Mason. The first combat employing the Swallows occurred on August 17, 1926, when the two aircraft attacked a Mexican ship, the *Concon,* with rifle fire and dynamite bombs. The Mexican vessel was unloading supplies for the Liberal forces at Corinto. This air attack was repeated the next day by a single Swallow as the *Concon* left the port. In the following weeks, the two aircraft performed reconnaissance missions over the Cosigüina stratovolcano peninsula along the Gulf of Fonseca. In addition, the Swallows performed "utility" missions, transporting mail and other communications to government troops operating in the area. The US government authorized the sale of a third Swallow to Nicaragua, and it was shipped directly from the factory. Mario Overall, "The Origins of Close Air Support: Nicaragua's 'Constitutional War,'" trans. Doug MacPhail, *Air and Space Power Journal-Español* (online, accessed May 6, 2017).

87. The town of Chinandega originated as a *poblado* (settlement) in 1796 and became a major commercial center. It lies in northwestern Nicaragua, on the Pacific coast near Corinto. In 1842 Chinandega was the capital of the United Provinces of Central America, but with the collapse of the federal union, Chinandega became the administrative center of the Chinandega Department.

88. One aircraft was holed fourteen times and the other ten. Gerald Martin, "Yank Air Raid in Nicaragua Beats Rebels," *Chicago Daily Tribune,* February 8, 1927. See also "Chinandega Battle as Seen from Plane," *New York Times,* March 5, 1927; "American Fliers Take Own Risk," *New York Times,* March 24, 1927. In the end, the Conservatives won the battle for Chinandega, also recovering Matagalpa and Jinotega from the Liberals. See Augusto Sandino, *Sandino: The Testimony of a Nicaraguan Patriot, 1921–1934* (Princeton, NJ: Princeton University Press, 2014), 45.

89. Overall, "Origins of Close Air Support."

90. During the Battle of Muy Muy (north of Lake Nicaragua in the Matagalpa Department), the homemade bombs used by Mason and Brooks failed to explode, and their aircraft suffered severe damage from ground fire. "In fact, they were barely able to flutter back to an emergency air strip in deferred forced landings." Vernon Megee, "The Genesis of Air Support in Guerrilla Operations," *Proceedings,* June 1965, 50–51.

91. Ross Rowell, "The Air Service in Minor Warfare," *Proceedings,* October 1929, 871–72. Rowell wrote several essays about his experiences in Nicaragua and lectured on the topic as well, including one delivered to the Army War College in 1929. See Ross Rowell, "Marine Air in Nicaragua," ed. Edwin Simmons, *Marine Corps Gazette* 69, no. 5 (May 1985): 80–91.

92. Rowell, "Air Service in Minor Warfare," 872.

93. Ibid. Rowell would later tell an Army War College audience in 1929, "At first we were getting hit daily, but we kept data on the ranges. Pretty soon we found out where they could hit us and where they could not. All of this was very valuable training for us." Rowell, "Marine Air in Nicaragua," 84.

94. They were fired on near Murra, after which they strafed the area and returned to base. Lamson-Scribner retired as a major general in 1961. He served in World War II and then during the Korean War as assistant commanding general, First Marine Aircraft Wing, where he was instrumental in developing the technique of using marine artillery to suppress enemy antiaircraft artillery. Pat Meid and James Yingling, *US Marine Operations in Korea, 1950–1953,* vol. 5, *Operations in West Korea* (Create Space Independent Publishing

Platform, 2014). Corporal Larry Pabst left the Marine Corps and became a pilot for Eastern Air Transport, later Eastern Airlines. Clark, *With the Old Corps in Nicaragua,* 179, n. 8.

95. The new governor was not comfortable with the small force guarding him and the town. Consequently, in early July, reinforcements arrived with Captain Grover Darnall, USMC, commanding the First Company (forty-eight men) of the Guardia. They were soon joined by two additional marine officers and twenty-eight enlisted marines.

96. Captain Archibald would later take temporary command of VO-7M while Major Rowell was away. Archibald was killed in a plane crash, and the airfield at Managua was named Archibald Field in his honor. According to his nomination for the Navy Cross, he "laid out and supervised the construction of all flying fields on Nicaragua, seventeen in number [and] in nearly every case he voluntarily landed in the fields before they were safe for use in order to hasten the completion of the work." Ross Rowell to the Major General Commandant, "Archibald, R. J., Captain, USMC, Commendation of," September 15, 1928, MCHD, Second Brigade Files.

97. As early as 1928, Marine Corps F8C Falcons and 02U Corsairs were using SE 1375B radios, employing a wind-driven generator as a power source. Larger transport planes (Fokker TA1s and TA2s) employed the heavier and more powerful SE 1385. When available, marines on the ground used the US Army's SCR 127 or 130 radio set. Wind, motor noise, and other interference made air-ground communication by radio problematic at best. Moreover, the aircraft employed trailing wire some 150 to 300 feet long and could not fly low without first reeling in the wire. As a result, aircrews on patrol used Very pistols with red, white, or green stars; dropped messages; used hand or arm signals; waggled the wings; and employed engine noise (throttled up or down, "blipping" the engine) to communicate with troops on the ground. Marine patrols on the ground often used panels painted with codes to identify their point of origin. They also used large panels made of orange and white cloth in the shape of squares, triangles, circles, semicircles, and stars, which could be arranged to provide information to aircraft overhead ("code groups"). The pilot or observer would acknowledge the message sent with a Very pistol, and when the exchange was complete, a panel signaling "no further need of you" was laid out. Francis Pierce, "Infantry-Air Communication," *Marine Corps Gazette* 13, no. 4 (December 1928): 266–68. Captain Pierce was one of the few marine aviators in Nicaragua to be wounded in action. On March 19, 1928, he was an observer in an 02U-1 flown by Gunner Michael Wodarczyk, leading a two-ship patrol in the vicinity of Murra, near Ocotal. Northeast of Murra they came under fire from guerrillas hiding in a large house. As Wodarczyk maneuvered to attack, a bullet hit the bottom of the airplane and passed through Captain Pierce's left foot. Although he was bleeding quite heavily, Pierce kept his machine gun in action until it became clear he needed medical attention, and Wodarczyk flew to Ocotal. "Private Murphy, Fifth Regiment, who had never been in an airplane before," volunteered to replace Pierce, and the airplanes returned to bomb and strafe the guerrillas, after which they returned to Managua. Ross Rowell to Commanding Officer, Second Brigade, subject: "Recommendation for Awards and Citations in Connection with Aerial Bombardment of Bandit Forces in Murra Region on 18–19 March, 1928," March 24, 1928, MCHD, Second Brigade Files.

98. The message pickup technique described was devised by Francis Pierce and Arthur Page Jr. when they were at Quantico together. Kaufman, *1912–2012,* 88. According to Pierce, "In practice the observer's hand line consists of thirty feet of light woven sash cord with a

lead weight of about one and a half pounds securely fastened to the end. The other end of the line is secured [by] five feet of signal halliard or similar rope knotted at intervals of one foot to afford hand holds for the observer. The line is lowered over the side of the plane in flight, the knotted portion being held in the hand. The pilot then flies up wind at a sufficiently low altitude so that the lead weight fouls the message cord. Both lines are then hauled into the cockpit and the message secured." Pierce, "Infantry-Air Communication," 269.

99. "Geography of Nicaragua," 5. Hatfield was born and reared in New Mexico and had spent considerable time in Mexico; he had also served in the Dominican Republic. Consequently, it was believed that he understood "Latin American psychology, and was fitted for the task." Ibid.

100. Ibid. Sandino made it a habit to write to the commanders of marine garrisons. For example, the marines translated a letter dated February 7, 1928, and received by the commander of the garrison at Matagalpa as follows: "I have the honour to advise you that I am already here and that up to date I have not killed anybody nor set anything on fire. I wish to demonstrate that you are the destructors, as you have distinguished yourselves in the Segovias as cowards and bandits. Today I stay in a zone where it might hurt you and it would be good to destroy it in the same way as you have done with the poor and defenceless countrymen in Nueva Segovia. Neither you nor your companions can imagine the streams of blood which will run as long as you don't deoccupy our territory." MCHD, Second Brigade Files: Adversaries.

101. Macaulay, *Sandino Affair,* 76.

102. "Protection of American Interests," 179.

103. "Mike" Wodarczyk was a gunnery sergeant in the Fifth Regiment when he volunteered for flying duty. By the end of World War II, he was a lieutenant colonel. While in Nicaragua he received the Distinguished Flying Cross for actions in February and March 1928. Clark, *With the Old Corps in Nicaragua,* 179, n. 13.

104. Ross Rowell, "A Skirmish with Rebels," *Popular Aviation-Aeronautics* 8, no. 3 (March 1931): 10.

105. Rowell argued for a joint air-ground attack but was overruled.

106. Although larger bombs were available, Rowell opted for 17-pound bombs to reduce the weight for the long flight to Ocotal.

107. Rowell, "Air Service in Minor Warfare," 873. Rowell's description of the Sandinistas' reaction to the air attack at Ocotal recalls the air attack by Mason and Brooks at Chinandega some weeks earlier. According to Brooks, "After I had figured out where the sharpshooters were hidden, I heaved a bomb at them. The traffic jam that followed that explosion was probably the worst ever known in Chinandega. Some one must have told those people that the place to meet bombs was on the street. Men, women, and children dashed up and down the streets, through the squares and back again. They seemed to be crazy, they ran so fast and so aimlessly." Quoted in Overall, "Origins of Close Air Support."

108. Rowell, "Skirmish with Rebels," 10.

109. Johnson, *Marine Corps Aviation,* 56.

110. Rowell, "Skirmish with Rebels," 11.

111. Joseph Alexander, *A Fellowship of Valor: The Battle History of the United States Marines* (New York: HarperCollins, 1997), 57. See also Clark, *United States Marine Corps Generals of World War II,* 128.

112. Hatfield claimed that on one street alone there were 50 dead. According to another account, at least 100 of the guerrillas who had laid siege to Ocotal were killed by the air attack. Yet another claimed that some 300 guerrillas had been killed. An accurate count will probably never be achieved.

113. Schroeder, "Social Memory and Tactical Doctrine," 509.

114. Letter from Commanding Officer, Marine Detachment, Ocotal, to Commanding General, Second Brigade, July 20, 1927, MCHD, Second Brigade Files.

115. "Geography of Nicaragua," 6.

116. Nalty, *United States Marines in Nicaragua,* 62.

117. Probably so named in reference to El Chipote Mountain, near Murra, Nueva Segovia. El Chipote Mountain is 3,774 feet at its peak.

118. O'Shea was a Naval Academy graduate who would rise to the rank of colonel in World War II.

119. Rowell, "Skirmish with Rebels," 12.

120. Many reports state that Thomas's DH burned upon crashing, but some do not mention a fire. One document claims that Lieutenant Thomas set fire to the airplane himself.

121. Ross Rowell to Major General Logan Feland, "Statement re: Heroic Conduct under Fire of Second Lieutenant Earl A. Thomas and Sergeant Frank E. Dowdell," August 21, 1930, MCHD, Second Brigade Files. Major Rowell wrote the letter years after the event because he had been away when Thomas's airplane went down, and Captain Archibald, in temporary command, was killed in an airplane crash before he could submit the award nomination. Colonel Gulick nominated the two fallen aviators for the Navy Cross. Because details were unavailable at the time, the Navy Crosses were reduced to letters of commendation.

122. Ibid., 2.

123. Some accounts claim his left arm was severed; others claim he was struck on the head on the right side and his right arm was severed.

124. Rowell to Feland, 2–3.

125. Carleton Beals to Brigadier General Logan Feland, July 15, 1930, MCHD, Second Brigade Files. Other accounts claim that Thomas was killed by a "dynamite bomb."

126. Ibid. According to Rowell, Beals quoted Sandino as saying that "the two aviators were the bravest men his forces had ever fought against." It must be noted, however, that Rowell's claims were in the context of requesting that Thomas and Dowdell be posthumously awarded the Medal of Honor (which they did not receive; nor did they receive the Navy Cross). General Feland concurred with the nomination, but in his letter to the secretary of the navy he used Beals's description of events, noting that "Sergeant Dowdell gave his own life in defending his wounded officer and comrade." Regarding Lieutenant Thomas's death, Feland's comments reflected Rowell's claim that the marines of VO-7M had vowed not to be taken alive: "His sacrifice averted the serious blow to the pacification which would have resulted from his capture and holding by the Sandino forces." Major General Logan Feland to the Secretary of the Navy, "Recommends Awards Posthumously of Medals of Honor to Second Lieutenant Earl A. Thomas and Sergeant Frank Dowdell," September 8, 1930, MCHD, Second Brigade Files. Yet another source claims that both marine aviators were captured, "court-martialed," convicted, tortured, and hung. Clark, *With the Old Corps in Nicaragua,* 52. The truth will probably never be known.

127. Of course, such a tale could not go unexploited, and a fictionalized account appeared in the story "Air Patrol," in John Thomason, *Marines and Others* (New York: Charles Scribner's Sons, 1929), 197–229. The story of the crash and the subsequent rescue attempt was also the basis of the Marvel comic *Semper Fi, Tales of the Marine Corps,* in April 1988.

128. Hogaboom graduated from the Naval Academy in 1925 and was commissioned into the Marine Corps. After completing his initial training at the Philadelphia Navy Yard, he joined the Fifth Regiment and was sent to Nicaragua. He also saw service in China. During World War II he saw action in the Aleutian Islands off Alaska and in the Pacific, where he was chief of staff for the Third Marine Division in the battle for Iwo Jima. After World War II the Fleet Marine Force Organization and Composition Board, better known as the Hogaboom Board, convened at Quantico to "conduct a thorough and comprehensive study of the Fleet Marine Force and make recommendations . . . for the optimum organization, composition, and equipping of the FMF in order to best perform its mission." The board was formed to address how the Marine Corps would respond to new developments such as nuclear weapons, missiles, electronics, supersonic aircraft, and the helicopter. William Jones, "The Hogaboom Board," *Marine Corps Gazette* 84, no. 8 (August 2000): 51. Lieutenant General Hogaboom retired in October 1959 and was advanced to general. See General Robert E. Hogaboom, Manpower and Reserve Affairs, US Marine Corps (online, accessed April 22, 2017).

129. The rescue of Bat 21 Bravo—the call sign for US Air Force Lieutenant Colonel Iceal "Gene" Hambleton—from behind North Vietnamese lines during the so-called Easter Offensive of 1972 was the largest, longest, and most complex combat search-and-rescue mission of the Vietnam War. Hambleton was the only survivor of his EB-66, shot down by a North Vietnamese SA-2 surface-to-air missile. See Stanley Busboom, "Bat 21: A Case Study" (master's thesis, US Army War College, 1990). See also Darrel Whitcomb, *The Rescue of Bat 21* (Annapolis, MD: Naval Institute Press, 1998).

130. After the Ocotal fight, Sandino divided his forces into three groups at Las Cruces, Zapotillo Ridge, and Jabalines, all of which were close to San Albino and Quilali.

131. Clark, *With the Old Corps in Nicaragua,* 55.

132. John Lejeune, "Testimony of the Marine Corps Commandant before the Senate Committee on Foreign Relations, February 18, 1928," *Marine Corps Gazette* 13, no. 1 (March 1928): 45–66.

133. Rowell, "Skirmish with Rebels," 12.

134. "Record of Events, Fifth Regiment," December 18–24, 1927, MCHD, Second Brigade Files.

135. "Intelligence Report, Second Brigade," December 18–24, 1927, MCHD, Second Brigade Files. It was claimed at the time that two marine deserters who had joined Sandino had planned the ambush, but Marine Corps Headquarters publicly denied this. Clark, *With the Old Corps in Nicaragua,* 181, n. 16. It is noteworthy that during the 1912 intervention there was no regimental staff organization; therefore, a formalized intelligence function did not exist. However, during the second campaign, formal intelligence billets were "set up at brigade (B-2), regimental (R-2), battalion (Bn-2), and Guardia Nacional (GN-2) levels." Letter to Mr. R. F. Nichols, Adjutant, VFW Post No. 2794, July 20, 1954, MCHD, Second Brigade Files: Miscellaneous.

136. This act was immortalized in the distinctive badge and seal of the Sandinistas, showing a guerrilla with a machete held high, preparing to decapitate a marine.

137. These were no ragtag *cacos* fighting with sticks and elderly smoothbore firearms. As William "Ironman" Lee recalled, "Some of the writers and historians describe the bandits down there in Nicaragua as poor peons in baggy pants and poorly armed, with no shoes. This is not true. They had good equipment and gear. In fact, they had Browning Automatic Rifles and Lewis machine guns, and they were using 1927 ammunition. The date was stamped on the cartridges. . . . The Marines were using ammunition dated 1918, and the rounds would crack or crimp. It all had to be hand culled. About every third round of our machine gun ammo would cause a stoppage because the cartridge would crimp or crack. We got so we'd take the ammo off a dead bandit because it was newer and more dependable than our own." Bartlett, "The Ironman," pt. 2, 28.

138. Message transcript quoted by Ross Rowell in "Annual Report of Aircraft Squadrons, Second Brigade, US Marine Corps, July 1, 1927, to June 20, 1928," *Marine Corps Gazette* 13, no. 4 (December 1928): 254 (emphasis in original).

139. As described in chapter 3, the two-seat Vought Corsair was powered by a Pratt & Whitney Wasp radial engine and had a top speed of over 150 miles per hour but a low landing speed of only 50 miles per hour, which proved crucial to operations from unimproved airstrips. Christian Schilt called the Corsair "an outstanding combat plane," one that the marines were very pleased to receive in Nicaragua "because of [its] outstanding performance, ease in handling, [and] quick takeoffs and landings." General Christian Schilt, USMC, Ret., oral history transcript, November 17 and 20, 1969, 57, 74. Oral History Collection, Headquarters, US Marine Corps, History and Museums Division, Washington, DC. The Corsair was in such demand that the entire November 1928 production was sent to the marines in Nicaragua, shipped there "under urgent Navy Department orders." See "Navy Ships Latest Model Vought Planes to Marines in Nicaragua," *Aviation,* January 23, 1928, 203. Schilt flew a plane from this batch during the evacuation of wounded marines from Quilali, "one of the greatest feats known in military aviation." See "Marines Use Vought Corsairs for Rescue Work in Nicaragua," *Aviation,* January 30, 1928, 262.

140. C. Frank Schilt, "Marines in Nicaragua Saved by Airplanes," *Aero Digest* 12, no. 2 (February 1928): 173.

141. Ibid.

142. Ibid. Schilt is also quoted (but not exactly) in Lejeune Cummins, *Quijote on a Burro: Sandino and the Marines; a Study in the Formulation of Foreign Policy* (Mexico City: Distrito Federal, La Impresora Azteca, 1958), 62.

143. Schilt, "Marines in Nicaragua Saved by Airplanes," 295.

144. Ibid., 173, 295. According to Schilt, "The [Wasp] engine pulled the plane out of the field almost like a helicopter." Not surprisingly, this quote found its way into Pratt & Whitney advertising; see, for example, *Aviation,* January 30, 1928, 263. On his eighth landing, the "tail skag" of the Corsair broke off, and marines on the ground had to lift and carry the tail assembly to reposition the airplane before takeoff. Schilt "took off without [the] skag, landing on the rudder." On the ninth landing, a strut was bent, straightened with an axe, and wrapped with wire. Schilt, "Marines in Nicaragua Saved by Airplanes," 295. See also Frederick Neely, "Schilt, 'Corsair' and 'Wasp' in Nicaragua," *US Air Services* 13, no. 2 (February 1928): 35–36.

145. Mersky, *Marine Corps Aviation,* 22. See also John Elliott, "Marine Aviation in Nicaragua: A Time of Pioneering," *Leatherneck* 92, no. 9 (September 2009).

146. See "Schilt Receives from the President Unique Honor," *US Air Services* 13, no. 7 (July 1928): 40. Born in Richland County, Illinois, Christian Schilt enlisted in the Marine Corps in June 1917 and sailed to the Azores with the First Aeronautic Company as an aerial gunner. He returned to the United States as a corporal and began flight training at Miami. He graduated in June 1919, was commissioned, and was sent to the Dominican Republic the following October as a member of Squadron D. He returned to the United States in 1920 and was then sent to Haiti with Squadron E. He returned to the Dominican Republic to make an aerial survey and mosaic map of the coastline (see chapter 3). After completing that assignment, he was posted to Brown Field at Quantico for the next five years. While at Quantico he won second place in the Schneider International Seaplane Race at Norfolk, Virginia, in November 1926. A year later he was ordered to Nicaragua. He returned to the United States in August 1929 as the commander of a squadron at Quantico. In 1930 he became chief test pilot and aerological officer at the Naval Aircraft Factory in Philadelphia. He returned to Quantico in 1932 and attended the US Army Air Corps Tactical School at Maxwell Field, Alabama, in 1933. He returned to Quantico to become a squadron commander with Aircraft One of the Fleet Marine Force. With the outbreak of World War II, Major Schilt was assigned to the US embassy in London as the assistant naval attaché for air. He was sent to Guadalcanal in September 1942 as assistant chief of staff, First Marine Aircraft Wing. By the end of the war, he was a brigadier general and commander of the Second Marine Aircraft Wing on Okinawa. He commanded the First Marine Aircraft Wing again during the Korean War. After Korea he was promoted to major general and served in numerous capacities, becoming director of aviation and a lieutenant general in 1955. He retired in April 1957 and was promoted to general. He died in January 1987 and is buried at Arlington National Cemetery. Clark, *United States Marine Corps Generals of World War II,* 134–36.

147. Clark, *United States Marine Corps Generals of World War II,* 134–36.

148. See Pierce, "Infantry-Air Communication," 266. Pierce described air-ground communications as "one of the most important duties assigned an aviation unit on active field duty." Rowell described infantry missions as "the means by which the ground commander may keep contact and exchange information with the advanced elements of his organization." According to Rowell, "It is of great importance because often it is the only means by which organized effort can be obtained under the circumstances prevailing." The number of aircraft providing this support varied from one (over friendly territory) to three (over hostile territory where trouble was expected). "For such missions the most experienced pilot (not the highest ranking) should be the flight leader and he should have an equally experienced observer in the rear cockpit. Coordination with the ground element should be accomplished before the mission is undertaken and a report given to the ground commander upon completion, followed by a briefing and written report provided to squadron personnel." Rowell, "Aircraft in Bush Warfare," 188. See also *Small Wars Manual* (1940), chap. 9, "Aviation," sec. 5, "Employment of Reconnaissance Aviation," para. 9-21, "Infantry Mission."

149. The recently graduated recruits assigned to the Eleventh Regiment were horribly undertrained. Ironman Lee recalled, "In the first part of 1928, I was assigned 12 Marines on a combat patrol. When we got a mile and a half out of town I said, 'Let's hold up here and load our weapons.' One young, pink-cheeked lad came up and held his rifle up to me.

I took a look at him and I asked, 'What the hell do you want?' He said, 'I want you to show me how to load my rifle.' Well, I must say! If you're on a combat patrol and somebody comes up and asks how to load their rifle, well, I didn't know what to say. I stood there with my mouth open. I counted to 10 before swinging at him. And then I took another look at him. He looked intelligent enough. . . . So I asked how many more wanted their rifles loaded, and I had four more in the group who had never loaded rifles before and had never fired on the rifle range. They were taken out of boot camp at Parris Island and shipped to Nicaragua, assigned to a unit, and here they were! I thought they were trying to pull a dog wash on me, but they were serious. We set up a range out there, with targets about 100 yards away, and I taught them all to load and shoot. I tell you, that's a hell of a way to begin a combat patrol!" Quoted in Bartlett, "The Ironman," pt. 2, 28–29.

150. Stores ships were originally a class of ships so designated before the age of steam. During the Mexican-American War and later the US Civil War, captured enemy ships that were considered unworthy of prize money were often used for storage purposes when there was no nearby port. In modern parlance, stores ships (or combat stores ships) are cargo ships used to transport supplies.

151. "Report of Commanding General, Second Brigade to the Major General Commandant, for the Period January 15 to February 27, 1928," MCHD, Second Brigade Files.

152. Clark, *With the Old Corps in Nicaragua,* 61. Upon his arrival, General Feland divided Nicaragua into three "areas of command" to facilitate operations in the field. Sandino's operations were usually in the Northern Area of Command, which included all of western Nicaragua north of a line from Somotillo to Jinotega; this area was the responsibility of Colonel Dunlap. The Southern Area of Command included western Nicaragua south of the Somotillo-Jinotega line and was the responsibility of the Fifth Regiment. The Eastern Area of Command included the entire east coast and territory inland, commanded by Major Harold Utley in Puerto Cabezas.

153. Rowell, "Skirmish with Rebels," 12. It is uncertain why Sandino called them *chula* guns. The word can mean many things in Spanish, including "poser," "pimp," and even "pretty." As Rowell noted, perhaps it was the rockets' pyrotechnic display and the exploding dynamite that caused Sandino to remark on how delightfully pretty the result was.

154. "Aircraft in Nicaragua," *Aero Digest* 12, no. 5 (May 1928): 760.

155. Rowell, "Annual Report of Aircraft Squadrons, Second Brigade," 253. Also see Rowell, "Air Service in Minor Warfare," 875. According to VO-7M records, the attacking aircraft dropped four 50-pound bombs and eighteen 17-pound bombs and expended almost 3,000 rounds of machine gun ammunition. Six hits were registered on the attacking planes. Observation Squadron Seven-M, "Record of Events, January 15, 1928," MCHD, Second Brigade Files.

156. "Aircraft in Nicaragua," 760.

157. Rowell, "Skirmish with Rebels," 62.

158. Schroeder, "Social Memory and Tactical Doctrine," 508–49. In many ways, religious groups led the charge against the intervention and especially the use of airplanes. Following the rout of Sandino's forces at Ocotal, the *Christian Advocate* published an essay entitled "Fighting in Nicaragua," bemoaning the "slaughter" that had occurred. In response, Quartermaster Sergeant Allan Titus wrote a letter to the editor taking "vigorous exception" to the use of that term. He wrote: "The word, 'slaughter,' suggests that a force of

Marines attacked a helpless crowd of natives and shot them down in cold blood and without mercy. Very little is made of the fact that these Marines and members of the Constabulary were besieged for seventeen hours by a vastly superior force . . . and were fighting for their lives. . . . It should be considered that these young men . . . many of them, no doubt, from good Methodist homes, and, dare I say, the parents of these same boys are not calling the effective work of the airplanes a 'slaughter,' but a timely deliverance." Summing up, Sergeant Titus wrote that the small force "could not have held out" and asked, "had not the planes come to the rescue, what would the headlines of the news papers blazoned forth to the civilized world?" Allan Titus, letter to the editor, *Christian Advocate,* July 27, 1927, MCHD, Second Brigade Files.

159. Harold Campbell, "Aviation in Guerrilla Warfare," pt. 2, *Marine Corps Gazette* 15, no. 5 (May 1931): 36–37. Undoubtedly this notion came from Campbell's study of *Small Wars* by British colonial officer C. E. Callwell. As Colonel Callwell wrote: "It is so often the case that the power which undertakes a small war desires to acquire the friendship of the people which its armies are chastising, that the system of what is called 'military execution' is ill-adapted to the end in view. The most satisfactory way of bringing such foes to reason is by the rifle and the sword, for they understand this mode of warfare and respect it. Sometimes, however, the circumstances do not admit of it, and then their villages must be demolished and granaries destroyed." Callwell, *Small Wars,* 41.

160. Rowell, "Aircraft in Bush Warfare," 191–192.

161. Ibid., 193.

162. Ibid., 192.

163. Campbell, "Aviation in Guerrilla Warfare," pt. 2, 40.

164. Edwin Brainard, "The Marines Take Wings," *Leatherneck* 11, no. 8 (August 1928): 32.

165. Rowell, "Annual Report," 254.

166. Ross Rowell, "Report of Air Mission, April 10, 1928," National Archives, Washington, DC.

167. During the period of British "air control" following World War I, the Royal Air Force routinely bombed villages, and Wing Commander J. A. Chamier insisted that airplanes be used to carry out relentless attacks "on houses, inhabitants, crops, and cattle." The French likewise had no moral qualms about attacking civilians and even used poison gas on occasion. See J. A. Chamier, "The Use of Air Power for Replacing Military Garrisons," *Journal of the Royal United Services Institute,* February–November 1921, 210; William Dean, "The Colonial Armies of the French Third Republic: Overseas Formation and Continental Deployment, 1871–1920" (PhD diss., University of Chicago, 1999), 315–24.

168. Quoted in Schroeder, "Social Memory and Tactical Doctrine," 511.

169. Ibid., 511–512.

170. Rowell, "Annual Report," 253.

171. See Wray Johnson, "Airpower and Restraint in Small Wars: Marine Corps Aviation in the Second Nicaraguan Campaign, 1927–1933, *Aerospace Power Journal,* Fall 2001. See also Corum and Johnson, *Airpower in Small Wars.* chaps. 1 and 2.

172. Conferences were held in London in 1909 to codify rules related to trade during wartime. The result, known as the Declaration of London, was signed by all the major countries that would fight in World War I, but only the United States ratified the document. As a result, shortly after the war began, Great Britain violated almost every rule laid

out, including the seizing of food and other goods from ships en route to German ports. Winston Churchill, then First Lord of the Admiralty, admitted that the purpose was to "starve the whole population—men, women, and children, old and young, wounded and sound—into submission." Quoted in Ralph Raico, "The Blockade and Attempted Starvation of Germany," a review of C. Paul Vincent, *The Politics of Hunger: Allied Blockade of Germany, 1915–1919* (Ohio University Press, 1985), http://mises.org/library/blockade-and-attempted-starvation-germany, accessed April 20, 2017. See also Justus Doenecke, *Nothing Less than War: A New History of America's Entry into World War I* (Lexington: University Press of Kentucky, 2011).

173. Rowell, "Annual Report," 253.

174. Cummins, *Quijote on a Burro*, 54.

175. After the battle for El Chipote, even the sound of approaching airplanes would cause the guerrillas to dash for cover or attempt to portray themselves as ordinary peasants, removing their red and black badges from their collars and hats. According to one Second Brigade report, a Guardia patrol was ambushed near Los Cruces, and its leader, a marine lieutenant, was wounded in both feet; several Guardia soldiers were also wounded. But shortly after they were fired on, an airplane could be heard approaching, and the guerrillas "ceased firing immediately and disappeared at once." Ironically, according to the report, the pilot never saw the firefight. Nevertheless, the incident confirmed "that bandits mortally dread the airplane, and that their morale is shattered merely by its appearance." US Navy, Bureau of Aeronautics, News Letter no. 262 (August 1931), MCHD, Second Brigade Files: Aviation.

176. Sandino divided his forces into two main groups. One moved northward toward Jalapa, and the other southwesterly toward Jinotega. This second group was concentrated in the Yali–San Rafael del Norte area by February, where American journalist Beals interviewed Sandino.

177. "Record of Events," March 24, 1928, MCHD, Second Brigade Files.

178. Merritt "Red Mike" Edson (a nickname he got because of his flaming red hair) was born in Rutland, Vermont, and attended the University of Vermont while serving in the National Guard. He was commissioned into the Marine Corps in 1917 and was sent to France in 1918, arriving too late to see any combat. He returned to the United States in 1919 and volunteered for flying duty. He graduated from flight school at Pensacola in 1922 and was ordered to Guam for duty with VS-1, remaining there until July 1925. At the US Army's Advanced Flying School at Kelly Field, he was diagnosed with a condition that affected his depth perception, which effectively ended his flying career He returned to Quantico and was assigned to the USS *Denver* as detachment commander. He went ashore to lead the famous Coco River patrols, which he described in several articles for the *Marine Corps Gazette*. He returned to the United States in 1929 and was posted to China in the late 1930s. He helped author the 1940 edition of the *Small Wars Manual*. While at Quantico he met Captain Victor Krulak, aide-de-camp to Brigadier General Holland McT. Smith, commander of the First Division. Smith was forming the First Raider Battalion, an American commando unit, from the First Battalion of the Fifth Regiment. Edson volunteered to form, train, and lead the new Raider battalion; he commanded the battalion during the battle for Guadalcanal, earning the Medal of Honor for his defense of Henderson airfield. He was promoted ahead of officers with more seniority and became assistant

division commander of the Second Division during the fight for Tarawa atoll. After the war, Edson was a leading defender of an autonomous Marine Corps during the unification debate that led to the creation of the Department of Defense and a separate US Air Force. Believing he could speak his mind only as a civilian, Edson retired in August 1947. He returned home to Vermont and became the state's first commissioner of police. He committed suicide by carbon monoxide poisoning on August 14, 1955. Clark, *United States Marine Corps Generals of World War II,* 45–47. See also "Major General Merritt Austin Edson, USMC," *Who's Who in Marine Corps History* (online, accessed May 5, 2017).

179. Mulcahy, "Marine Corps Aviation in Second Nicaraguan Campaign," 127.

180. Alexander, *Fellowship of Valor,* 60. Despite advances in technology over the decades, airdrops similar to those carried out by the marines in Nicaragua continue today. For example, the Kenya Wildlife Service Air Wing supports antipoaching patrols on the ground, including the interdiction of Somali *shifta* gangs. The Air Wing at one time comprised four Aviat A-1 Huskys, two Piper PA-18-150 Super Cubs (formerly belonging to the Israeli air force), two Cessna C-180s, and one American Champion 8K-CAB Super Decathlon. A principal challenge is air-dropping water to ground patrols during the dry season. Over time, the Air Wing developed a delivery system using 2.5-gallon plastic "jerry cans" manufactured in Canada and a modified "Amit" parachute manufactured by APCO Aviation in Israel (the same parachute is used to recover Israeli miniature drones). The procedure for delivery calls for the pilot to enter into a left-hand turn over the objective area. Once downwind, speed is reduced to 60 knots indicated airspeed with 20 degrees of flaps. The right-side door is opened, and the pilot releases the parachute-equipped jerry can at about 200 feet above ground level. This delivery method has been very successful, and the Air Wing continues operations today. Interview with William Clark, pilot, Kenya Wildlife Service Air Wing, 2005.

181. Merritt Edson, "The Coco River Patrol: Operations of a Marine Patrol along the Coco River in Nicaragua," pt. 1, *Marine Corps Gazette* 19, no. 3 (August 1936): 44.

182. Thompson .45-caliber submachine guns had been issued to marines guarding mail trains in the United States, but they had not yet become standard issue throughout the Corps. The Thompson was issued in Nicaragua as the ideal weapon for jungle warfare.

183. Edson recalled that, during the first trip, he and his men subsisted on the three Bs: bananas, beans, and canned beef. The beef was in short supply, so they occasionally added monkey meat to their diet. With regular aerial resupply, the marines could travel light and fast and not go hungry.

184. Today, an airdrop entails the use of parachutes. However, the marines in Nicaragua simply flew low over the objective area and threw packages out of the airplane. For parachute drops, see *Airdrop of Supplies and Equipment: Reference Data for Airdrop Platform Loads,* Marine Corps Reference Publication 4-11.3L, Army FM 4-20.116 (FM 10–516), Air Force TO 13C7-1-13 (Headquarters, Departments of the Army and Air Force, August 2001).

185. "Geography of Nicaragua," 10.

186. Operations Journal, Eleventh Regiment, September 1928, MCHD, Second Brigade Files.

187. "Up to the end of 1928, aviation had 84 contacts in which the planes were struck 82 times by fire from the ground; in 1929, the number of contacts dropped to 26; in 1930,

there were but 5; in 1931, 7; in 1932, 9; and from July 1 to December 15, 1932, 1." Mulcahy, "Marine Corps Aviation in the Second Nicaraguan Campaign," 128–29.

188. Rowell, "Air Service in Minor Warfare," 876.

189. Mulcahy, "Marine Corps Aviation in the Second Nicaraguan Campaign," 131.

190. The vice secretary of the commission was a young US Army captain of infantry, Matthew Ridgway. See American Electoral Commission in Nicaragua, executive memorandum no. 8, July 20, 1928, 2, MCHD, Second Brigade Files: Elections.

191. Some 133,000 votes were cast, almost 30,000 more than in 1924. Nalty, *United States Marines in Nicaragua,* 27.

192. Consolidated Distribution Report, January 4, 1929, MCHD, Second Brigade Files.

193. "Translation of Nicaraguan Press," *La Prensa,* April 25 and 30, 1932, MCHD, Second Brigade Files.

194. "News of the Air Services: First Non-stop Flight US to Nicaragua," *Aero Digest,* February 1928, 204. The Fokker departed Miami at 5:31 a.m. on January 14 and landed at Managua twelve hours later.

195. Johnson, *Marine Corps Aviation,* 57.

196. "Supply Plane in Nicaragua Invaluable," *Aviation,* February 6, 1928, 351.

197. The second Fokker trimotor was flown to Nicaragua from Miami by Major Edwin Brainard, Gunnery Sergeant Millard Shepard, and Corporal N. M. Winchester. En route to Managua, Major Brainard stopped at Tela, Honduras. Shepard would later receive the Distinguished Flying Cross. As a pilot for the Aircraft Squadrons, Second Brigade, he flew more than 970 hours in OC landplanes, the OL-8 amphibian, and the TA-1. As a transport pilot, he flew missions that carried approximately 1,000 passengers, including wounded marines and Guardia personnel. He also transported more than 850,000 pounds of freight, which "taxed [his skill] to the utmost when heavy tropical storms were encountered." In addition, he flew missions transporting Nicaraguan civilians and prisoners. R. H. Dunlap to the Major General Commandant, subject: "Recommendation for Award of the Distinguished Flying Cross, Case of Gunnery Sergeant Millard T. Shepard, US Marine Corps," April 6, 1929, MCHD, Second Brigade Files. The third trimotor was flown nonstop to Nicaragua on February 4 by Lieutenant George Tower, Lieutenant James McHugh, and a Fokker company mechanic, Robert Wenc. The second flight was accomplished in eleven hours, lifting off from Miami at 5:15 a.m. Two days earlier, the same crew had made the trip from Washington, DC, to Miami in a little over nine hours. "2nd Non-stop Flight US to Nicaragua," *Aero Digest* 12, no. 3 (March 1928): 384.

198. "Air mobility" is defined as the rapid movement of personnel and material by air. Today, this includes both airlift and aerial refueling. For a useful history of air mobility, see Robert Owen, *Air Mobility: A Brief History of the American Experience* (Washington, DC: Potomac Books, 2013).

199. *Anything, Anywhere, Anytime: An Illustrated History of the Military Airlift Command, 1941–1991* (Scott Air Force Base, IL: Military Airlift Command, Office of History, 1991), 1.

200. The US Army's Fiftieth Aero Squadron was formed in August 1917 and performed observation and reconnaissance missions over France in 1918, flying the DH-4. In early October nine companies of the 308th Infantry Regiment were cut off and surrounded by

German forces. Able to communicate with Seventy-Seventh Division headquarters only by carrier pigeon, the battalion-sized force gave the incorrect coordinates for its location. Nevertheless, pilots of the Fiftieth Aero Squadron located the "lost battalion," and the division commander, Major General Robert Alexander, ordered the squadron to resupply the surrounded soldiers with ammunition, rations, and medical supplies. The force held out until a relief force broke through on October 8. See Julius Adler, ed., *History of the Seventy Seventh Division, August 25th, 1917–November 11th, 1918* (New York: 77th Division Association, 1919), 199–207.

201. *Anything, Anywhere, Anytime,* 2.

202. One of these aircraft, dubbed the "Question Mark" and piloted by army officers Carl Spaatz and Ira Eaker, set a world record for flight endurance (150 hours) on January 7, 1929.

203. Having transitioned from an observation to a transportation mission, the commandant approved "administrative movement"—that is, on paper only—of Marine Utility Squadron Six (VJ-6M) to Nicaragua and the "return" of VO-6M to Quantico. VO-6M would then train new pilots for Nicaraguan service. The chief of naval operations approved the administrative movement, and on September 1, 1928, VO-6M and VJ-6M exchanged locations. Parker and Batha, *History of Marine Observation Squadron Six,* 3–4.

204. E. R. Johnson, *American Military Transport Aircraft since 1925* (Jefferson, NC: McFarland, 2013), "Series I, 1925–1962."

205. Louis Bourne Jr. to the Commanding Officer, Second Brigade, subject: "Navy Cross, Recommendation for," November 26, 1929, MCHD, Second Brigade Files. Archie Paschal was born in Glendon, North Carolina. He left home in 1908 and enlisted in the Marine Corps at the age of eighteen—not telling anyone where he was going and not writing home until 1917. He saw action during the occupation of Veracruz in 1914 and served in France during World War I. Paschal became one of the earliest enlisted pilots in the Marine Corps, earning numerous honors and accolades. He was well liked by his brothers in arms, officer and enlisted alike. During World War I he was attached to No. 218 Squadron, Royal Air Force. He participated in the airdrop mission to aid trapped French troops and was cited for heroism. Officially, he was not a pilot at the time, not acquiring his "Nappy" wings until 1921 (No. 3, behind Benjamin Belcher and Neil Abbott). By then, he had almost 1,000 hours of flying time. In 1922 Paschal flew a VE-7 Bluebird from the deck of the aircraft carrier USS *Langley.* While posted to Santo Domingo in 1924, he flew DH-4Bs. He had his share of brushes with death while flying for the Marine Corps. For example, while formation flying over Quantico, his airplane made contact with the tail of another airplane, nearly shearing off his upper wing. The pilot of the other plane parachuted to safety, but Paschal managed to land his airplane and received a commendation for his "coolness and skill." As noted in chapter 3, Paschal participated in the transcontinental transfer of FB-3s from the East Coast to the West Coast of the United States, a mission commanded by Major "Rusty" Rowell. In addition to flying transports in Nicaragua, he flew combat missions in other aircraft, displaying "great courage and skill in attacks on hostile bandit forces." After Nicaragua, Archie Paschal left the Marine Corps and became a pilot for Pan American Airlines. His last logged flight was on July 28, 1936, flying a DC-2 from Mexico to Brownsville, Texas. However, he continued to fly, and on October 10, 1936, he crashed in bad weather near Guatemala City, Guatemala, en route to the Canal

Zone from Brownsville. He and two other Pan American employees were killed. Paschal is buried in Arlington National Cemetery. John Chappell, "The Runaway Pilot from Glendon: Archie Paschal Led Storied Career in Aviation," ThePilot.com, May 10, 2017, accessed May 10, 2017.

206. Citation for the Navy Cross awarded to Master Technical Sergeant Archie Paschal, February 4, 1930, MCHD, Second Brigade Files.

207. When the transport crashed, a propeller blade pierced the fuel tank, and the hot engine ignited the fuel. H. O. Martin to Commanding Officer, Second Brigade, subject: "Commendatory Action on the Part of Sergeant R. V. Burns, US Marine Corps," September 20, 1930, MCHD, Second Brigade Files. See also F. L. Bradman to Commanding Officer, Second Brigade, subject: "Recommendation for Award of Distinguished Flying Cross for Staff Sergeant Robert V. Burns, US Marine Corps," November 21, 1930, ibid. In lieu of the Distinguished Flying Cross, Staff Sergeant Burns was awarded the Cross of Valor by the president of Nicaragua and received a special letter of commendation from the secretary of the navy.

208. Rowell, "Annual Report," 252.

209. According to a Navy Department newsletter, aerial "dusting" was performed with "sixteen hundred pounds of Paris Green mixture." US Navy, Bureau of Aeronautics, News Letter no. 275 (March 1932), MCHD, Second Brigade Files: Aviation.

210. Mulcahy, "Marine Corps Aviation in the Second Nicaraguan Campaign," 129.

211. Johnson, *Marine Corps Aviation,* 78.

212. As part of the licensing agreement, Pitcairn agreed to use Cieva's copyrighted name for the airplane, Autogiro, as opposed to the more common spelling Autogyro (which Pitcairn had coined earlier to avoid using Cieva's spelling).

213. See Peter Brooks, *Cierva Autogiros: The Development of Rotary-Wing Flight* (Washington, DC: Smithsonian Institution Press, 1988); Charles Gablehouse, *Helicopters and Autogiros: A History of Rotating-Wing and V/STOL Aviation* (Philadelphia: J. B. Lippincott, 1969).

214. For an in-depth discussion of the marines' acquisition of the Autogiro and its deployment to Nicaragua, see Lyn Montross, "The Marine Autogiro in Nicaragua, *Marine Corps Gazette* 37, no. 2 (February 1953): 56–61.

215. "Autogiro Lands on Big Ship's Deck, *Popular Science* 119, no. 6 (December 1931): 61. The Royal Air Force Fleet Air Arm also evaluated the Pitcairn Autogiro, and in 1940 the Royal Naval Air Service purchased six PA-18s (redesignated the Pitcairn PA-39) for convoy escort duty. Pitcairn, AGA, Pitcairn-Cierva, Pitcairn-Larsen, *Aerofiles* (online, accessed May 10, 2017).

216. "Translation of Nicaraguan Press," *La Prensa,* August 13, 1932, MCHD, Second Brigade Files.

217. Ibid., July 5, 1932.

218. Ibid., July 28, 1932.

219. Smith et al., *Review of the Organizations and Operations of the Guardia Nacional.*

220. "Record of Events, Fifth Regiment," January 21, 1929, MCHD, Second Brigade Files.

221. Marion Dawson, "The Nicaraguan Voluntarios," n.d. (circa 1939), 1–5, MCHD, Second Brigade Files.

222. Ibid., 7.
223. Ibid.
224. Ibid.
225. Ibid., 8.
226. Macaulay, *Sandino Affair,* 132. The disbandment of the *voluntarios* does not mean that locally raised paramilitary units are not useful. In fact, they are often the key to success in counterinsurgency, as demonstrated during the Malayan emergency, in the Philippines, and elsewhere.
227. Lewis Burwell "Chesty" Puller is the most decorated US marine in history. He was born in West Point, Virginia. He attended the Virginia Military Institute but, inspired by the marines at Belleau Wood, left school to fight in France during World War I. However, he saw no combat action. He returned to the United States and was commissioned into the reserves in 1919. But due to the postwar drawdown, he was returned to the enlisted ranks as a corporal. He was then ordered to Haiti as a Gendarmerie lieutenant and participated in more than forty engagements against the *cacos.* Puller returned to the United States and was recommissioned in 1924. He served in a variety of assignments until 1928, when he was assigned to the Guardia Nacional in Nicaragua. He returned to the United States in 1931 and was posted to the American Legation in China, where he served until 1936. He went back to China in 1940 as the commanding officer of the Second Battalion, Fourth Regiment. Upon returning to the United States in August 1941, he took command of the First Battalion, Seventh Regiment, First Marine Division. Puller went on to carve out his iconic status as a heroic and aggressive leader in World War II on Guadalcanal and Peleliu; during the Korean War he fought at the Battle of Chosin Reservoir. It was at "Frozen Chosin" that Puller famously remarked, "We've been looking for the enemy for some time now. We've finally found him. We're surrounded. That simplifies things." In July 1954 Major General Puller took command of the Second Marine Division, but he fell ill and retired in November 1955. He died in 1971 and is buried in Christ Church Parish Cemetery, Saluda, Virginia. See Hoffman, *Chesty.*
228. Clark, *With the Old Corps in Nicaragua,* 117.
229. Guardia Nacional, "Guardia Newsletter," December 1932, MCHD, Second Brigade Files.
230. Ibid., December 31, 1930.
231. The description provided is derived from John Hendrickson, "El Terremoto," *Leatherneck* 70, no. 4 (April 1987).
232. "Marines at Managua," *Outlook and Independent,* April 15, 1931, 1, MCHD, Second Brigade Files.
233. "Weekly Operations Report," Commanding Officer, Aircraft Squadrons, Second Brigade, to the Bureau of Aeronautics, Navy Department, Washington, DC, April 4, 1931, MCHD, Second Brigade Files.
234. According to the after-action report, "Shortly after the quake, arrangements were made with the Pan American Airways to use their spare transmitter on the amateur band. . . . Pvt Swift sent out eighty-four messages to station W3AFT located at Quantico and operated by Major W. C. Hawthorne, USMC. All of the messages were messages to the families of Marine Corps personnel stationed in Managua." "Weekly Operations Report, Earthquake," 7, MCHD, Second Brigade Files.

235. In 1925 Army Air Service aviator Major Henry "Hap" Arnold (later commander of the US Army Air Force during World War II) was an intelligence officer posted in Washington, DC. He read a report about an airline established in Colombia known as SCADTA (Sociedad Colombo Alemana de Transportes Aéreos, or Colombian-German Air Transport Society). Though alarmed that a German aviation concern was located so close to the Panama Canal, Arnold also saw a business opportunity. He took a map and sketched a notional American airline that would fly from Key West, Florida, to Havana, Cuba, on to the Yucatán peninsula of Mexico, then southward to British Honduras, through Nicaragua, and ending at the Canal Zone. He shared his idea with another Air Service officer, Carl "Tooey" Spaatz (later commander of American strategic air forces in World War II and the first chief of staff of the independent US Air Force), and they, along with two other officers, drew up a prospectus for such an airline and tried to find investors in New York City. They called the project Pan American Airways. Unfortunately, all four officers became embroiled in the court-martial of Brigadier General William "Billy" Mitchell. Arnold and Spaatz received official reprimands, and with this cloud over their heads, they withdrew from the project. However, their names remained on the prospectus, and the project went forward without them. Two years later, Juan Trippe gathered some wealthy investors, formed his own company in New York, and called it Pan American Airways Inc. Daly, *American Saga,* 27–28.

236. "Weekly Operations Report, Earthquake." The report refers to "OL-S's," but no such airplane existed at the time, and the *Lexington*'s aircraft complement in June 1931 did not list any such aircraft. However, Loening OL-8 amphibians (belonging to VJ-1B) did serve aboard the *Lexington* (so it was probably a typographical error). In 1931 the *Lexington* also carried seventeen TM4-1s. Larkins, *US Navy Aircraft* [and] *US Marine Corps Aircraft,* 69, 99 (US Navy aircraft section). The Martin TM, a single-engine biplane torpedo bomber, was the US Navy's standard torpedo bomber throughout much of the 1930s. Deliveries began in August 1928 to the aircraft carriers *Saratoga* and *Lexington.* The TM4-1 (referred to in the report as "14-M-1s") was powered by a Pratt & Whitney R-1690-24 radial engine. See Gordon Swanborough and Peter Bowers, *United States Navy Aircraft since 1911,* 2d ed. (London: Putnam, 1976).

237. "Weekly Operations Report, Earthquake," 4.

238. The Fokker Universal, or Standard, was first developed in 1925. It had a 200 hp Wright J-4 radial engine. Later models were upgraded with the 220 hp J-5 and the 246 hp J-6 engines. The Universal was a rugged and reliable airplane used by small air carriers hauling cargo and passengers. It had a unique shock absorber system made of bungee cords, which enabled the airplane to land easily on unimproved airstrips. See Marc Dierikx, *Fokker: A Transatlantic Biography* (Washington, DC: Smithsonian Institution Press, 1997).

239. Commander, Special Service Squadron, to the Chief of Naval Operations, "Managua Earthquake, Special Report on," April 21, 1931, MCHD, Second Brigade Files.

240. The USS *Chaumont* was built for the US Army in 1920 but was transferred to the US Navy in 1921. It served mostly in the Pacific, deploying marines of the Fourth Regiment to the international settlement in Shanghai, China, to protect American interests there. It also delivered US Army soldiers from the Thirty-First Regiment to Shanghai from the Philippines when the city was attacked by Japanese forces early in 1932. Five years

later, the *Chaumont* would rush the Sixth Marine Regiment to Shanghai to reinforce the Fourth Regiment during the all-out Japanese effort to take the city. During World War II the elderly transport made runs between Seattle, Washington, and Alaska. In 1943 it was selected to be converted to a hospital ship and returned to active service as the USS *Samaritan*. After the war it was sold for scrap. Naval History and Heritage Command, *Dictionary of American Naval Fighting Ships*.

241. "Weekly Operations Report, Earthquake," 4.

242. Ernest Swift, "The Red Cross Flies to Managua," *Red Cross Courier*, September 1931, 454–56.

243. "Weekly Operations Report, Earthquake," 5.

244. "US Marine Goes Mad in Managua, Slain by Guard," *Chicago Tribune*, April 5, 1931. As the headline suggests, some marines were unable to face the horror of the Managua earthquake. In this particular instance, a young marine sergeant "lost his mind under the strain of rescue work" and was shot by a Guardia soldier.

245. Cummins, *Quijote on a Burro*, 45.

246. *Current History*, January 1931, 600.

247. The pilot of the amphibian, Lieutenant Colin Coffman, was flying to Puerto Cabezas to meet his wife, who had just arrived in Nicaragua that day. "Translation of Nicaraguan Press," *Diario Moderno*, August 20, 1932, MCHD, Second Brigade Files. Coffman was accompanied by Sergeant W. A. Schoffield and Corporal Raymond Townsend, riding as mechanics. Coffman's plane was not the only one that went down in the area. Another amphibian (commonly referred to by marines as a "Goose") crashed the next day near the coast. The pilot of that plane was quickly rescued. *La Nacion*, August 23, 1932. Unfortunately, although the use of parachutes had become common and improvements had made them safer, they did not always work. For example, a plane piloted by Captain William Byrd was struck by a buzzard, and he and his observer bailed out. Both were killed. Rodney Dutcher, "First Complete Story of Sandino's Battle with the Marines," *Sunday Star* (Washington, DC), September 7, 1930.

248. Citation accompanying the award of the Distinguished Flying Cross to Raymond P. Rutedge, Hall of Valor, *Military Times*, valor.militarytimes.com, accessed May 10, 2017.

249. "Translation of Nicaraguan Press," *Diario Moderno*, August 20, 1932, MCHD, Second Brigade Files.

250. Ibid., *Diario Moderno* and *El Commercio*. Sergeant Simmons had been involved in an earlier crash of an amphibian. In that incident, a Loening piloted by Staff Sergeant Gordon Heritage crashed while flying in support of Captain Merritt Edson's Coco River patrols. Heritage and Simmons survived the crash, burned their aircraft, and made their way toward the coast. After an arduous trek, the two men encountered a friendly Miskito Indian who agreed to take them to Sandy Bay in a canoe, traveling down the Ulana River. There, they rested for a while before being taken by dugout to Puerto Cabezas. Robert Hucker, "The Coco River Patrol," *Air Classics* 15, no. 4 (1979): 16–18.

251. Some thought was given to using the Autogyro to rescue the downed crew, but the idea was dropped because, although the plane could descend, it "could not go straight up again," and there was not enough space for a rolling start. Moreover, the ground was soft and swampy in some areas. "Translation of Nicaraguan Press," *La Nacion*, August 20, 1932, MCHD, Second Brigade Files.

252. Most of the officers and noncommissioned officers sold their furniture and other belongings, including the brigade commander. "Translation of Nicaraguan Press," *La Nueva Prensa,* October 5, 1932, MCHD, Second Brigade Files.

253. When the marines began evacuating their garrisons on the east coast during the drawdown, Guardia reinforcements were sent there, usually by air. On one occasion two trimotors, a Ford and a Fokker, flew Guardia troops to Puerto Cabezas. According to a Second Brigade report, "The trip is perhaps the most dangerous flight in Nicaragua. The course lies over a jungle, mostly uninhabited, 250 miles long. There is no possible landing field other than the field at the destination. The East Coast boasts the trifling amount of 240 inches of rain a year, and the Coast is frequently cloud banked and rainy." To improve their chances of making it, the crews reduced the load (passengers and equipment) and fueled the airplanes for a round-trip. US Navy, Bureau of Aeronautics, News Letter no. 258 (June 1931), MCHD, Second Brigade Files: Aviation.

254. "Annual Report," January 6, 1933 (aboard the USS *Henderson,* en route to Norfolk), MCHD, Second Brigade Files.

255. Major Bourne succumbed to a brief illness in January 1935. Ralph Mitchell, like others who served in Nicaragua, would go on to greater things. Mitchell had graduated from the Naval Academy and been commissioned into the Marine Corps in 1915. He first went to Guam and then to Texas, where the First Brigade was monitoring the border. He was sent to flight school in November 1920 and became a naval aviator in 1921. He went back to Guam for a time and then returned to the United States to attend the Army Air Corps Tactical School, graduating in 1927. He then attended the Command and General Staff School at Fort Leavenworth, Kansas. After a short tour in San Diego, he took command of the Aircraft Squadrons, Second Brigade, in Nicaragua. He returned to the United States in 1931, handing over command to Pat Mulcahy. Following several routine assignments, he took over as director of Marine Corps aviation, a post he held until 1942. During World War II he took command of the First Marine Aircraft Wing following Roy Geiger's departure. He followed Geiger as commander of Air Solomons. He was relieved in March 1944 by Army Air Force General Hubert Harmon and was named commander of Air South Pacific. He returned to the United States at the end of the war and took command of the Second Marine Aircraft Wing at Cherry Point, North Carolina. He retired in 1948 and was promoted to lieutenant general. He died in 1970. Clark, *United States Marine Corps Generals of World War II,* 96–97.

256. Francis Patrick "Pat" Mulcahy attended Notre Dame University and was commissioned as a marine in 1917. He attended flight school at Miami in 1918 and served with the Northern Bombing Group in France. On September 29 he shot down a German Fokker D.VII over Coremarch, Belgium, the first marine aerial victory in World War I. He also participated in the aerial resupply effort to encircled French forces, dropping food and other supplies from 100 feet under heavy enemy fire. He returned to the United States after the war and was sent to Haiti, where he remained until 1921. He later went back to Haiti and served there until 1925. During his second tour in Haiti, he took command of the observation squadron. Upon returning to the United States, he attended the Army Air Corps Tactical School and then the Command and General Staff School. From there, he was ordered to Nicaragua and commanded the Aircraft Squadrons, Second Brigade. During World War II Mulcahy commanded the "Cactus Air Force" on Guadalcanal from

December 1941 to February 1943. He became chief of staff for Air Solomons and then served as commander of the Second Marine Aircraft Wing until March 1944. In November of that year he took command of the Tenth Tactical Air Force. Owing to illness, he was sent to San Diego in June 1945 and was medically retired in April 1946, whereupon he was promoted to lieutenant general. He died in December 1973. Ibid., 99–101.

257. "Translation of Nicaraguan Press," *El Commercio,* October 27, 1932, MCHD, Second Brigade Files.

258. Navy press release, December 27, 1932. MCHD, Second Brigade Files.

259. The Vought aircraft in the first group were crewed by Lieutenant Hayne Boyden and Gunnery Sergeant A. J. Pasczkiewicz, A. W. Kreiser and Staff Sergeant L. Cartwright, Lieutenant J. A. Timmons and Private J. T. Duvall, Lieutenant F. H. Wirsig and Private First Class H. R. Hacker, and Gunnery Sergeant J. S. Carter and Sergeant M. E. Julson. The Ford trimotors were flown by Lieutenant P. O. Parmelee (assisted by Staff Sergeant Gordon Heritage and Master Technical Sergeant H. L. Blackwell and accompanied by a lieutenant and four enlisted men) and Lieutenant Samuel S. Jack (assisted by Master Technical Sergeant Horace Geer and accompanied by four enlisted marines). Ibid.

260. The Curtiss aircraft of the second group were crewed by Captain Mulcahy and Master Technical Sergeant Morris Kurtz, Lieutenant Frank Dailey and Sergeant Curtis Goehring, Captain E. G. Farrell and Private C. C. Mintling, Lieutenant Paul Putnam and Gunnery Sergeant Ike Smith, Lieutenant William Lemly and Corporal Fred Brothers, Lieutenant Mark Heaney and Private Joseph Trautman, Lieutenant Frank June and Corporal Walter Puishis, Lieutenant Frank Schwable and Private A. D. Godwin, and Staff Sergeant F. H. Smith and Private R. W. Greenwood. The Ford trimotor was flown by Lieutenant W. D. Saunders (assisted by Gunnery Sergeant R. E. A. Lillie and Master Technical Sergeant H. R. Jordan and accompanied by a navy medical officer and three enlisted marines). Ibid.

261. The Sikorsky transport was piloted by Captain Hal Major (assisted by Gunnery Sergeant Neal Williams and Master Technical Sergeant Charles Campbell and accompanied by two enlisted marines). The Loenings were crewed by Lieutenant P. E. Conradt and Gunner K. F. Bubier, Lieutenant K. H. Weir and Sergeant A. T. King, Lieutenant A. F. Binney and Private L. F. Smith, and Staff Sergeant I. V. Masters and Private S. C. Manle. Ibid.

262. "From the Halls of Montezuma . . .," US Navy, Bureau of Aeronautics, News Letter no. 297 (February 1933), 1–2, MCHD, Second Brigade Files: Aviation.

263. Cummins, *Quijote on a Burro,* 54.

264. "Annual Report of the Secretary of the Navy, Fiscal Year 1928" (Washington, DC, 1929), 50, cited in ibid., 54.

265. Ibid., 55.

266. Rowell, "Aircraft in Bush Warfare," 180.

267. Megee, "Genesis of Air Support in Guerrilla Operations," 59.

268. Megee, "Guerrilla Lessons from Nicaragua," 36, 38. Vernon Megee served in Haiti from 1923 to 1925. He was then ordered to China, where he remained until 1928, at which time he entered preliminary flight training at San Diego. His training was interrupted in January 1929 when he deployed to Nicaragua as quartermaster, Aircraft Squadrons, Second Brigade. He completed his flight training in Pensacola in 1931 and was assigned to Aircraft Squadrons, West Coast Expeditionary Forces. Following that tour he taught at the

Marine Corps schools in Quantico, where he coauthored the first edition of the *Small Wars Manual.* From 1939 to 1940 he commanded a fighter squadron, and from 1940 to 1943 he was the executive officer of the US Naval Aviation Mission to Peru. From there, he became the chief of staff for the Third Marine Aircraft Wing at Cherry Point, which deployed to Hawaii in the spring of 1944. As commander of the Landing Force Air Support Control Unit One, he deployed for combat during the battle for Iwo Jima. During the battle for Okinawa he commanded all marine landing force air control units. Following World War II, Megee was an instructor at the Naval War College, where he was promoted to brigadier general. From 1947 to 1950 he served as assistant director of Marine Corps aviation and then as commander of the First Marine Aircraft Wing during the Korean War. He was promoted to lieutenant general in 1956 and became the first aviator to serve as assistant commandant. Megee retired from service in 1959 and was advanced to general, the first aviator to achieve that rank. After retiring, he attended graduate school at the University of Texas at Austin, writing a thesis entitled "United States Military Intervention in Nicaragua, 1902–1932." He then served as superintendent of the Marine Military Academy in Harlingen, Texas, until 1968. He retired for good to Albuquerque, New Mexico, and died there in 1992. He is buried in Arlington National Cemetery. See "General Vernon E. Megee, USMC," *Who's Who in Marine Corps History*" (online, accessed May 5, 2017). See also Megee, *Memoirs of a Marine,* a book he would not allow to be published until after his death.

269. Regarding the role of aviation in supporting ground operations during the conflict in South Vietnam, Megee wrote: "The currently reported difficulties in providing effective close air support for the Vietnamese forces engaged in guerrilla operations against infiltrating Viet Cong units may strike a responsive chord in the memories of older officers who served under similar conditions in the jungled mountains of Nicaragua from 1927 to 1932. For those younger officers now actually or potentially concerned with so-called counter-insurgency activities, a review of the early development of air support techniques against elusive irregulars may possibly prove to be of more than passing historical interest." Megee, "Genesis of Air Support in Guerrilla Operations," 49.

270. *Small Wars Manual,* 1-6-8.

271. Ibid., 1-16-31.

Conclusion

1. John Keegan, introduction to Alan Wykes, *Hitler's Bodyguards: SS Leibstandarte* (New York: Random House, 1974), 6.

2. Ibid.

3. B. H. Liddell Hart, *Why Don't We Learn from History?* (New York: Hawthorn Books, 1971), 15.

4. Specifically, "the ability to airlift army and police units to remote locations and keep them supplied by airdrop and helicopter has proven decisive. Such was the case of the US Marines' intervention in Nicaragua in the late 1920s. Marine Corps transports and other aircraft sustained deep-penetration patrols and remote outposts as well as moved government forces to concentrate against guerrilla formations." Corum and Johnson, *Airpower in Small Wars,* 427.

5. Chalmers Johnson, "Revolution in the Social System," in *Hoover Institution Studies 3* (Washington, DC: Hoover Institution on War, Revolution, and Peace, 1964), 94–95.

6. Freiherr von der Heydte, *Modern Irregular Warfare,* 94.

7. Callwell, *Small Wars,* 85, 33.

8. Bernard Fall, "A Portrait of the 'Centurion,'" in Roger Trinquier, *Modern Warfare—A French View of Counterinsurgency* (New York: Frederick A. Praeger, 1964), xvii.

9. Bernard Fall, *Street without Joy: Indochina at War, 1946–1954,* 4th ed. (Harrisburg, PA: Stackpole, 1961), 266. In South Vietnam, "the use of massive bomb attacks and napalm drops on villages is not only militarily stupid, but it is inhuman and likely to backfire very badly on the psychological level." Indeed, in 1963 officials claimed that more than 23,000 Communist Vietcong had been killed, some 7,500 of them by fixed-wing strike aircraft of the South Vietnamese air force. "One might want to ponder the question," Fall wrote: "How many of those 7,500 were innocent bystanders?" Ibid., 266–67.

10. Callwell, *Small Wars,* 23.

11. *Small Wars Manual,* 1-6-9.

12. Ibid., 1-6-8.

13. According to many analysts today, the proliferation of state-of-the-art information and weapons technologies has contributed to global subversive warfare conducted via the Internet and using cybernetic weapons to strike worldwide. And so-called hybrid warfare has enabled states to engage in what amounts to "big guerrilla warfare," such as that conducted by Ukraine's Azov Regiment. Globalism has engendered low-level urban terrorism, mass migration, and other effects, all converging to provoke a new form of insurgency. In response, the US Defense Advanced Research Projects Agency has called for "metabolic dominance," that is, creating soldiers with superior physical and cognitive performance, ably assisted by bioengineering, cybernetics, and nanotechnology—so-called fifth-generation warfare. These "superwarriors" will be able to lead paramilitary forces against the new guerrillas and defeat them—or so it is claimed.

14. For a useful discussion of air policing by the British and their tendency to bomb and strafe recalcitrant peoples, see "Colonial Air Control: The European Powers Develop New Concepts of Air Warfare," chap. 2 in Corum and Johnson, *Airpower in Small Wars.*

15. Instead of British soldiers (and, in particular, English soldiers), large numbers of Indian and other colonial troops were brought in to complement the aircraft squadrons.

16. Civic actions conducted by military forces are intended to convey friendship to local populations through short- and long-term programs such as the construction of schools, the digging of wells, and the provision of medical, dental, and veterinary care. Civil affairs encompasses developmental programs regarded as nation building, such as supervising elections; establishing, equipping, and training police forces; and improving services such as sanitation and electrical production. See *Joint Doctrine for Civil-Military Operations,* Joint Publication 3-57 (Washington, DC: Joint Chiefs of Staff, 2001). See also *Civil Affairs Tactics, Techniques, and Procedures,* Field Manual 3-05.401, Marine Corps Reference Publication 3-33.1A (Washington, DC: Headquarters, Department of the Army, 2003).

17. The first major airlift of an entire army did not occur until mid-1936, when Ju-52s of the German Luftwaffe transported General Franco's army from Morocco to Spain at the commencement of the Spanish Civil War.

18. The Marine Corps' emphasis on close air support is legendary, and marine aviators were the only American fliers who had a practical conception of and experience in how ground forces could and should be provided with close support at the outbreak of World War II. From its earliest years, the *Marine Corps Gazette* has published numerous articles on the subject, and in 1968 the historical branch of Marine Corps Headquarters published an annotated bibliography on the development of close air support in the Marine Corps. See *An Annotated Bibliography of the United States Marine Corps' Concept of Close Air Support* (Washington, DC: Headquarters, US Marine Corps, 1968). Technically, "armed overwatch" is a type of close air support. In Iraq and Afghanistan, concerns about the dense mix of forces were generally but not completely offset by the use of precision munitions delivered by fast-moving aircraft linked to controllers on the ground via ROVER communications laptops streaming real-time video between cockpits and ground controllers. Although US Central Command Air Forces categorized such missions as close air support, they are best described as overwatch. Overwatch improves the ground commander's situational awareness by providing persistent and responsive surveillance; it improves the security of the ground force by offering rapid and precise delivery of aerial fires; and it exerts a kind of psychological dominance over the enemy, something the marines well understood, as described in this book. For a useful discussion of armed overwatch, see Clint Hinote, "Armed Overwatch: Key to Successful COIN Operations in Urban Terrain," *Air Land Sea Application Center Bulletin 2008-1,* 9–12 (online, accessed May 12, 2017).

19. Assigning aircraft to watch over ground patrols did not mean that Marine Corps aviators disavowed the concept of centralized control of aviation resources. Ross Rowell believed that, at least within a deployed Marine Corps force, aircraft should be centrally controlled at the force commander level. He wrote: "The senior air officer should have the same dual staff and command status that is given the artillery commander in the infantry division. In other words, the senior air officer should actively command the air organization and at the same time serve as the advisor to the commander on air matters. . . . The air squadrons will operate in support of the ground organizations and also independently. In certain special situations, planes may be attached temporarily to ground units. As a general rule this practice should be discouraged. Better support can be given in most cases if the control is centralized." Rowell, "Aircraft in Bush Warfare," 203. Although it would be going too far to say that Rowell was advocating what amounts to a joint force air component commander (a modern echelon authorized by the Goldwater-Nichols legislation of 1986), his words show that even Marine Corps aviators of the small wars era understood the advantages of centralized control of aviation.

20. The marines may have been rather loose with their rules of engagement, but never to the extent that the European air forces were. The marines never used poison gas or gas of any sort, although Rowell and others suggested the use of nonlethal chemicals: "a sneezing gas, a lachrymatory gas, a laughing gas, a cholic-producing gas or even a harmless anaesthetic." See Rowell, "Aircraft in Bush Warfare," 195; Denny [Harold] Campbell, "Aviation in Guerrilla Warfare," pt. 3, *Marine Corps Gazette* 16, no. 3 (November 1931): 33. French imperial policy permitted the use of lethal gases, and aerial bombardment of civilians with toxic gases such as phosgene was the norm. In that regard, the French made little distinction between combatants and noncombatants in punitive operations, and the use of gas was not regarded as particularly unethical or immoral or even counterproductive.

According to Dr. Bill Dean, a professor at the US Air Force Air Command and Staff College, Maxwell Air Force Base, Alabama, "the French had no qualms about bombing villages that were strictly civilian targets." Indeed, the Escadrille Cherifienne often used gas to attack towns that had already submitted to French authority. Dean, "Colonial Armies of the French Third Republic," 315–24.

21. *Small Wars Manual,* 1-17-32.

22. Ibid. One can certainly argue that the marines did not leave Haiti, the Dominican Republic, or Nicaragua with "the lasting friendship and respect of the native population." However, such a goal was accomplished in the Philippines, and it was the marines' intent on Hispaniola and in Nicaragua.

23. Rowell, "Air Service in Minor Warfare," 872.

24. Restraint as a feature of modern counterinsurgency doctrine can be found in many military publications, most notably in the first edition of the US Army Field Manual (FM 3-24), *Counterinsurgency* (December 2006). In appendix E, devoted to "airpower in counterinsurgency," the manual makes it clear that "counterinsurgents must take care to minimize civilian casualties." Unfortunately, the US Air Force's response to the manual and the appendix was undisguised outrage. Indeed, the commander of the Air Force Doctrine Center claimed in an interview that the manual exhibited "a bit too much hand-wringing over the potential for collateral damage." See John Tirpak, "Washington Watch," *Air Force Magazine,* March 2007, 15.

25. Rowell, "Aircraft in Bush Warfare," 191.

26. As this book goes to print, the US Air Force is once again exploring the idea of acquiring aircraft like the A-29 as a light attack and reconnaissance aircraft (the OA-X). The air force initiative is intended to explore the pros and cons of buying a new, off-the-shelf light attack platform for the close air support role and for other missions in "permissive" and "semipermissive" environments, meaning that the threat of ground-based antiaircraft artillery and missiles is low to medium.

27. Using a bomber as a counterterrorism weapon might seem odd, but after the Libyan government was implicated in a left-wing terrorist attack on a Berlin disco (killing several American military personnel), Operation El Dorado Canyon was launched in April 1986, targeting the Gaddafi regime as the sponsor of the attack. The attack was made by F-111F Aardvark deep-strike bombers.

28. See John Akehurst, *We Won a War: The Campaign in Oman, 1965–1975* (The Chantry, UK: Michael Russell, 1982); John Cann, *Flight Plan Africa: Portuguese Airpower in Counterinsurgency, 1961–1974* (West Midlands, UK: Helion, 2015).

29. Brian Burridge, "Iraq 2003—Air Power Pointers for the Future," *Royal Air Force Air Power Review* 7, no. 3 (Autumn 2004): 2.

30. Norton Schwartz, letter to the editor, *Air Force Magazine,* March 2007, 4.

31. William Mitchell, *Winged Defense: The Development and Possibilities of Modern Air Power—Economic and Military* (1925; reprint, New York: Dover Publications, 1988), 3. See also William Mitchell, "Aeronautical Era," *Saturday Evening Post,* December 20, 1924.

Bibliography

Adler, Julius, ed. *History of the Seventy Seventh Division, August 25th, 1917–November 11th, 1918.* New York: 77th Division Association, 1919.

"Aircraft in Nicaragua." *Aero Digest* 12, no. 5 (May 1928).

Airdrop of Supplies and Equipment: Reference Data for Airdrop Platform Loads. Marine Corps Reference Publication 4-11.3L, Army FM 4-20.116 (FM 10-516), Air Force TO 13C7-1-13. Headquarters, Departments of the Army and Air Force, August 2001.

"Air Force in Minor Wars." May 1930 syllabus. Typescript. Maxwell Air Force Base, AL, US Air Force Historical Research Agency.

Akehurst, John. *We Won a War: The Campaign in Oman, 1965–1975.* The Chantry, UK: Michael Russell, 1982.

Alexander, Joseph. *A Fellowship of Valor: The Battle History of the United States Marines.* New York: HarperCollins, 1997.

Ameling, Glenn. "Admiral and Diplomat: William Banks Caperton, Agent of United States Naval Policy in Latin America, 1915–1919." Master's thesis, Brigham Young University, 1981.

American Electoral Commission in Nicaragua. Executive memorandum no. 8, July 20, 1928. Marine Corps History Division, Second Brigade Files: Elections.

"American Fliers Take Own Risk." *New York Times,* March 24, 1927.

Andrade, John. *US Military Aircraft Designations and Serials since 1979.* Leicestershire, UK: Mideland Counties Publications, 1979.

Angelucci, Enzo. *Great Aeroplanes of the World.* London: Hamlyn, 1973.

An Annotated Bibliography of the United States Marine Corps' Concept of Close Air Support. Washington, DC: Headquarters, US Marine Corps, 1968.

"Annual Report of General George Barnett to the Secretary of the Navy, Fiscal Year 1916." October 5, 1916. Marine Corps History Division, Haiti, Occupation.

"Annual Report of General George Barnett to the Secretary of the Navy, Fiscal Year 1919." October 10, 1919. Marine Corps History Division, Haiti: Occupation.

Anything, Anywhere, Anytime: An Illustrated History of the Military Airlift Command, 1941–1991. Scott Air Force Base, IL: Military Airlift Command, Office of History, 1991.

Arbon, Lee. *They Also Flew: The Enlisted Pilot Legacy, 1912–1942.* Washington, DC: Smithsonian Institution Press, 1992.

"Army Continued." N.d. (circa 1930s). Marine Corps History Division, Other Reports.

Astor, Gerald. *Semper Fi in the Sky: The Marine Air Battles of World War II.* New York: Random House, 2005.

Auliard, Gilles. "Maiden of the Skies." *Air Classics,* April 2009.

Austin, Lee. *Marine Aviation: World War I.* Quantico, VA: First Marine Aviation Force Veterans Association, 1945.

"Autogiro Lands on Big Ship's Deck." *Popular Science* 119, no. 6 (December 1931).

Aviation History and Research (Op-504f), Office of the Chief of Naval Aviation. "Historical Sketch of the Naval Aviation Pilot Program." September 3, 1952. Marine Corps History Division, Aviation: Enlisted Pilots.

"Aviators Pick out Federal Positions." *New York Times,* April 30, 1914.

Barnett, Brigadier General George (USMC). "Report of Affairs in the Republic of Haiti, June 1915 to June 30, 1920." October 20, 1920. Office of Naval Records and Library, Record Group 45, Subject File, 1911–1927, WA-7, National Archives, Washington, DC.

Barnett, Brigadier General George, to Secretary of the Navy. "Report on Affairs in the Republic of Haiti, June 1915 to June 30, 1920." October 11, 1920. Marine Corps History Division, First Brigade Files.

Barr, William. "Tells How Marine Fliers Hunt Down Bandits." *Recruiters' Bulletin* 5, no. 5 (June 1919).

Barry, John. *The Great Influenza: The Story of the Deadliest Pandemic in History.* London: Viking Penguin, 2005.

Bartlett, Tom. "The Ironman." 3 parts. *Leatherneck* 67, nos. 7–9 (July, August, September 1984).

Belcher, Michael. "The Flying Sergeants." *Proceedings,* February 1982.

Bemis, Samuel. *A Diplomatic History of the United States.* Rev. ed. New York: Holt, 1942.

———. *The Latin American Policy of the United States.* New York: Harcourt, Brace, 1943.

Bickel, Keith. *Mars Learning: The Marine Corps' Development of Small Wars Doctrine, 1915–1940.* Boulder, CO: Westview Press, 2001.

Biddle, Wayne. *Barons of the Sky: From Early Flight to Strategic Warfare; the Story of the American Aerospace Industry.* New York: Simon & Schuster, 1991.

Boot, Max. *The Savage Wars of Peace: Small Wars and the Rise of American Power.* New York: Basic Books, 2002.

Bourin, Monique, ed. *Pour une anthropologie du préléseigneurial dans les campagnes médiévales (XIe–XIVe siècles): réalités et representations paysannes.* Paris: Publications de la Sorbonne, 2004.

"Bourne, Louis, Navy Cross, Recommendation for." November 26, 1929. Marine Corps History Division, Second Brigade Files.

Bowers, Peter. *Boeing Aircraft since 1916.* 2d ed. London: Putnam Aeronautical Books, 1989.

———. *Curtiss Aircraft, 1907–1947.* London: Putnam, 1979.

Boyden, Hayne. "Aerial Adventures in Hispaniola." *Leatherneck* 8, no. 31 (August 1925).

———. "Aerial Adventures in Hispaniola, Part II." *Leatherneck* 8, no. 37 (October 1925).

———. "Aerial Mapping in Haiti." Marine Corps History Division, Haiti: Air.

———. ". . . and Santo Domingo." *Marine Corps Gazette* 56, no. 11 (November 1972).

———. "Some Forced Plane Landings in Santo Domingo." *Marine Corps Gazette* 7, no. 2 (June 1922).

Boyne, Walter, ed. *Air Warfare: An International Encyclopedia.* Santa Barbara, CA: ABC-CLIO, 2002.

Bradman, F. L. "Recommendation for Award of Distinguished Flying Cross for Staff Sergeant Robert V. Burns, US Marine Corps." November 21, 1930. Marine Corps History Division, Second Brigade Files.

Brainard, Edwin. "Marine Aviation—A Lecture." *Marine Corps Gazette* 11, no. 3 (September 1926).

———. "The Marines Take Wings." *Leatherneck* 11, no. 8 (August 1928).

Breckenridge, James Carson, Papers. Marine Corps Historical Research Center, Archives and Special Collections.

Breckenridge, Mary. "Lieutenant General James Carson Breckenridge, USMC (September 1877–March 1942)." *Quarterly Bulletin of the Frontier Nursing Service* 17, no. 4 (Spring 1942).

Breyton, W. "L'Aviation Sanitaire au Maroc en 1933." *Revue de L'Armée de L'Air* 56 (March 1934).

Brooks, Peter. *Cierva Autogiros: The Development of Rotary-Wing Flight.* Washington, DC: Smithsonian Institution Press, 1988.

Brown, Charles. *Agents of Manifest Destiny: The Lives and Times of the Filibusters.* Chapel Hill: University of North Carolina Press, 1980.

Bruce, J. M. *The Aeroplanes of the Royal Flying Corps.* London: Putnam, 1982.

Bruce, J. M., Michael Rolfe, and Richard Ward. *Aircam Aviation Series No. 9: Spad Scouts SVII–SXIII.* Canterbury, UK: Osprey, 1968.

Buckley, John. *Air Power in the Age of Total War.* Bloomington: Indiana University Press, 1999.

"Bullet-Evading Airplanes." *Aero Digest* 12, no. 6 (June 1928).

Burridge, Brian. "Iraq 2003—Air Power Pointers for the Future." *Royal Air Force Air Power Review* 7, no. 3 (Autumn 2004).

Busboom, Stanley. "Bat 21: A Case Study." Master's thesis, US Army War College, 1990.

Calder, Bruce. "Caudillos and Gavilleros versus the United States Marines: Guerrilla Insurgency during the Dominican Intervention, 1916–1924." *Hispanic American Historical Review* 58, no. 4 (November 1974).

———. "Some Aspects of the United States Occupation of the Dominican Republic." PhD diss., University of Texas, 1974.

Callwell, C. E. *Small Wars: Their Principles and Practice.* 3d ed. 1906. Reprint, Lincoln: University of Nebraska Press, 1996.

Campbell, Denny [Harold]. "Aviation in Guerrilla Warfare." Part 3. *Marine Corps Gazette* 16, no. 3 (November 1931).

Campbell, Harold. "Aviation in Guerrilla Warfare." Part 2. *Marine Corps Gazette* 15, no. 5 (May 1931).

Cann, John. *Flight Plan Africa: Portuguese Airpower in Counterinsurgency, 1961–1974.* West Midlands, UK: Helion, 2015.

Carpenter, Manson. "Contact with Bandits." July 28, 1919. Marine Corps History Division, Second Brigade Files.

Carter, C. B. "The Kentucky Feud in Nicaragua: Why Civil War Has Become Her National Sport." Typescript, n.d. Marine Corps History Division, Nicaragua: Guardia Nacional.

Chambers, Washington Irving, Papers. Naval Historical Foundation Collection, Manuscripts Division, Library of Congress, Washington, DC.

Chamier, J. A. "The Use of Air Power for Replacing Military Garrisons." *Journal of the Royal United Services Institute,* February–November 1921.

Chapman, Charles. *Republican Hispanic America: A History.* New York: Macmillan, 1937.

Chappell, John. "The Runaway Pilot from Glendon: Archie Paschal Led Storied Career in Aviation." ThePilot.com, May 10, 2017.

"Chinandega Battle as Seen from Plane." *New York Times,* March 5, 1927.

Citation for the Navy Cross awarded to Master Technical Sergeant Archie Paschal, February 4, 1930. Marine Corps History Division, Second Brigade Files.

Civil Affairs Tactics, Techniques, and Procedures. Field Manual 3-05.401, Marine Corps Reference Publication 3-33.1A. Washington, DC: Headquarters, Department of the Army, 2003.

Clark, George. *United States Marine Corps Generals of World War II: A Biographical Dictionary.* Jefferson, NC: McFarland, 2008.

———. *With the Old Corps in Nicaragua.* Novato, CA: Presidio Press, 2001.

Clausewitz, Carl von. *On War.* Edited and translated by Michael Howard and Peter Paret. Princeton, NJ: Princeton University Press, 1976.

Clifford, John. "History of the First Battalion of US Marines." 1930. Marine Corps Historical Research Center, Cochrane Collection, PC 1, box 15

Close Air Support. Joint Publication 3-3-09.3. Washington, DC: Joint Chiefs of Staff, November 25, 2014.

Collings, Kenneth. *Just for the Hell of It.* New York: Dodd, Mead, 1938.

———. "The Man Who Invented Dive-Bombing." *Liberty* 19, no. 17 (April 25, 1942).

"Collings Defied Death often in Flying Career." *New York Herald Tribune,* May 7, 1941.

Command and Control. Marine Corps Doctrine Publication 6. Washington, DC: Headquarters, US Marine Corps, 1996.

Commander, Special Service Squadron. "Managua Earthquake, Special Report on." April 21, 1931. Marine Corps History Division, Second Brigade Files.

Commanding Officer. "Weekly News Letter, for Week Ending January 15, 1921." Marine Corps History Division, Second Brigade Files.

Commanding Officer, Aircraft Squadrons, Second Brigade. "Weekly Report." April 4, 1931. Marine Corps History Division, Second Brigade Files.

Commanding Officer, First Air Squadron. "Weekly News Letter, January 8, 1921." Marine Corps History Division, Second Brigade Files.

Commanding Officer, First Division, Squadron D. "Weekly News Letter, for Week Ending October 9, 1920." Marine Corps History Division, Second Brigade Files.

Conrad, Charles. "A Year in Haiti's Customs and Fiscal Service." *Proceedings,* April 1923.

Consolidated Distribution Report. January 4, 1929. Marine Corps History Division, Second Brigade Files.

Constabulary Detachment, USMC, Headquarters, Port-au-Prince, Republic of Haiti. "Report of Activities, July 1, 1920 to June 30, 1921." July 15, 19212. Marine Corps History Division, Annual Reports.

Coogan, Anthony. "Northeast China and the Origins of the Anti-Japanese United Front." *Modern China* 20, no. 3 (July 1994).

"Cooking Outfits for an Army: A Chicago Inventor May Furnish Enough for 100,000 Men." *New York Times,* March 25, 1898.

Corbett, Julian. *Signals and Instructions, 1776–1794: Publications of the Navy Records Society.* Vol. 35. London: Navy Records Society, 1908.

Corum, James. *The Luftwaffe: Creating the Operational Air War, 1918–1940.* Lawrence: University Press of Kansas, 1997.

Corum, James, and Wray Johnson. *Airpower in Small Wars: Fighting Insurgents and Terrorists.* Lawrence: University Press of Kansas, 2003.

Coxe, Lewis. "Types and Missions of Surface Vessels, Submarines, and Aircraft." Lecture at Langley Field, VA, March 4–5, 1930. Typescript. Maxwell Air Force Base, AL, US Air Force Historical Research Agency.

Craig, Lieutenant General Edward, USMC, Ret. Oral history transcript, June 8, 1968. Oral History Collection, Headquarters, US Marine Corps, History and Museums Division, Washington, DC.

Craige, John. *Black Bagdad.* New York: Milton, Balch, 1933.

———. "Development of the Republic of Haiti." N.d. Marine Corps History Division, Marines in Haiti.

Cramer, Floyd. *Our Neighbor Nicaragua.* New York: Frederick A. Stokes, 1929.

Craven, Thomas. "History of Aviation in the United States Navy: From Its Beginning until the Spring of 1920." 1977. Thomas T. Craven Papers, File ZGU, Subject File, 1911–1927, Record Group 45, Library of Congress, Washington, DC.

Cummins, Lejeune. *Quijote on a Burro: Sandino and the Marines; a Study in the Formulation of Foreign Policy.* Mexico City: Distrito Federal, La Impresora Azteca, 1958.

Cunningham, Alfred. "Aviation in the Navy." *Marine Corps Gazette* 1, no. 4 (December 1916).

———. "Value of Aviation to the Marine Corps." *Marine Corps Gazette* 5, no. 3 (September 1920).

Daily Diary, Commanding Officer (Colonel Eli K. Cole, USMC), First Marine Brigade. Naval Records of the Office of Naval Records and Library, Record Group 45, box 632, National Archives, Washington, DC.

Daley, Robert. *An American Saga: Juan Trippe and His Pan Am Empire.* New York: Random House, 1980.

Davis, H. P. *Black Democracy: The Story of Haiti.* New York: Dial Press, 1928.

Davis, Richard. *Real Soldiers of Fortune.* 1906. Reprint, Ithaca, NY: Cornell University Library, 2009.

Davis, Thomas. "With No Thought of Aggression." *Military History Quarterly* (2007).

Dawson, Marion. "The Nicaraguan Voluntarios." N.d. (circa 1939). Marine Corps History Division, Second Brigade Files.

Day, Lieutenant General Karl, USMC, Ret. Oral history transcript, August 5, 1968. Oral History Collection, Headquarters, US Marine Corps, History and Museums Division, Washington, DC.

Dean, William. "The Colonial Armies of the French Third Republic: Overseas Formation and Continental Deployment, 1871–1920." PhD diss., University of Chicago, 1999.

Debekker, L. J. "The Massacre at Aux Cayes." *Nation,* March 1930.

del Castillo, Guillermo. *América Hispánica, 1492–1898.* Barcelona: Labor, 1985.

Denny, Harold. *Dollars for Bullets: The Story of American Rule in Nicaragua.* 1929. Reprint, Westport, CT: Greenwood Press, 1980.

Dierikx, Marc. *Fokker: A Transatlantic Biography.* Washington, DC: Smithsonian Institution Press, 1997.

District Commander. "Control of Field Forces by Regimental Headquarters, 15th Regiment." Marine Corps History Division, Second Brigade Files.

Dodge, R. A. "Massacre in Haiti." *Proceedings,* November 1994.

Doenecke, Justus. *Nothing Less than War: A New History of America's Entry into World War I.* Lexington: University Press of Kentucky, 2011.

Donald, David, ed. *Encyclopedia of World Aircraft.* Etobicoke, ON: Prospero Books, 1997.

Dutcher, Rodney. "First Complete Story of Sandino's Battle with the Marines." *Sunday Star* (Washington, DC), September 7, 1930.

Eden, Paul, and Soph Moeng. *The Complete Encyclopedia of World Aircraft.* London: Amber Books, 2002.

Edson, Merritt. "The Coco River Patrol: Operations of a Marine Patrol along the Coco River in Nicaragua." Part 1. *Marine Corps Gazette* 19, no. 3 (August 1936).

Ege, Lennart. *Balloons and Airships.* New York: Macmillan, 1974.

Elliott, John. "Early Marine Corps Aviators." *Naval Aviation News,* May 1977.

———. "The Longest Flight: Early Marine Aviators Make History." *Leatherneck* 91, no. 5 (May 2008).

———. "Marine Aviation in Nicaragua: A Time of Pioneering." *Leatherneck* 92, no. 9 (September 2009).

Elliott, John, and Clyde Gillespie. "MCAS Quantico." *Naval Aviation News,* May 1975.

Ellsworth, Harry. *One Hundred Eighty Landings of the United States Marines, 1800–1934.* Washington, DC: Government Printing Office, 1974.

Emmons, Roger. "Enlisted Marine Aviation Pilots." Marine Corps Aviation Association Historian Memorandum, August 15, 1976. Marine Corps History Division, Aviation: Enlisted Pilots.

———. *First Marine Aviation Force, 1917–1918.* Edited by George Clark. Pike, NH: Brass Hat, 1964.

———. "Navy Fliers Transferred to Marine Aviation, Marine Day Wing in France, 1918." First Marine Aviation Force Veterans Association Newsletter (Baltimore), 1971.

Encyclopædia Britannica. 11th ed. Cambridge: Cambridge University Press, 1911.

Estrada, Louie. "Marine Col. William A. 'Ironman' Lee Dies at 98." *Washington Post,* January 2, 1999.

"Evacuation of Wounded—Marine Aviation 1922." Marine Corps History Division, Miscellaneous.

"An Ex Marine Who Has Made Good." *Recruiters' Bulletin* 4, no. 3 (January 1918).

Executive memorandum no. 2, American Electoral Commission in Nicaragua, November 22, 1928. Marine Corps History Division, Second Brigade Files.

Fall, Bernard. *Street without Joy: Indochina at War, 1946–1954.* 4th ed. Harrisburg, PA: Stackpole, 1961.

Farber, M. A. "Harold W. Dodds, 91, Former Princeton President." *New York Times,* October 26, 1980.

Fegan, J. C. "After Nineteen Years We Leave Haiti." *Marine Corps Gazette* 19, no. 2 (August 1934).

Feifer, George. *Breaking Open Japan: Commodore Perry, Lord Abe, and American Imperialism in 1853.* Washington, DC: Smithsonian Institution Scholarly Press, 2006.

"Final Report of Arms Commission from Captain Julian P. Brown to Commanding General." June 10, 1927. Marine Corps History Division, Second Brigade Files.

Finney, Robert. *History of the Air Corps Tactical School, 1920–1940.* Washington, DC: Center for Air Force History, 1992.

First Division, Squadron D, M.A.F. "Santo Domingo Aerial Pilot." 1st ed., 1920. Marine Corps History Division, Second Brigade Files.

Fleming, Charles, et al. *Quantico: Crossroads of the Marine Corps.* Washington, DC: Headquarters, US Marine Corps, History and Museums Division, 1978.

Fombona, Horacio. *Crímenes del Imperialismo Norte-americano.* Mexico City: Ediciones Churubusco, 1927.

"The Formative Period, 1915–1920." Typescript, n.d. Marine Corps History Division, Haiti: Histories.

Fotakis, Zisis. *Greek Naval Strategy and Policy, 1910–1919.* Cass Series: Naval Policy and History. London: Routledge, 2005.

Foulois, Benjamin. "Report of the Operations of the First Aero Squadron, Signal Corps, with Punitive Expedition, USA for Period March 15 to August 15, 1916." N.d. Maxwell Air Force Base, AL, Historical Research Agency.

Freidel, Frank. *Franklin D. Roosevelt: The Ordeal.* 1954. Reprint, Charleston, SC: Nabu Press (BiblioBazar), 2011.

Freiherr von der Heydte, Friedrich. *Modern Irregular Warfare, in Defense Policy as a Military Phenomenon.* Translated by George Gregory. New York: New Benjamin Franklin House, 1986.

Friedman, Norman. *US Cruisers: An Illustrated Design History.* Annapolis, MD: Naval Institute Press, 1984.

Fry, John. "The First Seaplane: Glenn Curtiss' Arrival at North Island." Association of Naval Aviation, San Diego Squadron Newsletter, April 2010.

———. *USS* Saratoga, *CV-3: An Illustrated History of the Legendary Aircraft Carrier, 1927–1946.* Atglen, PA: Schiffer Publishing, 1996.

Fuller, Stephen, and Graham Cosmas. *Marines in the Dominican Republic: 1916–1924.* Washington, DC: Headquarters, US Marine Corps, History and Museums Division, 1974.

Futrell, Robert. "Development of Aeromedical Evacuation in the United States Air Force, 1904–1960." USAF Historical Study no. 23. Maxwell Air Force Base, AL, Albert F. Simpson Historical Research Center, 1960.

———. "The Development of Aeromedical Evacuation in the United States Air Force, 1909–1939." *Journal of the American Aviation Historical Society* 23, no. 3 (Fall 1978).

Gablehouse, Charles. *Helicopters and Autogiros: A History of Rotating-Wing and V/STOL Aviation.* Philadelphia: J. B. Lippincott, 1969.

Geiger, Roy, Personal Papers. Marine Corps Historical Research Center, PC 311, 312.

"Gen. Karl Day, 76, a Marine Aviator." *New York Times,* January 22, 1973.

"Geography of Nicaragua." Typescript, n.d. Marine Corps History Division, Secondary Literature.

George, H. L. "Bombardment Aviation." Lecture, n.d. Maxwell Air Force Base, AL, US Air Force Historical Research Agency.

Ginther, James. "Marine Aviator Number One: Alfred Austell Cunningham and the Development of Early Marine Corps Aviation." Master's thesis, Abilene Christian University, 1993.

Godinho, Antonio. "Marines in the Azores Islands in World War I: Diary of Walter S. Poague." *Fortitudine* 37, no. 1 (2012).

Goldwer, Marvin. *The Constabulary in the Dominican Republic and Nicaragua: Progeny and Legacy of United States Intervention.* Gainesville: University of Florida Press, 1962.

Graber, D. A. *Crisis Diplomacy: A History of U.S. Intervention, Policies and Practices.* Washington, DC: Public Affairs Press, 1959.

Graham, Captain Garrett H. "Origin of Dive Bombing." February 22, 1944. Marine Corps History Division, Aviation: Dive Bombing.

Gray, John. "The Second Nicaraguan Campaign." *Marine Corps Gazette* 17, no. 4 (February 1933).

Grossnick, Roy, ed. *Kite Balloons to Airships . . . the Navy's Lighter-than-Air Experience.* Washington, DC: Deputy Chief of Naval Operations, Air Warfare, n.d.

———. *United States Naval Aviation, 1910–1995.* 4th ed. Washington, DC: Government Printing Office, 1997.

Guangqui Xu. "Americans and Nationalist Chinese Military Aviation, 1929–1949." *Journal of the American Aviation Historical Society* 44, no. 1 (Spring 1999).

Guardia Nacional. "Guardia Newsletter." December 1932. Marine Corps History Division, Second Brigade Files.

"Haiti: Historical Outline of the Military Occupation." N.d. Marine Corps History Division, Haiti: Occupation.

"Haitian Curse Proves Blessing to Retiring Marine Traveler." *Washington Sunday Star,* October 28, 1934.

Hamill, Hugh, ed. *Caudillos: Dictators in Spanish America.* Norman: University of Oklahoma Press, 1992.

Hanna, Mark. *Pirate Nests and the Rise of the British Empire, 1570–1740.* Chapel Hill: University of North Carolina Press, 2015.

Hanst, Charles. "Marine Aviation in Santo Domingo." *Popular Aviation,* October 1928.

Harding, Richard. *The Emergence of Britain's Global Naval Supremacy: The War of 1739–1748.* Suffolk, UK: Boydell & Brewer, 2010.

Harned, Glenn. *Marine Corps Generals, 1899–1936: A Biographical Encyclopedia.* Jefferson, NC: McFarland, 2015.

Harrison, Lawrence. "Nicaraguan Anguish and Costa Rican Progress." *This World,* Fall 1983.

Hart, B. H. Liddell. *Why Don't We Learn from History?* New York: Hawthorn Books, 1971.

Headquarters Bulletin. September 1945. Marine Corps History Division, Miscellaneous.

Headquarters, First Provisional Brigade. General Order 17. July 18, 1919. Record Group 38, E6, box 13, National Archives, Washington, DC.

Healy, David. *Gunboat Diplomacy in the Wilson Era: The US Navy in Haiti, 1915–1916.* Madison: University of Wisconsin Press, 1976.

Heinl, Robert. *Soldiers of the Sea: The United States Marine Corps, 1775–1962.* 1962. Reprint, Mount Pleasant, SC: Nautical & Aviation Publishing Company of America, 1991.

Heinl, Robert, and Nancy Heinl. *Written in Blood: The Story of the Haitian People, 1492–1971.* 1978. Reprint, Lanham, MD: University Press of America, 2005.

Hendrickson, John. "El Terremoto." *Leatherneck* 70, no. 4 (April 1987).

Hennessey, Juliette. *The United States Army Air Arm: April 1861 to April 1917*. Washington, DC: Office of Air Force History, 1958.

Herbert, Frank. *Dune*. New York: G. P. Putnam's Sons, 1965.

Hinds, James. "Bombs over Mexico." *Aerospace Historian* 31, no. 2 (September 1984).

Hinote, Clint. "Armed Overwatch: Key to Successful COIN Operations in Urban Terrain." *Air Land Sea Application Center Bulletin 2008-1*.

"History of the Garde D'Haiti." Typescript, April 3–July 31, 1934. Marine Corps History Division, Haiti Garde.

Hoffman, Jon. *Chesty: The Story and Life of Lieutenant General Lewis B. Puller, USMC*. New York: Random House, 2001.

"A Homemade Statoscope." *Popular Mechanics* 39, no. 6 (June 1923).

Hoover Institution Studies 3. Washington, DC: Hoover Institution on War, Revolution, and Peace, 1964.

Hopper, Bruce. "When the Air Was Young: American Day Bombardment, A.E.F., France, 1917–1918" (unpublished manuscript, n.d.), Library of Congress, Washington, DC.

"Horse Marines." *Leatherneck* 5, no. 27 (May 1922).

House Documents, Otherwise Published as Executive Documents. Vol. 4. Delhi, India: S. N. (Reink) Books, 2017.

Hucker, Robert. "The Coco River Patrol." *Air Classics* 15, no. 4 (1979).

"Injured Man Carried on Airplane Wing." *Popular Science Monthly* 100 (January–June 1922).

"Intelligence Report, Second Brigade." December 18–24, 1927. Marine Corps History Division, Second Brigade Files.

"Interview with Major General Ross E. Rowell, USMC, on the Origin and Early Use of Dive-Bombing Tactics, Held in the Aviation History Unit on 24 October 1946." N.d. Marine Corps History Division, Aviation.

Interview with William Clark, pilot, Kenya Wildlife Service Air Wing, 2005.

Jacobs, James. "Alfred Austell Cunningham, 1882–1939." Marine Corps Historical Research Center, Cunningham Papers, PC 49, Personal Papers Collection.

James, C. L. R. *The Black Jacobins: Toussaint L'Ouverture and the San Domingo Revolution*. 2d ed. New York: Vintage Books, 1989.

Jessup, Philip. *Elihu Root*. New York: Dodd, Mead, 1938.

Johnson, E. R. *American Military Transport Aircraft since 1925*. Jefferson, NC: McFarland, 2013.

———. *United States Naval Aviation, 1919–1941*. Jefferson, NC: McFarland, 2011.

Johnson, Edward. *Marine Corps Aviation: The Early Years, 1912–1940*. Washington, DC: Headquarters, US Marine Corps, History and Museums Division, 1977.

Johnson, Wray. "Airpower and Restraint in Small Wars: Marine Corps Aviation in the Second Nicaraguan Campaign, 1927–1933." *Aerospace Power Journal*, Fall 2001.

———. "Terror Groups Are Not Invincible." *Marine Corps Gazette* 95, no. 10 (October 2011).

Joint Doctrine for Civil-Military Operations. Joint Publication 3-57. Washington, DC: Joint Chiefs of Staff, 2001.

Jomini, Baron de. *The Art of War*. Translated by G. H. Mendell and W. P. Craighill. Philadelphia: J. B. Lippincott, 1862.

Jones, William. "The Hogaboom Board." *Marine Corps Gazette* 84, no. 8 (August 2000).

Katz, Mark. *Revolution and Revolutionary Waves.* New York: Macmillan–St. Martin's Press, 1997.

Kaufman, Roxanne. *1912–2012: 100 Years of Marine Corps Aviation; an Illustrated History.* Washington, DC: Government Printing Office, n.d.

Keene, R. R. "The Battle for Cuzco Well." *Leatherneck* 81, no. 9 (September 1998).

———. "Battle of Cuzco Well, Guantanamo Bay, Cuba." *Leatherneck* 91, no. 9 (September 2008).

———. "Giants of the Marine Corps: John H. Quick." *Leatherneck* 58, no. 5 (May 1975).

———. "Guantanamo and the 1st Marine Battalion, 25 June 1898." *Marine Corps Gazette* 82, no. 7 (1998).

Kemp, P. K. [Christopher Lloyd]. *Brethren of the Coast: Buccaneers of the South Seas.* New York: St. Martin's Press, 1961.

Kingsbury, R. S. "Report against Captain Charles F. Merkel, M.C." September 30, 1918. Marine Corps History Division, Second Brigade Files.

Knapp, Walter. "The Marines Take Wing." *Aviation History,* May 2012.

Kopytoff, Barbara. "Guerrilla Warfare in Eighteenth Century Jamaica." *Expedition* 19, no. 2 (January 1977).

Lainé, Serge. "L'Aéronautique Militaire Française au Maroc (1911–1939)." *Revue Historique des Armées* 4 (1978).

———. "L'Aviation Sanitaire au Maroc en 1933." *Revue de l'Armée de l'Air,* March 1934.

Lamberton, W. M. *Reconnaissance and Bomber Aircraft of the 1914–1918 War.* Warwick, UK: Warwick Printing, 1962.

Lane, Rufus. "Santo Domingo." N.d. Marine Corps History Division, Second Brigade Files.

Langley, Lester. *The Banana Wars: United States Intervention in the Caribbean, 1898–1934.* Lexington: University Press of Kentucky, 1983.

———. *The United States and the Caribbean, 1900–1970.* Athens: University of Georgia Press, 1980.

Lansing, Robert. *War Memoirs of Robert Lansing: Secretary of State.* 1935. Reprint, Westport, CT: Greenwood Press, 1971.

Larimer, E. B. "Ammunition—Disposition of." June 13, 1934. Marine Corps History Division, First Brigade Files.

Larkins, William. *US Navy Aircraft, 1921–1941* [and] *US Marine Corps Aircraft, 1914–1959.* 1 vol. 1961 and 1959. Reprint, Atglen, PA: Schiffer Military History / Aviation History, 1995.

Lawton, Wilbur. *The Boy Aviators of Nicaragua; or, In League with the Insurgents.* New York: Hurst, 1910.

Layman, R. D. "Les Caproni Ca-5 de l'US Navy." *Avions* 4 (June 1993).

Lejeune, John. "Testimony of the Marine Corps Commandant before the Senate Committee on Foreign Relations, February 18, 1928." *Marine Corps Gazette* 13, no. 1 (March 1928).

Leyburn, James. *The Haitian People.* 1941. Reprint, New Haven, CT: Yale University Press, 1966.

"A List [of] Expeditions Formed and Landings Effected by the US Naval Forces in Central America, Mexico and the West Indies, from 1901 to May 1, 1929." Washington, DC: Naval Historical Center.

Lockhart, James. "Encomienda and Hacienda: The Evolution of the Great Estate in the Spanish Indies." *Hispanic American Historical Review,* 1969.

"Lutz Wins Curtiss Marine Trophy." *Aero Digest* 12, no. 6 (June 1928).

Macaulay, Neil. *The Sandino Affair.* 3d ed. 1967. Reprint, Micanopy, FL: Wacahoota Press, 1998.

MacMurray, John. *How the Peace Was Lost: The 1935 Memorandum; Developments Affecting American Policy in the Far East.* Edited by Arthur Weldon. Stanford, CA: Stanford University Press, 1992.

MacPhail, Doug. "The Origins of Close Air Support: Nicaragua's 'Constitutional War.'" *Air and Space Power Journal-Español.* www.airpower.au.af.mil/apjinternational/apj-s/2005/2ti05/overalleng.html, accessed June 28, 2018.

"Major Brainard, Chief of Marine Corps Aviation." *US Air Services* 12, no. 9 (September 1927).

"Major Brainard Joins Curtiss," *US Air Services* 14, no. 6 (June 1929).

Manual of Military Occupation Specialties. NAVMC 1006.PD (revised). Washington, DC: Headquarters, US Marine Corps, Personnel Department, Classification Division Detail Branch, 1945.

Mao Tse-tung. "Yu Chi Chan [Guerrilla Warfare]." In *Mao Tse-tung on Guerrilla Warfare.* Translated by Samuel Griffith. New York: Frederick A. Praeger, 1961.

"Marine Corps Aviation: Enough of Its History to Appreciate Its Accomplishments." *Headquarters Bulletin* 239 (September 1945).

"Marine Corps Aviation on Aircraft Carriers (Prior to World War II)." N.d. Marine Corps History Division, Miscellaneous.

Marine Corps Command and Staff College. Course card: "Small Wars (and Operations Other than War)." May 2005.

"Marine Corps Reserve Aviation in the Department of the Pacific." *Marine Corps Gazette* 19, no. 2 (August 1934).

"Marine Corps Reserve Notes." *Marine Corps Gazette* 14, no. 2 (June 1929).

"Marines at Managua." *Outlook and Independent,* April 15, 1931. Marine Corps History Division, Second Brigade Files.

"Marines Use Vought Corsairs for Rescue Work in Nicaragua." *Aviation,* January 30, 1928.

Martin, Gerald. "Yank Air Raid in Nicaragua Beats Rebels." *Chicago Daily Tribune,* February 8, 1927.

Martin, H. O. "Commendatory Action on the Part of Sergeant R. V. Burns, US Marine Corps." September 20, 1930. Marine Corps History Division, Second Brigade Files.

Matsusaka, Yoshihisa Tak. *The Making of Japanese Manchuria, 1904–1932.* East Asian Monographs 196. Boston: Harvard University Asia Center, 2003.

Matt, Paul. *United States Navy and Marine Corps Fighters, 1918–1962.* Edited by Bruce Robertson. Letchworth, UK: Harleyford Publications, 1962.

Mauer, Mauer. *Aviation in the U.S. Army, 1919–1939.* Washington, DC: Office of Air Force History, 1987.

May, Ernest. *The Making of the Monroe Doctrine.* Cambridge, MA: Harvard University Press, 1975.

McCarthy, Colman. "In Nicaragua, an Ex-Marine's Campaign of Conscience." *Washington Post,* March 2, 1986.

McClellan, Edwin. "American Marines in Nicaragua." *Marine Corps Gazette* 6, no. 1 (March 1921).

———. "The Birth and Infancy of Marine Aviation." *Marine Corps Gazette* 15, no. 5 (May 1931).

Megee, Vernon. "The Evolution of Marine Aviation." *Marine Corps Gazette* 49, no. 8 (August 1965).

———. "The Genesis of Air Support in Guerrilla Operations." *Proceedings,* June 1965.

———. "Guerrilla Lessons from Nicaragua." *Marine Corps Gazette* 49, no. 6 (June 1965).

———. *Memoirs of a Marine: Old Corps–New Corps, 1919–1959.* Dallas, TX: Atriad Press, 2011.

Megson, T. H. G. *Aircraft Structures for Engineering Students.* London: Edward Arnold, 1972.

Meid, Pat, and James Yingling. *US Marine Operations in Korea, 1950–1953.* Vol. 5, *Operations in West Korea.* Create Space Independent Publishing Platform, 2014.

"Memorandum, Major General Commandant [Barnett] to First Lieutenant Bernard L. Smith, MC, in Charge Marine Detachment, Aeronautic Section, USS *Mississippi.*" April 18, 1914. Marine Corps History Division, Aviation: Enlisted Pilots.

Mersky, Peter. *Marine Corps Aviation: 1912 to the Present.* 3d ed. Baltimore: Nautical & Aviation Publishing Company of America, 1997.

Metcalf, Clyde. *A History of the United States Marine Corps.* New York: G. P. Putnam's Sons, 1939.

Mets, David. "Dive-Bombing between the Wars." *Airpower Historian,* July 1965.

Metzger, Louis. "The Horse Marines." *Marine Corps Gazette* 87, no. 4 (April 2003).

Miller, Edward. *War Plan Orange: The US Strategy to Defeat Japan, 1897–1945.* Annapolis, MD: Naval Institute Press, 1991.

Miller, H. N. "Report of Skirmish with Native Bandits on 10 June, 1919." June 11, 1919. Marine Corps History Division, Second Brigade Files.

Miller, James. "The Passing of the Carrier Pigeon." *Popular Mechanics* 53, no. 2 (February 1930).

Miller, Roger. *A Preliminary to War: The 1st Aero Squadron and the Mexican Punitive Expedition of 1916.* Washington, DC: Air Force History and Museums Program, 2003.

Millett, Allan. *Semper Fi: The History of the United States Marine Corps.* New York: Macmillan, 1980.

Millett, Richard. *Guardians of the Dynasty: A History of the US Created Guardia Nacional de Nicaragua and the Somoza Family.* Maryknoll, NY: Orbis Books, 1977.

———. *Searching for Stability: The US Development of Constabulary Forces in Latin America and the Philippines.* Occasional Paper no. 20. Fort Leavenworth, KS: Combat Studies Institute, US Army Combined Arms Center, 2010.

Millspaugh, Arthur. *Haiti under American Control, 1915–1930.* Boston: World Peace Foundation, 1931.

Milton, Bart. "How Uncle Sam Hunts Bandits." *Popular Aviation* 11, no. 4 (October 1932).

Minor, Van Lieu. "A Brief Classified Bibliography Relating to United States Intervention in Nicaragua." *Hispanic American Historical Review* 11, no. 2 (May 1931).

Mitchell, William. "Aeronautical Era." *Saturday Evening Post,* December 20, 1924.

———. *Winged Defense: The Development and Possibilities of Modern Air Power—Economic and Military.* 1925. Reprint, New York: Dover Publications, 1988.

Montague, Ludwell. *Haiti and the United States, 1714–1938.* Durham, NC: Duke University Press, 1940.

Montross, Lyn. "The Marine Autogiro in Nicaragua." *Marine Corps Gazette* 37, no. 2 (February 1953).

Moore, James. "Crews and Planes of VO-9M, Traveling via Air from Port au Prince, Haiti, to M. B. Quantico, Va." N.d. Marine Corps History Division, First Brigade Files.

———. "Disposition of Aeronautical Material on Evacuation from Haiti," May 31, 1934. Marine Corps History Division, First Brigade Files.

———. "Evacuation." July 12, 1934. Marine Corps History Division, First Brigade Files.

———. "Memorandum for the Commanding General." June 29, 1934. Marine Corps History Division, First Brigade Files.

———. "Proposed Itinerary of VO Squadron 9M, via Air, from Port au Prince, Haiti, to M. B., Quantico, Va." N.d. Marine Corps History Division, First Brigade Files.

Moore, James, Henry Carr, and Ivan Miller. "Recommendation for Disposition of Government Property, Navy and Marine Corps, in Hands of Observation Squadron 9-M, on Withdrawal from Haiti." December 18, 1933. Marine Corps History Division, First Brigade Files.

Mulcahy, Francis. "Marine Corps Aviation in the Second Nicaraguan Campaign." *Proceedings,* August 1933.

Müniz, Humberto. "Sugar Land and Gavillero Warfare in Eastern Dominican Republic: The Case of Central Romana, 1910–1924." *Historia Y Sociedad* 12 (2000–2001).

Munro, Dana. *The Five Republics of Central America.* New York: Oxford University Press, 1918.

———. *Intervention and Dollar Diplomacy in the Caribbean, 1900–1921.* 1964. Reprint, Westport, CT: Greenwood Press, 1980.

———. *The United States and the Caribbean Area, 1921–1933.* 1934. Reprint, Princeton, NJ: Princeton University Press, 1974.

Murphy, Leo. *Flying Machines over Pensacola: An Early Aviation History from 1909 to 1929.* Gulf Breeze, FL: Pensacola Bay Flying Machine, 2003.

Murray, F. R. "Disposition of Aeronautical Material on Evacuation from Haiti." June 11, 1934. Marine Corps History Division, First Brigade Files.

Musicant, Ivan. *The Banana Wars: A History of the United States Military Intervention in Latin America from the Spanish-American War to the Invasion of Panama.* New York: Macmillan, 1990.

Nalty, Bernard. *The United States Marines in Nicaragua.* Washington, DC: Headquarters, US Marine Corps, History and Museums Division, 1968.

National Association of Manufacturers. *American Industries.* 1925.

"Nation's Press Commends Marine Corps Withdrawal from Haiti." *Army and Navy Journal,* August 18, 1934.

"Naval and Military Aeronautics." *Aerial Age Weekly* 13, no. 14 (June 13, 1921).

Navarez, Alfonzo. "Dana G. Munro, 97, a Retired Professor and Ex-Diplomat." *New York Times,* June 19, 1990.

Navarro-Génie, Marco. *August "César" Sandino: Messiah of Light and Truth*. Syracuse, NY: Syracuse University Press, 2002.

"Navy Ships Latest Model Vought Planes to Marines in Nicaragua." *Aviation*, January 23, 1928.

Neely, Frederick. "As Usual, the Marines Had the Situation in Hand." *US Air Services* 12, no. 1 (January 1927).

———. "Schilt, 'Corsair' and 'Wasp' in Nicaragua." *US Air Services* 13, no. 2 (February 1928).

Neimeyer, Charles. "First United States Marine Officer Killed in Combat: 'Shall I Board Her, Sir?'" *Leatherneck* 95, no. 11 (November 2012).

Nelson, Evelyn, and Frederick Nelson. *The Island of Guam (Description and History from a 1934 Perspective)*. Edited by Mary McCutcheon. 1934. Reprint, Washington, DC: Ana Publications, 1992.

Nelson, William. *Almost a Territory: America's Attempt to Annex the Dominican Republic*. Newark: University of Delaware Press, 1990.

Neufeld, Gabrielle, and James Santelli. "1912–1941 Squadrons of the Corps." *Marine Corps Gazette* 57, no. 11 (November 1973).

———. "Smedley Butler's Air Corps: The First Marine Aviators in China." *Proceedings*, April 1977.

"News of the Air Services: First Non-stop Flight US to Nicaragua." *Aero Digest*, February 1928.

Obituary of Neil W. Macauly Jr. *Gainesville (FL) Sun*, October 31, 2007.

"Official Commendatory Remarks About and Career Information Regarding Select Early Marine Corps Aviators." N.d. Marine Corps History Division, Aviation: Aviators (Early).

Operations Journal, Eleventh Regiment. September 1928. Marine Corps History Division, Second Brigade Files.

Operations Order no. 37. July 3, 1927. Marine Corps History Division, Second Brigade Files.

Operations Report, Eleventh Regiment. June 29 to July 30, 1927. Marine Corps History Division, Second Brigade Files.

"Outline of Bombing Training for Marine Corps Detachment at Miami, Florida." June 1918. Marine Corps History Division, Herman A. Peterson Papers, Accession no. 6B12, box 1.

Owen, Robert. *Air Mobility: A Brief History of the American Experience*. Washington, DC: Potomac Books, 2013.

Pace, Eric. "William A. Lee Is Dead at 98: Marines' Acclaimed 'Ironman.'" *New York Times*, January 2, 1999.

Page, Arthur. "Detail of Pilots for Aviation Duty in the Tropics." March 7, 1921. Marine Corps History Division, Haiti: Other Reports.

Paine, Ralph. "Naval Aviation Overseas." *Cross and Cockade Journal* 4, no. 1 (Spring 1963).

Papers Relating to the Foreign Relations of the United States, 1927. Vol. 2. Washington, DC: Government Printing Office, 1942.

Parker, Gary, and Frank Batha. *A History of Marine Observation Squadron Six*. Washington, DC: Headquarters, US Marine Corps, History and Museums Division, 1977.

Patillo, Donald. *A History in the Making: 80 Turbulent Years in the American General Aviation Industry.* New York: McGraw-Hill Professional, 1998.

"Paul Fuller Going to Haiti: Wilson Sending Him There to Report on Island's Affairs." *New York Times,* April 30, 1915.

Paulus-Sannon, Horace. *Histories de Toussaint Louverture.* Vol. 3. 2d ed. Port-au-Prince, Haiti: Presses Nationals, 2003.

Pauly, Roger. *Firearms: The Life Story of a Technology.* Santa Barbara, CA: Greenwood Press, 2004.

Pelletier, Alan. "Made in America: Thomas Morse MB-3 and Boeing MB-3A." *Air Enthusiast* 131 (September–October 2007).

Pierce, Francis. "Infantry-Air Communications." *Marine Corps Gazette* 13, no. 4 (December 1928).

Pike, Frederick. *FDR's Good Neighbor Policy: Sixty Years of Generally Gentle Chaos.* Austin: University of Texas Press, 1995.

Plantey, Capitaine, et le Médecin-Major Vincent. "Les Avions Sanitaires." *Aeronautique* 29 (October 1921).

Potts, John. "Origins of Dive Bombing." September 8, 1944. Marine Corps History Division, Aviation.

Presley, Russell. "Weekly News Letter, for Week Ending November 27, 1920." December 3, 1920. Marine Corps History Division, Second Brigade Files.

Press release. December 27, 1932. Marine Corps History Division, Second Brigade Files.

"Protection of American Interests." *Marine Corps Gazette* 12, no. 3 (September 1927).

Ragsdale, Kenneth. *Wings over the Border: Pioneer Military Aviation in the Big Bend.* Austin: University of Texas Press, 1984.

Raico, Ralph. "The Blockade and Attempted Starvation of Germany." http://mises.org/library/blockade-and-attempted-starvation-germany.

Reckner, James. *Teddy Roosevelt's Great White Fleet.* Annapolis, MD: Naval Institute Press, 2001.

"Recommendation for Awards and Citations in Connection with Aerial Bombardment of Bandit Forces in Mura Region on 18–19 March, 1928." March 24, 1928. Marine Corps History Division, Second Brigade Files.

"Record of Events." March 24, 1928. Marine Corps History Division, Second Brigade Files.

"Record of Events, Fifth Regiment." December 18–24, 1927. Marine Corps History Division, Second Brigade Files.

Reisman, Philip. "Sandinista Flags." Part 1. *Flag Bulletin* 22, no. 5 (September–October 1983).

Renda, Mary. *Taking Haiti: Military Occupation and the Culture of US Imperialism.* Chapel Hill: University of North Carolina Press, 2001.

"Report from the Commanding General to the Major General Commandant." March 12, 1927. Naval Forces Ashore in Nicaragua. Marine Corps History Division, Second Brigade Files.

"Report, Military Governor of Santo Domingo, to the Secretary of the Navy, Subject: Claim of Dugal McPhail, May 19, 1924." Record Group 38, E6, box 74, National Archives, Washington, DC.

"Report of Commanding General, Second Brigade to the Major General Commandant, for the Period January 15 to February 27, 1928." Marine Corps History Division, Second Brigade Files.

"Report of Operations, April 30, 1921." Marine Corps History Division, First Brigade Files.

"Report of Operations, for Period July 1, 1920, to June 30, 1921 (Confidential)." Marine Corps History Division, First Brigade Files.

"Report of Operations from September 21, 1930, to October 20, 1930." October 25, 1930. Marine Corps History Division, First Brigade Files.

"Report of Operations, May 31, 1921." Marine Corps History Division, First Brigade Files.

"Report on First Air Squadron, Marine Aviation Force." N.d. Marine Corps History Division, Second Brigade Files.

Reserve Officers of Public Affairs Unit 4-1. *Marine Aviation: World War I.* Washington, DC: Headquarters, US Marine Corps, Division of Reserve, 1966.

———. *The Marine Corps Reserve: A History.* Washington, DC: Headquarters, US Marine Corps, Division of Reserve, 1966.

Robie, Bill. *For the Greatest Achievement: A History of the Aero Club of America and the National Aeronautic Association.* Washington, DC: Smithsonian Institution, 1993.

Rogers, John. "The Haitianization of the Garde d'Haiti." *Leatherneck* 16, no. 10 (October 1933).

Rogers, Major General Ford O., USMC, Ret. Oral history transcript, December 3, 1970. Oral History Collection, Headquarters, US Marine Corps, History and Museums Division, Washington, DC.

Romero, Manuel. *La aviacion durante la revolucion Mexicana.* Mexico City: Sporte Aeronautico, 1988.

Rottman, Gordon. *US Marine Corps World War II Order of Battle: Ground and Air Units in the Pacific War, 1939–1945.* Military Book Club ed. Westport, CT: Greenwood Press, 2002.

Rowell, Ross. "Aircraft in Bush Warfare." *Marine Corps Gazette* 14, no. 3 (September 1929).

———. "Aircraft in Bush Warfare." January 1, 1931. Typescript. Maxwell Air Force Base, AL, US Air Force Historical Research Agency.

———. "The Air Service in Minor Warfare." *Proceedings,* October 1929.

———. "Annual Report of Aircraft Squadrons, Second Brigade, US Marine Corps, July 1, 1927, to June 20, 1928." *Marine Corps Gazette* 13, no. 4 (December 1928).

———. "Archibald, R. J., Captain, USMC, Commendation of." September 15, 1928. Marine Corps History Division, Second Brigade Files.

———. "Marine Air in Nicaragua." Edited by Edwin Simmons. *Marine Corps Gazette* 69, no. 5 (May 1985).

———. "Report of Air Mission, April 10, 1928." National Archives, Washington, DC.

———. "A Skirmish with Rebels." *Popular Aviation-Aeronautics* 8, no. 3 (March 1931).

Russell, John. "Russell Report to US Military Representative in Haiti." March 10, 1920. Marine Corps History Division, Personal Papers Collection.

Russell, Sandy, ed. *Naval Aviation, 1911–1986: A Pictorial Study.* Washington, DC: Deputy Chief of Naval Operations, Air Warfare, 1986.

Sanderson, L. H. M. "Dive Bombing, History of." August 19, 1946. Marine Corps History Division, Aviation: Dive Bombing.

———. "Origin of Dive Bombing as I Know It." September 1, 1944. Marine Corps History Division, Aviation: Dive Bombing.

Sanderson, Major General Lawson H. M., USMC, Ret. Oral history transcript, December 3, 1970. Oral History Collection, Headquarters, US Marine Corps, History and Museums Division, Washington, DC.

Sandino, Augusto. *Sandino: The Testimony of a Nicaraguan Patriot, 1921–1934.* Princeton, NJ: Princeton University Press, 2014.

Scheina, Robert. *Latin America's Wars.* Vol. 2, *The Age of the Professional Soldier, 1900–2001.* Sterling, VA: Potomac Books, 2003.

Schilt, C. Frank. "Marines in Nicaragua Saved by Airplanes." *Aero Digest* 12, no. 2 (February 1928).

Schilt, General Christian, USMC, Ret. Oral history transcript, November 17 and 20, 1969. Oral History Collection, Headquarters, US Marine Corps, History and Museums Division, Washington, DC.

"Schilt Receives from the President Unique Honor." *US Air Services* 13, no. 7 (July 1928).

Schmidt, Hans. *Maverick Marine: General Smedley D. Butler and the Contradictions of American Military History.* 1987. Reprint, Lexington: University Press of Kentucky, 1998.

———. *The United States Occupation of Haiti, 1915–1934.* 1971. Reprint, New Brunswick, NJ: Rutgers University Press, 1995.

Schmitz, David. *Henry L. Stimson: The First Wise Man.* Lanham, MD: Rowman & Littlefield, 2000.

Schroeder, Michael. "Social Memory and Tactical Doctrine: The Air War in Nicaragua during the Sandino Rebellion, 1927–1932." *International History Review* 29, no. 3 (September 2007).

Schwartz, Norton. "Letter to the editor. *Air Force Magazine,* March 2007.

Scott, James. "Revolution in the Revolution: Peasants and Commissars." *Theory and Society* 7 (January–May 1979).

"Sea Gives up Lost Writer." *Long Island Daily Press,* August 13, 1943.

"2d Non-stop Flight US to Nicaragua." *Aero Digest* 12, no. 3 (March 1928).

Selected Works of Mao Tse-tung. 5 vols. Peking: Foreign Language Press, 1963.

A Selection of Lectures and Essays from the Work of Officers Attending the First Course at the Royal Air Force Staff College, 1921–1923. London: Her Majesty's Stationery Office, Air Ministry, 1923.

Semper Fi, Tales of the Marine Corps. Marvel Comics, April 1988.

Senior Board Member of the Board for the Award of Medals of Honor, Distinguished-Service Medal, Navy Cross, Distinguished Flying Cross and Life Saving Medals. "Corporal Hilmer N. Torner, US Marine Corps—Extraordinary Achievement while in Aerial Flight—Award for, May 17, 1932." Marine Corps History Division, Second Brigade Files.

Shacochis, Bob. *The Immaculate Invasion.* New York: Viking, 1999.

Shepherd, General Lemuel, USMC, Ret. Oral history transcript, September 19, 1978. Oral History Collection, Headquarters, US Marine Corps, History and Museums Division, Washington, DC.

Sherrod, Robert. *History of Marine Corps Aviation in World War II.* Baltimore: Nautical & Aviation Publishing Company of America, 1987.

———. "Marine Corps Aviation: The Early Days." Part 1. *Marine Corps Gazette* 36, no. 5 (May 1952).

Shirley, Noel. "La Guardia, Caproni Bombers, and the US Navy." *Cross and Cockade Journal* 25, no. 2 (1984).

Shulimson, Jack, and Graham Cosmas. "Teddy Roosevelt and the Corps' Sea-Going Mission." *Marine Corps Gazette* 65, no. 11 (November 1981).

Silverthorn, Lieutenant General Merwin, USMC, Ret. Oral history transcript, 1978. Oral History Collection, Headquarters, US Marine Corps, History and Museums Division, Washington, DC.

Simmons, Edwin. "Ross Rowell: Aviator with a Flair." *Marine Corps Gazette* 69, no. 5 (1985).

Sitz, W. H. "A History of US Naval Aviation." Technical Note 160. Typescript. US Department of the Navy, Bureau of Aeronautics, April 1925.

Small Wars Manual. 1940. Reprint, Washington, DC: Department of the Navy, 1987.

Smith, Douglas. *One Hundred Years of US Navy Air Power.* Annapolis, MD: Naval Institute Press, 2010.

Smith, Julian, et al. *A Review of the Organizations and Operations of the Guardia Nacional de Nicaragua, 1927–1933.* 2 vols. Washington, DC: Headquarters, US Marine Corps, n.d. [circa 1934].

Smith, Newcomb. "Watching Bandits in Haiti from the Air." *Recruiters' Bulletin* 5, no. 9 (October 1919).

Smith, Peter. *Dive Bomber: An Illustrated History.* Ashbourne, UK: Moorland, 1982.

Smith, Richard. *First Across: The US Navy's Transatlantic Flight of 1919.* Annapolis, MD: Naval Institute Press, 1973.

Smock, Raymond, and Susan Hammonds, eds. *Masters of the House: Congressional Leadership over Two Centuries.* New York: Westview Press, 1998.

Stein, Stephen. *From Torpedoes to Aviation: Washington Irving Chambers and Technological Innovation in the New Navy, 1876–1913.* Tuscaloosa: University of Alabama Press, 2007.

Stern, Robert. *The Lexington Class Carriers.* Annapolis, MD: Naval Institute Press, 1993.

Stimson, Henry. *American Policy in Nicaragua.* New York: Charles Scribner's Sons, 1927.

Stimson, Henry, and McGeorge Bundy. *On Active Service in Peace and War.* 1948. Reprint, New York: Hippocrene Books, 1971.

Stuart, Graham. *Latin America and the United States.* New York: D. Appleton-Century, 1938.

Stubbs, Richard. *Hearts and Minds in Guerrilla Warfare: The Malayan Emergency, 1948–1960.* East Asia Historical Monographs. Oxford: Oxford University Press, 1990.

"Summary of Operations and Final Report of Commanding Officer, Nuevo Segovia Expedition." August 21, 1927. Marine Corps History Division, Second Brigade Files.

"Supply Plane in Nicaragua Invaluable." *Aviation,* February 6, 1928.

Swanborough, Gordon, and Peter Bowers. *United States Military Aircraft since 1909.* Washington, DC: Smithsonian Institution Press, 1989.

———. *United States Navy Aircraft since 1911.* New York: Funk & Wagnalls, 1968.

———. *United States Navy Aircraft since 1911.* 2d ed. London: Putnam, 1976.

Sweetman, Jack. *The Landing at Veracruz, 1914.* Annapolis, MD: Naval Institute Press, 1968.

Swift, Ernest. "The Red Cross Flies to Managua." *Red Cross Courier,* September 1931.

Taylor, Michael. *Jane's Encyclopedia of Aviation.* London: Studio Editions, 1989.

A Text on the Employment of Marine Corps Aviation. Quantico, VA: Marine Corps Schools, 1935.

Thaxton, Carlton, et al., eds. *A Roster of Spanish American War Soldiers from Georgia.* Americus, GA: Thaxton, 1984.

Thomason, John. *Marines and Others.* New York: Charles Scribner's Sons, 1929.

Tirpak, John. "Washington Watch." *Air Force Magazine,* March 2007.

Titus, Allan. Letter to the editor. *Christian Advocate,* July 27, 1927. Marine Corps History Division, Second Brigade Files.

Towers, John. "Naval Aviation." Lecture no. 4. February 28, 1929. Typescript. Maxwell Air Force Base, AL, US Air Force Historical Research Agency.

"Translation of Nicaraguan Press." Marine Corps History Division, Second Brigade Files.

Trask, Stephen. "Scopes that Shoot through Day and Dark." *Arms and the Man (American Rifleman)* 64, no. 3 (April 13, 1918).

Treadwell, Terry. *America's First Air War: The United States Army, Naval, and Marine Air Services in the First World War.* Osceola, WI: MBI Publishing, 2000.

Trimble, William. *Admiral William A. Moffett: Architect of Naval Aviation.* Washington, DC: Smithsonian Institution Press, 1994.

———. *Wings for the Navy: A History of the Naval Aircraft Factory, 1917–1956.* Annapolis, MD: Naval Institute Press, 1990.

Trinquier, Roger. *Modern Warfare—A French View of Counterinsurgency.* New York: Frederick A. Praeger, 1964.

Turnbull, Archibald, and Clifford Lee Lord. *History of United States Naval Aviation.* Manchester, NH: Ayer, 1971.

Turner, Thomas. "Aviation Notes." *Marine Corps Gazette* 6, no. 3 (September 1921).

US Congress. *Congressional Record.* Washington, DC: Government Printing Office, annual.

US Congress. Senate Select Committee on Haiti and Santo Domingo. *Inquiry into Occupation and Administration of Haiti and Santo Domingo.* 67th Cong., 1st and 2d sess. Washington, DC: Government Printing Office, 1922.

US Department of the Navy. *Annual Report of the Secretary of the Navy, 1920.* Washington, DC: Government Printing Office, 1921.

US Department of the Navy, Office of Naval Intelligence. "A List of Expeditions Formed and Landings Effected by the US Naval Forces in Central America, Mexico and the West Indies, from 1901 to May 1, 1929." May 1, 1929. Naval Historical Center, Washington, DC.

US Department of State. *A Brief History of the Relations between the United States and Nicaragua, 1909–1928.* Washington, DC: Government Printing Office, 1928.

US Marine Corps. *Marine Corps Aircraft: 1913–1965.* Washington, DC: Headquarters, US Marine Corps, Historical Branch, 1967.

US Marine Corps Radio Dispatch. July 12, 1934. Marine Corps History Division, First Brigade Files.

"US Marine Goes Mad in Managua, Slain by Guard." *Chicago Tribune,* April 5, 1931.

US Military Government of Santo Domingo. *Santo Domingo: Its Past and Its Present Condition.* Santo Domingo City, Dominican Republic, 1920.

US Navy, Bureau of Aeronautics. News Letter no. 258, June 1931; News Letter no. 262, August 1931; News Letter no. 275, March 1932; News Letter no. 297, February 1933. Marine Corps History Division, Second Brigade Files.

Utley, Harold. "An Introduction to the Tactics and Technique of Small Wars." *Marine Corps Gazette* 16, no. 1 (May 1931).

Valencia, Robert Himmerich. *The Encomenderos of New Spain, 1521–1555.* Austin: University of Texas Press, 1991.

Van Deurs, George. *Wings for the Fleet: A Narrative of Naval Aviation's Early Development, 1910–1916.* Annapolis, MD: Naval Institute Press, 1966.

Van Wyen, Adrian. *Naval Aviation in World War I.* 1969. Reprint, Honolulu, HI: University Press of the Pacific, 2005.

Webster's Ninth New Collegiate Dictionary. Springfield, MA: Merriam-Webster, 1985.

"Weekly Operations Report, Earthquake." Marine Corps History Division, Second Brigade Files.

Welles, Sumner. *Naboth's Vineyard: The Dominican Republic, 1844–1924.* Vol. 2. New York: Payson & Clarke, 1928.

"What Some of Our Reserve Officers Are Doing in Aviation." *Marine Corps Gazette* 19, no. 2 (August 1934).

Wheelan, Joseph. *Jefferson's War: America's First War on Terror, 1801–1805.* New York: Carroll & Graf, 2003.

Whitcomb, Darrel. *The Rescue of Bat 21.* Annapolis, MD: Naval Institute Press, 1998.

Whittaker, Robert. *Dragon Master: The Kaiser's One-Man Air Force on Tsingtau, China, 1914.* Cleveland, WI: Compass Books–Video Films, 1994.

Williams, Mary. *The People and Politics of Latin America.* New York: Ginn, 1945.

Williamson, Charles. *The US Naval Mission to Haiti: 1959–1963.* Annapolis, MD: Naval Institute Press, 1999.

Willock, Roger. *Unaccustomed to Fear: A Biography of the Late General Roy S. Geiger.* 1968. Reprint, Quantico, VA: Marine Corps Association, 1983.

Wirkus, Faustin, and Taney Dudley. *The White King of La Gonave: The True Story of the Sergeant of Marines Who Was Crowned King on a Voodoo Island.* Garden City, NY: Doubleday, Doran, 1931.

Wise, Frederic, and Meigs Frost. *A Marine Tells It to You.* 1929. Reprint, Quantico, VA: Marine Corps Association, 1981.

Wolmar, Christian. *Engines of War: How Wars Were Won and Lost on the Railways.* New York: Public Affairs, 2010.

Workers Party of America and the Young Workers League of America. Leaflet. March 23, 1928. Marine Corps History Division, Nicaragua: Adversaries.

World Aircraft Information Files. London: Bright Star Publishing, 2002.

Wykes, Alan. *Hitler's Bodyguards: SS Leibstandarte.* New York: Random House, 1974.

Yenne, Bill. *Seaplanes and Flying Boats: A Timeless Collection from Aviation's Golden Age.* New York: BCL Press, 2003.

Index

A Mitchell Institute Book

Aviation and Air Power

Series Editor: Brian D. Laslie

In his work *Winged Defense*, Brigadier General William "Billy" Mitchell stated, "Air power may be defined as the ability to do something in the air." Since Mitchell made this statement, the definition of air power has been contested and argued about by those on the ground, those in the air, academics, industrialists, and politicians.

Each volume of the Aviation and Air Power series seeks to expand our understanding of Mitchell's broad definition by bringing together leading historians, fliers, and scholars in the fields of military history, aviation, air power history, and other disciplines in the hope of providing a fuller picture of just what air power accomplishes.

This series offers an expansive look at tactical aerial combat, operational air warfare, and strategic air theory. It explores campaigns from the First World War through modern air operations, along with the heritage, technology, culture, and human element particular to the air arm. In addition, this series considers the perspectives of leaders in the US Army, Navy, Marine Corps, and Air Force, as well as their counterparts in other nations and their approaches to the history and study of doing something in the air.